Office of the Inspector General
U.S. Department of Justice

OVERSIGHT ★ INTEGRITY ★ GUIDANCE

Review of Four FISA Applications and Other Aspects of the FBI's Crossfire Hurricane Investigation

versight and Review Division 20-012

December 2019

[PAGE INTENTIONALLY LEFT BLANK]

Background

The Department of Justice (Department) Office of the Inspector General (OIG) undertook this review to examine certain actions by the Federal Bureau of Investigation (FBI) and the Department during an FBI investigation opened on July 31, 2016, known as "Crossfire Hurricane," into whether individuals associated with the Donald J. Trump for President Campaign were coordinating, wittingly or unwittingly, with the Russian government's efforts to interfere in the 2016 U.S. presidential election. Our review included examining:

- The decision to open Crossfire Hurricane and four individual cases on current and former members of the Trump campaign, George Papadopoulos, Carter Page, Paul Manafort, and Michael Flynn; the early investigative steps taken; and whether the openings and early steps complied with Department and FBI policies;

- The FBI's relationship with Christopher Steele, whom the FBI considered to be a confidential human source (CHS); its receipt, use, and evaluation of election reports from Steele; and its decision to close Steele as an FBI CHS;

- Four FBI applications filed with the Foreign Intelligence Surveillance Court (FISC) in 2016 and 2017 to conduct Foreign Intelligence Surveillance Act (FISA) surveillance targeting Carter Page; and whether these applications complied with Department and FBI policies and satisfied the government's obligations to the FISC;

- The interactions of Department attorney Bruce Ohr with Steele, the FBI, Glenn Simpson of Fusion GPS, and the State Department; whether work Ohr's spouse performed for Fusion GPS implicated ethical rules applicable to Ohr; and Ohr's interactions with Department attorneys regarding the Manafort criminal case; and

- The FBI's use of Undercover Employees (UCEs) and CHSs other than Steele in the Crossfire Hurricane investigation; whether the FBI placed any CHSs within the Trump campaign or tasked any CHSs to report on the Trump campaign; whether the use of CHSs and UCEs complied with Department and FBI policies; and the attendance of a Crossfire Hurricane supervisory agent at counterintelligence briefings given to the 2016 presidential candidates and certain campaign advisors.

OIG Methodology

The OIG examined more than one million documents that were in the Department's and FBI's possession and conducted over 170 interviews involving more than 100 witnesses. These witnesses included former FBI Director Comey, former Attorney General (AG) Loretta Lynch, former Deputy Attorney General (DAG) Sally Yates, former DAG Rod Rosenstein, former Acting AG and Acting DAG and current FBI General Counsel Dana Boente, former FBI Deputy Director Andrew McCabe, former FBI General Counsel James Baker, and Department attorney Bruce Ohr and his wife. The OIG also interviewed Christopher Steele and current and former employees of other U.S. government agencies. Two witnesses, Glenn Simpson and Jonathan Winer (a former Department of State official), declined our requests for voluntary interviews, and we were unable to compel their testimony.

We were given broad access to relevant materials by the Department and the FBI. In addition, we reviewed relevant information that other U.S. government agencies provided the FBI in the course of the Crossfire Hurricane investigation. However, because the activities of other agencies are outside our jurisdiction, we did not seek to obtain records from them that the FBI never received or reviewed, except for a limited amount of State Department records relating to Steele; we also did not seek to assess any actions other agencies may have taken. Additionally, our review did not independently seek to determine whether corroboration existed for the Steele election reporting; rather, our review was focused on information that was available to the FBI concerning Steele's reports prior to and during the pendency of the Carter Page FISA authority.

Our role in this review was not to second-guess discretionary judgments by Department personnel about whether to open an investigation, or specific judgment calls made during the course of an investigation, where those decisions complied with or were authorized by Department rules, policies, or procedures. We do not criticize particular decisions merely because we might have recommended a different investigative strategy or tactic based on the facts learned during our investigation. The question we considered was not whether a particular investigative decision was ideal or could have been handled more effectively, but rather whether the Department and the FBI complied with applicable legal requirements, policies, and procedures in taking the actions we reviewed or, alternatively, whether the circumstances surrounding the decision indicated that it was based on

inaccurate or incomplete information, or considerations other than the merits of the investigation. If the explanations we were given for a particular decision were consistent with legal requirements, policies, procedures, and not unreasonable, we did not conclude that the decision was based on improper considerations in the absence of documentary or testimonial evidence to the contrary.

The Opening of Crossfire Hurricane and Four Related Investigations, and Early Investigative Steps

The Opening of Crossfire Hurricane and Four Individual Cases

As we describe in Chapter Three, the FBI opened Crossfire Hurricane on July 31, 2016, just days after its receipt of information from a Friendly Foreign Government (FFG) reporting that, in May 2016, during a meeting with the FFG, then Trump campaign foreign policy advisor George Papadopoulos "suggested the Trump team had received some kind of suggestion from Russia that it could assist this process with the anonymous release of information during the campaign that would be damaging to Mrs. Clinton (and President Obama)." The FBI Electronic Communication (EC) opening the Crossfire Hurricane investigation stated that, based on the FFG information, "this investigation is being opened to determine whether individual(s) associated with the Trump campaign are witting of and/or coordinating activities with the Government of Russia." We did not find information in FBI or Department ECs, emails, or other documents, or through witness testimony, indicating that any information other than the FFG information was relied upon to predicate the opening of the Crossfire Hurricane investigation. Although not mentioned in the EC, at the time, FBI officials involved in opening the investigation had reason to believe that Russia may have been connected to the WikiLeaks disclosures that occurred earlier in July 2016, and were aware of information regarding Russia's efforts to interfere with the 2016 U.S. elections. These officials, though, did not become aware of Steele's election reporting until weeks later and we therefore determined that Steele's reports played no role in the Crossfire Hurricane opening.

The FBI assembled a Headquarters-based investigative team of special agents, analysts, and supervisory special agents (referred to throughout this report as "the Crossfire Hurricane team") who conducted an initial analysis of links between Trump campaign members and Russia. Based upon this

analysis, the Crossfire Hurricane team opened individual cases in August 2016 on four U.S. persons—Papadopoulos, Carter Page, Paul Manafort, and Michael Flynn—all of whom were affiliated with the Trump campaign at the time the cases were opened.

As detailed in Chapter Two, the Attorney General's Guidelines for Domestic Operations (AG Guidelines) and the FBI's Domestic Investigations Operations Guide (DIOG) both require that FBI investigations be undertaken for an "authorized purpose"—that is, "to detect, obtain information about, or prevent or protect against federal crimes or threats to the national security or to collect foreign intelligence." Additionally, both the AG Guidelines and the DIOG permit the FBI to conduct an investigation, even if it might impact First Amendment or other constitutionally protected activity, so long as there is some legitimate law enforcement purpose associated with the investigation.

In addition to requiring an authorized purpose, FBI investigations must have adequate factual predication before being initiated. The predication requirement is not a legal requirement but rather a prudential one imposed by Department and FBI policy. The DIOG provides for two types of investigations, Preliminary Investigations and Full Investigations. A Preliminary Investigation may be opened based upon "any allegation or information" indicative of possible criminal activity or threats to the national security. A Full Investigation may be opened based upon an "articulable factual basis" that "reasonably indicates" any one of three defined circumstances exists, including:

> An activity constituting a federal crime or a threat to the national security has or may have occurred, is or may be occurring, or will or may occur and the investigation may obtain information relating to the activity or the involvement or role of an individual, group, or organization in such activity.

In Full Investigations such as Crossfire Hurricane, all lawful investigative methods are allowed. In Preliminary Investigations, all lawful investigative methods (including the use of CHSs and UCEs) are permitted except for mail opening, physical searches requiring a search warrant, electronic surveillance requiring a judicial order or warrant (Title III wiretap or a FISA order), or requests under Title VII of FISA. An investigation opened as a Preliminary Investigation may be converted subsequently to a Full Investigation if

information becomes available that meets the predication standard. As we describe in the report, all of the investigative actions taken by the Crossfire Hurricane team, from the date the case was opened on July 31 until October 21 (the date of the first FISA order) would have been permitted whether the case was opened as a Preliminary or Full Investigation.

The AG Guidelines and the DIOG do not provide heightened predication standards for sensitive matters, or allegations potentially impacting constitutionally protected activity, such as First Amendment rights. Rather, the approval and notification requirements contained in the AG Guidelines and the DIOG are, in part, intended to provide the means by which such concerns can be considered by senior officials. However, we were concerned to find that neither the AG Guidelines nor the DIOG contain a provision requiring Department consultation before opening an investigation such as the one here involving the alleged conduct of individuals associated with a major party presidential campaign.

Crossfire Hurricane was opened as a Full Investigation and all of the senior FBI officials who participated in discussions about whether to open a case told us the information warranted opening it. For example, then Counterintelligence Division (CD) Assistant Director (AD) E.W. "Bill" Priestap, who approved the case opening, told us that the combination of the FFG information and the FBI's ongoing cyber intrusion investigation of the July 2016 hacks of the Democratic National Committee's (DNC) emails, created a counterintelligence concern that the FBI was "obligated" to investigate. Priestap stated that he considered whether the FBI should conduct defensive briefings for the Trump campaign but ultimately decided that providing such briefings created the risk that "if someone on the campaign was engaged with the Russians, he/she would very likely change his/her tactics and/or otherwise seek to cover-up his/her activities, thereby preventing us from finding the truth." We did not identify any Department or FBI policy that applied to this decision and therefore determined that the decision was a judgment call that Department and FBI policy leaves to the discretion of FBI officials. We also concluded that, under the AG Guidelines and the DIOG, the FBI had an authorized purpose when it opened Crossfire Hurricane to obtain information about, or protect against, a national security threat or federal crime, even though the investigation also had the potential to impact constitutionally protected activity.

Additionally, given the low threshold for predication in the AG Guidelines and the DIOG, we concluded that the FFG information, provided by a government the United States Intelligence Community (USIC) deems trustworthy, and describing a first-hand account from an FFG employee of a conversation with Papadopoulos, was sufficient to predicate the investigation. This information provided the FBI with an articulable factual basis that, if true, reasonably indicated activity constituting either a federal crime or a threat to national security, or both, may have occurred or may be occurring. For similar reasons, as we detail in Chapter Three, we concluded that the quantum of information articulated by the FBI to open the individual investigations on Papadopoulos, Page, Flynn, and Manafort in August 2016 was sufficient to satisfy the low threshold established by the Department and the FBI.

As part of our review, we also sought to determine whether there was evidence that political bias or other improper considerations affected decision making in Crossfire Hurricane, including the decision to open the investigation. We discussed the issue of political bias in a prior OIG report, *Review of Various Actions in Advance of the 2016 Election*, where we described text and instant messages between then Special Counsel to the Deputy Director Lisa Page and then Section Chief Peter Strzok, among others, that included statements of hostility toward then candidate Trump and statements of support for then candidate Hillary Clinton. In this review, we found that, while Lisa Page attended some of the discussions regarding the opening of the investigations, she did not play a role in the decision to open Crossfire Hurricane or the four individual cases. We further found that while Strzok was directly involved in the decisions to open Crossfire Hurricane and the four individual cases, he was not the sole, or even the highest-level, decision maker as to any of those matters. As noted above, then CD AD Priestap, Strzok's supervisor, was the official who ultimately made the decision to open the investigation, and evidence reflected that this decision by Priestap was reached by consensus after multiple days of discussions and meetings that included Strzok and other leadership in CD, the FBI Deputy Director, the FBI General Counsel, and a FBI Deputy General Counsel. We concluded that Priestap's exercise of discretion in opening the investigation was in compliance with Department and FBI policies, and we did not find documentary or testimonial evidence that political bias or improper motivation influenced his decision. We similarly found that, while the formal documentation opening each of the four individual investigations was approved by Strzok (as required by the DIOG), the

decisions to do so were reached by a consensus among the Crossfire Hurricane agents and analysts who identified individuals associated with the Trump campaign who had recently traveled to Russia or had other alleged ties to Russia. Priestap was involved in these decisions. We did not find documentary or testimonial evidence that political bias or improper motivation influenced the decisions to open the four individual investigations.

Sensitive Investigative Matter Designation

The Crossfire Hurricane investigation was properly designated as a "sensitive investigative matter," or SIM, by the FBI because it involved the activities of a domestic political organization or individuals prominent in such an organization. The DIOG requires that SIMs be reviewed in advance by the FBI Office of the General Counsel (OGC) and approved by the appropriate FBI Headquarters operational section chief, and that an "appropriate [National Security Division] official" receive notification after the case has been opened.

We concluded that the FBI satisfied the DIOG's approval and notification requirements for SIMs. As we describe in Chapter Three, the Crossfire Hurricane opening was reviewed by an OGC Unit Chief and approved by AD Priestap (two levels above Section Chief). The team also orally briefed National Security Division (NSD) officials within the first few days of the investigations being initiated. We were concerned, however, that Department and FBI policies do not require that a senior Department official be notified prior to the opening of a particularly sensitive case such as this one, nor do they place any additional requirements for SIMs beyond the approval and notification requirements at the time of opening, and therefore we include a recommendation to address this issue.

Early Investigative Steps and Adherence to the Least Intrusive Method

The AG Guidelines and the DIOG require that the "least intrusive" means or method be "considered" when selecting investigative techniques and, "if reasonable based upon the circumstances of the investigation," be used to obtain information instead of a more intrusive method. The DIOG states that the degree of procedural protection the law and Department and FBI policy provide for the use of a particular investigative method helps to determine its intrusiveness. As described in Chapter Three, immediately after opening the investigation, the

Crossfire Hurricane team submitted name trace requests to other U.S. government agencies and a foreign intelligence agency, and conducted law enforcement database and open source searches, to identify individuals associated with the Trump campaign in a position to have received the alleged offer of assistance from Russia. The FBI also sent Strzok and a Supervisory Special Agent (SSA) abroad to interview the source of the information the FBI received from the FFG, and also searched the FBI's database of CHSs to identify sources who potentially could provide information about connections between individuals associated with the Trump campaign and Russia. Each of these steps is authorized under the DIOG and was a less intrusive investigative technique.

Thereafter, the Crossfire Hurricane team used more intrusive techniques, including CHSs to interact and consensually record multiple conversations with Page and Papadopoulos, both before and after they were working for the Trump campaign, as well as on one occasion with a high-level Trump campaign official who was not a subject of the investigation. We found that, under Department and FBI policy, although this CHS activity implicated First Amendment protected activity, the operations were permitted because their use was not for the sole purpose of monitoring activities protected by the First Amendment or the lawful exercise of other rights secured by the Constitution or laws of the United States. Additionally, we found that under FBI policy, the use of a CHS to conduct consensual monitoring is a matter of investigative judgment that, absent certain circumstances, can be authorized by a first-line supervisor (an SSA). We determined that the CHS operations conducted during Crossfire Hurricane received the necessary FBI approvals and that, while AD Priestap knew about and approved of all of the operations, review beyond a first-level FBI supervisor was not required by Department or FBI policy.

We found it concerning that Department and FBI policy did not require the FBI to consult with any Department official in advance of conducting CHS operations involving advisors to a major party candidate's presidential campaign, and we found no evidence that the FBI consulted with any Department officials before conducting these CHS operations. As we describe in Chapter Two, consultation, at a minimum, is required by Department and FBI policies in numerous other sensitive circumstances, and we include a recommendation to address this issue.

Shortly after opening the Carter Page investigation in August 2016, the Crossfire Hurricane team discussed the possible use of FISA-authorized

electronic surveillance targeting Page, which is among the most sensitive and intrusive investigative techniques. As we describe in Chapter Five, the FBI ultimately did not seek a FISA order at that time because OGC, NSD's Office of Intelligence (OI), or both determined that more information was needed to support probable cause that Page was an agent of a foreign power. However, immediately after the Crossfire Hurricane team received Steele's election reporting on September 19, the team reinitiated their discussions with OI and their efforts to obtain FISA surveillance authority for Page, which they received from the FISC on October 21.

The decision to seek to use this highly intrusive investigative technique was known and approved at multiple levels of the Department, including by then DAG Yates for the initial FISA application and first renewal, and by then Acting Attorney General Boente and then DAG Rosenstein for the second and third renewals, respectively. However, as we explain later, the Crossfire Hurricane team failed to inform Department officials of significant information that was available to the team at the time that the FISA applications were drafted and filed. Much of that information was inconsistent with, or undercut, the assertions contained in the FISA applications that were used to support probable cause and, in some instances, resulted in inaccurate information being included in the applications. While we do not speculate whether Department officials would have authorized the FBI to seek to use FISA authority had they been made aware of all relevant information, it was clearly the responsibility of Crossfire Hurricane team members to advise them of such critical information so that they could make a fully informed decision.

The FBI's Relationship with Christopher Steele, and Its Receipt and Evaluation of His Election Reporting before the First FISA Application

As we describe in Chapter Four, Steele is a former intelligence officer ███████████████ ████████████████████ who, in 2009, formed a consulting firm specializing in corporate intelligence and investigative services. In 2010, Steele was introduced by Ohr to an FBI agent, and for several years provided information to the FBI about various matters, such as corruption in the International Federation of Association Football (FIFA). Steele also provided the FBI agent with reporting about Russian oligarchs.

In 2013, the FBI completed the paperwork allowing the FBI to designate Steele as a CHS. However, as described in Chapter Four, we found that the FBI and Steele held significantly differing views about the nature of their relationship. Steele's handling agent viewed Steele as a former intelligence officer colleague and FBI CHS, with obligations to the FBI. Steele, on the other hand, told us that he was a businessperson whose firm (not Steele) had a contractual agreement with the FBI and whose obligations were to his paying clients, not the FBI. We concluded that this disagreement affected the FBI's control over Steele during the Crossfire Hurricane investigation, led to divergent expectations about Steele's conduct in connection with his election reporting, and ultimately resulted in the FBI formally closing Steele as a CHS in November 2016 (although, as discussed below, the FBI continued its relationship with Steele through Ohr).

In June 2016, Steele and his consulting firm were hired by Fusion GPS, a Washington, D.C., investigative firm, to obtain information about whether Russia was trying to achieve a particular outcome in the 2016 U.S. elections, what personal and business ties then candidate Trump had in Russia, and whether there were any ties between the Russian government and Trump or his campaign. Steele's work for Fusion GPS resulted in his producing numerous election-related reports, which have been referred to collectively as the "Steele Dossier." Steele himself was not the originating source of any of the factual information in his reporting. Steele instead relied on a Primary Sub-source for information, who used his/her network of sub-sources to gather information that was then passed to Steele. With Fusion GPS's authorization, Steele directly provided more than a dozen of his reports to the FBI between July and October 2016, and several others to the FBI through Ohr and other third parties. The Crossfire Hurricane team received the first six election reports on September 19, 2016—more than two months after Steele first gave his handling agent two of the six reports. We describe the reasons it took two months for the reports to reach the team in Chapter Four.

FBI's Efforts to Evaluate the Steele Reporting

Steele's handling agent told us that when Steele provided him with the first election reports in July 2016 and described his engagement with Fusion GPS, it was obvious to him that the request for the research was politically motivated. The supervisory intelligence analyst who supervised the analytical efforts for the Crossfire Hurricane team (Supervisory Intel Analyst)

explained that he also was aware of the potential for political influences on the Steele reporting.

The fact that the FBI believed Steele had been retained to conduct political opposition research did not require the FBI, under either DOJ or FBI policy, to ignore his reporting. The FBI regularly receives information from individuals with potentially significant biases and motivations, including drug traffickers, convicted felons, and even terrorists. The FBI is not required to set aside such information; rather, FBI policy requires that it critically assess the information. We found that after receiving Steele's reporting, the Crossfire Hurricane team began those efforts in earnest.

We determined that the FBI's decision to receive Steele's information for Crossfire Hurricane was based on multiple factors, including: (1) Steele's prior work as an intelligence professional for ██████████████████████████; (2) his expertise on Russia; (3) his record as an FBI CHS; (4) the assessment of Steele's handling agent that Steele was reliable and had provided helpful information to the FBI in the past; and (5) the themes of Steele's reporting were consistent with the FBI's knowledge at the time of Russian efforts to interfere in the 2016 U.S. elections.

However, as we describe later, as the FBI obtained additional information raising significant questions about the reliability of the Steele election reporting, the FBI failed to reassess the Steele reporting relied upon in the FISA applications, and did not fully advise NSD or OI officials. We also found that the FBI did not aggressively seek to obtain certain potentially important information from Steele. For example, the FBI did not press Steele for information about the actual funding source for his election reporting work. Agents also did not question Steele about his role in a September 23, 2016 *Yahoo News* article entitled, "*U.S. intel officials probe ties between Trump advisor and Kremlin,*" that described efforts by U.S. intelligence to determine whether Carter Page had opened communication channels with Kremlin officials. As we discuss in Chapters Five and Eight, the FBI assessed in the Carter Page FISA applications, without any support, that Steele had not "directly provided" the information to *Yahoo News*.

The First Application for FISA Authority on Carter Page

At the request of the FBI, the Department filed four applications with the FISC seeking FISA authority targeting Carter Page: the first application on October █, 2016, and three renewal applications on January █, April █, and June █, 2017. A different FISC judge considered each application and issued the requested orders, collectively resulting in approximately 11 months of FISA coverage targeting Carter Page from October █, 2016, to September █, 2017. We discuss the first FISA application in this section and in Chapter Five.

Decision to Seek FISA Authority

We determined that the Crossfire Hurricane team's receipt of Steele's election reporting on September 19, 2016 played a central and essential role in the FBI's and Department's decision to seek the FISA order. As noted above, when the team first sought to pursue a FISA order for Page in August 2016, a decision was made by OGC, OI, or both that more information was needed to support a probable cause finding that Page was an agent of a foreign power. As a result, FBI OGC ceased discussions with OI about a Page FISA order at that time.

On September 19, 2016, the same day that the Crossfire Hurricane team first received Steele's election reporting, the team contacted FBI OGC again about seeking a FISA order for Page and specifically focused on Steele's reporting in drafting the FISA request. Two days later, on September 21, the FBI OGC Unit Chief contacted the NSD OI Unit Chief to advise him that the FBI believed it was ready to submit a formal FISA request to OI relating to Page. Almost immediately thereafter, OI assigned an attorney (OI Attorney) to begin preparation of the application.

Although the team also was interested in seeking FISA surveillance targeting Papadopoulos, the FBI OGC attorneys were not supportive. FBI and NSD officials told us that the Crossfire Hurricane team ultimately did not seek FISA surveillance of Papadopoulos, and we are aware of no information indicating that the team requested or seriously considered FISA surveillance of Manafort or Flynn.

We did not find documentary or testimonial evidence that political bias or improper motivation influenced the FBI's decision to seek FISA authority on Carter Page.

Preparation and Review Process

As we detail in Chapter Two, the FISC Rules of Procedure and FBI policy required that the Carter Page FISA applications contain all material facts. Although

the FISC Rules do not define or otherwise explain what constitutes a "material" fact, FBI policy guidance states that a fact is "material" if it is relevant to the court's probable cause determination. Additionally, FBI policy mandates that the case agent ensure that all factual statements in a FISA application are "scrupulously accurate."

On or about September 23, the OI Attorney began work on the FISA application. Over the next several weeks, the OI Attorney prepared and edited a draft application using information principally provided by the FBI case agent assigned to the Carter Page investigation at the time and, in a few instances, by an OGC attorney (OGC Attorney) or other Crossfire Hurricane team members. The drafting process culminated in an application that asserted that the Russian government was attempting to undermine and influence the upcoming U.S. presidential election, and that the FBI believed Carter Page was acting in conjunction with the Russians in those efforts. The application's statement of facts supporting probable cause to believe that Page was an agent of Russia was broken down into five main elements:

- The efforts of Russian Intelligence Services (RIS) to influence the upcoming U.S. presidential election;

- The Russian government's attempted coordination with members of the Trump campaign, based on the FFG information reporting the suggestion of assistance from the Russians to someone associated with the Trump campaign;

- Page's historical connections to Russia and RIS;

- Page's alleged coordination with the Russian government on 2016 U.S. presidential election activities, based on Steele's reporting; and

- Page's statements to an FBI CHS in October 2016 that that he had an "open checkbook" from certain Russians to fund a think tank project.

In addition, the statement of facts described Page's denials of coordination with the Russian government, as reported in two news articles and asserted by Page in a September 25 letter to then FBI Director Comey.

The application received the necessary Department approvals and certifications as required by law. As we fully describe in Chapter Five, this application received more attention and scrutiny than a typical FISA application in terms of the additional layers

of review and number of high-level officials who read the application before it was signed. These officials included NSD's Acting Assistant Attorney General, NSD's Deputy Assistant Attorney General with oversight over OI, OI's Operations Section Chief and Deputy Section Chief, the DAG, Principal Associate Deputy Attorney General, and the Associate Deputy Attorney General responsible for ODAG's national security portfolio. However, as we explain below, the Department decision makers who supported and approved the application were not given all relevant information.

Role of Steele Election Reporting in the First Application

In support of the fourth element in the FISA application—Carter Page's alleged coordination with the Russian government on 2016 U.S. presidential election activities—the application relied entirely on the following information from Steele Reports 80, 94, 95, and 102:

- Compromising information about Hillary Clinton had been compiled for many years, was controlled by the Kremlin, and had been fed by the Kremlin to the Trump campaign for an extended period of time (Report 80);

- During a July 2016 trip to Moscow, Page met secretly with Igor Sechin, Chairman of Russian energy conglomerate Rosneft and close associate of Putin, to discuss future cooperation and the lifting of Ukraine-related sanctions against Russia; and with Igor Divyekin, a highly-placed Russian official, to discuss sharing with the Trump campaign derogatory information about Clinton (Report 94);

- Page was an intermediary between Russia and the Trump campaign's then manager (Manafort) in a "well-developed conspiracy" of cooperation, which led to Russia's disclosure of hacked DNC emails to WikiLeaks in exchange for the Trump campaign's agreement to sideline Russian intervention in Ukraine as a campaign issue (Report 95); and

- Russia released the DNC emails to WikiLeaks in an attempt to swing voters to Trump, an objective conceived and promoted by Page and others (Report 102).

We determined that the FBI's decision to rely upon Steele's election reporting to help establish probable cause that Page was an agent of Russia was a judgment reached initially by the case agents on the

Crossfire Hurricane team. We further determined that FBI officials at every level concurred with this judgment, from the OGC attorneys assigned to the investigation to senior CD officials, then General Counsel James Baker, then Deputy Director Andrew McCabe, and then Director James Comey. FBI leadership supported relying on Steele's reporting to seek a FISA order on Page after being advised of, and giving consideration to, concerns expressed by Stuart Evans, then NSD's Deputy Assistant Attorney General with oversight responsibility over OI, that Steele may have been hired by someone associated with presidential candidate Clinton or the DNC, and that the foreign intelligence to be collected through the FISA order would probably not be worth the "risk" of being criticized later for collecting communications of someone (Carter Page) who was "politically sensitive." According to McCabe, the FBI "felt strongly" that the FISA application should move forward because the team believed they had to get to the bottom of what they considered to be a potentially serious threat to national security, even if the FBI would later be criticized for taking such action. McCabe and others discussed the FBI's position with NSD and ODAG officials, and these officials accepted the FBI's decision to move forward with the application, based substantially on the Steele information.

We found that the FBI did not have information corroborating the specific allegations against Carter Page in Steele's reporting when it relied upon his reports in the first FISA application or subsequent renewal applications. OGC and NSD attorneys told us that, while the FBI's "Woods Procedures" (described in Chapter Two) require that every factual assertion in a FISA application be "verified," when information is attributed to a FBI CHS, the Woods Procedures require only that the agent verify, with supporting documentation, that the application accurately reflects what the CHS told the FBI. The procedures do not require that the agent corroborate, through a second, independent source, that what the CHS told the FBI is true. We did not identify anything in the Woods Procedures that is inconsistent with these officials' description of the procedures.

However, absent corroboration for the factual assertions in the election reporting, it was particularly important for the FISA applications to articulate the FBI's knowledge of Steele's background and its assessment of his reliability. On these points, the applications advised the court that Steele was believed to be a reliable source for three reasons: his professional background; his history of work as an FBI CHS since 2013; and his prior non-election reporting,

which the FBI described as "corroborated and used in criminal proceedings." As discussed below, the representations about Steele's prior reporting were overstated and had not been approved by Steele's handling agent, as required by the Woods Procedures.

Due to Evans's persistent inquiries, the FISA application also included a footnote, developed by OI based on information provided by the Crossfire Hurricane team, to address Evans's concern about the potential political bias of Steele's research. The footnote stated that Steele was hired by an identified U.S. person (Glenn Simpson) to conduct research regarding "Candidate #1's" (Donald Trump) ties to Russia and that the FBI "speculates" that this U.S. person was likely looking for information that could be used to discredit the Trump campaign.

Relevant Information Inaccurately Stated, Omitted, or Undocumented in the First Application

Our review found that FBI personnel fell far short of the requirement in FBI policy that they ensure that all factual statements in a FISA application are "scrupulously accurate." We identified multiple instances in which factual assertions relied upon in the first FISA application were inaccurate, incomplete, or unsupported by appropriate documentation, based upon information the FBI had in its possession at the time the application was filed. We found that the problems we identified were primarily caused by the Crossfire Hurricane team failing to share all relevant information with OI and, consequently, the information was not considered by the Department decision makers who ultimately decided to support the applications.

As more fully described in Chapter Five, based upon the information known to the FBI in October 2016, the first application contained the following seven significant inaccuracies and omissions:

1. Omitted information the FBI had obtained from another U.S. government agency detailing its prior relationship with Page, including that Page had been approved as an "operational contact" for the other agency from 2008 to 2013, and that Page had provided information to the other agency concerning his prior contacts with certain Russian intelligence officers, one of which overlapped with facts asserted in the FISA application;

2. Included a source characterization statement asserting that Steele's prior reporting had been "corroborated and used in criminal proceedings,"

which overstated the significance of Steele's past reporting and was not approved by Steele's handling agent, as required by the Woods Procedures;

3. Omitted information relevant to the reliability of Person 1, a key Steele sub-source (who was attributed with providing the information in Report 95 and some of the information in Reports 80 and 102 relied upon in the application), namely that (1) Steele himself told members of the Crossfire Hurricane team that Person 1 was a "boaster" and an "egoist" and "may engage in some embellishment" and (2) ███████████████████████████████ ;

4. Asserted that the FBI had assessed that Steele did not directly provide to the press information in the September 23 *Yahoo News* article based on the premise that Steele had told the FBI that he only shared his election-related research with the FBI and Fusion GPS, his client; this premise was incorrect and contradicted by documentation in the Woods File—Steele had told the FBI that he also gave his information to the State Department;

5. Omitted Papadopoulos's consensually monitored statements to an FBI CHS in September 2016 denying that anyone associated with the Trump campaign was collaborating with Russia or with outside groups like WikiLeaks in the release of emails;

6. Omitted Page's consensually monitored statements to an FBI CHS in August 2016 that Page had "literally never met" or "said one word to" Paul Manafort and that Manafort had not responded to any of Page's emails; if true, those statements were in tension with claims in Report 95 that Page was participating in a conspiracy with Russia by acting as an intermediary for Manafort on behalf of the Trump campaign; and

7. Included Page's consensually monitored statements to an FBI CHS in October 2016 that the FBI believed supported its theory that Page was an agent of Russia but omitted other statements Page made that were inconsistent with its theory, including denying having met with Sechin and Divyekin, or even knowing who Divyekin was; if true, those statements contradicted the claims in Report 94 that Page

had met secretly with Sechin and Divyekin about future cooperation with Russia and shared derogatory information about candidate Clinton.

None of these inaccuracies and omissions were brought to the attention of OI before the last FISA application was filed in June 2017. Consequently, these failures were repeated in all three renewal applications. Further, as we discuss later, we identified 10 additional significant errors in the renewal applications.

The failure to provide accurate and complete information to the OI Attorney concerning Page's prior relationship with another U.S. government agency (item 1 above) was particularly concerning because the OI Attorney had specifically asked the case agent in late September 2016 whether Carter Page had a current or prior relationship with the other agency. In response to that inquiry, the case agent advised the OI Attorney that Page's relationship was "dated" (claiming it was when Page lived in Moscow in 2004-2007) and "outside scope." This representation, however, was contrary to information that the other agency had provided to the FBI in August 2016, which stated that Page was approved as an "operational contact" of the other agency from 2008 to 2013 (after Page had left Moscow). Moreover, rather than being "outside scope," Page's status with the other agency overlapped in time with some of the interactions between Page and known Russian intelligence officers that were relied upon in the FISA applications to establish probable cause. Indeed, Page had provided information to the other agency about his past contacts with a Russian Intelligence Officer (Intelligence Officer 1), which were among the historical connections to Russian intelligence officers that the FBI relied upon in the first FISA application (and subsequent renewal applications). According to the information from the other agency, an employee of the other agency had assessed that Page "candidly described his contact with" Intelligence Officer 1 to the other agency. Thus, the FBI relied upon Page's contacts with Intelligence Officer 1, among others, in support of its probable cause statement in the FISA application, while failing to disclose to OI or the FISC that (1) Page had been approved as an operational contact by the other agency during a five-year period that overlapped with allegations in the FISA application, (2) Page had disclosed to the other agency contacts that he had with Intelligence Officer 1 and certain other individuals, and (3) the other agency's employee had given a positive assessment of Page's candor.

Further, we were concerned by the FBI's inaccurate assertion in the application that Steele's prior reporting had been "corroborated and used in criminal

proceedings," which we were told was primarily a reference to Steele's role in the FIFA corruption investigation. We found that the team had speculated that Steele's prior reporting had been corroborated and used in criminal proceedings without clearing the representation with Steele's handling agent, as required by the Woods Procedures. According to the handling agent, he would not have approved the representation in the application because only "some" of Steele's prior reporting had been corroborated—most of it had not—and because Steele's information was never used in a criminal proceeding. We concluded that these failures created the inaccurate impression in the applications that at least some of Steele's past reporting had been deemed sufficiently reliable by prosecutors to use in court, and that more of his information had been corroborated than was actually the case.

We found no evidence that the OI Attorney, NSD supervisors, ODAG officials, or Yates were made aware of these issues before the first application was submitted to the court. Although we also found no evidence that Comey had been made aware of these issues at the time he certified the application, as discussed in our analysis in Chapter Eleven, multiple factors made it difficult for us to precisely determine the extent of FBI leadership's knowledge as to each fact that was not shared with OI and not included, or inaccurately stated, in the FISA applications. These factors included, among other things, limited recollections, the inability to question Comey or refresh his recollection with relevant, classified documentation because of his lack of a security clearance, and the absence of meeting minutes that would show the specific details shared with Comey and McCabe during briefings they received, beyond the more general investigative updates that we know they were provided.

FBI Activities After the First FISA Application and FBI Efforts to Assess Steele's Election Reporting

On October 31, 2016, shortly after the first FISA application was signed, an article entitled "A Veteran Spy Has Given the FBI Information Alleging a Russian Operation to Cultivate Donald Trump," was published by *Mother Jones*. Steele admitted to the FBI that he was a source for the article, and the FBI closed him as a CHS for cause in November 2016. However, as we describe below, despite having been closed for cause, the Crossfire Hurricane team continued to obtain information from Steele through Ohr, who met with the FBI on 13 occasions to pass along information he had been provided by Steele.

In Chapter Six, we describe the events that followed Steele's closing as a CHS, including the FBI's receipt of information from several third parties who had acquired copies of the Steele election reports, use of information from the Steele reports in an interagency assessment of Russian interference in the U.S. 2016 elections, and continuing efforts to learn about Steele and his source network and to verify information from the reports following Steele's closure.

Starting in December 2016, FBI staff participated in an interagency effort to assess the Russian government's intentions and actions concerning the 2016 U.S. elections. We learned that whether and how to present Steele's reporting in the Intelligence Community Assessment (ICA) was a topic of significant discussion between the FBI and the other agencies participating in it. According to FBI staff, as the interagency editing process for the ICA progressed, the Central Intelligence Agency (CIA) expressed concern about the lack of vetting for the Steele election reporting and asserted it did not merit inclusion in the body of the report. An FBI Intel Section Chief told us the CIA viewed it as "internet rumor." In contrast, as we describe in Chapter Six, the FBI, including Comey and McCabe, sought to include the reporting in the ICA. Limited information from the Steele reporting ultimately was presented in an appendix to the ICA.

FBI efforts to verify information in the Steele election reports, and to learn about Steele and his source network continued after Steele's closure as a CHS. In November and December 2016, FBI officials travelled abroad and met with persons who previously had professional contacts with Steele or had knowledge of his work. Information these FBI officials obtained about Steele was both positive and negative. We found, however, that the information about Steele was not placed in his FBI CHS file.

We further learned that the FBI's Validation Management Unit (VMU) completed a human source validation review of Steele in early 2017. The VMU review found that Steele's past criminal reporting was "minimally corroborated," and included this finding in its report that was provided to the Crossfire Hurricane team. This determination by the VMU was in tension with the source characterization statement included in the initial FISA application, which represented that Steele's prior reporting had been "corroborated and used in criminal proceedings." The VMU review also did not identify any corroboration for Steele's election reporting among the information that the Crossfire Hurricane team had collected. However, the VMU did not include this finding in its written validation report

and therefore members of the Crossfire Hurricane team and FBI executives were unaware of it.

We also found that the FBI's interviews of Steele, his Primary Sub-source, a second sub-source, and other investigative activity, revealed potentially serious problems with Steele's descriptions of information in his reports. For example, as detailed in Chapters Six and Eight, the Primary Sub-source made statements during his/her January 2017 FBI interview that were inconsistent with multiple sections of the Steele reports, including some that were relied upon in the FISA applications. Among other things, regarding the allegations attributed to Person 1, the Primary Sub-source's account of these communications, if true, was not consistent with and, in fact, contradicted the allegations of a "well-developed conspiracy" in Reports 95 and 102 attributed to Person 1.

We further determined that the Crossfire Hurricane team was unable to corroborate any of the specific substantive allegations regarding Carter Page contained in Steele's election reporting which the FBI relied on in the FISA applications. We were told by the Supervisory Intel Analyst that, as of September 2017, the FBI had corroborated limited information in the Steele election reporting, and much of that was publicly available information. Most relevant to the Carter Page FISA applications, the allegations contained in Reports 80, 94, 95, and 102, which were relied upon in all four applications, remained uncorroborated and, in several instances, were inconsistent with information gathered by the Crossfire Hurricane team.

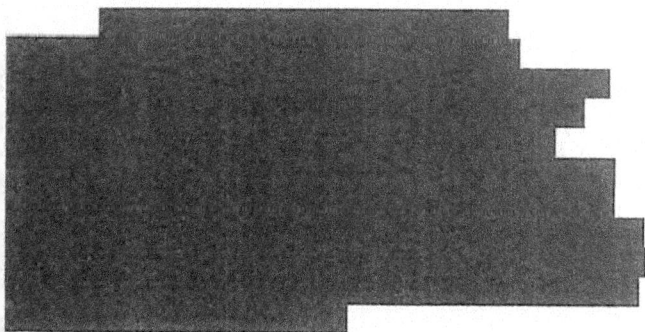

The Three Renewal Applications for Continued FISA Authority on Carter Page

As noted above, the FBI filed three renewal applications with the FISC, on January ▮, April ▮, and June ▮, 2017. In addition to repeating the seven significant errors contained in the first FISA application and outlined above, we identified 10 additional

significant errors in the three renewal applications, based upon information known to the FBI after the first application and before one or more of the renewals. We describe the circumstances surrounding these 10 errors in Chapter Eight, and provide a chart listing additional errors in Appendix One. As more fully described in Chapter Eight, the renewal applications:

8. Omitted the fact that Steele's Primary Sub-source, who the FBI found credible, had made statements in January 2017 raising significant questions about the reliability of allegations included in the FISA applications, including, for example, that he/she had no discussion with Person 1 concerning WikiLeaks and there was "nothing bad" about the communications between the Kremlin and the Trump team, and that he/she did not report to Steele in July 2016 that Page had met with Sechin;

9. Omitted Page's prior relationship with another U.S. government agency, despite being reminded by the other agency in June 2017, prior to the filing of the final renewal application, about Page's past status with that other agency; instead of including this information in the final renewal application, the OGC Attorney altered an email from the other agency so that the email stated that Page was "not a source" for the other agency, which the FBI affiant relied upon in signing the final renewal application;

10. Omitted information from persons who previously had professional contacts with Steele or had direct knowledge of his work-related performance, including statements that Steele had no history of reporting in bad faith but "[d]emonstrates lack of self-awareness, poor judgment," "pursued people with political risk but no intelligence value," "didn't always exercise great judgment," and it was "not clear what he would have done to validate" his reporting;

11. Omitted information obtained from Ohr about Steele and his election reporting, including that (1) Steele's reporting was going to Clinton's presidential campaign and others, (2) Simpson was paying Steele to discuss his reporting with the media, and (3) Steele was "desperate that Donald Trump not get elected and was passionate about him not being the U.S. President";

12. Failed to update the description of Steele after information became known to the Crossfire

Hurricane team, from Ohr and others, that provided greater clarity on the political origins and connections of Steele's reporting, including that Simpson was hired by someone associated with the Democratic Party and/or the DNC;

13. Failed to correct the assertion in the first FISA application that the FBI did not believe that Steele directly provided information to the reporter who wrote the September 23 *Yahoo News* article, even though there was no information in the Woods File to support this claim and even after certain Crossfire Hurricane officials learned in 2017, before the third renewal application, of an admission that Steele made in a court filing about his interactions with the news media in the late summer and early fall of 2016;

14. Omitted the finding from a FBI source validation report that Steele was suitable for continued operation but that his past contributions to the FBI's criminal program had been "minimally corroborated," and instead continued to assert in the source characterization statement that Steele's prior reporting had been "corroborated and used in criminal proceedings";

15. Omitted Papadopoulos's statements to an FBI CHS in late October 2016 denying that the Trump campaign was involved in the circumstances of the DNC email hack;

16. Omitted Joseph Mifsud's denials to the FBI that he supplied Papadopoulos with the information Papadopoulos shared with the FFG (suggesting that the campaign received an offer or suggestion of assistance from Russia); and

17. Omitted information indicating that Page played no role in the Republican platform change on Russia's annexation of Ukraine as alleged in the Report 95, which was inconsistent with a factual assertion relied upon to support probable cause in all four FISA applications.

Among the most serious of the 10 additional errors we found in the renewal applications was the FBI's failure to advise OI or the court of the inconsistences, described in detail in Chapter Six, between Steele and his Primary Sub-source on the reporting relied upon in the FISA applications. Although the Primary Sub-source's account of these communications, if true, was not consistent with and, in fact, contradicted the allegations of a "well-developed conspiracy" in Reports 95 and 102 attributed to Person 1, the FBI did not share this information with OI. The

FBI also failed to share other inconsistencies with OI, including the Primary Sub-source's account of the alleged meeting between Page and Sechin in Steele's Report 94 and his/her descriptions of the source network. The fact that the Primary Sub-source's account contradicted key assertions attributed to his/her own sub-sources in Steele's Reports 94, 95, and 102 should have generated significant discussions between the Crossfire Hurricane team and OI prior to submitting the next FISA renewal application. According to Evans, had OI been made aware of the information, such discussions might have included the possibility of foregoing the renewal request altogether, at least until the FBI reconciled the differences between Steele's account and the Primary Sub-source's account to the satisfaction of OI. However, we found no evidence that the Crossfire Hurricane team ever considered whether any of the inconsistencies warranted reconsideration of the FBI's assessment of the reliability of the Steele reports or notice to OI before the subsequent renewal applications were filed.

Instead, the second and third renewal applications provided no substantive information concerning the Primary Sub-source's interview, and offered only a brief conclusory statement that the FBI met with the Primary Sub-source "[i]n an effort to further corroborate Steele's reporting" and found the Primary Sub-source to be "truthful and cooperative." We believe that including this statement, without also informing OI and the court that the Primary Sub-source's account of events contradicted key assertions in Steele's reporting, left a misimpression that the Primary Sub-source had corroborated the Steele reporting. Indeed, in a letter to the FISC in July 2018, before learning of these inconsistencies from us during this review, the Department defended the reliability of Steele's reporting and the FISA applications by citing, in part, to the Primary Sub-source's interview as "additional information corroborating [Steele's] reporting" and noting the FBI's determination that he/she was "truthful and cooperative."

The renewal applications also continued to fail to include information regarding Carter Page's past relationship with another U.S. government agency, even though both OI and members of the Crossfire Hurricane expressed concern about the possibility of a prior relationship following interviews that Page gave to news outlets in April and May 2017 stating that he had assisted other U.S. government agencies in the past. As we describe in Chapter Eight, in June 2017, SSA 2, who was to be the affiant for Renewal Application No. 3 and had been the affiant for the first two renewals, told us that he wanted a definitive answer to whether Page

had ever been a source for another U.S. government agency before he signed the final renewal application. This led to interactions between the OGC Attorney assigned to Crossfire Hurricane and a liaison from the other U.S. government agency. In an email from the liaison to the OGC Attorney, the liaison provided written guidance, including that it was the liaison's recollection that Page had or continued to have a relationship with the other agency, and directed the OGC Attorney to review the information that the other agency had provided to the FBI in August 2016. As noted above, that August 2016 information stated that Page did, in fact, have a prior relationship with that other agency. The next morning, immediately following a 28 minute telephone call between the OGC Attorney and the OI Attorney, the OGC Attorney forwarded to the OI Attorney the liaison's email (but not the original email from the OGC Attorney to the liaison setting out the questions he was asking). The OI Attorney responded to the OGC Attorney, "thanks I think we are good and no need to carry it any further." However, when the OGC Attorney subsequently sent the liaison's email to SSA 2, the OGC Attorney altered the liaison's email by inserting the words "not a source" into it, thus making it appear that the liaison had said that Page was "not a source" for the other agency. Relying upon this altered email, SSA 2 signed the third renewal application that again failed to disclose Page's past relationship with the other agency. Consistent with the Inspector General Act of 1978, following the OIG's discovery that the OGC Attorney had altered and sent the email to SSA 2, who thereafter relied on it to swear out the third FISA application, the OIG promptly informed the Attorney General and the FBI Director and provided them with the relevant information about the OGC Attorney's actions.

None of the inaccuracies and omissions that we identified in the renewal applications were brought to the attention of OI before the applications were filed. As a result, similar to the first application, the Department officials who reviewed one or more of the renewal applications, including Yates, Boente, and Rosenstein, did not have accurate and complete information at the time they approved them.

We do not speculate whether or how having accurate and complete information might have influenced the decisions of senior Department leaders who supported the four FISA applications, or the court, if they had known all of the relevant information. Nevertheless, it was the obligation of the FBI agents and supervisors who were aware of the information to ensure that the FISA applications were "scrupulously accurate" and that OI, the Department's decision

makers, and ultimately, the court had the opportunity to consider the additional information and the information omitted from the first application. The individuals involved did not meet this obligation.

Conclusions Concerning All Four FISA Applications

We concluded that the failures described above and in this report represent serious performance failures by the supervisory and non-supervisory agents with responsibility over the FISA applications. These failures prevented OI from fully performing its gatekeeper function and deprived the decision makers the opportunity to make fully informed decisions. Although some of the factual misstatements and omissions we found in this review were arguably more significant than others, we believe that all of them taken together resulted in FISA applications that made it appear that the information supporting probable cause was stronger than was actually the case.

We identified at least 17 significant errors or omissions in the Carter Page FISA applications, and many additional errors in the Woods Procedures. These errors and omissions resulted from case agents providing wrong or incomplete information to OI and failing to flag important issues for discussion. While we did not find documentary or testimonial evidence of intentional misconduct on the part of the case agents who assisted OI in preparing the applications, or the agents and supervisors who performed the Woods Procedures, we also did not receive satisfactory explanations for the errors or problems we identified. In most instances, the agents and supervisors told us that they either did not know or recall why the information was not shared with OI, that the failure to do so may have been an oversight, that they did not recognize at the time the relevance of the information to the FISA application, or that they did not believe the missing information to be significant. On this last point, we believe that case agents may have improperly substituted their own judgments in place of the judgment of OI, or in place of the court, to weigh the probative value of the information. Further, the failure to update OI on all significant case developments relevant to the FISA applications led us to conclude that the agents and supervisors did not give appropriate attention or treatment to the facts that cut against probable cause, or reassess the information supporting probable cause as the investigation progressed. The agents and SSAs also did not follow, or appear to even know, the requirements in the Woods Procedures to re-verify the factual assertions from previous applications

that are repeated in renewal applications and verify source characterization statements with the CHS handling agent and document the verification in the Woods File.

That so many basic and fundamental errors were made by three separate, hand-picked teams on one of the most sensitive FBI investigations that was briefed to the highest levels within the FBI, and that FBI officials expected would eventually be subjected to close scrutiny, raised significant questions regarding the FBI chain of command's management and supervision of the FISA process. FBI Headquarters established a chain of command for Crossfire Hurricane that included close supervision by senior CD managers, who then briefed FBI leadership throughout the investigation. Although we do not expect managers and supervisors to know every fact about an investigation, or senior officials to know all the details of cases about which they are briefed, in a sensitive, high-priority matter like this one, it is reasonable to expect that they will take the necessary steps to ensure that they are sufficiently familiar with the facts and circumstances supporting and potentially undermining a FISA application in order to provide effective oversight, consistent with their level of supervisory responsibility. We concluded that the information that was known to the managers, supervisors, and senior officials should have resulted in questions being raised regarding the reliability of the Steele reporting and the probable cause supporting the FISA applications, but did not.

In our view, this was a failure of not only the operational team, but also of the managers and supervisors, including senior officials, in the chain of command. For these reasons, we recommend that the FBI review the performance of the employees who had responsibility for the preparation, Woods review, or approval of the FISA applications, as well as the managers and supervisors in the chain of command of the Carter Page investigation, including senior officials, and take any action deemed appropriate. In addition, given the extensive compliance failures we identified in this review, we believe that additional OIG oversight work is required to assess the FBI's compliance with Department and FBI FISA-related policies that seek to protect the civil liberties of U.S. persons. Accordingly, we have today initiated an OIG audit that will further examine the FBI's compliance with the Woods Procedures in FISA applications that target U.S. persons in both counterintelligence and counterterrorism investigations. This audit will be informed by the findings in this review, as well as by our prior work over the past 15 years on the Department's and FBI's use of

national security and surveillance authorities, including authorities under FISA, as detailed in Chapter One.

Issues Relating to Department Attorney Bruce Ohr

In Chapter Nine, we describe the interactions Department attorney Bruce Ohr had with Christopher Steele, the FBI, Glenn Simpson (the owner of Fusion GPS), and the State Department during the Crossfire Hurricane investigation. At the time of these interactions, which took place from about July 2016 to May 2017, Ohr was an Associate Deputy Attorney General in the Office of the Deputy Attorney General (ODAG) and the Director of the Organized Crime and Drug Enforcement Task Force (OCDETF).

Ohr's Interactions with Steele, the FBI, Simpson, and the State Department

Beginning in July 2016, at about the same time that Steele was engaging with the FBI on his election reporting, Steele contacted Ohr, who he had known since at least 2007, to discuss information from Steele's election reports. At Steele's suggestion, Ohr also met in August 2016 with Simpson to discuss Steele's reports. At the time, Ohr's wife, Nellie Ohr, worked at Fusion GPS as an independent contractor. Ohr also met with Simpson in December 2016, at which time Simpson gave Ohr a thumb drive containing numerous Steele election reports that Ohr thereafter provided to the FBI.

On October 18, 2016, after speaking with Steele that morning, Ohr met with McCabe to share Steele's and Simpson's information with him. Thereafter, Ohr met with members of the Crossfire Hurricane team 13 times between November 21, 2016, and May 15, 2017, concerning his contacts with Steele and Simpson. All 13 meetings occurred after the FBI had closed Steele as a CHS and, except for the November 21 meeting, each meeting was initiated at Ohr's request. Ohr told us that he did not recall the FBI asking him to take any action regarding Steele or Simpson, but Ohr also stated that "the general instruction was to let [the FBI] know...when I got information from Steele." The Crossfire Hurricane team memorialized each of the meetings with Ohr as an "interview" using an FBI FD-302 form. Separately, in November 2016, Ohr met with senior State Department officials regarding Steele's election reporting.

Department leadership, including Ohr's supervisors in ODAG and the ODAG officials who

reviewed and approved the Carter Page FISA applications, were unaware of Ohr's meetings with FBI officials, Steele, Simpson, and the State Department until after Congress requested information from the Department regarding Ohr's activities in late November 2017.

We did not identify a specific Department policy prohibiting Ohr from meeting with Steele, Simpson, or the State Department and providing the information he learned from those meetings to the FBI. However, Ohr was clearly cognizant of his responsibility to inform his supervisors of these interactions, and acknowledged to the OIG that the possibility that he would have been told by his supervisors to stop having such contact may have factored into his decision not to tell them about it.

We concluded that Ohr committed consequential errors in judgment by (1) failing to advise his direct supervisors or the DAG that he was communicating with Steele and Simpson and then requesting meetings with the FBI's Deputy Director and Crossfire Hurricane team on matters that were outside of his areas of responsibility, and (2) making himself a witness in the investigation by meeting with Steele and providing Steele's information to the FBI. As we describe in Chapter Eight, the late discovery of Ohr's meetings with the FBI prompted NSD to notify the FISC in July 2018, over a year after the final FISA renewal order was issued, of information that Ohr had provided to the FBI but that the FBI had failed to inform NSD and OI about (and therefore was not included in the FISA applications), including that Steele was "desperate that Donald Trump not get elected and was passionate about him not being the U.S. President."

FBI Compliance with Policies

The FBI's CHS Policy Guide (CHSPG) provides guidance to agents concerning contacts with CHSs after they have been closed for cause, as was the case with Steele as of November 2016. According to the CHSPG, a handling agent must not initiate contact with or respond to contacts from a former CHS who has been closed for cause absent exceptional circumstances that are approved by an SSA. The CHSPG also requires reopening of the CHS if the relationship between the FBI and a closed CHS is expected to continue beyond the initial contact or debriefing. Reopening requires high levels of supervisory approval, including a finding that the benefits of reopening the CHS outweigh the risks.

We found that, while the Crossfire Hurricane team did not initiate direct contact with Steele after his closure, it responded to numerous contacts made by Steele through Ohr. Ohr himself was not a direct witness in the Crossfire Hurricane investigation; rather, his purpose in communicating with the FBI was to pass along information from Steele. While the FBI's CHS policy does not explicitly address indirect contact between an FBI agent and a closed CHS, we concluded that the repeated contacts with Steele should have triggered the CHS policy requiring that such contacts occur only after an SSA determines that exceptional circumstances exist. While an SSA was present for the meetings with Ohr, we found no evidence that the SSAs made considered judgments that exceptional circumstances existed for the repeated contacts. We also found that, given that there were 13 different meetings with Ohr over a period of months, the use of Ohr as a conduit between the FBI and Steele created a relationship by proxy that should have triggered, pursuant to FBI policy, a supervisory decision about whether to reopen Steele as a CHS or discontinue accepting information indirectly from him through Ohr.

Ethics Issues Raised by Nellie Ohr's Former Employment with Fusion GPS

Fusion GPS employed Nellie Ohr as an independent contractor from October 2015 to September 2016. On his annual financial disclosure forms covering calendar years 2015 and 2016, Ohr listed Nellie Ohr as an "independent contractor" and reported her income from that work on the form. We determined that financial disclosure rules, 5 C.F.R. Part 2634, did not require Ohr to list on the form the specific organizations, such as Fusion GPS, that paid Nellie Ohr as an independent contractor during the reporting period.

In addition, for reasons we explain in Chapter Eleven, we concluded that the federal ethics rules did not require Ohr to obtain Department ethics counsel approval before engaging with the FBI in connection with the Crossfire Hurricane matter because of Nellie Ohr's prior work for Fusion GPS. However, we found that, given the factual circumstances that existed, and the appearance that they created, Ohr displayed a lapse in judgment by not availing himself of the process described in the ethics rules to consult with the Department ethics official about his involvement in the investigation.

Meetings Involving Ohr, CRM officials, and the FBI Regarding the MLARS Investigation

Ohr's supervisors in ODAG also were unaware that Ohr, shortly after the U.S. elections in November 2016, and again in early 2017, participated in discussions about a money laundering investigation of Manafort that was then being led by prosecutors from the Money Laundering and Asset Recovery Section (MLARS), which is located in the Criminal Division (CRM) at the Department's headquarters.

As described in more detail in Chapter Nine, in November 2016, Ohr told CRM Deputy Assistant Attorney General Bruce Swartz and Counsel to the CRM Assistant Attorney General Zainab Ahmad about information he was getting from Steele and Simpson about Manafort. Between November 16, 2016 and December 15, 2016, Ohr participated in several meetings that were attended, at various times, by some or all of the following individuals: Swartz, Ahmad, Andrew Weissmann (then Section Chief of CRM's Fraud Section), Strzok, and Lisa Page. The meetings involving Ohr, Swartz, Ahmad, and Weissmann focused on their shared concern that MLARS was not moving quickly enough on the Manafort criminal investigation and whether there were steps they could take to move the investigation forward. The meetings with Strzok and Page focused primarily on whether the FBI could assess the case's relevance, if any, to the FBI's Russian interference investigation. MLARS was not represented at any of these meetings or told about them, and none of attendees had supervisory responsibility over the MLARS investigation.

There were no meetings about the Manafort case involving Ohr, Swartz, Ahmad, and Weissmann from December 16, 2016 to January 30, 2017. On January 31, 2017, one day after Yates was removed as DAG, Ahmad, by then an Acting CRM Deputy Assistant Attorney General, after consulting with Swartz and Weissmann, sent an email to Lisa Page, copying Weissmann, Swartz, and Ohr, requesting a meeting the next day to discuss "a few Criminal Division related developments." The next day, February 1, Swartz, Ohr, Ahmad, and Weissmann met with Strzok, Lisa Page, and an FBI Acting Section Chief. None of the attendees at the meeting could explain to us what the "Criminal Division related developments" were, and we did not find any. Meeting notes reflect, among other things, that the group discussed the Manafort criminal investigation and efforts that the Department could undertake to investigate attempts by Russia to influence the 2016 elections. MLARS was not represented at, or told about, the meeting.

We are not aware of information indicating that any of the discussions involving Ohr, Swartz,

Weissmann, Ahmad, Strzok, and Lisa Page resulted in any actions taken or not taken in the MLARS investigation, and ultimately the investigation remained with MLARS until it was transferred to the Office of the Special Counsel in May 2017. We also did not identify any Department policies prohibiting internal discussions about a pending investigation among officials not assigned to the matter, or between those officials and senior officials from the FBI. However, as described in Chapter Nine, we were told that there was a decision not to inform the leadership of CRM, both before and after the change in presidential administrations, of these discussions in order to insulate the MLARS investigation from becoming "politicized." We concluded that this decision, made in the absence of concerns of potential wrongdoing or misconduct, and for the purpose of avoiding the appearance that an investigation is "politicized," fundamentally misconstrued who is ultimately responsible and accountable for the Department's work. We agree with the concerns expressed to us by then DAG Yates and then CRM Assistant Attorney General Leslie Caldwell. Department leaders cannot fulfill their management responsibilities, and be held accountable for the Department's actions, if subordinates intentionally withhold information from them in such circumstances.

The Use of Confidential Sources (Other Than Steele) and Undercover Employees

As discussed in Chapter Ten, we determined that, during the 2016 presidential campaign, the Crossfire Hurricane team tasked several CHSs, which resulted in multiple interactions with Carter Page and George Papadopoulos, both before and after they were affiliated with the Trump campaign, and one with a high-level Trump campaign official who was not a subject of the investigation. All of these CHS interactions were consensually monitored and recorded by the FBI. As noted above, under Department and FBI policy, the use of a CHS to conduct consensual monitoring is a matter of investigative judgment that, absent certain circumstances, can be authorized by a first-line supervisor (a supervisory special agent). We determined that the CHS operations conducted during Crossfire Hurricane received the necessary FBI approvals, and that AD Priestap knew about, and approved of, all of the Crossfire Hurricane CHS operations, even in circumstances where a first-level supervisory special agent could have approved the operations. We found no evidence that the FBI used CHSs or UCEs to interact with members of the Trump campaign prior to the opening of the Crossfire Hurricane investigation. After the opening of the investigation, we

found no evidence that the FBI placed any CHSs or UCEs within the Trump campaign or tasked any CHSs or UCEs to report on the Trump campaign. Finally, we also found no documentary or testimonial evidence that political bias or improper motivations influenced the FBI's decision to use CHSs or UCEs to interact with Trump campaign officials in the Crossfire Hurricane investigation.

Although the Crossfire Hurricane team's use of CHSs and UCEs complied with applicable policies, we are concerned that, under these policies, it was sufficient for a first-level FBI supervisor to authorize the domestic CHS operations that were undertaken in Crossfire Hurricane, and that there was no applicable Department or FBI policy requiring the FBI to notify Department officials of the investigative team's decision to task CHSs to consensually monitor conversations with members of a presidential campaign. We found no evidence that the FBI consulted with any Department officials before conducting these CHS operations. We believe that current Department and FBI policies are not sufficient to ensure appropriate oversight and accountability when such operations potentially implicate sensitive, constitutionally protected activity, and that they should require, at minimum, Department consultation. As noted above, we include a recommendation in this report to address this issue.

Consistent with current Department and FBI policy, we learned that decisions about the use of CHSs and UCEs were made by the case agents and the supervisory special agents assigned to Crossfire Hurricane. These agents told the OIG that they focused the CHS operations on the FFG information and the four investigative subjects, and that they viewed CHS operations as one of the best methods available to quickly obtain information about the predicating allegations, while preventing information about the nature and existence of the investigation from becoming public, and potentially impacting the presidential election.

During the meeting between a CHS and the high-level Trump campaign official who was not a subject of the investigation, the CHS asked about the role of three Crossfire Hurricane subjects—Page, Papadopoulos, and Manafort—in the Trump campaign. The CHS also asked about allegations in public reports concerning Russian interference in the 2016 elections, the campaign's response to ideas featured in Page's Moscow speech, and the possibility of an "October Surprise." In response, the campaign official made no comments of note about those topics. The CHS and the high-level campaign official also discussed ▪▪▪▪▪▪▪▪

▪▪▪▪▪▪▪▪ We found that the Crossfire Hurricane team made no use of any information collected from the high-level Trump campaign official, because the team determined that none of the information gathered was "germane" to the allegations under investigation. However, we were concerned that the Crossfire Hurricane team did not recall having in place a plan, prior to the operation involving the high-level campaign official, to address the possible collection of politically sensitive information.

As discussed in Chapter Ten, through the use of CHSs, the investigative team obtained statements from Carter Page and Papadopoulos that raised questions about the validity of allegations under investigation. For example, when questioned in August 2016 about other individuals who were subjects in the investigation, Page told a CHS that he had "literally never met" or "said one word to" Manafort and that Manafort had not responded to any of Page's emails. As another example, Papadopoulos denied to a CHS that anyone associated with the Trump campaign was collaborating with Russia or with outside groups like WikiLeaks in the release of emails. Papadopoulos stated that the "campaign, of course, [does not] advocate for this type of activity because at the end of the day it's...illegal" and that "our campaign is not...engag[ing] or reaching out to WikiLeaks or to the whoever it is to tell them please work with us, collaborate because we don't, no one does that...." Papadopoulos also said that "as far as I understand...no one's collaborating, there's been no collusion and it's going to remain that way." In another interaction, Papadopoulos told a CHS that he knew "for a fact" that no one from the Trump campaign had anything to do with releasing emails from the DNC, as a result of Papadopoulos's involvement in the Trump campaign. Despite the relevance of this material, as described in Chapters Five and Seven, none of Papadopoulos's statements were provided by the Crossfire Hurricane team to the OI Attorney and Page's statements were not provided to the OI attorney until June 2017, approximately ten months after the initial Carter Page FISA application was granted by the FISC.

Through our review, we also determined that there were other CHSs tasked by the FBI to attempt to contact Papadopoulos, but that those attempted contacts did not lead to any operational activity. We also identified several individuals who had either a connection to candidate Trump or a role in the Trump

campaign, and were also FBI CHSs, but who were not tasked as part of the Crossfire Hurricane investigation. One such CHS did provide the Crossfire Hurricane team with general information about Crossfire Hurricane subjects Page and Manafort, but we found that this CHS had no further involvement in the investigation.

We identified another CHS that the Crossfire Hurricane team first learned about in 2017, after the CHS voluntarily provided his/her handling agent with an ██████████████████████████████████ —and the handling agent forwarded the material, through his supervisor and FBI Headquarters, to the Crossfire Hurricane team. ████████████████████████████████ The handling agent told us that, when he subsequently informed the Crossfire Hurricane team that the CHS had access to ████████████ ████████████, a Crossfire Hurricane team intelligence analyst asked the handling agent to collect ████████ from the CHS, which the handling agent did. We found that the Crossfire Hurricane team determined that there was not "anything significant" in this ████ collection, and did not seek to task the CHS. While we found that no action was taken by the Crossfire Hurricane team in response to receiving ████████, we nevertheless were concerned to learn that the handling agent for the CHS placed ████████████ ████████████ into the FBI's files, and we promptly notified the FBI upon learning that they were still being maintained in the FBI's files. We further concluded that, because the CHS's handling agent did not understand the CHS's political involvement, no assessment was performed by the source's handling agent or his supervisors (none of whom were members of the Crossfire Hurricane team) to determine whether the CHS required re-designation as a "sensitive source" or should have been closed during the pendency of the campaign.

While we concluded that the investigative activities undertaken by the Crossfire Hurricane team involving CHSs and UCEs complied with applicable Department and FBI policies, we believe that in certain circumstances Department and FBI policies do not provide sufficient oversight and accountability for investigative activities that have the potential to gather sensitive information involving protected First Amendment activity, and therefore include recommendations to address these issues.

Finally, as we also describe in Chapter Ten, we learned during the course of our review that in August 2016, the supervisor of the Crossfire Hurricane investigation, SSA 1, participated on behalf of the FBI in a strategic intelligence briefing given by Office of the Director of National Intelligence (ODNI) to candidate Trump and his national security advisors, including Michael Flynn, and in a separate strategic intelligence briefing given to candidate Clinton and her national security advisors. The stated purpose of the FBI portion of the briefing was to provide the recipients "a baseline on the presence and threat posed by foreign intelligence services to the National Security of the U.S." However, we found that SSA 1 was selected to provide the FBI briefings, in part, because Flynn, who was a subject in the ongoing Crossfire Hurricane investigation, would be attending the Trump campaign briefing.

Following his participation in the briefing of candidate Trump, Flynn, and another Trump advisor, SSA 1 drafted an EC documenting his participation in the briefing, and added the EC to the Crossfire Hurricane investigative file. We were told that the decision to select SSA 1 to participate in the ODNI briefing was reached by consensus among a group of senior FBI officials, including McCabe and Baker. We noted that no one at the Department or ODNI was informed that the FBI was using the ODNI briefing of a presidential candidate for investigative purposes, and found no applicable FBI or Department policies addressing this issue. We concluded that the FBI's use of this briefing for investigative reasons could potentially interfere with the expectation of trust and good faith among participants in strategic intelligence briefings, thereby frustrating their purpose. We therefore include a recommendation to address this issue.

Recommendations

Our report makes nine recommendations to the FBI and the Department to assist them in addressing the issues that we identified in this review:

- The Department and the FBI should ensure that adequate procedures are in place for OI to obtain all relevant and accurate information needed to prepare FISA applications and renewal applications, including CHS information. In Chapter Twelve, we identify a few specific steps to assist in this effort.

- The Department and FBI should evaluate which types of SIMs require advance notification to a senior Department official, such as the DAG, in addition to the notifications currently required for SIMs, especially for case openings that implicate core First Amendment activity and raise policy considerations or heighten enterprise risk, and establish implementing policies and guidance, as necessary.

- The FBI should develop protocols and guidelines for staffing and administrating any future sensitive investigative matters from FBI Headquarters.

- The FBI should address the problems with the administration and assessment of CHSs identified in this report, including, at a minimum, revising the FBI's standard CHS admonishments, improving the documentation of CHS information, revising FBI policy to address the acceptance of information from a closed CHS indirectly through a third party, and taking other steps we identify in Chapter Twelve.

- The Department and FBI should clarify the terms (1) "sensitive monitoring circumstance" in the AG Guidelines and the DIOG to determine whether to expand its scope to include consensual monitoring of a domestic political candidate or an individual prominent within a domestic political organization, or a subset of these persons, so that consensual monitoring of such individuals would require consultation with or advance notification to a senior Department official, such as the DAG, and (2) "prominent in a domestic political organization" so that agents understand which campaign officials fall within that definition as it relates to "sensitive investigative matters," "sensitive UDP," the designation of "sensitive sources," and "sensitive monitoring circumstance."

- The FBI should ensure that appropriate training on DIOG § 4 is provided to emphasize the constitutional implications of certain monitoring situations and to ensure that agents account for these concerns, both in the tasking of CHSs and in the way they document interactions with and tasking of CHSs.

- The FBI should establish a policy regarding the use of defensive and transition briefings for investigative purposes, including the factors to be considered and approval by senior leaders at the FBI with notice to a senior Department official, such as the DAG.

- The Department's Office of Professional Responsibility should review our findings related to the conduct of Department attorney Bruce Ohr for any action it deems appropriate. Ohr's current supervisors in CRM should also review our findings related to Ohr's performance for any action they deem appropriate.

- The FBI should review the performance of all employees who had responsibility for the preparation, Woods review, or approval of the FISA applications, as well as the managers, supervisors, and senior officials in the chain of command of the Carter Page investigation for any action it deems appropriate.

TABLE OF CONTENTS

[PAGE INTENTIONALLY LEFT BLANK]

[PAGE INTENTIONALLY LEFT BLANK]

CHAPTER ONE
INTRODUCTION

I. Background and Overview

The Department of Justice (Department) Office of the Inspector General (OIG) undertook this review to examine certain actions by the Federal Bureau of Investigation (FBI) and the Department during an FBI investigation into whether individuals associated with the Donald J. Trump for President Campaign were coordinating, wittingly or unwittingly, with the Russian government. The FBI's counterintelligence investigation, known as "Crossfire Hurricane," was opened on July 31, 2016, weeks after the Republican National Convention (RNC) formally nominated Trump as its candidate for President, and several months before the November 8, 2016 elections, through which Trump was elected President of the United States. On May 17, 2017, the Crossfire Hurricane investigation was transferred from the FBI to the Office of Special Counsel upon the appointment of Special Counsel Robert S. Mueller III to investigate Russian interference with the 2016 presidential election and related matters.

The FBI opened Crossfire Hurricane in July 2016 following the receipt of certain information from a Friendly Foreign Government (FFG). According to the information provided by the FFG, in May 2016, a Trump campaign foreign policy advisor, George Papadopoulos, "suggested" to an FFG official that the Trump campaign had received "some kind of suggestion" from Russia that it could assist with the anonymous release of information that would be damaging to Hillary Clinton (Trump's opponent in the presidential election) and President Barack Obama. At the time the FBI received the FFG information, the U.S. Intelligence Community (USIC), which includes the FBI, was aware of Russian efforts to interfere with the 2016 U.S. elections, including efforts to infiltrate servers and steal emails belonging to the Democratic National Committee (DNC) and the Democratic Congressional Campaign Committee. The FFG shared this information with the State Department on July 26, 2016, after the internet site WikiLeaks began releasing emails hacked from computers belonging to the DNC and Clinton's campaign manager. The State Department advised the FBI of the information the next day.

Crossfire Hurricane was opened several weeks after the FBI's July 5, 2016 conclusion of its "Midyear Exam" investigation into Clinton's handling of government emails during her tenure as Secretary of State.[1] Some of the same FBI officials, supervisors, and attorneys responsible for the Midyear investigation were assigned to the newly opened Crossfire Hurricane investigation, but there was almost no

---

[1] *See* U.S. Department of Justice (DOJ) Office of the Inspector General (OIG), *A Review of Various Actions by the Federal Bureau of Investigation and Department of Justice in Advance of the 2016 Election*, Oversight and Review Division Report 18-04 (June 2018), https://www.justice.gov/file/1071991/download (accessed November 12, 2019), 2 (hereinafter *Review of Various Actions in Advance of the 2016 Election*).

overlap between the FBI agents and analysts assigned to the Midyear and Crossfire Hurricane investigations.

The FBI opened Crossfire Hurricane as an umbrella counterintelligence investigation, without identifying any specific subjects or targets. FBI officials told us that they did not immediately identify subjects or targets because it was unclear from the FFG information who within the Trump campaign may have received the reported offer of assistance and might be coordinating, wittingly or unwittingly, with the Russian government. By August 10, 2016, the FBI had assembled an investigative team of special agents, analysts, and supervisory special agents (the Crossfire Hurricane team) and conducted an initial analysis of links between Trump campaign members and Russia. Based upon this analysis, the FBI opened individual cases under the Crossfire Hurricane umbrella on three U.S. persons—Papadopoulos, Carter Page, and Paul Manafort—all of whom were affiliated with the Trump campaign at the time the cases were opened.[2] On August 16, 2016, the FBI opened a fourth individual case under Crossfire Hurricane on Michael Flynn, who was serving at the time as the Trump campaign's National Security Advisor.[3]

Two of the four Crossfire Hurricane subjects were already the subjects of other existing federal investigations. Carter Page was the subject of an ongoing counterintelligence investigation opened by the FBI's New York Field Office (NYFO) on April 4, 2016, relating to his contacts with suspected Russian intelligence officers. Manafort was the subject of an ongoing criminal investigation, supervised by the Money Laundering and Asset Recovery Section (MLARS) in the Department's Criminal Division, concerning millions of dollars Manafort allegedly received from the government of Ukraine.[4]

---

[2] According to public reporting, Carter Page ceased being associated with the Trump campaign as of September 26, 2016, and Manafort resigned as of August 19, 2016. As noted in Chapter Ten, accounts vary as to when Papadopoulos left the Trump campaign; according to The Special Counsel's Report on the Investigation into Russian Interference with the 2016 Presidential Election, Papadopoulos was dismissed from the campaign in early October 2016. See Special Counsel Robert S. Mueller III, Report on the Investigation Into Russian Interference in the 2016 Presidential Election, Vol. I (March 2019), 93 (hereinafter The Special Counsel's Report).

[3] Flynn remained on the Trump campaign through the election and was subsequently appointed as National Security Advisor. Flynn resigned that position on February 13, 2017. Papadopoulos, Manafort, and Flynn were later indicted in federal district court for crimes prosecuted by the Special Counsel. On October 5, 2017, and December 1, 2017, respectively, Papadopoulos and Flynn pleaded guilty to making material false statements and material omissions during interviews with the FBI. On August 21, 2018, Manafort was convicted after trial on tax and bank fraud charges, and on September 14, 2018, pleaded guilty to charges of conspiracy against the United States and conspiracy to obstruct justice.

The indictments and sentencing documents are publicly available and therefore we refer to these individuals by name in this report. We also refer to Carter Page by name in this report because the Department publicly released, in response to Freedom of Information Act (FOIA) requests, redacted versions of the Foreign Intelligence Surveillance Act (FISA) applications and orders that name him.

[4] Prior to January 2017, MLARS was named the Asset Forfeiture and Money Laundering Section.

Some of the early investigative steps taken by the Crossfire Hurricane team immediately after opening the investigation were to develop profiles on each subject; send names of, among others, individuals associated with the Trump campaign to other U.S. government intelligence agencies for any further information; and review FBI files for potential FBI Confidential Human Sources (CHSs) who might be able to assist the investigation. FBI witnesses we interviewed told us they believed that using CHSs in covert operations would be an efficient way to develop a better understanding of the information received from the FFG. We determined that the Crossfire Hurricane team tasked several CHSs and Undercover Employees (UCEs) during the 2016 presidential campaign, which resulted in interactions with Carter Page, Papadopoulos, and a high-level Trump campaign official who was not a subject of the investigation. All of these interactions were consensually monitored and recorded by the FBI. The interactions between CHSs and Page and Papadopoulos occurred both during the time Page and Papadopoulos were advisors to the Trump campaign, and after Page and Papadopoulos were no longer affiliated with the Trump campaign. We also learned that in August 2016, a supervisor of the Crossfire Hurricane investigation participated on behalf of the FBI in a strategic intelligence briefing given by the Office of the Director of National Intelligence (ODNI) to candidate Trump and his national security advisors, including investigative subject Flynn, and also participated in a separate strategic intelligence briefing given to candidate Clinton and her national security advisors. The FBI viewed the briefing of candidate Trump and his advisors as a possible opportunity to collect information potentially relevant to the Crossfire Hurricane and Flynn investigations. The supervisor memorialized the results of the briefing in an official FBI document, including instances where he was engaged by Trump and Flynn, as well as anything he considered related to the FBI or pertinent to the Crossfire Hurricane investigation. The supervisor did not memorialize the results of the briefing of candidate Clinton and her advisors.

An early investigative step considered but not initially taken by the Crossfire Hurricane team was to seek court orders under the Foreign Intelligence Surveillance Act (FISA) authorizing surveillance of Page and Papadopoulos. The U.S. Foreign Intelligence Surveillance Court (FISC) may approve FISA surveillance of an American citizen for a period of up to 90 days, subject to renewal, if the government's FISA application establishes probable cause to believe that the targeted individual is an agent of a foreign power by knowingly engaging in at least one of the five activities enumerated in the FISA statute.[5] The Crossfire Hurricane team initially considered seeking FISA surveillance of Papadopoulos as a result of his statement to the FFG and of Page based upon information the FBI had collected about his prior and more recent contacts with known and suspected Russian intelligence officers, as well as Page's financial, political, and business ties to the

---

[5] See 50 U.S.C. §§ 1801(b)(2)(A) through (E). In the case of the Carter Page FISA applications, the government relied upon the definition of an agent of a foreign power in Section 1801(b)(2)(E), which covers, among other things, any person who knowingly aids or abets any other person who knowingly engages in clandestine intelligence activities (other than intelligence gathering activities) that involve or are about to involve a violation of the criminal statutes of the United States, pursuant to the direction of an intelligence service or network of a foreign power, or knowingly conspires with other persons in such activities.

Russian government. Officials determined there was an insufficient basis to proceed with a FISA application concerning Papadopoulos, and the Crossfire Hurricane team never submitted a FISA application for Papadopoulos. With regard to Page, on August 15, 2016, the Crossfire Hurricane team requested assistance from the FBI's Office of the General Counsel (OGC) to prepare a FISA application for submission to the FISC. However, after consultation between FBI OGC and attorneys in the Office of Intelligence (OI) in the Department's National Security Division (NSD), which is responsible for preparing FISA applications and appearing before the FISC, the Crossfire Hurricane team was told in late August 2016 that more information was needed to establish probable cause for a FISA on Page.

A few weeks later, on September 19, 2016, the Crossfire Hurricane team received a set of six reports prepared by Christopher Steele concerning Russian interference in the 2016 U.S. election and alleged connections between this Russian effort and individuals associated with the Trump campaign.[6] Steele is a former intelligence officer ███████████████████████████████ who, following his retirement, opened a consulting firm and furnished information to the FBI beginning in 2010, primarily on matters concerning organized crime and corruption in Russia and Eastern Europe. In 2013, the FBI prepared paperwork to enable it to open Steele as an FBI CHS. In providing the first two election reports to his FBI handling agent in July 2016, Steele told the handling agent that he had been hired by an investigative firm, Fusion GPS, to collect information on the relationship between candidate Trump's businesses and Russia. Steele further informed the FBI handling agent that Fusion GPS had been retained by a law firm to conduct this research. According to the handling agent, it was obvious to him that the request for the research was politically motivated.

Two of the six Steele reports received by the Crossfire Hurricane team on September 19 referenced Carter Page by name. One stated that Page had held secret meetings with two high level Russian officials during Page's July 2016 trip to Moscow. This report also indicated that one of the alleged meetings included a discussion about the Kremlin potentially releasing compromising information about Democratic candidate Hillary Clinton to Trump's campaign team. Another report from Steele described "a well-developed conspiracy of co-operation" between the Russian government and Trump's campaign to defeat Clinton, using Carter Page and others as intermediaries.[7] On September 21, 2016, 2 days after the team received these reports, FBI OGC advised OI that the FBI believed it was ready to

---

[6] As described in this report, information from Christopher Steele's reports—sometimes collectively referred to as the "Steele dossier"—that pertained to Carter Page was relied upon in the Carter Page FISA applications. In those applications, Steele was referred to as "Source #1." We refer to Steele by name in this report because the Department and the FBI have publicly revealed Steele's identity as Source #1 in connection with FOIA litigation.

[7] A third report from Steele, which did not reference Carter Page, stated that Russian intelligence services had used concealed cameras to film Trump's alleged sexual activities with prostitutes at a Moscow hotel, and claimed that the Russians could blackmail Trump by threatening to release this compromising material. These allegations, which have come to be known publicly as the "salacious and unverified" portion of the reporting, were not included in the original Carter Page FISA application or any of the renewal applications.

submit a request for FISA authority on Carter Page, and OI and the FBI began drafting the first FISA application. Among the FBI's purposes in seeking a FISA order for Page was to obtain information about Page's trip to Russia in July 2016, when Page was still a member of the Trump campaign.

On September 23, 2016, *Yahoo News* published an article stating that U.S. intelligence officials had received reports regarding Carter Page's private meetings in Moscow with senior Russian officials. The article cited a "well-placed Western intelligence source," and contained details about Carter Page's activities in Russia that closely paralleled the information contained in the reporting that Steele had provided to the FBI. We found no evidence that anyone from the FBI asked Steele in September 2016 or at any other time, if he had spoken with the *Yahoo News* reporter. Steele had, in fact, spoken with the reporter prior to the article's publication, which the FBI would learn from public records after the submission of the first FISA application.

On October ▮▮, 2016, NSD submitted the Carter Page FISA application to the FISC, asserting that there was probable cause to believe that Page was an agent of the Russian government. The application relied on, among other things:

- The information provided by the FFG about its interaction with Papadopoulos;

- Information from the FBI's previously opened counterintelligence investigation relating to Page arising from his contacts with Russian intelligence officers;

- Information from Steele's reports that pertained specifically to Carter Page; and

- Information from a meeting between Page and an FBI CHS that was consensually monitored by Crossfire Hurricane investigators.

The application also stated in a footnote that the FBI "speculates that the [person who hired Steele] was likely looking for information that could be used to discredit [candidate Trump's] campaign." Further, the application advised the court of information reported in the September 23, 2016 *Yahoo News* article and stated that (a) the FBI "does not believe that Source #1 directly provided...to the press" the information in the article, (b) according to the article and other news articles, individuals affiliated with the Trump campaign made statements distancing the campaign from Carter Page, and (c) Page himself denied the accusations in the *Yahoo News* article and reiterated that denial in a September 25, 2016 letter to the FBI Director and in a September 26, 2016 media interview.

However, the application, as well as the renewal applications, did not include significant relevant information, and contained inaccurate and incomplete information, that was known to the Crossfire Hurricane team at the time but that it did not share with NSD attorneys. For example, when asked by an NSD attorney who was involved in helping to draft the first FISA application whether Page had provided information to another U.S. government agency or was a source for that other agency, a Crossfire Hurricane agent incorrectly told the NSD attorney that

Page's contact with the other U.S. government agency was "dated" and "outside scope." The Crossfire Hurricane agent made this statement despite the fact that the Crossfire Hurricane team had been told by the other agency in a written memorandum that Page had been approved as an operational contact for the other agency from 2008 to 2013 and that Page had provided information to the other agency that was relevant to the FISA application.[8] The Crossfire Hurricane team also failed to inform NSD attorneys about information obtained by the FBI during CHS operations and interviews that was inconsistent with the allegations contained in the Steele reporting that was being relied upon in the FISA application.

The FISA application was reviewed by numerous FBI agents, FBI attorneys, and NSD attorneys, and, as required by law, was ultimately certified by then FBI Director James Comey and approved by then Deputy Attorney General Sally Yates. The FISC granted the first FISA application on October ■, 2016, authorizing the use of FISA authority on Carter Page.

On October 31, 2016, *Mother Jones* magazine published an online news article titled "A Veteran Spy has Given the FBI Information Alleging a Russian Operation to Cultivate Donald Trump." The October 31 article quoted a "well-placed Western intelligence source," and described how that individual had provided reports to the FBI about connections between Trump and the Russian government. According to the article, the source was continuing to provide information to the FBI, and was quoted as saying "it's quite clear there was or is a pretty substantial inquiry going on." On November 1, 2016, Steele's FBI handling agent questioned Steele, who admitted speaking to the reporter who wrote the October 31 article. The handling agent advised Steele at that time that his relationship with the FBI would likely be terminated for disclosing his relationship with the FBI to the press, and the FBI officially closed Steele for cause on November 17, 2016. Steele was never paid by the FBI for any of the reports or information that he provided concerning Carter Page or connections between the Russian government and the Trump campaign.

After Steele was closed as an FBI CHS, Crossfire Hurricane agents continued to receive information from him through a conduit, Department attorney Bruce Ohr, who at the time was an Associate Deputy Attorney General in the Office of the Deputy Attorney General (ODAG). Ohr had known Steele, through work, since at least 2007 and, starting in July 2016, Steele had contacted Ohr on multiple occasions to discuss information from Steele's reports. At Steele's suggestion, Ohr also met in August and December 2016 with Glenn Simpson, the owner of Fusion GPS, which Ohr's wife had worked for as an independent contractor through September 2016. During those meetings, Simpson provided Ohr with several of

---

[8] According to the other U.S. government agency, "operational contact," as that term is used in the memorandum about Page, provides "Contact Approval," which allows the other agency to contact and discuss sensitive information with a U.S. person and to collect information from that person via "passive debriefing," or debriefing a person of information that is within the knowledge of an individual and has been acquired through the normal course of that individual's activities. According to the U.S. government agency, a "Contact Approval" does not allow for operational use of a U.S. person or tasking of that person.

Steele's election reports. Ohr also communicated with a senior State Department official concerning, among other matters, the Steele reporting. Between the date of Steele's closing as an FBI CHS in November 2016 and May 15, 2017, Ohr met with the FBI on 13 occasions. In his meetings with the FBI, Ohr provided the FBI with information that Steele had provided to him, the Steele election reports that Ohr had received from Simpson, as well as a thumb drive containing information Ohr had received from his wife that contained open source research she had compiled while working for Fusion GPS. Department leaders, including Ohr's supervisors within ODAG, were unaware of Ohr's meetings with Steele, Simpson, the FBI, or the State Department, or of Ohr's wife's connection to Fusion GPS, until late November 2017, when Congress requested information from the Department regarding Ohr's activities.

As the FBI's Crossfire Hurricane investigation proceeded, the Department submitted three renewal applications to the FISC seeking authority to continue FISA surveillance of Carter Page. Comey and Yates approved the first renewal application, Comey and then Acting Attorney General Dana Boente approved the second renewal, and then Acting FBI Director Andrew McCabe and then Deputy Attorney General (DAG) Rod Rosenstein approved the third renewal. In total, at the request of the FBI, the Department filed four FISA applications, each of which was granted by the FISC: the first FISA application on October ■, 2016, and three renewal applications on January ■, April ■, and June ■, 2017. A different FISC judge considered each application before issuing the requested orders, which collectively resulted in approximately 11 months of FISA coverage of Carter Page from October ■, 2016, until September ■, 2017.

Each of the FISA orders issued by the FISC authorized the U.S. government to conduct electronic surveillance ████████████████ targeting Carter Page for a period of up to 90 days. The authority permitted the government to, among other things, ██ by Carter Page. This included ████████████████████████████ during the 90-day period. The authority also permitted the government to ██ . The orders expressly limited the electronic surveillance ████████ to only ████████████████ specifically identified in the order and in the manner specified by the order. Further, the orders required the government to adhere to standard procedures designed to minimize the government's acquisition and retention of non-public information about a U.S. person that did not constitute foreign intelligence information. At the request of the government, the orders also included special procedures restricting access to acquired information to only those individuals assigned to the Crossfire Hurricane investigation (and their supervisors), which the Department interpreted to include Department attorneys and officials assisting in and overseeing the investigation. The orders also required higher approval than would normally be required before disseminating the information outside the FBI.

In April and May 2017, following news reports that the FBI had obtained a FISA for Carter Page, Page gave interviews to news outlets denying that he had collected intelligence for the Russian government and asserting instead that he had previously assisted U.S. government agencies. Shortly before the FBI filed the final renewal application with the FISC in mid-June 2017, and in response to concerns expressed by the investigative team and NSD about Page's claim, an FBI OGC Attorney emailed the U.S. government agency that had provided information to the FBI in August 2016, referenced above, about its prior interactions with Carter Page to inquire about Page's past status. The other U.S. government agency's liaison to the Crossfire Hurricane team responded by email to the FBI OGC attorney by directing the attorney to a memoranda previously sent to the FBI by the other U.S. government agency informing the FBI that Page had been approved as an operational contact for the other agency from 2008 to 2013. The email also stated, using the other agency's terminology, that it was the other agency liaison's recollection that Page had prior interactions with that other agency. However, when asked by one of the supervisory special agents (SSA) on the Crossfire Hurricane team (who was going to be the affiant on the final FISA renewal application) about Page's prior interactions with that other agency, the OGC Attorney advised the SSA that Page was "never a source" for the other U.S. government agency. In addition, the OGC Attorney altered the email that the other U.S. government agency had sent to the OGC Attorney so that the email inaccurately stated that Page was "not a source" for the other agency; the OGC Attorney then forwarded the altered email to the SSA. Shortly thereafter, on June ▇, 2017, the SSA served as the affiant on the final renewal application, which was again silent about Page's prior relationship with the other U.S. government agency.

On July 12, 2018, while the OIG's review was ongoing, NSD submitted a letter to the FISC advising the court of certain factual omissions in the Carter Page FISA applications that had come to NSD's attention after the final renewal application was filed on June ▇, 2017.[9] The Department's letter stated that, despite the omissions, it was the Department's view that the applications contained sufficient information to support the FISC's earlier probable cause findings as to Page.

On March 28, 2018, the OIG publicly announced that, in response to requests from the Attorney General and Members of Congress, it had initiated this review to examine:

- Whether the Department and the FBI complied with legal requirements and applicable policies and procedures in FISA applications filed with the FISC relating to surveillance of Carter Page;

- What information was known to the Department and FBI at the time the applications were filed about Christopher Steele; and

---

[9] At the time of this letter, NSD was unaware of the numerous factual assertions made in the FISA applications that were inaccurate, incomplete, or unsupported by appropriate documentation that the OIG identified during the course of our review and that we detail in this report.

- How the Department's and FBI's relationships and communications with Steele related to the FISA applications.[10]

In addition, during the OIG's *Review of Various Actions in Advance of the 2016 Election*, we discovered text messages and instant messages between some FBI employees, using FBI mobile devices and computers, which expressed statements of hostility toward then candidate Trump and expressed statements of support for then candidate Clinton.[11] Because some of the FBI employees responsible for those communications, including Section Chief Peter Strzok and FBI Attorney Lisa Page, also had involvement in the Crossfire Hurricane investigation, we examined whether their communications evidencing a potential bias affected investigative decisions made in Crossfire Hurricane.[12] We also examined, where available, the government emails, text messages, and instant messages of all Department and FBI employees who played a substantive role in Crossfire Hurricane to determine if there were any additional communications evidencing a potential bias and, if so, whether the views expressed influenced any investigative decisions.

The March 28, 2018 OIG announcement also stated that "if circumstances warrant, the OIG will consider including other issues that may arise during the course of the review." In May 2018, in response to Rosenstein's request, the OIG added to the scope of this review to determine whether the FBI infiltrated or surveilled the Trump campaign. Accordingly, we examined the FBI's use of CHSs in the Crossfire Hurricane investigation, up through November 8, 2016 (the date of the 2016 U.S. elections) to evaluate whether the FBI had placed any CHSs within the Trump campaign or tasked any CHSs to report on the Trump campaign, and, if so, whether any such use of CHSs was in violation of applicable Department and FBI policies or was politically motivated. We subsequently learned of and included in our review certain other CHS activities that took place after the 2016 election.

II.   Prior OIG Reports on FISA and Related Issues

In addition to the requests described above from the Attorney General, the Deputy Attorney General, and Members of Congress, our initiation of this review was informed by our prior work over the past 15 years on the Department's and FBI's use of national security and surveillance authorities, including authorities under FISA. This prior OIG work considered the challenges faced by the Department and the FBI as they utilized national security authorities while also striving to safeguard civil liberties and privacy. In every year since 2006, the OIG's

---

[10] As part of our review of this issue, the OIG examined the interactions between Ohr and the Crossfire Hurricane team as well as Ohr's communications with Steele and Simpson, both before and after the FBI closed Steele as a CHS. Our review also examined Ohr's interactions with Department attorneys regarding the Manafort criminal case.

[11] DOJ OIG, *Review of Various Actions in Advance of the 2016 Election*, 3.

[12] FBI Attorney Lisa Page is not related to Carter Page, the individual affiliated with the Trump campaign who was the subject of the FISA surveillance in Crossfire Hurricane.

annual report on "*Top Management and Performance Challenges Facing the Department of Justice* has highlighted the difficulty faced by the Department and the FBI in maintaining a balance between protecting national security and safeguarding civil liberties.

The OIG's prior oversight work, some of which was congressionally mandated, informed our decision to initiate this review. That prior oversight work included OIG reviews of the FBI's use of specific FISA authorities,[13] the FBI's use of other national security-related surveillance authorities,[14] and the FBI's or other Department law enforcement components' use of CHSs and administrative subpoenas.[15] We also conducted reviews that specifically examined the impact of

---

[13] DOJ OIG, *A Review of the FBI's Handling of Intelligence Information Related to the September 11 Attacks*, Oversight and Review Division (November 2004), https://oig.justice.gov/special/s0606/final.pdf (accessed November 12, 2019); DOJ OIG, *A Review of the Federal Bureau of Investigation's Activities Under Section 702 of the Foreign Intelligence Surveillance Act Amendments Act of 2008*, Oversight and Review Division (September 2012), https://oig.justice.gov/reports/2016/o1601a.pdf (accessed November 12, 2019); DOJ OIG, *A Review of the Federal Bureau of Investigation's Use of Section 215 Order for Business Records*, Oversight and Review Division (March 2007), https://oig.justice.gov/reports/2014/215-I.pdf (accessed November 12, 2019); DOJ OIG, *A Review of the FBI's Use of Section 215 Orders for Business Records in 2006*, Oversight and Review Division (March 2008), https://oig.justice.gov/reports/2016/215-2008.pdf (accessed November 12, 2019); DOJ OIG, *FBI's Use of Section 215 Orders: Assessment of Progress in Implementing Recommendations and Examination of Use in 2007 through 2009*, Oversight and Review Division Report 15-05 (May 2015), https://oig.justice.gov/reports/2015/o1505.pdf (accessed November 12, 2019); DOJ OIG, *A Review of the FBI's Use of Section 215 Orders for Business Records in 2012 through 2014*, Oversight and Review Division Report 16-04 (September 2016), https://oig.justice.gov/reports/2016/o1604.pdf (accessed November 12, 2019); DOJ OIG, *A Review of the FBI's Use of Trap and Trace Devices Under the Foreign Intelligence Surveillance Act in 2007 through 2009*, Oversight and Review Division 15-06 (June 2015), https://oig.justice.gov/reports/2015/o1506.pdf (accessed November 12, 2019).

[14] DOJ OIG, *A Review of the Federal Bureau of Investigation's Use of National Security Letters*, Oversight and Review Division (March 2007), https://oig.justice.gov/reports/2016/NSL-2007.pdf (accessed November 12, 2019); DOJ OIG, *A Review of the FBI's Use of National Security Letters: Assessment of Corrective Actions and Examination of NSL Usage in 2006*, Oversight and Review Division (March 2008), https://oig.justice.gov/reports/2014/s1410a.pdf (accessed November 12, 2019); DOJ OIG, *A Review of the Federal Bureau of Investigation's Use of National Security Letters: Assessment of Progress in Implementing Recommendations and Examination of Use in 2007 through 2009*, Oversight and Review Division (August 2014), https://oig.justice.gov/reports/2014/s1408.pdf (accessed November 12, 2019); DOJ OIG, *A Review of the Federal Bureau of Investigation's Use of Exigent Letters and Other Informal Requests for Telephone Records*, Oversight and Review Division (January 2010), https://oig.justice.gov/reports/2014/o1411.pdf (accessed November 12, 2019); DOJ OIG, *A Review of the Department of Justice's Involvement with the President's Surveillance Program*, Oversight and Review Division (July 2009), https://oig.justice.gov/reports/2016/PSP-01-08-16-vol-3.pdf (accessed November 12, 2019).

[15] DOJ OIG, *Audit of the Bureau of Alcohol, Tobacco, Firearms and Explosives' Management and Oversight of Confidential Informants*, Audit Division 17-17 (March 2017), https://oig.justice.gov/reports/2017/a1717.pdf (accessed November 12, 2019); DOJ OIG, *Audit of the Drug Enforcement Administration's Confidential Source Policies and Oversight of Higher-Risk Confidential Sources*, Audit Division 15-28 (July 2015), https://oig.justice.gov/reports/2015/a1528.pdf (accessed November 12, 2019); DOJ OIG, *Audit of the Drug Enforcement Administration's Management and Oversight of its Confidential Source Program*, Audit Division 16-33 (September 2016), https://oig.justice.gov/reports/2016/a1633.pdf (accessed November 12, 2019); DOJ OIG,

the FBI's use of investigative authorities on U.S. persons engaged in activities that are protected by the First Amendment of the U.S. Constitution.[16]

III. Methodology

During the course of this review, the OIG conducted over 170 interviews involving more than 100 witnesses. These interviews included former FBI Director Comey, former Attorney General Loretta Lynch, former DAG Yates, former Acting Attorney General and Acting DAG and current FBI General Counsel Dana Boente, former FBI Deputy Director McCabe, former DAG Rod Rosenstein, former FBI General Counsel James Baker, FBI agents, analysts, and supervisors who worked on the Crossfire Hurricane investigation, attorneys from the FBI's National Security and Cyber Law Branch, NSD attorneys who prepared or reviewed the FISA applications, Department attorneys from ODAG who reviewed the FISA applications, former and current members of the FBI's senior executive leadership, Department attorney Bruce Ohr and his wife, Nellie Ohr, and additional Department attorneys who supervised and worked with Ohr on matters relevant to this review.

The OIG also interviewed witnesses who were not current or former Department employees regarding their interactions with the FBI on matters falling with the scope of this review, including Christopher Steele and employees of other U.S. government agencies.[17] Steele provided the OIG with access to, but not copies of, memoranda regarding interactions he had with FBI personnel and Bruce Ohr in 2010, 2011, and 2016. Steele represented to us that he drafted the memoranda shortly after each interaction. In addition, we reviewed relevant information that other U.S. government agencies provided to the FBI in the course of the Crossfire Hurricane investigation. Because the activities of other agencies were not within the scope of this review, we did not seek to obtain records from them that the FBI never received or reviewed, except for a limited amount of State

---

Public Summary of the Addendum to the Audit of the Drug Enforcement Administration's Management and Oversight of its Confidential Source Program, Audit Division 16-33a (March 2017), https://oig.justice.gov/reports/2017/a1633a.pdf (accessed November 12, 2019); DOJ OIG, *A Review of the Drug Enforcement Administration's Use of Administrative Subpoenas to Collect or Exploit Bulk Data,* Oversight and Review Division 19-01 (March 2019), https://oig.justice.gov/reports/2019/o1901.pdf (accessed November 12, 2019); DOJ OIG, *The Federal Bureau of Investigation's Management of Confidential Case Funds and Telecommunication Costs,* Audit Division 18-03 (January 2008), https://oig.justice.gov/reports/FBI/a0803/final.pdf (accessed November 12, 2019).

[16] DOJ OIG, *A Review of the FBI's Investigative Activities Concerning Potential Protesters at the 2004 Democratic and Republican National Political Conventions,* Oversight and Review Division (April 2006), https://oig.justice.gov/special/s0604/final.pdf (accessed November 12, 2019); DOJ OIG, *A Review of the FBI's Investigations of Certain Domestic Advocacy Groups,* Oversight and Review Division (September 2010), https://oig.justice.gov/special/s1009r.pdf (accessed November 12, 2019).

[17] According to Steele, his cooperation with our investigation ███████████ ██████ .

Department records relating to Steele.[18] Additionally, our review also did not seek to independently determine whether corroboration existed for the Steele election reporting; rather, our review was focused on information that was available to the FBI prior to and during the pendency of the Carter Page FISAs that related to the Steele reporting.

Two witnesses, Glenn Simpson and Jonathan Winer (a former State Department official), declined our requests for voluntary interviews, and we were unable to compel their testimony.[19] The OIG does not have authority to subpoena for testimony former Department employees or third parties who may have relevant information about an FBI or Department program or operation.[20] Certain former FBI employees who agreed to interviews, including Comey and Baker, chose not to request that their security clearances be reinstated for their OIG interviews. Therefore, we were unable to provide classified information or documents to them during their interviews to develop their testimony, or to assist their recollections of relevant events.

We also received and reviewed more than one million documents that were in the Department's and FBI's possession. Among these were electronic communications of Department and FBI employees and documents from the Crossfire Hurricane investigation, including interview reports (FD-302s and Electronic Communications or ECs), contemporaneous notes from agents, analysts, and supervisors involved in case-related meetings, documents describing and analyzing Steele's reporting and information obtained through FISA coverage on

---

[18] In this review, we also did not seek to assess the actions taken by or information available to U.S. government agencies outside the Department of Justice, as those agencies are outside our jurisdiction.

[19] The OIG did not seek to interview Carter Page or any other subject in the Crossfire Hurricane investigation because their actions were not the focus of our review. Rather, consistent with the OIG's jurisdiction, we examined the actions of the FBI and Department. In response to a request from Page to review a draft of our report, the OIG advised Page in correspondence in November 2019 that the OIG would notify him of the report's anticipated release date shortly before the report is made public. This courtesy is consistent with the OIG's practice in other matters where the actions we reviewed affected the personal interests of a private citizen.

[20] In 2016, Congress passed the "Inspector General Empowerment Act" (IGEA) (P. L. 114-317). Timely completion of this review would not have been possible without the IGEA's statutory clarification that OIGs must be granted access to all agency records and information, including highly sensitive records, such as FISA materials. We note that the Department and the FBI gave us broad and timely access to all such material, and provided us with their full cooperation.

Earlier versions of the IGEA also included a provision to authorize all OIGs to issue testimonial subpoenas (the Department of Defense OIG already has such authority, as does the Health and Human Services OIG in certain circumstances), but the provision was removed from the IGEA prior to its passage. The OIG would have directly benefited from the ability to subpoena former government and non-government individuals in this review. In addition to being able to compel the testimony of the small number of individuals who did not testify voluntarily, the ability to subpoena witnesses would have expedited completion of the review, as multiple individuals only agreed to interviews at a late stage in the review. In September 2018, the House of Representatives unanimously passed legislation that would provide testimonial subpoena authority to OIGs. No similar legislation has been introduced in the current Congress.

Carter Page, and draft and final versions of materials used to prepare the FISA applications and renewals filed with the FISC.[21] We also obtained documents from attorneys and supervisors in NSD, Criminal Division (CRM), ODAG, and the Office of the Attorney General (OAG).

As with the OIG's *Review of Various Actions in Advance of the 2016 Election*, we obtained electronic communications between and among FBI agents, analysts, and supervisors, and FBI and Department officials to understand what happened during the investigation and identify what was known by the members of the Crossfire Hurricane team as the investigation progressed. In addition to a large volume of unclassified and classified emails, we received and reviewed hundreds of thousands of text messages and instant messages to or from FBI personnel who worked on the investigation.[22] We also were provided with and reviewed transcripts of testimony from numerous witnesses who participated in hearings jointly conducted during the 115th Congress by the House Committee on the Judiciary and the House Committee on Oversight and Government Reform.

Our review included the examination of highly classified information. We were given broad access to relevant materials by the Department and the FBI, including emails, text messages, and instant messages from both the FBI's Top Secret SCINet and Secret FBINet systems, as well as access to the FBI's classified Delta database, which FBI agents use to record their interactions with, and information received from, CHSs. Chapter Ten provides more information on the methodology we employed to examine the FBI's use of CHSs.

As with the OIG's handling of past reviews, we did not analyze all of the decisions made during the Crossfire Hurricane investigation. Rather, we reviewed the issues described below in Section IV of this chapter. Moreover, our role in this review was not to second-guess discretionary judgments by Department personnel about whether to open an investigation, or specific judgment calls made during the course of an investigation, where those decisions complied with or were authorized by Department rules, policies, or procedures. We do not criticize particular decisions merely because we might have recommended a different investigative strategy or tactic based on the facts learned during our investigation. The question we considered was not whether a particular investigative decision was ideal or could have been handled more effectively, but whether the Department and the FBI complied with applicable legal requirements, policies, and procedures in taking the actions we reviewed or, alternatively, whether the circumstances surrounding the

---

[21] We did not review the entirety of FISA ▮▮▮▮ obtained through FISA surveillance ▮▮ ▮▮▮▮▮ targeting Carter Page. We reviewed only those documents ▮▮▮▮ under FISA authority that were pertinent to our review.

[22] During our review, we identified a small number of text messages and instant messages, beyond those discussed in the OIG's *Review of Various Actions in Advance of the 2016 Election*, in which FBI employees involved in the Crossfire Hurricane investigation discussed political issues and candidates. Unlike the messages in the OIG's *Review of Various Actions in Advance of the 2016 Election*, the messages here did not raise significant questions of potential bias or improper motivation because of the potential connection to investigative activity.

decision indicated that it was based on inaccurate or incomplete information, or considerations other than the merits of the investigation. If the explanations we were given for a particular decision were consistent with legal requirements, policies and procedures, reflected rational investigative strategy and were not unreasonable, we did not conclude that the decision was based on improper considerations in the absence of documentary or testimonial evidence to the contrary.[23]

IV. Structure of the Report

This report consists of twelve chapters. The public version of this report contains limited redactions of information that the FBI and other agencies determined is classified or too sensitive for public release.[24] Following this introduction, Chapter Two summarizes relevant Department and FBI policies concerning counterintelligence investigations, including the policies governing the FBI's use of CHSs and FISA authority in the context of counterintelligence investigations.

In Chapter Three, we provide an overview of the Crossfire Hurricane investigation, including the information that predicated the investigation, the identification of the subjects of the investigation, the organization and staffing of the Crossfire Hurricane team, and the involvement of Department and FBI leadership. We also describe the context surrounding the Crossfire Hurricane investigation, in particular the conclusion by the USIC that the Russian government was attempting to interfere with the 2016 U.S. elections. In Chapter Four, we discuss the FBI's receipt and evaluation of information from Steele up and through the first Carter Page FISA application. In Chapter Five, we describe the preparation of the first FISA application which, once granted by the FISC, authorized FISA surveillance of Carter Page. We also describe instances in which information in the first FISA application was inaccurate, incomplete, or unsupported by appropriate documentation.

Chapter Six discusses the FBI's activities involving Steele after the first FISA application, including the FBI's decision to close Steele as a CHS and the FBI's efforts to assess Steele's election reports. Chapter Seven describes the three renewal applications for FISA surveillance of Carter Page as the Crossfire Hurricane investigation proceeded. In Chapter Eight, we discuss a letter NSD sent to the FISC

---

[23] As part of the standard practice in our reviews, we provided a draft copy of this report to the Department and the FBI to conduct a factual accuracy review. Also consistent with our standard practice, we contacted individuals who were interviewed as part of the review and whose conduct is addressed in this report, and certain other witnesses, to provide them an opportunity to review the portions of the report that pertain to their testimony to the OIG. With limited exceptions, these witnesses availed themselves of this opportunity, and we provided those who did conduct such a review with the opportunity to provide oral or written comments directly to the OIG concerning the portions they reviewed, consistent with rules to protect classified information.

[24] Consistent with our standard practice, we provided a draft copy of this report to the Department and the FBI, and as appropriate, other government agencies, for the purpose of conducting a classification review and providing final classification markings.

in July 2018, about one year after the final renewal application was filed, outlining omissions from the FISA applications. We also describe additional instances of inaccurate, incomplete, or undocumented information in the three FISA renewal applications that were not identified in NSD's letter.

In Chapter Nine, we discuss the interactions between Ohr and the Crossfire Hurricane team, Ohr's communications with Steele and Simpson, both before and after the FBI closed Steele as a CHS, and Ohr's interactions with Department attorneys regarding the Manafort criminal case. Chapter Ten discusses the FBI's use of CHSs other than Steele and its use of Undercover Employees (UCEs) as part of the Crossfire Hurricane investigation. We also describe several individuals we identified who had either a connection to candidate Trump or a role in the Trump campaign, and were also FBI CHSs, and provide the reasons such individuals were not tasked as part of the Crossfire Hurricane investigation. Finally, we describe the attendance of an SSA on the Crossfire Hurricane team at counterintelligence briefings given to the presidential candidates and certain campaign advisors.

Chapter Eleven contains our analysis of the factual information presented in Chapters Three through Ten. Chapter Twelve provides our conclusions and our nine recommendations.

Appendix One to this report contains a chart illustrating the results of our review of the FBI's compliance with the FISA "Woods Procedures" that are described in Chapter Two. Appendix Two is the FBI's official response to this report and the report's recommendations.

CHAPTER TWO
APPLICABLE LAWS AND DEPARTMENT AND FBI POLICIES

In this chapter, we describe the standards set forth in the Attorney General's Guidelines for Domestic FBI Operations (AG Guidelines) and implemented through the FBI's Domestic Investigations and Operations Guide (DIOG) and the Counterintelligence Division (CD) Policy Directive and Policy Guide (CDPG) for the opening of predicated counterintelligence investigations. We then describe the FBI's process for opening and overseeing Sensitive Investigative Matters (SIMs), such as those involving political candidates or officials. Next, we discuss relevant policies governing the use and handling of Confidential Human Sources (CHS), focusing on the validation process, the use of sub-sources, and the continued receipt of intelligence from a closed CHS.

We then summarize the legal standards for obtaining approval to conduct electronic surveillance and physical searches under the Foreign Intelligence Surveillance Act of 1978 (FISA), as well as the procedural steps, approval and certification standards, and accuracy requirements necessary to obtain such approvals. Because our review focuses on the process the FBI used to obtain authorization to conduct electronic surveillance and physical searches targeting Carter Page, the discussion of FISA in this chapter is limited to the provisions applicable to these authorities. We also describe government ethics regulations concerning conflicts of interests that apply to certain events discussed in Chapter Nine.

Finally, we discuss examples of other Department and FBI policies regulating investigative activity that could potentially impact civil liberties, including policies that address when someone acting on behalf of the FBI becomes a member of, or participates in, the activity of an organization without disclosing their FBI affiliation to an appropriate official of the organization, and when investigative actions involve members of the news media, White House personnel, and Members of Congress.

I.   FBI Counterintelligence Investigations

The FBI has the authority to investigate federal crimes that are not exclusively assigned to other agencies.[25] In addition, under Executive Order (EO) 12333 and various statutory authorities, the FBI has the primary domestic responsibility for investigating threats within the United States to the national security. Such threats are defined to include the following:

- International terrorism;
- Espionage and other intelligence activities, sabotage, and assassination, conducted by, for, or on behalf of foreign powers, organizations, or persons;

---

[25] *See* AG Guidelines § A.1; DIOG §§ 6.4.1, 7.4.1.

- Foreign computer intrusion; and
- Other matters determined by the Attorney General, consistent with E.O. 12333 or any successor order.

Beyond these investigative functions, the FBI also serves as a domestic intelligence agency and has the authority to collect and analyze foreign intelligence as a member of the U.S. Intelligence Community (USIC).[26]

The standards that the FBI must follow when conducting investigative and intelligence gathering activities are set forth in the AG Guidelines and implemented through the DIOG. The AG Guidelines and the DIOG both require that FBI investigations be undertaken for an authorized purpose—that is, "to detect, obtain information about, or prevent or protect against federal crimes or threats to the national security or to collect foreign intelligence."[27] The DIOG requires that the authorized purpose be "well-founded and well-documented," and states that this threshold requirement is a safeguard intended to ensure that FBI employees respect the constitutional rights of Americans. Under both the AG Guidelines and the DIOG, no investigation may be conducted for the sole purpose of monitoring activities protected by the First Amendment or the lawful exercise of other rights secured by the Constitution or laws of the United States.[28] However, the DIOG also recognizes that

> the law does not preclude FBI employees from observing and collecting any of the forms of protected speech and considering its content—as long as those activities are done for a valid law enforcement or national security purpose and are conducted in a manner that does not unduly infringe upon the ability of the speaker to deliver his or her message.[29]

Balancing individual rights and the FBI's legitimate investigative needs requires "a rational relationship between the authorized purpose and the protected speech to be collected such that a reasonable person with knowledge of the circumstances could understand why the information is being collected."[30]

The AG Guidelines recognize that activities subject to investigation as "threats to the national security" also may involve violations or potential violations of federal criminal laws, or may serve important purposes outside the ambit of normal criminal investigation and prosecution by informing national security decisions.[31] Given such potential overlaps in subject matter, the AG Guidelines

---

[26] *See* AG Guidelines §§ A.2, B.

[27] AG Guidelines § II.B.1; DIOG § 7.2.; *see also* AG Guidelines §§ I.B.1, II; DIOG §§ 2.2.1, 6.2.

[28] *See* AG Guidelines §§ I.B.1, I.C.3; DIOG § 4.1.2.

[29] DIOG § 4.2.1.

[30] DIOG § 4.2.1.

[31] *See* AG Guidelines § A.2.

state that the FBI is not required to differently label its activities as criminal investigations, national security investigations, or foreign intelligence collection, nor is it required to segregate FBI personnel based on the subject areas in which they operate. Rather, the AG Guidelines state that, where an authorized purpose exists, all of the FBI's legal authorities are available for deployment in all cases to which they apply.[32]

The AG Guidelines and the DIOG require that the "least intrusive" means or method be "considered" when selecting investigative techniques and, "if reasonable based upon the circumstances of the investigation," be used to obtain information instead of a more intrusive method.[33] In choosing whether an investigative method is appropriate, the DIOG requires FBI agents to balance the level of intrusion against the investigative needs, particularly where the information sought involves clearly established constitutional, statutory, or evidentiary rights, or sensitive circumstances. Considerations include the seriousness of the crime or national security threat; the strength and significance of the intelligence or information to be gained; the amount of information already known about the subject or group under investigation; and the requirements of operational security, including protection of sources and methods.[34] The DIOG states that the degree of procedural protection the law and Department and FBI policy provide for the use of a particular investigative method helps to determine its intrusiveness.[35] According to the DIOG, search warrants, wiretaps, and undercover operations are considered to be very intrusive, while database searches and communication with established sources are less intrusive.[36] The least intrusive method principle reflects an attempt to balance the FBI's ability to effectively conduct investigations with the potential negative impact an investigation can have on the privacy and civil liberties of individuals encompassed within an investigation.[37] However, the DIOG states that investigators "must not hesitate to use any lawful method consistent with the [AG Guidelines] when the degree of intrusiveness is warranted in light of the seriousness of the matter concerned."[38] According to the DIOG, "[i]n the final analysis, choosing the method that [most] appropriately balances the impact on privacy and civil liberties with operational needs, is a matter of judgment, based on training and experience."[39]

Where the authorized purpose involves a threat to the national security, the AG Guidelines require the FBI to coordinate with other Department components,

---

[32] See AG Guidelines § A, II.

[33] See AG Guidelines § I.C.2; DIOG § 4.4.1.

[34] See DIOG § 4.4.4.

[35] See DIOG § 4.4.3.

[36] See DIOG § 4.4.3.

[37] See DIOG § 4.4.4.

[38] See DIOG § 4.1.1(F).

[39] See DIOG § 4.4.5.

specifically including the National Security Division (NSD), and to share information with other agencies with national security responsibilities, including other USIC agencies, the Department of Homeland Security, and the White House. Section VI.D of the AG Guidelines governs the FBI's responsibility to provide information concerning threats to the national security to NSD and to the White House. Where there is "compromising" information about U.S. officials or political organizations, or information concerning activities of U.S. persons intended to affect the political process, the FBI may disseminate it to the White House with the approval of the Attorney General, based on a determination that the dissemination is needed for foreign intelligence purposes, to protect against international terrorism or other threats to the national security, or for the conduct of foreign affairs.[40]

A.   Predicated Investigations

Where the FBI has an authorized purpose and factual predication—that is, allegations, reports, facts or circumstances indicative of possible criminal activity or a national security threat, or the potential for acquiring information responsive to foreign intelligence requirements—it may initiate an investigation. The predication requirement is not a legal requirement but rather a prudential one imposed by Department and FBI policy.[41]

Predicated investigations that concern federal crimes or threats to the national security are divided into Preliminary Investigations and Full Investigations.[42] Preliminary Investigations may be opened on the basis of any "allegation or information" indicative of possible criminal activity or threats to the national security. Authorized investigative methods in Preliminary Investigations include all lawful methods (to include CHS and UCE operations) except mail opening, search warrants, electronic surveillance requiring a judicial order or warrant (Title III or FISA), or requests under Title VII of FISA. A Preliminary Investigation may also be converted to a Full Investigation if the available information provides predication for a Full Investigation.[43] As described in more detail in Chapter Three, both Crossfire Hurricane and an earlier counterintelligence investigation on Carter Page were initiated as Full Investigations, and thus we focus on the requirements for this level of predicated investigation.[44]

---

[40] *See* AG Guidelines § VI.D.2.b.

[41] For example, the Supreme Court has held that the Department and FBI can lawfully open a federal criminal grand jury investigation even in the absence of predication. *See United States* v. *Morton Salt*, 338 U.S. 632, 642-43 (1950) (a grand jury "can investigate merely on suspicion that the law is being violated, or even just because it wants assurance that it is not"); *see also United States* v. *R. Enterprises*, 498 U.S. 292, 297 (1991).

[42] *See* AG Guidelines § II.B.3.

[43] *See* AG Guidelines §§ II.B.3, II.B.4; DIOG §§ 6.1, 6.4, 6.6, 6.7.2, 6.9 (Preliminary Investigations); DIOG §§ 7.5, 7.6, 7.7.3, 7.9 (Full Investigations).

[44] In addition to predicated investigations, the AG Guidelines and the DIOG also authorize the FBI to use relatively non-intrusive means to conduct assessments when it receives or obtains allegations or other information concerning crimes or threats to the national security. Assessments

Under Section II.B.3 of the AG Guidelines and Section 7 of the DIOG, the FBI may open a Full Investigation if there is an "articulable factual basis" that reasonably indicates one of the following circumstances exists:

- An activity constituting a federal crime or a threat to the national security has or may have occurred, is or may be occurring, or will or may occur and the investigation may obtain information relating to the activity or the involvement or role of an individual, group, or organization in such activity;

- An individual, group, organization, entity, information, property, or activity is or may be a target of attack, victimization, acquisition, infiltration, or recruitment in connection with criminal activity in violation of federal law or a threat to the national security and the investigation may obtain information that would help to protect against such activity or threat; or

- The investigation may obtain foreign intelligence that is responsive to a requirement that the FBI collect positive foreign intelligence—*i.e.*, information relating to the capabilities, intentions, or activities of foreign governments or elements thereof, foreign organizations or foreign persons, or international terrorists.

The DIOG provides examples of information that is sufficient to initiate a Full Investigation, including corroborated information from an intelligence agency stating that an individual is a member of a terrorist group, or a threat to a specific individual or group made on a blog combined with additional information connecting the blogger to a known terrorist group.[45]

A Full Investigation may be opened if there is an "articulable factual basis" of possible criminal or national threat activity. When opening a Full Investigation, an FBI employee must certify that an authorized purpose and adequate predication exist; that the investigation is not based solely on the exercise of First Amendment rights or certain characteristics of the subject, such as race, religion, national origin, or ethnicity; and that the investigation is an appropriate use of personnel and financial resources. The factual predication must be documented in an electronic communication (EC) or other form, and the case initiation must be approved by the relevant FBI personnel, which, in most instances, can be a Supervisory Special Agent (SSA) in a field office or at Headquarters. As described in more detail below, if an investigation is designated as a Sensitive Investigative Matter, that designation must appear in the caption or heading of the opening EC, and special approval requirements apply.

---

require an authorized purpose but no particular factual predication, and are the lowest level of investigation permitted under the AG Guidelines and the DIOG. *See* AG Guidelines § II.A; DIOG § 5.2. The investigations opened on Carter Page were not assessments.

[45] DIOG § 7.5.

All lawful investigative methods may be used in a Full Investigation, including electronic surveillance and physical searches under FISA.[46] However, as described above, the FBI must consider the least intrusive means or method to accomplish the operational objectives of the investigation.

B.   Sensitive Investigative Matters (SIM)

The DIOG states that certain investigative matters, known as Sensitive Investigative Matters or SIMs, should be brought to the attention of FBI management and Department officials, as described in further detail below, because of the possibility of public notoriety and sensitivity.[47] Section 10.1.2.1 of the DIOG, in relevant part, defines a SIM as an assessment or predicated investigation of the activities of a domestic public official or domestic political candidate (involving corruption or a threat to the national security), or a domestic political organization or an individual prominent in such an organization. The term "domestic political candidate" includes an individual who is seeking nomination or election to federal or other political office, while the term "domestic political organization" includes, in relevant part, a committee or group formed to elect an individual to public office. Under the DIOG, if an assessment or predicated investigation concerns a person prominent in a "domestic political organization" but not the political organization itself, it nonetheless must be treated as a SIM.[48]

Section 10.1.3 of the DIOG states that the following factors are to be considered when deciding to open a SIM:

- The seriousness or severity of the violation or threat;
- The significance of the information sought to the violation or threat;
- The probability that the proposed course of action will be successful;
- The risk of public exposure, and if there is such a risk, the adverse impact or the perception of the adverse impact on civil liberties and public confidence; and
- The risk to the national security or the public welfare if the proposed course of action is not approved (*i.e.*, the risk of doing nothing).

The DIOG cautions that, when conducting a SIM, the FBI should take particular care to consider whether a planned course of action is the least intrusive method if reasonable, based upon the circumstances of the investigation.[49] As noted above, when balancing the needs of the investigation and the intrusiveness of an investigative method, the FBI must consider the seriousness of the crime or national security threat, the strength and significance of the intelligence or

---

[46] *See* AG Guidelines § II.B.4(b)(ii); *see also* DIOG §§ 7.9, 18.7.1.

[47] DIOG § 10.1.1

[48] *See* DIOG § 10.1.2.2.3.

[49] *See* DIOG § 10.1.3

information to be gained, the amount of information already known about the subject or group under investigation, and the requirements of operational security, including protection of sources and methods.[50]

The DIOG and CDPG impose special approval and notification requirements for initiating a Full Investigation of a U.S. person relating to a threat to the national security or any investigation involving a SIM. When a case is opened and designated a SIM by FBI Headquarters, these include review by the FBI Office of the General Counsel (OGC), approval by the FBI Headquarters operational Section Chief (SC), and notification to NSD.[51] At NSD, counterintelligence investigations fall within the purview of the Counterintelligence and Export Control Section (CES), which has the responsibility of supervising and coordinating, among other things, the criminal investigation and prosecution of national security cases, except counterterrorism cases, nationwide. CES receives a steady volume of investigation notifications from the FBI, referred to as letterhead memoranda or LHMs, and on counterintelligence matters CES officials meet regularly with officials from the FBI's Counterintelligence Division.

II. Department and FBI Policies Governing the Use of Confidential Human Sources (CHS)

CHSs play a crucial role in the FBI's efforts to combat crime and protect national security. CHSs provide the FBI with information and insights about the inner workings of criminal, terrorist, and espionage networks that otherwise would be unavailable. The intelligence that CHSs generate has enabled the FBI to thwart terrorist plots, combat intelligence gathering by malign foreign actors, and collect critical evidence for criminal prosecutions.

A. Risk Management Issues Related to CHSs

The operation of CHSs carries numerous risks, both for the CHSs and for law enforcement.[52] CHSs oftentimes place themselves in significant danger because

---

[50] *See* DIOG § 4.4.4.

[51] The DIOG states "an appropriate NSD official" should be notified and provides a general email account for notification. *See* DIOG §§ 7.7, 7.10, DIOG Appendix G § G.9.1 (classified); CDPG § 3.1.2.

[52] The OIG has conducted numerous reviews of the CHS Programs at the Department's law enforcement components, including most recently the OIG's *Audit of the Federal Bureau of Investigation's Management of its Confidential Human Source Validation Processes*, Audit Division Report 20-009 (November 2019), http://oig.justice.gov/reports/2019/a20009.pdf (accessed December 1, 2019). *See also* DOJ OIG, *Audit of the Bureau of Alcohol, Tobacco, Firearms and Explosives' Management and Oversight of Confidential Informants*, Audit Division 17-17 (March 2017), https://oig.justice.gov/reports/2017/a1717.pdf (accessed November 12, 2019); DOJ OIG, *Audit of the Drug Enforcement Administration's Confidential Source Policies and Oversight of Higher-Risk Confidential Sources*, Audit Division 15-28 (July 2015), https://oig.justice.gov/reports/2015/a1528.pdf (accessed November 12, 2019); DOJ OIG, *Audit of the Drug Enforcement Administration's Management and Oversight of its Confidential Source Program*, Audit Division 16-33 (September 2016), https://oig.justice.gov/reports/2016/a1633.pdf (accessed November 12, 2019); DOJ OIG,

disclosure of their cooperation with the FBI can result in retaliation by the persons on whom they are reporting, including physical abuse and even death. Maintaining the confidential nature of the FBI's relationship with its human sources consequently is a priority for the FBI and the Department. Without such secrecy, the safety of CHSs and the FBI's ability to recruit CHSs would be severely jeopardized.

Law enforcement agencies, including the FBI, also assume various risks when utilizing CHSs. Sources may fail to follow instructions and engage in criminal activities that are not authorized, or they may lie or otherwise provide inaccurate information. In light of these risks, the Department and the FBI have established detailed policies to govern the use of CHSs, which seek to mitigate the various risks that such use creates. The Department has established AG Guidelines for FBI CHSs (AG CHS Guidelines) and baseline risk and mitigation protocols for CHS operations.[53] The AG CHS Guidelines and protocols require, for example, that the FBI: (1) complete an initial suitability or validation review prior to operating a CHS; (2) admonish the CHS regarding the parameters of his or her service, such as a prohibition on unauthorized illegal activity, and the requirement to abide by the FBI's instructions; (3) maintain proper payment documentation; and (4) subject the CHS to an on-going validation review, to include quarterly and annual reporting on the CHS's activities.[54] Sources that the FBI operates outside of the United States are subject to further requirements under a separate set of Attorney General's Guidelines.[55]

The FBI's CHS policies provide additional guidance about source operation procedures and include the DIOG, the Confidential Human Source Policy Guide (CHSPG), and the Confidential Human Source Validation Standards Manual (VSM).[56] Under these policies, FBI case agents (handling agents) are responsible for recruiting and operating CHSs, as well as securing approvals for CHS activities and maintaining accurate CHS case files.[57] These policies expressly recognize that the "FBI must, to the extent practicable, ensure that the information collected from

---

Public Summary of the Addendum to the Audit of the Drug Enforcement Administration's Management and Oversight of its Confidential Source Program, Audit Division 16-33a (March 2017), https://oig.justice.gov/reports/2017/a1633a.pdf (accessed November 12, 2019);

[53] Alberto Gonzales, Attorney General's Guidelines Regarding the Use of FBI Confidential Human Sources ("AG CHS Guidelines") (Dec. 13, 2006); James M. Cole, Deputy Attorney General, Baseline Risk Assessment and Mitigation Policies for Law Enforcement Operations in Criminal Matters (December 7, 2013) at 6-10.

[54] AG CHS Guidelines §§ II.A, II.B, II.C & IV.C.4.

[55] William P. Barr, Attorney General's Guidelines on the Development and Operation of FBI Criminal Informants and Cooperative Witnesses in Extraterritorial Jurisdictions (January 15, 1993); See also Confidential Human Source Policy Guide (CHSPG) § 19.

[56] The FBI is in the process of drafting new guidance to replace the Confidential Human Source Validation Standards Manual ("VSM"), 0258PG (March 26, 2010). Witnesses we interviewed told the OIG that the FBI has changed its validation process, and no longer follows much of the VSM, but it has not yet been replaced by more recent guidance.

[57] DIOG § 18.5.5; CHSPG § 1.0; VSM § 1.0.

every CHS is accurate and current, and not given to the FBI in an effort to distract, mislead, or misdirect FBI organizational or governmental efforts."[58]

The CHSPG recognizes that the decision to open an individual as a CHS will not only forever affect the life of that individual, but that the FBI will also be viewed, fairly or unfairly, in light of the conduct or misconduct of that individual.[59] Accordingly, the CHSPG identifies criteria that handling agents must consider when assessing the risks associated with the potential CHS. ████████████████████

██

██████████[60] These risks must be weighed against the benefits associated with use of the potential CHS.[61]

Once a CHS has been evaluated and recruited, the CHSPG does not allow for tasking until after the CHS has been approved for opening by an FBI SSA; the required approvals for a specific tasking have been granted; and the CHS has met with the co-handling agent assigned to his or her file, who has the same duties, responsibilities, and file access as the handling agent.[62] The CHSPG requires additional supervisory approval by a Special Agent in Charge (SAC) and review by a Chief Division Counsel (CDC) to open CHSs that are "sensitive" sources, ██.[63]

Before a CHS may be tasked, the CHS must also be admonished by the handling agent regarding the nature and parameters of the CHS's relationship with

---

[58] VSM § 1.0.

[59] CHSPG § 3.1.

[60] CHSPG § 3.1.

[61] Criteria used by agents and analysts to weigh the risks and benefits are: ████████████

██

██

██

██. CHSPG § 3.1.

[62] CHSPG §§ 2.2.1, 4.2.

[63] CHSPG § 3.5.1.1. ████████████████████████████████

██

██

██████████████████████████

the FBI.[64] Admonishments must also be given to the CHS "whenever it appears necessary or prudent to do so, and at least annually."[65] The CHSPG contains a list of required admonishments, which include that the CHS's assistance to the FBI is voluntary; that the CHS must abide by the admonishments of the FBI and must not take any independent actions on behalf of the U.S. government; and that the CHS must provide truthful information to the FBI.[66] The required admonishments listed in the CHSPG do not include a specific statement that the CHS must keep his or her relationship with the FBI confidential.

Exceptions to the requirements of the CHSPG and the DIOG may be made in "extraordinary circumstances" and require the approval of the Assistant Director of the Directorate of Intelligence.[67]

B. Documenting CHS Activities

The FBI maintains an automated case management system for all CHS records, which the FBI refers to as "Delta."[68] The Delta file for each CHS contains

[69]

.[70] The handling agent also assigns the CHS a ▮▮▮▮▮▮▮▮▮, which enables the CHS to sign payment receipts, admonishments, and consent forms without indicating the CHS's true identity.[71] The FBI permanently retains its CHS files, as directed by the National Archives and Records Administration (NARA).[72]

Within Delta, handling agents are required to document information reported by the CHS, as well as a wide variety of other information, including interactions between the handling agent and the CHS, ▮▮▮▮▮▮▮▮▮▮

---

[64] CHSPG § 5.1.

[65] CHSPG § 5.1.

[66] CHSPG § 5.2.

[67] CHSPG § 1.5.2.

[68] CHSPG §§ 3.10.1, 16.1.1.

[69] CHSPG § 16.1.5. The FBI's CHS Policy requires case agents to enter all communications concerning their CHSs into Delta, unless an exemption for "compelling circumstances" has been granted. CHSPG § 16.1.2. Even if such an exemption is granted, however, all CHSs must nevertheless be "registered" in the FBI's Delta database in a source-opening communication. CHSPG §§ 16.1.2, 16.1.4.

[70] CHSPG § 16.2.

[71] CHSPG § 16.3.

[72] CHSPG § 16.1.8.

▮▮▮▮▮▮.[73] Handling agents are also specifically required to document derogatory information about the CHS, which the FBI broadly defines as "[i]nformation that detracts from the character or standing" of an individual.[74] Derogatory information can take many forms, including, for example, involvement in criminal activity, drug use or possession, financial delinquency or bankruptcy, shifts in beliefs and values, unfavorable comments from individuals who know the CHS, undisclosed allegiances, or inaccurate or incomplete reporting.[75] Documenting derogatory information is critical to the CHS risk management process because, as recognized by the CHSPG, "past activities and observable characteristics can provide insights that point to future control or handling issues, reliability problems, or lack of credibility" on the part of the CHS. The OIG has previously recommended that the FBI create a sub-section within each CHS Delta file that contains, in a single location, all of the information concerning the reliability of the CHS, including any red flags, derogatory reporting, anomalies, or other counterintelligence concerns. The FBI has not implemented this recommendation.[76]

The CHSPG prohibits FBI personnel from disclosing investigative information to a CHS, including "the identity of...actual or potential subjects" of an investigation "other than what is strictly necessary for operational reasons."[77] If an agent believes that the disclosure of classified information to a source is necessary, the agent is required to obtain authorization from an FBI Assistant Director before disclosing the classified information.

C.   Validation Process for CHSs

Validation is the process used by the FBI to measure the value and mitigate the risks associated with the operation of CHSs.[78] By design, the validation process

▮▮▮▮▮▮▮▮▮▮▮▮▮▮▮▮▮▮▮[79]

▮▮▮▮▮▮▮▮▮▮▮▮▮▮▮▮

- ▮▮▮▮▮ (▮▮▮▮▮▮▮▮▮▮▮);

---

[73] CHSPG §§ 5.1, 16.1.7.

[74] CHSPG § 16.1.7; FBI National Name Check Derogatory Information Policy Implementation Guide (FBI NNCPG), 0317PG (July 25, 2010), B-1.

[75] See, e.g., FBI NNCPG § 3.1.1.

[76] See DOJ OIG, A Review of the FBI's Handling and Oversight of FBI Asset Katrina Leung, Oversight and Review Division, Special Report (May 2006), 229.

[77] CHSPG § 2.3; see also AG CHS Guidelines § I.D.5.

[78] VSM § 2.1.1.

[79] VSM § 2.2.

- ██);
- ██████████████████████████████████████); and
- ██
  ██████████).[80]

Each year, the handling agent must complete a Field Office Annual Source Report (FOASR), ███████████████████████████████████████
██ .[81] FOASRs must be maintained in the CHS's Delta validation sub-file, where they are reviewed and approved by the SSA and an Assistant Special Agent in Charge (ASAC), then submitted to the FBI Headquarters' Validation Management Unit (VMU), which assesses each CHS for continued operation.[82]

SSAs are responsible for daily oversight of CHSs operated by handling agents on the SSA's squad. SSAs review all communications regarding those CHSs, and perform required reviews of documentation collected in each CHS's Delta file.[83] Every 90 days, the SSA must also complete a Quarterly Supervisory Source Report (QSSR) for each CHS operated by a handling agent under that SSA's supervisory authority.[84] As part of the QSSR, the SSA must review the Delta file for each CHS to note any significant anomalies (for example, potential derogatory information, sudden requests for money, or substantial changes in behavior, lifestyle, or viewpoint) that occurred in the last 90 days.[85]

VMU independently conducts Human Source Validation Reviews (HSVRs), which are separate evaluations of the CHS that are completed, among other reasons, because an FBI Field Office or Operational Division has requested enhanced review.[86] These HSVRs involve:

- Independent review and analysis of the ██████████████████████
  ██ ;[87]

- Appropriate traces to ████████████████████████ , criminal activities, or interactions with other intelligence services, terrorist groups, or criminal organizations;[88]

---

[80] VSM § 2.1.2.

[81] CHSPG § 16.7; VSM § 4.1.2.

[82] CHSPG §§ 16.7, 4.1.2.1.

[83] CHSPG §§ 2.1.1, 16.7 & 16.8.

[84] CHSPG § 16.8.

[85] CHSPG § 16.8.

[86] VSM §§ 4.1, 4.1.2, 4.1.3 & 4.1.4.

[87] VSM §§ 4.1.3, 4.1.4.

[88] VSM §§ 4.1.3, 4.1.4.

- ██ **;** [89] and

- ██ **.** [90]

In the validation context, the term "corroborated" has a specific meaning—that an independent source (for example, ████████████████████████ ██████████████ has provided the FBI with the same information. ██ ██ [91]

The FBI's validation process also addresses the use of sub-sources by a CHS. [92] For example, the VSM requires the FOASR to assess the CHS's access to information, ██ **.** [93] If the latter, the FOASR should ████████████████████████████████ ██ ██ ██ [94]

D. Closure and Re-Opening of CHSs

Closing a CHS requires documentation of the reason for the closure, which must be included in the CHS's Delta file. [95] A CHS may be closed for general reasons or for cause. General reasons include considerations such as a lack of productivity, poor health, or transfer of the handling agent. [96] However, a CHS must be closed for cause "if there is grievous action by the CHS or a discovery of previously unknown facts or circumstances that make the individual unsuitable for use as a CHS." [97] Reasons that justify closing a CHS for cause include commission

---

[89] VSM §§ 4.1.4, 4.1.4.1.

[90] VSM §§ 4.1.4., 4.1.4.2.

[91] VSM § 2.2.

[92] CHSPG § 10.12; VSM § 4.1.2.1.7.

[93] VSM § 4.1.2.1.7.

[94] VSM § 4.1.2.1.7.

[95] CHSPG § 18.1.

[96] CHSPG § 18.1.1.

[97] CHSPG § 18.1.2.

of unauthorized illegal activity, unwillingness to follow instructions, unreliability, or serious control problems.[98] The handling agent must advise the CHS that he or she has been closed, and document such notification in the CHS's validation sub-file, including a statement as to whether the CHS acknowledged or refused to acknowledge the closure.[99]

Absent exceptional circumstances that are approved (in advance, whenever possible) by an SSA, a handling agent must not initiate contact with or respond to contacts from a former CHS who has been closed for cause.[100] Where there is contact with a CHS following closure (whether or not for cause), new information "may be documented" to a closed CHS file.[101] However, the CHSPG requires reopening of the CHS if the relationship between the FBI and the CHS is expected to continue beyond the initial contact or debriefing.[102]

A request to reopen a CHS that has previously been closed for cause requires high levels of supervisory approval, ██████████████████████████████ ██████████████████████████████ A CHS who has been closed for cause █████████████████████████████████ [104]

E.   Use of CHSs in Sensitive Monitoring Circumstances

The CHSPG "emphasizes the importance of oversight and self-regulation to ensure that CHS Program activities are conducted within Constitutional and statutory parameters and that civil liberties and privacy are protected."[105] To protect such rights, the FBI must meet additional requirements for use of CHSs in what the AG Guidelines and the DIOG define as "sensitive monitoring circumstances."[106]

One of the investigative techniques that the FBI may use in predicated investigations is consensual monitoring, which means the monitoring and/or recording of conversations, telephone calls, and electronic communications based on the consent of one party involved, such as an FBI CHS.[107] SSAs may approve the use of CHSs for consensual monitoring in ordinary cases, so long as the consent

---

[98] CHSPG § 18.1.2.

[99] CHSPG § 18.2.

[100] CHSPG § 18.3.

[101] CHSPG § 18.3

[102] CHSPG § 18.3.

[103] CHSPG § 4.5.1.

[104] CHSPG § 4.5.1.

[105] CHSPG § 1.2.

[106] AG Guidelines § VII.O; DIOG § 18.6.1.6.3.

[107] AG Guidelines § V.A.4; DIOG §§ 18.6.1.2, 18.6.1.4.

of the CHS has been documented, and the CDC or OGC has determined that, given the facts of the case, the consensual monitoring is legal.[108]

For investigations concerning threats to national security, the FBI is required to obtain approval from the Department for consensual monitoring in a "sensitive monitoring circumstance."[109] A "sensitive monitoring circumstance" as defined by the AG Guidelines and the DIOG is not the same as a "sensitive investigative matter" or "SIM." As described in Section I.B of this chapter, DIOG § 10.1.2 defines a SIM to include predicated investigations of the activities of a domestic public official or political candidate (involving corruption or a threat to the national security), or a domestic political organization or an individual prominent in such an organization.[110] In contrast, a "sensitive monitoring circumstance" is defined more narrowly. As it pertains to this report, a "sensitive monitoring circumstance" arises only when the FBI seeks to record communications of officials who have already been elected or appointed, such as Members of Congress, federal judges, or high ranking members of the executive branch.[111]

The AG Guidelines and the DIOG do not mandate prior notice to, or approval by, the Department before the FBI conducts consensual monitoring of candidates for political office or prominent officials in domestic political organizations, including the most senior officials in a national presidential campaign. However, the definition of a sensitive monitoring circumstance provides that the Attorney General, the DAG, or an Assistant Attorney General (AAG) can require that the FBI obtain Department approval prior to conducting consensual monitoring for a specific investigation of which they are aware.[112] As described in Chapter Ten of this report, the consensual monitoring conducted in the Crossfire Hurricane investigation did not meet the definition of sensitive monitoring circumstances provided by the AG Guidelines and the DIOG.

F. Use of CHS Reporting in FISA Applications

The CHSPG allows the use of CHS reporting in FISA applications without revealing the identity of the CHS, so long as the handling agent provides the relevant FBI Headquarters operational unit (e.g., Counterintelligence, Counterterrorism) with the CHS file number, duration of service to the FBI, and a statement on whether the CHS is reliable and has provided reporting that has been corroborated.[113] The CHS handling agent must also be prepared to furnish information to NSD concerning the CHS's criminal history, payments, and any

---

[108] DIOG §§ 18.6.1.5.1, 18.6.1.5.1.7.

[109] AG Guidelines § VII.O; DIOG § 18.6.1.6.3.

[110] AG Guidelines §§ VII.N, VII.O; DIOG §§ 10.1.2, 18.6.1.6.3.

[111] AG Guidelines §§ VII.N, VII.O; DIOG §§ 10.1.2, 18.6.1.6.3.

[112] AG Guidelines § VII.O(4); DIOG § 18.6.1.6.3.

[113] CHSPG § 10.13.

impeachment information.[114] All information provided to support a FISA application must also be documented in the CHS's Delta file.[115]

Further, the FBI's Foreign Intelligence Surveillance Act and Standard Minimization Procedures Policy Guide (FISA SMP PG) requires that the FISA accuracy or "Woods" file, described in more detail in the next section, contains documentation from the CHS handling agent stating that the handling agent has reviewed the facts presented in the FISA application regarding the CHS's reliability and background, and that, based upon a review of the CHS file, the facts presented in the application concerning the CHS are accurate.

III. The Foreign Intelligence Surveillance Act (FISA)

The FBI identified Carter Page as a U.S. person during all times relevant herein.[116] Accordingly, in this section, we briefly describe the statutory requirements and Department policies and procedures for obtaining approval to conduct electronic surveillance and physical searches targeting a U.S. person under FISA.[117]

A. Statutory Requirements and the Foreign Intelligence Surveillance Court

FISA authorizes the U.S. government to apply for and obtain an order from the Foreign Intelligence Surveillance Court (FISC) to conduct electronic surveillance and physical searches for foreign intelligence purposes. The government's application for electronic surveillance must be approved by the Attorney General (or his or her designee) and contain certain specified information, including a statement of the facts and circumstances relied upon by the applicant to support the belief that the target is a foreign power or an agent of a foreign power, and that each facility or place at which the electronic surveillance is directed is being used,

---

[114] CHSPG § 10.13.

[115] CHSPG § 10.13.

[116] A U.S. person means a U.S. citizen, a lawful permanent resident (*i.e.*, a green card holder), an unincorporated association with a substantial number of members who are citizens of the United States or lawful permanent residents, or a corporation that is incorporated in the United States—provided such corporation does not constitute a foreign government or any component thereof, a faction of a foreign nation, or an entity that is openly acknowledged by a foreign government to be directed and controlled by the foreign government. *See* 50 U.S.C. § 1801(i). FISA treats U.S. persons and non-U.S. persons differently in various aspects, including by setting forth different definitions of an "agent of a foreign power" for non-U.S. persons, and authorizing initial electronic surveillance and physical searches targeting a non-U.S. person for a longer duration (120 days versus 90 days for a U.S. person).

[117] This report does not describe other FISA provisions not relevant here, including the statutory requirements for obtaining similar FISA authority on a non-U.S. person, *see* 50 U.S.C. §§ 1801-1805, 1821-1825; *see also* E.O. 12139 (May 23, 1979); E.O. 12949 (Feb. 9, 1995). Also not relevant here are the circumstances under which the U.S. government may conduct emergency electronic surveillance or physical searches without a court order (for not more than 7 days). For the emergency provisions, *see* 50 U.S.C. §§ 1805(e), 1824(e).

or is about to be used, by a foreign power or an agent of a foreign power; proposed minimization procedures; and a description of the nature of the information sought and the type of communications or activities subject to surveillance.

An application for physical searches requires substantially similar information, except that it also must state the facts and circumstances justifying the applicant's belief that the premises or property to be searched contains "foreign intelligence information" and "is or is about to be, owned, used, possessed by, or is in transit to or from" the target.[118] Electronic surveillance and physical searches targeting a U.S. person may be approved for up to 90 days, and subsequent extensions may be approved for up to 90 days provided the government submits another application that meets the requirements of FISA.[119] The approvals and certifications required for applications for electronic surveillance and physical searches are discussed in more detail below.

In addition, 50 U.S.C. § 1881d(b) allows the U.S. government to apply for and obtain concurrent authorization to continue targeting a U.S. person reasonably believed to be outside the United States when applying for authorization to conduct electronic surveillance and physical searches within the United States. Because the requirements for such applications are substantially similar to those for surveillance and searches within the United States, we discuss them together.

Probable Cause

The electronic surveillance and physical search provisions of FISA require the FISC to make a probable cause finding based on information submitted by the government. Specifically, the FISC must find probable cause to believe that: (1) the target of the electronic surveillance and physical searches is a foreign power or, as described in more detail below, the agent of a foreign power; (2) for electronic surveillance, that each of the facilities or places at which the surveillance is being directed is being used, or is about to be used, by the foreign power or agent of a foreign power; and (3) for physical searches, that each of the premises or property to be searched is or is about to be owned, used, possessed by, or is in transit to or from the foreign power or agent of a foreign power. In determining whether probable cause exists, a judge may consider the target's past activities, as well as the facts and circumstances relating to his current or future activities.[120] Where the

---

[118] *See* 50 U.S.C. §§ 1823(a)(1)-(8). Foreign intelligence information means information that relates to, and if concerning a U.S. person is necessary to, the ability of the United States to protect against actual or potential attack or other grave hostile acts of a foreign power or an agent of a foreign power; sabotage, international terrorism, or the international proliferation of weapons of mass destruction by a foreign power or an agent of a foreign power; or clandestine intelligence activities by an intelligence service or network of a foreign power or by an agent of a foreign power. *See, e.g.,* 50 U.S.C. § 1801(e)(1).

[119] An order for electronic surveillance or physical searches may be extended on the same basis as the original order. The extension for a U.S. person may not exceed 90 days, whereas for non-U.S. person who is an agent of a foreign power it may be for a period not to exceed 1 year. *See* 50 U.S.C. §§ 1801(b)(1)-(2), 1805(d), 1824(d).

[120] 50 U.S.C. §§ 1805(a)(2), 1805(b), 1824(a)(2), 1824(b).

FISC authorizes the electronic surveillance or physical search of a U.S. person, the Attorney General may authorize, for the effective period of the FISC's order, the targeting of the U.S. person for the purpose of acquiring foreign intelligence information while such person is reasonably believed to be located outside the United States.[121]

According to FISA guidance issued by OGC, probable cause means the following:

> "[P]robable cause" is reason to believe, based on the available facts and circumstances, as well as the logical inferences that can be drawn from them. It is determined by the totality of the facts and circumstances, as viewed from the perspective of a reasonable person. Probable cause [means] probability, not certainty, and, thus, is significantly lower than the "proof beyond a reasonable doubt" necessary to support a criminal conviction. It is also lower than the "preponderance of the evidence" required in most civil cases.

The FISA guidance also states:

> [OGC] recommends that a field agent seeking a FISA order focus on the *object* of the belief required, *i.e.*, the facts and circumstances demonstrating that the target of the proposed search or surveillance is an agent of a foreign power and that the premises to be surveilled...is used by that agent of a foreign power, rather than on the *quantum* of the belief involved. If you can show that a target is engaged in certain activities, and that he is engaged in them for or on behalf of a foreign power, you have won most of the battle.[122]

Unlike wiretap applications in a criminal case, which require the government to establish probable cause to believe that an individual is committing, has committed, or is about to commit a specific criminal offense, among other requirements, FISA does not require that the government show a nexus to criminality.[123] Rather, a probable cause finding under FISA "focuses on the status of the target as a foreign power or the agent of a foreign power," which is discussed in more detail below.[124] The Report of the Senate Select Committee on Intelligence

---

[121] *See* 50 U.S.C. § 1881b(c)(B)(i).

[122] FBI OGC, *What Do I Have to Do to Get a FISA?* ("FISA guidance"), Jan. 23, 2003 (emphasis in original); *see also United States v. Rosen*, 447 F. Supp. 2d 538, 549 (E.D. Va. 2006).

[123] *See, e.g., United States v. Daoud*, 761 F.3d 678, 681 (7th Cir. 2014); *United States v. Abu-Jihaad*, 630 F.2d 102, 122, 127 (2d Cir 2010); *United States v. Duka*, 671 F.3d 329, 339-41 (3d Cir. 2011); *United States v. Wen*, 477 F.3d 896, 898 (7th Cir. 2007); *In re Sealed Case*, 310 F.3d 717, 738 (Foreign Intel. Surv. Ct. Rev. 2002) (per curiam); *United States v. Cavanagh*, 807 F.2d 787, 790 (9th Cir. 1987).

[124] *See, e.g., United States v. El-Mezain*, 664 F.3d 467, 564 (5th Cir. 2011); *see also United States v. Duggan*, 743 F.2d 59, 72-73 (2d Cir. 1984).

(SSCI) that accompanied the 1978 passage of FISA explains the rationale for the different probable cause standards:

> [I]f electronic surveillance is to make an effective contribution to foreign counterintelligence, it must be available for use when necessary for the investigative process. The criminal laws are enacted to establish standards for arrest and conviction[,] and they supply guidance for investigations conducted to collect evidence for prosecution. Foreign counterintelligence investigations have different objectives. They succeed when the United States can insure that an intelligence network is not obtaining vital information, that a suspected agent's future access to such information is controlled effectively, and that security precautions are strengthened in areas of top priority for the foreign intelligence service.... Therefore, procedures appropriate in regular criminal investigations need modification to fit the counterintelligence context. [FISA] adopts probable cause standards that allow surveillance at an early stage in the investigative process by not requiring that a crime be imminent or that the elements of a specific offense exist.[125]

Given these differences, the FISA guidance notes that the strictures developed to assess the reliability of informants providing information used to support a wiretap application in criminal cases do not necessarily apply to FISA.[126] However, the FISA guidance nonetheless cautions that probable cause determinations should take into account "the same aspects of reliability...as in the ordinary criminal context, including the reliability of any informant, the circumstances of the informant's knowledge, and the age of the information relied upon." The FISA guidance instructs agents to "look to the totality of the information and consider its reliability on a case-by-case basis" when judging the information supporting a FISA application.[127]

Agent of a Foreign Power

As described above, the probable cause finding required under FISA focuses on the status of the target as a foreign power or the agent of a foreign power. Under FISA § 1801(b)(2), the definition of "agent of a foreign power" includes, in relevant part, "any person" (including any U.S. person) who engages in the following conduct:

A.   Knowingly engages in clandestine intelligence gathering activities for or on behalf of a foreign power, which activities

---

[125] Report of the Senate Select Committee on Intelligence, *Foreign Intelligence Surveillance Act of 1978*, S. Rep. No. 701, 95th Cong., 2d Sess. 34 (Mar. 14, 1978) (S. Rep. 95-701), 3981.

[126] The rules for assessing the reliability of information provided by confidential informants or sources in counterintelligence cases are discussed above in Section II.

[127] *See* FISA guidance, *supra* (*citing Illinois* v. *Gates*, 462 U.S. 213 (1983)).

34

involve or may involve a violation of the criminal statutes of the United States; or

B.   Pursuant to the direction of an intelligence service or network of a foreign power, knowingly engages in any other clandestine intelligence activities for or on behalf of such foreign power, which activities involve or are about to involve a violation of the criminal statutes of the United States.[128]

Further, under FISA § 1801(b)(2)(E), the provision the Department relied upon in the Carter Page FISA applications, an agent of a foreign power also includes any person who knowingly aids or abets any person, or conspires with any person, in the conduct described above.

FISA provides that a U.S. person may not be found to be a foreign power or an agent of a foreign power solely upon the basis of activities protected by the First Amendment.[129] Congress added this language to reinforce that lawful political activities may not serve as the only basis for a probable cause finding, recognizing that "there may often be a narrow line between covert action and lawful activities undertaken by Americans in the exercise of the [F]irst [A]mendment rights," particularly between legitimate political activity and "other clandestine intelligence activities."[130] The Report by SSCI accompanying the passage of FISA states that there must be "willful" deception about the origin or intent of political activity to support a finding that it constitutes "other clandestine intelligence activities":

If...foreign intelligence services hide behind the cover of some person or organization in order to influence American political events and deceive Americans into believing that the opinions or influence are of domestic origin and initiative and such deception is willfully maintained in violation of the Foreign Agents Registration Act, then electronic

---

[128] FISA does not define what constitutes "other clandestine intelligence activities." However, the 1978 House Permanent Select Committee on Intelligence (HPSCI) Report accompanying the passage of FISA states the following:

The term "any other clandestine intelligence activities" is intended to refer to covert actions by intelligence services of foreign powers. Not only do foreign powers engage in spying in the United States to obtain information, they also engage in activities which are intended to harm the Nation's security by affecting the course of our Government, the course of public opinion, or the activities of individuals. Such activities may include political action (recruiting, bribery or influencing of public officials to act in favor of the foreign power), disguised propaganda (including the planting of false or misleading articles or stories), and harassment, intimidation, or even assassination of individuals who oppose the foreign power. Such activity can undermine our democratic institutions as well as directly threaten the peace and safety of our citizens. Report of the House Permanent Select Committee on Intelligence, *Foreign Intelligence Surveillance Act of 1978*, H. Rep. No. 1283, 95th Cong., 2d Sess. 41 (Jun. 8, 1978) (H. Rep. 95-1283).

[129] See 50 U.S.C. §§ 1805(a)(2)(A), 1824(a)(2)(A).

[130] H. Rep. 95-1283 at 41, 79-80; FISA guidance at 7-8; *see also Rosen*, 447 F. Supp. 2d at 547-48 (probable cause finding may be based partly on First Amendment protected activity).

surveillance might be justified under ["other clandestine intelligence activities"] if all the other criteria of [FISA] were met.[131]

Approval and Certification Requirements

Each application for electronic surveillance or physical searches under FISA must be approved by the "Attorney General," defined to include the Attorney General, Acting Attorney General, DAG, or, upon designation, the AAG of NSD.[132] The Attorney General (or his or her designee) must provide written approval that an application satisfies the statutory requirements—namely, that the facts and circumstances set forth in the affidavit support a finding of probable cause, and that the application meets all other statutory criteria.[133] During times relevant herein, the general practice was to submit FISA applications to the NSD AAG for approval and, in instances where the NSD AAG was unavailable or in an acting position, to the DAG. Similarly, in the event the DAG was unavailable or in an acting position, the FISA application was submitted to the Attorney General for approval.

Applications submitted to the FISC must also include written certification by certain specified high-ranking executive branch officials. In the case of FISA applications for FBI investigations, the application is usually certified by the FBI Director or Deputy Director.[134] The written certification must include the following:

- A statement that the certifying official deems the information sought to be "foreign intelligence information;"

- A statement that a "significant purpose" of the electronic surveillance or physical searches is to obtain foreign intelligence information;

- A statement that such information cannot reasonably be obtained by normal investigative techniques;

- A designation of the type of foreign intelligence information being sought (*e.g.*, information concerning a U.S. person that is necessary to the ability of the United States to protect against clandestine

---

[131] *See* S. Rep. 95-701 at 24-25. The Foreign Agents Registration Act, 22 U.S.C. § 611 *et seq.*, is a disclosure statute that requires persons acting as agents of foreign principals such as a foreign government or foreign political party in a political or quasi-political capacity to make periodic public disclosure of their relationship with the foreign principal, as well as activities, receipts and disbursements in support of those activities.

[132] *See* 50 U.S.C. §§ 1801(g), 1804(a), 1821(1), 1823(a).

[133] *See generally* David S. Kris and J. Douglas Wilson, National Security Investigations and Prosecutions § 6:5 (2016). In certain cases, the Director of the FBI, the Secretary of Defense, the Secretary of State, the Director of National Intelligence (DNI), or the Director of the CIA may request that the Attorney General personally review a FISA application. This obligation is not delegable by the Attorney General (or any of the other officials mentioned) except "when disabled or otherwise unavailable." *See* 50 U.S.C. §§ 1804(d), 1823(d).

[134] *See* 50 U.S.C. §§ 1804(a)(6), 1823(a)(6); E.O. 12139 (May 23, 1979) (electronic surveillance); E.O. 12949 (Feb. 9, 1995) (physical search).

intelligence activities by an intelligence service or network of a foreign power or by an agent of a foreign power).

- A "statement of the basis" for the certification that the information sought is the type of foreign intelligence designated and that it cannot reasonably be obtained by normal investigative means.[135]

As described in more detail below, the FISC must find that an application includes all of the required statements and certifications (among other requirements) before issuing an order authorizing electronic surveillance or physical searches. Where the target is a U.S. person, the FISC must find that the certifications are not clearly erroneous.[136]

Foreign Intelligence Surveillance Court (FISC)

The FISC was established in 1978 to hear applications and grant orders for electronic surveillance.[137] Subsequent amendments to FISA expanded the FISC's jurisdiction to the collection of foreign intelligence information by other means, including physical searches.[138] The FISC consists of 11 federal district court judges, chosen by the Chief Justice of the United States, from at least 7 judicial circuits, with at least 3 judges required to reside within 20 miles of the District of Columbia.[139] Judges on the FISC sit for staggered 7-year terms, during which time they also continue to serve as judges in their home districts.[140] According to former FISC Presiding Judge John D. Bates, district court judges selected to sit on the FISC are typically experienced judges with significant national security or Fourth Amendment experience.[141]

The FISC's Rules of Procedure require the government to submit a proposed application for authorization to conduct FISA surveillance and physical searches no later than 7 days before the government seeks to have the matter entertained, except that the 7-day requirement is waived when submitting an application

---

[135] *See* 50 U.S.C. §§ 1804(a)(6)(A)-(E), 1823(a)(6); *see also* H. Rep. 95-1283 at 76.

[136] *See* 50 U.S.C. § 1881b(c)(1)(D). The certifications submitted in support of a FISA application are presumed valid. The certifications are upheld absent a "substantial preliminary showing" that the application knowingly and intentionally, or with reckless disregard for the truth, included a false statement, and that the allegedly false statement was "necessary" to the approval of the application. In 2002, the Foreign Intelligence Surveillance Court of Review stated: "We think the government's purpose...is to be judged by the national security official's articulation and not be a FISA [C]ourt inquiry into the origins of the investigation nor an examination of the personnel involved...." *In re Sealed Case*, 310 F.3d at 736.

[137] *See* National Security Investigations and Prosecutions § 5:3.

[138] *See In re Motion for Release of Court Records*, 526 F. Supp. 2d 484, 487-88 (FISA Ct. 2007).

[139] *See* 50 U.S.C. § 1803(a)(1); Rule 4, FISC Rules of Procedure (Nov. 1, 2010).

[140] *See* 50 U.S.C. § 1803(d).

[141] *See* Culper Rule of Law Series: Judge John Bates, Lawfare Podcast at 32:00, https://www.lawfareblog.com/lawfare-podcast-culper-partners-rule-law-series-judge-john-bates (accessed Dec. 2, 2019) (hereinafter Lawfare Podcast).

following emergency authorization (not applicable here) or when the court agrees to expedite its consideration of an application at the government's request.[142] The proposed application typically is referred to as the "read copy," which is prepared by an attorney in NSD's Office of Intelligence (OI) based upon information provided by the FBI. The FISC will review the read copy, evaluate whether it meets the requirements of the statute, and, through a legal advisor, discuss with the assigned OI attorney, any issues the legal advisor or judge identified. The read copy allows FISC legal advisors to have informal interaction with OI to convey any questions, concerns, or requests for additional information from the legal advisor or judge before a final application is filed.[143] The OI attorney then works with the FBI to provide additional information to the FISC legal advisor and makes any necessary revisions before submitting the final application to the FISC.[144]

Once a final application is submitted, the judge may request that the OI attorney present it at a scheduled hearing, or may approve the application based on the written submission.[145] The judge is authorized to enter an order approving electronic surveillance or physical searches if he or she finds that the facts presented in the application are sufficient to establish probable cause, as discussed above; that the application includes "minimization procedures" sufficient to minimize the acquisition and retention, and prohibit the dissemination, of non-public information about a U.S. person unless it meets certain criteria; and that the application includes all required statements and certifications.[146]

---

[142] See Rules 6(a), 9(a), FISC Rules of Procedure (2010). The FISC Rules specifically address emergency authorizations but do not address expedited applications. However, Rule 9(a) states that the 7-day requirement does not apply to emergency authorizations or "as otherwise permitted by the Court." According to NSD, in instances where the government seeks the court's expedited consideration of a FISA application, and the court is able to do so, the court will rely upon "as otherwise permitted by the Court" to waive the 7-day requirement.

[143] According to a 2013 letter explaining how the FISC operates, FISC legal advisors interact with NSD on a daily basis. See Letter from Judge Reggie Walton to Senator Patrick Leahy, U.S. Senate Committee on the Judiciary (Jul. 29, 2013) (2013 Judge Walton Letter), http://www.fisc.uscourts.gov/sites/default/files/Leahy.pdf (accessed Dec. 2, 2019).

[144] See 2013 Judge Walton Letter, at 6 & n.3.

[145] If the judge denies a final application, he or she is required to draft a statement of reasons explaining the basis for the denial. See 50 U.S.C. §§ 1803(a)(1), 1822(c). Denials of applications for electronic surveillance or physical searches may be appealed to the Foreign Intelligence Surveillance Court of Review. See 50 U.S.C. §§ 1803(b), 1822(d). Alternatively, if the judge indicates that he or she will deny a proposed or final application, NSD may decide not to submit a final application, or may withdraw a final application after submission. See 2013 Judge Walton Letter at 3.

[146] See 50 U.S.C. §§ 1805(a), 1824(a); see also 50 U.S.C. § 1881d(b) (concurrent authorization to conduct electronic surveillance and physical searches targeting a U.S. person inside and outside the United States). In addition to the standard minimization procedures, which apply to all information acquired through electronic surveillance and physical searches, each application may describe other minimization procedures that are appropriate for the particular surveillance or search in question. The FISC may modify the government's proposed minimization procedures if it concludes they do not meet the statutory requirements. See National Security Investigations and Prosecutions, § 9.1.

If the FISC approves a FISA application, it issues a primary order finding that the statutory requirements were met and authorizing the electronic surveillance or physical searches. The primary order also must direct the government to follow the minimization procedures proposed in the application.[147] Where assistance from a third party (such as an email provider, telephone company, or landlord) is required, the FISC also issues a secondary order directing the third party to "furnish...all information, facilities, or technical assistance necessary" to accomplish the search or surveillance "in such a manner as will protect its secrecy and produce a minimum of interference."[148]

In addition, under Rule 13(a) of the FISC Rules of Procedure, if the government subsequently identifies a misstatement or omission of material fact in an application or other document submitted to the FISC, the government, in writing, must immediately inform the judge to whom the submission was made of the following: (1) the misstatement or omission, (2) any necessary correction, (3) the facts and circumstances of the misstatement or omission, (4) any modifications the government has made or proposes to make to how it will implement any authority or approval granted by the FISC, and (5) the government's proposal for disposal of or treatment of any information obtained as a result of the misstatement or omission.[149]

B.   FBI and Department FISA Procedures

1.   Preparation and Approval of FISA Applications

The FBI's policies and procedures for the preparation and approval of applications for authorization to conduct electronic surveillance or physical searches under FISA are contained in the FBI's online FISA Management System (FISAMS), the FISA Verification Form (described below), the DIOG, and the FISA SMP PG. We will describe the typical preparation and approval process below. The preparation and approval process taken with respect to the four Carter Page FISA applications, including steps that were taken in addition to the steps typically completed during the FISA process, are discussed in Chapters Five and Seven.

The FBI's FISA process is initiated when a case agent begins drafting a FISA Request Form for submission to OI. The FISA Request Form requires that the case agent provide specific categories of information to OI, the most important of which is a description of the facts and circumstances that the agent views as establishing probable cause to believe the target of the application is a foreign power or an agent of a foreign power. In particular, the FISA Request Form states that the case agent should provide a complete description of all material facts regarding a target to justify FISA authority or, in the case of renewals, to justify continued FISA coverage. In the case of FISA renewals, the form also asks the case agent to describe in detail any previous information that requires modification or correction.

---

[147] See 50 U.S.C. §§ 1805(c)(2)(A), 1824(c)(2)(A).

[148] See 50 U.S.C. § 1805(c)(2)(B).

[149] See Rule 13(a), FISC Rules of Procedure.

The form does not specifically require the case agent disclose exculpatory facts or facts that, if accurate, would tend to undermine the factual assertions being relied upon to support the government's theory, in whole or in part, that the target is a foreign power or an agent of a foreign power.

After the case agent prepares the FISA Request Form, in ordinary circumstances, the supervisory chain in the relevant field office will receive the request for approval, including the SSA, CDC, ASAC, and the SAC, before the request is sent to the appropriate FBI Headquarters substantive division Unit Chief (UC). The UC reviews and approves the request, assigns it to the appropriate FBI Headquarters substantive division SSA Program Manager, and to OGC's National Security and Cyber Law Branch (NSCLB) for assignment and review. As described in Chapter Five, in the case of Carter Page, because the investigation was close-hold and being conducted from FBI Headquarters instead of a field office, the case agent submitted the FISA Request Form directly to the NSCLB line attorney assigned to Crossfire Hurricane.

Once the FISA Request Form is submitted to NSCLB, an NSCLB line attorney reviews the request and provides feedback to the case agent. Once the draft is finalized, the NSCLB line attorney approves the FISAMS request and routes the form to the appropriate FBI Headquarters Section Chief for review and approval. The FBI Headquarters Section Chief reviews the request and, if approved, submits the request to the appropriate Deputy Assistant Director (DAD) for approval in the case of an expedited request, or, if not, directly to OI. Once in OI, the request is then assigned to an OI line attorney from one of three units within OI's Operations Section: the Counterintelligence Unit, the Counterterrorism Unit, or the Special Operations Unit. In this instance, an OI attorney in the Counterintelligence Unit was assigned to the Carter Page FISA request.

The OI attorney prepares the read copy application using the information provided by the FBI and works with the NSCLB attorney and FBI case agent to obtain additional information, frequently resulting in a "back and forth" between OI and the FBI. According to NSD, as part of this back and forth process, OI will ask whether the FBI is aware of any "exculpatory" information that relates to the target of the application, as well as any derogatory information that relates to sources relied upon in the application. An OI supervisor, usually the relevant Unit Chief or Deputy Unit Chief, then reviews the draft read copy. Neither the FISA statute nor FISC procedures dictate who in the Department must approve the read copy before it is submitted to the FISC. In most instances, once the FBI case agent affirms the accuracy of the information in the read copy, the OI supervisor conducts the final review and approval before a read copy is submitted with the FISC. However, in some cases, multiple OI supervisors, or even senior NSD leadership, may review the read copy, particularly if it presents a novel or complicated issue or otherwise has been flagged by the OI supervisor for further review.

NSD's Deputy Assistant Attorney General (Deputy AAG) for Intelligence is responsible for, among other things, overseeing OI. According to the Deputy AAG for Intelligence at the time of the Carter Page FISA applications and renewals, not all FISA requests from the FBI culminate in the filing of an application with the

FISC. Sometimes the back and forth process between the OI attorney and the case agent does result in sufficient factual information for a showing of probable cause or sometimes investigative objectives and needs change during the drafting process, obviating the FBI's desire for FISA authority on a particular target.

However, as described previously, after a read copy is filed, OI may receive feedback from the court through the FISC legal advisor. The OI attorney will then work with the case agent to address any issues raised by the legal advisor, such as by providing additional information to the FISC legal advisor and making any requested revisions before preparing the final application. Occasionally, the feedback from the court leads the FBI, in consultation with OI, to decide not to submit a final application, or to limit the authorities sought in the final application.

At the same time the read copy is filed with the FISC, OI sends the completed FISA application (referred to as the "FISA Certification Copy" or "cert copy") and a one-page cover memorandum (cert memo) signed by the OI supervisor to the case agent for final review within the FBI. This process in OI is sometimes referred to as "signing out" a FISA.

After receiving the cert copy and cert memo, an FBI agent, not necessarily the case agent, is assigned to complete an accuracy review of the application, which is discussed in more detail in Section III.B.2 below. After any additional edits necessitated by the accuracy review are made, the agent and an SSA sign the FISA Verification Form, also known as the Woods Procedures (described further below) or "Woods Form," and send the application package to the FBI Headquarters substantive division Program Manager who, according to the FISA SMP PG, must review the FISA application and coordinate the FISA accuracy and approval process that takes place at FBI Headquarters.

The Headquarters Program Manager is responsible for ensuring that the supervisory personnel in the field office have completed and documented their reviews of the application; determining whether another field office should also review the application for factual accuracy; verifying and providing documentation for any factual assertions identified by the field office as requiring Headquarters verification; and notifying OI and NSCLB of any factual assertions in the application that could not be verified so that the necessary action is taken to remove the unverified information from the declaration. If all factual assertions have been verified and documented, the Headquarters Program Manager will sign the affidavit in the application declaring under penalty of perjury that the information in the application is true and correct. The Program Manager then submits the application package to NSCLB for final legal review and approval by an NSCLB line attorney and Senior Executive Service-level supervisor. Witnesses told us that usually the Senior Executive Service-level supervisor is an NSCLB Section Chief or a Deputy General Counsel, but that, on occasion, the role is delegated to a GS-15 Unit Chief.

FBI procedures do not specify what steps must be taken during the final legal review. As described in Chapter Five, the FBI's Deputy General Counsel at the time of the Carter Page FISA applications told us that she typically reviewed the cert memo and FISA Verification Form to determine whether the FISA application package was complete, all the steps of the Woods Procedures were completed, the probable cause standard was met, and there were no outstanding issues.[150] Ultimately, if the NSCLB line attorney and a Senior Executive Service-level supervisor approve the FISA cert copy, they both sign the cert memo, and the complete application package is then taken to the FBI Director's Office for review and approval. If the FBI Director signs the cert copy, the paper copy of the signed application is delivered to OI. OI then provides the signed application package to the final signatory who, as discussed above, is usually the NSD AAG but can sometimes be the DAG or Attorney General.

In addition to receiving the final application and cert memo, the NSD AAG (or DAG or Attorney General) typically receives an oral briefing from senior OI managers. The NSD AAG receives the application for the first time during or shortly before the oral briefing, unless the application was submitted for his or her review beforehand, which is not typical. During the oral briefing, senior OI managers present all the FISA applications awaiting final Department approval, which, according to NSD, in 2016 generally ranged from 20 to 30 total applications in any given week (though the quantity sometimes varied outside that range). Once the FISA application is approved and signed by the NSD AAG, OI will submit it to the FISC for its final consideration.

2. "Woods Procedures"

In April 2001, the FBI implemented FISA verification procedures (known as "Woods Procedures") for applications for electronic surveillance or physical searches under FISA.[151] These procedures were adopted following errors in numerous FISA applications in FBI counterterrorism investigations, virtually all of which "involved information sharing and unauthorized disseminations to criminal investigators and prosecutors."[152]

To address these concerns, the procedures focused on ensuring accuracy in three areas: (1) the specific factual information supporting probable cause, (2) the existence and nature of any related criminal investigations or prosecutions involving the target of the FISA authorization, and (3) the existence and nature of any ongoing asset relationship between the FISA target and the FBI. The procedures required FBI agents and supervisors to undertake specific steps before filing a FISA application, which included a determination of whether the target is the subject of a

---

[150] As discussed in Chapter Five, the then Deputy General Counsel told us that she would sometimes read the FISA application if she determined, based on the cert memo or otherwise, that there was a reason to do so.

[151] Memorandum from Michael J. Woods, Unit Chief, FBI Office of the General Counsel, National Security Law Unit, to FBI Field Offices (Apr. 5, 2001). https://fas.org/irp/agency/doj/fisa/woods.pdf (accessed Dec. 2, 2019); see generally National Security Investigations and Prosecutions § 6.3.

[152] In re All Matters Submitted to the Foreign Intelligence Surveillance Court, 218 F. Supp. 2d 611, 620-21 (FISA Ct. 2002), rev'd, In re Sealed Case, 310 F.3d at 736.

past or current criminal investigation, negative or positive search results in FBI databases on the target, and a review of the affidavit for factual accuracy.

The Woods Procedures in the original memorandum were subsequently expanded and incorporated into other policy documents, including the 2016 FISA SMP PG, which was the applicable FBI policy guide in effect during the period relevant to this review, and a 2009 joint NSD-FBI guidance memorandum on FISA application accuracy (2009 Accuracy Memorandum).[153] Both the FISA SMP PG and 2009 Accuracy Memorandum state that the U.S. government's ability to obtain FISA authority depends on the accuracy of applications submitted to the FISC and that because FISA proceedings are *ex parte*, the FISC relies on the U.S. government's "full and accurate presentation of the facts to make its probable cause determinations." The FISA SMP PG further states that it is the case agent's responsibility to ensure that statements contained in applications submitted to the FISC are "scrupulously accurate."

Like the original procedures, the accuracy procedures in the FISA SMP PG require relevant FBI personnel to conduct database searches ▆▆▆▆▆▆▆▆▆▆▆▆▆▆▆▆▆▆▆▆▆▆▆▆to identify any previous or ongoing criminal investigations and to determine the target's immigration status; ▆▆▆▆▆▆▆▆▆▆▆▆▆▆▆▆▆▆▆▆▆▆▆; and identify the source of every fact asserted in a FISA application. The results of these steps must be documented in the FISA Verification or Woods Form and must be reviewed for accuracy and verified by relevant FBI personnel, with the results of the factual review documented and included in the final FISA package.

The FISA SMP PG requires that the case agent who requested the FISA application create and maintain an accuracy sub-file (known as a "Woods File") that contains: (1) supporting documentation for every factual assertion contained in a FISA application, and (2) supporting documentation and the results of the required searches and verifications. The Woods File must include the documented results of the required database and CHS file searches, as well as copies of the "most authoritative documents" supporting the facts asserted in the application. The FISA SMP PG advises that while there is some "latitude" as to what documents meet this requirement, the case agent "should endeavor to obtain the original documentation and/or best evidence of any given fact."

Further, as described earlier in this chapter, where a FISA application contains reporting from a CHS, the Woods File must contain a memorandum, email, or other documentation from the handling agent, CHS coordinator, or either of their immediate supervisors, stating that: (1) this individual has reviewed the facts presented in the FISA application regarding the CHS's reliability and background,

---

[153] Foreign Intelligence Surveillance Act and Standard Minimization Procedures, 0828PG, Aug. 11, 2016; Matthew G. Olsen, NSD Acting Assistant Attorney General and Valerie Caproni, FBI General Counsel, Memorandum for All Office of Intelligence Attorneys, All National Security Law Branch Attorneys, and All Chief Division Counsels, Guidance to Ensure the Accuracy of Federal Bureau of Investigation Applications under the Foreign Intelligence Surveillance Act, February 11, 2009; *see also* previous FBI policy guide, FBI FISA Accuracy Policy Implementation Guide, 0394PG, Mar. 31, 2011 (superseded by 0828PG).

and (2) based on this review of the CHS file documentation, the facts presented in the FISA application are accurate. Common accuracy documentation for a CHS include, among other things, ██████████████████████████████████████ ██ ██████████████ and reliability of the CHS.

After the Woods File is created, the case agent is responsible for verifying each factual assertion in the FISA application and ensuring that the supporting documentation is in the Woods File. In the case of renewal applications, the case agent must re-verify the accuracy of each factual assertion that is carried over from the first application and also verify and obtain supporting documentation for any new factual assertions that are added. After the case agent completes this process, the agent signs the Woods Form affirming the accuracy and documentation of every factual assertion in the application. The case agent then submits the Woods Form and Woods File to his or her SSA. The SSA is responsible for reviewing the Woods File and confirming that it contains supporting documentation of every factual assertion in the application. After the SSA completes this process, the SSA signs the Woods Form, and then the Woods Form, but not the Woods File, is transmitted to Headquarters. As described previously, one of the responsibilities of the Headquarters Program Manager is to verify any factual assertions that require Headquarters verification and provide supporting documentation for the Woods File. After doing so, the Program Manager signs the Woods Form affirming that he or she has verified the accuracy of those factual assertions and has transmitted the necessary documentation to the field office for inclusion in the Woods File.

According to FBI training materials, "everyone in the FISA process" relies on the case agent's signature on the Woods Form verifying that the factual assertions contained in the application are accurate. According to the FISA SMP PG, the Headquarters Program Manager, who signs the FISA application under penalty of perjury certifying that the information in the application is true and correct, does not typically have the personal or programmatic knowledge of the factual information necessary for a FISA application and therefore must rely on the field office for the accuracy of the information in the application. The case agent's signature allows the Program Manager to sign and swear to the application and the Director or Deputy Director to certify the application. Further, OI, NSD, the approving official (NSD AAG, DAG, or Attorney General), and the FISC rely on the Headquarters Program Manager, or declarant, that the application contains a complete and accurate recitation of the relevant facts.

The FISA SMP PG states that information in a FISA application that cannot be verified as true and correct must be removed from the application, or the entire application must be delayed until the information is verified and the verification is documented. According to FBI and NSD officials, in the case of information provided by a CHS, the verification process does not require that the FBI establish the accuracy of the CHS's information before that information may be relied upon in a FISA application. The OGC Unit Chief who supervised the attorney assigned to assist the Carter Page FISA applications told us that the Woods Procedures require that the case agent identify documentation stating what the CHS told the FBI, but does not require the agent to corroborate the underlying accuracy of the information. Similarly, according to NSD supervisors, although the Woods Procedures require that every factual assertion in a FISA application be "verified," when a particular fact is attributed to a source, an agent must only verify that the fact came from the source and that the application accurately states what the source said. The Woods Procedures do not require that the FBI have corroboration from a second source for the same information. According to the Deputy AAG who had oversight over OI at the time of the Carter Page FISA applications, the FISC is aware of how the FBI "verifies" information that is attributed to a CHS, and the court has not requested a change to their Woods Procedures. Further, NSD officials told us that in all instances, a FISA application will include an FBI assessment of the reliability of the CHS's information, which may come from factual corroboration or, in the absence of factual corroboration, from information about the CHS's general reliability.

IV. Ethics Regulations

Government ethics regulations, specifically those providing guidance on conflicts of interests pertain to the events discussed in Chapter Nine concerning Department attorney Bruce Ohr.

The Standards of Ethical Conduct for Employees of the Executive Branch (Standards of Ethical Conduct), 5 C.F.R. § 2635, is a comprehensive set of regulations that set forth the principles of ethical conduct to which all executive branch employees must adhere. In addition to the basic obligations of public service, the regulations address such ethical issues as gifts from outside sources and impartiality in performing official duties. Specifically, 5 C.F.R. § 2635.502 seeks to avoid any appearance of the loss of impartiality in the performance of official government duties by an employee due to a financial interest that the employee may have. It applies in circumstances:

> [w]here an employee knows that a particular matter involving specific parties is likely to have a direct and predictable effect on the financial interest of a member of his household...and where the employee determines that the circumstances would cause a reasonable person with knowledge of the relevant facts to question his impartiality in the matter....

Another portion of the regulations, 5 C.F.R. § 2635.402(b)(1), defines "direct and predictable effect" as "a close causal link between any decision or action to be taken in the matter and any expected effect of the matter on the financial interest."

Section 502 also includes a catch-all provision, which states:

> An employee who is concerned that circumstances other than those specifically described in this section would raise a question regarding his impartiality should use the process described in this section to

determine whether he should or should not participate in a particular matter. 5 C.F.R. § 2635.502(a)(2).

The process referenced in this section is for the employee to describe the circumstances that would raise an impartiality question to a Department ethics officer for the purpose of receiving guidance on how to address potential conflicts of interest, including whether the employee should be disqualified from participation. 5 C.F.R. § 2635.502(c).

V.   Examples of Other Department and FBI Policies Regulating Investigative Activity that Could Potentially Impact Civil Liberties

On occasion, the Department and the FBI investigate alleged illegal activity that is intertwined with, or take investigative steps with the potential to implicate, what is otherwise constitutionally protected activity. Examples include investigations of allegations of illegal campaign finance activity, allegations of violations of the Foreign Agent Registration Act, or the use of legal process to obtain information about the media or Members of Congress. The Department and the FBI have promulgated specific policies intended to ensure appropriate oversight of and accountability for many of these investigative activities. Some of these policies, such as the notification requirement described above for a "Sensitive Investigative Matter," applied to the Crossfire Hurricane investigation. In this section, we provide examples of other Department and FBI policies and procedures, not applicable to the Crossfire Hurricane investigation, that establish senior-level approval requirements and other procedures to regulate certain investigative activity capable of implicating civil liberties and constitutional concerns.

A.   Undisclosed Participation

Undisclosed Participation (UDP) takes place when anyone acting on behalf of the FBI, including a CHS, becomes a member of, or participates in, the activity of an organization on behalf of the U.S. government without disclosing their FBI affiliation to an appropriate official of the organization.[154] A CHS who participates in an organization entirely on his or her own behalf and who is not tasked by the FBI to obtain information or undertake other activities in that organization is not engaging in UDP—regardless of whether the CHS volunteers information to the FBI and regardless of whether the CHS's affiliation with the FBI is known. However, if the CHS is tasked by the FBI to join an organization, obtain specific information through participation in the organization, or take specific actions, those activities are on behalf of the FBI, and require compliance with the UDP policies set forth in the DIOG.[155]

---

[154] DIOG § 16.1.

[155] DIOG §§ 16.2.3.1, 16.3.

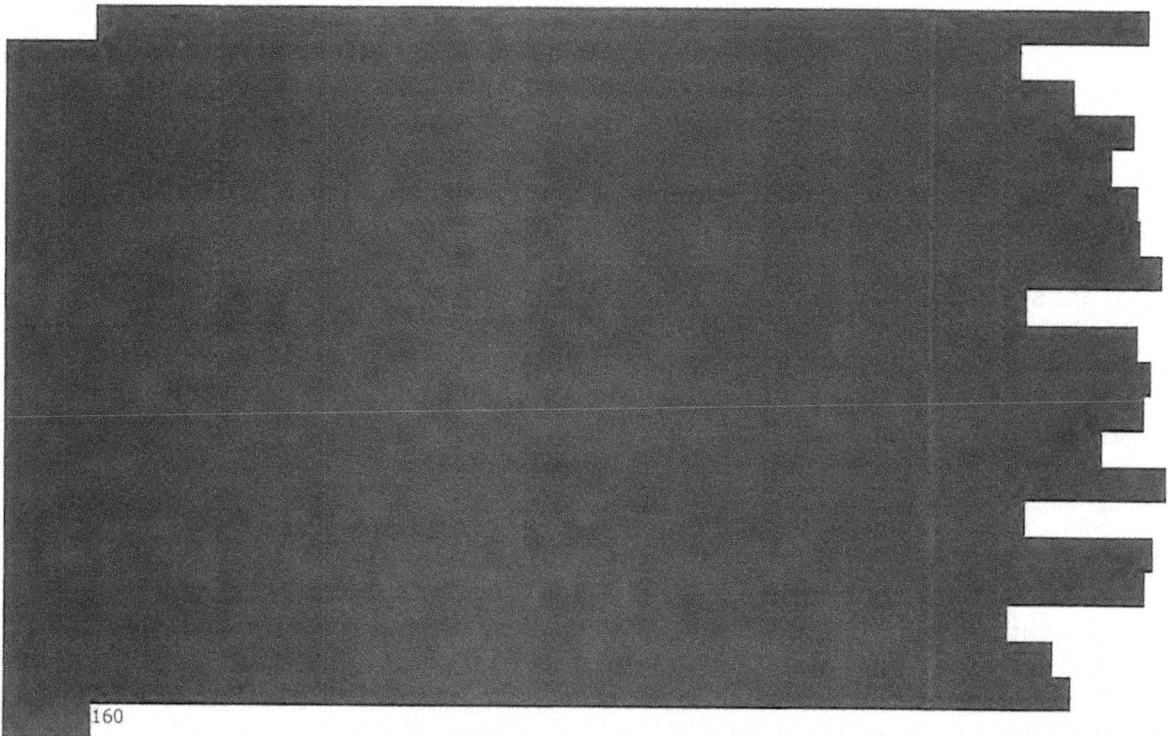

In our review, we identified an FBI CHS who, months after the presidential campaign was concluded, ▓▓▓▓▓▓▓▓▓▓▓▓▓▓▓▓▓▓▓▓▓▓▓▓ ▓▓▓▓▓▓▓▓▓▓▓▓▓▓▓▓▓▓ to the FBI, without being tasked by the FBI to gather that information, or directed by the FBI to participate in the campaign. This type of voluntary activity does not meet the definition of UDP and therefore does not implicate the FBI's requirements for approval of UDP.

B. Investigative Activities Concerning Members of the News Media, White House and Executive Branch Personnel, and Members of Congress

The Department and the FBI have policies to ensure appropriate oversight and accountability for investigative activities involving members of the news media, White House personnel, and Members of Congress.

1. Members of the News Media

The Department and the FBI have numerous regulations and policies regarding investigations that involve members of the news media that relate to events arising from their profession. For example, 28 C.F.R. § 50.10 and the

---

[156] DIOG § 16.2.3.5.

[157] DIOG § 16.4(A).

[158] DIOG § 16.3.1.5.1(B).

[159] DIOG § 16.2.3.2.

[160] DIOG § 16.3.1.5.3(C).

Department's Justice Manual § 9-13.400 govern obtaining information from, or records of, members of the news media and questioning, arresting, or charging members of the news media. The rules require, with certain exceptions, the Attorney General to approve subpoenas issued to members of the news media; warrants to search premises, properties, communications records, or business records of a member of the news media; and questioning, arresting, or charging members of the news media.

Pursuant to DIOG § 18.5.9.3.1, FBI agents must obtain higher-level authority, consistent with 28 C.F.R. § 50.10, when seeking the issuance of a subpoena for records relating to members of the news media. Similarly, DIOG § 18.6.4.3.4.3 requires the FBI to obtain the Attorney General's approval when using an administrative subpoena directed to a telecommunications provider for toll records associated with members of the news media.

2. White House and Executive Branch Personnel

The Department's Justice Manual states that any monitoring of oral communications without the consent of all parties, when it is known that the monitoring concerns an investigation into an allegation of misconduct committed by a senior member of the executive branch, must be approved by a Deputy AAG from the Department's Criminal Division.[161]

DIOG § 18.5.6.4.7 states that an FBI agent may only initiate contact with White House personnel as part of an investigation after consulting with the FBI OGC and obtaining SAC and appropriate FBI Assistant Director approval.

3. Members of Congress and Their Staff

The Department's Justice Manual states that any monitoring of oral communications without the consent of all parties when it is known that the monitoring concerns an investigation into an allegation of misconduct committed by a Member of Congress must be approved by a Deputy AAG from the Department's Criminal Division.[162]

DIOG § 18.5.6.4.6 requires FBI agents to obtain SAC and appropriate FBI Assistant Director approval, along with notice to the AD for the Office of Congressional Affairs, when seeking to interview a Member of Congress or Congressional staff in connection with a public corruption matter or a foreign counterintelligence matter.

---

[161] Section 9-7.302.

[162] Sections 9-7.302, 9-85.110.

CHAPTER THREE
THE OPENING OF CROSSFIRE HURRICANE, STAFFING, AND THE EARLY STAGES OF THE INVESTIGATION

On July 31, 2016, the FBI opened a counterintelligence investigation known as "Crossfire Hurricane." In this chapter, we provide an overview of the opening and initial steps of the Crossfire Hurricane investigation and its related cases. We first summarize the intelligence available to the FBI in the summer of 2016 regarding the Russian government's efforts to interfere with the 2016 U.S. elections. We then describe the events that led to the opening of the Crossfire Hurricane umbrella investigation and the related counterintelligence investigations of George Papadopoulos, Carter Page, Paul Manafort, and Michael Flynn. We also describe the structure and oversight of these investigations, including the FBI's staffing of the cases and the involvement of senior FBI and Department officials. Finally, we describe the early investigative steps taken in furtherance of the investigations.

I.   Intelligence Community Awareness of Attempted Russian Interference in the 2016 U.S. Elections

At the time the Crossfire Hurricane investigation was opened in July 2016, the U.S. Intelligence Community (USIC), which includes the FBI, was aware of Russian efforts to interfere with the 2016 U.S. elections. The Russian efforts included cyber intrusions into various political organizations, including the Democratic National Committee (DNC) and Democratic Congressional Campaign Committee (DCCC). Throughout spring and early summer 2016, the FBI became aware of specific cyber intrusions for which the Russian government was responsible, through ongoing investigations into Russian hacking operations conducted by the FBI's Cyber Division and the FBI's Counterintelligence Division (CD).

In March and May 2016, FBI field offices identified a spear phishing campaign by the Russian military intelligence agency, known as the General Staff Intelligence Directorate (GRU), targeting email addresses associated with the DNC and the Hillary Clinton campaign, as well as efforts to place malware on DNC and DCCC computer networks. In June and July 2016, stolen materials were released online through the fictitious personas "Guccifer 2.0" and "DCLeaks." In addition, in late July 2016, WikiLeaks released emails obtained from DNC servers as part of its "Hillary Leak Series." By August 2016, the USIC assessed that in the weeks leading up to the 2016 U.S. elections, Russia was considering further intelligence operations to impact or disrupt the elections.

In addition to the Russian infiltration of DNC and DCCC computer systems, between March and August 2016, the FBI became aware of numerous attempts to hack into state election systems. These included confirmed access into elements of multiple state or local electoral boards using tactics, techniques, and procedures associated with Russian state-sponsored actors.[163] The FBI learned that Russian efforts also included cyber-enabled scanning and probing of election related infrastructure in several states.

It was in this context that the FBI received information on July 28, 2016, about a conversation between Papadopoulos and an official of a Friendly Foreign Government (FFG) in May 2016 during which Papadopoulos "suggested the Trump team had received some kind of suggestion" from Russia that it could assist this process with the anonymous release of information during the campaign that would be damaging to candidate Clinton and President Obama. As described below, the FBI opened the Crossfire Hurricane investigation 3 days after receiving this information.

II. The Friendly Foreign Government Information and the FBI's Decision to Open Crossfire Hurricane and Four Related Counterintelligence Investigations

On July 31, 2016, the FBI opened the Crossfire Hurricane counterintelligence investigation to determine whether individuals associated with the Donald J. Trump for President Campaign were coordinating or cooperating, wittingly or unwittingly, with the Russian government to influence or interfere with the 2016 U.S. elections. According to the opening Electronic Communication (EC), the investigation was predicated on intelligence from an FFG. In this section, we describe the receipt of the information from the FFG and the decisions to open the Crossfire Hurricane

---

[163] Beginning in January 2017 and continuing into 2019, several U.S. government agencies, as well as senior intelligence officials, reported on Russia's efforts to interfere with the 2016 U.S. elections. For example, the Intelligence Community Assessment (ICA) titled "Assessing Russian Activities and Intentions in Recent U.S. Elections," published on January 6, 2017, concluded that Russian President Vladimir Putin and the Russian government conducted an influence campaign followed by a Russian messaging strategy that blended covert intelligence operations, such as cyber activity, with overt efforts in order to undermine public faith in the U.S. democratic process, denigrate then candidate Clinton, and harm Clinton's electability and potential presidency. Additionally, in June 2017, during a Senate Select Committee on Intelligence Hearing on Russian Interference in the 2016 U.S. Elections, USIC leadership concurred with the ICA and acknowledged that the Russian government was responsible for compromises of and leaks from political figures and institutions, among other activities, as part of its efforts to influence and interfere in U.S. elections. Similarly, the Senate Select Committee on Intelligence in 2019 and the House Permanent Select Committee on Intelligence in 2018 found, in part, that the Russian government historically has attempted to interfere in U.S. elections and attempted to interfere in the 2016 U.S. elections through attacks on state voter registration databases, cyber operations targeting governments and businesses using tactics such as spear phishing, hacking operations to include the DNC network, and social media campaigns. U.S. House Permanent Select Committee on Intelligence, *Report on Russian Active Measures*, 115th Cong., 2d sess., 2018, 114-130. U.S. Senate Select Committee on Intelligence, *Russian Active Measures Campaigns and Interference in the 2016 U.S. Election, Volume 1: Russian Efforts Against Election Infrastructure with Additional Views*, 116th Cong., 1st sess., 2019, 1-10. Further, Special Counsel Robert S. Mueller III concluded that the Russian government interfered with the 2016 U.S. elections through a social media campaign that favored then candidate Trump and disparaged then candidate Clinton, and through cyber intrusion operations against entities and individuals working on the Clinton Campaign. *See The Special Counsel's Report*, Vol. I at 1, 4-7.

counterintelligence investigation and the related investigations of Papadopoulos, Page, Manafort, and Flynn.

A. Receipt of Information from the Friendly Foreign Government and the Opening of Crossfire Hurricane

By March 2016, Papadopoulos, Page, and Flynn were among several individuals serving as foreign policy advisors for the Trump campaign. Manafort joined the Trump campaign in March 2016 as the campaign convention manager. In the weeks that followed, Papadopoulos met with officials of an FFG in a European city that had arranged several meetings in May 2016 to engage with members of the Trump campaign. During one of these meetings, Papadopoulos reportedly "suggested" to an FFG official that the Trump campaign "received some kind of a suggestion from Russia" that it could assist the campaign by anonymously releasing derogatory information about presidential candidate Hillary Clinton.[164] However, the FFG did not provide information about Papadopoulos's statements to the U.S. government at that time.

On July 26, 2016, 4 days after WikiLeaks publicly released hacked emails from the DNC, the FFG official spoke with a U.S. government (USG) official in the European city about an "urgent matter" that required an in-person meeting. At the meeting, the FFG official informed the USG official of the meeting with Papadopoulos. The FFG official also provided ███████████████ information from ████ FFG officials ██████ following the May 2016 meeting (hereinafter referred to as the FFG information). ████████ stated, in part, that Papadopoulos

---

[164] During October 25, 2018 testimony before the House Judiciary and House Committee on Government Reform and Oversight, Papadopoulos stated that the source of the information he shared with the FFG official was a professor from London, Joseph Mifsud. Papadopoulos testified that Mifsud provided him with information about the Russians possessing "dirt" on Hillary Clinton. Papadopoulos raised the possibility during his Congressional testimony that Mifsud might have been "working with the FBI and this was some sort of operation" to entrap Papadopoulos. As discussed in Chapter Ten of this report, the OIG searched the FBI's database of Confidential Human Sources (CHS), and did not find any records indicating that Mifsud was an FBI CHS, or that Mifsud's discussions with Papadopoulos were part of any FBI operation. In Chapter Ten, we also note that the FBI requested information █ ██

We refer to Joseph Mifsud by name in this report because the Department publicly revealed Mifsud's identity in The Special Counsel's Report (public version). According to The Special Counsel's Report, Papadopoulos first met Mifsud in March 2016, after Papadopoulos had already learned that he would be serving as a foreign policy advisor for the Trump campaign. According to The Special Counsel's Report, Mifsud only showed interest in Papadopoulos after learning of Papadopoulos's role in the campaign, and told Papadopoulos about the Russians possessing "dirt" on then candidate Clinton in late April 2016. The Special Counsel found that Papadopoulos lied to the FBI about the timing of his discussions with Mifsud, as well as the nature and extent of his communications with Mifsud. The Special Counsel charged Papadopoulos under Title 18 U.S.C. § 1001 with making false statements. Papadopoulos pled guilty and was sentenced to 14 days in prison. *See The Special Counsel's Report*, Vol. 1, at 192-94.

suggested the Trump team had received some kind of suggestion from Russia that it could assist this process with the anonymous release of information during the campaign that would be damaging to Mrs. Clinton (and President Obama). It was unclear whether he or the Russians were referring to material acquired publicly of [sic] through other means. It was also unclear how Mr. Trump's team reacted to the offer. We note the Trump team's reaction could, in the end, have little bearing of what Russia decides to do, with or without Mr. Trump's cooperation.

On July 27, 2016, the USG official called the FBI's Legal Attaché (Legat) and ███████████████████████████ in the European city to her office and provided them with the FFG information.[165] The Legat told us he was not provided any other information about the meetings between the FFG and Papadopoulos.[166] The Legat also told us that he did not know under what FBI case number the FFG information should be documented and transmitted. At the recommendation of the European city Assistant Legal Attaché (ALAT) for Counterintelligence, the Legat contacted a former ALAT who at the time was an Assistant Special Agent in Charge (ASAC) in the FBI's Philadelphia Field Office. The ASAC told the Legat that he believed the FFG information was related to the hack of DNC emails and identified a case number for that investigation for the Legat to use to transmit the information. The following day, on July 28, 2016, the Legat sent an EC documenting the FFG information to the Philadelphia Field Office ASAC. The same day, the information in the EC was emailed to the Section Chief of the Cyber Counterintelligence Coordination Section at FBI Headquarters.

From July 28 to July 31, officials at FBI Headquarters discussed the FFG information and whether it warranted opening a counterintelligence investigation. The Assistant Director (AD) for CD, E.W. "Bill" Priestap, was a central figure in these discussions. According to Priestap, he discussed the matter with then Section Chief of CD's Counterespionage Section Peter Strzok, as well as the Section Chief of CD's Counterintelligence Analysis Section I (Intel Section Chief); and with representatives of the FBI's Office of the General Counsel (OGC), including Deputy General Counsel Trisha Anderson and a unit chief (OGC Unit Chief) in OGC's National Security and Cyber Law Branch (NSCLB). Priestap told us that he also discussed the matter with either then Deputy Director (DD) Andrew McCabe or then Executive Assistant Director (EAD) Michael Steinbach, but did not recall discussing the matter with then Director James Comey. Comey told the OIG that he did not recall being briefed on the FFG information until after the Crossfire Hurricane investigation was opened, and that he was not involved in the decision to open the case. McCabe said that although he did not specifically recall meeting with Comey immediately after the FFG information was received, it was "the kind of thing that would have been brought to Director Comey's attention immediately." McCabe's

---

[165] A Legal Attaché (Legat) is the FBI Director's personal representative in a country in which the FBI has regional responsibility.

[166] According to the Legat, the ███████████████████ stated at the meeting with the USG official that the FFG information "sounds like an FBI matter."

contemporaneous notes reflect that the FFG information, Carter Page, and Manafort, were discussed on July 29, after a regularly scheduled morning meeting of senior FBI leadership with the Director. Although McCabe told us he did not have an independent recollection of this discussion, he told us that, based upon his notes, this discussion likely included the Director. McCabe's notes reflect only the topic of the discussion and not the substance of what was discussed.

McCabe told us that he recalled discussing the FFG information with Priestap, Strzok, then Special Counsel to the Deputy Director Lisa Page, and Comey, sometime before Crossfire Hurricane was opened, and he agreed with opening a counterintelligence investigation based on the FFG information. He told us the decision to open the case was unanimous. McCabe said the FBI viewed the FFG information in the context of Russian attempts to interfere with the 2016 U.S. elections in the years and months prior, as well as the FBI's ongoing investigation into the DNC hack by a Russian Intelligence Service (RIS). He also said that when the FBI received the FFG information it was a "tipping point" in terms of opening a counterintelligence investigation regarding Russia's attempts to influence and interfere with the 2016 U.S. elections because not only was there information that Russia was targeting U.S. political institutions, but now the FBI had received an allegation from a trusted partner that there had been some sort of contact between the Russians and the Trump campaign. McCabe said that he did not recall any discussion about whether the FFG information constituted sufficient predication for opening a Full Investigation, as opposed to a Preliminary Investigation, but said that his belief at the time, based on his experience, was that the FFG information was adequate predication.[167]

According to Priestap, he authorized opening the Crossfire Hurricane counterintelligence investigation on July 31, 2016, based upon these discussions. He told us that the FFG information was provided by a trusted source—the FFG—and he therefore felt it "wise to open an investigation to look into" whether someone associated with the Trump campaign may have accepted the reported offer from the Russians. Priestap also told us that the combination of the FFG information and the FBI's ongoing cyber intrusion investigation of the DNC hacks created a counterintelligence concern that the FBI was "obligated" to investigate. Priestap said that he did not recall any disagreement about the decision to open Crossfire Hurricane, and told us that he was not pressured to open the case.

We interviewed all of the senior FBI officials who participated in these discussions about their reactions to the FFG information and assessments of it as

---

[167] As detailed in Chapter Two, the DIOG provides for two types of predicated investigations, Preliminary Investigations and Full Investigations. A Preliminary Investigation may be opened based upon "any allegation or information" indicative of possible criminal activity or threats to the national security; a Full Investigation may be opened based upon an "articulable factual basis" of possible criminal activity or threats to the national security. In cases opened as Preliminary Investigations, all lawful investigative methods (including CHS and UCE operations) may be used except for mail opening, physical searches requiring a search warrant, electronic surveillance requiring a judicial order or warrant (Title III wiretap or a FISA order), or requests under Title VII of FISA. A Preliminary Investigation may be converted to a Full Investigation if the available information provides predication for a Full Investigation.

predication for Crossfire Hurricane. Each of these officials told us the information warranted opening a counterintelligence investigation. For example, Anderson told us that when the information from the Legat arrived it was "really disturbing," and that she told Priestap the information needed to be reviewed by the Deputy Director immediately (Anderson and Priestap, in fact, briefed McCabe that day, July 28). She also told us that the decision to open the case was based upon the concern that the U.S. democratic process could be manipulated by a foreign power. Anderson also told us that "[the FBI] would have been derelict in our responsibilities had we not opened the case," and that a foreign power allegedly colluding with a presidential candidate or his team members was a threat to our nation that the FBI was obligated to investigate under its counterintelligence mission.

Similarly, then FBI General Counsel James Baker told us that everyone was in agreement about opening an investigation because the information came from a trusted intelligence partner, and it concerned a "Russian connection to the Trump campaign." He told us the FBI had information about the Russian's hacking activities, which they considered "a threat." Baker could not specifically recall whether Crossfire Hurricane was opened as a Preliminary Investigation or a Full Investigation, but told us that a Full Investigation "would have been justified under these facts."

The Intel Section Chief also told us that he recalled the discussions about the FFG information when it arrived and said no one disagreed with opening a counterintelligence investigation based on the information. The Intel Section Chief also said that in the context of what was occurring with the DNC hacks and the release of the DNC emails, there was a possibility that the Russians reached out to a campaign to offer their assistance, and the FBI needed to investigate the allegation. The OGC Unit Chief had the same recollection, telling us that there was no real question about whether to investigate and that her impression was everyone thought the FFG information was so serious that the FBI had to investigate the allegations: "[T]his is not something we were looking to do, but given the allegations, we thought they were serious enough [that] we had to investigate."

Like Priestap, these officials told us that their evaluation of the FFG information was informed by the FBI's ongoing cyber investigation involving Russia and the DNC hack. According to the Intel Section Chief and Strzok, when the FFG information arrived, the FBI already had strong corroborating information indicating that senior officials in the Russian government were responsible for directing attacks on the 2016 U.S. elections, including the hack of the DNC. Anderson said the FBI's ongoing cyber investigation supported the decision to open a counterintelligence case based on the FFG information. Anderson stated:

> ...I don't remember exactly when we felt, you know, the moment in time when we felt that we had Russian attribution, not just to the hack, but also to the release of the emails. So though that was suspected or we had some information to support that theory for quite some time, but whether you...can attribute that to the Russians with a

high degree of certainty or...not, it sort of puts the whole thing together. On the one hand you've got the Russian efforts to obtain material that could be used as part of a foreign influence campaign and then on the other hand you've got [this] information about the possibility of collusion between the Russians and members of a presidential candidate's campaign.

Priestap told the OIG that before arriving at a final decision, he considered whether to provide a "defensive briefing" to any member of the Trump campaign in lieu of opening an investigation. According to Priestap, defensive briefings occur when U.S. government or corporate officials are being targeted by a foreign adversary and the FBI determines the officials should be alerted to the potential threat. Priestap did not recall who first raised the issue of defensive briefings, but said he discussed the subject collaboratively with other FBI officials. Priestap told us that he ultimately decided not to conduct defensive briefings and explained his reasoning:

> While the Counterintelligence Division does regularly provide defensive briefings to U.S. government officials or possible soon to be officials, in my experience, we do this when there is no indication, whatsoever, that the person to whom we would brief could be working with the relevant foreign adversary. In other words, we provide defensive briefings when we obtain information indicating a foreign adversary is trying or will try to influence a specific U.S. person, and when there is no indication that the specific U.S. person could be working with the adversary. In regard to the information the [FFG] provided us, we had no indication as to which person in the Trump campaign allegedly received the offer from the Russians. There was no specific U.S. person identified. We also had no indication, whatsoever, that the person affiliated with the Trump campaign had rejected the alleged offer from the Russians. In fact, the information we received indicated that Papadopoulos told the [FFG] he felt confident Mr. Trump would win the election, and Papadopoulos commented that the Clintons had a lot of baggage and that the Trump team had plenty of material to use in its campaign. While Papadopoulos didn't say where the Trump team had received the "material," one could reasonably infer that some of the material might have come from the Russians. Had we provided a defensive briefing to someone on the Trump campaign, we would have alerted the campaign to what we were looking into, and, if someone on the campaign was engaged with the Russians, he/she would very likely change his/her tactics and/or otherwise seek to cover-up his/her activities, thereby preventing us from finding the truth. On the other hand, if no one on the Trump campaign was working with the Russians, an investigation could prove that. Because the possibility existed that someone on the Trump campaign could have taken the Russians up on their offer, I thought it wise to open an investigation to look into the situation.

McCabe said that he did not consider a defensive briefing as an alternative to opening a counterintelligence case. He said that based on the FFG information, the FBI did not know if any member of the campaign was coordinating with Russia and that the FBI did not brief people who "could potentially be the subjects that you are investigating or looking for." McCabe told us that in a sensitive counterintelligence matter, it was essential to have a better understanding of what was occurring before taking an overt step such as providing a defensive briefing.[168]

We also asked those FBI officials involved in the decision to open Crossfire Hurricane whether the FBI received any other information, such as from members of the USIC, that the FBI relied upon to predicate Crossfire Hurricane. All of them told us that there was no such information and that predication for the case was based solely on the FFG information.[169] We also asked Comey and McCabe about then CIA Director John Brennan's statements reported in several news articles that he provided to the FBI intelligence on Russian contacts with U.S. persons that predicated or prompted the opening of Crossfire Hurricane. Comey told us that while Brennan shared intelligence on the overarching efforts by the Russian government to interfere in the 2016 U.S. elections, Brennan did not provide any information that predicated or prompted the FBI to open Crossfire Hurricane. McCabe said that he did not recall Brennan providing the FBI with information before the FBI's decision to open an investigation about any U.S person potentially cooperating with Russia in the efforts to interfere with the 2016 U.S. elections. Priestap and the Intel Section Chief also told us that Brennan did not provide the FBI any intelligence that predicated the opening of Crossfire Hurricane. We did not find information in FBI or Department electronic communications, emails, or other documents, or through witness testimony, indicating otherwise.

On July 31, 2016, the FBI opened a full counterintelligence investigation under the code name Crossfire Hurricane "to determine whether individual(s) associated with the Trump campaign are witting of and/or coordinating activities with the Government of Russia." As the predicating information did not indicate a specific individual, the opening EC did not include a specific subject or subjects. As described in Chapter Two, the factual predication required to open a Full Investigation under the Attorney General's Guidelines for Domestic Operations (AG

---

[168] McCabe told us that the decision to brief the DNC and Clinton campaign about the DNC hack was a different situation than the decision not to brief the Trump campaign about allegations of Russian efforts to assist the Trump campaign. He said that the DNC was a victim of hacking and the FBI had known that the DNC was not responsible for the hacks for some time.

[169] As we describe in Chapter Four, although the FBI first received reporting from Christopher Steele regarding alleged Russian interference in the 2016 U.S. elections in early July 2016, the agents and analysts investigating the FFG information (the Crossfire Hurricane team) did not become aware of the Steele reporting until September 19, 2016. We found no evidence the Steele election reporting was known to or used by FBI officials involved in the decision to open the Crossfire Hurricane investigation.

In the OIG's *Review of Various Actions in Advance of the 2016 Election*, we describe in Classified Appendix One certain information that the FBI was in possession of in 2016 but the vast majority of which the FBI had not reviewed by June 2018. Given that timing, we did not see any evidence that any of that information was considered for or part of the predication for the opening of Crossfire Hurricane.

Guidelines) and the FBI's Domestic Investigations and Operations Guide (DIOG) is an "articulable factual basis" that reasonably indicates that one of several circumstances exist:

- An activity constituting a federal crime or a threat to the national security has or may have occurred, is or may be occurring, or will or may occur and the investigation may obtain information relating to the activity or the involvement or role of an individual, group, or organization in such activity;

- An individual, group, organization, entity, information, property, or activity is or may be a target of attack, victimization, acquisition, infiltration, or recruitment in connection with criminal activity in violation of federal law or a threat to the national security and the investigation may obtain information that would help to protect against such activity or threat; or

- The investigation may obtain foreign intelligence that is responsive to a requirement that the FBI collect positive foreign intelligence—*i.e.*, information relating to the capabilities, intentions, or activities of foreign governments or elements thereof, foreign organizations or foreign persons, or international terrorists.

The opening EC describing the predication for Crossfire Hurricane relied exclusively on Papadopoulos's statements to the FFG ████████████ in the FFG information.

Crossfire Hurricane was opened by CD and was assigned a case number used by the FBI for possible violations of the Foreign Agents Registration Act (FARA), Title 18 U.S.C. § 951, which makes it a crime to act as an agent of a foreign government without making periodic public disclosures of the relationship.[170] As described in Chapter Two, the AG Guidelines recognize that activities subject to investigation as "threats to the national security" may also involve violations or potential violations of federal criminal laws, or may serve important purposes outside the ambit of normal criminal investigation and prosecution by informing national security decisions. Given such potential overlap in subject matter, neither the AG Guidelines nor the DIOG require the FBI to differently label its activities as criminal investigations, national security investigations, or foreign intelligence collections. Rather, the AG Guidelines state that, where an authorized purpose exists, all of the FBI's legal authorities are available for deployment in all cases to which they apply.[171]

The opening EC also designated Crossfire Hurricane as a "sensitive investigative matter," or SIM, which as described in Chapter Two, includes matters

---

[170] The FARA statute defines an "agent of a foreign government" as an individual who agrees to operate in the United States subject to the direction or control of a foreign government or official. 18 U.S.C. § 951(d).

[171] *See* AG Guidelines § A, II.

involving the activities of a domestic public official or political candidate (involving corruption or a threat to the national security), or a domestic political organization or an individual prominent in such an organization.[172] The term "domestic political organization" includes, in relevant part, a committee or group formed to elect an individual to public office. According to David Laufman, then Chief of the National Security Division's (NSD) Counterintelligence and Export Control Section (CES), the case was designated a SIM because it involved a campaign and "people associated with a campaign." The DIOG requires that cases opened and designated as SIMs by FBI Headquarters be reviewed by OGC and approved by the appropriate FBI Headquarters operational section chief. The DIOG also requires that the FBI provide an "appropriate NSD official" with written notification of the opening of a SIM.[173] The DIOG does not impose any additional special requirements on SIMs, but does state particular care should be taken when considering whether a planned course of action is the least intrusive method and if reasonable based upon the circumstances of the investigation.[174]

After Priestap authorized the opening of Crossfire Hurricane, Strzok, with input from the OGC Unit Chief, drafted and approved the opening EC.[175] Strzok told us that the case agent normally drafts the opening EC for an investigation, but that Strzok did so for Crossfire Hurricane because a case agent was not yet assigned and there was an immediate need to travel to the European city to interview the FFG officials who had met with Papadopoulos. With respect to the DIOG's notification requirement to NSD, we located in the Crossfire Hurricane case file a Letterhead Memorandum (LHM) dated August 3, 2016, addressed to NSD. However, NSD officials told us that NSD has no record showing it received the LHM, and we were unable to determine whether the FBI in fact provided the LHM to NSD.[176]

In addition to being designated a SIM, witnesses told us that, because the information being investigated related to an ongoing presidential election campaign, the Crossfire Hurricane case file was designated as "prohibited" meaning that access to the file was restricted and viewable to only those individuals assigned to

---

[172] The DIOG requires that if a case is designated as a SIM at the time of opening, the title or case caption must contain the words "Sensitive Investigative Matter." The opening EC for Crossfire Hurricane met this DIOG requirement.

[173] There is no requirement under the AG Guidelines or the DIOG that a senior Department official approve of or be consulted prior to the opening of an investigation designated a SIM.

[174] The DIOG requires that the least intrusive means or method be considered and—if reasonable based upon the circumstances of the investigation—used to obtain intelligence or evidence in lieu of a more intrusive method. The concept of least intrusive method applies to the collection of all information.

[175] Strzok was promoted to a CD Section Chief in February 2016, and later to Deputy Assistant Director (DAD) of CD's Operations Branch I on September 4, 2016.

[176] According to FBI documents, although the FBI usually provides an LHM to NSD, "due to the extreme sensitivity of both predication and subject of [Crossfire Hurricane], NSD was orally briefed." Notes and testimony reflect that in early August, NSD officials were briefed on at least two occasions at FBI Headquarters about the Crossfire Hurricane investigation.

work on the investigation. Agents and analysts referred to the investigation as "close-hold" and, as discussed later in this chapter, used covert investigative techniques to ensure information about the investigation remained known only to the team and FBI and Department officials.

B. The FBI Opens Counterintelligence Investigations on Papadopoulos, Carter Page, Manafort, and Flynn

On August 1, 2016, Strzok and a supervisory special agent (SSA 1) traveled to the European city to interview the FFG officials who met with Papadopoulos in May 2016.[177] According to Strzok and SSA 1, during the interview they learned that Papadopoulos did not say that he had direct contact with the Russians; that while his statement did not include him, it did not exclude him either; and that Papadopoulos stated the Russians told "us." Strzok and SSA 1 also said they learned that Papadopoulos did not specify any other individual who received the Russian suggestion. Strzok, the Intel Section Chief, the Supervisory Intelligence Analyst (Supervisory Intel Analyst), and Case Agent 2 told the OIG that, based on this information, the initial investigative objective of Crossfire Hurricane was to determine which individuals associated with the Trump campaign may have been in a position to have received the alleged offer of assistance from Russia.

After conducting preliminary open source and FBI database inquiries, intelligence analysts on the Crossfire Hurricane team identified three individuals—Carter Page, Paul Manafort, and Michael Flynn—associated with the Trump campaign with either ties to Russia or a history of travel to Russia. On August 10, 2016, the team opened separate counterintelligence FARA cases on Carter Page, Manafort, and Papadopoulos, under code names assigned by the FBI. On August 16, 2016, a counterintelligence FARA case was opened on Flynn under a code name assigned by the FBI. The opening ECs for all four investigations were drafted by either of the two Special Agents assigned to serve as the Case Agents for the investigation (Case Agent 1 or Case Agent 2) and were approved by Strzok, as required by the DIOG.[178] Each case was designated a SIM because the individual subjects were believed to be "prominent in a domestic political campaign."[179]

As summarized below, the opening ECs for the investigations provided similar descriptions of the predicating information relied upon to open the cases. The ECs

---

[177] Email exchanges reflect that the FBI planned to interview the FFG officials by telephone; however, the Legat told Strzok that a Senior Executive Service-level (SES) FBI official from CD should make the trip and meet with the FFG officials. Emails also reflect that a USG official advised the FBI that one of the FFG officials the FBI planned to interview would be unavailable on August 9 and suggested the interview take place prior to that date.

[178] Although the opening ECs identified Strzok, SSA 1, and the OGC Unit Chief as approvers, the OGC Unit Chief said that she provided legal review of the opening ECs only. As we described in Chapter Two, when a case is opened and designated a SIM by FBI Headquarters, the case opening requires review by OGC and approval by the FBI Headquarters operational Section Chief (SC).

[179] We did not locate any records that indicated the FBI provided written notification to NSD about the opening of these cases. However, as we described earlier in this chapter, the FBI orally briefed NSD officials on at least two occasions in August 2016 about the Crossfire Hurricane investigation to include Papadopoulos, Manafort, Flynn, and Carter Page.

differed in their descriptions of the particular activities of the subjects that gained the FBI's attention.

- The opening EC for the Carter Page investigation stated that there was an articulable factual basis that Carter Page "may wittingly or unwittingly be involved in activity on behalf of the Russian Federation which may constitute a federal crime or threat to the national security." The EC cross-referenced the predication for Crossfire Hurricane and stated that Page was a senior foreign policy advisor for the Trump campaign, had extensive ties to various Russia-owned entities, and had traveled to Russia as recently as July 2016. The EC also noted that Carter Page was the subject of an open, ongoing counterintelligence investigation assigned to the FBI's New York Field Office (NYFO), which we describe in the next section.

- The opening EC for the Manafort investigation stated that there was an articulable factual basis that Manafort "may wittingly or unwittingly be involved in activity on behalf of the Russian Federation which may constitute a federal crime or threat to the national security." The EC cross-referenced the predication for Crossfire Hurricane and stated that Manafort was designated the Delegate Process and Convention Manager for the Trump campaign, was promoted to Campaign Manager for the Trump campaign, and had extensive ties to pro-Russian entities of the Ukrainian government.

- The opening EC for the Papadopoulos investigation stated that there was an articulable factual basis that Papadopoulos "may wittingly or unwittingly be involved in activity on behalf of the Russian Federation which may constitute a federal crime or threat to the national security." The EC cross-referenced the predication for Crossfire Hurricane and stated that Papadopoulos was a senior foreign advisor for the Trump campaign and had "made statements indicating that he is knowledgeable that the Russians made a suggestion to the Trump team that they could assist the Trump campaign with an anonymous release of information during the campaign that would be damaging to the Clinton Campaign."

- The opening EC for the Flynn investigation stated that there was an articulable factual basis that Flynn "may wittingly or unwittingly be involved in activity on behalf of the Russian Federation which may constitute a federal crime or threat to the national security." The EC cross-referenced the predication for Crossfire Hurricane and stated that Flynn was an advisor to the Trump campaign, had various ties to state-affiliated entities of Russia, and traveled to Russia in December 2015.

C. The Pre-Existing FBI New York Field Office Counterintelligence Investigation of Carter Page

The OGC Unit Chief told us that of all the individuals associated with the Trump campaign best positioned to have received the alleged offer of assistance from Russia, Carter Page "quickly rose to the top" of the list because of his past connections to Russian officials and the FBI's previous contacts with Page. As reflected in the FISA applications described in Chapters Five and Seven, as well as in other FBI documents, NYFO had an interest in Carter Page for several years before August 2016 and had interviewed him on multiple occasions because of his relationships with individuals the FBI knew to be Russian intelligence officers.

An FBI counterintelligence agent in NYFO (NYFO CI Agent) with extensive experience in Russian matters told the OIG that Carter Page had been on NYFO's radar since 2009, when he had contact with a known Russian intelligence officer (Intelligence Officer 1). According to the EC documenting NYFO's June 2009 interview with Page, Page told NYFO agents that he knew and kept in regular contact with Intelligence Officer 1 and provided him with a copy of a non-public annual report from an American company. The EC stated that Page "immediately advised [the agents] that due to his work and overseas experiences, he has been questioned by and provides information to representatives of [another U.S. government agency] on an ongoing basis." The EC also noted that agents did not ask Page any questions about his dealings with the other U.S. government agency during the interviews.[180]

NYFO CI agents believed that Carter Page was "passed" from Intelligence Officer 1 to a successor Russian intelligence officer (Intelligence Officer 2) in 2013 and that Page would continue to be introduced to other Russian intelligence officers in the future.[181] In June 2013, NYFO CI agents interviewed Carter Page about these contacts. Page acknowledged meeting Intelligence Officer 2 following an introduction earlier in 2013. When agents intimated to Carter Page during the interview that Intelligence Officer 2 may be a Russian intelligence officer, specifically, an "SVR" officer, Page told them he believed in "openness" and because

---

[180] On or about August 17, 2016, the Crossfire Hurricane team received a memorandum from the other U.S. government agency detailing its prior relationship with Carter Page, including that Page had been approved as an operational contact for the other agency from 2008 to 2013 and information that Page had provided to the other agency concerning Page's prior contacts with certain Russian intelligence officers. We found no evidence that, after receiving the August 17 Memorandum, the Crossfire Hurricane team requested additional information from the other agency prior to submission of the first FISA application in order to deconflict on issues that we believe were relevant to the FISA application. According to the U.S. government agency, "operational contact," as that term is used in the August 17 Memorandum, provides "Contact Approval," which allows the agency to contact and discuss sensitive information with a U.S. person and to collect information from that person via "passive debriefing," or debriefing a person of information that is within the knowledge of an individual and has been acquired through the normal course of that individual's activities. According to the U.S. government agency, a "Contact Approval" does not allow for operational use of a U.S. person or tasking of that person.

[181] CI agents refer to this as "slot succession," whereby a departing intelligence officer "passes" his or her contacts to an incoming intelligence officer.

he did not have access to classified information, his acquaintance with Intelligence Officer 2 was a "positive" for him. In August 2013, NYFO CI agents again interviewed Page regarding his contacts with Intelligence Officer 2. Page acknowledged meeting with Intelligence Officer 2 since his June 2013 FBI interview.

In January 2015, three Russian intelligence officers, including Intelligence Officer 2, were charged in a sealed complaint, and subsequently indicted, in the Southern District of New York (SDNY) for conspiring to act in the United States as unregistered agents of the Russian Federation.[182] The indictment referenced Intelligence Officer 2's attempts to recruit "Male-1" as an asset for gathering intelligence on behalf of Russia.

On March 2, 2016, the NYFO CI Agent and SDNY Assistant United States Attorneys interviewed Carter Page in preparation for the trial of one of the indicted Russian intelligence officers. During the interview, Page stated that he knew he was the person referred to as Male-1 in the indictment and further said that he had identified himself as Male-1 to a Russian Minister and various Russian officials at a United Nations event in "the spirit of openness." The NYFO CI Agent told us she returned to her office after the interview and discussed with her supervisor opening a counterintelligence case on Page based on his statement to Russian officials that he believed he was Male-1 in the indictment and his continued contact with Russian intelligence officers.

The FBI's NYFO CI squad supervisor (NYFO CI Supervisor) told us she believed she should have opened a counterintelligence case on Carter Page prior to March 2, 2016 based on his continued contacts with Russian intelligence officers; however, she said the squad was preparing for a big trial, and they did not focus on Page until he was interviewed again on March 2. She told us that after the March 2 interview, she called CD's Counterespionage Section at FBI Headquarters to determine whether Page had any security clearances and to ask for guidance as to what type of investigation to open on Page.[183] On April 1, 2016, the NYFO CI Supervisor received an email from the Counterespionage Section advising her to open a ▮▮▮▮▮▮ investigation on Page. The NYFO CI Supervisor said that ▮▮▮ In addition, according to FBI records, the relevant CD section at FBI Headquarters, in consultation with OGC, determined at that time that the Page investigation opened by NYFO was not a SIM, but also noted, "should his status change, the appropriate case modification would be made." The NYFO CI Supervisor told us that based on what was documented in

[182] Intelligence Officer 3 pled guilty in March 2016. The remaining two indicted Russian intelligence officers were no longer in the United States.

[183] CI agents in NYFO told us that the databases containing security clearance information were located at FBI Headquarters. When a subject possesses a security clearance, the FBI opens an espionage investigation; if the subject does not possess a security clearance, the FBI typically opens a counterintelligence investigation.

the file and what was known at that time, the NYFO Carter Page investigation was not a SIM.

Although Carter Page was announced as a foreign policy advisor for the Trump campaign prior to NYFO receiving this guidance from FBI Headquarters, the NYFO CI Supervisor and CI Agent both told the OIG that this announcement did not influence their decision to open a case on Page and that their concerns about Page, particularly his disclosure to the Russians about his role in the indictment, pre-dated the announcement. However, the NYFO CI Supervisor said that the announcement required noting his new position in the case file should his new position require he obtain a security clearance.

On April 6, 2016, NYFO opened a counterintelligence ███████ investigation on Carter Page under a code name the FBI assigned to him (NYFO investigation) based on his contacts with Russian intelligence officers and his statement to Russian officials that he was "Male-1" in the SDNY indictment. Based on our review of documents in the NYFO case file, as well as our interview of the NYFO CI Agent, there was limited investigative activity in the NYFO investigation between April 6 and the Crossfire Hurricane team's opening of its investigation of Page on August 10. The NYFO CI Agent told the OIG that the steps she took in the first few months of the case were to observe whether any other intelligence officers contacted Page and to prepare national security letters seeking Carter Page's cell phone number(s) and residence information. The NYFO CI agent said that she did not use any CHSs to target Page during the NYFO investigation. The NYFO investigation was transferred to the Crossfire Hurricane team on August 10 and became part of the Crossfire Hurricane investigation.

III. Organization and Oversight of the Crossfire Hurricane Investigation

The FBI conducted and oversaw the Crossfire Hurricane investigation from July 31, 2016, to May 17, 2017, at which time it was transferred to the Special Counsel's Office. Over that 10-month period, three different teams of agents and analysts were assigned to the case: the first team worked out of FBI Headquarters from the opening of the case through December 2016; the second team worked out of three FBI field offices and FBI Headquarters from approximately January 2017 through April 2017; and the third team worked, like the second team, out of the three FBI field offices and FBI Headquarters from April 2017 to May 17, 2017. In this section, we describe the organization and staffing of the three investigative teams and the FBI's reasons for making changes as to how the investigation was organized. We also describe the role played by FBI and Department senior leadership in the investigation.

63

A.   FBI Staffing of the Crossfire Hurricane Investigation

1.   The Management and Structure of the Crossfire Hurricane Team

Witnesses told us that because of the sensitivity of the investigation, CD officials originally decided to conduct the investigation out of FBI Headquarters, under the program management of Operational Branch I, Section CD-4, rather than out of one or more field offices, which is more typical. The original team consisted of intelligence analysts, special agents, and SSAs from multiple field offices who were assigned to Headquarters for 90-day temporary duty assignments (TDYs). CD assigned the original team to the same office space at Headquarters, with both agents and analysts working together in close proximity. Agents and analysts on the Crossfire Hurricane team told the OIG that the decision to conduct the investigation out of FBI Headquarters instead of a field office presented multiple challenges, such as difficulties in obtaining needed investigative resources, including surveillance teams, electronic evidence storage, technically trained agents, and other investigative assets standard in field offices to support investigations. We were told that these were known risks consciously taken by CD officials, including Priestap, in order to minimize the potential for unauthorized public disclosure of the investigation and allow for better coordination with Headquarters and interagency partners.

Priestap told us that although he was ultimately responsible for the investigation, Strzok and the Intel Section Chief managed Crossfire Hurricane. Following the opening of the case, the team held meetings three times a week to discuss and determine the next investigative and analytical steps. The agents and analysts told us that the investigative and analytical decisions for the investigation were made at these meetings by the agents and analysts and then presented to the supervisors. Priestap said that while Strzok managed the operational side of Crossfire Hurricane, Priestap also sought the opinions of the Intel Section Chief and the OGC Unit Chief on operational decisions. Priestap also told us that he originally wanted to assign the investigation to a Deputy Assistant Director (DAD) other than Strzok because, although he had confidence in Strzok's counterintelligence capabilities, he had concerns about Strzok's personal relationship with Lisa Page affecting the Crossfire Hurricane team. According to Priestap, he told Steinbach about his concerns and Steinbach was supportive of his decision to remove Strzok from the team, but his decision was overruled by McCabe. Steinbach told us that he had concerns about Strzok and Lisa Page working together because he was aware of instances where they bypassed the chain of command to advise McCabe about case related information that had not been provided to Priestap or Steinbach. Priestap and Steinbach said they did not know why McCabe kept Strzok assigned to the investigation. Strzok told the OIG he did not ask McCabe to keep him on the investigation and does not know whether Lisa Page requested Strzok remain on the investigation in conversations with McCabe. We found no evidence that Page made any such request of McCabe.

McCabe told us that he recalled separate conversations with Steinbach and Priestap about Strzok's work on Crossfire Hurricane, but he said that in neither conversation did he (McCabe) overrule a decision by Priestap to remove Strzok from the case. According to McCabe, Steinbach said that he wanted to remove Strzok from his role on Crossfire Hurricane after Strzok became DAD (in September 2016) so that Strzok could have a "traditional DAD experience," rather than spending too much attention on a single, major sensitive case. McCabe told us that he did not disagree with Steinbach, and he saw it as a decision for Steinbach and Priestap to make on their own. McCabe said that in a separate conversation with Priestap, Priestap raised a concern about Strzok and Page, but that it was not about any personal relationship between the two, which McCabe said he did not know about at the time. According to McCabe, Priestap expressed frustration about the amount of time Page and Strzok were spending together talking about casework and that it was interfering with Strzok's ability to carry out his other responsibilities. McCabe told us that he did not recall Priestap requesting that Strzok be removed from the case because of this concern, but McCabe said that he talked to Page about reducing the amount of time she was interacting with Strzok.

Over a dozen agents, analysts, and one Staff Operations Specialist (SOS) were originally assigned on a full-time basis to the Crossfire Hurricane team. Only one of the team members on Crossfire Hurricane, Case Agent 3, had previously been assigned to the team that conducted the investigation, known as "Midyear Exam" or "Midyear," of Secretary of State Hillary Clinton's use of personal email for official purposes. However, the supervisory chain of DAD Strzok, the Intel Section Chief, AD Priestap, EAD Steinbach, Deputy Director McCabe, and Director Comey was the same for the Midyear and Crossfire Hurricane investigations. EAD Steinbach retired in February 2017 and was succeeded by Carl Ghattas. The Crossfire Hurricane team members were selected by Strzok, the Intel Section Chief, and SSA 1. The agents reported to SSA 1 and the analysts reported to the Supervisory Intel Analyst. SSA 1 reported operational activities to Strzok. The Supervisory Intel Analyst reported analytical findings to the Intel Section Chief. In addition, an OGC line attorney (OGC Attorney) was supervised by the OGC Unit Chief and provided legal support to the team.[184] The OGC Unit Chief reported to Anderson, who reported to Baker.

Case Agent 1 and the SOS were the original Crossfire Hurricane team members who had primary responsibility over the Carter Page investigation. They were joined by Case Agent 3 and Case Agent 4 who worked on the Papadopoulos and Manafort investigations, respectively.

Following the November 2016 U.S. elections, the 90-day TDY assignments ended for the agents and analysts on the original investigative team, and many of the team members, including SSA 1, returned to their field offices. In addition, in January 2017, CD reorganized the structure of the Crossfire Hurricane investigation by transferring the day-to-day operations of the four individual investigations to three field offices, and dividing oversight of the investigations between two operational branches at FBI Headquarters—Operations Branch I and Operations Branch II. According to Priestap, he transferred the cases to the field offices

---

[184] Both of these attorneys were also assigned to the Midyear team to provide legal support.

because of the need to conduct investigative activities in cities where the subjects of the investigations were located and to do so efficiently. Priestap told us that he also wanted to incorporate Operations Branch II into the program management of some of the Crossfire Hurricane cases for its expertise on RIS.

With respect to the four individual investigations, CD transferred the Carter Page investigation to NYFO, and it remained assigned to Case Agent 1, who returned to that office following his 90-day TDY. DAD Jennifer Boone and SSA 3 of Operations Branch II at FBI Headquarters assumed program management responsibilities over the case. The Papadopoulos investigation was transferred to the Chicago Field Office and assigned to Case Agent 3. The Flynn investigation was transferred to the Washington Field Office (WFO) and assigned to Case Agent 4. Strzok and SSA 2 of Operations Branch I retained program management responsibilities over both of these investigations. The Manafort investigation was transferred to a white collar criminal squad at WFO.[185]

The Supervisory Intel Analyst told us that the shifting makeup of the teams and the changing leadership created a divide between the analysts and the agents, which resulted in less interaction between the two groups. In April 2017, CD again reorganized the Crossfire Hurricane investigation by restructuring the day-to-day operations of the cases at FBI Headquarters to recentralize the case. Officials told us that the investigation had become too decentralized and that the reason to restructure the investigation at Headquarters was to impose greater structure on the team's investigative and analytical efforts. In addition, in March 2017, Comey notified Congress about the existence of the Crossfire Hurricane investigation. Witnesses told us that this created a need for a more cohesive effort by the Crossfire Hurricane team to keep Priestap regularly informed of case activities so that he was better able to respond to Congressional inquiries.

At the end of this chapter, Figure 3.1 illustrates the FBI chain of command for the Crossfire Hurricane investigation from the opening of the case on July 31, 2016 through December 2016. Figure 3.2 illustrates the chain of command from January 2017 through April 2017, and Figure 3.3 from April 2017 until the cases were transferred to the Special Counsel's Office on May 17, 2017.

2. The Role of Peter Strzok and Lisa Page in Crossfire Hurricane and Relevant Text Messages

In the OIG's June 2018 *Review of Various Actions in Advance of the 2016 Election*, we described text messages between Strzok and Lisa Page expressing statements of hostility toward then candidate Trump and statements of support for then candidate Clinton, and several text messages that appeared to mix political opinions with discussions of the investigation into candidate Clinton's email use and references to the Crossfire Hurricane investigation. One such exchange occurred on July 31, 2016, the date of the opening of the Crossfire Hurricane investigation,

---

[185] As described further in Chapter Nine, in January 2016, the FBI initiated a money laundering and tax evasion investigation of Manafort predicated on his activities as a political consultant to members of the Ukrainian government and Ukrainian politicians.

when Strzok texted Page: "And damn this feels momentous. Because this matters. The other one did, too, but that was to ensure we didn't F something up. This matters because this MATTERS. So super glad to be on this voyage with you." (Emphasis in original).

The following week, in an exchange on August 6, 2016, Lisa Page forwarded to Strzok a news article relating to Trump's criticism of a Gold Star family who appeared at the Democratic National Convention. The text message stated, in part, "And Trump should go f himself." Strzok responded favorably to the article and added, "And F Trump." Page replied, "So. This is not to take away from the unfairness of it all, but we are both deeply fortunate people." She then forwarded another news article and texted, "And maybe you're meant to stay where you are because you're meant to protect the country from that menace." Strzok responded, "Thanks. It's absolutely true that we're both very fortunate. And of course I'll try and approach it that way. I just know it will be tough at times. I can protect our country at many levels, not sure if that helps...."

Two days later, on August 8, 2016, Lisa Page texted Strzok, "[Trump's] not ever going to become president, right? Right?!" and Strzok replied, "No. No he's not. We'll stop it." In Chapter Twelve of the OIG's June 2018 *Review of Various Actions in Advance of the 2016 Election*, we detail additional text messages by Strzok and Page and the explanations that they provided to the OIG for these and the other text messages and our findings regarding them. *See* https://www.justice.gov/file/1071991/download.

In that review, we found that Strzok led the Midyear investigation shortly after its opening through its conclusion, and that he was deeply and actively involved in investigative decision making throughout the course of that investigation. We further found that Lisa Page served as a liaison between the investigative team and McCabe, and that she also regularly participated in team meetings and in investigative decision making.

As part of this review, in order to determine whether there was any bias in the investigative activities for Crossfire Hurricane that we reviewed, we asked agents and analysts assigned to the case about the roles Strzok and Page played in the Crossfire Hurricane investigation and their level of involvement in decision making. With respect to Strzok, these witnesses told us that while he approved the team's investigative decisions during the time he was in the supervisory chain of command for the investigation, he did not unilaterally make any decisions or override any proposed investigative steps. Priestap, in addition to telling us that it was his (Priestap's) decision to initiate the investigation, told us that to his knowledge, Strzok was not the primary or sole decision maker on any investigative step in Crossfire Hurricane. Further, as described above, in January 2017, the Crossfire Hurricane cases were divided between two operational branches within CD, and Strzok no longer supervised the Carter Page investigation, which was transferred to Operations Branch II, CD-1, under the supervision of then DAD Boone. In this report, we describe those occasions when Strzok was involved in investigative decisions.

With respect to Lisa Page, witnesses told us that she did not work with the team on a regular basis or make any decisions that impacted the investigation. Priestap told us that Lisa Page was "not in charge of anything" and that he never witnessed her attempt to steer the investigation or dictate investigative actions. Baker said that Lisa Page attended high-level meetings and knew the facts of the case, but was not in a "decision making position" and had no "decision making authority." Lisa Page told us that she did not have a formal role in the Crossfire Hurricane investigation but may have participated in team meetings to keep McCabe aware of the status of the investigation. McCabe also told us that she was the "facilitation point" between CD and his office during the investigation. As with Strzok, when we learned in this review of Lisa Page's presence at meetings or involvement in any investigative activity, we include that information in this report.

B. The Role of Senior FBI and Department Leadership in the Crossfire Hurricane Investigation

As part of our review, we examined the role that senior FBI and Department leaders played in Crossfire Hurricane, as well as their knowledge of critical events in the case, including its opening, the use of CHSs to gather information, and the decision to seek authority to conduct electronic surveillance. Throughout the chapters of this report, we highlight and describe this involvement and knowledge, where relevant. In this section, we summarize the role of FBI leadership and Department officials in the early stages of the investigation until May 2017 when the Papadopoulos, Carter Page, Manafort, and Flynn cases were transferred to the Special Counsel's Office.

1. FBI Leadership

We learned that CD officials briefed the Crossfire Hurricane investigation to FBI senior leadership throughout the investigation. Comey told the OIG that the FBI had "hundreds of thousands" of counterintelligence cases opened while he was Director, and he would not be involved in a counterintelligence case unless the chain of command made a judgment call about whether the nature of the case required the Director's involvement. He said the decision to brief the Director was based on several things, including whether the case required engagement with Department leadership or whether it was of interest to Congress. Comey said his level of involvement in Crossfire Hurricane was similar to some cases and dissimilar to others. He said:

> I would put [cases in] three buckets. One, cases they'd never tell me about because of a judgment by the leadership chain that it wasn't for the Director to know. Cases that I would be told about, simply to be aware of. And then cases, the third category would be cases that I was told about and, in some detail, and kept informed of as the investigation went on. Crossfire Hurricane was in that third bucket.

According to records reviewed by the OIG, Comey received his first, formal briefing on August 15, 2016, though, as described previously, McCabe's contemporaneous notes suggest Comey may have been told about the FFG information on July 29. Comey told us that he was updated on the status of the investigation every 2 to 4 weeks. These status updates were provided at the end of his regularly scheduled morning national security briefings conducted by, among others, McCabe, Steinbach, Priestap, and Strzok. According to Comey, these briefings did not typically include discussions about investigative strategy, but he was often briefed on specific investigative actions the Crossfire Hurricane team had taken or planned to take. Comey said that he did not recall playing a role in making any significant investigative decisions and did not have any concerns or disagreements with the investigative actions described by senior CD officials during briefings.

Comey told us that he recalled a discussion with the briefers about taking precautions to keep the case close-hold. Comey said he was mindful that the investigation involved a political campaign, and he advised the team to keep in mind that, "[although] it's smoke that we see, we don't know whether there's fire there." McCabe also told us the FBI wanted "to keep our inquiry as quiet as we could." He said that it was important to keep the investigation covert to avoid alerting the subjects of the investigation or others, and, specifically in this case, it was important due to the pending election.

McCabe told us he received regular briefings on the progress of Crossfire Hurricane and discussed the investigation with Comey at regular briefings. Strzok told us the team briefed McCabe approximately 5-10 times during the investigation, and the OGC Unit Chief told us McCabe was briefed every few weeks until the election in November and less frequently thereafter. According to both Strzok and the OGC Unit Chief, these briefings provided updates on the team's investigative activities and typically were not discussions about what steps to take. The OGC Unit Chief also said that McCabe directed the team to "get to the bottom of this as quickly as possible, but with a light footprint."

Priestap told us that Strzok, the Intel Section Chief, and the OGC Unit Chief frequently briefed him on the investigation and kept him apprised of significant developments. In addition to approving the opening of the Crossfire Hurricane cases, Priestap told us that he was involved in discussions as to whether to seek authority under FISA to conduct electronic surveillance ███████████ targeting Carter Page, a subject we describe in detail in Chapter Five. Priestap said he briefed Steinbach nearly every day on the case and provided Comey or McCabe with updates on an as-needed basis.

2. Department of Justice

a. National Security Division

The Department was first notified about the opening of Crossfire Hurricane on August 2, 2016, when Priestap and the Intel Section Chief briefed several representatives from NSD, including Deputy Assistant Attorney General (Deputy AAG) George Toscas, Deputy AAG Adam Hickey, and David Laufman, who as described previously was the CES Section Chief.[186] According to Laufman and his contemporaneous notes of the briefing, FBI officials described the FFG information and the four individuals the FBI had identified through its initial investigative work who were members of the campaign and had ties to Russia. Laufman told us that his impression was that the information from the FFG had "raised obvious alarm bells in the FBI" and he said the information "resonated" with him. He also said that the information the FBI provided at the briefing presented the question of whether someone in the Russian government was working with the campaign of a major party candidate to influence the U.S. elections. Laufman told us that "we certainly understood the significance of the matter and the need for further investigation" and that it would have been "a dereliction of duty and responsibility of the highest order not to commit the appropriate resources as urgently as possible to run these facts to the ground, and find out what was going on."

After this initial briefing, Toscas contacted Deputy AAG Stuart Evans who oversaw NSD's Office of Intelligence (OI), which prepares and files FISA applications. Evans told us that he met with Toscas, Hickey, and FBI representatives on or about August 11, 2016, concerning the opening of Crossfire Hurricane. Evans said he believed the FBI described the information from the FFG that led to the opening of the case and the FBI's preliminary assessment that led the team to focus on the four individuals associated with the Trump campaign. He said the basis for the investigation did not strike him as "thin" at the time of this briefing or in retrospect, and the steps the FBI had taken up to that point were not dissimilar to how he had seen the FBI handle other counterintelligence cases involving insider threat information reported by a credible source. Evans told the OIG that he did not recall anyone raising the issue of seeking FISA authority targeting Carter Page at this August briefing.

Following these initial briefings, the FBI invited NSD to attend weekly meetings with the Crossfire Hurricane team. According to Evans, he and Toscas attended some of the meetings, as did representatives from CES, including Laufman, and OI. Laufman's notes reflect that Hickey attended some of the meetings as well. According to Evans, CES and OI maintained "loose involvement and knowledge" of the status of the investigation in case the FBI requested assistance from CES on criminal legal process or from OI on a FISA application. However, Evans told us that his reaction to these meetings was that the investigation seemed "pretty slow moving," with not much changing week-to-week in terms of the updates the FBI was providing to NSD.

According to Laufman and his deputy, the FBI did not ask CES to assist with criminal legal process at any time before the 2016 U.S. elections. In December 2016, the FBI briefed NSD officials on the status of the Crossfire Hurricane cases, and, according to Laufman's notes, advised NSD of CD's reorganization of the investigation. According to his notes, the FBI decided that it would be establishing a new unit or team to focus on Russian influence activities and that none of the

---

[186] Lisa Page was the other FBI representative who attended this briefing. As described earlier, Strzok was meeting with the FFG officials about their conversations with Papadopoulos on this date.

Crossfire cases had been closed "so far." Laufman told us that he advised the FBI that CES wanted to be in a position to provide input should the FBI decide to close any of the Crossfire Hurricane cases, just to be sure the FBI had exhausted all investigative steps, but he did not recall this ever arising.

Mary McCord was NSD's Principal Deputy AAG when Crossfire Hurricane was opened. She told us that she received a comprehensive briefing from the FBI on the investigation in January 2017, by which time she was the Acting AAG of NSD.[187] She said that prior to that time, she was involved in certain aspects of the investigation through OI's assistance with the first Carter Page FISA application in September and October 2016, as well as through meetings she attended in November and December 2016 about aspects of the Manafort and Flynn cases. She said that she neither attended nor received long debriefs about the weekly Crossfire Hurricane meetings attended by other NSD officials before the election. According to McCord, as a general matter, it was typical for Department attorneys not to become directly involved in a counterintelligence investigation until the case required legal guidance or legal process.

According to McCord, by January 2017, developments in some of the cases, particularly the Flynn and Manafort cases, led to the need for a comprehensive briefing for Department officials on the different cases the FBI was pursuing, as well as for the greater involvement of prosecutors moving forward. In late February 2017, Laufman assigned a CES trial attorney (CES Trial Attorney) to assist the FBI's Crossfire Hurricane team by providing legal guidance as needed on any of the cases. Laufman told us, and his notes reflect, that CES did not receive regular briefings on the investigation from the FBI between December 2016 and March 2017.[188] As we described earlier in this chapter, during this period of time, the Crossfire Hurricane investigation was decentralized, with the individual cases being handled by three different FBI field offices. Witnesses from NYFO who worked on the Carter Page investigation told us that as a result of this, there were no regular team meetings with officials at FBI Headquarters.

b.   Office of the Deputy Attorney General

Sally Yates was the Deputy Attorney General (DAG) when Crossfire Hurricane was opened on July 31, 2016. Yates told the OIG that she did not specifically recall receiving a formal briefing from the FBI in the summer of 2016 about the case, or at any time before she left the Department on January 30, 2017, though she left open the possibility that such a briefing could have occurred. According to Yates, her office was typically less involved in counterintelligence investigations than criminal investigations.[189] Yates said that although she and others in the Office of

---

[187] McCord became the acting AAG in mid-October 2016 and continued in both roles until Dana Boente became the Acting AAG for NSD in April 2017.

[188] Laufman did not attend the meetings in January, February, and March 2017 that were attended by Boente, McCord, and other senior Department officials.

[189] Matthew Axelrod, then Principal Assistant Deputy Attorney General, told us that ODAG had less involvement in counterintelligence investigations than criminal investigations because most

the Deputy Attorney General (ODAG) attended Monday, Wednesday, and Friday morning threat intelligence briefings with the FBI Director on national security issues, typically those briefings focused on matters involving imminent national security threats and criminal cases. According to Yates, the primary counterintelligence issue for ODAG in the summer of 2016 was the broader issue of Russian interference in the elections and the possible infiltration of voting machines.

Yates told us that she did recall that following one of the morning threat intelligence briefings, Comey pulled her aside to discuss the FFG information the FBI had received regarding Papadopoulos. Yates did not recall specifically when this conversation took place, except that it was some time before she received the first Carter Page FISA application for approval.[190] Yates told us that she did not recall the specific details Comey provided, but did recall that they discussed why the FFG had not notified U.S. officials sooner. She said she recalled learning during that conversation that the FFG did not determine the significance of the information about Papadopoulos until the WikiLeaks release of DNC emails in July 2016. She also said that she did not recall whether Comey told her the FBI had opened an investigation in response to the FFG information. However, she said that an investigation "would be the natural consequence of that," and "[i]t would be strange not to" open an investigation given that what Papadopoulos said in May 2016 would happen, i.e., the release of information damaging to then candidate Clinton, did, in fact, happen in July 2016.

We asked Comey and McCabe about any discussions they had with Yates about the FFG information. Comey told us that he did not recall providing any briefing to Yates, but that the topic was likely discussed at one of the threat intelligence briefings. Comey also told us that the FBI generally tried to keep Department leadership informed about all significant activities to include important public corruption or espionage cases concerning Russian efforts to interfere with the 2016 U.S. elections. McCabe told us that he did not recall briefing Crossfire Hurricane to Yates; however, his contemporaneous notes of a regularly scheduled meeting with the DAG on August 10 reflect that Yates was briefed on the FFG information at that time. According to McCabe, the FBI did not provide regular briefings to Yates on Crossfire Hurricane after this meeting, but the FBI provided updates on developments in the investigation to ODAG following the Attorney General's morning briefings, which Yates typically attended.

Yates told us that she did not recall specific discussions about any of the Crossfire Hurricane cases after her initial conversation with Comey, though she said she was confident that such discussions took place and thought that Tashina Gauhar, the Associate Deputy Attorney General responsible for ODAG's national security portfolio, likely had such discussions with NSD or the FBI. Yates did recall

---

counterintelligence investigations do not lead to prosecution and can last for years while agents gather intelligence.

[190] As described in Chapter Five, ODAG received the first FISA application on or about October 14, 2016.

having a conversation with McCabe regarding the ongoing money laundering investigation of Manafort (described in more detail in Chapter Nine) and about not taking any overt investigative steps before the election. She told us that even though Manafort was no longer chair of the Trump campaign at the time of this conversation, she and McCabe agreed that they did not want to do anything that could potentially impact candidate Trump. She said she did not recall having a similar conversation with McCabe or Comey about the Crossfire Hurricane cases and thought that this was because, to her knowledge, the FBI was not contemplating any overt steps in those cases before the election.

Gauhar told the OIG that she was sure she attended discussions about the Crossfire Hurricane cases, likely during regularly scheduled meetings ODAG held with NSD officials, or possibly during the regularly scheduled morning threat intelligence briefings, but she did not recall any discussions specifically. According to Gauhar, discussions she attended before the election about Russia tended to focus on the broader topic of what Russia was trying to do to influence the upcoming election. She said she did not recall the Crossfire Hurricane cases being an ongoing topic of conversation from her vantage point, until issues came up in the Flynn case in early January 2017. Gauhar also told us that she learned more about the individual Crossfire Hurricane cases and the investigation after Boente requested regular briefings in February 2017.

On January 30, 2017, Boente became the Acting Attorney General after Yates was removed, and ten days later became the Acting DAG after Jefferson Sessions was confirmed and sworn in as Attorney General. Boente simultaneously served as the Acting Attorney General on the FBI's Russia related investigations after Sessions recused himself from overseeing matters "arising from the campaigns for President of the United States." Boente told the OIG that after reading the January 2017 Intelligence Community Assessment (ICA) report on Russia's election influence efforts (described in Chapter Six), he requested a briefing on Crossfire Hurricane. That briefing took place on February 16, and Boente said that he sought regular briefings on the case thereafter because he believed that it was extraordinarily important to the Department and its reputation that the allegations of Russian interference in the 2016 U.S. elections were investigated. Boente told us that he also was concerned that the investigation lacked cohesion because the individual Crossfire Hurricane cases had been assigned to multiple field offices. In addition, he said that he had the impression that the investigation had not been moving with a sense of urgency—an impression that was based, at least in part, on "not a lot" of criminal legal process being used. To gain more visibility into Crossfire Hurricane, improve coordination, and speed up the investigation, Boente directed ODAG staff to attend weekly or bi-weekly meetings with NSD for Crossfire Hurricane case updates.

Boente's calendar entries and handwritten notes reflect multiple briefings in March and April 2017. Boente's handwritten notes of the March meetings reflect that he was briefed on the predication for opening Crossfire Hurricane, the four individual cases, and the status of certain aspects of the Flynn case. Boente told us that when he was briefed on the predication for the investigation, he did not question it and did not have any concerns about the decision to open Crossfire

73

Hurricane. Boente's handwritten notes of the meetings focused on the Flynn investigation and potential criminal violations of the Logan Act, the FBI's efforts to corroborate information contained in the source reporting that we describe in Chapters Four and Six, and the FBI's investigative efforts in the Carter Page and Manafort cases.[191] According to Boente's handwritten notes, he was last briefed on Crossfire Hurricane the day after Rod Rosenstein was sworn in as DAG on April 26, 2017.

Rosenstein told us that he recalled being briefed three times during his initial two weeks as DAG on aspects of the investigation and Russian efforts to influence the 2016 U.S. elections. The first briefing occurred within a day or two of being sworn in and was provided by Boente and then Principal Associate Deputy Attorney General James Crowell. That briefing was followed by a meeting with Comey, McCord, and several others from the FBI and NSD. Rosenstein said he also received a briefing from representatives of the USIC that included an overview of Russian interference with the U.S. elections.

Rosenstein told us that during the initial Department briefings he was most focused on information that had developed into criminal investigations, which he believed were going to be more immediately relevant to his work as DAG. Rosenstein said he did not recall the details provided during the briefings regarding Carter Page other than Page was suspected of being a foreign agent. Rosenstein said he also did not recall the details of what was explained to him about the predication for opening the Crossfire Hurricane investigation.[192] He said he would have been focused on the status and direction of the cases at the time of the briefings, and not as much on any historical information concerning their initiation.

In Chapters Five and Seven, we describe ODAG's role in the four Carter Page FISA applications. As described in Chapter Seven, Yates approved the first Carter Page FISA application on October ▇, 2016 and FISA Renewal Application No. 1 on January ▇, 2017, Boente approved FISA Renewal Application No. 2 on April ▇, 2017, and Rosenstein approved the FISA Renewal Application No. 3 on June ▇, 2017.

c. Office of the Attorney General

Loretta Lynch was sworn in as Attorney General on April 27, 2015. Lynch told the OIG that she did not recall receiving a briefing on the Crossfire Hurricane investigation. Lynch's National Security Counselor told us that she did not receive any briefing on the case and did not know if Lynch received a briefing. Lynch said

---

[191] The Logan Act, Title 18 U.S.C. § 953, makes it a crime for a citizen to confer with foreign governments against the interest of the United States. Specifically, it prohibits citizens from negotiating with other nations on behalf of the United States without authorization.

[192] Rosenstein told us that at some later point—most likely in 2018—FBI officials represented to him that the basis for opening Crossfire Hurricane was the FFG information concerning Papadopoulos, and nothing else. He told us that he did not receive any information from the FBI indicating otherwise. He also told us that he did not have an opinion about whether the FFG information provided a sufficient basis to open the case.

she did not recall providing any guidance or direction to the FBI on the investigation, or having any awareness of the Carter Page FISA applications before she left the Department on January 20, 2017. She told us that her office generally did not oversee counterintelligence investigations, but that sometimes counterintelligence issues were raised during morning threat intelligence briefings. She said that she remembered knowing that Papadopoulos was a concern for the FBI, but she did not recall learning the specific information that came from the FFG relating to him.

Office of the Attorney General (OAG) officials told us that they did not read the Carter Page FISA applications or provide any feedback to OI, but email communications reflect that they were aware the FBI was seeking FISA authority targeting Carter Page before the first application was filed. These officials included Lynch's Chief of Staff and her National Security Counselor. The Chief of Staff told us she had no recollection of the email that referenced the FISA application. The National Security Counselor told us that she believed she would have advised the Attorney General of the application, but she did not have any specific recollection of having done so.

Lynch told the OIG that after one of her weekly security meetings at FBI Headquarters in the spring of 2016, Comey and McCabe pulled her aside and provided information about Carter Page, which Lynch believed they learned from another member of the Intelligence Community. According to Lynch, Comey and McCabe provided her with information indicating that Russian intelligence reportedly planned to use Page for information and to develop other contacts in the United States, and that they were interested in his affiliation with the campaign. Lynch told us that her understanding was that this information from Comey and McCabe was "preliminary" in that they did not state that any decisions or actions needed to be taken that day. She said that they discussed the possibility of providing a defensive briefing to the Trump campaign, but she believed it was "preliminary" and "something that might happen down the road." According to Lynch, she did not recall receiving any further updates on this issue following this conversation. Lynch's recollection of what Comey and McCabe told her is consistent with information referenced in connection with the 2015 SDNY indictment and subsequent conviction of a Russian intelligence officer referenced earlier in this chapter.

Comey told the OIG that he did not recall having such a conversation with Lynch, and that he did not think it was possible for such conversation to have occurred in the spring of 2016 because the FBI did not receive the FFG information concerning Papadopoulos until late July (as we described earlier in this chapter). He also said that he did not recall himself having any knowledge of Carter Page's existence until the middle of 2016.[193] Similarly, McCabe told us that he did not

---

[193] The OIG was unable to question Comey further using classified details Lynch described to us because, as noted in Chapter One, Comey chose not to have his security clearances reinstated for our interview. Internal email communications reflect that in April 2016 NYFO prepared summaries of the information that ultimately led NYFO to open a counterintelligence investigation on Carter Page on

recall having any knowledge of Carter Page at this time. He told us he had no recollection of briefing Lynch in the spring of 2016 about Carter Page and did not know Carter Page was the subject of an open investigation in NYFO.

3.   White House Briefings

Lynch told us that in her interactions with the White House in 2016, she did not recall substantive discussions about the Crossfire Hurricane investigations but did recall discussions about the broader topic of Russian interference in the 2016 U.S. elections. Lynch said that the FBI, and not the Attorney General, would brief the White House on the investigation if the FBI was able to share information it received, but she did not recall that occurring. Yates also told us she did not attend any White House briefings where Crossfire Hurricane or the Carter Page FISA application was briefed or discussed, and she had no knowledge of whether any such meetings occurred.

Priestap told the OIG that the FBI does not routinely brief ongoing cases to the White House with the exception of mass shootings, major terrorist attacks, or intelligence that suggests an imminent attack on the United States. Priestap said that due to certain national security considerations, information from ongoing investigations may also need to be briefed to the White House by the Director.

Comey told us that he received no requests from the White House to investigate members of the Trump campaign or inquiries about whether the campaign was involved with the efforts by the Russians to interfere in the 2016 U.S. elections. Comey said that he recalled generally the administration's interest in what the FBI was doing as a member of the USIC to understand and defeat Russia's efforts to interfere with the elections. In fact, according to Strzok, the White House requested a briefing from the USIC in the fall of 2016 about actions the Russians were taking to interfere in the elections. On September 2, 2016, Lisa Page and Strzok exchanged the following text:

> 9:41 a.m., Strzok to Lisa Page: "Checkout my 9:30 mtg on the 7th"
>
> 9:42 a.m., Lisa Page to Strzok: "I can tell you why you're having that meeting."
>
> 9:42 a.m., Lisa Page to Strzok: "It's not what you think."
>
> 9:49 a.m., Strzok to Lisa Page: "TPs [Talking Points] for D [Director]?"
>
> 9:50 a.m., Lisa Page to Strzok: "Yes bc POTUS wants to know everything we are doing."

Strzok told us that these texts referred to the request by the White House to know everything the USIC knew about what Russia was doing to interfere in the 2016 U.S. elections and did not refer to the Crossfire Hurricane cases investigating

---

April 6, 2016 (described previously), and provided them to CD officials at Headquarters to be used for a "Director's note" and a separate "Director's Brief" to be held on April 27, 2016.

U.S. subjects. Strzok told us that he never attended any White House briefings about Crossfire Hurricane.

McCabe's notes from a morning meeting with Comey and others in late July 2016 reflect that McCabe learned from Comey during the meeting that another U.S. government agency had briefed President Obama on intelligence that agency had suggesting that a RIS was engaged in covert actions to influence the U.S. presidential election in favor of Trump. McCabe told us he did not attend this White House briefing; however, based on his notes, he said he did not believe the FFG information would have been discussed during this meeting, and our review of his notes did not indicate otherwise. According to McCabe's notes of what he had been told by Comey, President Obama stated that the FBI should think about doing "defensive briefs." The notes do not provide any further details about what Obama said regarding defensive briefings, and McCabe told us he did not recall that any further details were provided to him. However, McCabe said he surmised from his notes that the briefings under discussion were to be given to the Trump campaign. As more fully described in Chapter Ten, the FBI participated in ODNI strategic intelligence briefings that were provided to members of both the Trump campaign and the Clinton campaign, including the candidates, in August and September 2016. However, those were not defensive briefings and did not address the allegations contained in the FFG information.

When we asked Comey about meetings with the White House concerning Crossfire Hurricane, he said that although he did not brief the White House about the investigation, he did mention to President Obama and others at a meeting in the Situation Room that the FBI was trying to determine whether any U.S. person had worked with the Russians in their efforts to interfere in the 2016 U.S. election.[194] Comey said he thought it was important that the President know the nature of the FBI's efforts without providing any specifics. Comey said although he did not recall exactly what he said, he may have said there were four individuals with "some association or connection to the Trump campaign." Comey stated that after he provided this information, no one at the meeting responded or followed up with any questions. Comey did not recall specifically when this meeting took place, but believed it may have been in August 2016. We were unable to determine whether this meeting was part of the same meeting reflected in McCabe's notes discussed above.

IV. Investigative Steps in Crossfire Hurricane Prior to Receipt of Christopher Steele Reporting on September 19

According to FBI officials, the early investigative steps taken in Crossfire Hurricane were structured to maintain a close-hold on the investigation and avoid any impact on the 2016 U.S. elections. FBI officials told us that no steps were

---

[194] Comey told us that this meeting was attended by then Chief of Staff Dennis McDonough, then National Security Advisor Susan Rice, then Director of National Intelligence (DNI) James Clapper, then CIA Director John Brennan, and then Director of the National Security Agency Michael Rogers.

taken to investigate anyone associated with the Trump campaign prior to the opening of Crossfire Hurricane on July 31.[195] Department officials including Rosenstein, Evans, Laufman, and Gauhar said they did not learn anything at any time suggesting otherwise. We reviewed emails of senior CD officials from the 2 months prior to the opening of Crossfire Hurricane and did not find any communications suggesting any investigative actions relating to Trump campaign personnel were taken prior to July 31, 2016, with the exception of the pre-existing Page and Manafort cases discussed previously.

Anderson told us that the investigation began on July 31 with covert investigative techniques to be "very quiet" prior to the election. We were told that the team's concern was that if the information about the investigation became public, it would disrupt the investigative efforts and could potentially impact the 2016 U.S. elections. Anderson also told us that counterintelligence investigations are typically "conducted in the dark" because any public confirmation of the existence of the investigation "might alert the hostile foreign power...that we were onto them." She also said that early on in the investigation, FBI managers overseeing the Crossfire Hurricane team "took off the table any idea of legal process" in conducting the investigation, because the FBI was "trying to move very quietly." The FBI did not use national security letters or compulsory process prior to obtaining the first FISA orders.

At the outset of the investigation, as described earlier in this chapter, Strzok and SSA 1 traveled to verify the FFG information while analysts conducted open source and database research on the Crossfire Hurricane subjects and monitored their travel. Analysts also developed profiles on each of the four subjects and reviewed FBI files for information and to identify potential FBI CHSs with useful contacts for the investigation.[196] Additionally, almost immediately after opening the Page, Papadopoulos, and Manafort investigations on August 10, the case agent assigned to the Carter Page investigation, Case Agent 1, contacted OGC about the possibility of seeking FISA authority for Carter Page. As we discuss in Chapter Five, FBI documents indicate that by late August, Case Agent 1 had been told that he had not yet presented enough information to support a FISA application targeting Carter Page.

The FBI also sent names of individuals associated with the Trump campaign to other U.S. government agencies and a foreign intelligence agency and requested any information about those individuals. McCabe said that requesting a name trace from other U.S government agencies is a standard step in counterterrorism and counterintelligence cases that assists investigators by providing information on the

---

[195] As referenced in Chapter Nine, prior to his involvement with the Trump campaign, Manafort was the subject of a federal criminal investigation by the Department for alleged white collar offenses. Further, as referenced earlier in this chapter, prior to his involvement with the Trump campaign, Carter Page was the subject of a NYFO counterintelligence investigation for his contacts with Russian intelligence officers.

[196] As described in Chapter Ten, early in the investigation, the Crossfire Hurricane team discovered that they had an existing FBI CHS who had previously interacted with three of the named subjects of the investigation.

kind of network surrounding a person in whom the FBI is interested. He told us that the FBI requests a name check on an individual who is the subject of an investigation, or who the FBI is considering as a subject, but is not certain that an investigation is warranted. McCabe said that the FBI also uses the information received from such name checks to eliminate individuals as subjects. The FBI received information from the name trace requests and serialized that information to the Crossfire Hurricane case file.

As we describe in Chapter Five, on or about August 17, 2016, the Crossfire Hurricane team received information from another U.S. government agency advising the team that Carter Page had been approved as an operational contact for the other agency from 2008 to 2013 and detailing information that Page had provided to the other agency regarding Page's past contacts with certain Russian intelligence officers. However, this information was not provided to NSD attorneys and was not included in any of the FISA applications. We also found no evidence that the Crossfire Hurricane team requested additional information from the other agency prior to submission of the first FISA application in order to deconflict on issues that were relevant to the FISA application.

FBI officials told us that the early steps in the investigation focused on developing information about the four subjects and conducting CHS operations to obtain relevant subject specific information. According to McCabe, using sources is a logical first step in an investigation to learn what information the FBI may have access to that could be of value in the investigation. Agents told us that CHS operations can be an effective tool for quickly obtaining information, including, for example, the telephone numbers and email addresses of the named subjects. In determining how to use CHSs in the Crossfire Hurricane investigation, SSA 1 and the case agents told the OIG that they focused their CHS operations on the predicating information and the four named subjects. Case Agent 1 told the OIG that the team "had a very narrow mandate" and that was "a mandate to look at these four individuals...and see if there's any potential cooperation between themselves and the Russian government...that was our goal in that investigation." He added that they were focused on the information provided by the FFG and "we wanted to prove or disprove it, [as] best we could" but also "wanted to make sure that it didn't get broadcast out and we didn't harm the electoral process." Case Agent 2 stated that the core of the investigation was "literally looking at the predication and saying, okay, who reasonably could have had been in a position to receive suggestions from the Russians?"

As summarized in Chapter Ten, the Crossfire Hurricane team conducted three CHS operations prior to the team's initial receipt of Steele's reporting on September 19, 2016. All three CHS operations were with individuals who were still with the Trump campaign. The first was a consensually recorded meeting in August 2016 between Carter Page and an FBI CHS. During the meeting, Page discussed his recent trip to Moscow, a pending "October Surprise" discussed further in Chapters Five, Seven, and Ten, and his involvement with the Russian energy company Gazprom. Page also told the CHS that he had "literally never met" Paul Manafort, had "never said one word to him," and that Manafort had not responded to any of

Carter Page's emails.[197]   SSA 1 and Case Agent 1 told the OIG that this meeting was important for the investigation as it helped the team determine where Page lived and what he was currently working on as well as developing a successful contact between an established FBI source and one of the Crossfire Hurricane targets.

The second CHS operation took place in September 2016, between an FBI CHS and a high-level official in the Trump campaign who was not a subject of the investigation.   Case Agent 1 told the OIG that the plan for this operation was for the CHS to ask the high-level official about Papadopoulos and Carter Page "because they were...unknowns" and the Crossfire Hurricane team was trying to find out how "these two individuals who are not known in political circles...[got] introduced to the campaign," including whether the person responsible for those introductions had ties to RIS.   During the consensually recorded meeting, the CHS raised a number of issues that were pertinent to the investigation, but received little information from the high-level official in response.[198]

The third CHS operation took place in September 2016, and involved Papadopoulos.   The Crossfire Hurricane case agents told the OIG that, during this CHS operation, they were trying to recreate the conditions that resulted in Papadopoulos's comments to the FFG official about the suggestion from Russia that it could assist the Trump campaign by anonymously releasing derogatory information about then candidate Clinton, which we described earlier in this chapter.   Among other things, when the CHS asked Papadopoulos whether help "from a third party like WikiLeaks for example or some other third party like the Russians, could be incredibly helpful" in securing a campaign victory, Papadopoulos responded that the "campaign, of course, [does not] advocate for this type of activity because at the end of the day it's...illegal."   Papadopoulos also stated that the campaign is not "reaching out to WikiLeaks or to whoever it is to tell them please work with us, collaborate because we don't, no one does that...."[199]

Thereafter, on September 19, 2016, the Crossfire Hurricane team received information from an FBI source (Christopher Steele) on election matters that became an important part of the Crossfire Hurricane investigation and the FBI seeking FISA authority targeting one of the Crossfire Hurricane subjects, Carter Page.   The information the Crossfire Hurricane team received from Steele and the team's use of the information is described in the next chapter.

---

[197] As we discuss later in this report, Carter Page's comment about his lack of a relationship with Manafort was relevant to one of the allegations in the Steele reporting that was relied upon in the Carter Page FISA applications, but information about the August 2016 CHS meeting was not shared with the OI attorneys handling the FISA applications until June 2017.

[198] We found no evidence that the information learned at this meeting was put to use by the Crossfire Hurricane team or disclosed to the OI attorneys handling the Carter Page FISA applications.

[199] The Crossfire Hurricane team did not provide information about this meeting to OI attorneys handling the Carter Page FISA applications. As described in Chapter Eight, OI learned of the information from ODAG in May 2018.

Figure 3.1
FBI Chain of Command and Legal Support
for the Crossfire Hurricane Investigation
July 31, 2016 to December 2016

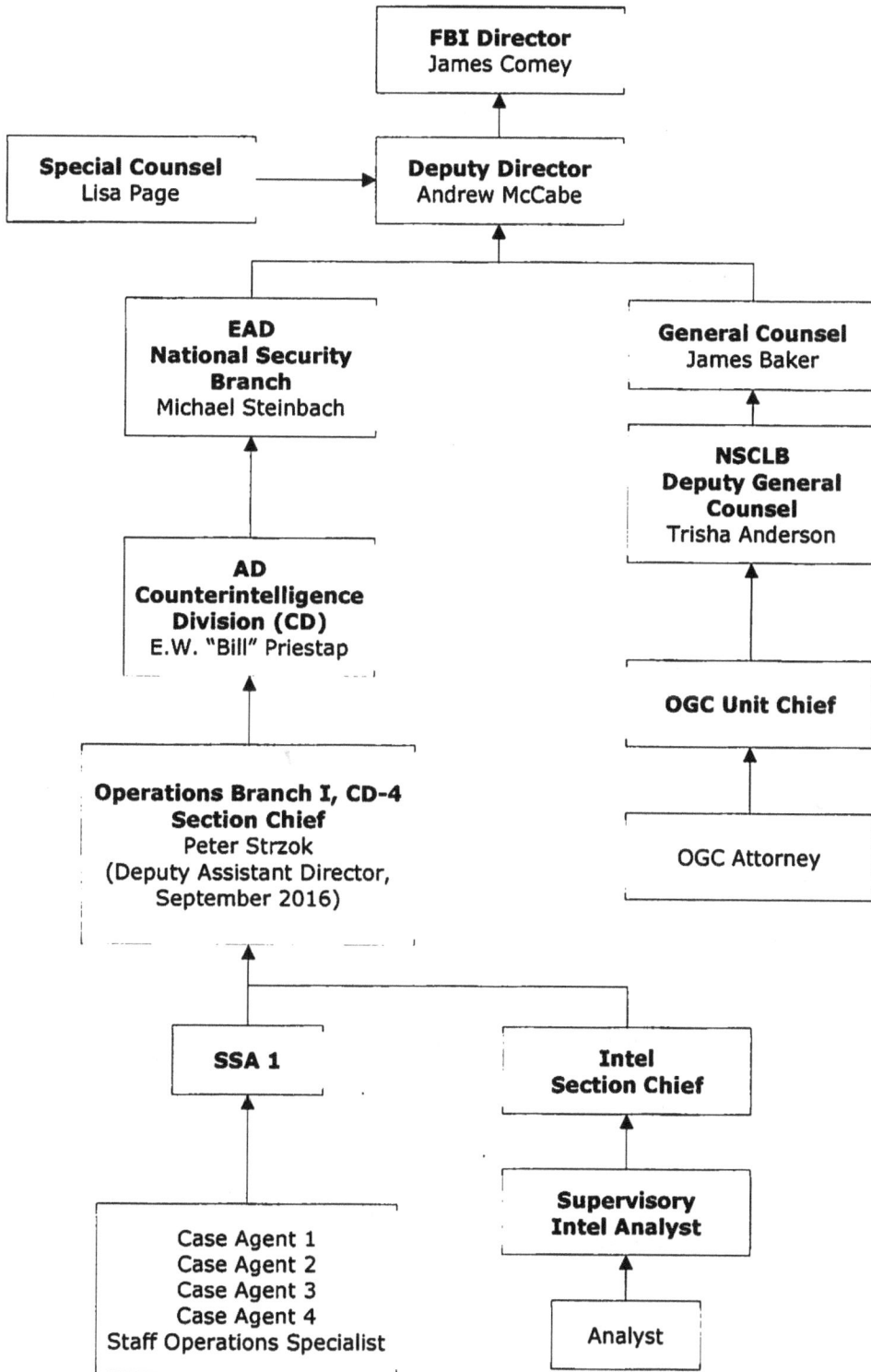

FBI Director
James Comey

Special Counsel
Lisa Page

Deputy Director
Andrew McCabe

EAD
National Security
Branch
Michael Steinbach

General Counsel
James Baker

NSCLB
Deputy General
Counsel
Trisha Anderson

AD
Counterintelligence
Division (CD)
E.W. "Bill" Priestap

OGC Unit Chief

Operations Branch I, CD-4
Section Chief
Peter Strzok
(Deputy Assistant Director,
September 2016)

OGC Attorney

SSA 1

Intel
Section Chief

Case Agent 1
Case Agent 2
Case Agent 3
Case Agent 4
Staff Operations Specialist

Supervisory
Intel Analyst

Analyst

81

Figure 3.2
FBI Chain of Command and Legal Support
for the Crossfire Hurricane Investigation
January 2017 to April 2017

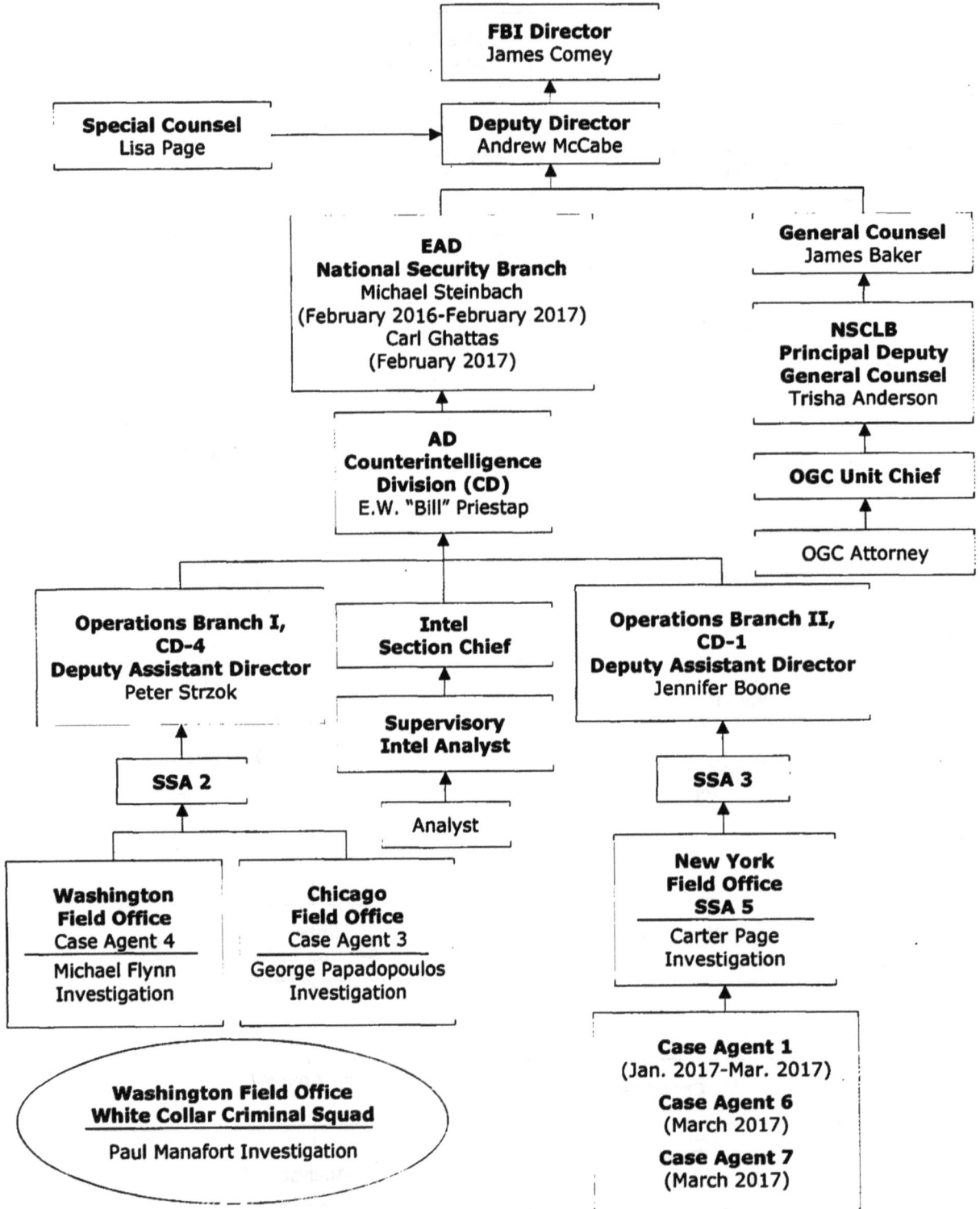

FBI Director
James Comey

Special Counsel
Lisa Page

Deputy Director
Andrew McCabe

EAD
National Security Branch
Michael Steinbach
(February 2016-February 2017)
Carl Ghattas
(February 2017)

General Counsel
James Baker

NSCLB
Principal Deputy
General Counsel
Trisha Anderson

AD
Counterintelligence
Division (CD)
E.W. "Bill" Priestap

OGC Unit Chief

OGC Attorney

Operations Branch I,
CD-4
Deputy Assistant Director
Peter Strzok

Intel
Section Chief

Operations Branch II,
CD-1
Deputy Assistant Director
Jennifer Boone

Supervisory
Intel Analyst

SSA 2

SSA 3

Analyst

Washington
Field Office
Case Agent 4

Michael Flynn
Investigation

Chicago
Field Office
Case Agent 3

George Papadopoulos
Investigation

New York
Field Office
SSA 5

Carter Page
Investigation

Washington Field Office
White Collar Criminal Squad

Paul Manafort Investigation

Case Agent 1
(Jan. 2017-Mar. 2017)

Case Agent 6
(March 2017)

Case Agent 7
(March 2017)

Figure 3.3
FBI Chain of Command and Legal Support
for the Crossfire Hurricane Investigation
April 2017 to May 17, 2017

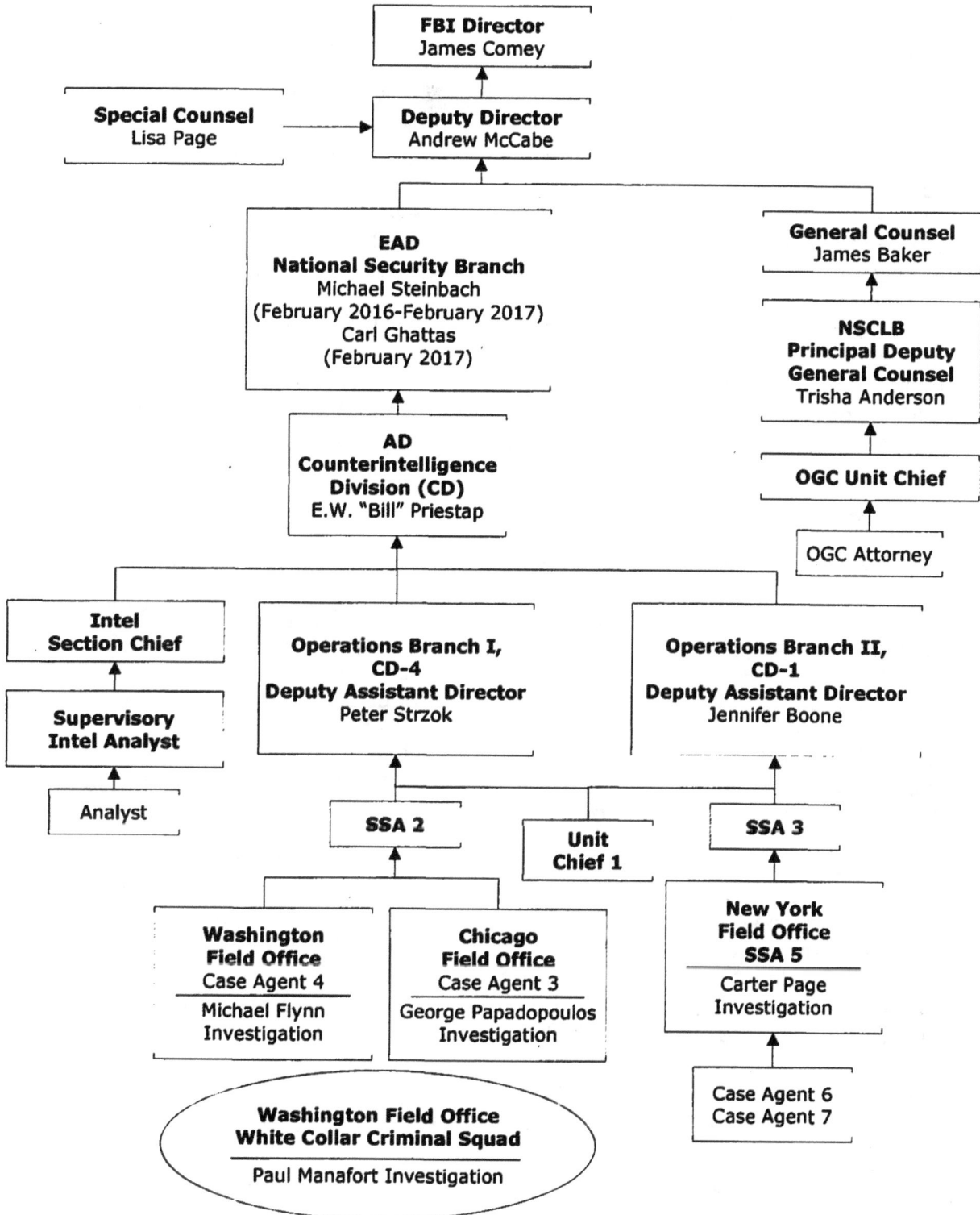

FBI Director
James Comey

Special Counsel
Lisa Page

Deputy Director
Andrew McCabe

EAD
National Security Branch
Michael Steinbach
(February 2016-February 2017)
Carl Ghattas
(February 2017)

General Counsel
James Baker

NSCLB
Principal Deputy
General Counsel
Trisha Anderson

AD
Counterintelligence
Division (CD)
E.W. "Bill" Priestap

OGC Unit Chief

OGC Attorney

Intel
Section Chief

Operations Branch I,
CD-4
Deputy Assistant Director
Peter Strzok

Operations Branch II,
CD-1
Deputy Assistant Director
Jennifer Boone

Supervisory
Intel Analyst

Analyst

SSA 2

Unit
Chief 1

SSA 3

Washington
Field Office
Case Agent 4

Michael Flynn
Investigation

Chicago
Field Office
Case Agent 3

George Papadopoulos
Investigation

New York
Field Office
SSA 5

Carter Page
Investigation

Washington Field Office
White Collar Criminal Squad

Paul Manafort Investigation

Case Agent 6
Case Agent 7

CHAPTER FOUR
THE FBI'S RECEIPT AND EVALUATION OF INFORMATION FROM CHRISTOPHER STEELE PRIOR TO THE FIRST FISA APPLICATION

In this chapter, we describe the FBI's relationship with Christopher Steele, who furnished information that was used in the Carter Page FISA applications (Steele is referred to in those applications as "Source #1"). Steele is a former intelligence officer ███████████████████████████████████ who, following his retirement, opened a consulting firm and furnished information to the FBI beginning in 2010, primarily on matters concerning organized crime and corruption in Russia and Eastern Europe. In 2013, the FBI prepared paperwork to enable it to open Steele as an FBI CHS.[200] We examine the considerations that led the FBI to conclude that Steele was a reliable CHS before submitting the first FISA application. According to FBI personnel we interviewed, these considerations included Steele's past record of furnishing information to the FBI; recommendations from persons familiar with his work; Steele's extensive experience with matters involving Russia; and the assessment by Steele's FBI handling agent. We also examine Steele's development of reporting concerning the 2016 U.S. elections, his initial production of that information to the FBI, the FBI's early efforts to assess the reporting, and Steele's contacts with the media prior to the first FISA application.

I.   Steele and His Assistance to the FBI Prior to June 2016

A.   Introduction to Handling Agent 1 and Early Assistance

Steele is a former intelligence officer of ███████████████████████████████ ████████████████████████ who, following his retirement, was enrolled by the FBI as a CHS furnishing information to the FBI primarily on matters concerning organized crime and corruption in Russia and Eastern Europe. Steele told the OIG that during his service as an intelligence officer ███████████████████████████, he developed a particular expertise on Russia and was stationed for a period in Moscow. Steele stated that, after he stopped ████████████████████████████, he formed a consulting firm specializing in corporate intelligence and investigative services.

Steele's introduction in 2010 to the FBI agent who later became Steele's primary handling agent (Handling Agent 1) was facilitated by Department attorney Bruce Ohr, who was then Chief of the Organized Crime and Racketeering Section in the Department's Criminal Division in Washington, D.C. Ohr told the OIG that he first met Steele in 2007 when he attended a meeting hosted by a foreign government during which Steele addressed the threat posed by Russian organized crime. Ohr said that, after this first meeting with Steele, he probably met with him less than once a year, and after Steele opened his consulting firm, Orbis Business Intelligence, he furnished Ohr with reports produced by Orbis for its commercial clients that he thought may be of interest to the U.S. government. Ohr said that he

---

[200] As we describe below, Steele contends that he was never a CHS for the FBI but rather that his consulting firm had a contractual relationship with the FBI.

eventually put Steele in contact with Handling Agent 1, with whom Ohr had previously worked.

Handling Agent 1 told the OIG that he first met Steele in the spring of 2010 during a trip abroad with Ohr.[201] He recalled that prior to the meeting, Ohr described Steele's background, including his work as an intelligence officer, assignment to Moscow, and Russia expertise. Based on his past experiences working with Ohr, Handling Agent 1 said he respected Ohr's judgment and had no reason to doubt his representations about Steele. Handling Agent 1 told us that Steele had relationships with reputable clients, and this fact bolstered Handling Agent 1's view of Steele's credibility. He also said that he had met with some of Steele's clients and knew of others, and that a representative of one of Steele's clients informed him that Steele "was solid and that his reporting was very interesting and good." Handling Agent 1 stated, however, that with the exception of Steele's work for Fusion GPS, a Washington, D.C. investigative firm, he did not request information from Steele about his firm's clients.[202]

Handling Agent 1 said he came away from his first meeting with Steele favorably impressed. Handling Agent 1 told the OIG that Steele was very professional and knowledgeable and "clearly an expert on Russia," including the activities of Russian oligarchs and Russian criminal networks. Handling Agent 1 told the OIG that although he was interested in the information from Steele, as of 2010 he was not yet prepared to enter into a formal CHS relationship with Steele. Handling Agent 1 explained that it is administratively burdensome to open a CHS who resides overseas and that prior to 2013 he was not receiving a "steady stream" of information from Steele. Handling Agent 1 said that following their initial meeting, Steele would provide information only every couple of months and that he met with him only infrequently, such as when Steele visited the United States. Steele was not compensated by the FBI during this period. Steele told us that this information originated from work performed for Orbis's private clients.

Handling Agent 1 stated that in the summer of 2010 Steele introduced him to a contact who had allegedly obtained information about corruption in the International Federation of Association Football (FIFA). According to Handling Agent 1, but for Steele's assistance in arranging this meeting, the FBI would not have had the impetus to open the FIFA investigation in 2010. The lead FBI agent assigned to the FIFA matter told us that after Russia won the right to host the 2018 World Cup in September 2012, he approached Handling Agent 1 to request permission to examine possible corruption in the bidding process. According to the agent, Handling Agent 1 recalled his earlier interview with the contact that he met through Steele, retrieved a copy of the FBI FD-302 form memorializing the interview, and instructed the agent to open a case. The agent said that Steele's

---

[201] Steele told us that he believed he met Handling Agent 1 and Ohr together at a conference in Europe before he left government service. Handling Agent 1 stated that his first meeting with Steele did not occur at a conference.

[202] Handling Agent 1 said he expected Steele to alert him if any of the clients were "bad actors," such as organized crime figures or others that would be of concern to the FBI. Handling Agent 1 stated that Steele never provided any such notification to him.

role in the FIFA investigation was limited to recommending to Handling Agent 1 that the FBI talk to the contact, whose information eventually proved valuable and helped predicate the opening of the investigation. The agent said he did not recall having any communication with Steele after the investigation's opening.

Additionally, Handling Agent 1 told us that Steele provided two other investigative leads to the FBI in connection with the FIFA investigation. First, in July 2011, Steele provided a report that summarized an alleged conversation between then Russian President Dmitry Medvedev and then Prime Minister Vladimir Putin in which, according to the report, Putin acknowledged that a Russian oligarch had bribed the President of FIFA so that Russia could win the right to host the World Cup tournament in 2018. Second, in 2012, Steele introduced the FBI to two British officials with information concerning Russia's alleged efforts to bribe FIFA executives. Our review of Steele's Delta file also revealed that Steele furnished the FBI with a report dated June 2015 that quoted a Kremlin official as having admitted that the Kremlin bribed FIFA executives in order to secure rights to host the 2018 World Cup.[203]

According to the U.S. Attorney's Office for the Eastern District of New York, as of December 2019, the FIFA investigation has resulted in 26 individual guilty pleas, 2 trial convictions, 4 corporate guilty pleas, and one corporate deferred prosecution agreement. Total forfeitures in the matter exceed $120 million. The OIG interviewed a prosecutor on the FIFA case who told us that Steele did not provide testimony in any court proceeding. Handling Agent 1 also told the OIG that Steele's information was not used to obtain any compulsory legal process in the FIFA case.

In addition to leads provided for the FIFA investigation, we were advised by the FBI that Steele furnished information about Russian oligarchs, some of whom were under investigation by the FBI. For example, we learned that, in October 2013, Steele provided lengthy and detailed reports to the FBI on three Russian oligarchs, one of whom was among the FBI's most wanted fugitives. According to an FBI document, an analyst who reviewed Steele's reporting on this fugitive found the reporting "extremely valuable and informative" and determined it was corroborated by other information that the FBI had obtained.

B.   The FBI Opens Steele as a CHS in October 2013

Handling Agent 1 told the OIG that in late October 2013, he concluded that the FBI needed to enroll Steele as a CHS. By that time, Steele had been providing information to the FBI intermittently for 3 years without compensation. According to Handling Agent 1, the volume of Steele's reporting had increased and involved persons of interest to the FBI, such as the oligarchs noted above, and Handling Agent 1 wanted to task Steele to collect additional information. Handling Agent 1

---

[203] As described in Chapter Two, the FBI maintains an automated case management system for all CHS records, which the FBI refers to as "Delta." The Delta file for each CHS contains all of the personal and administrative information about the CHS, as well as sub-files for unclassified reporting, classified reporting, validation documentation, and payment records.

said that he also wanted to compensate Steele for his fruitful lead in the FIFA investigation. Another consideration for Handling Agent 1 was Handling Agent 1's pending transfer in late spring 2014 to an FBI office in a European city to serve as the Legal Attaché (Legat). Handling Agent 1 said that the logistics of obtaining and using information from Steele while Handling Agent 1 was stationed abroad would be easier if Steele was formally opened as a CHS.

Steele told us that after Handling Agent 1 indicated he wanted to begin tasking Steele to collect information and provide compensation, Steele explained to Handling Agent 1 that ███████████████████████████ ██ ████ ████ and that any relationship would need to be between the FBI and Steele's consulting firm. Steele said that Handling Agent 1 contacted ██ ████████████ ██████████████████████ and obtained a "green light" to proceed. Prior to opening Steele as a CHS, Handling Agent 1 contributed information to a memorandum from the FBI's Legal Attaché (Legat) in Steele's home country notifying █████████ ███████ of Steele's proposed relationship with the FBI. The memorandum to ████████████████████████ included the following:

> Our New York Office is currently working with Christopher Steele, ███ ██. Mr. Steele is providing the FBI with information to support several ongoing criminal investigations involving transnational organized crime organizations. This information, provided primarily through Mr. Steele's privately owned company, Orbis Business Intelligence, is necessary to support our efforts to fully identify subjects with ties to European, Eurasian and Asian organized crime organizations and whose activities directly impact the United States.

> In order to properly protect this information and Mr. Steele's relationship with the FBI, our New York Office will treat any material provided as information obtained through a Confidential Human Source.

Handling Agent 1 told us that he did not recall seeing a draft of the memorandum before it was sent by the Legat. The author of the memorandum, an FBI Assistant Legal Attaché (ALAT 1), told us that Handling Agent 1 probably provided him with the text of the memorandum because he was not familiar with the FBI's use of Steele.

In addition, Steele made available for our review a letter on his consulting firm's letterhead from Steele ████████████████ dated approximately around the same time as the FBI's memorandum ███████████████████. The letter explained that Steele's consulting firm is expected to enter into "a proposed commercial relationship" with the FBI. A substantial portion of the letter described the consulting firm and its work, and the letter stated that information furnished to the U.S. government would come from the firm.

On October 30, 2013, Handling Agent 1 and another agent completed the paperwork to open Steele as an FBI CHS. As required by FBI policy, Handling Agent 1 provided the FBI's standard "admonishments" to Steele at the outset of

Steele's enrollment as a CHS and on an annual basis thereafter. The admonishments advised Steele, for example, that he was not authorized to commit illegal acts, that he must provide truthful information to the FBI, and that he must follow the instructions of the FBI. According to FBI records, Steele signed paperwork captioned "CHS admonishments" acknowledging his receipt of the admonishments for the period covering Crossfire Hurricane, and signed CHS payment receipts using an FBI assigned payment codename.[204]

Handling Agent 1 told the OIG that he instructed Steele not to divulge his relationship with the FBI to others, although the FBI's standard written CHS admonishments do not include such an instruction. According to Handling Agent 1, he told Steele not to share the information he was providing to the FBI with others, with one caveat. Handling Agent 1 explained that Steele would sometimes share with the FBI reports he had generated for his consulting firm's clients, and in that circumstance the clients would also be privy to the information that the FBI had obtained. Handling Agent 1 said he did not provide a specific instruction to Steele that he was not to disclose information that he was sharing with the FBI to the media. According to Handling Agent 1, he did not need to give that specific instruction because that prohibition was addressed by instructing Steele not to share the information he was providing to the FBI with others except for clients.

Steele told us, however, that he was never a CHS for the FBI, and that he advised Handling Agent 1 that he could not be a "clandestine source" due to his prior service as an intelligence officer of another country. Steele made available for the OIG's review documentation referring to such a prohibition. Steele stated that he never recalled being told that he was a CHS and that he never would have accepted such an arrangement, despite the fact that he signed FBI admonishment and payment paperwork indicating that he was an FBI CHS.[205] He also said that his relationship with the FBI was not that of a "confidential human source" because he would meet with Handling Agent 1 at Steele's office as well as in the presence of third parties, which included at times his Orbis business partner. Instead, he explained that the relationship with the FBI was "contractual" with his firm and that he was paid by the FBI "on a results basis" for information his firm furnished in response to taskings.[206] Steele said that he was told by Handling Agent 1 that such a relationship with the FBI was "unorthodox and groundbreaking," and that Handling Agent 1 was interested in similar relationships with others. Steele told us that he discussed with Handling Agent 1 how the FBI could be a client of his firm.

---

[204] The FBI-1057 memorializing Steele's receipt of admonishments in 2016 states that Handling Agent 1 "verbally admonished the CHS with CHS admonishments, which the CHS fully acknowledged, signed and dated." The FBI could not locate the signed admonishment form, however.

[205] During his time as an FBI CHS, Steele received a total of $95,000 from the FBI. We reviewed the FBI paperwork for those payments, each of which required Steele's signed acknowledgment. On each document, of which there were eight, was the caption "CHS's Payment" and "CHS's ▮▮▮▮▮▮▮▮" A signature page was missing for one of the payments.

[206] FBI records that we reviewed included an invoice dated January 25, 2016, from Steele's consulting firm requesting payment "[f]or consultancy services, including 7 meetings with contact, briefing, and reports" as well as for travel and accommodations. The FBI paid Steele (not the consulting firm) $15,000 in May 2016 for services rendered from July 2015 through February 2016.

According to Steele, the issue of the nature of his relationship with the FBI "was never really resolved and both sides turned a blind eye to it. It was not really ideal." However, he said that because the FBI "was keen to stay in touch and draw upon our work" the relationship continued without fully resolving the question of his status.

Among the material that Steele made available to the OIG for review prior to and after his OIG interview were three memoranda written by Steele, that Steele said he maintained in his firm's files, which summarized meetings in 2010 involving Steele, Handling Agent 1, and Ohr. The memoranda reflect that Steele indicated during those meetings that he was not amenable to becoming a CHS and that he wanted the FBI to enter into a consulting agreement with his firm. However, also included in the materials was an undated draft letter from Steele to Handling Agent 1 describing events that post-dated the three earlier memoranda, and stating that although Steele preferred that the FBI enter into a contract with his firm, he was prepared to sign a contract with the FBI as an individual. According to Steele, he did not recall sending the letter but the letter reflected his willingness to accommodate the FBI's administrative requirements. He stated that his firm would not handle the FBI's work as anything other than as an account with the firm. We did not find a copy of these memoranda or the letter in Steele's Delta file. Handling Agent 1 told us that Steele never presented him with copies of these materials.

In light of Steele's assertions, we asked Handling Agent 1 whether Steele ever advised him that he was prohibited from working for the FBI as a CHS and whether the FBI ever had a contract with Steele's firm. Handling Agent 1 responded "no" to both questions. We also asked Handling Agent 1 about the memorandum described above that was sent by ALAT 1 in 2013 to ███████████ ███████, especially its description that information from Steele would be "provided primarily through [Steele's] privately owned company," and that the FBI would "treat any material provided as information obtained through a Confidential Human Source." We wanted to know the rationale for including these statements if in fact the purpose of the memorandum was to alert ██████████████ that Steele was going to be working as a CHS for the FBI. Handling Agent 1 told us that he believed the FBI was trying to be as inclusive as possible in its description of Steele and therefore referenced information about Steele's firm, even though the FBI never had a relationship with the firm. Handling Agent 1 said that he did not know why the memorandum stated that material obtained from Steele would be "treated as information from a CHS" if in fact Steele was an FBI CHS. According to Handling Agent 1, there was no ambiguity in Steele's status as a CHS by late 2013. Handling Agent 1 said that he expressly informed Steele that he was a CHS, he provided Steele with CHS admonishments each year, and that Steele signed CHS payment paperwork using his CHS codename on multiple occasions. In the view of Handling Agent 1, Steele's contention that he was not a CHS is not credible.

We also asked ALAT 1 about the memorandum from the FBI to ████████ ███████████. He said that the purpose of the memorandum was to notify ███████████████████ that Steele would be a CHS for the FBI, and that the memorandum's reference to the FBI's "working with [Steele]" and explanation that material from him would be handled as information from a CHS were sufficient to notify ██████████████ of Steele's status as a CHS. He further stated, however, that the memorandum alerted ████████████████ that the FBI was going to have "some interaction with [Steele's] firm as well as [Steele]" given that the memorandum states that information from Steele would be furnished primarily through his firm. ALAT 1 said that this language was included in the memorandum to make clear that the information obtained from the firm would be treated as information from a CHS. ALAT 1 did not believe that he received any response to the memorandum from ████████████, and we did not find any such response in Steele's Delta file.

C. Steele's Work for the FBI During 2014-2015

Handling Agent 1 said that during 2014 and 2015 he communicated with Steele more regularly and met with him several times in Steele's home country and in a city in Europe. Steele furnished intelligence information that the FBI disseminated, including in four Intelligence Information Reports (IIRs) sent throughout the U.S. Intelligence Community (USIC) concerning the activities of Russian oligarchs.[207] Handling Agent 1 recalled receiving positive feedback from the USIC in response to some of the IIRs containing Steele's information before Steele began delivering election related information in 2016. Handling Agent 1 said that the response to the IIRs was that the information was "really good" and there were requests for additional reporting from Steele. By the time Steele was closed by the FBI as a CHS in November 2016, the FBI had disseminated 10 IIRs based on Steele's reporting.

Ohr told us that, during this time period, he and Handling Agent 1 asked Steele to inquire whether Russian oligarchs would be interested in entering into discussions with them. Handling Agent 1 stated that he did not recall tasking Steele to contact Russian oligarchs though he ███████████████ ████████████████████. According to Handling Agent 1, Steele originally proposed the idea of having him approach Russian oligarchs for the purpose of arranging meetings between the oligarchs and representatives of the U.S. government. In our review of Steele's CHS file, other pertinent documents, and interviews with Handling Agent 1, Ohr, and Steele, we observed that Steele had multiple contacts with representatives of Russian oligarchs with connections to Russian Intelligence Services (RIS) and senior Kremlin officials.[208] For example, in

---

[207] Each of the IIRs noted the limitations on the reporting and included the following standard warning: "WARNING: This is a raw information report, not finally evaluated intelligence. It is being shared for informational purposes, but has not been fully evaluated, integrated with other information, interpreted or analyzed."

[208] ████████████████████████ written by the FBI's Transnational Organized Crime Intelligence Unit (TOCIU) ████████████████████████████████ ██████████ Steele. Steele's ███████████████████████████████ recommended that a validation review be completed on Steele ████████████████. The FBI's Validation Management Unit did not perform such an assessment on Steele until early 2017 after, as described in Chapter Six, the Crossfire Hurricane team requested an assessment in the context of Steele's election reporting. Handling Agent 1 told us he had seen the TOCIU report and was not concerned about its findings concerning Steele because he was aware of Steele's ██████████████████████. We found

late November 2014, Handling Agent 1 met with Steele who advised Handling Agent 1 that he had received overtures from "interlocutors" for several Russian oligarchs seeking to arrange FBI interviews of the oligarchs.

Handling Agent 1 told the OIG that Steele facilitated meetings in a European city that included Handling Agent 1, Ohr, an attorney of Russian Oligarch 1, and a representative of another Russian oligarch.[209] Russian Oligarch 1 subsequently met with Ohr as well as other representatives of the U.S. government at a different location. Ohr told the OIG that, based on information that Steele told him about Russian Oligarch 1, such as when Russian Oligarch 1 would be visiting the United States or applying for a visa, and based on Steele at times seeming to be speaking on Russian Oligarch 1's behalf, Ohr said he had the impression that Russian Oligarch 1 was a client of Steele.[210]

We asked Steele about whether he had a relationship with Russian Oligarch 1. Steele stated that he did not have a relationship and indicated that he had met Russian Oligarch 1 one time. He explained that he worked for Russian Oligarch 1's attorney on litigation matters that involved Russian Oligarch 1 but that he could not provide "specifics" about them for confidentiality reasons. Steele stated that Russian Oligarch 1 had no influence on the substance of his election reporting and no contact with any of his sources. He also stated that he was not aware of any information indicating that Russian Oligarch 1 knew of his investigation relating to the 2016 U.S. elections.[211]

Steele's prior reporting to the FBI addressed issues other than Russian oligarchs. For example, we reviewed FBI records reflecting that he provided information on the hack of computer systems of an international corporation, and corruption involving former Ukrainian President Viktor Yanukovych. In addition, Steele told us he introduced Handling Agent 1 to sources with knowledge of Russian athletic doping and obtained samples of material for the FBI to analyze. Handling Agent 1 could not recall meeting with these sources or obtaining samples for analysis, though he did remember obtaining information from Steele concerning Russian athletic doping. Handling Agent 1 said he forwarded the information to the FBI New York Field Office (NYFO) which had an open investigation concerning doping.

Handling Agent 1 also recounted for us a situation involving Steele that reinforced his view that Steele was "very professional" and primarily motivated by a

---

that the TOCIU report was not included in Steele's Delta file. Handling Agent 1 said that he found preparation of the TOCIU report "curious" because he believed that TOCIU was aware of Steele's ▮▮▮▮▮▮▮▮ and fully supported them.

[209] Handling Agent 1 told us that he was aware that Steele had a relationship with Russian Oligarch 1's attorney and assumed it may have been a business relationship.

[210] As we discuss in Chapter Six, members of the Crossfire Hurricane team were unaware of Steele's connections to Russian Oligarch 1. ▮▮▮▮▮▮▮▮▮▮▮

[211] ▮▮▮▮▮▮▮▮▮▮▮▮▮▮▮▮▮▮▮

desire to counter threats posed by Russia. According to Handling Agent 1, on two occasions Steele made arrangements for a meeting between the FBI and a ▮▮▮▮ individual who had potentially important information. In both instances the meetings did not occur due to the FBI's failure to attend. According to Handling Agent 1, the FBI's failure to meet with the individual was the FBI's fault, cost Steele financially in the short term, and likely caused a loss of reputation with the intermediaries who arranged the individual's attendance at the meeting. Handling Agent 1 told the OIG that Steele's professionalism in seeking to arrange the meeting and then not seeking to "nickel and dime" the FBI in the process impressed him. Steele was eventually reimbursed by the FBI for his expenses, but it was over a year later.

We asked Handling Agent 1 about what information the FBI had corroborated from Steele's reporting prior to spring 2016 and whether Steele had been proven to be a reliable source. Handling Agent 1 said that Steele provided reliable information to the FBI in the past, but that not all of the information Steele furnished had been corroborated and verified. Handling Agent 1 cited several examples of information from Steele that the FBI had been able to corroborate prior to the spring of 2016, such as corruption in FIFA's bid selection process, information regarding ▮▮▮▮▮▮ Russian oligarchs, and corruption involving Yanukovych, but could not recall more. He also told the OIG that he was not aware of any information Steele provided prior to 2016 that had been shown to be false, inaccurate, or problematic. Handling Agent 1 said that the FBI found Steele's information to be valuable and that it warranted compensation. As a result, in 2014 and 2015, the FBI made five payments to Steele totaling $64,000. By the time the FBI closed Steele in November 2016, his cumulative compensation totaled $95,000, including reimbursement for expenses. Steele was not compensated by the FBI for the election reporting we discuss below.

We asked Steele how he would characterize his relationship with the FBI prior to furnishing reports on the 2016 election. He told us it was "good" except for the tardiness of the FBI's payments to him. He stated that he had confidence in Handling Agent 1.

We also inquired whether Steele's work for the FBI intruded on his work for his private clients. Steele told us that overall his work could be categorized in one of two ways. The first was work he performed for other clients of his consulting firm. He called this work "Pipeline 1." Steele stated however that he sometimes provided his work product from these engagements to the FBI at no cost, which he said he did because he believed the information possibly could be helpful to the U.S. government. The second category was work Steele performed for the FBI in response to taskings and for which the FBI provided compensation. Steele referred to this work as "Pipeline 2." According to Steele, Pipeline 1 and Pipeline 2 were mutually exclusive and did not overlap. Steele explained that his Pipeline 1 work for his clients was not affected by his Pipeline 2 work for the FBI, and he therefore was at liberty to discuss his work for his clients with his clients and with third parties, as necessary, without gaining permission from the FBI. He stated that any promises or commitments he made to the FBI did not affect the work of his consulting firm for its clients and that his FBI commitments only applied to work where the FBI was the client (*i.e.,* Pipeline 2).

II. Steele Provides the FBI with Election Reporting in 2016

A. Steele's Engagement by Fusion GPS in June 2016

Steele said that in approximately June 2016, he was hired for a short-term assignment by Fusion GPS, a Washington, D.C., investigative firm founded by former journalist Glenn Simpson and a partner.[212] Steele told us that he first met Simpson in 2010 and had completed a number of projects for him, some of which related to Russia. In May 2016, Simpson met Steele at a European airport and inquired whether Steele could assist in determining Russia's actions related to the 2016 U.S. elections, whether Russia was trying to achieve a particular election outcome, whether candidate Donald Trump had any personal and business ties in Russia, and whether there were any ties between the Russian government and Trump and his campaign.[213] Steele stated that he began work for Fusion GPS on the 2016 election assignment after Fusion GPS had completed a similar Trump related assignment for an entity connected to the Republican Party.

Steele told us he had a source network in place with a proven "track record" that could deliver on Fusion GPS's requirements. Steele added that this source network previously had furnished intelligence on Russian interference in European affairs.[214] Steele said he understood from Simpson that his assignment would end with the election in November 2016. He also stated that, prior to this request, he had not conducted any research on Trump.

We asked Steele when he learned who had retained Fusion GPS to obtain information concerning Trump and the Trump campaign. He told us he could not recall when he first learned that it was the law firm Perkins Coie and the Democratic National Committee (DNC), though he was certain that it was not at the outset of the engagement with Fusion GPS. Steele further stated that, by late July 2016, Steele had met with Simpson and an attorney from Perkins Coie, which

---

[212] Simpson declined the OIG's request to be interviewed. According to testimony that Simpson provided to Congress, the *Washington Free Beacon* retained Fusion GPS from approximately September or October 2015 to April/May 2016 to take "an open-ended look at Donald Trump's business career and his litigation history and his relationships with questionable people, how much he was really worth, how he ran his casinos, [and] what kind of performance he had in other lines of work." *See Testimony of Glenn Simpson before the House Permanent Select Committee on Intelligence, U.S. House of Representatives* (November 8, 2017) (hereinafter *Simpson House Testimony*) at 7, 12.

[213] According to interrogatory responses Steele provided in foreign litigation, Fusion GPS retained Steele "to investigate and report, by way of preparing confidential Intelligence Memorandum, on Russian efforts to influence the U.S. Presidential election process in 2016 and on links between Russia and the then Republican candidate and now President Donald Trump."

[214] Steele told us that this source network did not involve sources from his time as a ▮▮▮▮▮ ▮▮▮▮▮▮▮▮▮▮▮▮▮▮▮▮▮▮▮▮ and was developed entirely in the period after he retired from government service.

represented the DNC, and Steele said that by that time he was aware of the DNC's role. He stated that he could not remember whether he provided Perkins Coie's name to the FBI but believed it was probable that he did so, but not in July 2016.

Steele stated that he finalized arrangements with Simpson over the terms of his engagement a few weeks after their meeting at the European airport and that he started to collect information in June 2016. According to FBI records, Steele thereafter produced ▮ reports related to the 2016 U.S. elections, ▮ of which he provided to the FBI and ▮ others that were provided to the FBI by third parties, as described in Chapter Six.[215] The FBI obtained reports directly from Steele during the time period of July through October 2016.

Steele told us that the reports he generated were not designed to be "finished products" and instead were "to be briefed off of orally versus consumed as a written product." He said that the reports were "mostly single source reporting" and were uncorroborated intelligence "up to a point," but were informed by background research and his judgment as an intelligence professional. Steele explained that it was his firm's practice to faithfully report everything a reliable source provided and not to withhold information because it was controversial. He denied "tailoring" his reporting to meet the needs of his clients and explained that doing so ultimately was not a good business practice because it would result in loss of reputation. We also asked Steele whether his research was "opposition research" and biased. He provided a similar response and explained that his firm would not be in business if it provided biased information.[216] Steele called the allegation that he was biased against Trump from the start "ridiculous."[217] He stated that if anything he was "favorably disposed" toward the Trump family before he began his research because he had visited a Trump family member at Trump Tower and "been friendly" with [the family member] for some years. He described their relationship as "personal" and said that he once gifted a family tartan from Scotland to the family member.

---

[215] One report that was not provided to the FBI directly or via third parties was published by *BuzzFeed*. One of the reports provided to the FBI by third parties was a near duplicate of a report that Steele previously had furnished to the FBI. Steele also provided the FBI, from July through October 2016, with several reports that addressed Russian activities but were not election related.

[216] We also asked about obvious errors in the reporting, such a misspellings and the reference to a Russian consulate in Miami which did not exist. Steele told us that such errors are typical in intelligence work and were a function, in part, of the fast turnaround between his receipt of information from his sources and the dissemination of the reporting. He explained that he was accountable for any errors as the election reporting was "his baby."

[217] As we describe in Chapter Six, however, according to an FBI FD-302, when the FBI interviewed Steele in September 2017, he and a colleague from his firm described Trump as their "main opponent." Ohr also advised SSA 1 that Steele was "desperate that Donald Trump not get elected and was passionate about him not being the U.S. President." As we describe in Chapter Nine, SSA 1 met with Ohr on November 21, 2016, and memorialized Ohr's statements in a FBI FD-302 report. When we interviewed Steele, he told us that he did not state that he was "desperate" that Trump not be elected and thought Ohr might have been paraphrasing his sentiments. Steele told us that he was concerned that Trump was a national security risk, and he had no particular animus against Trump otherwise.

The first election report that Steele provided to the FBI, which, as described in Chapters Five and Seven, was one of four of Steele's reports that the FBI relied upon to support probable cause in the Carter Page FISA applications, is captioned "Company Intelligence Report 2016/080—U.S. Presidential Election: Republican Candidate Donald Trump's Activities in Russia and Compromising Relationship with the Kremlin," and is dated June 20, 2016 (Report 80). It was provided to Handling Agent 1 on July 5, 2016, and contains numerous allegations about the presidential candidates, including that: (1) the "Russian regime has been cultivating, supporting, and assisting [Trump] for at least 5 years;" (2) "[Trump] and his inner circle have accepted a regular flow of intelligence from the Kremlin, including on his Democratic and other political rivals;" (3) Trump's activities in Moscow, including "perverted sexual acts," make him vulnerable to blackmail; (4) Russian Intelligence Services have collected "compromising material" on Hillary Clinton; and (5) the Kremlin has been "feeding" information to Trump's campaign for an extended period of time. Steele said that he debated with his business colleague whether to include the sexual material in Report 80 but refused to omit it because he felt that as a matter of professional practice, when reporting information from a source, "we have to be faithful to all of the information the source provided" and not avoid material because it is controversial. Then Director James Comey later described this aspect of Steele's reporting as "salacious and unverified."[218]

Steele explained that shortly after drafting Report 80 he had discussions with his business partner and Simpson about what to do with the information. He said that he and his partner considered the contents of the report to have national security implications and that the report therefore needed to be shared with the FBI. He said that Simpson agreed to Steele's proposal, and thereafter, Steele contacted the FBI.[219]

B. Steele Informs Handling Agent 1 in July 2016 about his Election Reporting Work

Shortly before the Fourth of July 2016, Handling Agent 1 told the OIG that he received a call from Steele requesting an in-person meeting as soon as possible. Handling Agent 1 said he departed his duty station in Europe on July 5 and met with Steele in Steele's office that day. During their meeting, Steele provided Handling Agent 1 with a copy of Report 80 and explained that he had been hired by Fusion GPS to collect information on the relationship between candidate Trump's businesses and Russia. Handling Agent 1 said Steele had become concerned about the possibility of the Russians compromising Trump in the event Trump became

---

[218] We further discuss Comey's views of this information in Chapter Six.

[219] Simpson has testified before Congress that he assented to Steele's request to provide the information to the FBI, and that he viewed the situation as "potentially a crime in progress" that needed to be reported. *Simpson House Testimony* at 61; *Testimony of Glenn Simpson before the Senate Judiciary Committee*, United States Senate (August 22, 2017) (hereinafter *Simpson Senate Testimony*) at 160.

President.[220] According to Handling Agent 1, Steele informed him that Fusion GPS had been hired by a law firm to conduct research, though Steele stated that he did not know the law firm's name or its political affiliation.[221] Handling Agent 1 told the OIG, however, that he did not have to ask Steele to know that the request for the research was politically motivated as the connection to politics was obvious to Handling Agent 1 from the circumstances. Handling Agent 1 also told us that he asked Steele to try to identify the law firm. However, Handling Agent 1 said that he did not "continually ask" Steele about the firm's identity as his work with Steele progressed. When asked by the OIG about an October 2016 email from a member of the Crossfire Hurricane team stating that Handling Agent 1 had avoided tasking Steele to obtain the name of the law firm, Handling Agent 1 told us that information was incorrect and that he would never avoid asking a material question. When we asked the email's author about the email, he stated that it accurately represented what Handling Agent 1 had told him during a telephone call in October 2016.

We reviewed what Steele represented were his contemporaneous notes of his July 5 meeting with Handling Agent 1. Steele told us these notes were written within a day or two of the meeting. The notes reflect that Steele told Handling Agent 1 that Steele was aware that "Democratic Party associates" were paying for Fusion GPS's research, the "ultimate client" was the leadership of the Clinton presidential campaign, and "the candidate" was aware of Steele's reporting. Steele told us that he was "pretty candid" with Handling Agent 1. He also said it was clear that Fusion GPS was backed by Clinton supporters and senior Democrats who were supporting her. When we asked Handling Agent 1 about the information contained in Steele's notes, Handling Agent 1 told us that he did not recall Steele mentioning these facts to him during their meeting.

After being provided with a copy of Report 80 at the July 5 meeting, Handling Agent 1 said he asked Steele whether he was still collecting information for Fusion GPS. Handling Agent 1 said Steele responded that he was working on another report for Simpson. Handling Agent 1 said that, at that point, he advised Steele that Steele was not working on behalf of the FBI to collect the information Fusion GPS was seeking: "I said we are not asking you to do it and I'm not tasking you to do it." Steele provided the OIG with a similar interpretation of these events. He told us that Report 80, as well as all his other election reports, was "Pipeline 1" information and not subject to FBI controls. Handling Agent 1 said that he also advised Steele that because a law firm was involved there could be privilege issues that Handling Agent 1 would need to evaluate. Handling Agent 1 told the OIG that he returned to his duty station the same day with a copy of the reports Steele provided him, only one of which was election related.

---

[220] Handling Agent 1's records indicate that, during this meeting, Steele also provided Handling Agent 1 with reporting on Russian doping in athletics, Russian cyber activities, and Russian interference in European political affairs.

[221] As described earlier, Steele told us that by late July 2016, he had met with Simpson and an attorney from Perkins Coie, which represented the DNC, and by that time he was aware of the DNC's role.

Steele told us that Handling Agent 1 was "taken aback" by the contents of Report 80, and that Handling Agent 1 said he needed to send the Report back to the U.S. and would contact Steele at a later time after Handling Agent 1 had conferred with others about how to handle it. Steele said that he waited approximately one week and then contacted Handling Agent 1 to inquire whether he wanted to receive additional reports. According to Steele, Handling Agent 1 responded, "[N]ot yet. I'm still dealing with this. I'll get back to you." Steele said it was not until mid-August that he heard back from Handling Agent 1 and that Handling Agent 1 told him at that time that he wanted to receive additional reports.

Handling Agent 1 said he discussed Steele's reporting with his supervisor, the Legat, and both agreed that Handling Agent 1 should try to determine where to send the information in FBI Headquarters. However, due to the sensitivity of the reporting, Handling Agent 1 said that he wanted to be discrete and avoid a situation where he was "broadcasting" the information. Handling Agent 1 said that he informed his supervisor that he wanted to consult with NYFO (where Handling Agent 1 previously had worked) before taking further action, and that his goal was to put the information directly in the hands of people who needed to see it. According to Handling Agent 1, his supervisor approved, stating "Good idea. Call whoever you have to call. Do whatever you have to do."[222]

The Legat told us that he recalled Handling Agent 1's proposal to contact NYFO, which he concurred with, but that his expectation was that Handling Agent 1 would provide Steele's reporting to the Counterintelligence Division (CD) at FBI Headquarters within a matter of days. The Legat stated that he recalled inquiring about the handling of the reporting when Handling Agent 1 obtained another report from Steele, Report 94 described below, on July 19, 2016, as well as prior to a meeting members of the Crossfire Hurricane team had with Steele in October 2016. The Legat said that during this time, "I just assumed [Handling Agent 1] was handling it...[and] had sent it off."

Approximately 1 week after his July 5 meeting with Steele, Handling Agent 1 contacted an Assistant Special Agent in Charge (ASAC 1) in NYFO, whom Handling Agent 1 had known for many years and described as having experience with "sensitive matters." Handling Agent 1 said that he described the "gist" of the situation to ASAC 1, who responded that he would assess what to do and contact Handling Agent 1 later. ASAC 1 told us that the information that Handling Agent 1 explained to him "[c]learly [was] something that needs to be handled immediately" and "definitely of interest to the Counterintelligence folks." ASAC 1 said that after hearing from Handling Agent 1, he spoke with his Special Agent in Charge (SAC 1) the same day. ASAC 1's notes from his July 13 call with Handling Agent 1 closely track the contents of Report 80, identify Simpson as a client of a law firm, and include the following: "law firm works for the Republican party or Hillary and will

---

[222] Handling Agent 1 said that he did not contact the International Operations Division (IOD) at FBI Headquarters, which supports the Legats, about the reporting.

use [the information described in Report 80] at some point."[223] ASAC 1 told us that he would not have made this notation if Handling Agent 1 had not stated it to him.

On July 19, 2016, Steele sent an email to Handling Agent 1 that included another report, Report 94, which was captioned "Company Intelligence Report 2016/94—Russia: Secret Kremlin Meetings Attended by Trump Advisor Carter Page in Moscow (July 2016)." Report 94, which as described in Chapters Five and Seven was one of 4 reports the FBI relied upon to support the probable cause in the Carter Page FISA applications, alleged that during a visit to Moscow in July 2016, Page met with: (1) Igor Sechin, Chairman of Russian energy conglomerate Rosneft, and discussed the "lifting of western sanctions against Russia over Ukraine;" and (2) Igor Divyekin, a staff member in the Russian Presidential Administration, who informed Page of compromising information the Kremlin possessed on Hillary Clinton and its possible release to the Republican campaign. Report 94 further alleged that Divyekin advised Page that the Russians had derogatory information on Trump, which the candidate should bear in mind in future dealings with Russian leadership. Report 94 described conversations involving a limited number of persons (*e.g.*, Sechin confided the details of a secret meeting with Page; Sergei Ivanov confided in a compatriot that Divyekin had met secretly with Page).

Handling Agent 1 said that when he read Report 94 for the first time he recognized Sechin's name from intelligence reporting but did not recognize the other names, including Carter Page. He told the OIG that he was in no position to assess the reliability of the reporting and for that reason he was eager to forward the reporting to persons who could evaluate it. Steele's reporting, however, did not reach investigators at FBI Headquarters until 2 months later, a circumstance we describe further below.

C.   The Crossfire Hurricane Team Receives Steele's Reports on September 19

On July 28, 2016, three days prior to the opening of the Crossfire Hurricane investigation, Handling Agent 1 sent Reports 80 and 94 to ASAC 1 in NYFO, who forwarded them to SAC 1.[224] Handling Agent 1's sharing of the reports with ASAC 1 resulted in a meeting in NYFO on August 3 among ASAC 1, the Chief Division Counsel (CDC), an Associate Division Counsel (ADC), and a Supervisory Special Agent (SSA). Notes taken by the ADC show that the meeting participants discussed

---

[223] As we summarize in Chapter Ten, at approximately the same time that Handling Agent 1 was reporting information about Simpson to ASAC 1, an FBI agent from another FBI field office sent an email to his supervisor stating that he had been contacted by a former CHS who "was contacted recently by a colleague who runs an investigative firm. The firm had been hired by two entities (the Democratic National Committee as well as another individual...not name[d]) to explore Donald J. Trump's longstanding ties to Russian entities." On or about August 2, 2016, this information was shared by a CD supervisor with the Section Chief of CD's Counterintelligence Analysis Section I (Intel Section Chief), who provided it that day to members of the Crossfire Hurricane team (then Section Chief Peter Strzok, SSA 1, and the Supervisory Intel Analyst).

[224] ASAC 1 told us that he was not sure why nothing happened with the reports between July 13, the date he first spoke with Handling Agent 1, and July 28.

in general terms the information contained in Reports 80 and 94 and the relationship between Steele, Simpson, and a "law firm."

The ADC told the OIG that he was assigned the responsibility of reading Steele's reports and determining whether they were pertinent to any crimes involving public corruption. The ADC said he spoke with Handling Agent 1 on August 4, and Handling Agent 1 emailed Reports 80 and 94 to him the next day. Handling Agent 1 stated that, prior to sending the reports, ASAC 1 had contacted him to explain that the reports would be placed in a sub-file in NYFO and thereby "walled off" from agents in NYFO, and that the Assistant Director in Charge of NYFO and the "Executive Assistant Director (EAD) level" at FBI Headquarters were aware of the reports' existence. Handling Agent 1 stated that the ADC informed him in August that he was conferring with management in NYFO about how to handle the reports and would notify him after a determination had been made. Handling Agent 1 also stated that the engagement of an EAD was significant to him because he believed that "appropriate people were communicating" about the reports as a result and that he therefore should wait for further guidance about how to handle the reports.

As we discuss in detail in Chapter Nine, Handling Agent 1 also told us that, in mid to late August, he heard from Ohr "out of the blue," who inquired whether Handling Agent 1 had seen Steele's reports. According to Handling Agent 1, Ohr contacted him to confirm that the FBI was aware of the reports and was "handling" them. Handling Agent 1 told the OIG that he advised Ohr that news of the reports had reached the "EAD level" at FBI Headquarters and that executive management at NYFO was aware of the reports and trying to determine where to forward them. Ohr stated that he recalled Handling Agent 1 telling him this, but that at some later date Ohr said he became concerned that the right people at FBI Headquarters did not know about the reporting.

On August 25, 2016, according to a Supervisory Special Agent 1 (SSA 1) who was assigned to the Crossfire Hurricane investigation, during a briefing for then Deputy Director Andrew McCabe on the investigation, McCabe asked SSA 1 to contact NYFO about information that potentially could assist the Crossfire Hurricane Investigation.[225] SSA 1 said he reached out to counterintelligence agents and analysts in NYFO within approximately 24 hours following the meeting. Instant messages show that on September 1, SSA 1 spoke with a NYFO counterintelligence supervisor, and that the counterintelligence supervisor was attempting to set up a call between SSA 1 and the ADC.

On September 2, 2016, Handling Agent 1, who had been waiting for NYFO to inform him where to forward Steele's reports, sent the following email to the ADC and counterintelligence supervisor: "Do we have a name yet? The stuff is burning a hole." The ADC responded the same day explaining that SSA 1 had created an electronic sub-file for Handling Agent 1 in the Crossfire Hurricane case and that he

---

[225] During his interview with the OIG, McCabe told us that he did not remember asking SSA 1 to contact NYFO, and he said he did not remember knowing in August 2016 that NYFO had information relevant to the Crossfire Hurricane investigation.

should forward the Steele reports to it. However, SSA 1 told us that there was a problem with his attempt to send an email to Handling Agent 1 in early September. SSA 1 said he did not recognize the problem until September 13 and emailed Handling Agent 1 that day with the case information necessary to upload the reports.

On September 19, 2016, the Crossfire Hurricane team received the Steele reporting for the first time when Handling Agent 1 emailed SSA 1 six reports for SSA 1 to upload himself to the sub-file: Reports 80 and 94, and four additional reports (Reports 95, 100, 101, and 102) that Handling Agent 1 had since received from Steele.[226] FBI officials we interviewed told us that the length of time it took for Steele's election reporting to reach FBI Headquarters was excessive and that the reports should have been sent promptly after their receipt by the Legat. Members of the Crossfire Hurricane team told us that their assessment of the Steele election reporting could have started much earlier if the reporting had been made available to them.

As described in Chapters Five and Seven, the FBI relied upon Report 95 to support probable cause in the Carter Page FISA applications. Report 95 was entitled "Russia/US Presidential Election: Further Indications of Extensive Conspiracy Between Trump's Campaign Team and the Kremlin" and cited repeatedly to information provided by "Source E." Report 95 alleged the existence of "a well-developed conspiracy of co-operation" between the Trump campaign and Russian leadership, and claimed that the campaign's manager, Manafort, used Carter Page and others as "intermediaries" to further the conspiracy. According to Source E, the "Russian regime" was behind the leak of DNC emails to WikiLeaks with the "full knowledge and support" of Trump and his campaign team, and the WikiLeaks platform was used by Russia to afford it "plausible deniability" of its involvement in the leak. Also, as we describe in Chapter Eight, Report 95 included an allegation that Page and possibly others agreed to sideline Russian intervention in Ukraine as a campaign issue in exchange for Russia's disclosure of hacked DNC emails to WikiLeaks. The FBI used this information in all of the Carter Page FISA applications to support its assessment that Page helped influence the Republican Party to change its platform to be more sympathetic to Russia's interests by eliminating language from the Republican platform about providing weapons to Ukraine.

Report 102, as described in Chapters Five and Seven, was also one of the 4 reports relied upon to support probable cause in the Carter Page FISA applications. The Report was titled, "Russia/US Presidential Election: Reaction in Trump Camp to Recent Negative Publicity About Russian Interference and Likely Resulting Tactics Going Forward." Report 102 alleged that the purpose of the recent DNC email leaks was to shift votes from Bernie Sanders to Trump following Clinton's nomination.

---

[226] Additional reports included the following information: Report 100 (Premier Medvedev's office was furious over DNC hacking and associated anti-Russian publicity) and Report 101 (The Kremlin is supporting various U.S. political figures and indirectly funding their travel to Moscow). Reports 95 and 102 are described below.

Report 102 also alleged that Carter Page conceived of and promoted the idea that the release of the DNC emails would shift voter support to Trump.

D. The Crossfire Hurricane Team's Initial Handling of the Steele Reporting in September 2016

As described in Chapter Three, by the date the Crossfire Hurricane team received the six Steele reports on September 19, the investigation had been underway for approximately 6 weeks and the team had opened investigations on four individuals: Carter Page, George Papadopoulos, Paul Manafort, and Michael Flynn. In addition, during the prior 6 weeks, the team had used CHSs to conduct operations against Page, Papadopoulos, and a high-level Trump campaign official, although those operations had not resulted in the collection of any inculpatory information. Further, as described in Chapter Five, the team had discussions about the possibility of obtaining FISAs targeting Page and Papadopoulos, but it was determined that there was insufficient information at the time to proceed with an application to the court.

As also described in Chapter Three, the FBI had an ongoing cyber counterintelligence investigation into the Russian hacking of the DNC and was aware of other Russian efforts to interfere with the upcoming 2016 U.S. elections. We were told by several FBI witnesses that certain broad themes of the Steele reporting were consistent with information already known by the FBI and other U.S. government intelligence agencies. These themes included that the Russian government was seeking to sow discord and disunity within the United States and Trans-Atlantic alliance, that the Russian government was working to support Trump's election as President, and that Russian state-sponsored cyber operations were responsible for hacking activity focused on the Clinton campaign. Comey told the OIG that, in his view, the "heart of the [Steele] reporting was that there's a massive Russian effort to influence the American election and weaponize stolen information." Comey said he believed those themes from the Steele reporting were "entirely consistent with information developed by the [USIC] wholly separate and apart from the [Steele] reporting," as well as consistent with what "our eyes and ears could also see."

After obtaining the six Steele reports on September 19, analysts on the Crossfire Hurricane team immediately began to evaluate the information in the reports. By the next day, they had completed a draft Intelligence Memorandum that summarized key points from the reports and identified actions that needed to be taken to assess the information. For example, Report 95 stated that Russian diplomatic staff in the United States were rewarding assets (cooperators) using the émigré pension distribution system as cover, and the Intelligence Memorandum described ██

The FBI's analytical efforts also included developing various diagrams, charts, and timelines to document relationships and events pertinent to the Crossfire Hurricane investigation. In order to analyze the Steele election reports, the FBI developed a spreadsheet of excerpts from the reports with analyst notes indicating the source of the excerpt and verification information, such as whether information contained in the excerpt had been corroborated.[227] We discuss in Chapter Six these efforts by the FBI over time to assess the Steele election reporting.

Assistant Director (AD) E.W. "Bill" Priestap and then Deputy Assistant Director (DAD) Peter Strzok told the OIG that the FBI's assessment of Steele's information was not different from the approach the FBI typically uses in evaluating CHS information. They explained that the assessment involved determining the credibility of Steele, including understanding his record of furnishing reliable information, motivation, and possible biases; and verifying the information he provided through independent sources. Priestap described the FBI's approach to the reporting in the following terms:

> [W]e did not ever take the information he provided at face value.... We went to great lengths to try to independently verify the source's credibility and to prove or disprove every single assertion in the dossier.... We absolutely understood that the information in the so-called dossier could be inaccurate. We also understood that some parts could be true and other parts false. We understood that information could be embellished or exaggerated. We also understood that the information could have been provided by the Russians as part of a disinformation campaign.

The Supervisory Intelligence Analyst (Supervisory Intel Analyst) assigned to Crossfire Hurricane told the OIG that an early focus of the FBI's analytical effort to assess Steele's reporting was trying to identify Steele's sources. According to the Supervisory Intel Analyst, it was important to determine whether the reporting of those individuals matched their access to information. The Supervisory Intel Analyst said that, in order to evaluate that issue and fully assess the reporting, the FBI sought assistance from other USIC agencies by, for example, vetting Russian names identified in the reports.

We asked the Supervisory Intel Analyst whether the FBI sought to determine who was financing Steele's election related research. He said that the focus of the analysts was on Russian interference in the campaign and on any connections between Russia and the Trump campaign. He stated that he was aware of the potential for political influences on the reporting. He said that, because of that awareness, whether the reporting was "opposition research" that was politically motivated was not an issue that occupied his or his analysts' attention and that further research on the issue was nearly "immaterial." He explained that because "opposition research can be true, it can be false," his focus was on vetting the reporting to determine whether its contents were accurate.

---

[227] The OIG was advised that the spreadsheet does not include highly classified material, and therefore its presentation of information known to the FBI about corroboration of the Steele election reporting is partial.

On September 23, 2016, Case Agent 1, the lead case agent for the Carter Page investigation, emailed Handling Agent 1 to inquire about Steele. Handling Agent 1 responded: "[CHS] has been signed up for 3 years and is reliable. [CHS] responds to taskings and obtains info from a network of sub sources. Some of the [CHS'] info has been corroborated when possible."[228] This outreach was followed shortly thereafter by a request to Handling Agent 1 from one of the Crossfire Hurricane investigation supervisors, SSA 1, to participate in a video conference call with members of the Crossfire Hurricane team on September 27. According to participants on the call, the purpose of the call was to set a meeting with Steele to discuss his reports, learn about his source network, and gain his cooperation to collect additional information in support of the Crossfire Hurricane investigation.[229]

We asked Strzok who made the decision to use Steele as a source in the Crossfire Hurricane investigation. He said that McCabe and Comey were briefed on Steele's reporting and "okayed" the Crossfire Hurricane team's approach to use Steele in the investigation. Comey told us that he recalled being briefed about Steele but did not have a specific recollection beyond obtaining copies of Steele's reports and learning about Steele's background; his prior record of furnishing information to the FBI, including FIFA; and his work for political entities (first Republican, then Democratic).[230] McCabe told us that although he was sometimes present during discussions about the use of CHSs in Crossfire Hurricane, he left decisions about which sources to use and how to use them to the team.

As we describe below, in early October 2016 a meeting was held between members of the Crossfire Hurricane team and Steele in a European city. Unknown to the FBI at the time, Steele was working with his client, Fusion GPS, to alert select media outlets about his reporting concerning Russian interference with the 2016 U.S elections and allegations regarding the Trump campaign and candidate Trump. Additionally, the FBI was unaware at the time that Steele had not made available to the FBI all of the reports he prepared as of mid-September concerning Russia.[231] As described in Chapter Six, these and other reports were provided to

---

[228] We did not find this communication in Steele's Delta file.

[229] We found that the first time the Crossfire Hurricane team accessed Steele's Delta file was in November 2016. The Supervisory Intel Analyst told us that the team was in contact with Handling Agent 1 beginning in September and relied on him for information about Steele. Handling Agent 1 expressed surprise that the Crossfire Hurricane team did not access Steele's Delta file earlier. He said that the team should have "turned the file upside down" looking for information 2 months earlier and that he assumed that some members of the team had thoroughly reviewed the file.

[230] As noted earlier, Steele told us that he began work for Fusion GPS on the 2016 election assignment after Fusion GPS had completed a similar Trump related assignment for a Republican Party connected entity.

[231] The following are reports with select highlights that Steele did not furnish to the FBI, which range in date from July 30 to September 14, 2016:

- Report 97 (the Kremlin is concerned that political fallout from the DNC hacking operation is spiraling out of control; a source close to the Trump campaign confirms that the regular exchange of intelligence between the Trump team and the Kremlin had existed for at least 8 years; the Kremlin had determined not to use compromising

the FBI in November and December 2016 by a journalist, Senator John McCain, and Ohr. When we asked Steele why he failed to provide all of his then-existing reports to the FBI, he could not provide us with an explanation and said that he should have given them to the FBI at the time.

E. Steele Discusses His Reporting with Third Parties in Late September 2016 and the *Yahoo News* Article

During late September 2016, with Fusion GPS's authorization, Steele met with numerous persons outside the FBI to discuss the intelligence he had obtained, as part of his paid work for Fusion GPS, concerning Russian interference with the 2016 U.S. elections and allegations regarding the Trump campaign and candidate Trump.[232] For example, as we discuss in Chapter Nine, emails exchanged between Steele and Ohr show that Steele visited Washington, D.C., beginning around September 21, 2016, and met with Ohr on September 23, at which time the two discussed multiple issues involving election related intelligence that Steele had collected. Steele told us that during this visit he also met with an attorney from Perkins Coie, who was general counsel to the Clinton campaign.[233]

Steele also met with journalists during his September trip to Washington, D.C. According to a filing that Steele made in 2017 in foreign litigation, at Fusion GPS's instruction, he briefed reporters from *The New York Times, The Washington*

---

information against Trump given how cooperative his team had been over several years and of late);

- Report 105 (during a secret meeting between Putin and ex-Ukrainian President Yanukovych, Yanukovych confided to Putin that he did authorize and order substantial kick-back payments to Manafort but reassured Putin that no documentary trail was left behind; Putin and Russian leadership were skeptical of the ex-President's assurances that there were no traces of the payments; Manafort's departure from the Trump campaign was attributable to Ukrainian corruption revelations as well as infighting with campaign advisors);

- Report 112 (the leading figures of the Alpha group of businesses led by three Russian oligarchs are on very good terms with Putin; Alpha held compromising information on Putin and his corrupt business activities from the 1990s); and

- Report 113 (sources based in St. Petersburg reported that Trump has paid bribes and engaged in sexual activities in St. Petersburg, including participating in sex parties, but that witnesses had been "silenced," *i.e.*, bribed or coerced to disappear).

[232] This was not the first time that information included in Steele's reports concerning the Trump campaign was known to individuals outside the FBI. For example, Handling Agent 1 emailed an FBI supervisor on July 28, 2016, explaining that Steele had advised him that information from Reports 80 and 94 "may already be circulating at a 'high level' in Washington, D.C." Two days earlier, according to a text between Carter Page and a *Wall Street Journal* reporter (that Page has since made public), the reporter contacted Page inquiring whether Page had met with Sechin and Divyekin. The FBI also received correspondence from Members of Congress in August 2016 that described information included in the Steele reports. Additionally, then Assistant Secretary of State for European and Eurasian Affairs Victoria Nuland publicly stated during an interview in 2018 that Steele's election reporting was first provided to the State Department in July 2016.

[233] Steele told us that he had a second meeting with this attorney in October 2016, and that he had met with another attorney from Perkins Coie in July 2016.

Post, Yahoo News, The New Yorker, and CNN. The filing states that the briefings were verbal, occurred at the end of September, and "involved the disclosure of limited intelligence regarding indications of Russian interference with the U.S. election process and the possible coordination of members of Trump's campaign team and Russian government officials."

Steele told us that the press briefings were taskings from his client, Fusion GPS, that his firm had to honor, and Simpson has testified that Simpson attended the briefings.[234] Steele said that they were "off-the-record" and, while he made mention of the reports, Steele did not distribute them to the journalists. Steele explained that he discussed "general themes" from his reporting that lacked sufficient specificity to identify his sources, and that he avoided answering questions about whether he had reported his findings to authorities.[235]

We asked Steele whether he believed his participation in the press briefings was contrary to any admonishments that he had received previously from Handling Agent 1. He said that he did not recall the FBI telling him he could not talk to journalists about work that he performed on behalf of his firm's clients. According to Steele, the election reporting was a "Pipeline 1" assignment and therefore the FBI did not have a role in setting terms for his interactions with third parties, such as news organizations. He said that if the FBI had tried to interfere in his assignment for Fusion GPS, he would have objected and that such an attempt would have been a "showstopper." Steele stated that Orbis' client for the election reporting was Fusion GPS, which controlled and directed the terms for interactions with third parties.

Handling Agent 1 told us that he understood why Steele would believe in September 2016 that he did not have an obligation to discuss his press contacts with him given that: (1) Steele's work resulted from a private client engagement; and (2) Handling Agent 1 told Steele on July 5 that he was not collecting his election reporting on behalf of the FBI. However, Handling Agent 1's view was that while it was obvious that Fusion GPS would want to publicize Steele's election information, it was not apparent that Steele would be conducting press briefings and otherwise interjecting himself into the media spotlight. Handling Agent 1 told us that he would have recommended that Steele be closed in September 2016 if he had known about the attention that Steele was attracting to himself. According to Handling Agent 1, Steele should have had the foresight to recognize this fact and the professionalism to afford Handling Agent 1 an opportunity to assess the situation. However, we are unaware of any FBI admonishments that Steele violated by speaking to third parties, including the press, about work that he had

---

[234] *Simpson Senate Testimony*, at 207.

[235] According to a book co-authored by a *Yahoo News* reporter who was present for a Steele September 2016 press briefing, Steele told him at the meeting that he had provided his election reporting to the FBI and that there were "people in the [FBI] taking this very seriously." *See Russian Roulette: The Inside Story of Putin's War on America and the Election of Donald Trump* (New York: Grand Central Publishing, 2018), 226.

done solely for his firm's clients and where he made no mention of his relationship with the FBI.

On September 23, 2016, *Yahoo News* published an article entitled, "*U.S. Intel Officials Probe Ties Between Trump Advisor and Kremlin.*" The September 23 article described efforts by U.S. government intelligence agencies to determine whether Carter Page had opened communication channels with Kremlin officials. Steele told us that because his briefing with *Yahoo News* was "off-the-record," he did not believe that he was the source for the article. He stated that it was his understanding based on discussions with Simpson that the sourcing for the article came from within the U.S. government.[236] However, portions of the article align with information contained in Steele's Report 94. For example, the article stated that U.S. officials had received intelligence reporting that Page had met with Igor Sechin, Chairman of Rosneft, and Igor Divyekin, Deputy Chief in the Russian Presidential Administration. The article cited "a well-placed Western intelligence source" for this information, and the article's author has confirmed that Steele contributed information for the article and that Steele was the "Western intelligence source."[237]

We asked FBI agents and analysts assigned to the Crossfire Hurricane investigation whether, following publication of the *Yahoo News* article, they had concerns that Steele was briefing the press about the reports that he had provided to the FBI, and they expressed varying points of view. The Supervisory Intel Analyst told us that it was unclear to him in September 2016 whether Steele was briefing the press. He stated that because Steele was providing his reporting to Fusion GPS, the Supervisory Intel Analyst's view at the time was that it could have been Fusion GPS or its clients who were discussing the reporting with news outlets. The supervisory attorney from the FBI Office of the General Counsel assigned to the Crossfire Hurricane investigation (the OGC Unit Chief) stated that she and others assumed that Steele's clients, or others with whom the clients had shared the information, were responsible for the press stories, but that the Crossfire Hurricane team would not have been surprised if Steele's reporting was the basis for the *Yahoo News* article. In contrast, Case Agent 1 sent instant messages indicating his belief that Steele was the "Western intelligence source" mentioned in the *Yahoo News* article and Steele "was selling his stuff to others." Case Agent 1 told us that the Crossfire Hurricane team later assessed that Simpson or someone else who had the Steele information, rather than Steele himself, was responsible for furnishing the information to *Yahoo News*. However, as we describe below, the team had no factual basis to support this assessment.

SSA 1 told us that his first concern was that someone from inside the FBI had disclosed information to the media. He stated that there was a "paranoia with leaks" inside the FBI in light of recent problems with leaks, and that it seemed

---

[236] *Yahoo News* has reported that the author of the September 23 article relied on a "senior U.S. law enforcement official" for information. *See* "*Yahoo News'* Michael Isikoff Describes Crucial Meeting Cited in Nunes Memo," *Yahoo News* (February 2, 2018).

[237] *Russian Roulette*, at 227.

"foreign" that Steele—as ████████████████████—would be involved in such a breach. However, SSA 1's notes from a meeting on September 30 contain the following notation: "control issues—reports acknowledged in *Yahoo News*." We asked SSA 1 whether he was concerned at the time that there were control issues with Steele. He stated that he was concerned but that he was not sure that Steele was responsible for providing information to *Yahoo News*. In addition, he said he was focused on Steele's discussions with the State Department about his work with the FBI.[238] SSA 1 stated that an important objective of the planned meeting with Steele in early October was to obtain "exclusivity" in Steele's reporting relationship, meaning that Steele would provide his intelligence related to the election exclusively to the FBI.

As we describe in Chapter Five, drafts of the Carter Page FISA application stated, until October 14, 2016, that Steele was responsible for the leak that led to the September 23 *Yahoo News* article. One of the drafts specifically stated that Steele "was acting on his/her own volition and has since been admonished by the FBI." In contrast, the final version of the first FISA application stated:

> Given that the information contained in the September 23rd News Article generally matches the information about Page that Source #1 discovered during his/her research, the FBI assesses that Source #1's business associate or the law firm that hired the business associate likely provided this information to the press. The FBI also assesses that whoever gave the information to the press stated that the information was provided by a 'well-placed Western intelligence source.' The FBI does not believe that Source #1 directly provided this information to the Press.

The OI Attorney told us that at some point during the drafting process, the FBI assured him that Steele had not spoken with *Yahoo News* because the source was "a professional." As we discuss in greater detail in Chapter Five, no one at the FBI or the National Security Division (NSD) was able to explain to us the source of the information that resulted in, or supported, either the draft language that existed until October 14 or the final language regarding the *Yahoo News* article.

Steele told us that he did not recall the FBI ever asking him whether he was the source for the *Yahoo News* story, no one from the FBI recalled having asked Steele if he was the source of the *Yahoo News* story, and we found no documentary evidence to suggest that Steele had ever been asked this question by the FBI. As described in Chapters Seven and Eight, even after receiving additional information about Steele's media contacts, the Crossfire Hurricane team did not change the language in any of the three renewal applications regarding the FBI's assessment of Steele's role in the September 23 article.

---

[238] SSA 1 had been forwarded an email on September 30 from the State Department's Bureau of European and Eurasian Affairs indicating that senior staff there, including Assistant Secretary Nuland, were aware of a planned meeting between Steele and the FBI in early October in a European city, and that FBI officials from Headquarters were flying to Europe to participate in the meeting.

F.   The FBI's Early October Meeting with Steele

Handling Agent 1 told us that he took the lead in organizing the logistics for a meeting in early October between Steele and members of the Crossfire Hurricane team in a European city. An Acting Section Chief from CD (Acting Section Chief 1), Case Agent 2, and the Supervisory Intel Analyst, attended the meeting for the Crossfire Hurricane team. Case Agent 2 had extensive experience in counterintelligence and managing CHSs, including previously holding a supervisory training position where he provided instruction on those topics. The Supervisory Intel Analyst was one of the FBI's leading experts on Russia.

Case Agent 2 and SSA 1 told the OIG that the FBI had several objectives for the meeting, the most important of which were learning about Steele's source network; persuading Steele to work collaboratively with the Crossfire Hurricane team in the future; and, as noted above, obtaining assurances from Steele that he would provide the intelligence that the FBI was seeking exclusively to the FBI. According to Case Agent 2, the task for him was a difficult one because he was asking Steele—an experienced intelligence professional—to reveal how he gathered intelligence. Case Agent 2 stated that he needed to be careful to avoid use of heavy-handed tactics that would cause Steele to walk out. We also were told by Case Agent 2 that the team's primary objectives for the meeting came from discussions he had with Strzok and SSA 1. Strzok said that he discussed the goals of the early October meeting with the team and recalled attending meetings where taskings for Steele were discussed in anticipation of the meeting. However, Strzok said he was not involved in developing the taskings and left that effort to the Crossfire Hurricane team. He also stated that he was not asked to authorize the team's taskings for Steele. SSA 1 said that the team had specific objectives for the early October meeting with Steele and that he provided guidance to the team before they left, but he did not recall his specific instructions. SSA 1 stated that he trusted Case Agent 2, Acting Section Chief 1, and the Supervisory Intel Analyst to do their job when meeting with Steele.

The meeting was set for early October. According to Handling Agent 1, Steele contacted him three days prior to the meeting and advised Handling Agent 1 that Steele had previously shared the reports he had given to the FBI with then State Department official Jonathan Winer. Handling Agent 1 said that Steele also informed him that Winer was aware of the upcoming FBI meeting in October.

Handling Agent 1 stated that the Crossfire Hurricane team arrived in the European city the day before the meeting and that he conferred with them about Steele.[239] Handling Agent 1 said he recalled providing advice to the team to ask Steele "anything and everything.... Don't hold back." Handling Agent 1 also remembered that at least one member of the team asked Handling Agent 1 if Steele had said anything about the *Yahoo News* article. Handling Agent 1 said that he responded "no" and that he was not familiar with the article in question.

---

[239] After reviewing this report, the Supervisory Intel Analyst told us that he believed that the Crossfire Hurricane team arrived in the European city the morning of the meeting with Steele.

Handling Agent 1 also recalled the team discussing that the State Department was aware of the Steele reporting and that the team would need to discuss that with Steele.[240] Handling Agent 1 told us that he advised the team that Steele had contacted Jonathan Winer at the State Department. Case Agent 2 said that Handling Agent 1 did not mention to him that Steele had possible connections to Russian Oligarch 1 and that he would have wanted to know that information because it could have indicated that Steele was being used in a Russian "controlled operation" to influence perceptions (*i.e.*, a disinformation campaign). Handling Agent 1 did not recall if he told the Crossfire Hurricane team about Steele's connection to Russian Oligarch 1; however, he said he did inform the team that Steele collected intelligence on Russian oligarchs and had tried to arrange meetings between the FBI and Russian oligarchs.

The day of the meeting, Handling Agent 1 met with Steele prior to introducing him to the Crossfire Hurricane team and explained to Steele that he would be asked questions about his source network. Handling Agent 1 said that he encouraged Steele to be forthcoming with the Crossfire Hurricane team. Handling Agent 1 told the OIG that he attended the meeting but that Case Agent 2 did the majority of the talking for the FBI with the Supervisory Intel Analyst asking questions primarily about the source network.

The meeting lasted approximately 2.5 to 3 hours, according to the Supervisory Intel Analyst. According to Case Agent 2's written summary of the meeting, Case Agent 2 provided Steele with a "general overview" of the Crossfire Hurricane investigation, which included a description of events involving Papadopoulos and the Friendly Foreign Government (FFG) information that furnished the predication for the investigation. Case Agent 2's written summary also states that Case Agent 2 informed Steele that Papadopoulos's actions had resulted in a "small analytical effort" that had expanded to include Manafort, Flynn, and Carter Page.

Case Agent 2 told the OIG that he informed Steele that the FBI was interested in obtaining information in "3 buckets." According to Case Agent 2's written summary of the meeting, as well as the Supervisory Intel Analyst's notes, these 3 buckets were:

> (1) Additional intelligence/reporting on specific, named individuals (such as [Page] or [Flynn]) involved in facilitating the Trump campaign-Russian relationship;[241] (2) Physical evidence of specific individuals involved in facilitating the Trump campaign-Russian relationship (such as emails, photos, ledgers, memorandums etc); [and] (3) Any individuals or sub sources who [Steele] could identify

---

[240] According to Case Agent 2's written summary of the meeting with Steele in early October, Steele disclosed to the participants that he was furnishing information to the State Department "to ensure that the information was reaching the proper elements of the [U.S. government]."

[241] The written summary used codenames to identify Page and Flynn.

who could serve as cooperating witnesses to assist in identifying persons involved in the Trump campaign-Russian relationship.[242]

Case Agent 2's written summary of the meeting also indicates that Case Agent 2 explained that the FBI was willing to compensate Steele "significantly" for information concerning the "3 buckets" and that Steele would be paid $15,000 for his trip to the European city for the early October meeting.[243]

Case Agent 2 told the OIG that Steele sat throughout the meeting with his arms folded and he could tell from Steele's body language that he was "going to be difficult to handle." According to Case Agent 2, Steele was not "excited" to hear what information the FBI was hoping to obtain, and Case Agent 2's notes indicate that Steele was "caught off guard" with the tasking request. Case Agent 2 stated that Steele was focused instead during the meeting on candidate Trump and recalled that Steele responded to the "3 buckets" by stating "maybe I can go back to the hotel [in Russia] and get the manager for you to meet to talk about the prostitutes being there."

Notes taken by Case Agent 2 and the Supervisory Intel Analyst show that Steele provided some information during the meeting about his source network and furnished several other names that could be of interest to the FBI. For example, Steele identified a sub-source (Person 1) who Steele said was in direct contact with Steele's primary source (Primary Sub-source).[244] The notes further reflect that Steele described some of Person 1's reporting but caveated this information by explaining that Person 1 is a "boaster" and "egotist" and "may engage in some embellishment." As described in Chapters Five and Eight, the FBI did not provide this description of Person 1 to NSD's Office of Intelligence (OI) for inclusion in the Carter Page FISA applications despite relying on Person 1's information to establish probable cause in the applications.

The Supervisory Intel Analyst's notes also indicate that Steele explained that the information he obtained about Carter Page resulted from research he had been retained to conduct related to a litigation matter concerning debts allegedly owed by Paul Manafort.[245]

---

[242] The FBI advised the OIG that the Crossfire Hurricane investigation was a national security investigation, and these activities therefore involved national security ███████████ CHS operations ███.

[243] As we discuss below, after the FBI learned in November that Steele had disclosed information to *Mother Jones* in late October 2016, the FBI declined to make this payment.

[244] Person 1 ███

[245] At the time, according to FBI records that we reviewed, Manafort was involved in litigation with Russian Oligarch 1, and Steele had a relationship with one or more of the attorneys representing Russian Oligarch 1. In his interview with the OIG, Steele denied that his reporting on Carter Page resulted from work he performed on Russian Oligarch 1's behalf. Steele described as "ridiculous" any claim that Russian Oligarch 1 was involved in his reporting or influenced it.

Lastly, Steele provided the name of a Russian national, who he said may have connections with a Russian energy company, and who Steele claimed may be acting as Carter Page's possible "handler" for Russian intelligence. As noted in Chapter Three, Carter Page previously had a relationship with another U.S. government agency; Page had provided that agency with information on the same Russian national that Steele reported was Page's possible handler. According to an Assistant Legal Attaché (ALAT 2), Steele's allegations about the Russian national were investigated ███████████████████████████████, but no information was uncovered to substantiate the allegations.[246]

We were told by the Crossfire Hurricane team members that Steele refrained from providing the level of detail about his source network that the FBI had hoped to obtain. Steele told the team members that he did not want to identify his sources because he was concerned about their safety and security. He explained that he was ████████████████████████████Primary Sub-source, and that due to leaks, his source network was "drying up." According to Case Agent 2, Steele complained to the FBI during the meeting about these leaks.

We were also told by Case Agent 2 that Steele did not disclose information about the identity of Fusion GPS's client, a law firm which was funding Steele's work due to a confidentiality agreement that prevented him from sharing that information.[247] We asked Steele what he told the FBI during the meeting about his client. He said that his notes from the meeting, which he told us he prepared two days after the meeting, and are dated that day, were the best source for that information. We reviewed Steele's notes, which show that Steele stated during the meeting that Simpson was an "intermediary" and that Simpson had been retained by "people seeking to prevent Trump becoming President." The notes did not reflect that any additional information had been provided by Steele during the meeting regarding the identity of Fusion GPS's client. Steele told us that the FBI did not press him to identify Fusion GPS's client.

During the meeting, Case Agent 2 said he advised Steele of the need to establish an exclusive reporting relationship with the FBI concerning the information that he was being tasked to collect. Case Agent 2 drafted an Electronic

---

[246] Steele also reiterated some of the information in his election reporting identified other U.S. persons that he believed may be involved in or have knowledge of Russia and Trump connections. Additionally, he told the FBI that he was personal friends with a Trump family member and that the FBI may become aware of email communications concerning their friendship. Steele stated that he could not see the Trump family member being involved in any nefarious activities concerning the Trump-Russia matter.

[247] On October 14, 2016, Case Agent 2 wrote in an email to SSA 1, Case Agent 1, the Intel Section Chief, and Strzok, among others stating that Handling Agent 1 did not believe Steele knew the identity of the Fusion GPS client which was responsible for funding Steele's work. As we described in Section II.B. above, Steele told Handling Agent 1 in July that he did not know the precise identity of the client; however, it is unclear whether Handling Agent 1 subsequently asked Steele whether he had acquired that information. Handling Agent 1 told us that he did not "continually ask" Steele about the firm's identity after his meeting with Steele on July 5, 2016.

Communication (EC) following the early October meeting that was serialized into the Crossfire Hurricane case file and described the FBI request for exclusivity:

> [T]he CHS was admonished that if the CHS and FBI were going to have a reporting relationship regarding specific items of interest to the CROSSFIRE HURRICANE team (*i.e.*, [Manafort] and [Page]), that the CHS must have an exclusive reporting relationship with the FBI, rather than providing that information to the clients that hired the CHS's firm to provide reporting on Trump and [Manafort].

Recollections of the Crossfire Hurricane team members who attended the meeting varied about Steele's response to this request, except all agreed that Steele did not affirmatively disagree with it. Handling Agent 1 told us that Steele was told at the meeting "you do not talk to anybody else including anybody else in the United States government" about information Steele collected for the three buckets and that Steele agreed. Handling Agent 1 said that Steele left him with the impression that he would assist the FBI following the meeting and would abide by the FBI's instruction on exclusivity, and that he "did not buy for one second" the notion that Steele was not a CHS at this time with an obligation to follow FBI instructions. The Supervisory Intel Analyst said he could not recall Steele's response, but said that by the end of the meeting he was left with the impression that Steele would abide by the FBI's request. He further stated that, if Steele had rejected the FBI's request, it would have been documented. Case Agent 2 said that Steele never committed to share information regarding the "3 buckets" exclusively with the FBI. According to Case Agent 2, Steele's response instead was that he would consider ways to help the FBI.

Steele told us that the FBI indicated at the meeting in early October that the FBI wanted to take over the "election project" and control it, alternatively describing the FBI's actions as an attempt to get Steele to convert a "Pipeline 1" project into a "Pipeline 2" project. Steele recalled that, in response, he made it clear that was not going to happen because he was obligated to his client and was "not dumping the client" in favor of the FBI. He stated, however, that he wanted to be as helpful to the FBI as he could. According to Steele, the FBI accepted his position though they requested that he not share his election intelligence with other U.S. government agencies or with third-party clients (other than the client that retained him initially). Steele said he did not know whether he agreed to this request and pointed out that his notes from the meeting do not reflect his response.[248] We asked whether he would have recorded a response in the notes if he had rejected the request. He responded "yes," and said the lack of a response in his notes suggested he did not agree or disagree.

We asked Handling Agent 1 and members of the Crossfire Hurricane team whether it was realistic for the FBI to expect that Steele would abide by the FBI's request given that his consulting firm had been retained by a paying client to perform this work. Handling Agent 1 told us that he thought it was realistic

---

[248] The notes that Steele made available to the OIG to review, which Steele told us he prepared two days after the meeting, were consistent with his testimony to the OIG.

because Steele "was now being offered compensation to go forward from the United States government." Acting Section Chief 1 said he was not sure at the time how realistic the request was because he did not know how many clients Steele had, though he "rationalized" that given Steele's intelligence background his business probably "was wide to a lot of audiences" and he could afford to have an exclusive reporting relationship with the FBI on certain issues.

We also asked the FBI team members who attended whether there was any discussion during the meeting about the September 23 *Yahoo News* article. Case Agent 2 told the OIG that he could not remember asking Steele about the *Yahoo News* article during the meeting, and that he was more focused on getting Steele to "play ball." The Supervisory Intel Analyst also said he did not recall Steele being asked whether he was a source of the *Yahoo News* article. Handling Agent 1 stated that he could not recall if the article was raised during the meeting with Steele. According to Steele, he did not recall any discussion of the media during the early October meeting, and none was reflected in his notes. Steele further told us that if the issue of the media had been raised he would have recorded it in his notes given that he already had met with media groups in September.

According to the Crossfire Hurricane team members, the outcome of the early October meeting was less than desired. Case Agent 2 said he could not recall Steele agreeing to anything during the meeting. Both Case Agent 2 and the Supervisory Intel Analyst told the OIG that, although Steele continued to provide written reports to Handling Agent 1 after the meeting, Steele did not provide information specifically addressing the "3 buckets."[249] Case Agent 2 also expressed skepticism after the meeting as to whether Steele would abide by the FBI's request for exclusivity in his reporting. In response to an inquiry in mid-October from the OI Attorney who was drafting the first Carter Page FISA application, about whether Steele was refraining from providing information to Simpson that was relevant to the Crossfire Hurricane investigation, Case Agent 2 responded in an email that "we need to be realistic about that." Case Agent 2 wrote:

> We made a good faith effort and admonished the CHS [at the early October meeting] that any further information that s/he developed in regard to our subjects, Page[,] Manafort, Papadopoulos, Flynn should be exclusively provided to the FBI for further evaluation. Whether or not that happens remains to be seen.

Handling Agent 1 told us that after the early October meeting Steele failed to abide by the FBI's instructions when he continued to meet with the media and the State Department about issues over which the FBI had sought to establish an exclusive reporting relationship at the early October meeting. According to Handling Agent 1, while Steele appeared to follow the directions of Fusion GPS, he did not treat his other client – the FBI – fairly. According to Handling Agent 1, if Steele "had been straight with the FBI," he would not have been closed as a CHS. Handling Agent 1 added that it "blew his mind" that, given Steele's intelligence

---

[249] As we describe below, Steele did provide some limited information in mid-October 2016 concerning Carter Page.

background, Steele was meeting with the press and taking actions that endangered the safety of those in his source network. Case Agent 2 told the OIG that he thought it was "terrible" for Steele to complain to the FBI about leaks during the early October meeting given that he had been meeting with media outlets in September and had provided information that was used in the *Yahoo News* article. According to Case Agent 2, in hindsight, "[c]learly he wasn't truthful with us. Clearly."

We asked Steele whether during the early October meeting he lied or otherwise misled the FBI. He responded "no" and that he did not believe he ever lied to the FBI.

G.   FBI Disclosures to Steele during the Early October Meeting

In addition to inquiring about Steele's conduct at the early October meeting, we also asked whether the Crossfire Hurricane team members provided too much information to Steele during the meeting, including classified information. According to Case Agent 2's written summary of the meeting, Case Agent 2 provided Steele with a "general overview" of the Crossfire Hurricane investigation, which included a description of events involving Papadopoulos and the FFG, which furnished the predication for the investigation. Case Agent 2's written summary also states that Case Agent 2 informed Steele that Papadopoulos's actions had resulted in a "small analytical effort" that had expanded to include Manafort, Flynn, and Page.[250] FBI attendees at the meeting confirmed that Case Agent 2 led the discussion on these points, though Case Agent 2 told us that his written summary does not present the actual words he used in his explanations to Steele. The contents of both the "analytical effort" and the FFG's notice to the U.S. government are classified.

Handling Agent 1 told the OIG that he agreed it was peculiar that Case Agent 2 gave Steele an overview of the Crossfire Hurricane investigation, including providing names of persons related to the investigation. As an example, Handling Agent 1 explained that during the FIFA investigation he never informed Steele that the FBI was investigating FIFA. The Supervisory Intel Analyst told the OIG that he was concerned that Case Agent 2 had divulged too much information to Steele and that he notified his supervisor about his concern upon returning to Washington D.C.

---

[250] The relevant text from Case Agent 2's summary reads:

The CHS was then given a general overview of the FBI's CROSSFIRE HURRICANE investigation and told that it was a small cell that was exploring a small piece of the overall problem of Russian interference in the U.S. Electoral process. CHS was advised that the CH team was made aware of [Papadopoulos's] May 2016 comments in the U.K in late July by a friendly foreign service and that [Papadopoulos] had predicated a small analytical effort that eventually expanded to include [Manafort, Flynn, and Page]. CHS advised that he was not aware of [Papadopoulos].

The Supervisory Intel Analyst stated that he was concerned that Case Agent 2 had shared names as well as information related to the FFG information.[251]

Case Agent 2 said that he believed he had authority from CD to discuss classified information with Steele, though he agreed that in the "heat of the moment" he made a mistake and provided more information than he should have provided about the role of the FFG. He explained that his disclosure resulted from "trying in good faith to accomplish the mission." He stated that he remembered telling Steele that the FBI was investigating possible Russian penetrations of the Trump campaign but did not recall telling Steele that Papadopoulos, Manafort, Flynn, and Page were being investigated by the FBI. Rather, he recalled asking for information about those persons in light of press coverage that they had received. Steele told us that he did not believe the Crossfire Hurricane team members told him whether there was an open investigation on those persons. Case Agent 2 further stated that there was no effort on his part to conceal what he had said to Steele from his supervisors. After the meeting concluded, Case Agent 2 circulated a written summary of the meeting that included a description of the information he provided to Steele. Acting Section Chief 1 also attended the meeting in the European city and did not object at the time or afterwards to Case Agent 2's conduct.

We asked Case Agent 2's supervisors—Strzok and Priestap—about the information that the Crossfire Hurricane team communicated to Steele and whether Case Agent 2 had been authorized to disclose classified information during the early October meeting.[252] Priestap said that he did not recall being briefed beforehand about what information the team intended to convey to Steele. He explained, however, that given Steele's background in intelligence work, it was necessary to provide him with sufficient contextual information to understand the taskings. Priestap also said that there is an "art" to deciding how much information to convey to a CHS so that the CHS can be effective without divulging the sensitive details of an investigation. Strzok stated that he did not recall authorizing Case Agent 2 to disclose the specific information presented in Case Agent 2's written summary though Strzok said he recalled general discussions with the Crossfire Hurricane team members who were meeting with Steele about how much information to share with Steele. Strzok explained that "[y]ou provide as much information as needed to give effective direction, and as little as possible to compartment and protect what we're doing." After reading Case Agent 2's written summary of the information he presented to Steele, both Priestap and Strzok said that it appeared that Case Agent 2 provided more information than was necessary to Steele.

---

[251] Steele informed Simpson about the content of the discussions during the early October meeting, including that the FBI had information from "an internal Trump campaign source" that corroborated Steele's reporting, according to Simpson's testimony to the Senate Judiciary Committee. *Simpson Senate Testimony*, at 175.

[252] FBI Security staff told us that the Assistant Director for CD can authorize the disclosure of classified information. We found that the CHS Policy Guide (CHSPG) does not address the disclosure of sensitive or classified information to CHSs and that the FBI has not otherwise developed guidance on the issue.

H. Steele's Reporting to the FBI Following the Early October Meeting and Continuing Media Contacts

Steele continued to furnish the FBI with written reports following the early October meeting. Handling Agent 1 told us that he became a "middleman" between Steele and the Crossfire Hurricane team and forwarded Steele's reports to the team. According to Handling Agent 1's records, during October 2016, Steele communicated with him four times and provided seven written reports, one of which concerned Carter Page and thus was responsive to the FBI's request for information concerning Page's activities.[253]

On October 19, 2016, Steele also forwarded to Handling Agent 1 a report that Steele said he had obtained from State Department official Jonathan Winer. Steele included a notation on the report explaining that Winer had been given the report by a friend of a well-known Clinton supporter, and that the friend had obtained the report from a Turkish businessman with strong links to Russia, including the Federal Security Service of the Russian Federation (FSB).[254] The report included numerous allegations attributed to an FSB source, including that (1) a "'pervasive' and 'sophisticated' intelligence operation" was focused in part on

---

[253] These seven reports, with selected highlights, were:

- Report 130 (Putin and his colleagues were surprised and disappointed that leaks of Clinton's emails had not had a greater impact on the campaign; a stream of hacked Clinton material had been injected by the Kremlin into compliant western media outlets like WikiLeaks and the stream would continue until the election);

- Report ████████████████████████████████████;

- Report 134 (a close associate of Rosneft President Sechin confirmed a secret meeting with Carter Page in July; Sechin was keen to have sanctions on the company lifted and offered up to a 19 percent stake in return);

- Report 135 (Trump attorney Michael Cohen was heavily engaged in a cover up and damage control in an attempt to prevent the full details of Trump's relationship with Russia being exposed; Cohen had met secretly with several Russian Presidential Administration Legal Department officials; immediate issues were efforts to contain further scandals involving Manafort's commercial and political role in Russia/Ukraine and to limit damage from the exposure of Carter Page's secret meetings with Russian leadership figures in Moscow the previous month);

- Report 136 (Kremlin insider reports that Cohen's secret meeting/s with Kremlin officials in August 2016 was/were held in Prague);

- Report ██;

  and

- Report ██.

[254] According to open source reporting, the FSB serves as Russia's domestic intelligence and security service that retains a broad mission of counterintelligence, counterterrorism, cyber defense, border security, and economic security, in addition to overseeing Russia's vast technical monitoring system known as SORM.

Trump and was an "open secret" in Putin's government; (2) sex videos existed of Trump; and (3) the FSB funneled payments to Trump through an Azerbaijani family. According to Steele's notation to the report, Steele did not have a way to verify the source(s) or the information but noted that, even though the reporting originated from a different source network, some of it was "remarkably similar" to Steele's reporting, especially with regard to the alleged 2013 Ritz Carlton incident involving Trump and prostitutes, Trump's compromise by the FSB, and the Kremlin's funding of the Trump campaign by way of the Azerbaijani family. The Supervisory Intel Analyst characterized the report as "yet another report that would need to be evaluated."

In addition to continuing to provide reporting to the FBI, Steele also was, unbeknownst to the FBI at the time, continuing his outreach to the media concerning alleged contacts between the Trump campaign and the Russian government. According to information from the foreign litigation noted above, Steele returned to Washington, D.C., in mid-October and provided additional briefings to *The New York Times*, *The Washington Post*, and *Yahoo News*. We asked Steele why he did not advise the FBI of his engagements with the media. He stated that he did not alert the FBI because the media briefings were part of his contract with Fusion GPS and were set up and attended by Simpson. As noted above, Steele did not believe that the FBI had raised the issue of media contacts with him at the early October meeting, and his contemporaneous notes from that meeting do not mention the issue.

Further, Steele met on October 11 at the State Department with Winer and Deputy Assistant Secretary Kathleen Kavalec, who was a deputy to then Assistant Secretary Victoria Nuland. Steele told us that Winer had originally contacted him to request that he meet with Nuland, who ultimately did not attend.[255] Notes of the meeting taken by State Department staff reflect that Steele addressed a wide array of topics during the meeting, including:

- Derogatory information on Trump;

- Manafort's role as a "go-between" with the campaign and Kremlin;

- The role of Alfa Bank, one of Russia's largest privately owned banks, as a conduit for secret communications between Manafort and the Kremlin;

- Manafort's debts to the Russians;

- Carter Page's meeting with Sechin;

- The Russian Embassy's management of a network of Russian émigrés in the United States who carry out hacking and recruiting operations; and

---

[255] Steele told us that he was delayed from the airport and arrived late for the meeting, by which time Nuland had departed.

- The Russian cyber penetration of the DNC.[256]

The notes also indicate that Steele explained that the information his firm collected on the connection between Trump and Russia came from ███████████, ██ According to the notes, Steele stated that ██ The notes also state that Steele's firm had ███████████████████████████████████

We asked Kavalec about the meeting with Steele. She stated that Nuland did not ask to meet with Steele and that Nuland requested she attend the meeting because Nuland did not want to devote time to it. It was Kavalec's understanding that Steele sought the meeting with Nuland as part of a wider effort to disseminate his election report findings to persons in Washington, D.C. She stated that during the meeting Steele expressed frustration that the FBI had not acted on his reporting and explained that when he first offered information to the FBI he found a lack of interest.

Kavalec told us that shortly after the meeting with Steele, she encountered the FBI's liaison to the State Department and mentioned the meeting to him. According to Kavalec, she explained to the liaison that she was willing to be interviewed by the FBI regarding her meeting with Steele, though Steele had informed her that he had already been in contact with the FBI to share his reporting. The FBI liaison told us that Kavalec also informed him that a particular piece of information in Steele's reporting appeared to be incorrect. She explained to the FBI liaison that Russia did not have a consulate in Miami as indicated by Steele's reporting, which claimed that a cyber-hacking operation was being run, in part, out of the Russian consulate in Miami.[257] The FBI liaison informed SSA 1 and Case Agent 1 via email on November 18 that Kavalec had met with Steele, she had taken notes of their meeting, the liaison could obtain information from Kavalec about the meeting, and, according to Kavalec, the information from Steele's reporting about a Russian consulate being located in Miami was inaccurate.[258] The

---

[256] Much of the information presented by Steele at the State Department briefing can be found in Reports 130 and 132, both of which Steele provided to the FBI in October.

[257] Kavalec's typed notes from Steele's October 11, 2016 briefing stated that Steele told her that a Russian cyber hacking operation targeting the 2016 U.S. elections was making payments to involved persons from "the Russian [c]onsulate in Miami." Steele's election Report 95 contained similar, but not fully consistent, information. Report 95 did not explicitly state that there was a Russian consulate in Miami. Instead, Report 95 stated that Russian consular officials and diplomatic staff in Miami were making payments in order to facilitate a secret exchange of intelligence between persons affiliated with Trump and the Russian government.

[258] After reviewing a portion of our draft report and his November 18, 2016 email to SSA 1 and Case Agent 1, the FBI liaison told us that he believes that he first learned about Kavalec's meeting with Steele on or about November 18, 2016.

118

FBI liaison told us that he received no directives from the Crossfire Hurricane team to gather information from Kavalec regarding her contact with Steele.

In anticipation of an FBI interview, Kavalec said she prepared a typewritten summary of the meeting within 1 to 2 weeks after talking with the liaison. The typed summary began by noting that Steele said at the meeting that he had undertaken the investigation "at the behest of an institution he declined to identify that had been hacked." The summary also noted that Steele told the attendees that the "institution...is keen to see this information come to light prior to November 8." However, the FBI did not interview Kavalec nor did they seek her notes.

Two days after the meeting with Steele, Kavalec emailed an FBI CD Section Chief a document that Kavalec received from Winer discussing allegations about a linkage between Alfa Bank and the Trump campaign, a topic that was discussed at the October 11 meeting.[259] Kavalec advised the FBI Section Chief in the email that the information related to an investigation that Steele's firm had been conducting. The Section Chief forwarded the document to SSA 1 the same day.

We asked Steele why he did not inform the FBI of the meeting at the State Department and why he did not abide by the FBI's request for exclusivity. He said he did not think it was appropriate to turn down a meeting request from an Assistant Secretary of State, which he said he received on short notice. He also stated that, at the time he received the meeting request, the meeting agenda was unclear, and he was uncertain what topics he would be asked to discuss. He said it was his understanding that the FBI did not object to his discussing general themes with other agencies as opposed to "details" about his intelligence and source network.

Handling Agent 1 told us that he believed Steele should have alerted him to both his media contacts in September and October and his meeting with State Department staff in October. As noted above, the Crossfire Hurricane team first learned of Steele's October meeting with the State Department from the FBI liaison on November 18, by which date the FBI had already closed Steele as a CHS because of his *Mother Jones* disclosure, which we discuss in Chapter Six. Handling Agent 1 explained that Steele should have recognized the need to provide this notice to the FBI, especially given the discussions that took place with the Crossfire Hurricane team in early October.

---

[259] Steele separately wrote in Report 112, dated September 14, 2016, that Alfa Bank allegedly had close ties to Putin. The Crossfire Hurricane team received Report 112 on or about November 6, 2016, from a *Mother Jones* journalist through then FBI General Counsel James Baker. Additionally, Ohr advised the FBI on November 21, 2016, according to an FBI FD-302, that Steele had told Ohr that the Alfa Bank server was a link to the Trump campaign and that Person 1's Russia/American organization in the U.S. had used the Alfa Bank server two weeks prior. Steele told us that the information about Alfa Bank was not generated by Orbis. The FBI investigated whether there were cyber links between the Trump Organization and Alfa Bank, but had concluded by early February 2017 that there were no such links. The Supervisory Intel Analyst told us that he factored the Alfa Bank/Trump server allegations into his assessment of Steele's reporting.

In the next chapter we describe the first Carter Page FISA application, filed on October ■, 2016, which relied significantly on Steele's reporting.

CHAPTER FIVE
THE FIRST APPLICATION FOR FISA AUTHORITY ON CARTER PAGE

At the request of the FBI, the Department filed four applications with the Foreign Intelligence Surveillance Court (FISC) seeking FISA authority to conduct electronic surveillance ███████████████████ targeting Carter Page: the first application on October ██, 2016, and three renewal applications on January ██, April ██, and June ██, 2017. A different FISC judge considered each application and issued the requested orders, collectively resulting in approximately 11 months of FISA coverage targeting Carter Page from October ██, 2016, to September ██, 2017.

In this chapter, we describe the first of the four FISA applications, beginning with the early consideration of a potential FISA targeting Carter Page in August 2016, shortly after the FBI opened the Crossfire Hurricane investigation, and the FBI's eventual submission of a FISA request to the Office of Intelligence (OI) in the National Security Division (NSD) in September 2016, a few days after the Crossfire Hurricane team received Christopher Steele's reporting. We discuss the significance of the Steele reporting to the decision of FBI attorneys to proceed with the FISA request. We also describe the development of the first FISA application and the attention it received during the review and approval process from the FBI, OI, NSD management, and the Office of the Deputy Attorney General (ODAG). We further describe the filing of the read copy with the FISC, the feedback OI received from the court, revisions made to the application to address that feedback, and the last steps taken before the final application was filed and the orders were issued. These last steps included the completion of the Woods Procedures described in Chapter Two, then FBI Director James Comey's certification of the application, and the oral briefing provided to, and final approval given by, then Deputy Attorney General (DAG) Sally Yates. Finally, we describe the most significant instances in which information in the FISA application was inaccurately stated, incomplete at the time the application was filed, or unsupported by documentation in the Woods File.

I. Decision to Seek FISA Authority

A. Early Consideration of a Potential FISA

As described in Chapter Three, on August 10, 2016, under the umbrella of Crossfire Hurricane, FBI Headquarters opened a new full counterintelligence investigation on Carter Page. The pre-existing counterintelligence case on Page was then transferred from the FBI's New York Field Office (NYFO) to FBI Headquarters and merged into the new case. At about the same time, the Crossfire Hurricane team began planning for Confidential Human Source (CHS) operations (discussed later in this chapter and in Chapter Ten) targeting Carter Page and George Papadopoulos. Also at about the same time, the case agent assigned to the Carter Page investigation, Case Agent 1, contacted FBI's Office of the General Counsel (OGC) about the possibility of seeking FISA authority targeting Carter Page to conduct electronic surveillance ███████████████. This was the first potential use of FISA authority considered by the Crossfire Hurricane team.

The Crossfire Hurricane team told us that the proposal for FISA coverage targeting Carter Page originated from the team, not an instruction from management. The team also told us that its interest in obtaining a FISA was based upon Page's prior contacts with known Russian intelligence officers, which the team believed made him most receptive to receiving the offer of assistance from the Russians reported in the FFG information (described in Chapter Three) provided to the FBI in late July 2016. Case Agent 1 said that he had hoped that emails and other communications obtained through FISA electronic surveillance would help provide valuable information about what Page did while in Moscow in July 2016 and the Russian officials with whom he may have spoken.

For these reasons, on August 15, 2016, Case Agent 1 emailed a written summary on Carter Page to the OGC Unit Chief, stating that he thought the information provided "a pretty solid basis" for requesting FISA authority. This summary, which a Staff Operations Specialist (SOS) prepared, briefly described Page's Russian business and financial ties, his prior contacts with Russian intelligence officers, and his recent travel to Russia. According to Case Agent 1, both he and the SOS believed that they had enough information to establish the probable cause necessary to request FISA authority on Carter Page. Case Agent 1 told us that Page's contacts with known Russian intelligence officers (described in Chapter Three) provided a "pretty good link" for a FISA.

Later the same day, the OGC Unit Chief responded to Case Agent 1 with requests for additional information about what Page had previously told the FBI regarding his relationship with Russian intelligence officers in order to compare it with information the FBI had from other reporting sources. She said that this information would be helpful to determine whether Page had a clandestine relationship with Russia. The OGC Unit Chief added that she would reach out to her OI counterparts to get their thoughts, "but I think we'll need more for PC," meaning probable cause.

The next day, on August 16, the OGC Unit Chief contacted Stuart Evans, then NSD's Deputy Assistant Attorney General with oversight responsibility over OI, stating:

> We have some facts which may lead to a FISA on one of our subjects—mostly past contacts and connections to [Russian Intelligence Services] and a financial interest in [a] Russian-government controlled gas business. I don't think we're quite there yet, but given the sensitivity and urgency of this matter, I would like to get OI involved as early as possible.

The OGC Unit Chief told Evans he had permission to brief a small group of OI attorneys into Crossfire Hurricane, including the Operations Section Chief, Gabriel

Sanz-Rexach; the Deputy Section Chief; the Counterintelligence Unit Chief (OI Unit Chief); and one line attorney.[260]

The OGC Unit Chief and OGC Attorney assigned to assist the Crossfire Hurricane team met with the OI Unit Chief the same day to brief him on Crossfire Hurricane and the four individual subjects. During his OIG interview, the OI Unit Chief recalled that the OGC attorneys mentioned the possibility of seeking FISA authority targeting Carter Page, but he did not recall a decision being made at the meeting about whether to do so.[261] The OI Unit Chief said that, at the request of Evans, he advised OGC that the FBI would need to submit a formal FISA request before OI would begin the back-and-forth process with the FBI on a potential application. He told us that it was over a month later when OGC told him for the first time that the FBI was ready to move forward with the request.

While FISA discussions were ongoing, on or about August 17, 2016, the Crossfire Hurricane team received information from another U.S. government agency relating to Page's prior relationship with that agency and prior contacts with Russian intelligence officers about which the agency was aware. We found that, although this information was highly relevant to the potential FISA application, the Crossfire Hurricane team did not engage with the other agency regarding this information until June 2017, just prior to the final Carter Page FISA renewal application.[262] As we discuss later in this chapter, when Case Agent 1 was explicitly asked in late September 2016 by the OI Attorney assisting on the FISA application about Page's prior relationship with this other agency, Case Agent 1 did not accurately describe the nature and extent of the information the FBI received from the other agency.

Also in August, while FISA discussions were ongoing, the Crossfire Hurricane team conducted a consensually monitored meeting between an FBI CHS and Carter Page in an attempt to obtain information from Page about links between the Donald J. Trump for President Campaign and Russia. During the operation, which we describe in greater detail below, Page made statements to the CHS that would have, if true, contradicted the notion that Page was conspiring with Russia. Page

---

[260] OI's Operations Section is divided into three units: Counterintelligence, Counterterrorism, and Special Operations. Among other responsibilities, all three units prepare and file FISA applications with the FISC. Because the Carter Page investigation was a counterintelligence matter, the Counterintelligence Unit handled the Carter Page FISA applications.

[261] The OI Unit Chief did not recall providing specific feedback concerning a potential Carter Page FISA application during or in response to this meeting. He said they did not discuss at that time the specific information the Crossfire Hurricane team had to support a FISA application. He recalled only a general discussion about the case that included a heads up that they believed that at some later point they would want to move forward on a FISA request targeting Carter Page. The OGC Unit Chief and OGC Attorney told us they also did not recall the feedback from OI, if any, at this time. The OGC Attorney did not recall attending the meeting at all, even though the OI Unit Chief's meeting notes indicate he was present.

[262] We describe in Chapter Eight the circumstances surrounding the FBI's engagement with the other agency in June 2017 and the FBI's failure to include the information in the final FISA renewal application.

also made statements that contradicted the Steele reporting received by the team in September, in particular the assertion that Manafort was using Page as an intermediary with Russia. However, as we detail later in this chapter, we found no evidence the FBI made Page's statements from this CHS meeting available to OI or NSD until mid-June 2017.

FBI documents reviewed by the OIG indicate that by late August 2016, Case Agent 1 had been told that he had not yet presented enough information to support a FISA application targeting Carter Page. Case Agent 1's handwritten notes dated August 22, 2016 state: "Not there yet: OI" below a reference to a FISA request targeting Carter Page.[263] Case Agent 1 told us that he remembered being told that he had not yet presented enough information to support probable cause, but he could not recall whether OGC or OI, or both, had made that assessment.

Handwritten notes taken by David Laufman, then Chief of NSD's Counterintelligence and Export Control Section (CES), indicate that on August 25, 2016, FBI and NSD officials discussed the status of FISA coverage targeting Carter Page during a weekly Crossfire Hurricane meeting and that someone at the meeting conveyed that there was "[n]o FISA up on Page; currently no PC." Laufman told us that he did not remember who conveyed this information, but he thought it was probably one of the FBI officials in attendance, which included the OGC Unit Chief, the Section Chief of CD's Counterintelligence Analysis Section I (Intel Section Chief), and Assistant Director E.W. "Bill" Priestap.

As discussed below, the FBI OGC Unit Chief contacted the NSD OI Unit Chief on September 21, 2016, two days after the Crossfire Hurricane team received six of Steele's reports, to advise that the FBI believed it was ready to submit a formal FISA request to OI. As the OGC Unit Chief stated in an October 19, 2016 email to members of the Crossfire Hurricane team, "we first raised the issue of [a] potential FISA [targeting Carter Page] early on—maybe the 2nd or 3rd week of the case. But we didn't have serious discussions until we got the actual [Steele] reports (maybe the day after?)."

B. The FBI's Submission of a FISA Request Following Receipt of the Steele Reporting

As described in Chapter Four, the Crossfire Hurricane team received the first set of Steele's reports on September 19, 2016. Upon receipt of these reports, the team immediately began the process of evaluating Steele and the information he provided. For example, that same day, SSA 1 sent an email to Handling Agent 1 and others, stating, "Our team is very interested in obtaining a source symbol number/source characterization statement and specifics on veracity of past reporting, motivations, last validation, how long on the books, how much paid to

---

[263] It is unclear whether Case Agent 1 took this note during a meeting or at some other time. Case Agent 1 told us that the team had regular discussions during this time period, but did not specifically recall this particular discussion.

date, etc." SSA 1 told us that he did not receive a response from Handling Agent 1 to this email, and we did not find one during the course of our review.

Also on September 19, the team began discussions with OGC to consider Steele's reporting as part of a FISA application targeting Carter Page. In an email to the OGC Unit Chief and OGC Attorney, the Supervisory Intelligence Analyst (Supervisory Intel Analyst) forwarded an excerpt from Steele's Report 94 (described in more detail below) concerning Page's alleged secret meeting with Igor Divyekin in July 2016 and asked, "Does this put us at least *that* much closer to a full FISA on [Carter Page]?" (Emphasis in original). The Supervisory Intel Analyst told us that, earlier that day, he had researched information on Divyekin that "elevated" the significance of this particular allegation. He said that he wondered whether OGC would find that this information, along with the totality of the other information on Carter Page, brought them closer to probable cause on Page. Similarly, Case Agent 1 told us that the team's receipt of the reporting from Steele supplied missing information in terms of what Page may have been doing during his July 2016 visit to Moscow and provided enough information on Page's recent activities that Case Agent 1 thought would satisfy OI.

Two days later, on September 21, the OGC Attorney and OGC Unit Chief requested a meeting with the OI Unit Chief to discuss, among other things, a potential FISA application targeting Carter Page. The OGC Unit Chief told the OIG that the receipt of the Steele reporting changed her mind on whether they could establish probable cause. She said that although there could be differing opinions, she thought it was a "close call" when they first discussed a FISA targeting Page in August, and that the Steele reporting in September "pushed it over" the line in terms of establishing probable cause. She explained that the Steele reporting presented information that Page had recent contact with the Russians and that this contact was consistent with the information received from the FFG that someone on the campaign had received an offer or suggestion of assistance from the Russians. She said that before the Steele reporting, the FBI did not have information concerning what Page's current activities with the Russians might have been or information suggesting a connection between Page and the FFG information. Similarly, the OGC Attorney told us that he thought probable cause was "probably 50/50" before the Steele reporting; however, in his view, it was a combination of the Steele reporting, Carter Page's historical contacts with Russian intelligence officers, and statements Page made in October 2016 during a consensually monitored meeting with an FBI CHS (described later in this chapter and in Chapter Ten) just before the FISA application was filed with the court, that made the OGC Attorney comfortable about establishing probable cause.[264]

---

[264] We asked then Deputy Director Andrew McCabe about the testimony attributed to him in the January 18, 2018 House Permanent Select Committee on Intelligence Memorandum from Majority Staff on *Foreign Intelligence Surveillance Act Abuses at the Department of Justice and the Federal Bureau of Investigation* (HPSCI Majority Memorandum) that "Deputy Director McCabe testified before the Committee in December 2017 that no surveillance warrant would have been sought from the FISC without the Steele dossier information." *See* HPSCI Majority Memorandum at 3, declassified on February 2, 2018, and available at https://republicans-

On September 21, the OGC attorneys met with the OI Unit Chief and described the reporting from Steele concerning Carter Page that the team had recently received. According to notes of the meeting, the OGC Attorney and OGC Unit Chief told the OI Unit Chief about the allegations contained in the Steele reporting that Page had a secret meeting with a high-level Russian official in July 2016, that Page may have received a Russian dossier on Hillary Clinton, and that there was a "well-developed conspiracy" between associates of the Trump campaign and Russian leadership being managed, in part, by Carter Page. The OI Unit Chief told us that he recalled that the Steele reporting was "what kind of pushed it over the line" in terms of the FBI being ready to pursue FISA authority targeting Page. He recalled thinking that if the information bears out during the drafting process, there would probably be sufficient information to support a FISA application targeting Page. Conversely, he said that without the Steele reporting concerning Page, he would not have thought they could establish probable cause based on the other information the FBI presented at that time (Page's historical contacts with Russia).

On September 22, the OI Unit Chief assigned a line attorney (OI Attorney) to work on the Carter Page FISA, and he and the OI Attorney met with the OGC Unit Chief to brief the OI Attorney into the case and discuss the essential points for the FISA. The same day, OGC submitted a FISA request form to OI providing, among other things, a description of the factual information to establish probable cause to believe that Carter Page was an agent of a foreign power, the "facilities" to be targeted under the proposed FISA coverage, and the FBI's investigative plan.[265] Case Agent 1 said he prepared the FISA request form, and the OGC Attorney said he may have provided a "very quick review" before sending it to OI. The OGC Attorney told us that the FISA request form was not as "robust" as it could have been because the FBI wanted to submit it to OI as soon as possible.

The FISA request form drew almost entirely from Steele's reporting in describing the factual basis to establish probable cause to believe that Page was an agent of a foreign power, including the secret meeting between Carter Page and Divyekin alleged in Steele's Report 94 and the role of Page as an intermediary between Russia and the Trump campaign's then manager, Paul Manafort, in the "well-developed conspiracy" alleged in Steele's Report 95. The only additional information cited in the FISA request form to support a probable cause finding as to Page was (1) a statement that Page was a senior foreign policy advisor for the

intelligence.house.gov/uploadedfiles/memo_and_white_house_letter.pdf (last accessed December 2, 2019). McCabe told us that he did not recall his exact testimony, but that his view was that the FBI would have "absolutely" sought FISA authority on Carter Page, even without the Steele reporting, based upon Page's historical interactions with known Russian intelligence officers and the fact that Page told known Russian intelligence officers about the FBI's knowledge of those interactions. However, McCabe also told us that he was not privy to the discussions that took place between attorneys in FBI OGC and Case Agent 1 on the sufficiency of the evidence to establish probable cause before the Crossfire Hurricane team received Steele's election reports. McCabe said he could not speculate as to whether the FBI would have been successful in obtaining FISA authority from the FISC without the inclusion of the Steele reporting.

[265] "Facilities" are ████████████████████████

Trump campaign and had extensive ties to various state-owned or affiliated entities of the Russian Federation, (2) Papadopoulos's statement to the FFG in May 2016, and (3) open source articles discussing Trump campaign policy positions sympathetic to Russia, including that the campaign's tone changed after it began to receive advice from, among others, Manafort and Page.

The FISA request form submitted to OI did not include information that the FBI obtained as a result of CHS meetings in August and September referenced in Chapter Three and summarized in Chapter Ten. These meetings were an attempt by the FBI to better understand what Papadopoulos meant when he advised the FFG about the alleged offer of assistance from the Russians, to probe Page and Papadopoulos about links between the campaign and Russia and to determine whatever Page and Papadopoulos may have known about Russia's use of emails to benefit the Trump campaign. The first meeting involved a consensually monitored conversation between an FBI CHS and Page in August 2016, and the second involved consensually monitored conversations between an FBI CHS████ ███████████████████ and Papadopoulos in September 2016.

During the meeting in August, Carter Page stated, among other things, that he had "literally never met" or "said one word to" Paul Manafort, and that Manafort had not responded to any of Page's emails. Page made other statements that did not add support to the notion that Page was conspiring with Russia. During the meetings in September, Papadopoulos stated, among other things, that to his knowledge no one associated with the Trump campaign was collaborating with Russia or with outside groups like WikiLeaks in the release of emails. As described in Chapter Eight, the OI Attorney told us that he did not think the FBI told him about these meetings before the FISA application was filed with the court. We found no information suggesting otherwise.

The FISA request form also did not include information the Crossfire Hurricane team received from another U.S. government agency on August 17, 2016, relating to Page's prior relationship with that agency and prior contacts with Russian intelligence officers.

Finally, the FISA request form referred to Steele as a "reliable source, whose previous reporting to the FBI has been corroborated and used in criminal proceedings." As noted later in this chapter, while Steele had previously provided information to the FBI that helped the FBI further criminal investigations, his reporting had never been used in a criminal proceeding.

After receiving clarifying questions from OI in response to the FISA request form, the FBI submitted a revised, formal request for an expedited FISA application on September 30. As described in Chapter Two, an expedited FISA application seeks to have the FISC waive the requirement in its Rules of Procedure that the government submit a proposed application no later than 7 days before it seeks to have the matter considered by the FISC. Requests by the FBI that OI seek an expedited FISA application require the approval of a Deputy Assistant Director (DAD) or higher. In this instance, the expedited request was approved by DAD Strzok. Strzok told the OIG that he approved the request to expedite the FISA because there was a sense of urgency to complete the investigation as quickly and thoroughly as possible. According to Strzok, the team was not given an explicit instruction to finish the investigation before Election Day or Inauguration Day, but everyone involved understood the importance of moving quickly.

At the same time the Crossfire Hurricane team moved forward with a FISA request targeting Carter Page, FBI documents reflect that the team was also interested in a FISA request targeting George Papadopoulos to further the investigation. However, FBI OGC was not supportive. Instant messages between the OGC Attorney and the OGC Unit Chief indicate that they, the Intel Section Chief and Strzok, agreed that there was not a sufficient basis for FISA surveillance targeting Papadopoulos. The instant messages also show that the Intel Section Chief and Strzok were much more interested in pursuing the request for FISA coverage targeting Page.

The OGC Unit Chief told the OIG that she recalled that the difference between these two subjects with respect to a potential FISA application was that Carter Page had previous connections with Russian intelligence officers as well as the recent allegations in the Steele reporting that Page was an intermediary between Russia and the Trump campaign. With respect to Papadopoulos, the Crossfire Hurricane team had the information from the FFG that mentioned him, but no specific information that Papadopoulos was a person being directed by the Russians. Ultimately, the Crossfire Hurricane team did not seek FISA authority targeting Papadopoulos.

II. Preparation and Approval of the First FISA Application

Following receipt of the FISA request form on September 22, the OI Attorney immediately began work on the FISA application, preparing the initial drafts with information provided by the FBI. The preparation and approval process for the application took four weeks to complete. We were told that the application received more attention and scrutiny than the typical FISA application in terms of additional layers of review and the number of high-level officials who read the application. We describe this process in detail below.

A. Initial Drafts

On or about September 23, the OI Attorney began work on the initial draft FISA application. At this early stage of the drafting process, Evans told us that he instructed the OI Attorney and OI Unit Chief to handle the Carter Page FISA application as they would any other FISA application—to make sure the work was as thorough as possible so that NSD could answer the legal question of whether the facts meet the probable cause standard—and leave any policy questions to the decision makers down the road.

As described in Chapter Two, the read copy of a FISA application is prepared by an OI attorney using information provided by the FBI, primarily the case agent. The OI attorney relies heavily on the case agent to supply the necessary information and identify significant issues. NSD officials told us that the nature of FISA practice requires that OI rely on the FBI agents who are familiar with the investigation to provide accurate and complete information. Unlike federal prosecutors, OI attorneys are usually not involved in an investigation, or even aware of a case's existence, unless and until OI receives a request to initiate a FISA application. Once they receive a request, OI attorneys generally interact with field offices remotely and do not have broad access to FBI case files or sensitive source files. According to NSD officials, even if OI received broader access to FBI case files, the number of FISA requests that OI attorneys are responsible for handling makes it impracticable for an OI attorney to become intimately familiar with an FBI case file, particular one about which they have had little to no prior awareness.[266] In addition, NSD told us that OI attorneys are not in the best position to sift through a voluminous FBI case file because they do not have the background knowledge and context to meaningfully assess all the information.

In this case, based upon the information the FBI initially provided in the September 22 draft FISA request, the OI Attorney sent his first questions to the OGC Attorney on September 23. Case Agent 1 sent back responses the same day. Over the course of the next two weeks, the OI Attorney exchanged various emails and telephone calls with the FBI and prepared initial drafts using information principally provided by Case Agent 1 and, in a few instances, by the OGC Attorney or other Crossfire Hurricane team members. The culmination of this process led to the first drafts of the FISA application being shared with OI and NSD management on October 5 and 6, 2016.

In these initial drafts, the statement of facts in support of probable cause asserted that the Russians were attempting to undermine and influence the upcoming U.S. presidential election, and that the FBI believed Carter Page was acting in conjunction with the Russians in those efforts. The statement of facts supporting probable cause was broken down into four main elements:

(1) The efforts of Russian Intelligence Services (RIS) to influence the upcoming 2016 U.S. presidential election;

(2) The Russian government's attempted coordination with members of the Trump campaign, which was based on the FFG information concerning the alleged offer or suggestion of assistance from the Russians to someone associated with the Trump campaign;

(3) Page's historical connections to Russia and RIS, which included his business dealings with the Russian energy company Gazprom, his professional relationships with known Russian intelligence officers, and his disclosure to the FBI and a Russian Minister that he was Male-1 in an indictment against Russian intelligence officers; and

---

[266] NSD officials cautioned further that it is not unusual for OI to receive requests for emergency authorizations with only a few hours to evaluate the request.

(4) Page's alleged coordination with the Russian government on 2016 U.S. presidential election activities, based on some of the reporting from Steele.

In addition, the statement of facts described Page's denials of coordination with the Russian government as reported in two news articles and as asserted by Page in a September 25 letter to the FBI Director. Except for the addition of new information from an October 2016 CHS operation discussed later, the read copy and final application submitted to the FISC were organized in the same way.

In support of the fourth element concerning Carter Page's alleged coordination with the Russian government on 2016 U.S. presidential election activities, the drafts of the application—and later the read copy and final application—relied entirely on information from Steele that Steele said was provided to him by his Primary Sub-source. Specifically, the following aspects of Steele's Reports 80, 94, 95, and 102 were used to support the application:

- Compromising information about Hillary Clinton had been compiled for many years, was controlled by the Kremlin, and the Kremlin had been feeding information to the Trump campaign for an extended period of time (Report 80);

- During his July 2016 trip to Moscow, Carter Page attended a secret meeting with Igor Sechin, Chairman of Rosneft and close associate of Putin, to discuss future cooperation and the lifting of Ukraine-related sanctions against Russia; and a secret meeting with Igor Divyekin, another highly placed Russian official, to discuss sharing compromising information about Clinton with the Trump campaign (Report 94);

- Page was an intermediary between Russia and the Trump campaign's then manager (Manafort) in a "well-developed conspiracy" of cooperation, which led, with at least Page's knowledge and agreement, to Russia's disclosure of hacked DNC emails to WikiLeaks in exchange for the Trump campaign's agreement to sideline Russian intervention in Ukraine as a campaign issue (Report 95);[267] and

- Russia released the DNC emails to WikiLeaks in an attempt to swing voters to Trump, an objective conceived and promoted by Carter Page and others (Report 102).

The development of the statement of facts concerning Steele's reporting resulted from the back-and-forth exchange described above between the OI Attorney and the FBI, during which the OI Attorney asked many questions about

---

[267] In further support of this allegation from Report 95, the FISA application described two news articles from July and August 2016 reporting that the Trump campaign had worked behind the scenes to change the Republican Party's platform on providing weapons to Ukraine to fight Russian and rebel forces and that candidate Trump appeared to have adopted a "milder" tone on Russia's annexation of Crimea.

Page, as well as about Steele's reporting and the structure and access of his source network.

Among the questions regarding Carter Page, on September 29, the OI Attorney asked the Crossfire Hurricane team, "do we know if there is any truth to Page's claim that he has provided information to [another U.S. government agency]—was he considered a source/asset/whatever?" According to the OI Attorney, it would have been a significant fact to disclose to OI if Page had interactions with the other U.S. government agency that overlapped in time with his interactions with known Russian intelligence officers described in the FISA applications because it would raise the issue of whether Page interacted with the Russian intelligence officers at the behest of the other U.S. government agency or with the intent to assist the U.S. government. In response to the OI Attorney's question, Case Agent 1 advised him that Page did meet with the other U.S. government agency, but that the interactions took place while Page was in Moscow (which was between 2004 and 2007) and were "outside scope." Based upon this response, the OI Attorney did not include information about Page's prior interactions with the other U.S. government agency in the application. However, as fully described later in this chapter, the information Case Agent 1 provided to the OI Attorney was incomplete, inaccurate, and in certain respects contrary to the information the other agency provided to the Crossfire Hurricane team on August 17, 2016 and that Carter Page had provided to the FBI in 2009 and 2013. This information indicated that Page had a prior relationship with the other U.S. government agency and that his interactions with the other agency occurred more recently than the 2004-2007 time period and actually overlapped with information alleged in the FISA application concerning his alleged ties to Russian intelligence officers.

With respect to Steele, when the drafting process began, the Crossfire Hurricane team had only just begun the process of conducting the evaluation process (described in Chapters Four and Six) to assess Steele, his source network, and the information provided in his reports. That source evaluation process and the FISA drafting process were taking place simultaneously, and the FBI had not corroborated the Steele information being considered for the FISA application. Evans and other witnesses told us that the fact that the source information in the FISA application had not yet been corroborated was not unusual in the FISA context.[268] Officials told us that a significant fact in their consideration of the Steele information for the FISA application was that the Steele reporting on Carter Page appeared to be consistent with the information from the FFG that came from an independent reporting stream.[269]

---

[268] As described in Chapter Two, corroboration of source information is not required by the FBI's Woods Procedures. Although the Woods Procedures require that every fact in a FISA application be "verified," when a particular fact is attributed to a source, an agent must only verify that the fact came from the source and the application accurately states what the source said. The Woods Procedures do not require that the FBI have a second source for the same information.

[269] The Crossfire Hurricane team had information available to it by early October 2016 that the two reporting streams could have connectivity because they had learned that Person 1, an

131

Evans and other witnesses also emphasized that in the absence of corroboration, it was particularly important for the FISA application to articulate to the court the reliability of the source as assessed by the FBI. As the OGC Unit Chief advised Case Agent 1 on September 22 during the drafting of the FISA request form, "One last thing—we probably need a little bit more on the source— ██████ ███████████████████████ Since this is essentially a single source FISA, we have to give a fulsome description of the source." Therefore, on September 29, during the early drafting phase, Case Agent 1 provided OI with the following characterization of Steele for inclusion in the FISA application:

> This information comes from a sensitive FBI source whose reporting has been corroborated and used in criminal proceedings, and who obtains information from a number of ostensibly well-positioned sub-sources. The scope of the source's reporting is from 20 June 2016 through 20 August 2016.

The OI Attorney incorporated this information with other information the case agent provided to draft the following in the application:

> [Steele] has been an FBI source since in or about October 2013. [Steele's] reporting has been corroborated and used in criminal proceedings and the FBI assesses [Steele] to be reliable. [Steele] has been compensated approximately $95,000 and the FBI is unaware of any derogatory information pertaining to [Steele].

The final Carter Page application included this source characterization statement:

> [Steele] is a former ███████████████ ███████████ ██████████ and has been an FBI source since in or about October 2013. [Steele's] reporting has been corroborated and used in criminal proceedings and the FBI assesses [Steele] to be reliable. [Steele] has been compensated approximately $95,000 by the FBI and the FBI is unaware of any derogatory information pertaining to [Steele].

The OI Attorney told us that he does not have access to the CHS files of FBI sources and, therefore, tries to adhere closely to what a case agent sends him when he drafts a source characterization statement for a FISA application. He stated that he also relies on the fact that the Woods Procedures require that the source handling agent approve the language. However, as described later in this chapter, the source characterization statement in the application overstated the significance of Steele's past reporting and was not approved by the FBI agent who served as Steele's handling agent.

To further address reliability, the OI Attorney sought information from the FBI to describe the source network in the FISA application. On multiple occasions, the OI Attorney asked the FBI questions about the sub-sources, including in a September 30, 2016 email in which he asked Case Agent 1 and the Crossfire

---

important Steele election reporting sub-source, had been engaging in "sustained" contact with Papadopoulos since at least August 2016.

Hurricane team: "If the reporting is being made by a primary source, but based on sub-sources, why is it reliable—even though second/third hand?" The OIG did not find a written response to this specific question, and the OI Attorney did not recall a response. However, the OI Attorney told us that the Crossfire Hurricane team eventually briefed him on the sub-source information they learned from Steele after their early October meeting with him (described in Chapter Four). He also received a written summary of this information that the Supervisory Intel Analyst prepared shortly after the October meeting. The OI Attorney told us that based on the information the FBI provided, he thought at the time that some of the sub-sources were "definitely" in a position to have had access to the information Steele was reporting.

Ultimately, the initial drafts provided to OI management, the read copy, and the final application submitted to the FISC contained a description of the source network that included the fact that Steele relied upon a Primary Sub-source who used a network of sub-sources, and that neither Steele nor the Primary Sub-source had direct access to the information being reported. The drafts, read copy, and final application also contained a separate footnote on each sub-source with a brief description of his/her position or access to the information he/she was reporting. The Supervisory Intel Analyst assisted the case agent in providing information on the sub-sources and reviewed the footnotes for accuracy. According to the OI Attorney, the application contained more information about the sources than is typically provided to the court in FISA applications. According to Evans, the idea was to present the source network to the court so that the court would have as much information as possible.

B.   Review and Approval Process

As described in Chapter Two, once an FBI case agent affirms the accuracy of the information in the read copy of an application, an OI Unit Chief or Deputy Unit Chief is usually the final and only approver before a read copy is submitted to the FISC. The Unit Chief or Deputy is also usually the final approver that "signs out" the final application (cert copy) to the FBI for completion of the Woods Procedures and Director's certification before presentation to either the Assistant Attorney General (AAG) of NSD, the DAG, or Attorney General for final signature. The final signatory receives an oral briefing, the cert copy, and a cover memorandum (cert memo) describing each application. In most cases, the start of the oral briefing, or shortly beforehand, is the first time the application is presented to the final signatory. According to NSD, most FISA applications do not get singled out for additional review and, to place that in perspective, there are approximately 1,300 applications submitted to the FISC each year and roughly 25-40 final applications go to the AAG, DAG, or the Attorney General for signature in any given week.

However, in some cases, according to NSD, a FISA application will receive additional review and scrutiny, particularly if it presents a novel or complicated issue or otherwise has been flagged for further review. In this case, as described immediately below, documents and witness testimony reflect that the first Carter Page FISA application underwent a lengthy review and editing process within NSD, the FBI, and ODAG. According to Evans and other witnesses, this application had heightened sensitivity and therefore received additional attention because of the apparent effort by a foreign power to influence the upcoming 2016 U.S. elections and the prior connection of the FISA target (Carter Page) to one of the presidential campaigns.

1. Initial Feedback and NSD Concerns over Steele's Potential Motivation and Bias

Sanz-Rexach, Chief of OI's Operations Section, and his Deputy Section Chief were the first layers above the OI Unit Chief to receive a draft of the Carter Page application. After they provided feedback, the OI Attorney provided the draft on October 6, 2016 to Evans and, at the request of FBI OGC, to FBI General Counsel James Baker for concurrent review.

Baker told us that a review by the General Counsel was not a necessary step in the FBI's FISA approval process, but said that he would sometimes review an application when he thought it was warranted. Baker said that in this case, he asked to read the application because he recognized its sensitivities, including that the target had been associated with a presidential campaign and that the whole case was about Russian efforts to influence the presidential election and whether those efforts included any interactions with the Trump campaign. He said that he expected that the FBI would be called upon after-the-fact to justify its actions, and he wanted to ensure that his significant FISA experience was "brought to bear" on the application.[270]

For these reasons, Baker said he asked his Deputy General Counsel, Trisha Anderson, to give him the draft application before it was "too gelled" so that he could have influence over the drafting without disrupting the process. FBI documents indicate that Baker reviewed the draft on October 6 or 7. Baker told us that he read the probable cause section of the application, as well as the description in the Director's certification section of the foreign intelligence purpose of the requested FISA authority. He said that he thought it was important that the foreign intelligence purpose of the FISA authority was made clear in the application by focusing on the FBI's objective of learning the capabilities and tradecraft of Russia. He stated that he remembered being satisfied that the foreign intelligence purpose was properly articulated in the draft he reviewed.

Baker told us that he also remembered being satisfied at the time that there was probable cause articulated in the draft application to believe that Carter Page was an agent of a foreign power. He said that it was difficult for him to fully explain to us the basis for his assessment without reviewing the entire application again, but that he recalled Page's continuing relationships with Russian intelligence officers, even after the FBI made Page aware that they were Russian intelligence

---

[270] In addition to serving as the FBI's General Counsel from 2014 to 2018, Baker had held positions in OI's predecessor office, the Department's Office of Intelligence Policy and Review, from 1996 to 2007, and later as an Associate Deputy Attorney General in ODAG responsible for national security matters from 2009 to 2011.

officers, being "key" facts in his mind.[271] Further, he said that, in retrospect, he thought that Page's knowing interactions with Russian intelligence officers could have established probable cause even without reliance on the reporting from Steele. However, Baker did not recall being involved in the FISA discussions the team was having before the Steele reporting came in, and because of the redactions in the public version of the FISA application, he was unable to speak to how recent Page's interactions with Russian intelligence officers had been at the time the application was filed.

Baker said that he did not recall his specific line edits to the draft, but that another theme of his comments was to ensure that the court was fully apprised of all material factual information regarding Steele and his reliability as well as any derogatory information about Steele, so that the court could make its own assessment of the Steele reporting. Questions attributed to Baker in an October 7 draft reflect that he, among other things, asked the FBI to provide more information about Steele's prior employment to help establish his credibility and explain why he would have a source network. He also asked questions regarding Carter Page in an apparent attempt to clarify some of the facts regarding Page's travel history and past relationships with Russian intelligence officers. According to Baker, he did not read the application a second time before it was submitted to the court, but Anderson told him that his comments were adequately addressed.

Anderson also reviewed a draft of the application; however, we could not determine the timing of her review. Documents indicate that Anderson requested the draft on October 5 and received it the next day, but Anderson told us she recalled reading the draft after Baker, and closer in time to ODAG's review of the draft, which was almost 2 weeks later. Anderson said that she did not recall providing feedback on the draft and explained that Baker and the OGC Unit Chief were directly involved in the review process. Anderson did recall that she made sure the draft incorporated Baker's previous edits in some fashion, but she did not recall what those edits were.[272]

Review or approval of the FISA application by senior Counterintelligence Division (CD) officials was not a required step in the FBI's FISA procedures. Priestap, Strzok, and the Intel Section Chief told us that they did not play roles in the preparation or approval of the Carter Page FISA application. These officials told us that they were aware that FISA authority was being sought and, as described previously, Strzok provided DAD approval of the team's request for an expedited FISA application, as required by FBI procedures. Further, as described later in this chapter, Strzok had conversations with Evans about the status of the application.

---

[271] Because Baker requested not to have his security clearance reinstated for his OIG interview, Baker was unable to review the entire FISA application before or during the interview, and we were unable to ask questions that would reveal classified information.

[272] Similar to Baker, Anderson did not typically review FISA applications. The OGC Unit Chief said that she worked with the OGC Attorney and OI during the FISA process and was more involved in this FISA application than she was in some others. She told us that she did not recall providing or suggesting specific edits for this application.

However, we found no information suggesting that senior CD officials contributed to the substance of the application.

Evans shared his own feedback with the OI Unit Chief and OI Attorney, which included, among other issues, asking the Crossfire Hurricane team whether Steele "is affiliated with either campaign and/or has contributed to either campaign." On October 7, the OI Unit Chief emailed Evans's question to the team, and on October 10, Case Agent 1 addressed the second part of Evans's question, stating that Steele was most likely a foreign national and therefore unable to contribute to either campaign. Because Case Agent 1 did not fully address Evans's question, the OI Unit Chief asked the agent again, on October 11, whether Steele was affiliated with and/or had contributed to either presidential campaign. Again the case agent answered only the second part of the question, confirming that Steele had not contributed to any campaign and was not a U.S. person. Evans told us that he remembered being somewhat frustrated and annoyed by this answer and asked the question a third time to be sure that nothing was missed in terms of any potential political bias on the part of the source.

According to Evans, later in the day on October 11, after OI circulated a new draft application and, in response to his questions, he and OI learned for the first time from the FBI that Steele had been paid to develop political opposition research. He told us that he recalled that he, the OI Unit Chief, and the OI Attorney were all quite surprised by this new information and that it was frustrating that they had not been informed sooner. Evans said that the new information, coupled with the sensitive nature of the case, made him concerned that the source might have a bias that needed to be disclosed to the court. Consequently, Evans placed a temporary hold on the application so that OI could further explore and evaluate with the FBI the information OI had just learned.

Evans told the OIG, and emails and instant and text messages reflect, that over the next three days, he and OI asked additional questions about Steele to better understand his potential motivations, bias, and overall reliability. Before being asked these questions, the Crossfire Hurricane team had expected that the October 11 draft would be the final version submitted to the court as the read copy. However, on the evening of October 11, Evans had a telephone conversation with his counterpart at the FBI, DAD Strzok, to discuss Evans's concerns and let him know that OI needed more time to understand and evaluate the information it had just learned concerning Steele.[273] According to Evans, there was frustration expressed on both sides, with Strzok frustrated that the FISA process was not moving at the desired pace and Evans responding to the effect that "it doesn't help that just now, at the eleventh hour, I have for the first time learned that information about Steele." As detailed below, text messages between Strzok and the OGC Attorney reflect that Strzok believed the FBI had previously informed OI

---

[273] Evans said he also contacted Baker to let him know that OI needed time to explore the new information. Baker told us that he did not specifically recall whether Evans told him that OI needed more time to explore the FBI's information regarding Steele. However, Baker said that he remembered having a telephone conversation with Evans about this particular application, the substance of which we describe in the next section.

about Steele's source of payment. The conversation ended with Strzok agreeing to allow the Crossfire Hurricane team to answer whatever questions about the source OI needed to ask. Similarly, during her OIG interview, then NSD Principal Deputy Assistant Attorney General Mary McCord recalled that she had a telephone conversation with then Deputy Director Andrew McCabe during which she advised him that she believed the FISA application needed to include more information about who hired Steele, and that McCabe did not push back.[274] McCabe told us that he did not recall any specific conversations with McCord about this FISA application.

Internal FBI emails, as well as instant messages and text messages, reflect the FBI's discussions with Evans and reactions to his concerns. For example, following his telephone call with Evans on the evening of October 11, Strzok reached out to Lisa Page and advised her that support from McCabe might be necessary to move the FISA application forward:

> 6:21 p.m., Strzok to Lisa Page: "Currently fighting with Stu [Evans] for this fisa."

> 6:50 p.m., Strzok to Page: "Hey—The FISA will probably not go forward without a call from the [Deputy Director]. Even as is, the court may not hear it this week."

At the same time, Strzok also had communications with the OGC Attorney:

> 6:56 p.m., Strzok to OGC Attorney: "Stu is nervous. Didn't help that he just found out today about [Steele's] source of payment/direction for this particular reporting. I thought we had told OI earlier?"

> 6:56 p.m., OGC Attorney to Strzok: "Yes, we absolutely informed [OI Unit Chief] and [OI Attorney] about the source." "Multiple meetings, actually, with [Case Agent 1] and [the SOS]."

> 6:57 p.m., Strzok to OGC Attorney: "Ok—including the named intermediary, with the unnamed client (presumed to be connected to the campaign in some way)? Well, they didn't tell Stu..."

> 6:59 p.m., OGC Attorney to Strzok: "Yes, we provided source descriptions for all of the sub-sources, sources, etc. That is confusing because that seemed to be what put [OI Unit Chief] and [OI Attorney] at ease."

> 6:59 p.m., OGC Attorney to Strzok: "Is he going to hold the FISA?"

> 7:06 p.m., Strzok to OGC Attorney: "no, but I'm concerned about how they preload the Court/court advisor"

> 7:06 p.m., Strzok to OGC Attorney: "I think he wants more words in there about it...."

---

[274] McCord became the Acting AAG for NSD upon the departure of AAG John Carlin, which occurred in this timeframe.

7:07 p.m., OGC Attorney to Strzok: "Roger. I'll reach out to [OI Unit Chief] to see if he is in the office by chance.

Later the same evening, Strzok communicated with the OGC Unit Chief:

7:34 p.m., OGC Unit Chief to Strzok: "So Stu called you about his concerns about the [Page] FISA? Not sure why he didn't reach out to the [FBI General Counsel/Deputy General Counsel] or the [Deputy Director]/Director, as they've all approved moving forward with this. What was the point of his [sic]? Was he trying to get you to pull it?"

7:53 p.m., OGC Unit Chief to Strzok: "I got further clarification from [OI Unit Chief]. I think it's all good. We should have more from DOJ tomorrow."

7:53 p.m., Strzok to OGC Unit Chief: "Ok. Stu is very nervous."

7:54 p.m., Strzok to OGC Unit Chief: "He said he wasn't aware of the fact until a few hours ago that [Steele] was employed to find this information by a named client, in turn hired by an unnamed client presumably affiliated with the Clinton campaign in some manner."

Between 7:54 p.m. and 7:59 p.m., [Strzok and the OGC Unit Chief exchanged messages on an unrelated topic.]

7:59 p.m., Strzok to OGC Unit Chief: "Is OI still sending copy to FISC tomorrow?"

7:59 p.m., Strzok to OGC Unit Chief: "I'm worried about what Stu whispers in Court Advisors ear."

7:59 p.m., OGC Unit Chief to Strzok: "Yeah. I think so. Stu's going to think about it overnight. Not for attribution, but apparently he's the only one over there worried about it."

7:59 p.m., OGC Unit Chief to Strzok: "Yeah, me too."

8:00 p.m., Strzok to OGC Unit Chief: "Jim [Baker] or [Deputy Director] or someone may need to weigh in with [NSD Assistant Attorney General John] Carlin."

8:00 p.m., Strzok to OGC Unit Chief: "I'll bring it up at the prep SVTC tomorrow."

8:00 p.m., OGC Unit Chief to Strzok: "If it goes beyond noon, I would tend to agree."

The next morning, at 7:44 a.m., the OGC Attorney sent the following text message to Strzok:

Pete, I talked to [OI Unit Chief] last night. It doesn't sound like Stu is concerned about the FISA itself, but more of fleshing out the details of [Steele] (*e.g.*, how he began his reporting). All of that information was obtained from [Case Agent 1]. We should be in good shape once OI bats it around a little more internally this AM.

Although the OGC Attorney stated in these text messages that the OI Unit Chief and the OI Attorney had been briefed before October 11 on who had commissioned Steele's reporting, the OI Unit Chief told the OIG that he believed they did not learn about the potential political connections to Steele's reporting until after Evans raised his questions. The OI Attorney told us that he did not recall exactly when he learned about them, but that it was later in the drafting process, and that Evans's inquiries led to a better understanding of the nature of Steele's research. The OI Attorney told us that he did not recall asking the agent any specific questions about who Steele's clients were. Case Agent 1 told us that he did not recall any conversations with the OI Attorney about the source reporting's connection to political opposition research before OI asked questions about it. He explained that the Crossfire Hurricane team only suspected, but did not know in mid-October 2016, that Steele's reporting was generated through political opposition research.

The OIG did not find any written communications indicating that anyone on the Crossfire Hurricane team advised OI about the potential or suspected political connections to Steele's reporting before Evans raised his questions on October 11, and nothing to that effect appeared in the October 11 draft FISA application. Further, the emails described above containing Evans's questions about Steele's campaign affiliation or contributions suggest that OI did not have prior knowledge.

2. FBI Leadership Supports Moving Forward with the FISA Application and OI Drafts Additional Disclosures Concerning Steele

On October 12, 2016, Evans's concerns about Steele were briefed to Comey and McCabe in a meeting attended by at least Priestap, Strzok, Lisa Page, and the OGC Unit Chief. According to notes of the meeting, the group discussed that Evans was concerned Steele may have been hired by someone associated with Hillary Clinton or the Democratic National Committee (DNC) and that the read copy of the FISA application would not be filed with the court that day so that Evans could further assess the potential bias. The notes reflect that the group discussed that Evans was also concerned that the foreign intelligence to be collected through the FISA would not be "worth [the] risk." Following the meeting, the OGC Unit Chief emailed Anderson and the OGC Attorney on October 12 and advised them that the concerns Evans had raised were discussed with Comey and McCabe and that both were "supportive" of moving forward despite those concerns.

During his OIG interview, Evans told us that he thought he did not raise the concern about the potential value of the collection outweighing the risk until sometime after OI worked through the bias issue with the FBI. According to Evans, he raised on multiple occasions with the FBI, including with Strzok, Lisa Page, and later McCabe, whether seeking FISA authority targeting Carter Page was a good idea, even if the legal standard was met. He explained that he did not see a compelling "upside" to the FISA because Carter Page knew he was under FBI investigation (according to news reports) and was therefore not likely to say anything incriminating over the telephone or in email. On the other hand, Evans saw significant "downside" because the target of the FISA was politically sensitive

139

and the Department would be criticized later if this FISA was ever disclosed publicly. He told the OIG that he thought there was no right or wrong answer to this question, which he characterized as a prudential question of risk vs. reward, but he wanted to make sure he raised the issue for the decision makers to consider. According to Evans, the reactions he received from the FBI to this prudential question were some variations of—we understand your concerns, those are valid points, but if you are telling us it's legal, we cannot pull any punches just because there could be criticism afterward.

Baker told us that he recalled having a telephone conversation with Evans after learning about Evans's prudential concerns from Anderson and the OGC Unit Chief. According to Baker, he told Evans that he understood the matter was sensitive but that he (Baker) thought there was probable cause and that the FBI was seeking the FISA for a legitimate purpose and thought the application should go forward. Baker told us that he did not think he had persuaded Evans, and Baker said he was left with the impression that Evans planned to raise the issue with others in the Department.

Evans told us that he discussed this prudential question with Tashina Gauhar, the Associate Deputy Attorney General responsible for ODAG's national security portfolio, and McCord. According to Evans, Gauhar seemed to share his concern, but Gauhar said that she did not think anyone was going to tell the FBI not to pursue the FISA if the legal standard was met. Gauhar told us that ODAG's position was first to ensure that the legal standard for the FISA application was met, and that everyone, including NSD, thought that it was. She said that there was a separate question about the "policy decision to go forward," and on that question she understood that FBI leadership believed strongly that the application should go forward. She said that although it was possible, she did not remember stating ODAG's position in terms of deferring to the FBI or not being inclined to overrule the FBI if the FBI wanted to move forward.

According to Evans, McCord said that she would discuss the prudential issue with McCabe, but the discussion did not happen before Evans raised the issue directly with McCabe after a regularly scheduled meeting on October 19.[275] According to Evans, McCabe told Evans on October 19 something to the effect of, "I hear you. I understand. [B]ut we can't pull any punches and we've got to do it, and...let the chips fall where they may." McCabe told us that he did not recall the specific words he used with Evans, but he believed he conveyed to Evans that the FBI "felt strongly" that the FISA application should move forward. McCabe said that he understood at the time that the FBI would likely be criticized no matter what the

---

[275] McCord told us that she spoke to McCabe almost every day on various matters and had more than one conversation with him about the Carter Page FISA application, but she did not specifically recall whether she had a conversation with McCabe on or about October 17, and if she did, what specific issue would have prompted a conversation at that time. She said that she believed her most significant conversation with McCabe about the first FISA occurred in October. She said it was the telephone call described earlier, before or during the drafting of the Steele footnote, in which she and McCabe discussed Steele and the need to include more information about the source in the application. McCabe told us that he did not specifically recall any conversations with McCord about this application.

team did or did not do, but he believed that the team had to get to the bottom of this potentially serious threat to national security. He said that if the FBI had not sought FISA authority under the circumstances presented here simply because the team was afraid of the "political nature" of the information, the FBI would have failed to do its job.

The email on October 12, referenced above, from the OGC Unit Chief to Anderson and the OGC Attorney following the meeting with Comey and McCabe, said that Lisa Page would inform Evans of the FBI's decision to move forward with the FISA application. Text messages from Lisa Page to McCabe indicate that Page communicated with Evans later that same day:

> 3:11 p.m., Lisa Page to McCabe: "OI now has a robust explanation re any possible bias of the chs in the package. Don't know what the holdup is now, other than Stu's continued concerns. Strong operational need to have in place before Monday if at all possible, which means ct tomorrow.[276] I communicated you and boss's green light to Stu earlier, and just sent an email to Stu asking where things stood. This might take a high-level push. Will keep you posted.

> 3:13 p.m., Page to McCabe: "If I have not heard back from Stu in an hour, I will invoke your name to say you want to know where things are, so long as okay with you."

Later the same day, Page sent a text message to McCabe stating that she "[s]poke to Stu. Let's talk in the morning." Available text message records are unclear as to whether McCabe responded directly to this text or to the previous text message at 3:13 p.m., but to one or the other, McCabe responded, "Ok."[277]

Shortly before Lisa Page's first text to McCabe above, the Crossfire Hurricane team provided to OI additional information regarding Steele that the OI Attorney had requested. In an email on October 12, OI asked the FBI team what Steele had been specifically hired to do, what the FBI knew about the motivation of the individual who hired Steele, including whether that individual was a supporter of Hillary Clinton or the Democratic Party, and if the FBI could "articulate why it deems [Steele's] reporting to be credible notwithstanding [Steele] did the investigation based on [a] private citizen's motivation to help [Hillary Clinton/Democratic Party]." Through SSA 1, the team advised OI that based on information from Steele, Steele was specifically hired by an individual to provide information on candidate Trump's business affairs and contacts in Russia, Steele was never advised of the motivation of the individual who hired him, the individual who hired him was hired by an unidentified law firm in Washington, D.C., and

---

[276] As described below, it appears the desire to have FISA authority in place before ██████████ ████████, was due, at least in part, to the fact that ██████████████████████ ████████████████████████, and the Crossfire Hurricane team wanted FISA coverage targeting Carter Page ██████████████.

[277] We did not find evidence of any further involvement by Lisa Page in the FBI's efforts to file the FISA application, other than receiving a telephone call on October 18 from ODAG, described later in this chapter, to advise FBI leadership regarding the status of ODAG's review of the application.

"anything further would be speculation." In response to OI's final question about Steele's credibility, SSA 1 responded that: (1) the FBI has had an established relationship with the source since 2013; (2) the source was generating reporting well before the opening of Crossfire Hurricane and the leaks concerning the DNC emails, and therefore this was not a situation where a source was attempting to steer an ongoing investigation; and (3) Steele was not a U.S. citizen and therefore had no vested interest in the outcome of the election. The OI Attorney forwarded this information to the OI Unit Chief, noting that, "This creates more questions for me now...."

During further back and forth over a 3-day period, the Crossfire Hurricane team advised OI that Steele was hired by Glenn Simpson of Fusion GPS, they did not know Simpson's motivations, and they did not know the name of the law firm that retained Fusion GPS or its connections to Hillary Clinton or the Democratic Party because Steele did not believe asking Simpson about his client was appropriate. However, we found no evidence that Steele advised the FBI that he believed asking Simpson about the name of his client would be inappropriate. Rather, as described in Chapter Four, we obtained conflicting testimony as to whether Steele was even requested by the FBI to ask Simpson for the name of the law firm. Steele's FBI handler (Handling Agent 1) told us that he informed Steele during their July 5 meeting that the FBI would be interested in finding out the name of the law firm. SSA 2 told us that he understood Handling Agent 1 "stayed away from tasking [Steele] about the identity of the U.S. law firm." During his OIG interview, Steele told us that he did not know the identity of the law firm when he met with Handling Agent 1 on July 5. Steele said that he learned of it later in July and probably told the FBI the law firm's name at some later date, but he did not specifically recall.

The Crossfire Hurricane team further advised OI that Steele's Primary Sub-source recently provided unrelated information that was found by ▮▮▮▮▮▮▮▮ ▮▮▮▮▮▮▮▮▮ to be consistent with other reporting on the same topic. OI asked the team what the FBI knew about the September 23, 2016 Yahoo News article that quoted a "well-placed Western intelligence source" for information ostensibly coming from Steele's reporting about Carter Page's alleged meetings with Sechin and Divyekin. The team responded that they did not have any additional details regarding the leak.

On October 14, the OI Attorney consolidated in writing for Evans and OI management the additional details concerning Steele, described above, that the FBI provided over the previous 3 days. According to Evans, at this point, he and the others in OI believed that they had received all the information the FBI had on Steele.[278] The OI Attorney and the OI Unit Chief then revised the footnote in the draft application on Steele to address the potential that Steele, or those who hired

---

[278] This is consistent with an instant message from Strzok to Lisa Page on October 14, 2016, 11:45 a.m.: "I'm going to email Stu and let him know we've gotten all the info we're going to get re [Steele] and sourcing questions."

him, had a bias. Specifically, they added the following paragraph, which became part of Footnote 8 in the read copy and final application:

> [Steele], who now owns a foreign business/financial intelligence firm, was approached by an identified U.S. person, who indicated to [Steele] that a U.S.-based law firm had hired the identified U.S. person to conduct research regarding Candidate #1's ties to Russia (the identified U.S. person and [Steele] have a long-standing business relationship). The identified U.S. person hired [Steele] to conduct this research. The identified U.S. person never advised [Steele] as to the motivation behind the research into Candidate #1's ties to Russia. The FBI speculates that the identified U.S. person was likely looking for information that could be used to discredit Candidate #1's campaign.[279]

According to Evans, the use of the term "speculates" in the footnote was intended to convey that even though the FBI did not know at the time who Simpson's and the U.S. law firm's ultimate client was, the FBI believed it was likely that it was someone who was seeking political opposition research against candidate Trump. The FBI represented to Evans and OI that the Crossfire Hurricane team assumed, but did not know, that someone associated with the Hillary Clinton campaign or the Democratic Party paid for the research.[280] According to Evans, the use of "speculates" in a FISA application was unusual, but, in this context, he believed it was necessary to fully advise the court of the potential for bias. Evans told us that this additional information made him comfortable with the way that Steele was described in the application, specifically by making clear to the court that Steele had conducted opposition research on behalf of someone who appeared to have the intention of discrediting the Trump campaign.[281]

---

[279] The Carter Page FISA application did not identify by name Steele's clients or the presidential candidates, which is consistent with the Department's general practice of not disclosing the true identities of U.S. persons who are not the surveillance targets in FISA applications.

[280] McCabe told us that he thought he had heard by the time of the first FISA application that Simpson had been working first for a Republican client and then later for a Democratic client. However, McCabe also told us that his memory on the timing of events is not always reliable, and other FBI officials told us that the team did not know who hired Simpson until after the first FISA application. As described in Chapter Nine, documentation we reviewed indicates that FBI officials obtained greater clarity on who Glenn Simpson was working for through interviews with Bruce Ohr in November and December 2016. Documentation indicates that by February and March 2017 it was broadly known among FBI officials that Simpson was hired first by a candidate during the Republican primaries and then later by someone related to the Democratic Party. Further, at least some team members knew by early 2017 that Simpson was hired by the DNC and another unidentified entity to research candidate Trump's ties to Russia.

[281] As described in Chapter Ten, in early August 2016, before the Crossfire Hurricane team became aware of Steele's election reports, information from a former FBI CHS was shared with members of the Crossfire Hurricane team indicating that the former CHS was recently contacted "by a colleague who runs an investigative firm. The firm had been hired by two entities (the Democratic National Committee [DNC] as well as another individual he did not name) to explore Donald Trump's

Evans told us that sources often have "baggage" and can have a bias, but that does not necessarily make their information unreliable, especially if the FBI has a long history of assessing the source's reporting as reliable. In his experience, the important thing is to make sure that enough information is presented to the court so that the judge understands the issue. His general approach with this particular footnote was to exceed "what was even legally required and just mak[e] sure there was nothing...left on the table about this source that we could be open to criticism on afterwards, based on what the FBI was giving us."

After OI made this revision to the footnote, OI submitted an updated draft application to McCord for her review on October 14.[282] McCord remembered reading an early draft of the probable cause section and believed she probably read an updated probable cause section at least one more time before the read copy was filed focused on the questions OI asked the FBI and the revisions that were made to address those questions. Based upon our review of relevant emails, it appears that McCord provided comments on the October 14 draft. She said her strongest memory was asking about Steele's fee arrangement with Fusion GPS, which is also reflected in an October 18 email from the OI Unit Chief to his supervisors. McCord also remembered discussions within NSD and with ODAG about the prudential question described earlier as to whether to file the application even if it was legally supportable. She said the collective thinking was that filing the application was a legitimate investigative step even though it may later be criticized unfairly.

3. Other Substantive Changes to the Application before ODAG Review

In addition to the revisions made to the Steele footnote, the October 14 draft application contained another substantive change from earlier drafts, concerning the FBI's assessment of whether Steele was the source for the September 23 *Yahoo News* article described earlier in this chapter.

The draft FISA applications, and later the read copy and final application, advised the court that the *Yahoo News* article reported that U.S. intelligence officials were investigating Carter Page's involvement in suspected efforts by the Russian government to influence the U.S. presidential election and that a "well-placed Western intelligence source" told *Yahoo News* about Carter Page's alleged secret meetings with Sechin and Divyekin. The applications stated that, based on statements made in the *Yahoo News* article and in other news articles, individuals affiliated with the Trump campaign made statements distancing the campaign from

---

longstanding ties to Russian entities." The Supervisory Intel Analyst told us that he did not recall making a connection when the Steele reporting came in between this investigative firm hired by the DNC and the firm that hired Steele to conduct his election-related research. FBI emails reflect that he and SSA 1 made that connection by January 11, 2017, at the latest. We found no evidence that this information was shared with OI.

[282] As noted previously, on or about October 17, 2016, McCord became the Acting AAG for NSD. She replaced AAG John Carlin who left the Department on October 14, 2016. Evans told us that Carlin had very limited involvement in the Carter Page FISA prior to his departure and did not review a draft of the application. We found no information suggesting otherwise and therefore did not seek to interview Carlin.

Carter Page. Further, the applications noted that Page himself denied the accusations in the *Yahoo News* article and reiterated that denial in a September 25 letter to the FBI Director and in a September 26 media interview.

Evans told the OIG that OI included the reference to the September 23 *Yahoo News* article in the FISA application solely because it was favorable to Carter Page and not as corroboration for the Steele reporting in the application. According to Evans, the application's treatment of the article was favorable to Page in three respects: (1) the application described statements in the article that the campaign distanced itself from Page and minimized his role as an advisor; (2) the application stated that Page denied the allegations in the news article in a letter to the Director; and (3) as described below, the application made clear that the people who financed Steele's reporting were likely the same source for the information in the article.

The drafts of the FISA application that preceded the October 14 draft—including the October 11 draft that the FBI expected would be submitted to the FISC as the final read copy—stated that the FBI "believes that the 'well-placed Western intelligence source' is Steele." After reviewing the initial drafts, Evans asked OI to "drill down" on why Steele disclosed information to the media. For example, in an October 11 email to OI staff, Evans asked "does the FBI know why the source provided this info to the press.... Is there anything about his decision to speak to the press that suggests he's got a bias?"

The result of this effort culminated in new language in the October 14 draft stating that the FBI believed it was Glenn Simpson or the law firm who hired Simpson, and not Steele, who provided Steele's reporting to the media. With respect to the basis for the FBI's assessment, the language that appeared in Footnote 18 of the read copy and final application stated the following:

> As discussed above, [Steele] was hired by a business associate to conduct research into Candidate #1's ties to Russia. [Steele] provided the results of his research to the business associate, and the FBI assesses that the business associate likely provided this information to the law firm that hired the business associate in the first place. [Steele] told the FBI that he/she only provided this information to the business associate and the FBI. Given that the information contained in the September 23rd News Article generally matches the information about Page that [Steele] discovered during his/her research, the FBI assesses that [Steele's] business associate or the law firm that hired the business associate likely provided this information to the press. The FBI also assesses that whoever gave the information to the press stated that the information was provided by a "well-placed Western intelligence source." The FBI does not believe that [Steele] directly provided this information to the press.

Case Agent 1 told the OIG that he did not recall why the October 11 draft stated that Steele was the "well-placed Western intelligence source" or the reason the language was changed in the updated draft to state that the FBI did not believe

Steele directly provided the information in the article. He said he did not recall the details regarding what he was told, or what he told OI, about whether Steele was the source for the *Yahoo News* article leak. The OGC Attorney told us that he was not familiar with how the change between drafts occurred.

The OI Attorney said he could not recall the circumstances that led to the change in the drafts, including whether the Crossfire Hurricane team originally told him that Steele had disclosed the information to *Yahoo News*. The OI Attorney said that it was possible he had assumed that that was the case and wrote the initial drafts in that manner for the FBI's consideration. The OI Attorney told us that at some point during the drafting process, the FBI assured him that Steele had not spoken with *Yahoo News* because the source was "a professional."

We did not find any evidence that the FBI asked Steele whether he was a source for the information in the September 23 *Yahoo News* article. As described later in this chapter, the basis the FBI asserted in the application for its assessment that Steele was not a source was inaccurate and the documentation in the Woods File did not support it.

Another change from the early drafts of the first FISA application was the addition of particularized minimization procedures (PMPs) at the request of Evans. The final PMPs restricted access to the information collected through FISA authority to the individuals assigned to the Crossfire Hurricane team and required the approval of a DAD or higher before any FISA-derived information could be disseminated outside the FBI. In normal circumstances, the FBI is given more latitude to disseminate FISA-derived information that appears to be foreign intelligence information or evidence of a crime. Evans told us that he believed these added restrictions were warranted here because of the possibility that the FISA collection would include sensitive political campaign related information.

4. October Meeting between Page and an FBI CHS

As we summarize in Chapter Ten, in October 2016, before the FBI obtained the initial FISA authority targeting Carter Page, an FBI CHS had a consensually monitored meeting with Page. During the meeting, among other things, Page said that he wanted to develop a research institute and, in talking about how he would fund the institute, Page said, "I don't want to say there'd be an open checkbook, but the Russians would definitely...." According to the partial transcript, the sentence trailed off as Carter Page laughed. The CHS then stated "they would fund it—yeah you could do alright there" and Page responded "Yeah, but that has its pros and cons, right?" At another point in the conversation, Page noted that he had "a longstanding constructive relationship with the Russians going back throughout" his life. When asked about the link between the Russians and WikiLeaks, Page said that, "[as he has] made clear in a lot of...subsequent discussions/interviews...I know nothing about that—on a personal level, you know no one's ever said a word to me." With regard to the platform committee during the Republican National Convention, Page said that he "stayed clear of that—there was a lot of conspiracy theories that I was one of them...[but] totally off the record...members of our team were working on that, and...in retrospect it's way better off that I...remained at arms length."

Carter Page also told the CHS during the meeting that the "core lie" against him in the media "is that [Page] met with these sanctioned Russian officials, several of which I've never met in my entire life." Page said that the "core lie" concerned "Sechin [who] is the main guy, the head of Rosneft...[and] there's another guy I had never even heard of, you know he's like, in the inner circle." When asked about that person's name, Page said "I can't even remember, it's just so outrageous."

The Crossfire Hurricane team provided to OI some, but not all, of the information obtained during this meeting for inclusion in the first FISA application. According to the description in the FISA application, Page met with the FBI CHS on a particular date in October and made statements that led the FBI to believe that Page continued to be closely tied to Russian officials, including the suggestion that "the Russians" would be giving him an "open checkbook" to fund a foreign policy think tank project. The description also stated that Page told the CHS that he may be appearing in a televised interview to discuss the potential for change in U.S. foreign policy toward Russia and Syria in the event Trump wins the presidential election. However, as discussed later in this chapter, the application filed with the court did not fully or accurately describe the information obtained by the FBI as a result of this meeting because the FBI did not advise OI that Page denied meeting with Sechin and Divyekin, as alleged in Report 94, or that Page denied knowing anything about the disclosure by WikiLeaks of hacked DNC emails, as alleged in Report 95.

In addition, the FBI did not advise OI that Carter Page denied having been involved with the Republican Platform Committee. Page's statements to the FBI CHS, if true, would have been inconsistent with the FBI's assessment in the FISA application that Page helped influence the Republican Party to change its platform to be more sympathetic to Russia's interests by eliminating language in the Republican platform about providing weapons to Ukraine. The FBI's assessment was based in part on Report 95's allegation that Page and possibly others agreed to sideline Russian intervention in Ukraine as a campaign issue in exchange for Russia's disclosure of hacked DNC emails to WikiLeaks. The assessment also drew upon news articles in July and August 2016 reporting that the Trump campaign influenced the Republican Party to change its platform to not call for giving Ukraine weapons to fight Russian and rebel forces.

5. Feedback from ODAG and Submission of the Read Copy

At the time OI submitted the October 14 draft application to McCord, OI simultaneously sent the draft to ODAG for review. Over the next few days, the application was reviewed by Gauhar, an OI attorney on detail in ODAG, Principal Associate Deputy Attorney General Matthew Axelrod, and later Yates, who ultimately approved and signed the final application.

As noted previously, in instances where the DAG approves and signs FISA applications, OI typically submits the application package to ODAG as a finished product after the read copy has been filed with the court and shortly before or during the oral briefing on the final application. However, in cases with heightened sensitivity, which can occur for a variety of reasons, OI may proactively flag the application for ODAG earlier in the process for special attention, which OI did in this case. Further, although sometimes NSD will ask ODAG whether it wants to read a flagged application in advance, Evans told us that in this case NSD decided that it would not submit the read copy to the FISC until Yates had personally read it and said she was comfortable moving forward.

Gauhar and the OI attorney on detail, both of whom had prior FISA experience in OI before joining ODAG, were the first to review the draft Carter Page application.[283] On October 18, the two met with OI to discuss specific suggestions they had for the probable cause section, and later in the day, OI circulated an updated draft incorporating new edits to address ODAG's suggestions. According to Gauhar, and as reflected in the October 18 updated draft, her office had suggested edits to add more emphasis and focus on Carter Page in the probable cause section, while at the same time making changes in tone to characterize the Trump campaign in a more neutral manner.[284] She explained that ODAG wanted to make sure that the court was not left with the misimpression that the FBI had information indicating that there were current members of the Trump campaign who were wittingly conspiring with Russia. Gauhar said she did not think that OI intentionally drafted the application in that direction, and she thought that some additional changes would help ensure that there was no misimpression.

Axelrod said he read the October 18 draft the next morning and had some suggested edits to further address the theme of the edits from the day before. ODAG sent NSD the additional suggested changes, and NSD and the FBI accepted the changes and incorporated them into the read copy.

ODAG's edits did not suggest significant changes to the Steele information in the application. Gauhar said that she was in communication with Evans when he

---

[283] Immediately before Gauhar joined ODAG, from 2009 to 2014, she was the Deputy Assistant Attorney General in NSD with responsibility over OI (the position Evans held at the time of the Page FISA applications). Gauhar joined the Department in 2001 as an attorney in OIPR, which, as described previously, was OI's predecessor office. In OIPR, she was responsible for preparing FISA applications and later oversaw the FISA process as a supervisor and Deputy Chief of OI's Operations Section. The OI attorney on detail had served as an attorney in OIPR starting in late 2006 where she prepared FISA applications and then later oversaw the FISA process when she became the Deputy Chief and then Chief of the Counterterrorism Unit in OI's Operations Section.

[284] Examples of the edits addressing tone included describing Carter Page as *an individual associated with* the Trump campaign, rather than as a member of the Trump campaign, and describing the conspiracy alleged in Steele's Report 95 as between Russia and *individuals involved in* the Trump campaign, rather than the campaign itself.

was asking his questions about Steele and by the time that she reviewed the draft, she knew that Evans and others had drilled down on the source.[285]

On October 18, Gauhar reached out to Lisa Page, her contact in the Deputy Director's office, to advise her that the Carter Page FISA application was under review in ODAG. According to Gauhar, she was aware at the time that the FBI had been pushing OI to complete the process on the application, and she wanted McCabe to know that the application was now with ODAG and they were working on it.[286] Page advised Gauhar that it was possible that McCabe might ask Yates about the status of application during a regularly scheduled meeting the following morning on October 19. We did not find any evidence reflecting that McCabe asked Yates during that morning meeting on October 19 about the status of the application, and McCabe told us that he did not have a specific recollection of having done so.

As noted earlier, Evans told the OIG that he discussed the issue of whether this FISA application was a good idea with McCabe after a regularly scheduled meeting on October 19. Gauhar told us that sometime around this date, she believes that Yates may have had a similar discussion with McCabe. According to Gauhar, she advised Axelrod that Evans had raised his prudential question with the FBI, and she said she had a general recollection that Yates may have had direct conversations with McCabe to discuss FBI leadership's position on moving forward with the application. Gauhar said she was not present during any such conversations between Yates and FBI leadership and did not recall the details, but she believed Yates was told that FBI leadership felt strongly that the FISA was an important investigative step.

Yates told the OIG that she did not specifically recall any conversations with either McCabe or Comey about the Carter Page FISA application, but that such conversations could have happened. Yates said she had a general recollection that the FBI believed that they really needed to take this investigative step, but whether that understanding was the result of a specific conversation or just by virtue of the fact that Comey was prepared to sign off on the FISA application, she did not recall. Comey and McCabe told us that they did not recall a discussion with Yates about the FISA application.

On October 19, after incorporating Axelrod's edits, OI finalized the read copy of the Carter Page FISA application and sent it to the Crossfire Hurricane team for final review. Late in the evening, Strzok notified Evans that the FBI was

---

[285] Emails indicate that on October 17, Gauhar asked a question about Steele, specifically how the FBI reconciled its belief that Steele did not disclose information in the September 23 *Yahoo News* article given the article's reference to a "well-placed Western intelligence source." OI advised that Steele told the FBI that he only provided information to his business associate and the FBI, and that the FBI believed that the business associate or the law firm disclosed the information to the media.

[286] For example, on October 17, Strzok had emailed Evans to advise him of upcoming operations in the investigation of Carter Page that would be assisted by the requested FISA coverage. Case Agent 1 told us that he became frustrated with the pace of the FISA application process and asked Strzok to do whatever he could to help move it along.

comfortable with its accuracy and content. Separately, Evans received notice from ODAG that, as he requested, Yates had read the application and had cleared NSD to file the read copy with the court. OI filed the read copy with the FISC the next day.

The OIG found no indication that then Attorney General Loretta Lynch or anyone in the Office of the Attorney General (OAG) was involved in the preparation, review, or approval of the Carter Page FISA application. Gauhar told us that she had brief conversations with Lynch's National Security Counselor and Chief of Staff to advise them for their situational awareness that a FISA application targeting Carter Page was expected to be filed. Neither the National Security Counselor nor the Chief of Staff read the application prior to its filing with the court. Lynch also said she did not read the application and did not recall any conversations about it.

III. Feedback from the FISC on the Read Copy, Completion of the Woods Procedures, and Final Briefing and Signatures

A. Feedback from the FISC and Revisions to the Application

On October 20, 2016, the FISC legal advisor assigned to the Carter Page application provided OI with four comments and questions regarding the read copy. Two related to information in the footnote about Steele, and two related to certain facilities believed to be used by Carter Page:

- The FISC legal advisor inquired about a sentence in the footnote that stated, "In addition to the specific information pertaining to Page reported in this application, [Steele] has provided other information, which the FBI is currently investigating." To clarify, the final application was revised to state, "In addition to the specific information pertaining to Page reported in this application, [Steele] has provided other information relating to the Russian Government's efforts to influence the election that do not directly pertain to Page, including the possibility of the Russian's [sic] also possessing a dossier on Candidate #1, which the FBI is currently investigating."

- The legal advisor asked how it was that Steele had a network of sub-sources, and the OI Attorney provided additional information to him regarding Steele's past employment history. At the request of the legal advisor, OI included the additional information in the final application, including the identity of ████████████████

- The legal advisor asked OI for clarification regarding the information used to establish Carter Page's use of a particular email account, and OI corrected an error in the description of the supporting documentation.

- The legal advisor requested additional information to establish the ███████ of Carter Page's ████████████████. The FBI provided the OI Attorney with some additional information; however, the information was somewhat stale, and the FBI elected instead to remove ██

████████████████████████████, rather than hold up the final application to investigate ████████████████ further.

According to the OI Attorney, the FISC legal advisor raised no other issues and did not further question the application's reliance on Steele's reporting.

B. The FBI's Completion of the Factual Accuracy Review ("Woods Procedures")

On October 19, the OI Unit Chief "signed out" the cert copy of the application and cert memo, so that the FBI could complete the FISA verification process known as the Woods Procedures, described in Chapter Two. Case Agent 1 was the agent responsible for compiling the supporting documentation into a Woods File, performing the field office database checks on Carter Page, and completing the accuracy review of each fact asserted in the FISA application. His supervisor for the Carter Page investigation, SSA 1, was responsible for confirming that the Woods File was complete and for double checking the factual accuracy review to confirm that the file contained appropriate documentation for each of the factual assertions in the FISA application.

With respect to the factual accuracy review, Case Agent 1 told us that he personally compiled the supporting documentation in the Woods File and then went through the factual statements in the cert copy one-by-one and made sure that each factual assertion was verified by a corresponding document in the Woods File. After he completed his review of all the factual information, he said he turned the Woods File over to SSA 1, and SSA 1 and Case Agent 1 then performed a second factual accuracy review of the same information together. SSA 1 said he found that each factual assertion was supported by documentation in the Woods File, and he had no concerns with how the Woods Procedures were completed. SSA 1 told us that he relied on Case Agent 1 to highlight each relevant fact in the supporting document in the Woods File, and that once he verified that each highlighted fact corresponded to a factual assertion in the application, he would move on to the next fact, without necessarily reviewing the entire document.[287] On the evening of October 20, Case Agent 1 and SSA 1 signed the "FISA Verification Form" or "Woods Form" affirming the verification and documentation of each factual assertion in the application.[288]

---

[287] We do not believe that this process, even when faithfully executed, is sufficient to ensure that all factual assertions in the application had adequate supporting documentation.

[288] As discussed in detail in Section IV below, we examined the completeness of the Woods File by comparing the facts asserted in the first FISA application to the documents maintained in the Woods File. Our comparison identified instances in which facts asserted in the application were not supported by documentation in the Woods File. Specifically, we found facts asserted in the FISA application that have no supporting documentation in the Woods File, facts that have purported supporting documentation in the Woods File but the documentation does not state the fact asserted in the FISA application, or facts that have purported supporting documentation in the Woods File but the documentation shows the fact asserted is inaccurate. The three most significant Woods errors, which are among the five problematic issues we describe later in Section IV, were: (1) the failure to seek and document Handling Agent 1's approval of the source characterization statement for Steele; (2)

After Case Agent 1 and SSA 1 signed the Woods Form, they passed the Woods Form, cert copy, and cert memo (collectively referred to as the FISA or application "package") to a Headquarters Program Manager assigned the responsibility of signing the final application under oath attesting that the factual information was true and correct. The Headquarters Program Manager was an SSA in the CD's Counterespionage Section. His official duties at the time did not include supervising the Carter Page investigation, contrary to what was stated in boilerplate language in the FISA application. Instead, he was briefed into the Crossfire Hurricane investigation on or about September 23 for the purpose of swearing out the Carter Page FISA.[289] The Headquarters Program Manager told us that after he was briefed, he attended some of the team meetings and had multiple conversations with Case Agent 1, SSA 1, and the OGC attorneys for updates on the status of and changes to the application. He said he read the entire application before it was final and, as changes were made to the application, he reviewed the changes. He said he had no specific memory of reviewing the Woods Form or Woods File (as described in Chapter Two, the Woods Procedures do not require the affiant to review the Woods File), but he believes that he would have done both since the Woods File was compiled at Headquarters, and thus he would have had access to it. However, he said he trusted that the case agent verified the accuracy of the factual assertions, as the case agent was required to do as part of the Woods Procedures. Further, the Headquarters Program Manager said that he was not independently aware of any information suggesting that the information in the application was inaccurate. After the Headquarters Program Manager signed the affidavit in the application declaring under penalty of perjury that the information in the application was true and correct, he submitted the application package to the OGC Attorney.

The OGC Attorney and Deputy General Counsel Anderson reviewed the application package on behalf of OGC's National Security and Cyber Law Branch. However, as discussed in Chapter Two, FBI procedures do not specify what steps must be taken during the final OGC legal review.[290] The OGC Attorney, who had participated in the drafting process and was familiar with the content of the application, told us that he reviewed the Woods Form with the Headquarters Program Manager. After the OGC Attorney confirmed that all of the Woods Procedures had been completed, he signed the cert memo below the OI Unit Chief's signature and submitted the package to Anderson.

---

the fact that documentation in the Woods File used to support the FBI's statement that Steele only shared his election related information with Glenn Simpson actually stated that Steele also shared the information with the State Department; and (3) the fact that documentation in the Woods File used to support the FBI's assertion that Carter Page did not refute his alleged contacts with Sechin and Divyekin to an FBI CHS in actuality stated that Page specifically denied meeting with Sechin and Divyekin to the CHS. We provide examples of other Woods related errors in Appendix One.

[289] According to the Headquarters Program Manager, because the investigation was closely-held and being run out of Headquarters, it was initially not assigned to a specific unit in the Counterintelligence Division and therefore did not have an assigned program manager.

[290] We make a recommendation in Chapter Eleven that addresses this issue.

Anderson told us that she reviewed the cert memo and Woods Form and determined that the application package was complete, all the steps of the Woods Procedures were represented to have been taken, the probable cause standard was met, and there were no outstanding issues. She then signed the cert memo below the other signatures, signifying that the application was ready for certification, and she gave the application package to the OGC Unit Chief for submission to the FBI Director.[291]

C.   FBI Director's Certification

Comey certified the Carter Page application on behalf of the FBI. In Chapter Two, we described the elements of the certification required by the FBI Director or Deputy Director, including that the information sought through the requested FISA authority is foreign intelligence information that cannot reasonably be obtained by normal investigative techniques and is necessary to protect the United States against clandestine intelligence activities. In this regard, the Director's certification is different from the approval of the NSD AAG, DAG, or the Attorney General, which requires that the signatory find that the application satisfies the FISA's statutory requirements.

Comey told the OIG that when he was Director his practice varied in terms of whether he would read a FISA application itself before certifying an application, or whether he would rely solely on the description of the application in the cert memo. He said that he would read applications if they required special attention, but that from time to time he would also select others to read for quality control purposes. In this instance, Comey said he read the application because of its sensitivity. He further stated that he read the application once, after Baker presented the final package to him. He said he did not recall any conversations with Baker or with others about the application.

Baker told us that he presented the final package to Comey because he wanted to discuss the foreign intelligence purpose with Comey before Comey signed the certification. Baker said that in addition to explaining the foreign intelligence purpose to Comey, he wanted to make sure that Comey knew that he (Baker) had read the FISA and was satisfied that the probable cause standard was met. According to Baker, Comey told him that he understood, was satisfied with the foreign intelligence purpose, and was glad Baker read the application.

Comey told us that the application seemed factually and legally sufficient when he read it, and he had no questions or concerns before he signed. When we

---

[291] Anderson told us that she did not read the FISA application at this stage in the process, which she said was not unusual. She said that her general practice was to rely upon the cert memo's description of the probable cause, unless there was a reason to dig deeper into the application based on her review of the cert memo or if she was familiar with the case from an earlier stage. As described previously, in this case, Anderson had read the Carter Page FISA application once before during the review process and she believed that both Baker and the OGC Unit Chief had also read and provided feedback on the application. As described previously, Baker provided comments on a draft of the application. The OGC Unit Chief told us that she read the application and was involved in discussions about it, but she said she did not recall requesting edits.

asked him why the FBI moved forward with an application on a target who was formerly connected to a presidential campaign, based in part on source reporting that may have been funded by the opposing political party and had not yet been corroborated, Comey said that the reason was because there was probable cause to believe that Page was an agent of a foreign power. He said that simply because the information regarding Page was uncorroborated at the time of the application did not mean that it was unreliable. He stated that in this case, he understood that the FBI assessed that Steele was a credible source, with a network of sub-sources in positions to receive information, and the core of the Steele reporting was consistent with other information the FBI had at the time.

Comey signed the application on October 20, and the application package was presented to Yates on October 21.

D.   DAG Oral Briefing and Approval

Yates told the OIG that she did not recall the discussion that took place at the October 21 oral briefing when NSD presented the final application package to her. Evans said that he recalled that because Yates had already read the FISA application and was familiar with its contents, the OI Attorney used the oral briefing to advise her of the FISC legal advisor's questions and the changes made in the final application to address those questions. Evans said that he recalled little discussion during the oral briefing on this application before Yates signed the application.

The OIG asked Yates about her views on the application. Yates told us that, in her view, the application did not present a close call from a legal sufficiency standpoint, and she was comfortable that it was an appropriate investigative step to take. In terms of the specific reasons she approved the application, Yates stated:

> Well, several things here. First, the context of the issue that we're talking about here, which is the Russian attempt to interfere in the 2016 presidential election, and the potential involvement of U.S. persons in that, is obviously a critically important topic. This is not some tangential run-of-the-mill crime. This is, to state the obvious here, critically important to the country. So we start sort of with the premise of, this is a topic that we need to get to the bottom of.

> Secondly, Carter Page is not someone who just popped up out of the blue on the FBI's radar, with respect to his relationship with the Russian government. He is someone who had been on the radar for quite some time, both in terms of, and I think it's laid out in the FISA, the attempts to recruit him that had been laid out in a prior criminal case, and the FBI's knowledge of interaction that he had had in the past, and was continuing to have, with high-level people in the Russian government. So, it's not as if, just some guy who had never had any relationship with Russia has been alleged to be involved in the Russians' interference in the election.

154

[T]hat's also against the backdrop of the information that Papadopoulos had provided, and that then was corroborated to the extent that then WikiLeaks did do the email dump, as predicted there, and identified that a person in the campaign that was coordinating that.

Combined with [Steele], who had been someone with whom the FBI had worked for many years, both in an official capacity at [███████ ███████], and then afterwards, whom they had found to be credible. I believe criminal cases had been made, or he had participated in criminal cases[.] So again, not just somebody out of the blue. And he was also very knowledgeable of Russia, which is not an easy place to break into, in terms of getting information.

...[I]t may have been, the information that [Steele] had acquired, may have been at the behest of the Clinton campaign or the DNC. I guess I would emphasize the word "may" there. That again, my understanding was that the FBI did not know who he was working for. In fact, and this is one of these things I have a hard time teasing out, what I knew then versus what I may know now, or have learned since, is that [Steele], my understanding is at one point, was actually working for someone connected with the Republican Party. I don't know, again, whether I knew that at the time, or not. I'm not at all sure about that. So, while certainly there was [an] implication that he was doing opposition research, it's gotta be for somebody. I mean, he's been hired by someone. My understanding was that the FBI didn't know who. And that is a factor to consider in this.[292]

But that was not the determinative factor, when you're talking about gathering foreign intelligence, not when it's against the backdrop of all of the other information there. And the FBI, who are experts in this, who have people who do this all day, every day, and the folks in DOJ who work with them on that, all believed that this was an important FISA to get, and to get now. So it's against the back-drop of that, of believing that it met the legal standards for a FISA, which appear to be borne out, given that it's been signed and reauthorized a number of times through the FISA court. It, I believed then and I believe now, it was the appropriate step to take. They're not all easy decisions that you make when you're DAG.

---

[292] FBI officials told us that the Crossfire Hurricane team did not know who hired Fusion GPS (which hired Steele) until after the first FISA application was filed, though, as described previously, the Crossfire Hurricane team and Steele's handling agent suspected Steele had been hired to conduct political opposition research. Documents indicate that by February and March 2017 it was broadly known among FBI officials involved with the investigation, and shared with senior NSD and ODAG officials, that Fusion GPS was hired first by a candidate during the Republican primaries and then later by someone related to the Democratic Party. Yates was removed as Acting Attorney General on January 30, 2017.

Following OI's presentation, Yates signed the application, and OI submitted the application to the FISC the same day. By her signature, and as stated in the application, Yates found that the application satisfied the criteria and requirements of the FISA statute and approved its filing with the court.[293]

E.   Final Orders

The final FISA application included proposed orders, which were signed by then Chief Judge of the FISC, Rosemary Collyer, on October ██, 2016. According to NSD, the Chief Judge signed the final orders as proposed by the government in their entirety, without holding a hearing.

The primary order and warrant stated that the court found, based upon the facts submitted in the verified application, that there was probable cause to believe that Russia is a foreign power and that Carter Page was an agent of Russia under 50 U.S.C. § 1801(b)(2)(E). The court also found that the ███████████ ██ ██. The court authorized the requested electronic surveillance ██████████ for 90 days ████████████ to effectuate the electronic surveillance ██████████ authorized by the court. The authorization permitted the government to, among other things, ███ by Carter Page. This included █████████████ ████████████████████████████████ during the 90-day period. The authorization also permitted the government to █████████████ ██ ██

IV.   Inaccurate, Incomplete, or Undocumented Information in the First FISA Application

Our review revealed instances in which factual assertions relied upon in the first FISA application targeting Carter Page were inaccurate, incomplete, or unsupported by appropriate documentation, based upon information the FBI had in its possession at the time the application was filed. We describe the most significant instances below and provide additional examples in a chart in Appendix One. We found no evidence that the OI Attorney, NSD supervisors, ODAG officials, or Yates were made aware of these issues by the FBI before the first FISA application was submitted to the court. Although we also found no evidence that Comey had been made aware of these issues at the time he certified the application, as more fully discussed in our analysis in Chapter Eleven, multiple factors made it difficult for us to precisely determine the extent of Comey's or

---

[293] Her signature also specifically authorized ██████████████ ████████████████████████████████

McCabe's knowledge as to each fact that was not shared with OI and not included, or inaccurately stated, in the FISA applications. These factors included, among other things, limited recollections, the inability to question Comey about classified material because of his lack of a security clearance, and the absence of meeting minutes that would show the specific details shared with Comey and McCabe during briefings they received, beyond the more general investigative updates that we know they were provided.

A. Information about Page's Prior Relationship with Another U.S. Government Agency and Information Page Provided to the Other Agency that Overlapped with Facts Asserted in the FISA Application

The OI Attorney told us that it is relevant to know if the target of a FISA is or had been working on behalf of another U.S. government agency to "make sure that the left hand knows what the right hand is doing" when seeking FISA authority. As noted previously, according to the OI Attorney, it would have been a significant fact if Page had a relationship with the other U.S. government agency that overlapped in time with his interactions with known Russian intelligence officers described in the FISA applications because it would raise the issue of whether Page interacted with the Russian intelligence officers at the behest of the other agency or with the intent to assist the U.S. government. Evans told us that information about a FISA target's relationship with another U.S. government agency is typically included in a FISA application. Evans also stated that OI would work with the FBI to fully understand any such relationship and describe it accurately in the relevant application.

Toward that end, on September 28, 2016, the OI Attorney emailed Case Agent 1 a draft of the FISA application, copying other members of the Crossfire Hurricane team. In a comment in the draft application, the OI Attorney asked "do we know if there is any truth to Page's claim that he has provided information to [another U.S. government agency]—was he considered a source/asset/whatever?" In response to the OI Attorney's question, on September 29, Case Agent 1 inserted the following comment in the draft:

> "He did meet with [the other U.S. government agency], however, it's dated and I would argue it was/is outside scope, I don't think we need it in. It was years ago, when he was in Moscow. If you want to keep it, I can get the language from the [August 17 Memorandum] we were provided [by the other U.S. government agency]."[294]

Based upon this response, the OI Attorney did not include information about Page's prior relationship with the other agency in the FISA application.

However, the information Case Agent 1 provided to the OI Attorney was inaccurate. As described in the August 17 Memorandum from the other U.S.

---

[294] As noted previously, on or about August 17, 2016, the Crossfire Hurricane team received information from another U.S. government agency detailing Carter Page's relationship with that other agency.

government agency to the FBI, Page first met with the other agency in April 2008, after he left Moscow (Page had lived in Moscow from 2004 to 2007), and he had been approved as an operational contact for the other agency from 2008 to 2013. Additionally, rather than being outside the scope of the FISA application, the FISA application included allegations about meetings that Page had with Russian intelligence officers that Page had disclosed to the other agency. Specifically, according to the August 17 Memorandum, Page provided information to the other agency in October 2010 about contacts he had with a Russian intelligence officer (Intelligence Officer 1), which the other agency assessed likely began in 2008. Page's contacts with Intelligence Officer 1 in 2007 and 2008 were among the historical connections to Russian intelligence officers that the FBI relied upon in the first FISA application (and subsequent renewal applications) to help support probable cause.[295] The August 17 Memorandum stated that Page told the other agency that he met with Intelligence Officer 1 four times, characterized him as a "compelling, nice guy," and described Intelligence Officer 1's alleged interest in contacting an identified U.S. person. According to the August 17 Memorandum, the employee of the other U.S. government agency who met with Page assessed that Page "candidly described his contact with" Intelligence Officer 1. Page's relationship with the other agency was not mentioned in any of the four FISA applications.

Further, the FBI had information in its own files indicating that Page had told the FBI about meeting with the other U.S. government agency after the period he lived in Moscow and during the period alleged in the FISA application. For example, according to the FBI Electronic Communication (EC) documenting a June 18, 2009 FBI interview of Page, Page had informed the FBI agents that "due to his work and overseas experiences, he has been questioned by and provides information to representatives of the [other U.S. government agency] on an ongoing basis," and that the "interviewing agents acknowledged this fact, and stated to Page that no questions would be asked about Page's dealings with the other U.S. government agency during the interview." According to another FBI EC, Page told the FBI during a June 2013 interview that, although he had not spoken to the other U.S. government agency for "about a year or so" Page had spoken to them "since his last interview with the FBI."

The Woods File for the first FISA application, which was prepared by Case Agent 1, included the EC documenting the 2009 FBI interview of Page. Additionally, Case Agent 1 received an email on August 10, 2016, containing an attachment titled "Carter Page-Profile," which had been prepared by a Crossfire Hurricane Staff Operations Specialist (SOS). The profile, dated August 1, 2016, quoted the 2009 EC regarding Page's statements to the FBI about his contact with the other U.S. government agency. We did not find any electronic communications indicating that the FBI provided OI with this Carter Page profile.

---

[295] The other agency did not provide the FBI with information indicating it had knowledge of Page's reported contacts with another particular intelligence officer. The FBI also relied on Page's contacts with this intelligence officer in the FISA application.

We asked Case Agent 1 about his knowledge in 2016 of Page's historical contacts with the other U.S. government agency and Case Agent 1's response to the OI Attorney's question on September 29, 2016, about any such contacts. Case Agent 1 told us that he did not recall his state of knowledge in 2016 regarding Page's history with the other U.S. government agency, but said he believed that he likely would have reviewed the August 17 Memorandum about Page sent to the Crossfire Hurricane team by the other U.S. government agency. He said he recalled believing that Page's involvement with the other U.S. government agency was "dated." After reviewing a synopsis of the information contained in the August 17 Memorandum during his OIG interview, Case Agent 1 reiterated to the OIG that he believed the information was dated, but also said that he "probably saw it." According to Case Agent 1, "I think I would have reviewed it with the team. I think that it would have been, you know, as we looked at it. It wasn't just me. But, we, you know, there was a determination made that it was dated." Case Agent 1 also said it was possible that he never reviewed the August 17 Memorandum from the other U.S. government agency.

The OI Attorney told us that he could not recall much about the issue of Page's historical contacts with the other U.S. government agency. After being shown his exchange with Case Agent 1 on September 29, 2016, the OI Attorney stated that if Case Agent 1 told him that Page's contacts with the other U.S. government agency were "out of scope" and dated, then he would have deferred to Case Agent 1's assessment on this issue. The OI Attorney also told us, after being informed about information in the August 17 Memorandum from the other U.S. government agency, that if OI had been aware of this information at the time the application was being prepared, OI would have discussed it internally and likely would have disclosed the information to the FISC to "err on the side of disclosure." When we discussed the information in the August 17 Memorandum with Evans, he responded similarly and told us "I think it would go in the application somewhere, be it in a footnote or elsewhere, if for no other reason than it also goes to the question of where the person's loyalties lie."

As described later in Chapters Seven and Eight, none of the three renewal applications described Page's prior historical contacts and relationship with the other U.S. government agency, even after the FBI received additional information from the other agency in June 2017. In April and May 2017, following news reports that the FBI had obtained a FISA targeting Carter Page, Page gave interviews to news outlets denying that he had collected intelligence for the Russian government and asserting instead that he had previously shared information that he had learned with the U.S. intelligence community. In mid-June 2017, in response to concerns expressed by members of the Crossfire Hurricane team, the OGC Attorney contacted the other U.S. government agency by email to seek clarification about Page's past status with that agency. The other U.S. government agency responded by email to the FBI OGC attorney by directing the attorney to memoranda previously sent to the FBI by the other U.S. government agency that informed the FBI that Page did previously have a relationship with that other agency and that the last contact occurred in July 2011. The email also stated, using the other agency's terminology, that Page had a relationship with that other agency. However, when asked about Page's prior status with that other agency by a Crossfire Hurricane supervisor, SSA 2, who was going to be the affiant on the final FISA renewal application, the OGC Attorney told SSA 2 that Page had never had a relationship with the other U.S. government agency. In addition, the OGC Attorney altered the email that the other U.S. government agency had sent to the OGC Attorney so that the email stated that Page had not been a source for the other agency; the OGC Attorney then forwarded the altered email to SSA 2, who told us he relied on the email. Shortly thereafter, SSA 2 served as the affiant on the final renewal application, which was again silent on Page's prior relationship with the other U.S. government agency.

B.   Source Characterization Statement

As described earlier, because the FBI did not have information corroborating the Steele reporting relied upon in the Carter Page FISA application, it was particularly important for the application to articulate to the court the FBI's assessment of the reliability of the source. Toward that end, the final application included in a footnote the following source characterization statement regarding Steele:

> [Steele] is a former ███████████ ████████ ███████ and has been an FBI source since in or about October 2013. [Steele's] reporting has been corroborated and used in criminal proceedings and the FBI assesses [Steele] to be reliable.[296] [Steele] has been compensated approximately $95,000 by the FBI and the FBI is unaware of any derogatory information pertaining to [Steele].[297]

The OIG found no documentation in the Woods File indicating that Steele's handling agent, Handling Agent 1, approved this language, as required by Foreign Intelligence Surveillance Act and Standard Minimization Procedures Policy Guide (FISA SMP PG) discussed in Chapter Two. Case Agent 1, who as described earlier compiled the Woods File and completed the Woods Procedures, told us that he was not aware of this requirement.[298] Handling Agent 1 told the OIG that he did not approve this language, and that his OIG interview was the first time he ever saw it. Further, Handling Agent 1 said that although he found Steele to be reliable in the past, only "some" of Steele's past reporting had been corroborated and most of it

---

[296] Although Case Agent 2's summary of the early October meeting with Steele states that Steele described his ███████████ in a manner consistent with the footnote in the FISA application, other documentation (discussed in Chapter Eight) indicates that Steele's ███████████ told the FBI in November 2016, after the first application was filed, that Steele had ███████████ ███████████████████████████████████████.

[297] As described later in Chapter Seven, after Steele admitted to a disclosure of information to *Mother Jones* in late October 2016, the renewal applications removed the reference to no derogatory information concerning Steele and stated that the FBI continued to assess that Steele was reliable "as previous reporting from Steele has been corroborated and used in criminal proceedings."

[298] Case Agent 1 told us that his experience with previous FISA applications had always involved CHSs for whom he (Case Agent 1) was the handling agent, and that, therefore, he never had the need to seek approval from a separate handling agent.

had not. He also stated that Steele's reporting had never been used in a criminal proceeding.

Handling Agent 1 also told us, and FBI emails and instant messages reflect, that he had provided language on September 23 to Case Agent 1 for the source characterization statement that was substantively different from the final language used in the FISA application:

> CHS has been signed up for 3 years and is reliable. CHS responds to taskings and obtains info from a network of sub sources. Some of the chs' info has been corroborated when possible.

Case Agent 1 provided this language from Handling Agent 1 to the OGC Unit Chief, who had requested that he reach out to the handling agent for a description of Steele's reliability and corroboration. However, the language Case Agent 1 provided to the OI Attorney on September 29, which was later used to draft the reliability footnote 8, differed from the language provided by Handling Agent 1 and instead stated the following:

> This information comes from a sensitive FBI source whose reporting has been corroborated and used in criminal proceedings, and who obtains information from a number of ostensibly well-positioned sub-sources. The scope of the source's reporting is from 20 June 2016 through 20 August 2016.

Case Agent 1, the OGC Unit Chief, and the OGC Attorney told us that they did not recall or know the specific circumstances that led to the use of "corroborated and used in criminal proceedings" in the final application instead of language that more closely tracked what Handling Agent 1 had provided. Emails and other FBI documents reflect that Case Agent 1 borrowed the exact language used in the final application from an Intelligence Memorandum on the Steele reporting, which the Supervisory Intel Analyst and Staff Operations Specialist (SOS) had prepared in late September 2016.[299] Case Agent 1 told us that he most likely wanted to make sure that the language in the FISA application was consistent with how Steele was described in that document, which he believed had been vetted by analysts.

The Supervisory Intel Analyst told us that the phrase "corroborated and used in criminal proceedings" was a reference to Steele's reporting in the FIFA investigation. He said that neither he nor anyone else on the team reviewed any of the documents or court filings in the FIFA case file, and he did not "dig into" exactly how Steele's reporting was used in the FIFA case. He said that his entire knowledge about Steele's role in and significance to the FIFA investigation came from Handling Agent 1, though he said he did not recall what he specifically learned from Handling Agent 1 regarding how Steele's information was used in the FIFA

---

[299] The Supervisory Intel Analyst told us that he did not specifically recall developing this specific language for the Intelligence Memorandum, but he said that metadata on the document itself reflected that he personally added the information.

investigation. Handwritten notes documenting conversations with Handling Agent 1 indicate that the Crossfire Hurricane team was left with the understanding that Steele was the original source for the FIFA investigation. SSA 1 told the OIG that the team "speculated" that Steele's information was corroborated and used in criminal proceedings because they knew Steele had been "a part of, if not predicated, the FIFA investigation" and was known to have an extensive source network into Russian organized crime. SSA 1 told us that the email he sent to Handling Agent 1 and others on September 19, requesting a "source characterization statement," among other information on Steele, reflected his "intent" as the case supervisor to provide accurate information in the FISA application about Steele's history with the FBI. As noted in Chapter Four, in connection with the FIFA matter, Steele had provided leads to the FBI, namely that the FBI should talk to a contact who had information on corruption in the FIFA organization. It was the contact's information, in part, that led to the opening of the FIFA investigation. However, the FIFA case agent and a prosecutor on the case told us that, to their knowledge, Steele did not have any role in the investigation itself, he did not provide court testimony, and his information did not appear in any indictments, search warrants, or other court filings. According to Handling Agent 1, he was clear with the Crossfire Hurricane team concerning Steele's role and that Steele had provided leads and not evidence in the FIFA case.

Witnesses gave us different understandings as to the meaning and scope of the phrase, "used in criminal proceedings." Handling Agent 1 told us that he never told the Crossfire Hurricane team that Steele's past reporting was "used in criminal proceedings," and he was bothered that the team used that phrase. Other witnesses said that the phrase could include providing a lead that helped bring about a criminal investigation, such as Evans who told us that a tip that leads to evidence of criminal wrongdoing could meet the "spirit" of "used in criminal proceedings." However, some witnesses, including attorneys who served in FBI OGC, NSD, and ODAG, interpreted the phrase to mean that the source information was used in some sort of formal court proceeding or legal process. In particular, Baker told us that, in his view, the phrase implies that the information "wasn't just a tip," but that it was used as evidence in a trial, in an affidavit, or in some other court filing or legal process.

Given the importance of a source's bona fides to a court's determination of credibility—particularly in cases where, as here, the source information supporting probable cause is uncorroborated—we believe the failure to comply with FBI policy requiring that Steele's handling agent review and approve the language in the source characterization statement was an important one. This failure may have resulted in the court being left with the misimpression that Steele's past reporting (or at least some of it) had been deemed worthy by prosecutors of being relied upon in court or that more of his information had been corroborated than was actually the case. Further, as we describe in Chapters Six and Eight, additional documentation became available to the Crossfire Hurricane team subsequent to the first FISA application that provided information contrary to the characterization of Steele in the first FISA application, including the finding of a formal FBI source validation review in March 2017 that Steele's past reporting on criminal matters, which included the FIFA case, was "minimally corroborated." Despite this information, the description of Steele in the FISA renewal applications did not change.

C.   Information about a Steele Sub-Source Relied Upon in the FISA Application (Person 1)

As described earlier in this chapter, the information in the FISA application relied upon to establish probable cause to believe that Carter Page was coordinating with the Russian government on 2016 U.S. presidential election activities was based upon certain aspects of Steele's reporting. This reporting included the alleged secret meetings between Page and Russian officials in July 2016 described in Steele's Report 94. We found that the most descriptive information in the FISA application of alleged coordination between Page and Russia came from Steele's Report 95, which attributed the information to "Source E."

The FISA application stated that, according to this sub-source, Carter Page was an intermediary between Russian leadership and an individual associated with the Trump campaign (Manafort) in a "well-developed conspiracy of co-operation" that led to the disclosure of hacked DNC emails by WikiLeaks in exchange for the Trump campaign team's agreement, which the FBI assessed included at least Carter Page, to sideline Russian intervention in Ukraine as a campaign issue. The application also stated that this same sub-source provided information contained in Steele's Report 80 that the Kremlin had been feeding information to Trump's campaign for an extended period of time and that the information had reportedly been "very helpful," as well as information contained in Report 102 that the DNC email leak had been done, at least in part, to swing supporters from Hillary Clinton to Donald Trump.[300] Because the FBI had no independent corroboration for this information, as witnesses have mentioned, the reliability of Steele and his source network was important to the inclusion of these allegations in the FISA application.

Before the initial FISA application was filed, FBI documents and witness testimony indicate that the Crossfire Hurricane team had assessed, particularly following the information Steele provided in early October, that Source E was most likely a person previously known to the FBI, referred to hereinafter as Person 1.[301] The Supervisory Intel Analyst's written summary of the early October meeting with Steele specifically attributed the information in Report 95 to Person 1 and also described information that Steele provided to the FBI team about Person 1, including that Person 1 "is a 'boaster' and an 'egoist' and may engage in some embellishment." The day after the early October meeting, the Supervisory Intel Analyst emailed this written summary to the Crossfire Hurricane team, as well as Strzok and the Intel Section Chief. The OIG found no documents or written communications in which the Crossfire Hurricane team evaluated Steele's statement characterizing Person 1 as a boaster or embellisher. SSA 1, who received the

---

[300] In Report 80, this sub-source was referred to as "Source D" and in Report 102 as an "associate" of candidate Donald Trump.

[301] As discussed in Chapter Four, Person 1 ████████████████████████████

written summary from the Supervisory Intel Analyst, told us that he did not recall any such conversations.

The footnote describing this sub-source in the FISA application did not include any information about how Steele had described Person 1 as a boaster or embellisher. Documents reflect that, on or about October 12, the OI Attorney received the Supervisory Intel Analyst's written summary of the early October meeting that attributed the information in Report 95 to Person 1 and stated that Steele had described Person 1 as a boaster and embellisher. The OI Attorney made handwritten notes on the written summary when he met with members of the Crossfire Hurricane team to learn more about the source network. The OI Attorney told us that he did not recall the team flagging this issue for him or that he independently made the connection between the sub-source in the FISA application and Steele's characterization of Person 1. Case Agent 1 and the OI Attorney told the OIG that they did not recall any conversations about Steele's statement about Person 1 at the time of the FISA application. We found no evidence that Steele's characterization of Person 1 was shared with Evans or the OI managers involved in the FISA application, and they told us that they did not recall being made aware of it. Evans and the OI Attorney told us that they would have wanted to discuss the issue internally in NSD and with the FBI and likely would have, at a minimum, disclosed the information to the court.

In addition, we learned that Person 1 ███████████████████████ ███████████████████████.[302] We also were concerned that the FISA application did not disclose to the court the FBI's belief that this sub-source was, at the time of the application, ████████████████████████. We were told that the Department will usually share with the FISC the fact that ████████████████ ███████████████. The OI Attorney told us he did not recall knowing this information at the time of the first application, even though NYFO opened the case after consulting with and notifying Case Agent 1 and SSA 1 prior to October 12, 2016, nine days before the FISA application was filed. Case Agent 1 said that he may have mentioned the case to the OI Attorney "in passing," but he did not specifically recall doing so.[303]

We believe the FBI should have specifically and explicitly advised OI about the FBI's assessment that this particular sub-source relied upon in the FISA application was Person 1, that Steele had provided derogatory information

---

[302] According to a document circulated among Crossfire Hurricane team members and supervisors in early October 2016, Person 1 had ███████████████████████ ███. The document described reporting ████████████████████████ ███████████████████████ In addition, in late December 2016, Department Attorney Bruce Ohr told SSA 1 that he had met with Glenn Simpson and that Simpson had assessed that Person 1 was ████████████ who was central in connecting Trump to Russia.

[303] Although an email indicates that the OI Attorney learned in March 2017 that ████████████ ██████████████████, the subsequent renewal applications did not include this fact. According to the OI Attorney, and as reflected in Renewal Application Nos. 2 and 3, the FBI expressed uncertainty about whether this sub-source was Person 1. However, other FBI documents in the same time period reflect that the ongoing assumption by the Crossfire Hurricane team was that this sub-source was Person 1.

regarding Person 1, and that ███████████████████████████████
████████████. Those facts were relevant to OI's assessment of the strength of the information in the FISA application and, based on what we were told was the Department's practice, likely would have been included by OI in the application so that the FISC could consider the information in deciding whether to grant the requested FISA authority.

D.   September 23 Media Disclosure

As described earlier, the final FISA application included the FBI's assessment in Footnote 18 that the FBI "does not believe that [Steele] directly provided...to the press" the information in the September 23 *Yahoo News* article concerning the investigation of Carter Page and his alleged meetings with Sechin and Divyekin. The basis for this assessment, as asserted in the application, was that Steele told the FBI that he "only provided this information to the business associate and the FBI." However, this assertion of what Steele said was inaccurate, and the documentation in the Woods File did not support it.

The documentation in the Woods File relied upon for this assertion was a written summary of the meeting in early October with Steele. The summary was drafted by Case Agent 2 and, as noted above, was emailed to the Crossfire Hurricane team a day after the meeting. This Woods document, however, did not state or otherwise indicate that Steele only provided the information to his business associate and the FBI. Indeed, the Woods document noted that Steele told the team that he also had provided his election reports to his contacts at the State Department. Neither Case Agent 1 nor SSA 1, who performed the Woods Procedures on this application, noted this error, and it is not clear upon what basis they believed they had verified the factual assertion in the footnote about the FBI's assessment of who provided information to the media for the September 23 news article. Both Case Agent 1 and SSA 1 told the OIG that they may have mistakenly been thinking the footnote said Steele gave the information to the "U.S. government" rather than "the FBI."

As described in Chapter Six, during his OIG interview, Steele told us that in September he and Simpson gave an "off-the-record" briefing to a small number of journalists about his reporting. Steele said he did not have permission to disclose to the OIG who attended this briefing but acknowledged that *Yahoo News* was identified in one of the court filings in the foreign litigation as having been present.[304] The author of the *Yahoo News* article reported publicly in February 2018 that he received a briefing from Steele on the information discussed in the article

---

[304] Steele told us that he did not know if the "Western intelligence source" cited in the September 23 *Yahoo News* article was a reference to him. He said he had understood that the media briefing he gave was "off-the-record." He said that he believed that *Yahoo News* had a source in the FBI or otherwise in the U.S. government who provided the information in the article. As we described in Chapter Four, the author of the *Yahoo News* article has written that Steele was the "Western intelligence source." *See Russian Roulette: The Inside Story of Putin's War on America and the Election of Donald Trump* (New York: Grand Central Publishing, 2018), 227.

before the article was published, although the author also stated that he did not rely solely on Steele in his reporting.[305]

Neither of the FBI's two written summaries of the meeting in early October 2016 with Steele indicate that Steele was asked specifically about the article or generally about contacts with the media. During our interview with Steele, he told us that he was "fairly sure" the FBI team did not ask him at the meeting or at any other time, but that had they asked, he would have told them about his interactions with the media. The OI Attorney surmised in an October 14 email to the OI Unit Chief that the FBI team had not asked Steele those questions. The OI Attorney told us that he did not recall whether he sought or received clarity on whether the FBI team had specifically asked Steele about the Yahoo News disclosure. He said that he probably would have included more information in the application if he had additional clarity on that point.

As detailed in Chapter Four, we found no documentation demonstrating that Steele was asked by the FBI whether he was the source of the Yahoo News article disclosure or told the FBI he was not. Handling Agent 1 told us that he had no idea how the FBI made its assessment that Steele's business associate or the law firm likely provided the information to the media. We found that the basis for that assessment was neither accurate nor supported by appropriate documentation, demonstrating a failure in the Woods process. Further, as we describe in Chapter Seven, as the FBI learned new information about Steele's disclosures to the media—from the source himself, from Department attorney Bruce Ohr, and from media reports of the source's admissions in court filings in the foreign litigation— the FBI did not make changes in any of the three later FISA renewal applications to reflect this new information.

E.   Papadopoulos's Denials to an FBI CHS in September 2016

As described earlier, one of the main elements relied upon by the FBI in support of its probable cause showing was the FFG information concerning George Papadopoulos and the reported offer or suggestion of assistance from the Russians to someone associated with the Trump campaign. Specifically, the government stated the following in the FISA application:

> In or about March 2016, George Papadopoulos [footnote omitted] and Carter Page (the target of this application) were publicly identified by Candidate #1 as part of his/her foreign policy team. Based on reporting from a friendly foreign government, which has provided reliable information in the past...the FBI believes that the Russian Government's efforts are being coordinated with Page and perhaps other individuals associated with Candidate #1's campaign. In or about July 2016, the above-referenced friendly foreign government provided information to a senior official within the U.S. [government]

---

[305] See "Yahoo News' Michael Isikoff Describes Crucial Meeting Cited in Nunes Memo," Yahoo News, February 2, 2018, www.yahoo.com/news/yahoo-news-michael-isikoff-describes-crucial-meeting-cited-nunes-memo-231005733.html (accessed Dec. 2, 2019).

regarding efforts made by the Russian Government to influence the 2016 U.S. Presidential election. Specifically, according to this information, during a meeting in or about April 2016 between officials of the friendly foreign government and George Papadopoulos...Papadopoulos suggested that Candidate #1's campaign had received some kind of suggestion from Russia that Russia could assist with the anonymous release of information during the campaign that would be damaging to another candidate for U.S. President (Candidate #2). It was unclear whether Papadopoulos or the Russians were referring to material acquired publicly or through other means. It was also unclear from this reporting how Candidate #1's campaign reacted to the alleged Russian offer. Nevertheless, as discussed below, the FBI believes that election influence efforts are being coordinated between the RIS and Page, and possibly others.[306]

However, during a September 2016 CHS meeting conducted by the FBI, which was consensually monitored, Papadopoulos told an FBI CHS that, to his knowledge, no one associated with the Trump campaign was collaborating with Russia or with outside groups like WikiLeaks in the release of emails. The FISA application did not include the statements Papadopoulos made to this CHS that were in conflict with information included in the FISA application.

Case Agent 1 told us that he did not recall whether he advised the OI Attorney about Papadopoulos's denial in September 2016 but that, if he did not, it may have been an oversight. He also said that the Crossfire Hurricane team's assessment was that the Papadopoulos denial was a rehearsed response, and that he did not view the information as particularly germane to the investigation of Carter Page.[307] We were advised by NSD that it did not know about this denial by Papadopoulos until May 2018, after ODAG found the information while reviewing documents for possible production to Congressional committees. The OI Attorney told us that he had no memory of being aware of this CHS meeting at any time before May 2018.

As described in Chapter Eight, in July 2018, after learning this information, NSD submitted a letter to the FISC under Rule 13(a) of the Court's Rules of Procedure, notifying the court of additional information relevant to the Carter Page FISA applications. The Rule 13(a) letter included Papadopoulos's statements to the

---

[306] Although the application stated that the meeting between the FFG and Papadopoulos occurred in April 2016, FBI documents indicate the meeting occurred in May 2016.

[307] After reviewing a draft of this report, Case Agent 1 told the OIG that he and the team discounted Papadopoulos's denials for several reasons, but that, in hindsight, he now realizes that those denials, and the team's assessment of those denials, should have been shared with OI "in order for [OI] to make the determination whether [those denials] should be in the application."

FBI CHS in September 2016, as well as similar statements Papadopoulos made to a CHS in late October 2016, after the first application was filed.[308] The letter stated:

> The above-described additional background information concerning Papadopoulos's September 2016 meeting with [an FBI CHS] and October 2016 discussion with a separate CHS would have been included in the applications had it been known to NSD at the time, as Papadopoulos's statements relate to the question of whether Papadopoulos was aware of or involved in coordination of election influence efforts between the RIS and members of Candidate #1's campaign. Even had this information been included, the totality of information submitted in these applications concerning Page's activities was sufficient to support the Court's finding of probable cause that Page was acting as an agent of a foreign power. [Footnote omitted].

Evans told the OIG that a FISA target's denial of facts asserted in a FISA application should be included in the application, even in instances where the FBI makes an assessment that the target making the denial is not being candid or truthful. According to Evans, there was no question in his mind that the Papadopoulos denial to the CHS in September 2016 was relevant to the court's consideration of the first application. In fact, later renewal applications advised the court of denials made by Papadopoulos to the FBI over the course of several interviews in 2017, as well as the FBI's belief that Papadopoulos provided misleading and incomplete information.[309]

F. Carter Page's Denials to an FBI CHS in August and October 2016

As described earlier in this chapter, the FBI conducted CHS meetings involving Carter Page in August and October 2016. We found that statements made by Page during these meetings, which conflicted with information included in the first FISA application, were not provided by the FBI to OI, and were not disclosed in the first FISA application.

In August 2016, as we describe in Chapter Ten, the FBI consensually monitored and recorded a meeting between Carter Page and an FBI CHS, during which Page said that he had "literally never met" or "said one word to" Paul Manafort, and that Manafort had not responded to any of Page's emails. Page

---

[308] In a footnote, the letter also advised the court that Papadopoulos made similar statements to the FBI during an interview in late January 2017, after Renewal Application No. 1 was filed and before Renewal Application No. 2.

[309] As described later in Chapter Eight, in February 2017, the FBI interviewed Joseph Mifsud who the FBI believed communicated to Papadopoulos the alleged offer from the Russians. According to FBI documents, Mifsud denied having advance knowledge that Russia was in possession of DNC emails and denied passing any offers or proffers to Papadopoulos. As described in Chapter Eight, this information was not included in the later renewal applications.

made similar statements during one of his interviews with the FBI in March 2017.[310] Although the first Carter Page FISA application and subsequent renewal applications alleged that Page was acting as an intermediary between Manafort and the Russian government as part of a "well-developed conspiracy" (from Report 95), none of the applications included statements from Carter Page to the CHS that conflicted with the conspiracy allegation.

The statements made by Page in August 2016 were not provided to OI prior to the filing of the first FISA application. The OI Attorney told us that, like the September 2016 CHS meeting involving Papadopoulos, he had no memory of being made aware of Page's August 2016 statements regarding Manafort before the first FISA application was filed. Case Agent 1 told us that he did not discuss these statements with the OI Attorney because he did not view them as contrary to the allegations in Report 95, in that it was possible that Manafort used Page as an intermediary without communicating directly with Page.[311]

We found that information about the August 2016 meeting was first shared with the OI Attorney on or about June 20, 2017, when Case Agent 6 sent the OI Attorney a 163-page document containing the statements made by Page during the meeting. As described in Chapter Seven, Case Agent 6, to bolster probable cause, had added to the draft of FISA Renewal Application No. 3 statements that Page made during this meeting about an "October Surprise" involving an "email dump" of "33 thousand" emails. The OI Attorney told us that he used the 163-page document to accurately quote in the final renewal application Page's statements concerning the "October Surprise," but that he did not read the other aspects of the document and that the case agent did not flag for him the statements Page made about Manafort. The OI Attorney told us that these statements, which were available to the FBI before the first application, should have been flagged by the FBI for inclusion in all of the FISA applications because they were relevant to the court's assessment of the allegations concerning Manafort's use of Page as an intermediary with Russia. Case Agent 6 told us that he did not know that Page made the statement about Manafort because the August 2016 meeting took place before he was assigned to the investigation. He said that the reason he knew about the "October Surprise" statements in the document was that he had heard about them from Case Agent 1 and did a word search to find the specific discussion of that topic.

Regarding the similar statement Page made during one of his March 2017 interviews with the FBI, the OI Attorney told us that Case Agent 6 also did not flag this statement for him, but added that he (OI Attorney) should have noticed the

---

[310] According to Evans, Page's statement concerning Manafort in August 2016 "arguably carries more significance" than Page's later statements because the August 2016 statements took place before Page would have learned from the media that he was under investigation by the FBI.

[311] After reviewing a draft of this report, Case Agent 1 told the OIG that, because the Crossfire Hurricane team did not receive Report 95 until several weeks after Page told the CHS that he had "literally never met" Manafort, Case Agent 1 "may have overlooked" this statement when the FISA application was being prepared. He acknowledged that he should have provided the information to the OI attorney.

statement himself in the interview summary Case Agent 6 forwarded to him on March 24, 2017, since it was only five pages, and the OI Attorney had read the entire document.

As described previously, the FISA application contained several statements Carter Page made to an FBI CHS during a consensually monitored and recorded meeting in October 2016, before the first FISA application was filed. In an email sent the same day as the CHS meeting to Case Agent 1 and other members of the Crossfire Hurricane team, the OGC Attorney asked the team to promptly send OI information about the meeting, including, among other things, any "exculpatory" statements made by Carter Page during this meeting, which was "probably the most important" information to provide to OI. Case Agent 1 thereafter provided to OI, on the same day as the October 2016 meeting, some of the statements made by Page to the CHS.

We determined, however, that the information Case Agent 1 provided to OI, which was incorporated into the first FISA application, did not fully or accurately describe the information obtained by the FBI as a result of the meeting. According to the first FISA application, Page told the CHS during the meeting that the Russians would be giving him an "open checkbook." The application further stated that Page did not "provide [the CHS] any specific details to refute, dispel, or clarify the media reporting" regarding Page's contacts with Russian officials Sechin and Divyekin, but that he made "vague statements that minimized his activities." However, the application failed to include Page's statement during the meeting in which Page specifically denied meeting with Sechin and Divyekin, and denied even knowing who Divyekin was. The application did not contain these denials even though the application relied upon the allegations in Report 94 that Page had secret meetings with both Sechin and Divyekin while in Moscow in July 2016. The application also failed to include the fact that Page denied to the CHS knowing anything about the disclosure by WikiLeaks of hacked DNC emails, which was contrary to the information from Report 95 in the application. Further, the application alleged that "Page helped influence" the Republican Party "to alter [its] platform to be more sympathetic to the Russian cause." However, it did not reference the fact that Page said to the CHS during their meeting that he "stayed clear of that—there was a lot of conspiracy theories that I was one of them...[but] totally off the record...members of our team were working on that, and...in retrospect it's way better off that I...remained at arms length."[312]

When we asked Case Agent 1 why he failed to provide this information from the October CHS meeting to the OI Attorney in advance of the first FISA application, he told us that he did not think that Page's statements on these issues were specific. We noted, however, Case Agent 1 used the transcripts of the recording as the support in the Woods File for the statements in the FISA

---

[312] Page made other statements denying culpability to a FBI CHS during a consensually recorded meeting in January 2017, in which he generally criticized the Steele reports that had recently been published by *BuzzFeed*, calling them "complete lies," and said that the FBI was provided "false" evidence against him. We found no evidence that the FBI provided this information to OI for its consideration.

applications. We further noted that the documents in the Woods File specifically stated that Page "denied meeting with Sechin/Divyekin," and said he "stayed clear" of the efforts of the Republican platform committee and knew "nothing about" WikiLeaks. Neither Case Agent 1 nor SSA 1 noted the inconsistency during the Woods Procedures, even though instant messages show that SSA 1 also knew as of October 17 that Page denied ever knowing Divyekin. This inconsistency was also not noted during the Woods Procedures on the subsequent FISA renewal applications, and none of the three later FISA renewal applications included Page's denials to the CHS.

We found no information indicating that the FBI provided OI with the documents containing Page's denials before finalizing the first FISA application. Instead, Case Agent 1 provided a summary that did not contain those denials to the OI Attorney and that the OI Attorney relied upon that summary in drafting the first application. Evans told us that had NSD known of Page's denials regarding Sechin and Divyekin, it was the kind of information that would have been included in the application.

Before FISA Renewal Application No. 1, was filed in January 2017, the OI Attorney did receive the documents containing the denials Page made to the CHS in October 2016. Yet, the information about the meeting remained unchanged in the renewal applications. The OI Attorney told us that he did not recall the circumstances surrounding this, but he acknowledged that he should have updated the descriptions in the renewal applications to include Page's denials.

In the next chapter, we describe the FBI's activities involving Steele after the first FISA application, including the FBI's decision to close Steele as a CHS and the FBI's efforts to assess Steele's election reporting in 2016 and 2017.

CHAPTER SIX
FBI ACTIVITIES INVOLVING CHRISTOPHER STEELE AFTER THE FIRST FISA AND FBI EFFORTS TO ASSESS STEELE'S ELECTION REPORTING

As detailed in this chapter, shortly after the Foreign Intelligence Surveillance Court (FISC) issued orders under FISA authorizing surveillance of Carter Page by the FBI, the FBI closed Steele as a Confidential Human Source (CHS) because Steele disclosed his relationship with the FBI to a reporter. Following the FBI's closure of Steele, which we describe below, several other individuals provided the FBI with reports prepared by Steele, some of which the FBI had not previously received. Among the individuals who provided Steele's information to the FBI were Department attorney Bruce Ohr, who we discuss below and in more detail in Chapter Nine.

Additionally, following Steele's closure, the FBI disseminated the Steele election reporting to the U.S. Intelligence Community (USIC) and sought to have it included in the January 2017 Intelligence Community Assessment (ICA) relating to Russian interference with the U.S. elections, in large part because the FBI believed the information in Steele's reports to be credible, although the FBI made clear to the USIC that the information in the reports had not been fully corroborated. The FBI also made attempts in 2016 and 2017 to further assess the reliability of Steele's reports. Through those efforts, as we discuss in this chapter, the FBI discovered discrepancies between Steele's reporting and statements sub-sources made to the FBI, which raised doubts about the reliability of some of Steele's reports. The FBI also assessed the possibility that Russia was funneling disinformation to Steele, and the possibility that disinformation was included in his election reports.

As we describe in this chapter, the FBI concluded, among other things, that although consistent with known efforts by Russia to interfere in the 2016 U.S. elections, much of the material in the Steele election reports, including allegations about Donald Trump and members of the Trump campaign relied upon in the Carter Page FISA applications, could not be corroborated; that certain allegations were inaccurate or inconsistent with information gathered by the Crossfire Hurricane team; and that the limited information that was corroborated related to time, location, and title information, much of which was publicly available.

I. Steele's Briefing to *Mother Jones* and the FBI's Closure of Steele as a CHS in November 2016

At the end of October 2016, Steele provided a briefing to a *Mother Jones* reporter in which Steele disclosed that he had provided the FBI with information showing connections between candidate Trump and his campaign and the Russian government. On October 31, 2016, three days after then FBI Director James Comey's public announcement that the FBI was reopening its investigation into then Secretary Clinton's use of a private email server based on the receipt of new evidence, *Mother Jones* published an article titled "A Veteran Spy Has Given the FBI Information Alleging a Russian Operation to Cultivate Donald Trump." The article described the work of a "well-placed Western intelligence source" with a background in Russian intelligence who was sharing information with the FBI. The article presented information contained in Report 80, and quoted the officer as stating that, based on his interactions with the FBI, "[i]t's quite clear there was or is a pretty substantial inquiry going on."

Steele's handling agent, Handling Agent 1, told the OIG that he first learned of the *Mother Jones* article on November 1 when SSA 1 emailed him a copy. Handling Agent 1 telephoned Steele that day and asked him if he had spoken with the author of the article. According to Handling Agent 1's records, Steele confirmed that he had spoken with the author. Handling Agent 1's notes state that Steele was "concerned about the behavior of [the FBI] and was troubled by the actions of [the FBI] last Friday" (*i.e.*, Comey's announcement concerning the discovery of additional Clinton emails). The notes also state that Handling Agent 1 advised Steele that he must cease collecting information for the FBI, and it was unlikely that the FBI would continue a relationship with him. Handling Agent 1 told us he had no further contact with Steele after the November 1 telephone call.

Upon learning of Steele's actions, then Assistant Director E.W. "Bill" Priestap decided that Steele had to be closed immediately. Senior leaders in the FBI's International Operations Division concurred with this decision during a meeting on November 3 and advised the FBI's Legal Attaché (Legat) in the European city where, as described in Chapter Four, members of the Crossfire Hurricane team met with Steele in early October, that the decision to close Steele was "non-negotiable." Handling Agent 1 finalized the necessary paperwork on November 17, 2016, which stated that Steele was closed on November 1 and was being closed for cause due to his disclosure of his confidential relationship with the FBI to a third party.[313] Strzok told the OIG that the FBI closed Steele "because he was a control problem. We did not close him because we thought he was [a] fabricator." According to Strzok, Steele's decisions to discuss his reporting with the media and to disclose his relationship with the FBI were "horrible and it hurt what we were doing, and no question, he shouldn't have done it."

As a consequence of his closing, Handling Agent 1 halted payment of $15,000 to Steele. Handling Agent 1 told the OIG that the FBI never paid Steele for information related to the 2016 U.S. elections. FBI records show that Steele's last payment occurred on August 12, 2016, and was for information furnished to the FBI's Cyber and Counterintelligence Divisions (CD) that was unrelated to the 2016 U.S. elections.

Steele told us that by the time of the *Mother Jones* interview, he and Glenn Simpson of Fusion GPS had decided not to continue with the FBI because the FBI

---

[313] The Source Closing Communication document included the following: "Was the individual aware of his/her status as a CHS? Yes." As we described in Chapter Four, Steele told us he was not a CHS for the FBI and was never advised by Handling Agent 1 that he was a CHS—a claim that Handling Agent 1 disputes.

"was being deceitful." In particular, Steele stated that he had asked Ohr and possibly Handling Agent 1 prior to late October 2016 why the U.S. government had not announced that the FBI was investigating allegations concerning the Trump campaign. Steele said that he was told in response that the Hatch Act made it a criminal offense for a federal official to make a public statement within 90 days of an election to the detriment or benefit of a candidate.[314] Both Ohr and Handling Agent 1 told us that they had no recollection of discussing the Hatch Act with Steele. Steele explained that he became frustrated with the FBI at the end of October when Comey notified Congress close to the election that the FBI was reopening the Clinton email investigation and *The New York Times* quoted law enforcement officials as saying that they had found no direct link between Trump and the Russian government.[315] Steele said that he, his firm, and his clients believed it was not appropriate for the FBI to make announcements in violation of the Hatch Act while at the same time not disclosing its investigative activity concerning the Trump campaign. According to Steele, the FBI's conduct compelled him to choose between his client and the FBI, and he chose his client because he believed that the FBI had misled him. Steele said that Simpson arranged for the video conference interview with *Mother Jones* and Simpson actively participated in the call along with Steele. Steele told us that he believed the interview was "off the record" and under the same rules as his other interviews arranged by Simpson. He does not know whether Simpson either before or after the interview may have changed the rules.

According to FBI officials, knowledge of Steele's disclosure to *Mother Jones* did not cause the team to reassess whether Steele was also the source of the disclosures to *Yahoo News* in September 2016. As described in Chapter Seven, the language in the Carter Page FISA Renewal Application No. 1 regarding the September 23 *Yahoo News* article remained unchanged, again stating that the FBI "does not believe that Source #1 [Steele] directly provided this information to [*Yahoo News*]." The National Security Division's (NSD) Office of Intelligence (OI) Unit Chief's notes from a November 29 meeting with the OI Attorney drafting the Carter Page FISA renewal application and the FBI Office of the General Counsel (OGC) Attorney stated "[Steele] was not the leaker to *Yahoo*" and noted "DD [Deputy Director] has signed off on requesting the FISA renewal."[316] The OI Unit Chief told us that the OGC Attorney made this statement, but that the OGC Attorney did not provide a basis for the assertion regarding the *Yahoo News* article. During his OIG interview, we asked the OGC Attorney if he knew the reason for the FBI's belief that Steele was not the leaker to *Yahoo News* and he said he was under the impression that Simpson was sharing the information with other entities. SSA 1

---

[314] The Hatch Act is codified at 5 U.S.C. §§ 7321-7326. Section 7323(a)(1) provides that "an employee may not use his official authority or influence for the purpose of interfering with or affecting the result of an election."

[315] "Investigating Donald Trump, F.B.I. Sees No Clear Link to Russia," *The New York Times*, October 31, 2016.

[316] As described in Chapter Seven, then Deputy Director Andrew McCabe told us that as Deputy Director he did not approve FISA requests before they were submitted to OI, but following the disclosures to *Mother Jones*, the FBI was comfortable seeking a FISA renewal targeting Carter Page.

and Case Agent 1 told us they did not recall any discussions about changing the FBI's assessment in the FISA application concerning the *Yahoo News* disclosure after learning Steele was responsible for the disclosure to *Mother Jones*. On December 19, 2016, Case Agent 1 interviewed then FBI General Counsel James Baker regarding his interactions with a *Mother Jones* reporter and Baker told Case Agent 1 that the reporter advised Baker that a former intelligence official "was passing information 'around town'" about Trump. Case Agent 1 said that by this time, the team had also heard rumors that Steele's reporting had been "floated around," so it was not clear to them who made the *Yahoo News* disclosure. Further, we were told that, after the FBI closed Steele as a CHS, the team was not going to have further communications with Steele.

II.   The FBI Receives Additional Steele Reporting Post-Election

Following the November 2016 U.S. elections, several third parties provided the FBI with additional Steele election reporting, which the FBI included in its validation efforts. Baker told the OIG that a *Mother Jones* reporter contacted him and furnished him with nine reports from Steele, four of which Steele had not previously provided to the FBI.[317] As described above, Baker was interviewed by Case Agent 1 and Baker's discussion with the *Mother Jones* reporter was documented in an FBI FD-302 report. According to the FD-302, Baker received a collection of Steele's reports from the *Mother Jones* reporter, which Baker forwarded to Priestap for analysis.[318]

Several weeks later, on December 9, 2016, Senator John McCain provided Comey with a collection of 16 Steele election reports, 5 of which Steele had not given the FBI.[319] McCain had obtained these reports from a staff member at the McCain Institute. The McCain Institute staff member had met with Steele and later acquired the reports from Simpson. Steele told the OIG that a former European Ambassador to Russia who generally was familiar with Steele's election reporting informed Steele that the former Ambassador would be meeting with Senator McCain at a conference in Nova Scotia in November, and asked Steele whether he wanted the former Ambassador to talk with McCain about the election reporting. Steele said he replied that he did, which resulted in the McCain Institute staff member visiting Steele in Europe in late November. According to deposition testimony the McCain Institute staff member provided in foreign litigation, during

---

[317] The nine Steele reports were Reports 80, 94, 95, 97, 105, 111, 112, 134, and 136. The FBI had not previously obtained Reports 97, 105, and 112 from Steele. According to an FBI FD-302, in a conversation later that month, the *Mother Jones* reporter advised Baker that the Steele reports also had been furnished to two Members of Congress, and that Steele was surprised that his reporting had not received more attention in the media.

[318] The *Mother Jones* reporter has stated publicly that he provided Steele reports to Baker. See "A New Right-Wing Smear Campaign Targets a Former FBI Official to Distract From Russia Scandal," *Mother Jones*, www.motherjones.com/politics/2019/01/a-new-right-wing-smear-campaign-targets-a-former-fbi-official-to-distract-from-russia-scandal/ (accessed November 22, 2019).

[319] These were Steele Reports 80, 86, 94, 95, 97, 100, 101, 102, 105, 111, 112, 113, 130, 134, 135, and 136. FBI records show that the FBI had not previously received Reports 86, 97, 105, 112 and 113 from Steele.

this visit Steele discussed his reporting with the staff member and showed the staff member a piece of paper on which Steele had written the true names of his sub-sources, although the staff member could not recall them. Steele told us that he shared some of the sub-source names with the staff member because the staff member was a "Russia expert" and had been tasked by Senator McCain to determine whether Steele's reporting was serious. The staff member also testified that Steele explained to him that the information in the reports needed to be corroborated and verified and that Steele was not in a position "to vouch for everything that was produced...."

Additionally, as we detail in Chapter Nine, on December 10, Department attorney Bruce Ohr received a thumb drive from Simpson containing some of Steele's election reports and provided the thumb drive to the FBI.[320] Included among the reports on the thumb drive was a document that the Crossfire Hurricane team had not previously seen, which recounted that a senior official in the Russian Ministry of Foreign Affairs had reported that a rumor was circulating that President-elect Trump's delay in appointing a new Secretary of State was the result of an "intervention" by Putin and the Kremlin, and that they had requested Trump appoint a "Russia-friendly" figure who was prepared to lift sanctions against Russia.

Finally, by early January 2017, *BuzzFeed* had obtained copies of some of the Steele election reports during a meeting with the McCain Institute staff member and published them as part of an article titled "These Reports Allege Trump Has Deep Ties to Russia."[321] Included in this collection was Report 166, another report that previously had not been shared with the FBI. It included allegations that Trump attorney Michael Cohen had held secret discussions in Prague in late summer 2016 with representatives of the Kremlin and "associated operators/hackers," and that the "anti-Clinton hackers" had been paid by the "[Trump] team" and Kremlin.[322] The FBI eventually concluded that these allegations against Cohen and the "Trump team" were not true.

---

[320] These were the same Steele reports that Senator McCain gave to Comey on December 9, except that the thumb drive did not include Report 130.

[321] Steele testified in foreign litigation that he did not provide his reports to journalists or media organizations and did not authorize anyone to share them. According to the McCain Institute staff member's testimony in the same litigation, Steele requested that the staff member meet with *BuzzFeed*, and that Steele neither requested nor prohibited the staff member from sharing the reports with *BuzzFeed*. Additionally, the staff member testified that Steele was aware that the staff member was furnishing Steele's reports to *The Washington Post*. Steele told the OIG that he trusted the staff member to handle his reports discretely and that the staff member betrayed that trust. Steele explained that the staff member had spent his career handling sensitive intelligence. Steele also said he understood from a former Ambassador that Senator McCain requested that Steele trust the staff member. Steele said he was "absolutely flabbergasted" when *BuzzFeed* published his election reports.

[322] On January 10, 2017, following the media release of the Steele election reports, Strzok texted Lisa Page:

6:09 p.m.: "Sitting with Bill watching CNN. A TON more out."

III. The FBI Disseminates the Steele Reporting to the U.S. Intelligence Community and Seeks to Have It Included in the January 2017 Intelligence Community Assessment

According to the Supervisory Intelligence Analyst (Supervisory Intel Analyst), the FBI first shared Steele's reporting with other U.S. government intelligence agencies in December 2016, when the FBI provided it to an interagency ICA drafting team that was set up in response to a request from President Obama to complete a comprehensive assessment of the Russian government's intentions and actions concerning the 2016 elections.[323] Members of the interagency ICA drafting team from the FBI, National Security Agency (NSA), and Central Intelligence Agency (CIA), with oversight from the Office of the Director of National Intelligence (ODNI), worked jointly to prepare a report known as the Intelligence Community Assessment (ICA). As part of these efforts, both Priestap and the FBI's Section Chief of CD's Analysis Section 1 (Intel Section Chief) wrote to the CIA in separate correspondence and described Steele as "reliable."

Whether and how to present Steele's reporting in the ICA was a topic of significant discussion within the FBI and with the other agencies participating in drafting the ICA. On December 16, 2016, the Intel Section Chief explained in an email to the FBI:

> DD [Deputy Director] wants the [Steele] reporting included in the submission with some level of detail, to include the newest stuff that [Supervisory Intel Analyst] can send you on the red side. Include details like the potential compromising material, etc. Can you please add a section (characterizing [Steele] obviously) in coordination with [Supervisory Intel Analyst]?

The Intel Section Chief told us that he asked then Deputy Director Andrew McCabe whether McCabe wanted to limit the FBI's submission to information concerning Russian election interference or to also include allegations against candidate Trump. The Intel Section Chief said that McCabe understood President Obama's request for the ICA to require the participating agencies to share all information relevant to Russia and the 2016 elections, and the Steele election reporting qualified at a minimum due to concerns over possible Russian attempts to blackmail Trump. That same day, the Intel Section Chief sent to Priestap, Strzok, and another senior official in CD an updated draft of the FBI's submission for the

---

6:18 p.m.: "Hey let me know when you can talk. We're discussing whether, now that this is out, we use it as a pretext to go interview some people."

Strzok told the OIG that he believed these texts were referencing the possibility of interviewing one of Trump's attorneys, Michael Cohen, and Manafort using the release of the Steele reports as the stated reason for seeking the interview, without revealing the ongoing investigation. Strzok said the media release of the reports would be a logical reason for the FBI to interview Cohen and Manafort without alerting them to the Crossfire Hurricane investigation.

[323] Strzok said that he believed that the FBI also may have furnished the Steele election reports to the intelligence service of a friendly foreign government but he did not have a specific recollection of it.

ICA with the following explanation: "Attached is the updated draft of [the] FBI's submission to the POTUS-tasked election targeting study. It now incorporates the [Steele] reporting at the DD's [Deputy Director's] request. This has obviously increased the sensitivity of the attached document." The Intel Section Chief said that the heightened sensitivity resulted from the reporting's allegations of collusion: "The minute we put the [Steele election reporting] in there, it goes from what you'd expect the FBI to be collecting in a counterintelligence context to direct allegations about collusion with the Trump campaign."

The following day, December 17, Comey completed his review of the FBI's draft submission for the ICA and emailed Priestap, McCabe, Strzok, the Intel Section Chief, the FBI Director's Chief of Staff, and Baker describing a call he had with then Director of National Intelligence (DNI) James Clapper:

> Thanks. Looks okay to me. FYI: During a secure call last night on this general topic, I informed the DNI that we would be contributing the [Steele] reporting (although I didn't use that name) to the IC [Intelligence Community] effort. I stressed that we were proceeding cautiously to understand and attempt to verify the reporting as best we can, but we thought it important to bring it forward to the IC effort. I told him the source of the material, which included salacious material about the President-Elect, was a former [███████████████ ███████████] who appears to be a credible person with a source and sub-source network in position to report on such things, but we could not vouch for the material. (I said nothing further about the source or our efforts to verify).

> I added that I believed that the material, in some form or fashion, had been widely circulated in Washington and that Senator McCain had delivered to me a copy of the reports and Senator Burr had mentioned to me the part about Russian knowledge of sexual activity by the President-Elect while in Russia. The DNI asked whether anyone in the White House was aware of this and I said "not to my knowledge." He thanked me for letting him know and we didn't discuss further.

According to the Intel Section Chief and Supervisory Intel Analyst, as the interagency editing process for the ICA progressed, the CIA expressed concern about using the Steele election reporting in the text of the ICA. The Supervisory Intel Analyst explained that the CIA believed that the Steele election reporting was not completely vetted and did not merit inclusion in the body of the report. The Intel Section Chief stated that the CIA viewed it as "internet rumor."

On December 28, 2016, McCabe wrote to the then ODNI Principal Deputy Director objecting to the CIA's proposal to present the Steele information in an appendix to the ICA. McCabe wrote:

> I would also like to speak with you tomorrow about my concerns about where the [Steele] references will appear in the joint report, notwithstanding the fact that it is officially part of the assessment. We

178

oppose CIA's current plan to include it as an appendix; there are a number of reasons why I feel strongly that it needs to appear in some fashion in the main body of the reporting, and I would welcome the chance to talk to you about it tomorrow.

McCabe told the OIG that he had three reasons for believing that the Steele election reporting needed to be included in the ICA: (1) President Obama had requested "everything you have relevant to this topic of Russian influence"; (2) the Steele election reporting was not completely vetted, but was consistent with information from other sources and came from a source with "a good track record" that the FBI had "confidence in"; and (3) McCabe believed the FBI, as an institution, needed to advise the President about the Steele election reporting because it had been widely circulated throughout government and media circles, and was likely to leak into the public realm. McCabe said he felt strongly that the Steele election reporting belonged in the body of the ICA, because he feared that placing it in an appendix was "tacking it on" in a way that would "minimiz[e]" the information and prevent it from being properly considered.

McCabe's view did not prevail. The final ICA report was completed early in the first week of January 2017, and included a short summary and assessment of the Steele election reporting, which was incorporated in an appendix. In the appendix, the intelligence agencies explained that there was "only limited corroboration of the source's reporting" and that Steele's election reports were not used "to reach analytic conclusions of the CIA/FBI/NSA assessment." The Intel Section Chief told us that the reference to "limited corroboration" was addressed to the "whole body" of Steele's reporting and not just those portions concerning Trump. He said that there was corroboration of certain facts as well as "the thrust" of the reporting regarding Russia's actions to disrupt the election and cause discord in the western alliance.

We asked Comey whether he recalled having any conversations with then CIA Director John Brennan or other members of the USIC about how the Steele election reports should be presented to the President. Comey stated:

> I remember being part of a conversation, maybe more than one conversation, where the topic was how the [Steele] reporting would be integrated, if at all, into the IC assessment. And I don't remember participating in debates about that. I think I was just told, in, I think, in a meeting with Clapper and Brennan and Rogers [then NSA Director], that the IC analysts found it credible on its face and gravamen of it, and consistent with our other information, but not in a position where they would integrate it into the IC assessment. But they thought it was important enough and consistent enough that it ought to be part of the package in some way, and so they had come up with this idea to make an [appendix]. I remember, I don't think I was part of a debate about that, as I said, but I remember a conversation where I was told that's how it would be handled and my reaction was, okay, that's reasonable.

According to Comey, the inclusion of the Steele election reporting as an appendix to the ICA was not a value judgment about the quality of the information. Instead, it reflected the relatively uncorroborated and incomplete status of the FBI's assessment. Comey told the OIG that the Steele election reporting was "not ripe enough, mature enough, to be in a finished intelligence product."

On January 5, 2017, Clapper, then NSA Director Michael Rogers, Brennan, and Comey briefed the ICA report to President Obama and his national security team, followed by a briefing for Congressional leadership on the morning of January 6, 2017, and finally a briefing for then President-elect Trump and his national security team on the afternoon of January 6, 2017. Comey told the OIG that the plan for the ICA briefing of President-elect Trump had two parts. The first part of the briefing, jointly conducted by Clapper, Brennan, Rogers, and Comey, involved advising Trump and his national security team of the overall conclusions of the ICA. The second part of the briefing involved notifying the President-elect of information from Steele's reporting that concerned Trump's alleged sexual activities in Moscow several years earlier. Comey stated that the other USIC Directors agreed that Trump had to be briefed on this information, and Clapper decided the briefing should be done by Comey in a small group or alone with the President-elect.

According to an email Comey sent to FBI officials on January 7, 2017, Comey mentioned during the initial portion of the briefing a piece of Steele's reporting that indicated Russia had files of derogatory information on both Clinton and the President-elect. Comey's email stated that a member of Trump's national security team asked during the briefing whether the FBI was "trying to dig into the sub-sources" to gain a better understanding of the situation, and Comey responded in the affirmative.

Comey's email reflects that, after the first portion of the meeting ended, Comey stayed behind to speak with President-elect Trump alone about the part of the Steele election reporting that dealt with Trump's alleged sexual activity. Comey's email reflects that he explained that according to Steele's sub-sources, the Russians had a file on the President-elect's alleged sexual activities while in Russia and possessed tapes of him with prostitutes at the Presidential Suite at the Ritz Carlton hotel in Moscow. The email further states that Comey explained that the material was "inflammatory stuff" and that a news organization "would get killed for reporting straight up from the source reports." In testimony before Congress, Comey has described this part of his email as communicating that "it was salacious and unverified material that a responsible journalist wouldn't report without corroborating in some way." Comey told the OIG that he informed President-elect Trump that the FBI did not know whether the allegations were true or false and that the FBI was not investigating them.[324]

---

[324] In the OIG's *Report of Investigation of Former Federal Bureau of Investigation Director James Comey's Disclosure of Sensitive Investigative Information and Handling of Certain Memoranda* (August 2019), we described Comey's creation of the January 7, 2017 email that memorialized his January 6, 2017 meeting with Trump. Prior to this meeting, Comey met with senior leaders of the FBI and the Crossfire Hurricane investigation and discussed a number of concerns about Comey meeting

After *BuzzFeed* published the Steele election reports on January 10, 2017, and news reports began describing the January 6 ICA briefing of President-elect Trump, Clapper informed Comey by email on January 11 that he had a telephone conversation with President-elect Trump that included discussion of the Steele "[election reporting]." Clapper included in the email to Comey a draft media statement by Clapper for public release, which stated that "[t]he IC [Intelligence Community] has not made any judgment that the information in [the Steele election reporting] is reliable, and we did not rely upon it in any way for our conclusions" in the ICA. Comey responded to the email with proposed revisions to Clapper's text:

> I just had a chance to review the proposed talking points on this for today. Perhaps it is a nit, but I worry that it may not be best to say "The IC has not made any judgment that the information in the document is reliable." I say that because we HAVE concluded that the source [Steele] is reliable and has a track record with us of reporting reliable information; we have some visibility into his source network, some of which we have determined to be sub-sources in a position to report on such things; and much of what he reports in the current document is consistent with and corroborative of other reporting included in the body of the main IC report. That said, we are not able to sufficiently corroborate the reporting to include in the body of the [ICA] report.

> That all rings in my ears as more complicated than "we have not made a judgment that the information in the document is reliable." It might be better to say that "we have not be [sic] able to sufficiently corroborate the information to include it in the body of our Russia report but, for a variety of reasons, we thought it important to include it in our report to our senior-most audience.

The ODNI released Clapper's media statement on January 11, 2017, which was captioned "DNI Clapper Statement on Conversation with President-elect Trump."[325] The sentence that Comey had raised concerns about in his email to Clapper remained unchanged and thus Clapper's statement included the following sentence regarding Steele's election reporting: "The IC has not made any

---

alone with Trump. One of the topics discussed was Trump's potential responses to being told about the "salacious" information, including that Trump might make statements, or provide information of value, to the Crossfire Hurricane investigation. Witnesses recalled agreeing that Comey should memorialize his meeting with Trump immediately after it occurred. Comey told the OIG that, in his view, it was important for the FBI executive managers to be "able to share in [Comey's] recall of the...salient details of those conversations" with Trump, and that if the meeting became "a source of controversy" it would be important to have a clear, contemporaneous record because Comey was concerned that Trump might "misrepresent what happened in the encounter."

[325] The statement can be found at https://www.dni.gov/index.php/newsroom/press-releases/item/1736-dni-clapper-statement-on-conversation-with-president-elect-trump (accessed Dec. 8, 2019).

judgment that the information in [the Steele election reporting] is reliable, and we did not rely upon it in any way for our conclusions" in the ICA.

IV.   FBI Validation Efforts Following Steele's Closure as a CHS

As described in Chapter Four, the FBI closed Steele as a CHS in November 2016 after he disclosed his relationship with the FBI to a news outlet. Although Steele was no longer a CHS, the FBI continued with its efforts to validate his reporting. This section describes those efforts.

A.   Information from Persons with Direct Knowledge of Steele's Work-Related Performance in a Prior Position

In mid-November and December 2016, FBI officials travelled abroad and met with persons who previously had professional contacts with Steele or had knowledge of his work.[326] According to Strzok, one of the purposes of the trips was to obtain information regarding Steele from persons with direct knowledge of Steele's work-related performance in a prior position in order to help the FBI assess Steele's reliability. Priestap said that it was not standard practice to take such a trip to assess a CHS, but in this case he believed it was important due to the nature of the information that the CHS provided and because the FBI was under a great deal of scrutiny. In his view, "[t]he bottom line is we had concerns about the reporting the day we got it.... [S]ome of it was so sensational, that we just, we did not take it at face value."

Priestap and Strzok took notes of the feedback that they received about Steele, some of which was positive and some of which was negative.[327] Their notes included positive comments such as "smart," "person of integrity," "no reason to doubt integrity" and "[i]f he reported it, he believed it." Priestap told us that his impression was that Steele's former colleagues considered Steele to be a "Russia expert" and very competent in his work. However, Priestap and Strzok also were provided with various negative comments concerning Steele's judgment. Their notes stated: "[d]emonstrates lack of self-awareness, poor judgment;" "[k]een to help" but "underpinned by poor judgment;" "Judgment: pursuing people with political risk but no intel value;" "[d]idn't always exercise great judgment— sometimes [he] believes he knows best;" and "[r]eporting in good faith, but not clear what he would have done to validate." Priestap told us that he understood the commentary on Steele's judgment to mean that Steele strongly believed in his convictions, which did not always align with management's convictions, leading to conflicts over priorities. Strzok described the feedback as follows:

> And many of them...almost without exception said, look, he is truthful.
> He has never been accused of, nor did anybody think he is an

---

embellisher, let alone a fabricator. That, if anything, he, to the extent there were negatives, it was that he was the type of person who would sometimes follow the shiny object without, perhaps, a deep set of judgment about the risk that may or may not be there in terms of following the shiny object. But in any event, he was not the type of person who would fabricate something or make something up or mischaracterize it, either intentionally or unintentionally.

Priestap said he interpreted the comments about Steele's judgment to mean that "if he latched on to something...he thought that was the most important thing on the face of this earth" and added that this personality trait doesn't necessarily "jump out as a particularly bad or horrible [one]" because, as a manager, it can be helpful if the "people reporting to [you] think the stuff they're working on is the most important thing going on" and use their best efforts to pursue it. Information from these meetings was shared with the Crossfire Hurricane team. However, we found that it was not memorialized in Steele's Delta file and therefore not considered in a validation review conducted by the FBI's Validation Management Unit (VMU) in early 2017.[328] In addition, as described in Chapter Eight, some of the relevant details about Steele's work-related performance in a prior position were not shared with OI and were not included in any of the Carter Page FISA renewal applications, even though the applications relied upon Steele's reporting.

B. The FBI's Human Source Validation Review of Steele in March 2017

Another method that the FBI utilized to evaluate Steele was the FBI's standard validation process. As we described in Chapter Two, the validation process ██ ██████████████████████████████████████. Throughout the FBI's operation of Steele as a CHS, Handling Agent 1 regularly submitted ███████████████ source reports that furnished information relevant to these factors. With the exception of Steele's last annual report, which described his disclosure of information to the media and resulted in his closure for cause, the reports depict Steele positively with no derogatory information noted. For example, the 2015 annual report states that "[s]ource provided relevant and significant intel on activities of Eurasian criminals to include OC [organized crime] members and associates, businessmen/oligarchs and politicians." The annual reports also noted that some of Steele's information had been corroborated.

The FBI continued its validation efforts into 2017 after SSA 1 requested that VMU perform a Human Source Validation Review (HSVR) on Steele.[329] SSA 1

---

[328] Priestap told the OIG that he recalled that he may have made a commitment to ████████ ██████████████.

[329] SSA 1 initially requested the HSVR in November 2016, which the Unit Chief of VMU confirmed. However, CD delayed the initiation of the HSVR due to the sensitivity of the subject matter and concerns over leaks. Strzok stated that another consideration was uncertainty about whether the assessment would add significant value. The HSVR was restarted in early February 2017.

explained that "I wanted to ensure that an independent asset validation was conducted by our Directorate of Intelligence, and not just the people that were working the Crossfire Hurricane case, to ensure the totality of his information was being looked at." SSA 3, who started work on the Crossfire Hurricane investigation in January 2017, and others recalled that there were multiple discussions about the need to complete an HSVR and that initiation of the review had been delayed for several weeks. VMU completed its report on March 23, 2017 after evaluating Steele's Delta file, conducting various database searches, and engaging in a limited email exchange with Handling Agent 1 as well as an agent on the Crossfire Hurricane team. The VMU assessment did not independently corroborate information in the Steele election reporting, but it did include searching inside FBI and U.S. government holdings, including Delta, for such corroboration.[330]

The validation report made a number of findings. The VMU found no issues regarding Steele's reliability or nothing to suggest that he had fabricated information, and determined that he was "suitable for continued operation" based on his authenticity and reliability. The report noted, however, that Steele was closed due to his disclosure of his FBI relationship to an online publication. The report also noted two compliance issues. First, ███. Second, the report noted that ██.

The "Summary" portion of the validation report included the following text:

VMU assesses it is likely [Steele] has contributed to the FBI's Criminal Program. VMU makes this assessment with medium confidence, based on the fact that [Steele's] reporting has been minimally corroborated; his or her access and placement is commensurate with his or her reporting; and on the presence of one major control issue [the disclosure to the media] noted in [Steele's] Delta file.

Handling Agent 1 told us that the finding that Steele's past criminal reporting was "minimally corroborated" was consistent with his understanding of the entire collection of Steele's reporting to the FBI. However, Priestap, who previously oversaw the work of VMU in his capacity as Deputy Assistant Director in the Directorate of Intelligence, explained that when he reviewed the Steele validation report it "jump[ed] out" to him that the report indicated that Steele's reporting was "minimally corroborated." He stated: "I had always understood that [Steele] had a long, successful track record of reporting, that had withstood, in effect, judicial or

---

[330] As noted above, Steele's Delta file did not include the views of persons with direct knowledge of Steele's work-related performance in a prior position, obtained by Strzok and Priestap in December 2016, or information generated by the Transnational Organized Crime Intelligence Unit, as described in Chapter Four, that raised questions about the extent of Steele's apparent connections to Russian oligarchs.

court-of-law scrutiny, and so when I saw 'minimally corroborated,' that was different than I had understood it."[331]

The validation report summary did not appear to assess Steele's counterintelligence and election reporting. We asked the Unit Chief of VMU (Validation SSA), about this and he told us "[w]e did not find corroboration for the [Steele election reporting]" from the holdings that VMU examined. He explained that, within the validation context, the term "corroboration" means that the FBI has received the same information from a separate source, and added that "uncorroborated" does not mean the information is untrue or provide a basis for closing the source. We asked why that finding did not appear in the validation report. The Validation SSA explained that "it's not common practice for us to go in and state the negative upfront," and "what we do is we speak to what we positively find."[332] He added: "I think it is a logical way to stay within the bounds of staying with what we know. As opposed to telling you all the things we don't know."

The VMU's decision to not include in the validation report that it did not find corroboration for Steele's election reporting came as a surprise to the FBI officials we interviewed. For example, Priestap told us that omitting that the "[Steele election reporting]" information was uncorroborated "defeats the whole purpose of us asking them to do the validation reporting." Priestap continued:

> [T]hat makes no sense to me. The whole point of having a human source validation section outside of the operational divisions is to provide an absolutely independent, unbiased, completely unbiased, look at the human sources. They have to do a report at the end. It's simply the way in which they document their findings. It is beyond me how somebody would undertake that effort and then not document their findings in that regard. That, to me, that goes against everything I stand for. It goes against what my organization stands for, it's like you are burying the results.

Strzok said that the validation report's lack of clarity was consistent with his past experience with VMU, and that VMU's work is "frequently ambiguous or perhaps not written with the level of precision and specificity and expertise that might be desired." He also stated that validation reports are "rarely helpful." Both the Intel Section Chief and Supervisory Intel Analyst said that they did not agree with the Validation SSA's conclusion that the Steele [election reporting] was "uncorroborated." They explained that there is a distinction between facts and

---

[331] We discuss in Chapters Five and Eight the FISA application's source characterization statement that Steele's reporting had been "corroborated and used in criminal proceedings."

[332] The OIG's Audit Division recently completed a review of the FBI's CHS validation processes finding, among other things, that FBI validation personnel were discouraged from documenting conclusions from CHS validation reviews in their written reports. The OIG report made numerous recommendations to the FBI to revise and improve the validation process. *See* U.S. Department of Justice (DOJ) Office of the Inspector General (OIG), *Audit of the Federal Bureau of Investigation's Management of its Confidential Human Source Validation Processes*, Audit Report 20-009 (November 2019), at 24-26.

allegations, and that it would not be appropriate to characterize all of the factual information in the Steele election reporting as "uncorroborated."[333]

Lastly, the validation report included a recommendation that ██████████ ██ ██ ██ ██ ██████████████████████████████████████ Source reporting must accurately describe the reliability of the information or its origin.

C. The FBI Identifies and Interviews the Primary Sub-Source in Early 2017

An important aspect of the FBI's assessment of Steele's election reporting involved evaluating Steele's source network, especially whether the sub-sources had access to reliable information. As noted in the first FISA application, Steele relied on a primary sub-source (Primary Sub-source) for information, and this Primary Sub-source used a network of sub-sources to gather the information that was relayed to Steele; Steele himself was not the originating source of any of the factual information in his reporting.[334] The FBI employed multiple methods in an effort to ascertain the identities of the sub-sources within the network, including meeting with Steele in October 2016 (prior to him being closed for cause) and conducting various investigative inquiries. For example, the FBI determined it was plausible that at least some of the sub-sources had access to intelligence pertinent to events described in Steele's election reporting. Additionally, the FBI's evaluation of Steele's sub-sources generated some corroboration for the election reporting (primarily routine facts about dates, locations, and occupational positions that was mostly public source information). Further, by January 2017 the FBI was able to identify and arrange a meeting with the Primary Sub-source.[335]

The FBI conducted interviews of the Primary Sub-source in January, March, and May 2017 that raised significant questions about the reliability of the Steele election reporting. In particular, the FBI's interview with Steele's Primary Sub-source in January 2017, shortly after the FBI filed the Carter Page FISA Renewal

---

[333] We discuss the FBI's conclusions about the reporting in Section V of this chapter.

[334] When interviewed by the FBI, the Primary Sub-source stated that ████████ ██ ████████████████████████████████████ The Primary Sub-source was ██

[335] Steele did not disclose the identity of the Primary Sub-source to the FBI.

Application No. 1 and months prior to Renewal Application No. 2, raised doubts about the reliability of Steele's descriptions of information in his election reports. During the FBI's January interview, at which Case Agent 1, the Supervisory Intel Analyst, and representatives of NSD were present, the Primary Sub-source told the FBI that he/she had not seen Steele's reports until they became public that month, and that he/she made statements indicating that Steele misstated or exaggerated the Primary Sub-source's statements in multiple sections of the reporting.[336] For example, the Primary Sub-source told the FBI that, while Report 80 stated that Trump's alleged sexual activities at the Ritz Carlton hotel in Moscow had been "confirmed" by a senior, western staff member at the hotel, the Primary Sub-source explained that he/she reported to Steele that Trump's alleged unorthodox sexual activity at the Ritz Carlton hotel was "rumor and speculation" and that he/she had not been able to confirm the story. A second example provided by the Primary Sub-source was Report 134's description of a meeting allegedly held between Carter Page and Igor Sechin, the President of Rosneft, a Russian energy conglomerate.[337] Report 134 stated that, according to a "close associate" of Sechin, Sechin offered "PAGE/TRUMP's associates the brokerage of up to a 19 percent (privatized) stake in Rosneft" in return for the lifting of sanctions against the company.[338] The Primary Sub-source told the FBI that one of his/her sub-sources furnished information for that part of Report 134 through a text message, but said that the sub-source never stated that Sechin had offered a brokerage interest to Page.[339] We reviewed the texts and did not find any discussion of a bribe, whether as an interest in Rosneft itself or a "brokerage."[340]

---

[336] David Laufman, then Chief of NSD's Counterintelligence and Export Control Section (CES), covered the first portion of the January interview and his Deputy Section Chief covered the remaining portions of the January interview. Laufman told us that he negotiated with the Primary Sub-source's counsel to facilitate the FBI's interview and sought to "build a cooperative relationship that could...result in the Bureau's being in a position to assess the validity of information in the [Steele election reporting] resulting from [the Primary Sub-source's] activities or the collection of [his/her] sub-subsources. So I saw my role as a broker to get that relationship consolidated." Laufman said that the portion of the interview he attended established the line of communication with the Primary Sub-source and, as he recalled, generally covered the facts in a "superficial" way. He said that after the completion of the interview, he never saw the FBI's written summary of the interview.

[337] According to the Supervisory Intel Analyst, the FBI was not able to prove or disprove Page's meeting with Sechin. The Analyst explained that Page did meet with a Rosneft official—Andrey Baranov, during his July 2016 trip to Moscow and that Page told the FBI that Baranov might have mentioned the possible sale of a stake in Rosneft. The Analyst stated that Report 134's mention of Sechin could be a "garble" for Baranov.

[338] Report 134 contained differing information on the alleged bribe offered by Sechin to Page. The Report first stated that Sechin offered Page a "large stake in Rosneft in return for lifting sanctions on Russia." Later, the same report stated that Sechin had offered Page a much smaller sum of money, "the brokerage of up to a 19 per cent (privatized) stake in Rosneft."

[339] The Primary Sub-source also told the FBI at these interviews that the sub-source who provided the information about the Carter Page-Sechin meeting ████████████████████████ ██

[340] According to a press report prior to the date of Report 134, a 19-percent stake in Rosneft could have sold for more than $10 billion. See https://www.cnbc.com/2016/06/08/russias-oil-giant-

The Primary Sub-source was questioned again by the FBI beginning in March 2017 about the election reporting and his/her communications with Steele. The Washington Field Office agent (WFO Agent 1) who conducted that interview and others after it told the OIG that the Primary Sub-source felt that the tenor of Steele's reports was far more "conclusive" than was justified. The Primary Sub-source also stated that he/she never expected Steele to put the Primary Sub-source's statements in reports or present them as facts. According to WFO Agent 1, the Primary Sub-source said he/she made it clear to Steele that he/she had no proof to support the statements from his/her sub-sources and that "it was just talk." WFO Agent 1 said that the Primary Sub-source explained that his/her information came from "word of mouth and hearsay;" "conversation that [he/she] had with friends over beers;" and that some of the information, such as allegations about Trump's sexual activities, were statements he/she heard made in "jest."[341] The Primary Sub-source also told WFO Agent 1 that he/she believed that the other sub-sources exaggerated their access to information and the relevance of that information to his/her requests. The Primary Sub-source told WFO Agent 1 that he/she "takes what [sub-sources] tell [him/her] with 'a grain of salt.'"

In addition, the FBI interviews with the Primary Sub-source revealed that Steele did not have good insight into how many degrees of separation existed between the Primary Sub-source's sub-sources and the persons quoted in the reporting, and that it could have been multiple layers of hearsay upon hearsay. For example, the Primary Sub-source stated to WFO Agent 1 that, in contrast to the impression left from the election reports, his/her sub-sources did not have direct access to the persons they were reporting on. Instead, the Primary Sub-source told WFO Agent 1 that their information was "from someone else who may have had access."

The Primary Sub-source also informed WFO Agent 1 that Steele tasked him/her after the 2016 U.S. elections to find corroboration for the election reporting and that the Primary Sub-source could find none. According to WFO Agent 1, during an interview in May 2017, the Primary Sub-source said the corroboration was "zero." The Primary Sub-source had reported the same conclusion to the Crossfire Hurricane team members who interviewed him/her in January 2017.

Following the January interview with the Primary Sub-source, on February 15, 2017, Strzok forwarded by email to Priestap and others a news article referencing the Steele election reporting; Strzok commented that "recent interviews and investigation, however, reveal [Steele] may not be in a position to judge the reliability of his sub-source network." According to the Supervisory Intel Analyst, the cause for the discrepancies between the election reporting and explanations

---

just-saw-its-profits-drop-75.html (accessed Dec. 8, 2019). We discuss below the issue of Steele or the sub-sources presenting their analyses as statements of Kremlin officials or others.

[341] According to WFO Agent 1, the Primary Sub-source told him that he/she spoke with at least one staff member at the Ritz Carlton hotel in Moscow who said that there were stories concerning Trump's alleged sexual activities, not that the activities themselves had been confirmed by the staff member as stated in Report 80.

later provided to the FBI by Steele's Primary Sub-source and sub-sources about the reporting was difficult to discern and could be attributed to a number of factors. These included miscommunications between Steele and the Primary Sub-source, exaggerations or misrepresentations by Steele about the information he obtained, or misrepresentations by the Primary Sub-source and/or sub-sources when questioned by the FBI about the information they conveyed to Steele or the Primary Sub-source.[342]

Another factor complicating the FBI's assessment of the Steele election reporting was the Primary Sub-source's statement to the FBI that he/she believed that information presented as fact in the reporting included his/her and Steele's "analytical conclusions" and "analytical judgments," and not just reporting from sub-sources. For example, Report 80 provides that:

> Speaking separately in June 2016, Source B (the former top-level Russian intelligence officer) asserted that TRUMP's unorthodox behavior in Russia over the years had provided the authorities there with enough embarrassing material on the now Republican presidential candidate to be able to blackmail him if they so wished.

The Primary Sub-source told the FBI that "the ability to blackmail Trump was [the sub-source's] 'logical conclusion' rather than reporting," even though it is presented as a statement from a sub-source. The Primary Sub-source noted another example of this practice in Report 135, which states:

> Referring back to the (surprise) sacking of Sergei IVANOV as Head of PA [Presidential Administration] in August 2016, his replacement by Anton VAINO and the appointment of former Russian premier Sergei KIRIYENKO to another senior position in the PA, the Kremlin insider repeated that this had been directly connected to the TRUMP support operation and the need to cover up now that it was being exposed by the USG and in the western media.

Report 111 also contains similar information to Report 135, namely that Ivanov was "sacked" due to his association with the Russian's U.S. election operation. The Primary Sub-source explained to the FBI that the connection between Ivanov's replacement and "fallout over Russia's influence efforts against the U.S. election" was the Primary Sub-source's "analytical conclusion." The Primary Sub-source told the FBI that he/she was careful to identify his/her

---

342

███
███
███
███
███

analytical conclusions to Steele and to offer a confidence level in them (*e.g.* possible vs. likely). We took note of the fact that, on December 1, 2016, ████████

██
██
██
██

The Supervisory Intel Analyst, as well as Steele, told us that blending judgments with assertions is not an appropriate way to report intelligence. Steele told us that he would hope that his reports were clear on what a source stated, what was assumed by the source, and what was analysis. However, Strzok told the OIG that the blending in Steele's reporting of analysis with statements from the sub-sources "posed problems" for the FBI. Strzok explained that "to understand what the individual source said we can no longer assume this guy said all of this. It's really [Steele] added on or [the Primary Sub-source] added on."

As discussed in Chapter Eight, Carter Page FISA Renewal Application Nos. 2 and 3 advised the court that following the January interview with the Primary Sub-source, "the FBI found the Russian-based sub-source to be truthful and cooperative." Renewal Application Nos. 2 and 3 continued to rely on the Steele information, without any revisions or notice to the court that the Primary Sub-source contradicted the Steele election reporting on key issues described in the renewal applications. We found no evidence that the Crossfire Hurricane team ever considered whether any of the inconsistencies warranted reconsideration of the FBI's previous assessment of the reliability of the Steele election reports, or notice to OI or the court for the subsequent renewal applications.

D. The FBI Obtains Additional Information about the Reliability of Steele's Reporting after FISA Renewal Application No. 3

Crossfire Hurricane team members told us that in the spring 2017 they determined that they needed to interview Steele more extensively about his election reporting and ask questions to account for new information that the Primary Sub-source had provided during his/her interview. The Supervisory Intel Analyst explained that the team members believed that an interview with Steele "would be a good way of potentially looking to see whether or not [the Primary Sub-source] is giving us accurate information [or] did [the Primary Sub-source] tell [Steele] something different." The FBI sought to obtain additional information about Steele's sub-sources prior to the interview and encountered some logistical delays in arranging it. The interview ended up occurring during two days in September 2017, following the Carter Page FISA Renewal Application No. 3.

The FBI's interview with Steele in September 2017 further highlighted discrepancies between Steele's presentation of information in the election reporting and the views of his Primary Sub-source.[343] For example, Steele told the interviewing agent and analyst that Reports 80, 95, 97, and 102, which range in date from June 20 to August 10, 2016, included information from a sub-source who was "close" to Trump.[344] Steele further advised the FBI staff that this sub-source was the same person who originally provided the Primary Sub-source with the information concerning Trump's alleged sexual activities at the Ritz Carlton hotel in Moscow, and that the Primary Sub-source met with this sub-source two or three times. However, we were told by WFO Agent 1 that the Primary Sub-source stated that he/she never met this sub-source and that other sub-sources were responsible for the Ritz Carlton reporting. The Primary Sub-source also told the FBI interviewers as well as WFO Agent 1 that he/she received a telephone call from an individual he/she believed was this sub-source but was not certain of the person's identity and that the person never identified him/herself during the call.[345] The FBI's written summary of the Primary Sub-source's interview describes this call as follows:

> [The Primary Sub-source] recalls that this 10-15 minute conversation included a general discussion about Trump and the Kremlin, that there was "communication" between the parties, and that it was an ongoing relationship. [The Primary Sub-source] recalls that the individual believed to be [Source E in Report 95] said that there was "exchange of information" between Trump and the Kremlin, and that there was "nothing bad about it." [Source E] said that some of this information exchange could be good for Russia, and some could be damaging to Trump, but deniable. The individual said that the Kremlin might be of help to get Trump elected, but [the Primary Sub-source] did not recall any discussion or mention of Wiki[L]eaks.

Report 95, however, attributes to this sub-source information concerning the release of DNC emails to WikiLeaks. Report 95 states: "Source E, acknowledged that the Russian regime had been behind the recent leak of embarrassing e-mail messages, emanating from the Democratic National Committee (DNC), to the WikiLeaks platform." Report 95 describes the relationship between the Trump campaign and "the Russian leadership" as a "well-developed conspiracy of co-operation." As described in Chapters Five, Seven, and Eight, all four Carter Page FISA applications relied on Report 95 to support probable cause.[346]

---

[343] The September interview was conducted by an FBI agent and analyst on assignment to the Special Counsel's Office.

[344] The reports describe this sub-source in varying ways: Report 80 ("Source D, a close associate of TRUMP...."); Report 95 ("Source E, an ethnic Russian close associate of Republican US presidential candidate Donald TRUMP...."); Report 97 ("a Russian émigré figure close to the Republican U.S. presidential candidate Donald TRUMP's campaign team...."); and Report 102 ("[A]n ethnic Russian associate of Republican US presidential candidate Donald TRUMP...").

[345] The Primary Sub-source told WFO Agent 1 that he/she found a YouTube video of the sub-source speaking and that it sounded like the person on the telephone call.

[346] The FISA applications also relied upon Reports 80, 94, and 102.

Report 97 contains four paragraphs of information with numerous allegations attributed to the sub-source (and hence is purportedly derived from the Primary Sub-source's 10-15 minute call). The information attributed to the sub-source includes that (1) the Kremlin was concerned that "political fallout from the DNC email hacking operation is spiraling out of control," (2) the Kremlin had intelligence on Clinton and her campaign but that the sub-source did not know when or if it would be released, and (3) that derogatory material possessed by the Russians would not be used against Trump "given how helpful and co-operative his team had been over several years, and particularly of late." Report 102 likewise contains numerous insights about the Trump campaign and Russian tactics. It includes allegations that the "aim of leaking the DNC e-mails to WikiLeaks during the Democratic Convention had been to swing supporters of Bernie SANDERS away from Hillary CLINTON and across to TRUMP," and that Carter Page "conceived and promoted" this "objective" and had discussed it directly with the sub-source.

The Supervisory Intel Analyst told the OIG that he found the Primary Sub-source's explanations about his/her contacts with this sub-source "peculiar" and that the Primary Sub-source could have been minimizing his/her relationship with the sub-source. The Supervisory Intel Analyst agreed that press reports discussing the sub-source's alleged contacts with the Trump campaign may have motivated the Primary Sub-source to minimize the extent of his/her relationship with the sub-source. We asked the Supervisory Intel Analyst whether he thought the Primary Sub-source had been truthful during his/her interview with the FBI. He said that he believed that there were instances where the Primary Sub-source was "minimizing" certain facts but did not believe that he/she was "completely fabricating" events. The Supervisory Intel Analyst stated that he did not know whether he could support a "blanket statement" that the Primary Sub-source had been truthful.

In Steele's September 2017 interview with the FBI, Steele also made statements that conflicted with explanations from two of his sub-sources about their access to Russian officials. For example, Steele explained that the Primary Sub-source had direct access to a particular former senior Russian government official and that they had been "speaking for a while." The Primary Sub-source told the FBI, however, that he/she had never met or spoken with the official. Steele also stated that one sub-source was ███ one of a few persons in a "circle" close to a particular senior official. The FBI obtained information from the sub-source that contradicted Steele's interpretation.

FBI documents reflect that another of Steele's sub-sources who reviewed the election reporting told the FBI in August 2017 that whatever information in the Steele reports that was attributable to him/her had been "exaggerated" and that he/she did not recognize anything as originating specifically from him/her.[347] The

---

347 ███

Primary Sub-source told the FBI that he/she believed this sub-source was "one of the key sources for the 'Trump dossier'" and the source for allegations concerning Michael Cohen and events in Prague contained in Reports 135, 136, and 166, as well as Report 94's allegations concerning the alleged meeting between Carter Page and Igor Divyekin. The Supervisory Intel Analyst told us that he believed this Steele sub-source may have been attempting to minimize his/her role in the election reporting following its release to the public.

Steele's September 2017 interview with the FBI, which was conducted 2 months after the final Carter Page FISA renewal application was submitted to the court, also revealed bias against Trump. According to the FBI FD-302 of the interview, Steele and his business colleague described Trump as their "main opponent" and said that they were "fearful" about the negative impact of the Trump presidency on the relationship between the United States and United Kingdom. The Supervisory Intel Analyst stated that he viewed Steele's description of Trump as the "main opponent" as an expression of "clear bias." Steele told us that he did not begin his investigation with any bias against Trump, but based on the information he learned during the investigation became very concerned about the consequences of a Trump presidency.

E. Crossfire Hurricane Team's Assessment of Potential Russian Influence on the Steele Election Reporting

Although an investigation into whether Steele's election reports, or aspects of them, were the product of a Russian disinformation campaign was not within the scope of this review, or within the scope of the OIG's oversight role, we examined the extent to which the Crossfire Hurricane team considered this possibility in its assessment of Steele's reporting. Priestap told us that he recognized that the Russians are "masters at disinformation" and that the Crossfire Hurricane team was aware of the potential for Russian disinformation to influence Steele's reporting. According to Priestap:

> [W]e had a lot of concurrent efforts to try to understand, is [the reporting] true or not, and if it's not, you know, why is it not? Is it the motivation of [Steele] or one of his sources, meaning [Steele's] sources?... [Or were they] flipped, they're actually working for the Russians, and providing disinformation? We considered all of that....

Steele told us that Russian intelligence is "sophisticated" and relies on disinformation. He said it can involve "planted information," which he described as "controlled information," and that often the information is true but with "bits missing and changed." For his part, Steele told us that he had no evidence that his reporting was "polluted" with Russian disinformation.

The Intel Section Chief told the OIG that the FBI's efforts to identify possible Russian disinformation in the Steele election reporting included trying to corroborate the reporting, learning as much as possible about Steele's sub-sources, and fully assessing Steele. According to an FBI memorandum prepared in December 2017 for a Congressional briefing, by the time the Crossfire Hurricane investigation was transferred to the Special Counsel in May 2017, the FBI "did not assess it likely that the [Steele] [election reporting] was generated in connection to a Russian disinformation campaign." Priestap told us that the FBI "didn't have any indication whatsoever" by May 2017 that the Russians were running a disinformation campaign through the Steele election reporting. Priestap explained, however, that if the Russians, in fact, were attempting to funnel disinformation through Steele to the FBI using Russian Oligarch 1, he did not understand the goal. Priestap told us that what he has

> tried to explain to anybody who will listen is if that's the theory [that Russian Oligarch 1 ran a disinformation campaign through [Steele] to the FBI], then I'm struggling with what the goal was. So, because, obviously, what [Steele] reported was not helpful, you could argue, to then [candidate] Trump. And if you guys recall, nobody thought then candidate Trump was going to win the election. Why the Russians, and [Russian Oligarch 1] is supposed to be close, very close to the Kremlin, why the Russians would try to denigrate an opponent that the intel community later said they were in favor of who didn't really have a chance at winning, I'm struggling, with, when you know the Russians, and this I know from my Intelligence Community work: they favored Trump, they're trying to denigrate Clinton, and they wanted to sow chaos. I don't know why you'd run a disinformation campaign to denigrate Trump on the side.

As discussed in Chapter Four, Steele performed work for Russian Oligarch 1's attorney on Russian Oligarch 1's litigation matters, and, as described later in Chapter Nine, passed information to Department attorney Bruce Ohr advocating on behalf of one of Russian Oligarch 1's companies regarding U.S. sanctions.[348] Priestap, the Intel Section Chief, and other members of Crossfire Hurricane told us that they were unaware of Steele's connections to Russian Oligarch 1, who was the subject of a Crossfire Hurricane case, and that they would have wanted to know about them.[349] Priestap, for example, told us "I don't recall knowing that there was

---

[348] An FBI FD-302 dated February 15, 2017, and written by an FBI agent assigned to the Crossfire Hurricane investigation, documented the FBI's interview of Ohr on February 14, and specifically stated that Steele's company was continuing to work for a particular attorney of Russian Oligarch 1.

[349] The Supervisory Intel Analyst and SSA 2 told us that they did not recall reviewing information in Steele's Delta file documenting Steele's frequent contacts with representatives for multiple Russian oligarchs in 2015. The Supervisory Intel Analyst explained that he did not recall doing a "deep dive" on Steele's past history as a source and relied in part on Handling Agent 1 for information about Steele. The first access of Steele's Delta file by a Crossfire Hurricane team member (the Supervisory Intel Analyst) occurred on November 18, 2016, after Steele had been closed as a CHS and a month after submission of the first Page FISA application. As described in Chapter Five,

any connectivity between [Steele] and [Russian Oligarch 1]." Priestap told us that he believed it was "completely fair" to say that the FBI should have assessed Steele's relationship with Russian Oligarch 1.

Stuart Evans, NSD's Deputy Assistant Attorney General who oversaw OI, stated that if OI had been aware of the information about Steele's connections to Russian Oligarch 1, it would have been evaluated by OI. He told us: "Counterintelligence investigations are complex, and often involve as I said, you know, double dealing, and people playing all sides.... I think that [the connection between Steele and Russian Oligarch 1] would have been yet another thing we would have wanted to dive into."[350]

V. The FBI's Efforts to Assess Steele's Election Reporting in 2016 and 2017

The FBI's assessment of the Steele election reporting began in mid-September 2016 and concluded approximately 1 year later, roughly 3 months after the submission of Carter Page FISA Renewal Application No. 3 to the Foreign Intelligence Surveillance Court (FISC). The FBI acquired the vast majority of its information about the Steele election reporting prior to the end of September 2017, when FISA surveillance of Carter Page expired.

To evaluate Steele's election reporting, intelligence analysts on the Crossfire Hurricane team created a spreadsheet identifying each statement that appeared in the Steele election reports in order to have a record of what the FBI learned during

---

the FISA application relied in part on Steele's reporting. In Chapter Four we noted that Steele's frequent contacts with Russian oligarchs in 2015 had raised concerns in the FBI Transnational Organized Crime Intelligence Unit. SSA 1 told us that he was unaware of these concerns, but said he would have found this information useful and would have wanted to know about it while supervising the Crossfire Hurricane investigation. Handling Agent 1 expressed surprise that the Crossfire Hurricane team did not access Steele's Delta file earlier. He said that the team should have "turned the file upside down" looking for information 2 months earlier and that he assumed that some members of the team had thoroughly reviewed the file.

[350] In addition to the information in Steele's Delta file documenting Steele's frequent contacts with representatives for multiple Russian oligarchs, we identified reporting the ████████

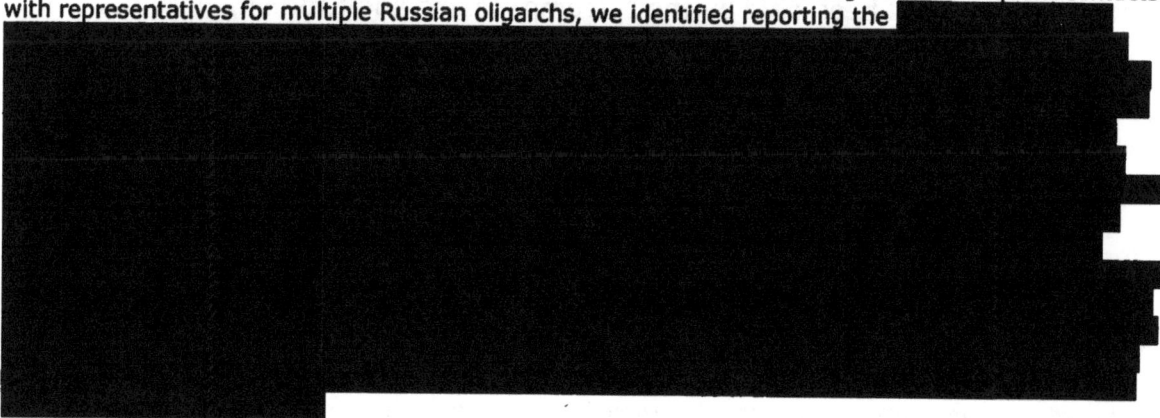

its assessment regarding those statements.[351] The intelligence analysts also attempted to determine the true identities of the sub-source(s) responsible for each statement in Steele's election reporting, and made assessments of each sub-source's likely access to the type of information described. FBI CD officials also travelled abroad and met with persons who previously had professional contacts with Steele to gather information about his reliability and the quality of his work.

According to FBI officials, it was challenging to corroborate the information in the Steele election reporting because much of it was "singular source intelligence," and thus could not be verified given the manner in which the events took place. For example, officials told us that a meeting or conversation between just a few people in Russia may only be known to the individuals involved. According to a Supervisory Special Agent who investigated the Steele election reporting, the Crossfire Hurricane team could not independently verify those types of allegations "without speaking to...folks that are high-level in Russia... ███████████████ ████████████ Strzok told us that, for this kind of information, the "frustration of it was...[the FBI] couldn't necessarily prove it and couldn't disprove it either."

Despite the FBI's efforts to corroborate and evaluate the Steele election reporting, we were told by the Supervisory Intel Analyst that, as of September 2017, the FBI had corroborated limited information in the Steele election reporting, and much of that information was publicly available.[352] Most relevant to the Carter Page FISA applications, the specific substantive allegations contained in Reports 80, 94, 95, and 102, which were relied upon in all four FISA applications, remained uncorroborated and, in several instances, were inconsistent with information gathered by the Crossfire Hurricane team. For example, as detailed in Chapters Five and Seven, these allegations included, among other things, that Page had secret meetings with Igor Sechin and Igor Divyekin in July 2016 and served as an "intermediary" between Manafort and the Russian government. As we describe in Chapters Five and Eight, certain information the FBI had obtained did not support these allegations or the theory in Steele's election reporting that Page was coordinating, or had coordinated, with Russian government officials on 2016 U.S. election activities. Additionally, the FBI determined that some of the allegations in the Steele reporting, including that Trump attorney Michael Cohen had traveled to Prague in late summer 2016 to meet with Kremlin representatives and that "anti-Clinton hackers" had been paid by the "[Trump] team" and Kremlin, were not true.

In the next two chapters, we describe the FBI's use of the Steele election reporting in the three Carter Page FISA renewal applications and the changes that were made, and not made, to the applications to reflect the additional information the FBI developed about Steele and his reporting.

---

[351] As we described in Chapter Four, the spreadsheet omitted certain highly classified information and therefore its scope was partial.

[352] Examples included that Carter Page was in Moscow as reported, that other individuals mentioned in the reporting existed, and that some individuals held the positions in the Russian government that were attributed to them in the reporting.

CHAPTER SEVEN
THE THREE RENEWAL APPLICATIONS FOR CONTINUED FISA AUTHORITYON CARTER PAGE

In this chapter, we describe the three FISA renewal applications to continue surveillance ███████████████ targeting Carter Page between January ██, 2017, when the FISA authority granted by the first FISA orders expired, and September ██, 2017, when the last renewal's authority expired. As described in Chapter Two, the Foreign Intelligence Surveillance Court (FISC) may approve FISA surveillance and physical searches targeting a U.S. person for a period of up to 90 days, subject to renewal, if the government's FISA application establishes probable cause to conclude that the targeted individual is an agent of a foreign power. A renewal permits the government to continue FISA authority targeting a U.S. person for an additional 90 days if the facts of the investigation continue to support a finding that there is probable cause to believe the targeted individual is an agent of a foreign power.[353]

The process to renew FISA authority, including who reviews and approves the renewal application, is the same process as with an initial application, which we described in Chapters Two and Five. When conducting the Woods Procedures for a renewal, the agent conducting the accuracy review must re-verify that factual assertions repeated from the prior FISA application remain true and must obtain supporting documentation for any new factual assertions. The National Security Division's (NSD) Office of Intelligence (OI) relies upon the FBI to accurately update the prior FISA application and conduct the accuracy review to determine whether factual information carried over from the prior FISA application remains true.

We describe in this chapter the facts asserted in the three renewal applications submitted to the FISC to demonstrate probable cause that Carter Page was an agent of a foreign power, including new information the FBI intercepted and collected during surveillance of Page. We also describe other factual assertions added to or modified in the renewal applications for the court's consideration. Finally, we discuss the completion of the Woods Procedures, including who reviewed, certified, and approved each of the three renewal applications, and the court's final orders. As we describe In Chapter Eight, we found instances in which factual representations made in the three Carter Page renewal applications were inaccurate, incomplete, or unsupported by appropriate documentation, based upon information in the FBI's possession at the time the applications were filed.

I. FISA Renewal Application No. 1 (January ██, 2017)

On January ██, 2017, a day before the initial FISA authority targeting Carter Page was set to expire, and at the request of the FBI, the Department filed an application with the FISC requesting an additional 90 days of FISA coverage

---

[353] The Office of Intelligence (OI) in the National Security Division (NSD) expects that the FBI will request a renewal on a targeted individual 45 days prior to the expiration of the existing FISA authority.

targeting Carter Page. A FISC judge reviewed and issued the requested orders resulting in an additional 90 days of surveillance ████████████████ targeting Carter Page from January ██, 2017 to April █, 2017.

A.   Investigative Developments and Decision to Seek Renewal

Emails and other communications reflect that in the first week of surveillance on Carter Page████████████, following the granting of the first FISA application in October 2016, the Crossfire Hurricane team collected ████████████ ████.[354] Based on our review of the Woods Files and communications between the FBI and OI, we identified a few emails between Page and members of the Donald J. Trump for President Campaign concerning campaign related matters. Emails between Supervisory Special Agent 1 (SSA 1) and Case Agent 1 show that during the initial weeks of FISA surveillance, they discussed several ████████████████████████ they believed were significant, including references to ████████ ██ ████████. The analysts and agents who reviewed the FISA ████████ prepared a packet ████████████████████████ that they believed demonstrated Carter Page's contacts with and references to Russia or Russian officials for OI to consider for a renewal application.

In addition to reviewing the FISA collection, the team continued its efforts (described in Chapter Six) to assess the accuracy of the information in Steele's election reports. According to the Supervisory Intelligence Analyst (Supervisory Intel Analyst), the team had not corroborated the reporting concerning Carter Page's activities by the time of Renewal Application No. 1 (or subsequent renewal applications), other than confirming Carter Page's travel to Russia in July 2016.

As detailed in Chapter Six, in November 2016, the FBI closed Steele as a Confidential Human Source (CHS) for his disclosures to *Mother Jones* concerning his election reports and relationship with the FBI. FBI officials told us that after these disclosures, they continued to assess that Steele was reliable. They said that they viewed the *Mother Jones* disclosure as a "control" issue, based on their understanding that it was a reaction to the letter then FBI Director James Comey sent to Congress in late October about the Clinton email investigation. Then Deputy Director Andrew McCabe recalled that Steele's disclosure to *Mother Jones* was viewed by the Crossfire Hurricane team as a control issue rather than a reliability issue, and the team was comfortable going forward with seeking a FISA renewal targeting Carter Page. SSA 1 told us that he believed the reason Steele provided for his disclosure to *Mother Jones* "politicized" Steele and identified an agenda. SSA 1 said that after Steele's disclosure to *Mother Jones*, he thought the team needed to have an independent validation review completed, which we discussed in Chapter Six.

---

[354] We did not review the entirety of FISA ████████ obtained through FISA surveillance ████ ████████ targeting Carter Page. We reviewed only those ████████████ under FISA authority that were relevant to our review.

However, to further assess Steele's reliability, as described in Chapters Six and Eight, senior Counterintelligence Division (CD) officials met with persons with direct knowledge of Steele's work-related performance in a prior position in mid-November 2016, and told us that they were reassured by the fact that the former employer said that Steele had no history of fabricating, embellishing, or otherwise "spinning" information in his reporting.[355] In addition, FBI officials told us that they were reassured by statements from Department attorney Bruce Ohr (described in Chapters Eight and Nine) that Ohr believed Steele was never untruthful in his reporting.

Case Agent 1's handwritten notes from a December 2016 Crossfire Hurricane team meeting reflect that the team discussed the information about Steele's prior work-related performance and Ohr and decided that they "can continue to rely on reporting for FISA." Case Agent 1 told us he did not recall this discussion or who said that they could continue to rely on Steele's reporting in the next FISA application.

Before this team meeting, and around 45 days prior to the expiration of the first FISA authority, Case Agent 1 notified the FBI's Office of the General Counsel (OGC) and OI that the Crossfire Hurricane team was interested in an additional 90 days of FISA authority targeting Carter Page. Case Agent 1 told us that the Crossfire Hurricane team sought a renewal to determine whether Carter Page had ongoing contact with Russia beyond the 90-day period covered by the first FISA orders. Case Agent 1 said that while it is not automatic to seek a renewal after a first application, there is an "understanding" that the FBI will typically seek a renewal because at the time they are required to notify OI, they have only had 45 days of surveillance, which is usually not sufficient time to gather enough information, or review the information collected, to determine whether or not there is evidence to continue the investigation. Case Agent 1 told us that the team had not reviewed all of the emails the first FISA application yielded and believed there were additional emails not yet collected. The OGC Unit Chief told us that unless there is no evidence collected with an initial FISA application, the FBI will usually seek a renewal to obtain more information.

B.   Preparation and Approval of Renewal Application No. 1

1.   Draft Renewal Application

Similar to the first Carter Page FISA application, Case Agent 1 and the OGC Attorney assisted the OI Attorney with the preparation of Renewal Application No. 1. However, the OGC Attorney told us that he was less involved in the preparation of this application as compared to the first application, which he said was typical of OGC involvement in renewal applications.

---

[355] We describe in Chapters Six and Eight the negative feedback received concerning Steele, including comments about his judgment. We found that the team did not share all relevant details about this feedback with OI.

Emails between OI, the OGC Attorney, and Case Agent 1 following the FISC's approval of the first FISA application on October ██, 2016, reflect that Case Agent 1 provided updates to OI on relevant FISA collections and case activities in the Carter Page investigation throughout the fall. The OI Attorney reviewed this information for inclusion into a renewal application and began drafting Renewal Application No. 1 in December. The OI Attorney told the OIG that, when drafting a renewal application, he relies on the FBI to provide him information relevant to the ongoing investigation, including any new information that may contradict or may be different from information presented to the FISC in prior FISA applications.

NSD officials told us that the drafting of Renewal Application No. 1 followed the same process and received the same level of scrutiny as the first FISA application signed in October, but because OI's questions about Steele and his election reporting were addressed in the first application, there were fewer discussions about the renewal application, as compared to the first application, and Renewal Application No. 1 was completed in less time. By December 28, 2016, the OI Attorney had completed a draft of Renewal Application No. 1, described below, and selected relevant FISA intercepts and results of the ongoing investigation to incorporate in the draft.

As in the first FISA application, the statement of facts in support of probable cause for the renewal stated that the Russians attempted to undermine and influence the 2016 presidential election, and that the FBI believed Carter Page was acting in conjunction with the Russians in those efforts. The statement of facts supported this assessment with the five main elements enumerated in the first application (described in Chapter Five) and added recent investigative results. Specifically, the elements that carried over from the first FISA application were:

(1) The efforts of Russian Intelligence Services (RIS) to influence the 2016 presidential election—the renewal application stated that although the elections had concluded, the FBI believed that the Russian government would continue efforts to use U.S. persons, such as Carter Page, to covertly influence U.S. foreign policy and support Russia's perception management efforts;

(2) The Russian government's attempted coordination with members of the Trump campaign, which was based on the Friendly Foreign Government (FFG) information concerning the offer or suggestion of assistance from the Russians to someone associated with the Trump campaign;

(3) Carter Page's historical connections to Russia and RIS, which included his business dealings with the Russian energy company Gazprom, his relationships with known Russian intelligence officers, and his disclosure to the FBI and a Russian Minister that he was Male-1 in an indictment against Russian intelligence officers;

(4) Carter Page's alleged coordination with the Russian government in 2016 U.S. presidential election activities, based on some of the reporting from Steele; and

(5) Carter Page's continued connections to Russian officials, based on the FBI's assessment of a consensually monitored October 17, 2016 conversation between Page and an FBI CHS.[356]

In addition, the recent investigative results section of the application included references to the following:

- ██

- ██

- ██

- ████████████████████████ Page ██████████ traveled ████████ to Russia in December 2016;

- ██ ;

- ██

- In December 2016, Carter Page made statements to an FBI CHS (summarized in Chapter Ten), distancing himself from his October suggestion of establishing a Russian-funded think tank, citing funding issues as a reason, which the FBI assessed was an indication that Page

---

[356] The statement of facts in Renewal Application No. 1 also carried over from the first application the description of Carter Page's denials of coordination with the Russian government, as reported in two news articles and asserted by Page in his September 25 letter to then FBI Director James Comey.

was likely trying to distance himself from Russia as a result of media reporting that continued to tie Page to Russia.

The renewal application stated that the FBI believed the recent investigative results demonstrated that Carter Page continued to try to influence U.S. foreign policy on behalf of Russia. The renewal application, like the first FISA application, failed to include information provided to the FBI by another U.S. government agency in August 2016 that Carter Page had a prior relationship with that other agency and had provided information to the other agency.

Renewal Application No. 1 included the same information from Steele's reporting that appeared in the first FISA application. However, the renewal application advised the court of Steele's disclosure to *Mother Jones* and that the FBI had "suspended" its relationship with Steele. Specifically, the source characterization statement for Steele in the renewal application stated the following:

> [Steele] is a ███████████████████████████ ████████ and has been an FBI source since in or about October 2013. [Steele] has been compensated approximately $95,000 by the FBI. **As discussed below in footnote 19, in or about October 2016, the FBI suspended its relationship with [Steele] due to [Steele's] unauthorized disclosure of information to the press. Notwithstanding the suspension of its relationship with [Steele], the FBI assesses [Steele] to be reliable as previous reporting from [Steele] has been corroborated and used in criminal proceedings. Moreover, the FBI notes that the incident that led to the FBI suspending its relationship with [Steele] occurred after [Steele] provided the reporting that is described herein.**[357] (Emphasis in original).

Later in the renewal application, footnote 19 referenced both the *Yahoo News* article, with the unsupported language from the first FISA application unchanged, and the *Mother Jones* article, and stated:

> As discussed above, [Steele] was hired by a business associate to conduct research into Candidate #1's ties to Russia. [Steele] provided the results of his research to the business associate, and the FBI assesses that the business associate likely provided this information to the law firm that hired the business associate in the first place. [Steele] told the FBI that he/she only provided this information to the business associate and the FBI. Given that the information contained in the September 23rd News Article generally matches the information about Page that [Steele] discovered during his/her research, the FBI assesses that [Steele's] business associate or the law firm that hired

---

[357] OI often indicates new information in a renewal application to the FISC by using a bold font. The text from the applications cited in this chapter is cited as it appears in the renewal FISA applications.

the business associate likely provided this information to the press. The FBI also assesses that whoever gave the information to the press stated that the information was provided by a "well-placed Western intelligence source." The FBI does not believe that [Steele] directly provided this information to the identified news organization that published the September 23rd News Article.

In or about late October 2016, however, after the Director of the FBI sent a letter to the U.S. Congress, which stated that the FBI had learned of new information that might be pertinent to an investigation that the FBI was conducting of Candidate #2, [Steele] told the FBI that he/she was frustrated with this action and believed it would likely influence the 2016 U.S. Presidential election. In response to [Steele's] concerns, [Steele] independently, and against the prior admonishment from the FBI to speak only with the FBI on this matter, released the reporting discussed herein to an identified news organization. Although the FBI continues to assess [that] [Steele's] reporting is reliable, as noted above, the FBI has suspended its relationship with [Steele] because of this disclosure. (Emphasis in original).

We found no evidence that the FBI "suspended" its relationship with Steele; rather, FBI paperwork reflects that Steele was closed for cause as an FBI CHS in November 2016.[358] However, as we describe in Chapters Six and Nine, as a practical matter, the FBI continued to collect information from Steele over a period of months through a conduit, Department attorney Bruce Ohr.

Additionally, as discussed in Chapter Five, contrary to FBI policy, the characterization of Steele's prior reporting had not been approved by his handling agent, who told us that the characterization was inaccurate—according to the handling agent, only some of Steele's prior reporting had been corroborated, most of it had not, and Steele's information had never been used in a criminal proceeding. This inaccuracy was not corrected in Renewal Application No. 1 or in the subsequent renewal applications, even after a formal FBI human source validation review of Steele in March 2017 found that his past contributions to the FBI's criminal program had been "minimally corroborated." Further, as described in Chapter Eight, the FBI did not reassess Steele's reliability in the renewal applications, or advise OI, after the Crossfire Hurricane team obtained additional information that was highly relevant to the reliability of his election reporting. This included information received before Renewal Application No. 1 about Steele's work-related performance in a prior position and before Renewal Application Nos. 2

---

[358] As described in Chapter Six, Handling Agent 1 told us that he informed Steele on November 1, 2016, that it was unlikely that the FBI would continue a relationship with him and that Steele must cease collecting information for the FBI. Handling Agent 1 completed a Source Closing Communication document on November 17, 2016, indicating that Steele had been closed for cause on November 1, 2016.

The disclosures of Steele's reports are further discussed in Chapters Four and Six.

and 3 from Steele's Primary Sub-source that contradicted the source reporting in the FISA applications. In addition, as we also discuss in Chapter Eight, Renewal Application No. 1 and the subsequent renewal applications did not describe information that the FBI obtained from Department attorney Bruce Ohr regarding Steele's possible motivations and bias.

Finally, the information in Renewal Application No. 1 regarding early CHS meetings remained unchanged from the prior application. The renewal application also did not include information about the August 2016 meeting between Carter Page and an FBI CHS or the September 2016 meetings between Papadopoulos and an FBI CHS, discussed in Chapters Five and Ten. It also did not include an accurate description of the October 2016 meeting between Page and an FBI CHS, also discussed in Chapters Five and Ten. In addition, as described in Chapters Eight and Ten, Renewal Application No. 1 and the subsequent renewal applications did not include information about an October 2016 CHS meeting involving an FBI CHS and Papadopoulos during which Papadopoulos said that he knew "for a fact" that the Trump campaign was not involved in releasing emails from the DNC.

2. Review and Approval Process

As described previously, according to Department and FBI procedures, once an FBI case agent affirms the accuracy of the information in the proposed FISA application (read copy), an OI Unit Chief or Deputy Unit Chief is usually the final and only approver before a read copy is submitted to the FISC. The Unit Chief or Deputy is also usually the final approver who "signs out" the final application (cert copy) to the FBI for completion of the Woods Procedures and Director's certification, before presentation to either the Assistant Attorney General (AAG) of NSD, the Deputy Attorney General (DAG), or the Attorney General for final signature. However, as reflected in Chapter Five, in some instances, FISA applications presenting novel issues or otherwise deemed to have heightened sensitivity will receive additional supervisory review within the FBI, the Department, or both. As described below, FISA Renewal Application No. 1 did not receive the same level of review in FBI OGC as the first Carter Page FISA application, but it did receive additional review within NSD and the Office of the Deputy Attorney General (ODAG).

a. Supervisory Review and Finalization of Read Copy

Unlike the first FISA application, then FBI General Counsel James Baker and then Deputy General Counsel, Trisha Anderson, did not review FISA Renewal Application No. 1 before the read copy was submitted to the court. Baker told us that he did not review any of the renewal applications. He said that, in general, if none of the relevant factual information had changed from the first application, and the foreign intelligence purpose for the FISA remained the same, he did not believe it was necessary to review renewal applications. In addition, he told us that in at least one instance, he did not know that the FBI was planning to seek a renewal on Carter Page until the application was already with the Director for certification. According to the OGC Unit Chief, OGC is usually less involved in renewal applications because they generally only require updates to the factual information already asserted in an initial FISA application. She said that the interactions on renewal applications mostly take place at the OI attorney and case agent levels. McCabe told us that, as the Deputy Director, he did not approve requests before they were submitted to OI for FISA application renewals, but he would have been briefed on the collections from the ongoing FISA surveillance. McCabe said that he understood that the first Carter Page FISA was "very productive" and the team wanted to pursue a renewal.

Within NSD, Renewal Application No. 1 received additional supervisory review above the OI Unit Chief. On December 28, after reviewing the draft, the OI Unit Chief emailed the OI Attorney to approve of the new information and assessments included in the draft. On December 29, the OI Attorney emailed a draft of Renewal Application No. 1 to Stuart Evans, NSD's then Deputy AAG for Intelligence, Gabriel Sanz-Rexach, the Chief of OI's Operations Section, and OI's Deputy Operations Section Chief for their review, advising them that the draft was "about 95% complete" and that an additional update would be added before the final draft was completed.

Sanz-Rexach told the OIG that he reviewed Renewal Application No. 1, but did not recall any specific comments he made to the read copy. He said that he recalled that prior to the renewal, the FBI ████████████████████████ ███. He also said that the evidence collected during the first FISA application time period demonstrated that Carter Page had access to individuals in Russia and he was communicating with people in the Trump campaign, which created a concern that Russia could use their influence with Carter Page to effect policy. The Deputy Operations Section Chief told us that she reviewed the new factual information in the renewal application, but did not recall as many meetings or discussions about the renewals and did not recall making any comments on any of the renewal applications.

Emails reflect that Evans reviewed the draft renewal application and provided two minor edits, one of which added more detail concerning Carter Page's December 2016 meeting with an FBI CHS. Evans told us that he focused his attention primarily on the footnote describing Steele's *Mother Jones* disclosure that led to a change in Steele's relationship with the FBI, and did not edit the footnote following his review.

On January 3, Evans emailed the read copy to NSD's then Acting AAG Mary McCord for her review with a request to discuss a few points in the renewal. Although the emails did not specify the points for discussion, McCord told us she recalled a discussion with Evans about the information the FBI collected from the FISA coverage targeting Carter Page up to that point and whether it was sufficient to sustain a renewal. McCord told us she also wanted to make sure that the renewal application described the closure of Steele after his disclosures to the media, which was already included in the read copy she reviewed.

b.   ODAG Review and Approval of Read Copy

Although not a required step in the FISA procedures, ODAG officials reviewed the read copy for Renewal Application No. 1 before it was submitted to the court. Similar to the first application, the renewal application was reviewed by Tashina Gauhar, the Associate Deputy Attorney General responsible for ODAG's national security portfolio, an OI attorney on detail in ODAG, Principal Associate Deputy Attorney General (PADAG) Matthew Axelrod, and DAG Sally Yates, who ultimately approved and signed the final application.

On December 30, 2016, the OI Unit Chief emailed the read copy of Renewal Application No. 1 to Gauhar, and the OI attorney on detail advising that it was "95% complete" with one question for ODAG to consider. Documents do not indicate that ODAG made any edits to the December 30 draft. The question for ODAG was whether to include an expansion to the particularized minimization procedures, or PMPs, restriction on who could access the FISA collections to include the agents and analysts investigating the ongoing perception management activities by Russia.[359] The final renewal application included the expanded PMPs, restricting access to the FISA collection to only those individuals assigned to investigate Russia's efforts to influence the 2016 U.S. elections and Russia's attempts at perception management and influence activities against the U.S.

On January 4, the OI attorney on detail in ODAG advised OI that the OI attorney had provided "a couple of suggestions...which we did not think (and hopefully are not) significant" and advised that Axelrod would want to review the read copy. We did not find documentation showing the suggestions ODAG recommended for the draft. According to Gauhar, ODAG did not make significant edits or have many questions after it reviewed Renewal Application No. 1. Gauhar also told us that she believed the first renewal was significant because it demonstrated that, despite the questions about whether to seek a Carter Page FISA prior to the first application, the surveillance yielded relevant and useful information. Gauhar said she recalled that the FISA collection included, among other things, ███
███
███████████████████████.

As with the first FISA application, NSD decided that although it was not a required step, it would not submit the read copy to the FISC until Yates had personally read it and said she was comfortable moving forward. According to Gauhar, Yates and Axelrod reviewed Renewal Application No. 1, and following Yates's review, OI submitted the read copy to the FISC. Yates and Axelrod told us that they did not have a specific recollection of reviewing Renewal Application No. 1 but said they may have done so.

---

[359] As described in Chapter Five, the PMPs in the first FISA application restricted access to the information collected through the FISA authority to the individuals assigned to the Crossfire Hurricane team and required the approval of a Deputy Assistant Director or higher before any FISA-derived information could be disseminated outside the FBI.

3. Feedback from the FISC, Completion of the Final Renewal Application and Woods Procedures, and Final Legal Review

On January 10, 2017, the OI Attorney advised Evans and OI management that the FISC judge reviewed the renewal application, had "no issue" with the application, and would sign the application without an appearance.

The day before, the OI Unit Chief "signed out" the cert copy of the application and cert memo to the FBI, so that the FBI could complete the Woods Procedures (previously described in Chapters Two and Five). Case Agent 1 was the agent responsible for compiling the supporting documentation into the Woods File and performing the field office database checks on Carter Page and the accuracy review of each fact asserted in the FISA application. His new supervisor at FBI Headquarters for the Carter Page investigation, SSA 3, was responsible for confirming that the Woods File was complete and double checking the factual accuracy review to confirm that the file contained appropriate documentation for the factual assertions in the FISA application.

As noted previously, in the case of renewal applications, the FISA Standard Minimization Procedures Policy Guide (FISA SMP PG) requires that a case agent re-verify the accuracy of each factual assertion from an initial application that is repeated in a renewal application and verify and obtain supporting documentation for any new factual assertions that are added to a renewal application. Case Agent 1 did not recall whether he reviewed every factual assertion or just the newly added information when he conducted the accuracy review for Renewal Application No. 1. Case Agent 1 told us that his general practice on a renewal application is not to necessarily review the factual information carried over from the prior application. He said that if the factual information does not materially change from the prior FISA application, he will review just the newly added information. According to Case Agent 6, Case Agent 1 told him that when he (Case Agent 1) performed the factual accuracy review on Renewal Application No. 1, he only reviewed the new factual assertions in the application, not the factual assertions that carried over from the prior application. At the time Case Agent 1 conducted the accuracy review of Renewal Application No. 1, he had been transferred back to the New York Field Office (NYFO) and was conducting the Carter Page investigation from that office. After he completed his review, he faxed the signed FISA Verification Form (Woods Form) to SSA 3 at FBI Headquarters.

SSA 3 reviewed the Woods File at Headquarters, signed the Woods Form on January 10, affirming the verification and documentation of each factual assertion in the application, and then sent the FISA application package containing the Woods Form, cert copy, and a cover memorandum (cert memo) to the Headquarters Program Manager assigned the responsibility, as the affiant, of signing the final application under oath that the factual information was true and correct. SSA 3 told us that when he signed the Woods Form, he was verifying that every fact contained in Renewal Application No. 1 had a supporting document confirming the accuracy of the statement. However, like Case Agent 1, SSA 3 also told us that, when he performs a Woods review, he does not re-verify the factual assertions carried over from previous applications, but only checks the new information, which is noted in bold font.[360]

The Headquarters Program Manager assigned as the affiant was SSA 2, who was assigned to the Crossfire Hurricane investigation in late December 2016.[361] He told us he received the renewal package from the OI Attorney and reviewed the first FISA application and the newly added information to Renewal Application No. 1. SSA 2 told us that he did not recall reviewing the Woods Form, but that it was his practice at the time to do so before signing a FISA application (as described in Chapter Two, the Woods Procedures do not require the affiant to review the Woods File, only the case agent and his or her supervisor). SSA 2 said that he believed everything in the application to be true and correct based on the Woods Verification completed by Case Agent 1 and SSA 3. SSA 2 told us that he identified no issues or questions after reviewing Renewal Application No. 1 and signed the affidavit affirming under penalty of perjury that the information in the package was true and correct. He then submitted the FISA application package to either the OGC Attorney or the OGC Unit Chief for final legal review.

As described in Chapter Two, after the affiant signs the affidavit, the application package is submitted to the FBI's National Security and Cyber Law Branch (NSCLB) for final legal review and approval by both a line attorney and Senior Executive Service-level supervisor. Once they approve the application, the line attorney and supervisor sign the cert memo. The OGC Attorney told the OIG that he did not recall reviewing any prior drafts of the application before he received the cert copy on January 10. He said that when he received the cert copy, he focused his legal review on the newly added material. We were advised that the FBI and NSD were unable to locate a fully signed copy of the cert memo that accompanied Renewal Application No. 1, and we were unable to independently determine who reviewed the FISA application package on behalf of OGC's NSCLB. Instant messages suggest that the OGC Attorney performed the line attorney review for NSCLB and submitted the package to Anderson for her review and signature.

4.   FBI Director's Certification

Comey reviewed and certified the Carter Page FISA Renewal Application No. 1 on behalf of the FBI on January 12. Chapter Two describes the elements of the

---

[360] The OIG examined the completeness of the Woods File by comparing the facts asserted in Renewal Application No. 1 to the documents maintained in the Woods File. Our comparison identified instances in which facts asserted in the application were not supported by documentation in the Woods File. Specifically, we found facts asserted in the FISA application that have no supporting documentation in the Woods File, facts that have purported supporting documentation in the Woods File but the documentation does not state the fact asserted in the FISA application, or facts that have purported supporting documentation in the Woods File but the documentation shows the fact asserted is inaccurate. We provide examples of specific errors in Appendix One.

[361] As described in Chapters Two and Five, the affiant for a FISA application is the Headquarters Program Manager in the relevant Operations Branch and Section. In the case of this renewal application, the investigation was conducted from Headquarters, and SSA 2 was one of the Supervisory Special Agents supervising aspects of the investigation.

certification required by the Director or Deputy Director, including that the information sought through the requested FISA authority is foreign intelligence information that cannot reasonably be obtained by normal investigative techniques and is necessary to protect the United States against clandestine intelligence activities. Comey told the OIG that he had no specific memory of reviewing or signing any of the Carter Page FISA renewal application packages. As we discussed in Chapter Five, Comey recalled reading the first Carter Page application before he certified it and being satisfied that the application seemed factually and legally sufficient when he read it, and he had no questions or concerns before he signed.

5. DAG Oral Briefing and Approval

Yates did not specifically recall the oral briefing on Renewal Application No. 1. OI's Deputy Operations Section Chief conducted the briefing and told the OIG that she did not recall anyone having any questions about Renewal Application No. 1. Yates told the OIG she did not recall if she read the entire renewal or just the additions and changes.

Yates told us that she did not have any concerns with the FBI seeking renewal authorization for the Carter Page FISA, although she wanted to make sure that the representation to the FISC was that the focus remained on Carter Page. Yates also told us that she had been briefed by McCabe prior to reviewing Renewal Application No. 1 on Steele's closure due to his disclosure to the media, and was aware that information would be included in the renewal. Yates said it was a brief discussion and she did not recall if McCabe told her whether there was an additional reason the FBI closed Steele or anything further about Steele. On January ██, Yates signed the application, and the application was submitted to the FISC the same day. By her signature, and as stated in the application, Yates found that the application satisfied the criteria and requirements of the FISA statute and approved its filing with the court.[362]

6. Final Orders

The final FISA application included proposed orders, which were signed by FISC Judge Michael W. Mosman, on January ██, 2017. According to NSD, the judge signed the final orders, as proposed by the government in their entirety, without holding a hearing.

The primary order and warrant stated that the court found, based upon the facts submitted in the verified application, that there was probable cause to believe that Russia is a foreign power and that Carter Page was an agent of Russia under 50 U.S.C. § 1801(b)(2)(E). The court also found that the ███████████ ██ ████████████████████████████ The court authorized the requested electronic surveillance ██████████████ for 90

---

[362] Her signature also specifically authorized ██████████████████████ ████████████████████████████.

days and ██
necessary to effectuate the electronic surveillance ██████████████████ that the
court authorized.

II.   FISA Renewal Application No. 2 (April █, 2017)

On April █, 2017, the day FISA coverage targeting Carter Page was set to
expire, and at the request of the FBI, the Department filed an application with the
FISC requesting an additional 90 days of FISA coverage targeting Carter Page. A
FISC judge reviewed and issued the requested orders resulting in an additional 90
days of electronic surveillance ██████████████ targeting Carter Page from
April █, 2017 to June █, 2017.

A.   Case Reorganization, Investigative Developments, and Decision to Seek Renewal

As described in Chapter Three, in January 2017, CD reorganized the Crossfire
Hurricane investigation and divided the cases among two of the three branches in
CD. As a result of the reorganization, there were new supervisory special agents
and case agents working on the Carter Page investigation. Deputy Assistant
Director (DAD) Jennifer Boone and SSA 3 were the supervisors at Headquarters
overseeing the Carter Page investigation, which was transferred to NYFO when the
cases were reorganized. In March 2017, Case Agent 1 was promoted to a
supervisory position, and Case Agent 6 became the new case agent handling the
Carter Page investigation in NYFO, with assistance from Case Agent 1 and SSA 5.

Email communications reflect that the Crossfire Hurricane team continued to
review evidence from the FISA collections after the court reauthorized FISA
authority in January 2017, targeting Carter Page. In January and February 2017,
the FBI provided updates to the OI Attorney, which were passed on to his
supervisors and ODAG. These updates included:

1. ███████████████████████████████████████
   ██████████ ;

2. ███████████████████████████████████████
   ███████████████████████████████████████
   ██████████ ; and

3. Page met with an FBI CHS regarding Page's think tank idea and
wanted help/insight from the CHS. Page revealed to the CHS that he
wanted the think tank to focus on countering anti-Western views on
Russia. He also revealed that a senior Russian government official
pledged a million dollars toward the project.

In addition, the team continued its efforts to corroborate the information in
Steele's reports, including identifying Steele's sub-sources. As described in Chapter

Six, after the FBI identified Steele's Primary Sub-source and in January 2017 (after Renewal Application No. 1 was signed), Case Agent 1 and the Supervisory Intel Analyst interviewed him/her. Following the January interview, the Supervisory Intel Analyst, with assistance from Case Agent 1, wrote a lengthy summary of the interview. As described in Chapter Six, the Primary Sub-source told the FBI that he/she provided Steele with some of the information in Steele's reports. The Supervisory Intel Analyst said that the information from the interview with the Primary Sub-source provided details used to identify sub-sources referenced in Steele's reports, which assisted the investigation. However, in some instances, statements the Primary Sub-source made about what his/her sources told him/her—and what he/she then provided to Steele—were inconsistent with information attributed to his/her sources in Steele's reporting, as well as in the first Carter Page FISA application and Renewal Application No. 1. As described in Chapter Eight, most team members told us that they either were not aware of the inconsistences or, if they were aware, did not make the connection that the inconsistencies affected aspects of the FISA applications. Further, Case Agent 1 and the Supervisory Intel Analyst told us that the Primary Sub-source may have been "minimizing" certain aspects of what he/she told Steele.

Further, in March 2017, Case Agent 1 and Case Agent 6 conducted five voluntary interviews with Carter Page. During those interviews, Carter Page provided the following: information about his July and December 2016 trips to Moscow; individuals he denied meeting to include Igor Sechin and Paul Manafort; a trip to Singapore in February 2017 for Gazprom Investor Day; and his lack of involvement in the Republican National Committee's (RNC) platform change on assistance to Ukraine. Carter Page also discussed his contacts with Gazprom, his assumption that he was under FBI surveillance, and he denied that anyone from Russia asked him to relay any messages to anyone in the campaign. Carter Page told the agents that he knew he had previously communicated with Russian intelligence officers in New York but stated his interactions were not a "back-channel," and he wanted nothing to do with espionage. He said that because of his interactions with these Russian intelligence officers, he knew he was "on the books" and understood that this meant RIS considered him a source, witting or unwitting. He also said that in mid-October 2016, while crossing a street in New York City, his cell phone fell out of his pocket and was smashed by a car, resulting in a loss of encrypted communications.

Following the interviews with Carter Page and review of the FISA collections, agents working on the Carter Page investigation discussed and had differing opinions about seeking a second renewal. Case Agent 6 told us that although he reviewed the FISA collections when he was assigned to the Carter Page investigation in February 2017, he had not reviewed enough information to make a determination as to whether seeking a renewal was necessary. He told us that he reviewed ███████████████████████████ in which Carter Page ████████ ████████ Case Agent 6 told us that although this email and Page's statement in an interview caused him to question whether it was worth seeking Renewal Application No. 2, he ultimately did not disagree with Case Agent 1 and SSA 5 who told him they wanted to continue the surveillance of Page. He also said that he discussed seeking the renewal with his NYFO Special Agent in Charge and did not recall any disagreement about seeking a second renewal from anyone working on the investigation.

SSA 3 told the OIG that there were discussions at Headquarters among members of the Crossfire Hurricane team, including SSA 2 and Boone, about Carter Page and whether he was a significant target at that point in the investigation. According to SSA 3, he and SSA 2 believed at the time they approached the decision point on a second FISA renewal that, based upon the evidence already collected, Carter Page was a distraction in the investigation, not a key player in the Trump campaign, and was not critical to the overarching investigation. SSA 2 told us that he questioned whether seeking a second renewal was the best use of FBI resources as Carter Page had "deviated from a consistent pattern of life" and was no longer communicating in the same way as he had in 2016. SSA 2 and SSA 3 told us that they did not know or recall who at the FBI ultimately made the decision to seek the second renewal or the reasons why.

Boone told us that the team discussed what further steps to take in the investigation of Carter Page and not solely whether or not to seek a second FISA renewal. Boone recalled a conversation with SSA 2 about whether a second renewal was necessary, but did not recall if she was directed from management to pursue a second renewal or if the team decided to seek a renewal after discussing whether it would add any value to the investigation. Boone did not recall who ultimately decided to move forward with Renewal Application No. 2, and available documents do not indicate.

B.   Preparation and Approval of Renewal Application No. 2

1.   Draft Renewal Application

Case Agent 6 and the OGC Attorney assisted the OI Attorney in the preparation of Renewal Application No. 2. On March 20, Case Agent 6 sent the OI Attorney an email with an attachment that included "my first round of additions so you can get started." The additions that Case Agent 6 sent included information Carter Page provided in his FBI interviews in March 2017 about his involvement with a Russian business, Page's discussion with Russian officials about a Southern District of New York (SDNY) indictment, Page's denials about meeting a Russian government official, and his lack of involvement in the drafting of the RNC's platform provision on Ukraine.[363] Emails reflect that on March 23 and March 29, Case Agent 6 sent a draft of Renewal Application No. 2 to Case Agent 1 for his review; however, we did not find a response from Case Agent 1 to Case Agent 6 about the draft.

---

[363] As discussed in Chapter Eight, all of the Carter Page FISA applications alleged that Page participated in drafting the RNC's platform change on providing lethal assistance to Ukraine. The FISA applications alleged that the platform change on Ukraine would not include a provision to provide weapons to Ukraine to fight Russian and rebel forces, controverting Republican Party policy.

On March 23, Case Agent 6 emailed the OI Attorney additional information from recent FISA collections, recent Carter Page interviews, and other information derived from the ongoing investigation for inclusion in Renewal Application No. 2. Case Agent 6 did not provide the OI Attorney with the written summary of the Primary Sub-source's interview in January 2017, but instead included in his March 20 write-up for the OI Attorney two brief references to aspects of the January interview, neither of which identified the key inconsistencies between the Primary Sub-source and Steele that we address in Chapter Eight. The OI Attorney completed an initial draft of Renewal Application No. 2 on March 23 and emails reflect that, over the next few days, Case Agent 6 and the OI Attorney edited the initial draft. On March 29, the OI Attorney sent the OGC Attorney a draft for his review and advised that, following the OGC Attorney's review, the OI Attorney would finalize the draft for an "up the chain review."

The statement of facts in the draft and final second renewal application contained the same information used to support probable cause as in Renewal Application No. 1. This included the assessment that post-election, the FBI believed that the Russian government would continue efforts to use U.S. persons, such as Carter Page, to covertly influence U.S. foreign policy and support Russia's perception management efforts. In addition, Renewal Application No. 2 advised the court of recent investigative results, including:

- ███ ;

- The results of recent FBI interviews with Carter Page in which he revealed that during his December 2016 travel to Russia, he met the Russian Deputy Prime Minister who asked him how to connect for "future cooperation," and in which Page also revealed that during travel to Singapore, he met a Vice President of Gazprombank, which the FBI assessed revealed Russia's continued interest in Page;[364]

- Carter Page's denial during a March 2017 FBI interview that he told Russian officials that he was "Male-1" in the indictment of three Russian intelligence officers, described in Chapter Three. When asked a second time about this statement, Page said he "forgot the exact statement," which the FBI assessed showed that Page was not completely forthcoming during this interview;

- ██ ;

- ███

_____

[364] As with other denials made by Carter Page (described in Chapters Five and Ten), Renewal Application No. 2 did not include denials Carter Page made during a meeting with an FBI CHS in January 2017 concerning Steele's election reports. During that recorded meeting, Carter Page characterized the Steele election reporting as "just so false" and "complete lies and spin."

- [REDACTED]

  and

- A February 2017 letter Carter Page sent to the Department of Justice, Civil Rights Division's Voting Section, urging the review of "severe election fraud in the form of disinformation, suppression of dissent, hate crimes and other extensive abuses" by members of the Clinton campaign, which the FBI assessed was self-serving and untrue.

Renewal Application No. 2 also included a new footnote stating that the FBI conducted several interviews of Papadopoulos, during which Papadopoulos confirmed he met with officials from the FFG but denied discussing anything related to the Russian government, which the FBI assessed were misleading or incomplete statements. The footnote did not include that Papadopoulos made other statements during these interviews, including statements that minimized Carter Page's role in the Trump campaign and a claim that Person 1 (whom the FBI assessed was the likely source for some of the Steele reporting relied upon in the applications, including the allegations against Page) told Papadopoulos that he/she (Person 1) had no knowledge of the information reported in "the recent Trump Dossier." Renewal Application Nos. 2 and 3 did advise the court of a news article claiming that Person 1 was a source for some of the Steele reports and that Person 1 denied having any compromising information regarding the President.[365]

The source characterization statement for Steele, reliance on Steele's reporting, and the information concerning the positions and access of the sub-sources remained the same as in the first FISA application and Renewal Application No. 1, with the exception of changing Steele's status with the FBI from "suspended" to "closed" as a result of the *Mother Jones* disclosure. The OI Attorney told us that there had been prior instances in other investigations where the FBI has closed a source, and OI disclosed it to the FISC as they did in the Carter Page Renewal Application No. 2. The OI Attorney told us that OI expects the FBI to assess the information provided by a closed source, and how closure of the source impacts the information from the source cited in an application. In this instance, he said the FBI told him that it continued to believe Steele was reliable.

---

[365] In Chapter Five, we describe how the FBI did not specifically and explicitly advise OI about the FBI's assessment before the first FISA application that Person 1 was the sub-source who provided the information relied upon in the application from Steele Reports 80, 95, and 102; that Steele had provided derogatory information regarding Person 1; and that [REDACTED]. As noted previously, in the next chapter, we describe the information from the Primary Sub-source interview concerning Person 1 and the information that was not shared with OI about inconsistences between the Primary Sub-source and Steele concerning information provided by Person 1.

Finally, the draft and final FISA Renewal Application No. 2 advised the court in a footnote that the FBI interviewed Steele's Primary Sub-source and found him/her to be "truthful and cooperative."

███ the application did not otherwise describe the information the Primary Sub-source provided to the FBI or identify any statements made by Primary Sub-source that contradicted or were inconsistent with information from Steele's reports relied on in the application. Emails reflect that on March 31, the OI Attorney drafted this footnote with feedback from the OGC Attorney. The OGC Attorney edited the footnote to reflect that the FBI was undertaking "additional investigative activity to further corroborate the information provide [sic] by [Steele]." The descriptor that the Primary Sub-source was "truthful and cooperative" was not edited by the OGC Attorney, who told us that although he did not receive a full briefing on the interview of the Primary Sub-source, he was present at meetings where the interview was discussed. The OGC Attorney said he recalled that he learned during these meetings that the information from the Primary Sub-source "echoed what the reporting was that [Steele] provided to us." We asked why the application did not include the information the Primary Sub-source provided during the interview and the OGC Attorney told us that he did not believe the OI Attorney was "looking to provide that level of detail in the application."

2.   Review and Approval Process

As described below, FISA Renewal Application No. 2 received supervisory review similar to Renewal Application No. 1, including review by NSD supervisors and ODAG.

a.   Supervisory Review and Finalization of Read Copy

As with Renewal Application No. 1, Baker told us that he did not review Renewal Application No. 2. Anderson was on leave during this time, and we found no evidence that anyone in OGC above the OGC Unit Chief level reviewed Renewal Application No. 2.

On March 30, the OI Attorney emailed a draft of Renewal Application No. 2 to Evans, Sanz-Rexach, OI's Deputy Operations Section Chief, and the OI Unit Chief for their review. Sanz-Rexach told us that he read Renewal Application No. 2 and did not have any concerns with the probable cause stated in the application. He said that with each renewal application, the FBI was obtaining "nuggets" of additional information that furthered the probable cause. The Deputy Operations Section Chief told us that she reviewed this renewal application and may have provided comments, but she did not recall any specific discussions about Renewal Application No. 2.

On April 3, Evans emailed McCord the draft application for her review and advised her that the read copy would be filed with the FISC later that day. McCord told us that while she did not have a specific recollection of Renewal Application No. 2, she did recall that after the first FISA renewal, there were ███████████

215

█████████ and more information developed in the investigation. Specifically, she recalled that the team had developed information confirming Carter Page's July trip, behavior by Page that was "at least suspicious," and that he made self-serving statements.

b.   ODAG Review and Approval of Read Copy

On January 30, 2017, Dana Boente became the Acting Attorney General. On February 9, 2017, following the confirmation of Jefferson Sessions to be the Attorney General, Boente became the Acting DAG, a position in which he served until April 25, 2017. On March 31, 2017, Boente became the Acting Attorney General with respect to the Crossfire Hurricane investigation by virtue of then Attorney General Sessions's recusal. Some of the personnel in ODAG also changed after January 30, and James Crowell became Acting PADAG. Gauhar remained in ODAG and continued in her position as the Associate Deputy Attorney General responsible for ODAG's national security portfolio.

On April 2, Gauhar gave the draft application to Boente and Crowell, along with a memorandum containing questions and notations to assist in their review of the renewal application. Gauhar said that because this was Boente's first review of a FISA application targeting Carter Page, Boente wanted to ensure he had "good visibility" into the application. Boente told us that he did not specifically recall reading the Gauhar memorandum or reviewing the read copy, although contemporaneous documents and emails reflect that Boente did, in fact, review the read copy prior to it being filed with the court.

Gauhar told us, and notes reflect, that after Boente reviewed the footnote in the renewal application concerning the closure of Steele as an FBI CHS, Boente asked whether there was concern about the potential bias of Steele. Gauhar told us that she did not recall the specific discussions they may have had on this issue, but she recalled that Boente was very engaged on the issue of Steele's potential bias, and said they had multiple discussions on that specific issue. Boente told us that he did not recall what information he was provided about Steele or what Boente knew about Steele or his reporting when Boente considered the second renewal application.

As with the previous two Carter Page FISA applications, OI waited for approval from ODAG before submitting the read copy to the FISC. On April 3, Gauhar notified Evans that Boente approved sending the read copy to the FISC.

3.   Feedback from the FISC, Completion of the Final Renewal Application and Woods Procedures, and Final Legal Review

On April 3, the read copy was filed with the FISC. On April 6, the OI Attorney advised Evans and the OI supervisors that the FISC judge reviewed the renewal application, had one non-substantive edit to a signature page, and would sign the application without an appearance.

On April 3, the OI Unit Chief "signed out" the cert copy of the application and cert memo to the FBI, so that the FBI could complete the Woods Procedures. Case Agent 6 asked Case Agent 1 to assist with the Woods Procedures because Case Agent 6 recently joined the investigation and was not familiar with all of the historical facts related to Carter Page. Case Agent 6 provided documents to Case Agent 1, who was the agent responsible for compiling the supporting documentation into the Woods File and performing the field office database checks on Carter Page and the accuracy review of each fact asserted in the FISA application. SSA 5 was responsible for confirming that the Woods File contained appropriate documentation for the factual assertions in the FISA application.

As noted previously, Case Agent 1 told us that his general practice on a renewal application is not to necessarily review the factual assertions carried over from the prior application. He said that if the factual information does not materially change from the prior FISA application, he will just review the newly added information. However, in this case, Case Agent 1 told us that he was "pretty sure" he reviewed the factual assertions from the prior renewal application in addition to the new factual assertions to confirm the Woods File contained the appropriate documentation for Renewal Application No. 2.[366] After Case Agent 1 completed the Woods process, he signed the Woods Form and gave the Woods Form and Woods File to SSA 5 who was his supervisor in NYFO. SSA 5 told us he made sure every fact in the application had a supporting document in the Woods File. SSA 5 then signed the Woods Form on April 4, affirming the verification and documentation of each factual assertion in the application, and sent the FISA application package containing the Woods Form, cert copy, and cert memo to the Headquarters Program Manager assigned the responsibility of signing the final application as the affiant under oath that the factual information was true and correct.[367]

As in the case of Renewal Application No. 1, SSA 2 served as the affiant for Renewal Application No. 2. SSA 2 told us that he reviewed the newly added information in Renewal Application No. 2 and identified no issues with any of the information in the application. SSA 2 told us that he believed everything in the application was true and correct. SSA 2 told us that he did not recall reviewing the Woods Form, but that it was his practice at the time to do so before signing a FISA application (as described in Chapter Two, the Woods Procedures do not require the

---

[366] As we noted previously, according to Case Agent 6, Case Agent 1 told him that when he (Case Agent 1) performed the factual accuracy review on Renewal Application No. 1, he only reviewed the new factual assertions in the application, not the factual assertions that carried over from the prior application. Case Agent 6 told us that they did not discuss how Case Agent 1 performed the factual accuracy review on Renewal Application No. 2.

[367] The OIG examined the completeness of the Woods File by comparing the facts asserted in Renewal Application No. 2 to the documents maintained in the Woods File. Our comparison identified instances in which facts asserted in the application were not supported by documentation in the Woods File. Specifically, we found facts asserted in the FISA application that have no supporting documentation in the Woods File, facts that have purported supporting documentation in the Woods File but the documentation does not state the fact asserted in the FISA application, or facts that have purported supporting documentation in the Woods File but the document shows the fact asserted is inaccurate. We provide examples of specific errors in Appendix One.

affiant to review the Woods File, only the case agent and his or her supervisor). After doing so, SSA 2 signed the affidavit affirming under penalty of perjury that the information in the package was true and correct before he submitted it to an OGC Attorney.

The OGC Attorney said that while he was aware of the FBI seeking renewal authority for the Carter Page FISA, he had less awareness of the specific issues in Renewal Application No. 2 and did not recall reviewing any drafts other than the cert copy. We were advised that the FBI and NSD were unable to locate a fully signed copy of the cert memo that accompanied Renewal Application No. 2, and we were therefore unable to independently determine who reviewed the FISA application package on behalf of OGC's NSCLB.

4. FBI Director's Certification

Comey signed FISA Renewal Application No. 2 on behalf of the FBI on April 5, 2017, certifying that the information sought was foreign intelligence information that could not reasonably be obtained by normal investigative techniques and was necessary to protect the United States against clandestine intelligence activities. Although Comey did not specifically recall reviewing FISA Renewal Application No. 2, for the reasons described in Chapter Five, Comey told us that he reviewed the first Carter Page application and was satisfied that the requested FISA authority had a sufficient foreign intelligence purpose.

5. Oral Briefing and Approval

Sanz-Rexach briefed Boente on Renewal Application No. 2 and told us that it was a short briefing, and Boente did not raise any questions before he signed the application. Boente had requested regular briefings on the investigation after he became the Acting Attorney General and was familiar with the case at the time he reviewed and approved Renewal Application No. 2.

Although, as noted above, contemporaneous documents and emails reflect that Boente read the application prior to it being filed with the court, Boente told us that he did not have an independent recollection of having read the application. After showing him the documentation indicating that he had read it, Boente said that he was sure he would have read the application provided to him. Boente told us that although he did not recall specific discussions about Steele in connection with this application, he remembered being aware that the origin of Steele's reports was opposition research, and he thought the footnote identifying Steele's reporting as political opposition research was "very clear." Boente told us when he signed the application following NSD's short oral briefing, he was satisfied that there was sufficient probable cause to believe Page was an agent of a foreign power. He also told us that he knew at the time that two different judges had previously found probable cause, and that it was important to acquire whatever evidence the Department could regarding Russia's interference with the 2016 U.S. elections.

On April ▮, Boente signed the application as Acting Attorney General, and the application was submitted to the FISC the same day. By his signature, and as stated in the application, Boente found that the application satisfied the criteria and requirements of the FISA statute and approved its filing with the court.[368]

6.   Final Orders

The final FISA application included proposed orders, which were signed by FISC Judge Anne C. Conway on April █, 2017. According to NSD, the judge signed the final orders, as proposed by the government in their entirety, without holding a hearing.

The primary order and warrant stated that the court found, based upon the facts submitted in the verified application, that there was probable cause to believe that Russia is a foreign power and that Carter Page was an agent of Russia under 50 U.S.C. § 1801(b)(2)(E). The court also found that █████████████ ██ The court authorized the requested electronic surveillance ██████ for 90 days and █████████████ necessary to effectuate the electronic surveillance ████████████ authorized by the court.

III.   FISA Renewal Application No. 3 (June █, 2017)

On June █, 2017, a day before FISA coverage on Carter Page was going to expire, and at the request of the FBI, the Department filed an application with the FISC requesting an additional 90 days of FISA coverage targeting Carter Page.[369] A FISC judge reviewed and issued the requested orders resulting in an additional 90 days of electronic surveillance ████████████ targeting Carter Page from June █, 2017 to September █, 2017.

A.   Investigative Developments and Decision to Seek FISA Renewal

After the second renewal of FISA authority, the FBI continued its FISA collection of communications and other evidence pertaining to Carter Page. In addition, available documents indicate that one of the focuses of the Carter Page investigation at this time was obtaining his financial records. NYFO sought compulsory legal process in April 2017 for banking and financial records for Carter Page and his company, Global Energy Capital, as well as information relating to two encrypted online applications, one of which Page utilized on his cell phone.

---

[368] Boente's signature also specifically authorized █████████████████████ ███████████████████████

[369] On May 17, 2017, the Crossfire Hurricane cases were transferred to the Office of the Special Counsel. Although agents and analysts were working with the Special Counsel, the FISA application was still subject to Department approval and notification requirements.

Documents reflect that agents also conducted multiple interviews of individuals associated with Carter Page.

Case Agent 6 told us, and documents reflect, that despite the ongoing investigation, the team did not expect to renew the Carter Page FISA before Renewal Application No. 2's authority expired on June 30. Case Agent 6 said that the FISA collection the FBI had received during the second renewal period was not yielding any new information. The OGC Attorney told us that when the FBI was considering whether to seek further FISA authority following Renewal Application No. 2, the FISA was "starting to go dark." During one of the March 2017 interviews, Page told Case Agent 1 and Case Agent 6 that he believed he was under surveillance and the agents did not believe continued surveillance would provide any relevant information. Case Agent 6 said ███████████████████████
███
███

SSA 5 and SSA 2 said that further investigation yielded previously unknown locations that they believed could provide information of investigative value, and they decided to seek another renewal. Specifically, SSA 5 and Case Agent 6 told us, and documents reflect, that ████████████████████████
██
█████████ they decided to seek a third renewal. █████
███
███

B. Preparation and Approval of Renewal Application No. 3

1. Draft Renewal Application

Case Agent 6 assisted the OI Attorney in the preparation of Renewal Application No. 3. Emails reflect that Case Agent 6 and the OI Attorney exchanged information on recent investigative findings and relevant FISA collections for the draft of Renewal Application No. 3.[370] On June 16, the OI Attorney emailed the OGC Attorney and Case Agent 6 the first draft of Renewal Application No. 3 for their review. On June 18, Case Agent 6 responded to the email by providing answers to the remaining questions in the draft application. Emails reflect that on June 19, the Supervisory Intel Analyst and SSA 2 received a copy of the renewal draft from Case Agent 6 for review; however, the Supervisory Intel Analyst did not recall reviewing the renewal application. SSA 2 said he had no comments, and we found no documentation indicating one way or the other.

The statement of facts in the third renewal application contained the same information used to support probable cause as in Renewal Application No. 2. This

---

[370] Although there were no recent relevant FISA collections the team found useful, we were told that the FBI was still reviewing FISA collections identified prior to Renewal Application No. 2.

included the assessment that post-election, the FBI believed that the Russian government would continue efforts to use U.S. persons, such as Carter Page, to covertly influence U.S. foreign policy and support Russia's perception management efforts. In addition, Renewal Application No. 3 advised the court of recent investigative results, including:

- A June 2017 interview by the FBI of an individual closely tied to the President of the New Economic School in Moscow who stated that Carter Page was selected to give a commencement speech in July 2016 because he was candidate Trump's "Russia-guy." This individual also told the FBI that while in Russia in July 2016, Carter Page was picked up in a chauffeured car and it was rumored he met with Igor Sechin. However, the FD-302 documenting this interview, which was included in the Woods File for Renewal Application No. 3, does not contain any reference to a chauffeured car picking up Carter Page. We were unable to locate any document or information in the Woods File that supported this assertion.[371]

- A June 2017 interview by the FBI of a different individual closely tied to the New Economic School in Moscow who told investigators that he did not think it likely that Carter Page and Sechin met during Page's visit to Moscow in July 2016. The FBI assessed that, because this individual was unaware of a meeting that Carter Page had with a different Russian official while in Moscow in July 2016, the individual did not know about all the meetings that Page had while in Moscow in July 2016, and the FBI assessed that, based on the rumored meeting between Page and Sechin described in the prior bullet point, Page likely met with Sechin prior to the time that Page joined this individual at the New Economic School;

- ████████████████████████████████████[372]

- ████████████████████████████████████

---

[371] We asked both agents that interviewed this individual, Case Agent 6 and Case Agent 7, if this individual stated during the interview that Page was picked up in a chauffeured car. Case Agent 6 told us he did recall the individual making this statement; Case Agent 7 did not recall and stated he may have made the statement during a telephone interview that occurred later.

[372] The third renewal application stated that ████████████████████████████████████

- ██;

- A statement by Carter Page during a March 30 interview with the FBI about the loss and destruction of his cell phone at the same time media reports were discussing the FBI's possible investigation of Page; and

- Carter Page's meetings with media outlets, which the FBI assessed may have been undertaken to promote his theories on U.S. foreign policy and refute claims of involvement with the Russian government's efforts to influence the 2016 U.S. election. The FBI believed Page was instructed by Russian officials to deny in the media Russian involvement with the election.

The application also stated the following:

██ Additionally, based on Page's history of willingness to assist Russian IOs, which as discussed above the FBI believes began as early as 2007..., and his comment to the FBI that he believes he is "on the [SVR] books," the FBI believes that Page remains favorable to future RIS taskings.

Steele's source characterization statement, reliance on Steele's reporting, and the information concerning the positions and access of Steele's sub-sources remained the same as in Renewal Application No. 2. The short description of the FBI's January 2017 interview with Steele's Primary Sub-source also remained the same. Renewal Application No. 3 also added ██

In support of probable cause, the FBI added statements Carter Page made during his first consensually monitored meeting with an FBI CHS in August 2016 (summarized in Chapter Ten). These statements included Page's response to a reference to "the 1980 October Surprise," where Page stated that there would be a "different October Surprise" this year and later stated that "well I want to have the conspiracy theory about the, uh, the Ru- the next email dump with these, uh, 33 thousand, you know." In the application, the FBI assessed that these statements, along with other evidence, indicated that Page was aware of the pending leak of DNC emails.[373] As previously described in Chapter Five, none of the applications advised the court of other statements Page made during this meeting, including

---

[373] On or about November 6, 2016, WikiLeaks released a second set of DNC emails.

that he had "literally never met" Manafort, had "never said one word to him," and that Manafort had not responded to any of Carter Page's emails.

As described in Chapter Five, we found that information about the August 2016 meeting was not included in any of the three prior FISA applications because it was not shared with the OI Attorney until on or about June 20, 2017, when Case Agent 6 sent the OI Attorney a 163-page document containing the statements made by Carter Page during the meeting. The OI Attorney told us that he used the 163-page document to accurately quote Page's statements concerning the "October Surprise" in the final renewal application but that the OI Attorney did not read the other aspects of the document and that the case agent did not flag for him the statements Page made about Manafort. The OI Attorney told us that these statements, which were available to the FBI before the first application, should have been flagged by the FBI for inclusion in the FISA applications at that time because the statements were relevant to the court's assessment of the allegations concerning Manafort using Page as an intermediary with Russia. Case Agent 6 told us that he did not know that Page made the statement about Manafort because the August 2016 meeting took place before he was assigned to the investigation. He said that the reason he knew about the "October Surprise" statements in the document was that he had heard about them from Case Agent 1 and did a word search to find the specific discussion on that topic. Case Agent 6 further told us that he added the "October Surprise" statements in consultation with the OI Attorney after the OI Attorney asked him if there was other information in the case file that would help support probable cause.

Case Agent 1 assisted in the preparation of the first application and told us that he did not recall why he did not include the "October Surprise" statements in the first application. He told us that he remembered that he thought it was an "odd exchange" between Page and the CHS at the time, and he said may have thought that it would have been difficult to convey to the court what Page's words meant.

Similar to the previous applications, Renewal Application No. 3 did not advise the court of information provided to the FBI in August 2016 regarding Carter Page's relationship with another U.S. government agency and information Page had shared with the other agency about his contacts with Russian intelligence officers, contacts that overlapped with facts asserted in the FISA application. This was so even though the FBI re-engaged with the other U.S. government agency in June 2017, following interviews that Page gave to news outlets in April and May 2017 during which Page stated that he had assisted the USIC in the past. SSA 2, who was to be the affiant for the third renewal and had been the affiant for the first two renewals, told us that he wanted a definitive answer as to whether Page had ever been a source for the other U.S. government agency before the final renewal application because he was concerned that Page could claim that he had been acting on behalf of the U.S. government in engaging with certain Russians. As we describe in Chapter Eight, this led to interactions between the FBI OGC Attorney and a liaison from the other U.S. government agency, who reconfirmed the information that the other agency had provided to the FBI in August 2016 that Page did have a prior relationship with that other agency. However, for reasons we detail in Chapter

Eight, that information was not accurately provided to either SSA 2 or OI by the OGC Attorney and was therefore not included in the third renewal application.

2. Review and Approval Process

As with Renewal Application Nos. 1 and 2, Baker told us he did not review Renewal Application No. 3. Baker told us that he questioned whether it was worthwhile to seek another renewal because Carter Page was no longer using the facilities the FBI was monitoring, and that from a management perspective, an additional renewal was not worth the expenditure of resources. Baker recalled discussions about whether the FISA was still productive and providing any foreign intelligence, but the decision was made to continue with the renewal because there was still an opportunity to obtain foreign intelligence information. Anderson did not recall whether she reviewed the third renewal application, and we found no evidence that anyone else in OGC above the OGC Unit Chief level did so.

On June 21, the OI Unit Chief sent the OI Attorney, Case Agent 6, and the OGC Attorney questions after reviewing the draft application. The OI Unit Chief's questions focused on whether there were updates to assessments from the prior renewals. On June 22, following email communications with Case Agent 6 to finalize the edits and questions from the OI Unit Chief, the OI Attorney emailed the read copy to Evans, Sanz-Rexach, the Deputy Operations Section Chief, and Case Agent 6. The OI managers and Evans told us that they did not recall their feedback, and Evans said he was not sure whether he reviewed this final application before it was filed.

On June 23, the same day the read copy was submitted to the court, Evans emailed Gauhar the application for ODAG's review. Unlike the read copy for the three prior Carter Page FISA applications, we found no information indicating that ODAG received and approved the read copy in advance of OI filing it with the court. With Renewal Application No. 3, it appears NSD followed the more typical practice of submitting the application to ODAG shortly before the DAG approved and signed the final application.

3. Feedback from the FISC, Completion of the Final Renewal Application and Woods Procedures, and FBI Director Certification

On June 28, the OI Attorney advised Evans, Sanz-Rexach, and OI's Deputy Operations Section Chief that, based on the read copy, the judge would approve Renewal Application No. 3. According to the OI Attorney's email to his supervisors, the judge "believed there was enough to let us go one more time and he will approve without a hearing." The OI Attorney told the OIG that the words, "let us go one more time" were his words and not the words of the judge. He said that he was not trying to imply that the judge said that the court would not approve another renewal.

Before the court's feedback, the OI Unit Chief "signed out" the cert copy of the application and cert memo to the FBI, so that the FBI could complete the

Woods Procedures. Emails reflect that a few additional minor edits were made to the cert copy after the read copy was filed and prior to the completion of the Woods Procedures.

Case Agent 7 was a relatively new FBI special agent who was responsible for compiling the supporting documentation into a Woods File and performing the field office database checks on Carter Page and the accuracy review of each fact asserted in the FISA application. Case Agent 7 told us that he had been assigned to assist in the Carter Page investigation sometime in spring 2017. Case Agent 7 was responsible for confirming that the file contained appropriate documentation for the factual assertions in the FISA application. Case Agent 7 told us that when he conducted the factual accuracy review on Renewal Application No. 3, he reviewed every fact to re-verify the accuracy of factual assertions carried over from prior applications and made sure every factual assertion had appropriate documentation in the Woods File. During the Woods process, Case Agent 6 and Case Agent 7, identified some documents that were missing from the Woods File, and added them in order to provide support for the pertinent factual assertions in Renewal Application No. 3. After Case Agent 7 completed the Woods process, he signed the Woods Form and gave the Woods Form and Woods File to SSA 5, who was Case Agent 7's supervisor in NYFO. SSA 5 told us he made sure every factual assertion in the application had a supporting document in the Woods File. SSA 5 signed the Woods Form on June 27, affirming the verification and documentation of each factual assertion in the application, and then sent the FISA application package containing the Woods Form, cert copy, and cert memo to the Headquarters Program Manager assigned the responsibility of signing the final application, as the affiant, under oath that the factual information was true and correct.[374]

As with the prior renewal applications, the Headquarters Program Manager assigned as the affiant for the final renewal application was SSA 2. SSA 2 told us that he believed he reviewed the newly added information in the renewal. In addition, SSA 2 said that as the affiant, it was his practice to review the Woods Form to make sure it was completed by the case agent and an SSA before signing off on the application and submitting it to an OGC attorney (as described in Chapter Two, the Woods Procedures did not require the affiant to review the Woods File, only the case agent and his or her supervisor). SSA 2 told us that he believed everything in the application was true and correct. SSA 2 signed the affidavit affirming under penalty of perjury that the information in the package was true and correct. He then submitted the FISA application package to the OGC Attorney for legal review.

---

[374] The OIG examined the completeness of the Woods File by comparing the facts asserted in Renewal Application No. 3 to the documents maintained in the Woods File. Our comparison identified instances in which facts asserted in the application were not supported by documentation in the Woods File. Specifically, we found facts that are asserted in the FISA application that have no supporting documentation in the Woods File, facts that have purported supporting documentation in the Woods File but the documentation does not state the fact asserted in the FISA application, or facts that have purported supporting documentation in the Woods File but the documentation shows the fact asserted is inaccurate. We provide examples of specific errors in Appendix One.

The OGC Attorney, who had participated in the drafting process and was familiar with the content of the application, told us that he reviewed the Woods Form with the Headquarters Program Manager. After the OGC Attorney confirmed that all of the Woods Procedures had been completed, he signed the cert memo below the OI Unit Chief's signature and submitted the package to OGC Unit Chief 2 who was assigned to perform the supervisory legal review.[375]

OGC Unit Chief 2 told us that he could not recall whether he read Renewal Application No. 3 in its entirety or just the probable cause portion. He said that his general practice is to rely upon the cert memo's description, and if something "triggers" his inclination to go further, he will read some or all of the application. OGC Unit Chief 2 told us that he was sure he reviewed the cert memo and Woods Form and, based on those documents, determined that the application package was complete, all the steps of the Woods Procedures were represented to have been taken, the probable cause standard was met, and there were no outstanding issues. He then signed the cert memo, signifying that the application was ready for certification and for submission to the FBI Director.

Then Acting Director McCabe signed Renewal Application No. 3 on June 28, certifying that the information sought was foreign intelligence information that could not reasonably be obtained by normal investigative techniques and was necessary to protect the United States against clandestine intelligence activities. McCabe told us that he did not recall whether he reviewed the entire FISA application package or whether he relied primarily upon the cert memo and his familiarity with the Carter Page investigation before he made the required certification. He told us that he understood at the time he signed the application that the FBI, Department, and FISC were comfortable with the application such that it was not "a great stretch" for him to sign the certification.

4. DAG Oral Briefing and Approval

On April 26, 2017, Rod Rosenstein was confirmed as the Deputy Attorney General. Gauhar remained the Associate Deputy Attorney General (ADAG) responsible for ODAG's national security portfolio and told us that she worked primarily with Crowell to complete the ODAG review of Renewal Application No. 3. Crowell told us he read the application but relied on Gauhar and NSD to advise Rosenstein on this application.

Shortly after he was sworn in as DAG, Rosenstein received briefings about the Crossfire Hurricane investigation. Rosenstein told us that, as a result, he was more familiar with the facts of the case than is typical for FISA applications. Rosenstein received a copy of the application in advance of NSD's oral briefing, and told us he "would have looked through it." Although he could not recall whether he

---

[375] Chapter Two describes the signature from NSCLB necessary for approval on the cert memo as Senior Executive Service (SES) level. Witnesses told us that usually the SES-level supervisor is an NSCLB section chief or a Deputy General Counsel, but that, on occasions, the role is delegated to a GS-15 Unit Chief.

reviewed the application in its entirety, he recalled reading enough to understand the substance of the allegations involved.

Rosenstein told us that he had reviewed FISA applications almost every day after his confirmation, and he believed Renewal Application No. 3 was "above average" in terms of the justification for the continued coverage in the renewal. He said that he was in a different position than those who considered the previous applications because by the time he received the application, many different Department officials had approved the prior ones and three different federal judges had found probable cause. He also said he had a conversation with Boente about the application in which Boente expressed the view that a DAG should not refuse to sign a FISA application that establishes probable cause, and when there is a legitimate basis for conducting the investigation, just because it could end up becoming "politically embarrassing" at some later point.[376] Further, Rosenstein told us that he did not view the application as being "particularly sensitive" when he received it in June 2017 because at that time the campaign was over, and Carter Page did not have any connection to the Trump Administration.

On June 29, OI's Deputy Operations Section Chief provided a briefing on the June renewal application to Rosenstein, and, according to Gauhar, Rosenstein brought his copy of Renewal Application No. 3 to the briefing. Gauhar and the Deputy Operations Section Chief did not recall any significant questions during the briefing about the renewal. However, Rosenstein told us that he recalled raising a question (at this briefing or immediately before it) about whether continued FISA coverage was going to produce useful information given that the FISA coverage targeting Carter Page had been leaked to the media. He said that he remembered being told that this renewal would likely be the last one unless new evidence was uncovered.

On June ██, Rosenstein signed the application, and the application was submitted to the FISC the same day. By his signature, and as stated in the application, Rosenstein found that the application satisfied the criteria and requirements of the FISA and approved its filing with the court.[377]

5. Final Orders

The final FISA application included proposed orders, which were signed by FISC Judge Raymond J. Dearie, on June ██, 2017. According to NSD, the judge signed the final orders, as proposed by the government in their entirety, without holding a hearing.

The primary order and warrant stated that the court found, based upon the facts submitted in the verified application, that there was probable cause to believe

---

[376] On June 26, Boente, who at the time was serving as the Acting Assistant Attorney General for NSD, received the read copy of Renewal Application No. 3. Boente told us he had no recollection of reading the application.

[377] Rosenstein's signature also specifically authorized ███████████████████

that Russia is a foreign power and that Carter Page was an agent of Russia under 50 U.S.C. § 1801(b)(2)(E). The court also found that ██. The court authorized the requested electronic surveillance ████████████ for 90 days and ████████████████████ necessary to effectuate the electronic surveillance ████████████████████ authorized by the court.

Approximately 1 year after this final FISA application, in July 2018, NSD submitted a letter to the FISC, advising the court of certain factual omissions in the Carter Page FISA applications that came to NSD's attention after the last renewal application was filed. In the next chapter we describe this compliance letter to the FISC and the omissions detailed in it, as well as other instances, not known to NSD at the time but identified by the OIG during this review, in which factual assertions relied upon in the three Carter Page renewal applications were inaccurate, incomplete, or unsupported by appropriate documentation, based upon information in the FBI's possession at the time the applications were filed.

CHAPTER EIGHT
MISSTATEMENTS, OMISSIONS, AND ERRORS IN THE FISA RENEWAL APPLICATIONS

As we describe in this chapter, the three Carter Page renewal applications contained a number of factual representations that were inaccurate, incomplete, or unsupported by appropriate documentation, based upon information in the FBI's possession at the time the applications were filed. On July 12, 2018, approximately one year after the final FISA renewal application, the National Security Division (NSD) sent a letter to the Foreign Intelligence Surveillance Court (FISC) advising the court of certain factual omissions in the Carter Page FISA applications that came to NSD's attention after the last renewal application was filed. The information, which had been in the FBI's possession, included certain statements made by George Papadopoulos to FBI confidential human sources (CHSs), information provided to the FBI by Department attorney Bruce Ohr as a result of Ohr's conversations with Christopher Steele, and admissions Steele made in court filings in foreign litigation regarding his interactions with the media. We found no evidence that officials in NSD had been told of this information or were aware of these omissions at the time the four FISA applications were filed with the court. Further, we found no evidence suggesting that the senior Department officials who approved the various FISA applications—Deputy Attorney General (DAG) Sally Yates (the first application and first renewal), Acting Attorney General Dana Boente (the second renewal), or DAG Rod Rosenstein (the third renewal)—were aware of these issues at the time they signed the FISA applications.

We also detail instances not described in the July 2018 letter to the FISC, but identified by the OIG during the course of this review, in which factual assertions made in the three renewal applications were inaccurate, incomplete, or unsupported by appropriate documentation, based upon information in the FBI's possession at the time the applications were filed. These included inconsistencies between Steele's reporting and information provided by his Primary Sub-source to the FBI; information provided to the FBI by another U.S. government agency about Page's prior relationship with that agency; information concerning Steele's past work-related performance; information regarding the connection between Steele's reporting and the Democratic Party, the Democratic National Committee (DNC), and the Hillary Clinton campaign; information from the FBI's human source validation report concerning Steele; denials by Joseph Mifsud to the FBI; and information about Carter Page's lack of involvement in the change in the Republican Party platform concerning Russia and Ukraine. We found no evidence that Yates was aware of these issues at the time she approved the first FISA renewal application. We found that Boente was also unaware of these issues when he approved the second renewal application, with one exception concerning information regarding the ties between Steele's reporting and the Democratic Party. Boente recalled knowing the information at the time he approved the second renewal. We found that Rosenstein was unaware of the issues we identified at the time he approved the third renewal application. With respect to the ties between Steele's reporting and the Democratic Party, Rosenstein told us he believes he learned that information from news media accounts, but did not recall whether he knew it at the time he approved the third renewal.

I. Omissions in the FISA Applications, as NSD Reported to the FISC in July 2018

Under Rule 13(a) of the FISC Rules of Procedure, the government has an obligation to correct any and all misstatements or omissions of material fact in its submissions to the court. Although the Rules do not define or otherwise explain what constitutes "material" facts or omissions, the FBI's Foreign Intelligence Surveillance Act and Standard Minimization Procedures Policy Guide (FISA SMP PG) states that a fact or omission is "material" if it is relevant to the court's probable cause determination. According to NSD supervisors, NSD will consider a fact or omission material if the information is capable of influencing the court's probable cause determination, but NSD will err on the side of disclosure and advise the court of information that NSD believes the court would want to know.

On July 12, 2018, about1 year after the last Carter Page FISA application was filed with the FISC, the NSD Assistant Attorney General submitted a letter to FISC Presiding Judge Rosemary Collyer under Rule 13(a), advising the court of certain factual omissions in the Carter Page FISA applications. These omissions included:

1. Statements made by George Papadopoulos to FBI CHSs in September and October 2016 denying that anyone involved in the Donald J. Trump for President Campaign was coordinating with Russia in the DNC hack or release of emails;

2. Information Department attorney Bruce Ohr provided to the FBI in November and December 2016 relevant to Steele's motivations and reliability; and

3. Admissions Steele made in April and May 2017 regarding his interactions with the news media in the summer and fall of 2016.

According to NSD supervisors, the Rule 13 Letter was initially prompted by NSD's receipt and review of the Ohr information in late January 2018. At about the same time, the FBI advised NSD and the Office of the Deputy Attorney General (ODAG) of admissions Steele made in court filings in foreign litigation in April and May 2017 concerning his media contacts. Later, in May 2018, while a draft of the letter was under review, NSD learned of Papadopoulos's September 2016 denial from ODAG, which ODAG had recently identified during a review of FBI documents. Then, in June 2018, NSD learned of Papadopoulos's October 2016 denial from the FBI, after asking the FBI to recheck its files for any other information that should be disclosed to the court.

In the Rule 13 Letter, NSD stated that, after the filing of the Carter Page FISA applications, NSD became aware of additional information relevant to the applications, and that some of this information was subject to Rule 13(a). The letter did not specify which information the government believed was material and therefore subject to Rule 13(a), and which information it believed was not. However, the letter stated that some of the additional information had been discussed publicly and that the government was providing all of the information "out of an abundance of caution" to ensure that the court had a complete understanding of the additional information.[378] The letter concluded by asserting that "even considering the additional information regarding Papadopoulos'[s] conversations with [an FBI CHS] and others, and regarding [Steele], the applications contained sufficient predication for the Court to have found probable cause that Page was acting as an agent of the Government of Russia."

According to NSD supervisors, as of October 2019, NSD had not received a formal response from the FISC to the Rule 13 Letter.[379] According to then Deputy Assistant Attorney General Stuart Evans, in his experience, although not in every case, there have been occasions in which the FISC has responded to Rule 13 letters, either by issuing a supplemental order, asking the government for more information, or holding a hearing. On January 31, 2019, Evans told the OIG that NSD had advised FISC Presiding Judge Rosemary Collyer that, through participation in OIG interviews, NSD Office of Intelligence (OI) officials learned of additional information that was possibly material to the Carter Page FISA applications, and that NSD planned to wait until after the OIG completed its review and provided its findings to the Department before determining whether to submit another Rule 13 letter to the court.[380] NSD supervisors told us that they believe the court may be waiting for the completion of the OIG's review, and the submission of any potential supplemental filings by NSD, before taking responsive steps, if any.

---

[378] Regarding the public discussion referenced in the letter, NSD cited to the memoranda from the House Permanent Select Committee on Intelligence (HPSCI) majority and HPSCI minority regarding the Carter Page FISA applications, and a memorandum from Senators Charles Grassley and Lindsey Graham to DAG Rosenstein and FBI Director Christopher Wray concerning Steele and his reporting, which were all publicly released in February 2018.

[379] On May 10, 2019, NSD sent a second letter to the FISC concerning the Carter Page FISA applications, advising the court of two incidents in which the FBI failed to comply with the Standard Minimization Procedures (SMPs) applicable ▮▮▮▮▮▮▮▮▮▮▮▮▮▮▮▮ pursuant to the final FISA orders issued by the court on June ▮, 2017. According to the letter, the FBI took and retained on an FBI-issued cell phone ▮▮▮▮▮▮▮▮▮▮▮ which NSD assessed did not comport with the SMPs. In addition, in a separate incident ▮▮▮▮▮▮▮▮▮▮▮▮▮▮▮▮▮▮▮▮ to an electronic folder on the FBI's classified secret network, which NSD assessed also did not comport with the SMPs. According to NSD, court staff contacted an NSD official in response to this letter and asked when the information at issue would be removed from non-compliant FBI systems, and asked about other cases that might be impacted by the same problem. On October 9, 2019, NSD sent another letter to the FISC advising the court that the FBI completed the remedial process for the information associated with the Page FISA applications and information from other cases impacted by the same problem.

[380] Later in the chapter, we discuss other instances, not described in the July 2018 Rule 13 Letter, in which the three Carter Page renewal applications were inaccurate, incomplete, or unsupported by appropriate documentation, based upon information in the FBI's possession at the time the applications were filed.

A. Papadopoulos's Denials to FBI Confidential Human Sources

In Chapter Five, we described how the first Carter Page FISA application did not include statements Papadopoulos made to an FBI CHS in September 2016 that were in tension with other information included in the application.[381] Specifically, in September 2016, Papadopoulos told the CHS that, to his knowledge, no one associated with the Trump campaign was collaborating with Russia or with outside groups like WikiLeaks in the release of emails. We were advised by NSD that it did not know about this denial by Papadopoulos until May 2018, after ODAG found the information while reviewing documents in response to Congressional information requests. Upon learning the information, NSD incorporated Papadopoulos's denial into the Rule 13 Letter.[382]

As described in Chapter Five, Case Agent 1 told us that he did not recall whether he advised the OI Attorney about Papadopoulos's denial in September 2016 but that, if he did not, it may have been an oversight. He also told us that the Crossfire Hurricane team's assessment was that Papadopoulos's denial to the CHS was a rehearsed response, and Case Agent 1 did not view the information as particularly germane to the investigation of Carter Page.[383] However, Evans told us that because Papadopoulos's denial was inconsistent with the theory that Papadopoulos had received (or was aware of) an offer from the Russians involving the release of emails, there was no question in Evans's mind that the information was material and would have been disclosed to the court had NSD known about it at the time of the FISA applications.

After NSD incorporated Papadopoulos's statements into the Rule 13 Letter, and before the final letter was submitted to the court, the FBI advised NSD of similar, previously undisclosed statements made by Papadopoulos to a CHS after the first Carter Page FISA application was filed but before the renewal applications.[384] Specifically, in October 2016, when asked if the Trump campaign was involved in the DNC email hack, Papadopoulos told the CHS that the campaign was not involved and that it would have been illegal to have done so. Papadopoulos also said that he did not think Russia was "playing" with the election

---

[381] We summarize the information this CHS obtained from Papadopoulos in Chapter Ten.

[382] In a footnote, NSD advised the court that Papadopoulos made similar statements directly to the FBI in a January 2017 interview. The renewal applications did not advise the court of these January 2017 statements, but did advise the court that Papadopoulos had been interviewed by the FBI and denied that he discussed anything related to the Russian government with FFG officials. As discussed in Chapter Seven, the renewal applications did not include that Papadopoulos made other statements during his interviews with the FBI, including statements that minimized Carter Page's role in the Trump campaign and statements that Person 1 (whom the FBI assessed was the likely source for some of the Steele reporting relied upon in the applications, including the allegations against Page) told Papadopoulos that he/she (Person 1) had no knowledge of the information reported in "the recent Trump Dossier."

[383] As noted previously, after reviewing a draft of this report, Case Agent 1 told us that he and the team discounted Papadopoulos's denials for several reasons, but that, in hindsight, he now realizes that the denials, and the team's assessment of those denials, should have been shared with OI.

[384] We summarize the information the CHS obtained from Papadopoulos in Chapter Ten.

or had any interest in it. Case Agent 1 received a document with these Papadopoulos statements included in it a few days after the October 2016 meeting (well before Renewal Application No. 1 was filed). Case Agent 1 told us that he was familiar with this CHS meeting at the time and probably reviewed the summary of the interview containing these statements, but Case Agent 1 said he did not recall why the statements were not shared with OI or included in the subsequent renewal applications. He said that the information would not have been purposely withheld from OI, but it may have been accidentally omitted from the information provided to OI for the renewal application.

In the Rule 13 Letter, NSD advised the court of these statements and added that Papadopoulos told the CHS in October 2016 that ████████████████ ███ ███ ███ ██. The letter further stated that by March 2017, Papadopoulos had denied any campaign involvement in the release of DNC emails on WikiLeaks during interviews conducted by the FBI and that those denials were included in Renewal Application Nos. 2 and 3.

The Rule 13 Letter stated that NSD would have included Papadopoulos' denials to the FBI CHSs in the Carter Page FISA applications had NSD known about them at the time. The letter further stated that, even if the information had been included in the FISA applications, it was the government's position that the "totality of information submitted in these applications concerning Page's activities was sufficient to support the Court's finding of probable cause that Page was acting as an agent of a foreign power." The letter included a footnote advising the court that Papadopoulos had been charged and pled guilty to making false statements and omissions that impeded the FBI's investigation. Evans told the OIG that the government's position was based in part on the fact that the FFG information concerning Papadopoulos was only one of many different pieces of information that supported the court's probable cause determination as to Carter Page. Further, according to Evans, this new information concerning Papadopoulos's denials was "cumulative" in that Renewal Application Nos. 2 and 3 had already advised the court that Papadopoulos had denied informing the FFG of any campaign involvement in the release of DNC emails on WikiLeaks during interviews with the FBI.

B. Information the FBI Received From Bruce Ohr Concerning Steele and His Reporting

In Chapter Nine, we describe the relationships and communications Ohr had with Steele and Glenn Simpson whose company, Fusion GPS, hired Steele to conduct the research on Trump's ties to Russia. We also describe the information Ohr passed to then Deputy Director Andrew McCabe in mid-October 2016 about Steele and his reporting, as well as the information Ohr passed to the Crossfire Hurricane investigative team beginning in November 2016 and continuing until the Special Counsel's appointment in mid-May 2017. At the time of these communications, Ohr was an Associate Deputy Attorney General (ADAG) and Director of the Organized Crime and Drug Enforcement Task Force (OCDETF) within ODAG. However, as we describe in the next chapter, Ohr's interactions with Steele and Simpson were outside Ohr's areas of responsibility, and he did not advise anyone in ODAG that he was meeting with Steele, Simpson, or the FBI about Steele's election reporting.

As described in Chapter Nine, the FBI interviewed Ohr on multiple occasions in 2016 and 2017 and those interviews were memorialized in FD-302s. Of particular relevance to the Carter Page FISA renewal applications, during the first interview of Ohr on November 21, 2016, which was attended by FBI officials overseeing the Crossfire Hurricane investigation—including Deputy Assistant Director (DAD) Peter Strzok, the Chief of the Counterintelligence Division's (CD) Analysis Section 1 (Intel Section Chief), and SSA 1—and by the FBI's Office of the General Counsel (OGC) Unit Chief, Ohr advised the FBI of the following:[385]

- Ohr met with Steele in July and September 2016 during which Steele advised Ohr of Steele's election reporting and who had hired him;

- Simpson, who hired Steele, was himself hired by a lawyer "who does opposition research," and Steele's reporting was going to Hillary Clinton's presidential campaign, an identified State Department official, and the FBI;

- Simpson was passing Steele's reporting to "many individuals or entities," and at times Steele would attend meetings with Simpson;

- Steele was "desperate that Donald Trump not get elected and was passionate about him not being the U.S. President;"

- Steele and Simpson could have met with *Yahoo News* or the author of the September 23 news article jointly, but Ohr did not know if they met jointly; and

- Ohr never believed Steele was "making up information or shading it."

Further, during subsequent interviews on December 5 and 12, 2016, Ohr advised members of the Crossfire Hurricane team that:

- Simpson directed Steele to speak to the press, which was part of what Simpson was paying Steele to do. Ohr did not know whether speaking with *Mother Jones* was Simpson's idea or not; and

- Simpson asked Steele to speak to *Mother Jones* as it was Simpson's "Hail Mary attempt."

---

[385] The FD-302 documenting this November 2016 interview stated that the interview took place on November 22, 2016, which SSA 1 told us was incorrect. Because the date noted on the FD-302 incorrectly stated that the interview took place on November 22, the Rule 13 Letter also incorrectly stated that the interview took place on November 22.

None of the Carter Page FISA renewal applications included any information obtained from Ohr during the course of the Crossfire Hurricane investigation, even though the interviews described above took place before Renewal Application No. 1 was filed in January 2017. In the Rule 13 Letter, NSD advised the court that NSD officials were not aware of the FBI's interviews of Ohr at the time of the renewal applications, and we found no documentation indicating otherwise. Further, Evans, the OI supervisors, and the OI Attorney who drafted the applications told us that they were not aware at the time of the renewal applications that Ohr had provided information to the FBI related to the Crossfire Hurricane investigation. Similarly, Yates, Boente, Rosenstein, and the ODAG officials who reviewed the renewal applications told us that they were also not aware that Ohr had provided the FBI with information related to the Crossfire Hurricane investigation.

As described in Chapter Nine, handwritten notes of an FBI briefing Boente received in February 2017 indicate that the FBI advised Boente and others at that time—including Evans, then Acting Assistant Attorney General Mary McCord, then Deputy Assistant Attorney General George Toscas from NSD, ADAG Tashina Gauhar, ADAG Scott Schools, and Principal ADAG James Crowell—that Ohr knew Steele for several years and remained in contact with him, and that Ohr's wife worked for Simpson as a Russian linguist. However, none of these handwritten notes—which include separate notes taken by Boente, Schools, and Gauhar—stated that the FBI had interviewed Ohr or that Ohr had provided the FBI with information regarding Steele's election reporting or Steele's feelings toward candidate Trump. Schools told us that he recalled a meeting in which the OGC Unit Chief referenced Ohr having contact with Simpson, but Schools was not sure if it was during this February 2017 briefing or another briefing. Further, he said that it was a "passing reference," and he never would have imagined that Ohr was having regular contact with the Crossfire Hurricane team and providing the information that appeared in the FD-302s. Boente and the other attendees of the February 2017 briefing told the OIG that they did not recall the FBI mentioning Ohr at any time during the investigation, and that they did not know about the FBI's interviews with Ohr at the time of the FISA applications. According to Gauhar, she was surprised to find a reference to Ohr in her notes, and, regardless, she "would never have dreamt" back then what she knows now concerning the extent of Ohr's interactions with Steele, Simpson, and the FBI on Steele's election reporting.

According to Gauhar, she first learned of Ohr's connections to the Crossfire Hurricane investigation from media reports in early January 2018. She said that around this same time, Schools gave her a copy of a January 4, 2018 letter from Senators Grassley and Graham to the Department, which referenced the FBI's interviews of Ohr. Emails reflect that on January 8, Gauhar forwarded this letter to Evans, and 2 days later Evans forwarded the letter to OI. According to Evans, this was the first time he learned about Ohr's interactions with the FBI on the Crossfire Hurricane investigation. Evans also said that when he consulted with the OI supervisors and OI Attorney who had worked on the Carter Page FISA applications, he learned that Ohr's involvement was "a surprise to all of us." Shortly thereafter, Evans requested and obtained the FD-302s documenting the Ohr interviews, and days later OI completed a first draft of the Rule 13 Letter.

Handwritten notes taken during a meeting in late January 2018 indicate that OGC's Deputy General Counsel Trisha Anderson told Gauhar, Evans, and OI supervisors that it had been reported to her that the FBI's New York Field Office (NYFO), which at the time had responsibility for the Carter Page investigation, had reviewed the FD-302s contemporaneously with Renewal Application No. 1 and decided that the information from Ohr was not relevant to the Carter Page FISA request. The notes further stated that the case agent handling the FISA request had been focused at that time on information relating to Carter Page's own activities and the FBI's termination of its source relationship with Steele.

Case Agent 1, who, as described previously in Chapter Seven, worked with OI in preparing Renewal Application No. 1 and later assisted Case Agent 6 with Renewal Application No. 2, told the OIG that he did not attend any of the interviews with Ohr. He also said that the information coming from Ohr was not a main focus for him personally. He told us, and documents reflect, that he received information about the Ohr interviews during at least one team meeting in December 2016 and through instant messages with SSA 1 that same month. Case Agent 1 told us that he recalled hearing about Steele being "desperate" about Trump, possibly during the team meeting in December 2016, but Case Agent 1 said he was unable to explain why that information was not included in the renewal applications. He said that he could not recall why he did not share the FD-302s of the Ohr interviews with OI. He said that he did not recall the details very well about the "desperate" comment or the discussions the team had about it, but he remembered thinking that the comment reflected the same potential bias as political opposition research, which was already articulated to the court. He further stated that, with respect to Ohr, he was primarily concerned with whether Ohr had any additional reports from Steele that the FBI did not possess. Because Case Agent 1 understood that there were no differences in the reporting Ohr and the FBI possessed, he said his thought was "unless [Ohr] gets more information that's germane to the investigation," he was going to keep his attention focused on other aspects of the investigation.

Other FBI officials responsible for helping OI draft the renewal applications or performing the Woods Procedures were also unable to explain why the FBI did not include any information from Ohr about Steele. SSA 3, who, as described previously, performed the supervisory factual accuracy review for Renewal Application No. 1 after Case Agent 1 completed the initial review, told us that he had just joined the case at the time he performed the Woods Procedures. SSA 3 said he had not been part of any discussions about what information to include or not to include in the renewal application and did not know why information from the Ohr interviews was not included. Case Agent 6, who helped OI draft the final two renewal applications, told us that he could not explain why information from Ohr was not included in the applications. Case Agent 6 said that no one told him about the Ohr interviews when he joined the case after Renewal Application No. 1 was filed. He said that he saw the FD-302s in the case file and glanced at them, but he did not think he knew at the time about the "desperate" comment or the information from Ohr about Steele's media contacts. His supervisor, SSA 5, who also joined the case after Renewal Application No. 1, said that he did not recall being aware at the time he performed the supervisory factual accuracy review on

Renewal Application Nos. 2 and 3 that Ohr had been interviewed by the FBI and had provided information about Steele.

The OGC Attorney did not attend the Ohr interviews or read the FD-302s, but he told us, and documentation reflects, that he attended the team meeting in December 2016 during which the first two Ohr interviews were discussed. He told us that although he recalled learning about the "desperate" comment, he did not believe at the time that it needed to be included in the renewal applications because the comment was only Ohr's opinion of Steele's feelings toward Trump. In addition, he said he believed that the renewal applications already addressed Steele's personal motivations through the new footnote advising the court of the circumstances that led to Steele's disclosures to *Mother Jones* and his closure as a CHS.

The OGC Unit Chief attended the first interview of Ohr in November 2016 and heard the information Ohr provided first hand. She said that the information did not change her perspective on Steele or cause her to believe the renewal applications needed to be updated. In particular, she explained that she was given the impression during Ohr's interview that Steele's research led to his views about Trump being elected president, rather than the other way around. She said she was reassured by Ohr's statements about Steele's truthfulness. She told the OIG that she believed at the time that the FBI had provided the FISC with all necessary information concerning Steele's potential bias and motivations through the footnotes describing the genesis of his research and the reasons the FBI eventually closed him as a CHS. For these reasons, she said it did not occur to her at the time to advise OI of the information Ohr provided, and that in any event, she would have deferred to the agents on the investigative team who were responsible for assisting OI with the application to advise OI. However, she said that given the "second-guessing" that occurred on that point after the Ohr interviews became more broadly known, she now believes that the investigative team should have provided the information to OI at the time of the renewal applications.

In the Rule 13 Letter, NSD advised the court that some of the information Ohr provided to the FBI during his November and December 2016 interviews

> goes beyond what was included in the applications. In particular, the Ohr information states specifically that the source's work was "going to" Candidate #2's [Hillary Clinton's] campaign. This information is consistent with, although goes somewhat further than the applications, which informed the Court, that "the FBI speculates that the identified U.S. person [who hired Source #1] was likely looking for information that could be used to discredit Candidate #1's [Donald Trump's] campaign." With respect to Ohr's statements concerning the strength of the Source's desire to see Candidate #1 lose and the Source's October 2016 media engagement, this information is additional to but consistent with the applications, already informing the Court that Source #1 spoke with the press in October 2016, in violation of the FBI's admonishment, and was motivated to do so because he was "frustrated" that the FBI Director's actions "would likely influence the

2016 U.S. Presidential election." The applications further stated that the FBI had suspended, and then closed its relationship with Source #1, and then closed him as a source, due to these actions. Moreover, during the November 22nd interview Ohr also stated that in his dealings with Source #1 he "never believed [Source #1] was making up information or shading it." Ultimately, none of the additional information altered the FBI's assessment of Source #1's reliability.

According to Evans, there was no question that OI would have included the Ohr information in the renewal applications had OI been made aware of it, because of its practice of erring on the side of disclosing information to the FISC. However, Evans told us that NSD ultimately did not believe that any of the information was material to the court's probable cause determination because the information was "largely cumulative" of other information in the applications concerning Steele's potential bias. He agreed, however, that the "desperate" comment provided "another strain of potential bias" because the "desperate" comment pertained specifically to Steele's own potential bias and motivations, whereas the disclosures in the FISA applications concerning the origins of Steele's research focused on the motivation of Simpson, who hired Steele, not Steele specifically.

C. Inaccuracies Regarding Steele's Disclosures to Third Parties and Admissions Concerning Steele's *Yahoo News* Contact

In Chapter Five, we described the footnote in the first Carter Page FISA application providing the FBI's assessment that Steele was not the direct source of the disclosure to *Yahoo News* in September 2016 about the FBI's investigation of Carter Page and Page's alleged meetings with Igor Sechin and Igor Divyekin. The basis for this assessment–that Steele told the FBI that he "only provided his information to [Simpson] and the FBI"–was neither accurate at the time nor supported by appropriate documentation. Nevertheless, the FBI repeated this error in all three renewal applications. In the Rule 13 Letter, NSD advised the FISC of this error, noting that the FBI knew before the first application that Steele also provided his information to a State Department official and knew before the first renewal that Steele provided his information to Ohr and Senator John McCain's office.

The Rule 13 Letter also advised the court of additional information the FBI obtained after the first FISA application—but that was not included in any of the renewal applications—that further undermined the FBI's assessment that Steele was not a direct source of the *Yahoo News* disclosure. Specifically, the Rule 13 Letter advised the court that in November 2016, Ohr told the FBI that it was possible that Steele and Simpson, who hired Steele, met jointly with *Yahoo News*, based on information Ohr learned from Steele in late September 2016. In addition, the letter advised that in December 2016, Ohr told the FBI that part of the work Simpson was paying Steele to do included speaking with the media. We found no evidence that the Crossfire Hurricane team, or any FBI officials overseeing the investigation, considered advising the court or OI of this information at the time of the renewal applications. As referenced above, FBI personnel involved in the FISA applications said they did not believe at the time that information from Ohr warranted any changes to the application.

However, by the time of Renewal Application No. 3, the FBI had learned information that more strongly indicated that Steele had directly provided information to *Yahoo News* around the time of the September 23 article. Yet, no revisions were made to the FBI's assessment, contained in Renewal Application No. 3, that Steele had not directly provided the information to the press. Media reporting in late April 2017 described statements Steele made in a court filing (pertinent to a lawsuit filed against him and others in a foreign court) concerning his interactions with the media. Specifically, one article excerpted a sworn statement dated April 3, 2017, in which Steele admitted that he gave "off-the-record briefings to a small number of journalists about the pre-election memoranda in late summer/autumn 2016." Emails reflect that on April 26, 2017, Strzok circulated this article to the Intel Section Chief and the Unit Chief assigned to take over the Crossfire Hurricane investigation in April 2017 (Unit Chief 1).

Other documentation indicates that the foreign lawsuit against Steele was discussed during a meeting with then Director James Comey on May 1, 2017.[386] The OGC Unit Chief took handwritten notes during the meeting, which stated "did not change our assessment, no need to update FISA" below references to the lawsuit. The OGC Unit Chief told us that she did not recall this discussion or who concluded that the FISC did not need to be updated with information from the foreign litigation. She also said that she did not recall specifically discussing or knowing prior to January 2018 that Steele admitted to talking to the media in these court filings and therefore she did not believe that the FBI advised OI of this information at the time of the Carter Page FISA applications. Comey told the OIG that he did not recall being advised of the court filings.

Approximately two weeks after the May 1, 2017 meeting, in a separate court filing submitted on his behalf, Steele admitted that he and Fusion GPS briefed journalists from five media outlets, including *Yahoo News*, at the end of September 2016, and also admitted the briefings involved "the disclosure of limited intelligence regarding indications of Russian interference in the U.S. election process and the possible co-ordination of members of Trump's campaign team and Russian government officials."

According to the Rule 13 Letter and FBI officials, although there had been open source reporting in May 2017 about Steele's statements in the foreign litigation, the FBI did not obtain Steele's court filings until the receipt of Senators Grassley and Graham's January 2018 letter to DAG Rosenstein and FBI Director Christopher Wray with the filings enclosed. We found no evidence that the FBI made any attempts in May or June 2017 to obtain the filings to assist a determination of whether to change the FBI's assessment concerning the

---

[386] The OGC Unit Chief's notes of the meeting do not reflect who else attended the meeting, but she told us that this meeting with the Director would have included a large group of FBI officials.

September 23 news article in the final renewal application.[387] However, the OGC Unit Chief's notes suggest that on May 1, without consulting OI, and relying only upon open source reporting concerning the filings, the FBI decided that Steele's April 3, 2017 sworn statement in the foreign litigation did not warrant any changes to Renewal Application No. 3.

We were unable to determine whether FBI personnel responsible for assisting OI on Renewal Application No. 3 were told about Steele's admissions in the foreign litigation regarding his media contacts. Case Agent 6 and the OGC Attorney told us that they did not recall whether they were aware of Steele's admissions in the foreign litigation before the final renewal application was filed. We are not aware of any other evidence on this point. The Supervisory Intelligence Analyst (Supervisory Intel Analyst) told us that although he was aware at the time, he did not recall making a connection between the open source reporting about Steele's court filings and the information in the FISA application concerning Steele's media contacts. He told us that if he had made such a connection, he would have made sure Case Agent 6 and the OGC Attorney were advised.

According to Evans, the failure to include this information in the prior FISA renewals was not the most significant error identified in the Rule 13 Letter. Evans told us that he was not sure an updated assessment would have been particularly relevant to the court's probable cause determination because whether Steele or the people who hired him were the source of the disclosure, the applications made clear that Steele's research was relied upon in the article. In addition, Evans said that as a result of the disclosure in the renewal applications concerning the *Mother Jones* article in October 2016, the court was already on notice that Steele had talked to one media organization when it approved the renewal of FISA authority.

In the Rule 13 Letter, NSD advised the court that the FBI should have updated its assessment in Renewal Application No. 3 about the source of the *Yahoo News* disclosure. The letter further stated that "irrespective of whether Source #1 directly spoke with the press in connection with the September 23 News Article, or was forthright with the FBI regarding his contacts with the press in September 2016," for the reasons described in the letter and in the FISA applications, "the FBI continued to assess that [Steele's] prior reporting was reliable."

II.   Other Inaccurate, Incomplete, or Undocumented Information in the Three FISA Renewal Applications

In addition to the issues raised in the July 2018 Rule 13 Letter to the FISC, our review revealed other instances in which the three Carter Page renewal applications were inaccurate, incomplete, or unsupported by appropriate documentation, based upon information in the FBI's possession at the time the

---

[387] The OGC Attorney told us that a later (unsuccessful) attempt to obtain the court filings may have been made in the summer of 2017, probably in August, as part of a continuing effort to validate Steele's reporting.

applications were filed. We describe the more significant instances below and identify other instances in Appendix One.

A.   Inconsistencies between Steele's Reporting and Information His Primary Sub-source Provided to the FBI

As described previously, all four Carter Page FISA applications relied upon the following aspects of Steele's reporting to support the government's position that there was probable cause to believe that Carter Page was an agent of a foreign power:

- From Report 80: Derogatory information about Hillary Clinton had been compiled for many years, was controlled by the Kremlin, and the Kremlin had been feeding information to the Trump campaign for an extended period of time;

- From Report 94: During his July 2016 trip to Moscow, Carter Page attended a secret meeting with Igor Sechin, Chairman of Rosneft and a close associate of Putin, and discussed future cooperation and the lifting of Ukraine-related sanctions against Russia; and a separate meeting Page attended with Igor Divyekin, a highly-placed Russian government official, and discussed sharing derogatory information about Clinton with the Trump campaign;

- From Report 95: Carter Page was an intermediary between Russia and the Trump campaign in a "well-developed conspiracy of co-operation," managed by Trump's then campaign manager, Paul Manafort, using Page as an intermediary, which led to Russia's disclosure of hacked DNC emails to WikiLeaks in exchange for the Trump team's agreement, to include at least Page, to sideline Russian intervention in Ukraine as a campaign issue; and

- From Report 102: Russia released the DNC emails to WikiLeaks in an attempt to swing voters to Trump, an objective conceived of and promoted by Page and others.

All four FISA applications clearly stated that Steele did not obtain the information described above directly from his source network. Instead, as described in the FISA applications, Steele received the information from a Primary Sub-source who obtained the information from his/her own source network.

In Chapter Six, we described the FBI's interview of the Primary Sub-source in January 2017, after FISA Renewal Application No. 1 was filed but before the last two renewal applications were filed. After the interview, the Supervisory Intel Analyst and Case Agent 1 memorialized the information in a lengthy written summary. As described in Chapter Six, the Primary Sub-source confirmed for the FBI that he/she provided Steele with some of the information in Steele's reports. However, in some instances, the information the Primary Sub-source told the FBI about what his/her sources told him/her—and what he/she then provided to Steele—was inconsistent with information attributed to his/her sources in Steele's reporting. Of particular relevance to the FISA applications, we found that the

Primary Sub-source's account to the FBI (based on the written interview summary) differed from Steele's reporting on the following points:

- With respect to the information from Reports 95 and 102 that the FBI assessed had come from Person 1 (described in prior chapters) concerning the alleged "conspiracy" between Russia and individuals associated with the Trump campaign, and Russia's release of DNC emails to WikiLeaks in an attempt to swing voters to Trump: the Primary Sub-source said, among other things, that he/she had no discussion with Person 1 concerning WikiLeaks and that there was "nothing bad" about the communications between the Kremlin and the Trump team;

- With respect to the alleged secret meeting between Carter Page and Sechin in July 2016: the Primary Sub-source said he/she was not told by his/her sub-source that this meeting had taken place until October 2016, well after Steele prepared and circulated Report 94, and that he/she only told Steele in July 2016 that he/she had heard that the meeting would be taking place; and

- With respect to the positions and access of the sub-sources: the Primary Sub-source's description of each of his/her sources indicated that their position and access to the information they were reporting was more attenuated than represented by Steele and described in the FISA applications.

Regarding the information in the first bullet above, in early October 2016, the FBI learned the true name of Person 1 (described in Report 95 as "Source E"). As described in Chapter Six, the Primary Sub-source told the FBI that he/she had one 10- to 15-minute telephone call with someone he/she believed to be Person 1, but who did not identify him/herself on the call. We found that, during his/her interview with the FBI, the Primary Sub-source did not describe a "conspiracy" between Russia and individuals associated with the Trump campaign or state that Carter Page served as an "intermediary" between Manafort and the Russian government. In addition, the FBI's summary of the Primary Sub-source's interview did not describe any discussions between the parties concerning the disclosure of DNC emails to WikiLeaks in exchange for a campaign platform change on the Ukrainian issue. To the contrary, according to the interview summary, the Primary Sub-source told the FBI that Person 1 told him/her that there was "nothing bad" about the communications between the Kremlin and Trump, and that Person 1 made no mention at all to WikiLeaks. Further, although Steele informed the FBI that he had received all of the information in Report 95 from the Primary Sub-source, and Steele told the OIG the same thing when we interviewed him, the

242

Primary Sub-source told the FBI that he/she did not know where some of the information attributed to Source E in Report 95 came from.[388]

Despite the inconsistencies between Steele's reporting and the information his Primary Sub-source provided to the FBI, the subsequent FISA renewal applications continued to rely on the Steele information, without any revisions or notice to the court that the Primary Sub-source had contradicted the Steele reporting on key issues described in the renewal applications. Instead, as described previously, FISA Renewal Application Nos. 2 and 3 advised the court:

> In an effort to further corroborate [Steele's] reporting, the FBI has met with [Steele's] ██████████ sub-source [Primary Sub-source] described immediately above. During these interviews, the FBI found the ██████████ sub-source to be truthful and cooperative. ██
>
> ████████████████████████████████ The FBI is undertaking additional investigative steps to further corroborate the information provide [sic] by [Steele] and ████████████████████
> ████████

NSD cited this language from the renewal applications in its July 2018 Rule 13 Letter as an example of information "corroborating" Steele's reporting, noting that "the FBI met with [Steele's] [Primary] sub-source, whom the FBI found to be truthful and cooperative." Evans and the OI officials who participated in the preparation of the renewal applications and Rule 13 Letter told us that they were not advised of the inconsistencies between Steele's reporting and the Primary Sub-source's interview, and that they did not believe that the FBI provided them with the lengthy written summary of the interview. We did not find any evidence indicating otherwise.

We found no evidence that the Crossfire Hurricane team ever considered whether any of the inconsistencies warranted reconsideration of the FBI's previous assessment of the reliability of the Steele reports or notice to OI or the court in the subsequent renewal applications. As described below, team members told us that they either were not aware of the inconsistencies or, if they were, did not make the connection that the inconsistencies affected aspects of the FISA applications.

Case Agent 1, who led the January 2017 interview of the Primary Sub-source, was closely familiar with the Carter Page FISA applications because, as described previously, he originally requested FISA authority targeting Carter Page and assisted OI with drafting the first two FISA applications. In addition, after the Carter Page investigation was reassigned to Case Agent 6 in early 2017, Case Agent 1 assisted Case Agent 6 with the completion of the Woods Procedures for Renewal

---

[388] According to Steele and his reports, Report 80 (dated June 20, 2016), Report 95 (dated July 28, 2016), Report 97 (dated July 30, 2016), and Report 102 (dated August 10, 2016) all contain information from Person 1. If these reports were accurate regarding Person 1's contributions to the reporting and the Primary Sub-source's estimate was accurate concerning his/her debrief of Person 1, then all of the information attributed to Person 1 came from a single, 10-to-15-minute telephone call between the Primary Sub-source and Person 1.

Application No. 2 by performing the factual accuracy review. The Woods File used during that review contained the interview summary of the Primary Sub-source. Case Agent 1 told us that he could not explain why changes had not been made to the renewal applications to account for the inconsistencies between the Primary Sub-source and Steele on facts asserted in the applications. Case Agent 1 said that although he thought the Primary Sub-source may have been minimizing the extent of his/her interactions with Person 1, it did not occur to Case Agent 1 at the time that the information from the Primary Sub-source contradicted information in the FISA applications. In particular, Case Agent 1 said that he did not know enough about some of the details concerning Person 1 to necessarily understand that the Primary Sub-source's account potentially conflicted with information in the FISA applications. For example, he said he did not know whether Steele had his own relationship with Person 1 such that Steele could have had another basis for attributing all the information in Report 95 to Person 1. Case Agent 1 added that he believed that someone else should have highlighted the issue for the agents working on the FISA application.

Case Agent 6 told us that he read the written summary of the Primary Sub-source's January 2017 interview before he assisted the OI Attorney with FISA Renewal Application No. 2, and Case Agent 6's written contributions to the draft application contain two references to information the FBI learned during the interview. However, Case Agent 6 did not identify for OI inconsistences between the Primary Sub-source and Steele on the facts asserted in the FISA application. Case Agent 6 did not participate in the Primary Sub-source's interview, which took place before he took over the Carter Page case from Case Agent 1. Case Agent 6 told us that he read the written summary of the interview after he took over and realized that he did not yet understand all the details of the case. He said that for this reason, he asked Case Agent 1 to assist him with the Woods Procedures for Renewal Application No. 2. Case Agent 6 told us that he did not recall Case Agent 1 or Supervisory Intel Analyst advising him during the Woods process of the inconsistencies.

Analytical documents prepared by, or with the assistance of, the Supervisory Intel Analyst after the Primary Sub-source interview identified inconsistences between Steele and the Primary Sub-source regarding some of the information contained in Reports 94 and 95. The Supervisory Intel Analyst told us that, after the January 2017 interview, his impression was that the Primary Sub-source's account did not line up completely with Steele's reporting, but the Supervisory Intel Analyst said he did not have any "pains or heartburn" about the accuracy of the Steele reporting based on what the Primary Sub-source had said. The Supervisory Intel Analyst said that his thinking at the time was focused instead on using the additional information learned from the Primary Sub-source, particularly the identity of his/her sub-sources, to see what other investigative leads could be generated for the team.

The Supervisory Intel Analyst told us that he played a supportive role for the agents preparing the FISA applications, including reading the probable cause section of the first application and providing the agents with some of the information on the identity of the sub-sources noted in the application. He said that he had some interaction with the agents preparing the renewal applications, but he believed those interactions were less extensive than his involvement in the first application. The Supervisory Intel Analyst did not recall anyone asking him whether he thought the Primary Sub-source was "truthful and cooperative," as noted in the renewal applications.[389] He told us it was his impression that the Primary Sub-source may not have been "completely truthful" and may have been minimizing certain aspects of what he/she told Steele. However, the Supervisory Intel Analyst told the OIG that, on the whole, he did not see any reason to doubt the information the Primary Sub-source provided about who he/she received his/her information from, which was the Supervisory Intel Analyst's focus.

SSA 5, who performed the supervisory factual accuracy review during the Woods Procedures for Renewal Application Nos. 2 and 3, told us that he did not recall whether he was briefed on the Primary Sub-source's interview, and he did not appear during his OIG interview to know anything about the Primary Sub-source. Similarly, Case Agent 7, who performed the Woods Procedures for Renewal Application No. 3, told us that he did not know, or have the case knowledge necessary to determine, that the Primary Sub-source provided information inconsistent with facts asserted in the FISA application.

Program managers supervising the investigation from FBI Headquarters—SSA 2 and SSA 3—were aware of the Primary Sub-source's interview and had read the written summary of it. However, we found no evidence that either of them identified issues with or raised any questions about how the Primary Sub-source's interview may have impacted the information in the FISA applications. As described previously, SSA 3 did not play a direct role in Renewal Application No. 2, but he was familiar with the prior FISA applications, having performed the supervisory factual accuracy review during the Woods Procedures for Renewal Application No. 1. SSA 3 told us that he did not recall noticing any information from the Primary Sub-source's interview that was inconsistent with information in the FISA application. SSA 2 was the affiant who declared, based on the completion of the Woods Procedures, that the information in Renewal Application Nos. 2 and 3 was true and correct. He told us that he did not recall any discussion about whether the Primary Sub-source's interview warranted revisions to the FISA applications, but said he had some recollection that the investigators believed at the time that the Primary Sub-source was holding something back about his/her interaction with Person 1.

The OGC Unit Chief and the OGC Attorney told us that they did not review or receive the written summary of the Primary Sub-source's January 2017 interview at

---

[389] Email communications reflect that in March 2017—after the first FISA application and first renewal were filed and before the last two renewals—the Supervisory Intel Analyst reviewed the first FISA application and the first renewal at OGC's request to assist with potential redactions before the Department responded to Congressional information requests. The Supervisory Intel Analyst provided comments to the OGC Attorney, including advising him that the Primary Sub-source was not ███████ ██████ as stated in the FISA applications, and asking whether a correction should be made. The Supervisory Intel Analyst did not provide any other comments relating to the Primary Sub-source, and he told us that he did not notice anything else potentially inaccurate or incomplete in the applications at that time.

any time before Renewal Application No. 2 was submitted to the court. However, they said that they knew the interview had taken place and had the general understanding from the team that the information provided to the FBI by the Primary Sub-source "essentially echoed," "was consistent with," or "corroborated" the information in Steele's reporting. The OGC Unit Chief said that her understanding was that the Primary Sub-source raised some questions about how Steele wrote his reports or the wording Steele used, and that the agents and analysts had looked into it but did not think the wording choices were substantively different. The OGC Attorney said that he had some vague recollection that the team thought Steele may have conflated some of his sourcing on WikiLeaks based on information provided by the Primary Sub-source. However, they both said that they did not recall the details of these discussions.

Although documents provided to the OIG indicate that senior FBI officials were told about some aspects of the Primary Sub-source's interview, the documents do not reflect that senior FBI officials were advised of the inconsistencies. For example, in late February 2017, the Supervisory Intel Analyst circulated a 2-page Intelligence Memorandum to CD Assistant Director E.W. "Bill" Priestap and other CD officials highlighting aspects of the Primary Sub-source's interview. In March 2017, Priestap forwarded the memorandum to Comey's and McCabe's offices. The memorandum stated that the Primary Sub-source told the FBI that Steele's reporting contained "some of [his/her] reporting, what appear to be [his/her] analytical conclusions, and what [he/she] believes to be [Steele's] analytical judgments." The memorandum provided some details concerning what the Primary Sub-source said about his/her own sources, but the memorandum did not describe the inconsistencies we noted earlier.[390]

Senior CD officials overseeing the Crossfire Hurricane investigation—including Priestap, Strzok, the Intel Section Chief, and CD DAD Jennifer Boone—told us that they did not recall being advised that the information from the Primary Sub-source significantly differed from the information in Steele's reporting. Boone told us that she recalled being told after the Primary Sub-source's interview that the team assessed that Steele may have gotten some of his information from a source other than the Primary Sub-source. Boone said that she did not recall being advised that the interview created inconsistencies between Steele and his Primary Sub-source as to facts relied upon in the FISA applications. Boone further stated that she would have expected to have been told that information. Strzok told us that he did remember learning as a result of the Primary Sub-source interview that Steele did not receive his reporting directly from the sub-sources, but rather solely through

[390] For example, the memorandum stated that, according to the Primary Sub-source, a particular person told the Primary Sub-source that the secret meeting between Carter Page and Sechin had taken place. However, the memorandum failed to note that the Primary Sub-source told the FBI that he/she was not told until October 2016 that the meeting had occurred, which was well after Steele drafted Report 94 in July 2016 (Report 94 asserted that the meeting had taken place, that Page and Sechin discussed the lifting of sanctions, and that Page reacted positively but was noncommittal). As the Primary Sub-source described to the FBI, he/she had only told Steele in July that he/she was aware of a rumor that Page was going to be meeting with Sechin. As noted previously, Page denied to an FBI CHS that he had met with Sechin in July 2016, and the FBI was unable to determine whether a meeting between Sechin and Page took place.

the Primary Sub-source as the intermediary. Strzok said he recalled having a "little bit of concern" about that. He later wrote to Comey's Chief of Staff, Priestap, and others that "[r]ecent interviews and investigation, however, reveal Steele may not be in a position to judge the reliability of his sub-source network."

Comey told us that he did not know whether the team interviewed any of Steele's sub-sources. Because Comey decided not to have his security clearance reinstated for his OIG interview, we were unable to question him further or refresh his recollection with relevant, classified documentation.

The NSD's Counterintelligence and Export Control Section (CES) representatives who attended the Primary Sub-source's January 2017 interview—Section Chief David Laufman and his Deputy Section Chief—told us that they did not recall discussing the interview with OI officials afterward. They told us that they did not have knowledge of the information in the Carter Page FISA applications at the time, and that they were not sufficiently familiar with the Steele reports to have understood that there were inconsistencies between the Primary Sub-source and Steele. We did not find any information to the contrary. They told us that they attended the interview because CES had helped negotiate the terms of the interview with the Primary Sub-source's attorney, and, as noted previously, their role during the interview was primarily to address any issues or concerns raised by the attorney during the interview.

The OI Attorney told the OIG that if had he known about the inconsistencies between the Primary Sub-source and Steele on the facts asserted in the FISA applications, he would have wanted an opportunity to ask questions and gather more information. In particular, after we asked the OI Attorney to read the written summary of the Primary Sub-source's interview regarding the telephone call with Person 1, the OI Attorney was surprised, agreed it was not consistent with the information in the FISA applications concerning Report 95, and said "it doesn't seem like the same story." Evans told us that OI would have sought to determine how the new information impacted the FISA applications, including obtaining the FBI's own assessment of how to reconcile the apparent inconsistencies. Evans said that at a minimum, OI would have advised the court of the inconsistencies and the FBI's assessment of those inconsistences. He further stated that, depending on the information from the FBI, OI may have decided to delay or abandon the filing of the next renewal application altogether.

B. Information about Page's Prior Relationship with Another U.S. Government Agency and Information Page Provided the Other Agency that Overlapped with Facts Asserted in the FISA Applications

As noted in Chapter Five, on or about August 17, 2016, while early FISA discussions were ongoing, the Crossfire Hurricane team received a memorandum (August 17 Memorandum) from another U.S. government agency relating to Page's prior relationship with that agency, including that Page had been approved for operational contact from 2008 to 2013. The information also described Page's prior interactions with Russian intelligence officers about which the agency was aware, including contacts Page had with a Russian intelligence officer (Intelligence Officer 1), which were among the historical connections to Russian intelligence officers that the FBI later relied upon in the first FISA application (and subsequent renewal applications) to help support probable cause.[391] We found that, although this information was highly relevant to the FISA application, the Crossfire Hurricane team did not engage with the other agency regarding this information. In addition, in response to a question from the OI Attorney in September 2016 as to whether Carter Page had a current or prior relationship with the other agency, Case Agent 1 provided the OI Attorney with inaccurate information that failed to disclose the extent and nature of Page's relationship with that agency. As a result, the first FISA application, and FISA Renewal Application Nos. 1 and 2, contained no information regarding Page's relationship with the other U.S. government agency, and did not reveal that his relationship with the other agency overlapped in part with facts asserted in the application regarding Page's ties to particular Russian intelligence officers.

Before Renewal Application No. 3 was submitted to the court, and following news reports about the Carter Page FISAs, Page conducted news interviews in April and May 2017 in which he publicly stated that he had assisted the USIC in the past. Thereafter, the FBI re-engaged with the other U.S. government agency about its prior relationship with Page. SSA 2, who had been the affiant for the first two renewals and would be the affiant for FISA Renewal Application No. 3, told the OIG that in June 2017 he wanted a definitive answer as to whether Page had a prior relationship with the USIC before SSA 2 signed the last renewal application. SSA 2 also told us that he was concerned that Page could claim that he had been acting on behalf of the U.S. government in engaging with certain Russians. SSA 2 stated that he contacted the OGC Attorney assisting with the Crossfire Hurricane investigation to help resolve this issue.[392] According to the OGC Attorney and SSA 2, the OGC Attorney was responsible for handling questions or concerns involving the other U.S. government agency for the Crossfire Hurricane team.

The OGC Attorney told us he recalled that the Supervisory Intel Analyst on the Crossfire Hurricane team had raised a concern that Page may have had a prior

---

[391] As described in Chapter Five, according to the August 17 Memorandum provided to the FBI by the other U.S. government agency, Page told the other agency in October 2010 that he met with Intelligence Officer 1 four times (which the other agency assessed began in 2008), characterized Intelligence Officer 1 as a "compelling, nice guy," and described Intelligence Officer 1's alleged interest in contacting an identified U.S. person. According to the August 17 Memorandum, the employee of the other U.S. government agency who met with Page assessed that Page "candidly described his contact with" Intelligence Officer 1.

As further described in Chapter Five, the other agency's memorandum did not provide the FBI with information indicating it had knowledge of Page's reported contacts with another particular intelligence officer. The FBI also relied on Page's contacts with this intelligence officer in the FISA application.

[392] On May 17, 2017, the Crossfire Hurricane investigation was transferred from the FBI to the Office of Special Counsel upon the appointment of Special Counsel Robert S. Mueller III to investigate Russian interference with the 2016 presidential election and related matters.

relationship with the other U.S. government agency in the past.[393] The OGC Attorney said it was "a big, big concern from both OI and from the FBI that we had been targeting [an individual with a prior relationship with the other agency], because that should never happen without us knowing about it." The OGC Attorney characterized the Crossfire Hurricane team as "spun up" about this concern, and said he knew that if it were true, they would "need to provide that to the court" because such information would "drastically change[] the way that we would handle...[the] FISA application." SSA 2 told the OIG that this issue was very important to resolve, because if Page

> was being tasked by another agency, especially if he was being tasked to engage Russians, then it would absolutely be relevant for the Court to know...[and] could also seriously impact the predication of our entire investigation which focused on [Page's] close and continuous contact with Russian/Russia-linked individuals.

In mid-June 2017, the OGC Attorney contacted the other U.S. government agency to seek additional information about Page's prior relationship with that other agency, and then communicated back to the OI Attorney and SSA 2. Because we determined that the OGC Attorney did not accurately convey, and in fact altered, the information he received from the other agency, we provide these communications in detail below.

1. June 15, 2017—FBI OGC Attorney Requests Information about Page from Other U.S. Government Agency

On June 15, 2017, the OGC Attorney emailed the liaison for the other U.S. government agency (Liaison) about Carter Page's past, stating:

> We need some clarification on Carter Page. There is an indication that he may be a "[digraph]" source.[394] This is a fact we would need to disclose in our next FISA renewal (we would not name the [U.S. government agency] of course).

> To that end, can we get two items from you?

> 1) Source Check/Is Page a source in any capacity?

> ...

---

[393] The Supervisory Intel Analyst said that he did not recall raising a concern about this issue, but that he did recall being aware that Page had been a "type of source" with this other agency in the past. Although the Supervisory Intel Analyst did not recall discussions about including this information in the FISA application, he did recall general discussions about Page's relationship with the other U.S. government agency.

[394] The Liaison told the OIG that the other U.S. government agency uses a specific two-letter designation, or digraph, to describe a U.S. person who has been approved by the other agency for operational contact.

2) If he is, what is a "[digraph]" source (or whatever type of source he is)?

If you would like to discuss more, please let me know.[395]

The Liaison responded that same day by providing the OGC Attorney with a list of documents previously provided by the other agency to the FBI mentioning Page's name, including the August 17 Memorandum. The Liaison also wrote that the U.S. government agency uses

> the [digraph] to show that the encrypted individual...is a [U.S. person]. We encrypt the [U.S. persons] when they provide reporting to us. My recollection is that Page was or is...[digraph] but the [documents] will explain the details. If you need a formal definition for the FISA, please let me know and we'll work up some language and get it cleared for use.

The OGC Attorney responded, "Thanks so much for this information. We're digging into the [documents] now, but I think the definition of the [digraph] answers our questions." That same day, the OGC Attorney forwarded the Liaison's email response to Case Agent 6 and an FBI SSA assigned to the Special Counsel's Office, without adding any explanation or comment. The SSA responded by telling Case Agent 6 that she would "pull these [documents] for you tomorrow and get you what you need." The OGC Attorney also sent an instant message to his supervisor, the OGC Unit Chief, stating that Carter Page was a "U.S. subsource of a source" and that "[digraph]=encrypted USPER."

We asked the OGC Attorney if he read the documents identified by the Liaison in her June 15, 2017 email. The OGC Attorney told the OIG that he "didn't know the details of...the content of the [documents]" and did not think he was involved in reviewing them. He also said he "didn't have access to the [documents] in the OGC space," but that the investigative team was provided the list of documents and that they would have been reviewing them. The OGC Attorney said he understood the Liaison's response to mean that Page had not been a source— which the OGC Attorney described as a "recruited asset"—but rather someone who had some interaction with a source for the other U.S. government agency, and not a direct relationship with the other agency. He stated his understanding was that the other U.S. government agency

> identified that [Page] was ["digraph"], and ["digraph"] refers to a U.S. person...who's incidentally picked up...[in] reporting out from a source of theirs. So their recruited asset is at a meeting, and [Page] happened to be there too. And then, in the reporting, the source mentions [Page] is there, so the agency protects [Page's] true name by using...["digraph" for Page].

---

[395] In an email sent to Case Agent 6 on June 13, 2017, and in an instant message sent to Case Agent 6 on June 15, 2017, the OGC Attorney referred to this request as "that source check" and "that [digraph] check," respectively.

The OGC Attorney told us that— his belief that Page had never been a source for the other U.S. government agency, but instead interacted with a source—was based on telephone conversations with the Liaison. He said he recalled the Liaison "saying that [Page] was not a source of theirs," but rather "incidentally reporting information via a source of theirs" and that they "ended up not actually opening him."[396]

When we asked the Liaison about the OGC Attorney's interpretation of the Liaison's email, the Liaison told us that her email stated just the opposite, namely that Page was a U.S. person who had provided direct reporting to the other U.S. government agency in the past. The Liaison also said that the reason she offered, in her email, to assist in providing language for the FISA application was because she was telling the OGC Attorney that, using the FBI's terminology, Page had been a source for the other agency. The Liaison also stated that she saw no basis for the OGC Attorney to have concluded, based on their communications and the August 17 Memorandum, that Page never had a direct relationship with the other agency.

The Liaison also said that she did not recall having any telephone discussions with the OGC Attorney on this issue. She added that, even if she had, she did not think the OGC Attorney would have been able to draw any conclusions from such a conversation. The Liaison explained that she would not have had the documents in front of her at the time of any such conversation, and therefore would not have given the OGC Attorney a definitive answer. She emphasized the need to read the documents in order to accurately understand the relationship between Page and the other U.S. government agency.

2. June 16, 2017—FBI OGC Attorney Provides the Liaison's Response to the OI Attorney

On the evening of June 15, 2017, the OGC Attorney contacted the OI Attorney to request a time to talk the next day. FBI telephone records confirm they spoke the next morning for approximately 28 minutes, until 11:46 a.m. Also at 11:46 a.m. on June 16, the OGC Attorney forwarded to the OI Attorney the Liaison's June 15 email response. However, in forwarding the Liaison's response to the OI Attorney, the OGC Attorney did not include the initial email that he sent to the Liaison inquiring about Page's status as a "[digraph] source." The OGC Attorney told us that he could not recall why he did not include the initial email, in which he asked, "Is Page a source in any capacity?"

The OI Attorney responded to the OGC Attorney's email, "thanks I think we are good and no need to carry it any further." The OGC Attorney replied, "Music to my ears."

The OI Attorney told us that he did not recall this email exchange with the OGC Attorney or the telephone call on June 16 with the OGC Attorney indicated in

---

[396] When questioned further on this point, the OGC Attorney told us that he only recalled engaging with the Liaison on this issue and not any other person from the other U.S. government agency.

FBI telephone records. When we asked the OI Attorney whether he reviewed the August 17 Memorandum, he said he did not recall if he had asked to see it, but also stated that he would have relied on the case agent's assessment of that document.

The OGC Attorney initially told us that he recalled providing a detailed briefing to the OI Attorney about Page's status, and telling him that the OGC Attorney had conferred with the Liaison and that Page had not been a source for the other agency. However, in a subsequent OIG interview months later, the OGC Attorney said he did not recall a specific conversation with the OI Attorney on this subject matter, but thought he would have conveyed to the OI Attorney the details of what the Liaison had told him.

3. June 19, 2017—FBI OGC Attorney Provides SSA 2 with Inaccurate Information

a. June 19, 2017 Instant Message Exchange

On June 19, 2017, the OGC Attorney and SSA 2 exchanged instant messages about Carter Page's past relationship with the other agency.[397] As described above, SSA 2 would be the affiant on Renewal Application No. 3 and was seeking a definitive answer as to whether Page had a prior relationship with the other agency. The relevant portions of the instant message exchange were as follows:

> 15:26:35, SSA 2: "Do we have any update on the [agency] CHS request? Also, [Case Agent 6] said [OI Attorney] is not so optimistic."
>
> 15:27:53, OGC Attorney: "[agency] CHS: You are referring to [Carter Page]?"
>
> 15:28:01, SSA 2: "Yes."
>
> 15:28:05, OGC Attorney: "He is cleared."
>
> 15:28:15, SSA 2: "Cleared to fly?"
>
> 15:28:16, OGC Attorney: "[digraph]=Masked USPER."
>
> 15:28:34, SSA 2: "So he was and the relationship officially ended?"
>
> 15:28:37, OGC Attorney: "So, essentially, the real...source was using [Carter Page] as a [Steele]-like subsource."
>
> 15:28:47, OGC Attorney: "[Carter Page] was never a source."
>
> 15:28:59, SSA 2: "You mean the [agency] officer?"
>
> 15:29:19, OGC Attorney: "Right. Whomever generated the reporting from the [documents]."

---

[397] These instant messages were exchanged on an internal FBINet application for FBI personnel. All instant messages produced to the OIG reflected Greenwich Mean Time. We have corrected the time stamps to reflect the time in the Eastern Time Zone. Some of the instant messages also contained emojis, which we omitted unless they affected the meaning of the message. We also do not include other intervening instant messages about unrelated topics unless they contributed to an understanding of the relevant messages.

15:29:45, OGC Attorney: "It was just liaison with [Carter Page] which resulted in reporting, eventually they closed it out as unhelpful."

15:30:39, OGC Attorney: "So, in discussing with [OI Attorney], he agreed we do not need to address it in the FISA."

15:31:16, OGC Attorney: "[OI Attorney] is always Eeyore in drafting these special FISA applications."

15:31:27, SSA 2: "So [Carter Page] was a [digraph] or [Carter Page] was a subsource of the [digraph]."

15:32:00, OGC Attorney: "It's [sic] sounds like a subsource of the [digraph]."

15:32:31, OGC Attorney: "And yes, [the other agency] confirmed explicitly he was never a source."

15:33:05, SSA 2: "Interesting."

15:33:21, OGC Attorney: "But like, interesting good, right?"

15:33:54, OGC Attorney: "I mean, at least we don't have to have a terrible footnote."

15:33:57, SSA 2: "Sure. Just interesting they say not a source. We thought otherwise based on the writing...I will re-read."

15:34:28, OGC Attorney: "At most, it's [the Supervisory Intel Analyst] being the CHS, and you talking to [the Supervisory Intel Analyst]."

15:34:54, SSA 2: "Got it. Thank you. Do we have that in writing."

15:35:19, OGC Attorney: "On TS. I'll forward/"

We asked the OGC Attorney about this instant message exchange with SSA 2 in which he told SSA 2 that Carter Page was never a source. The OGC Attorney stated, "That was my, the impression that I was given, yes." We also asked why he told SSA 2 in the instant message exchange that the other U.S. government agency "confirmed explicitly that he was never a source." The OGC Attorney explained that his statement was just "shorthand" for the information provided by the other agency about Page and that he had no particular reason to use the word "explicitly." As to his comment about a "terrible footnote" in the instant messages, the OGC Attorney told us that he was referring to how "laborious" it would be to draft such a footnote for the FISA application, not that such a footnote might undermine or conflict with the overall narrative presented in the FISA applications.

SSA 2 told us that the most important part of this interaction with the OGC Attorney was when the OGC Attorney told SSA 2 that the other agency had said "explicitly" that Page had never been a source. SSA 2 characterized that statement as "the confirmation that I need[ed]." SSA 2 also said that he understood the OGC Attorney's comment about not having to draft a "terrible footnote" to mean that the team could avoid having to explain in Renewal Application No. 3 that they had "just now come to determine that [Page] was an asset of the [other agency] and probably being tasked to engage...[with] Russians which is...why we opened a case on him." SSA 2 said that he understood the OGC Attorney to be saying that "the optic...would be terrible" if the prior FISA applications were "dubious" in light of a relationship between Page and the other agency, and the FBI was only becoming aware of that relationship in the third renewal application and after Page's public statements.

We showed the instant message exchange between the OGC Attorney and SSA 2 to the Liaison and the OI Attorney. Neither had previously been aware of this exchange. The OI Attorney told us that the OGC Attorney's description of Page as a sub-source did not sound familiar to him. He said:

> I feel like if the [OGC Attorney] would have said, well he was a sub-source, I mean to me that's like a flag.... [T]hat means he was being handled by somebody. That means that there was...something more; let's dig more into it.

The OI Attorney also focused on the portion of the exchange where SSA 2 expressed a belief that Page was a source and where the OGC Attorney mentioned not having to prepare a "terrible footnote." He told us that OI should have been made aware of any "internal debate" within the FBI about whether Page was a source for another U.S. government agency, because with the FISC there is no "defense counsel on the other side," and it is up to OI "to over tell the story."

The Liaison focused on the portion of the exchange in which the OGC Attorney stated that Page "was never a source." The Liaison told us that this statement was wrong, as was the OGC Attorney's statement that Page "was a U.S. sub-source of a source." The Liaison said that such an assertion is "directly contradictory to the [documents]" the agency provided to the FBI. The Liaison also said it was inaccurate to describe Carter Page as "like a sub-source of [a digraph]" and to state that the other agency had "confirmed explicitly that [Page] was never a source." We asked the Liaison whether the Liaison ever told the OGC Attorney that Page was not a source. The Liaison said that, to the best of the Liaison's recollection, the Liaison did not and would not have characterized the status of a "[digraph]" without either first reaching out to the other agency's experts responsible for the underlying reporting, or relying on the proper supporting documentation for an answer. The Liaison stated, "I have no recollection of there being any basis for [the OGC Attorney] to reach that conclusion, and it is directly contradicted by the documents."

b. The OGC Attorney Sends SSA 2 an Altered Version of the Liaison's June 15 Email

Immediately following the June 19 instant message exchange between the OGC Attorney and SSA 2, SSA 2 received an email from the OGC Attorney that appeared to be forwarding the Liaison's June 15 response email concerning Page's historical contact with the other U.S. government agency. However, the OIG determined that this forwarded version of the Liaison's response email had been altered. Specifically, the words "and not a 'source'" had been inserted in the

Liaison's June 15 response after the word "[digraph]." Thus, the Liaison's email was altered to read: "My recollection is that Page was or is and [sic] '[digraph]' **and not a 'source'** but the [documents] will explain the details." (Emphasis added). The OGC Attorney also did not include in the email sent to SSA 2 the initial email inquiry from the OGC Attorney to the Liaison about Page's status as a "[digraph] source."[398]

In response to the June 19 email, SSA 2 asked the OGC Attorney if SSA 2 could send the email to the FBI agents working on the matter. The OGC Attorney responded: "Yes. I actually already did on Friday when [the OI Attorney] said we're good to go. Sorry for not cc'ing you."[399]

We asked the OGC Attorney about the alteration in the email he sent to SSA 2. He initially stated that he was not certain how the alteration occurred, but subsequently acknowledged that he made the change. He also stated it was consistent with his impression of the information that he had been provided by the Liaison.

We discussed the altered email with SSA 2, who told us that the OGC Attorney was the person he relied upon to resolve the issue of whether Carter Page was or had been a source for the other U.S. government agency. SSA 2 told us that the statement inserted into the Liaison's email—that Page was "not a source"—was the most important part of the email for him. SSA 2 said "if they say [he's] not a source, then you know we're good." SSA 2 also said that if the email from the Liaison had not contained the words "not a source" then, for him, the issue would have remained unresolved, and he would have had to seek further clarification. SSA 2 stated: "If you take out 'and not a source,' it's not wrong, but it doesn't really answer the question." He also said that something lesser, such as a verbal statement from the Liaison through the OGC Attorney, would not have resolved the issue for him. SSA 2 also told us it was important to him that the OGC Attorney had first sent the Liaison's response email to the OI Attorney, because if they discussed the issue and they have "decided we don't have to do a footnote that he's not a source...we've resolved this. We're good to move forward." He also said that he "would assume that the [OI Attorney]...received exactly what [SSA 2] received since it was a forward."

We also showed the altered June 19, 2017 email to the Liaison. She told us that the combination of the omission of the OGC Attorney's question to the Liaison about Page's status as a "[digraph] source," along with the addition of the words "not a 'source'" to her response, was misleading. She explained that by omitting

---

[398] However, the email the OGC Attorney sent to SSA 2 did include header information from the June 16 email sent by the OGC Attorney to the OI Attorney, reflecting that the OI Attorney had been provided the Liaison's response email. It therefore appeared to SSA 2 that he and the OI Attorney had received the same information about Page's past status with the U.S. government agency. However, as described above, the email the OGC Attorney sent to the OI attorney did not contain the altered text that was included in the email that the OGC Attorney sent to SSA 2.

[399] The OGC Attorney did not alter the email he had previously forwarded to the other FBI agents.

how the OGC Attorney phrased his questions to her, it took away the context necessary to fully understand her response. We also asked the Liaison whether "not a 'source'" is language she would use to describe a "[digraph]." She said she would not have included the "not a 'source'" language in an email to the OGC Attorney because the Liaison's agency does "not call them sources." The Liaison added that the phrase "not a 'source'" is contradictory to the term "[digraph]," because "[digraph]" indicates that the person is providing information to the Liaison's agency.

Consistent with the Inspector General Act of 1978, following the OIG's discovery that the OGC Attorney had altered the email that he sent to SSA 2, who thereafter relied on it to swear out the final FISA application, the OIG promptly informed the Attorney General and the FBI Director, and provided them with the relevant information about the OGC Attorney's actions.[400]

C. Information Concerning Steele's Past Work-Related Performance

As described in Chapter Five, NSD told us that in the absence of information corroborating the facts from Steele's reporting asserted in the Carter Page FISA application, it was particularly important for the application to articulate to the court the FBI's assessment of the reliability of the source. Therefore, all four FISA applications articulated for the court the basis for the FBI's assessment that Steele was reliable. In all four applications, the FBI's source characterization statement began with the identification of Steele as a former ███████████████████ ███████████████. FBI and NSD officials told us that in assessing Steele's reliability, the FBI placed great weight on Steele's ███████████████. Additionally,

---

[400] Prior to the Crossfire Hurricane investigation, the OGC Attorney had been assigned to provide legal support to the FBI's "Midyear Exam" investigation, which concerned former Secretary of State Hillary Clinton's use of a private email server. In the OIG's June 2018 report, *Review of Various Actions in Advance of the 2016 Election*, we referred to the OGC Attorney as FBI Attorney 2. In that report, we described improper political instant messages that the OGC Attorney sent to other FBI employees using FBI information technology systems. For example, on the day after the 2016 U.S. elections, the OGC Attorney sent an instant message to another FBI employee regarding the election outcome, stating:

> I am so stressed about what I could have done differently...I just can't imagine the systematic disassembly of the progress we made over the last 8 years. ACA is gone. Who knows if the rhetoric about deporting people, walls, and crap is true. I honestly feel like there is going to be a lot more gun issues, too, the crazies won finally. This is the tea party on steroids. And the GOP is going to be lost, they have to deal with an incumbent in 4 years. We have to fight this again. Also Pence is stupid.

Two weeks later, the OGC Attorney sent an instant message to another FBI colleague about the amount of money the subject of an FBI investigation had been paid while working on the Trump campaign. The FBI colleague responded, "Is it making you rethink your commitment to the Trump administration?" The OGC Attorney replied, "Hell no," and then added "Viva le resistance."

We note that the OGC Attorney's alteration of the Liaison's email in connection with the Crossfire Hurricane investigation described in this report occurred in June 2017, one year prior to our June 2018 referral to the FBI of his actions in connection with the Midyear Exam investigation.

as described in Chapter Five, the FISC legal advisor asked NSD to explicitly identify ██████████████ in the source characterization statement.

As described in Chapter Six, after the first FISA application was filed, but before Renewal Application No. 1, Priestap and Strzok obtained information about Steele from persons with direct knowledge of his performance of his work duties in a prior position in an effort to further assess Steele's reliability. This was the first time anyone associated with the Crossfire Hurricane investigation discussed Steele with these persons, and it was prompted, at least in part, by Steele's disclosures to *Mother Jones* in late October 2016. Priestap and Strzok took handwritten notes of the feedback they received from the former employer about Steele. These notes referenced that Steele had held a "moderately senior" position in Moscow, as the Crossfire Hurricane team had originally thought and advised OI. Nothing in the notes indicated that Steele was "high-ranking" as stated in the applications. The notes described positive feedback about Steele, such as "smart," "person of integrity," "no reason to doubt integrity," and "[i]f he reported it, he believed it." Priestap told us that his impression was that Steele was considered to be a "Russia expert" and very competent in his work. However, Priestap and Strzok were also provided negative feedback concerning Steele's judgment, including "[d]emonstrates lack of self-awareness, [demonstrates] poor judgment;" "[k]een to help but underpinned by poor judgment;" "[j]udgment: pursuing people [with] political risk but no intel value;" "[r]eporting in good faith, but not clear what he would have done to validate;" and "[d]idn't always exercise great judgment—sometimes [he] believes he knows best."

Priestap and Strzok told us that they did not change their overall assessment of Steele's reliability after being provided this information because they were told that Steele was never untruthful. According to Priestap, he interpreted the negative feedback about Steele's judgment to mean that Steele was a person who strongly believed in his convictions and that those convictions did not always align with management's convictions. Priestap said he himself confronted similar disagreements over prioritization with his own staff, and what stood out more to Priestap were the statements indicating that Steele had never been intentionally dishonest in his prior work. Priestap also told us that, according to the feedback he received, Steele's past reporting accurately reflected what he was told, but Priestap said the question was the accuracy of what he was told, which could not addressed in this instance without knowing the identity of Steele's sources for the election reporting. Strzok interpreted the feedback regarding Steele's judgment to mean that Steele sometimes followed the "shiny object" without a judgment about whether the shiny thing was really worth pursuing given the risks involved, which was seen as a hindrance to his career progression, but that Steele had no history of fabricating, embellishing, or otherwise "spinning" information.

FBI officials told us, and documents reflect, that Strzok briefed the Crossfire Hurricane team regarding the information he received about Steele. Case Agent 1's handwritten notes from a December 2016 team meeting reflect that the team was told that Steele "may have some judgment problems" but that the team could "continue to rely on reports for FISA." Case Agent 1 did not recall this discussion or who said that they could continue to rely on Steele's reporting in the next FISA application.

Handwritten notes from the OI Unit Chief reflect that the OGC Attorney advised the OI Unit Chief and the OI Attorney at the end of November 2016 that the team had met with persons with direct knowledge of Steele's performance of his work duties in a prior position. According to the notes, the OGC Attorney told OI that Steele's past contacts said he "could be prone to rash judgments." The notes also indicate that the OGC Attorney advised OI that the FBI did an internal review and found no indication that any of Steele's reporting was false or misleading and that McCabe had signed off on requesting a FISA renewal targeting Carter Page.

The OI Attorney told us that he only vaguely recalled this discussion, but the OI Unit Chief said that he recalled being told that Steele was prone to rash judgment in his actions but not in his reporting. The OI Unit Chief told us he also recalled that the FBI believed it had no reason to question Steele's reporting and therefore had not changed its assessment of his reliability. Evans recalled that one or both of them later advised him, probably in December 2016, that the FBI had been told Steele had "questionable judgment" but was otherwise professional and reliable.

As for why Renewal Application No. 1 (and the subsequent renewal applications) did not include this information about Steele, Evans and the OI Unit Chief told us that, because the information did not change the FBI's assessment as to Steele's reliability, the circumstances leading to the FBI's closure of Steele as a CHS was the more critical update for the court. However, during their OIG interviews, Evans and the OI Unit Chief were shown Strzok's notes. After reviewing the notes, both Evans and the OI Unit Chief said that the notes contained more detail than what they recalled being told by the FBI, including the statement that it was "not clear what [Steele] would have done to validate" his reporting. Both said that they would have asked for more detail about that particular comment if they had known at the time. According to Evans, he would have considered whether to include information in the renewal application if he had known.

D. Information Regarding Steele Reporting's Ties to the Democratic Party, the Democratic National Committee, and the Hillary Clinton Campaign

As described in Chapter Five, the first Carter Page FISA application contained a footnote advising the court that Steele's election reporting may have originated from a request for political opposition research:

> [Steele], who now owns a foreign/business/financial intelligence firm, was approached by an identified U.S. person, who indicated to [Steele] that a U.S.-based law firm had hired the identified U.S. person to conduct research regarding Candidate#1's ties to Russia (the identified U.S. person and [Steele] have a long-standing business relationship). The identified U.S. person hired [Steele] to conduct this research. The

identified U.S. person never advised [Steele] as to the motivation behind the research into Candidate #1's ties to Russia. *The FBI speculates that the identified U.S. person was likely looking for information that could be used to discredit Candidate #1's campaign.* (Emphasis added).

According to FBI officials, and as represented to OI at the time of the first application, the Crossfire Hurricane team was told by Steele that he had been hired by Fusion GPS's Glenn Simpson to perform his election-related work, was advised by Steele that Fusion GPS had been retained by an unnamed law firm, and had not been informed by Steele of the motivation of Fusion GPS. Additionally, as we discuss in Chapter Four, the FBI assumed, but did not know at the time of the first application, that Steele was conducting opposition research. As described in Chapter Five, McCabe told us that he thought he had heard by the time of the first application that Simpson had been working first for a Republican and then later for a Democrat. However, McCabe also told the OIG that his memory on the timing of events is not always reliable. Other FBI officials told us that the team did not know who hired Simpson until after the first FISA application. We were told by Evans that the use of the term "speculates" in the footnote was intended to convey that even though the FBI did not know at the time the identity of Simpson's and the U.S. law firm's ultimate client, the FBI believed it was likely that it was someone who was seeking political opposition research against candidate Trump.[401]

According to FBI officials, the Crossfire Hurricane team did not investigate who ultimately paid for Steele's reporting. The OGC Unit Chief and the Supervisory Intel Analyst told us that the team focused instead on vetting the accuracy of the information in Steele's reporting because, if the reporting turned out to be true, it would not matter to the team who ultimately paid for the research.

Nevertheless, in the months following the first FISA application, information became known to the Crossfire Hurricane team that provided greater clarity about the political origins and connections of Steele's reporting. As described in Chapter Nine, by no later than November 21, 2016, Ohr had advised FBI officials that Steele's reporting had been given to the Hillary Clinton campaign (among other entities) and that Steele was "desperate" that Trump not be elected. SSA 1 and the Supervisory Intel Analyst told us, and email communications reflect, that by no later than January 11, 2017, SSA 1 and the Supervisory Intel Analyst understood that Fusion GPS had been hired by the DNC and another unidentified entity to research candidate Trump's ties to Russia. Finally, handwritten notes and other documentation reflect that in February and March 2017 it was broadly known among FBI officials working on and supervising the investigation, and shared with senior NSD and ODAG officials, that Simpson (who hired Steele) was himself hired first by a candidate during the Republican primaries and then later by someone

---

[401] As we describe in Chapter Five, OI officials told us that the FBI did not advise them of the FBI's belief that Steele was conducting political opposition research until October 11, 2016, when Evans asked the FBI three rounds of questions about Steele's political affiliations in connection with Evans's review of the first FISA application probing the FBI for information. Evans said that he expressed his frustration that the FBI had not informed OI of its belief earlier in the FISA process.

related to the Democratic Party. Nevertheless, the footnote in Renewal Application Nos. 1, 2 and 3, was not revised to reflect this additional information.

Case Agent 6 told us that after he took over the Carter Page investigation, he believed he had a conversation with Case Agent 1 about the identity of Steele's client, but he did not recall any details about what he was told. Case Agent 1 and the OGC Attorney told us that they did not recall when they learned who ultimately paid for the research, and Case Agent 1 said that it may have been sometime after he left the case. The OI Attorney told us that he did not recall being advised that the FBI had more clarity on who had paid for Steele's research.

By March 2017, Evans had received information indicating that Simpson was first hired by a Republican primary candidate and then later by someone related to the Democratic Party. Evans told us that he did not recall revisiting the language in the footnote after learning this information. He said that he interpreted the word "speculates" in the footnote to have the same meaning as the FBI "assesses" or "believes." Further, in his opinion, the footnote clearly advised the court of the potential for political bias, such that he could not see how the additional information would have made a real difference for the court. He said that he did not know that members of the Crossfire Hurricane team had learned that Fusion GPS was hired specifically by the DNC and that, if that were true, he would have wanted to update the court about that information, not because it was material, but just in the interest of candor with the court.

The OGC Unit Chief recalled the team briefing Comey that the research was conducted first for a Republican primary candidate and then later for the Democratic Party. We determined this briefing likely occurred in March 2017. Comey told us that he remembered being advised of this information. He also told us that he did not recall taking notice of the word "speculates" at the time he reviewed the FISA applications, but that in reviewing the language again he thought it "fairly conveyed" that the research originated from a biased source.

Yates told us that she remembered hearing that Steele's research was conducted first for a Republican and then later for a Democrat, but she said she did not recall whether she heard that before or after she left the Department in late January 2017. Yates was removed as Acting Attorney General on January 30, 2017, and we did not find evidence that she was informed of this information prior to that time. We identified notes indicating that by February and March 2017 it was broadly known that Simpson was hired first by a Republican primary candidate and then later by someone related to the Democratic Party. Boente told us that he remembered knowing before he approved Renewal Application No. 2 in April 2017 that Simpson had been hired by a Republican primary candidate and then a Democratic candidate, but Boente said he did not recall any discussion about whether to revise the language in the footnote. He said that whether, in hindsight, the FBI should have revised the language was not a question he could answer during his OIG interview without first having the benefit of an analysis. Rosenstein told us that he did not recall the FBI telling him about the political origins of Steele's reporting before he approved Renewal Application No. 3 in June 2017 or whether he just inferred that after reading the footnote. Rosenstein said that he did not recall the word "speculates" striking him at the time, but that if the FBI had information at the time of this final FISA application that the research had been funded by the Democratic Party, and that it was going to the Hillary Clinton campaign, he would have expected the FBI to revise the language to be more explicit. He said that if the FBI had such knowledge, the application should say that, or say that a witness told them that, because the additional clarity about the ultimate clients for Steele's reporting would be a relevant fact, though not necessarily dispositive. Similarly, although he did not read the renewal applications before they were filed, then FBI General Counsel James Baker told us that if the team had known the identity of Simpson's clients at the time, such that it was not speculation anymore, then Baker would have expected the language to have been updated.

E.   FBI's Source Validation Report Concerning Steele

To establish Steele's reliability, all four Carter Page FISA applications included the statement that Steele's reporting "has been corroborated and used in criminal proceedings." As described in Chapter Five, members of the Crossfire Hurricane team, including the Supervisory Intel Analyst and SSA 1, told us that the phrase "corroborated and used in criminal proceedings" was a reference to Steele's past reporting in the FIFA investigation. Although the team did not review the FIFA case file, SSA 1 stated that they "speculated" that Steele's information was corroborated and used in criminal proceedings because they knew Steele had been "a part of, if not predicated, the FIFA investigation" and was known to have had an extensive source network into Russian organized crime. However, as also described in Chapter Five, no one provided the source characterization statement to Steele's handling agent (Handling Agent 1) for approval, as required by the Woods Procedures. Handling Agent 1 told us that he would not have approved the statement because most of Steele's past reporting had not been corroborated and it had never been used in a criminal proceeding.

As we described in Chapter Six, the Crossfire Hurricane team requested that the FBI's Validation Management Unit (VMU) conduct a formal human source validation review of Steele in early 2017. VMU completed its evaluation and issued its report on March 23, 2017, which stated that Steele was "suitable for continued operation" ████████████████████████. However, the validation report stated that Steele's past reporting in support of the FBI's Criminal Program had been "minimally corroborated," which included Steele's contributions to the FIFA case.[402] Handling Agent 1 told us that "minimally corroborated" was consistent with his understanding of the entire collection of Steele's reporting to the FBI. Although this finding was different from the source characterization statement contained in

---

[402] As noted in Chapter Six, the validation report did not include the Validation Management Unit's (VMU) determination that Steele's election reporting was not corroborated. According to the Unit Chief of VMU, it is not common practice for VMU to include negative findings in its reports, only what they "positively find." The Unit Chief of VMU also said that within the validation context, the term "corroboration" means that the FBI has received the same information from a separate source, and added that uncorroborated does not mean the information is untrue or provide a basis for shutting down a source.

the Carter Page FISA applications, the two renewal applications filed after the March 2017 validation report did not revise the source characterization statement or at least advise the court of VMU's finding.

Although SSA 2 and SSA 3, the Headquarters Program Managers who supervised Crossfire Hurricane from FBI Headquarters, had received the validation report and were aware of its findings, we found no evidence that this information was circulated to NYFO, where the Carter Page investigation was being conducted at the time. Case Agent 1 and Case Agent 6, both of whom were working out of NYFO at the time, told us that they did not recall ever receiving the VMU report or being aware of its findings. Case Agent 6 told us that he would have wanted to know about the findings so that he could have asked questions, and he would have expected that the OI Attorney drafting the next FISA renewal application would have wanted to do the same. The OGC Unit Chief and OGC Attorney also told us they did not recall receiving the VMU report or learning its findings, though the OGC Unit Chief told us she had a general understanding that the FBI officials who reviewed the report thought the information was consistent with the FISA applications.

OI officials told us that they did not recall having been advised of VMU's findings at any time before the second and third renewals, and the OI Attorney said that, had he known, he would have sought additional information from the FBI about the validation that was undertaken. Further, Evans told us that the finding sounded like something he would have thought warranted an update to the court in the next FISA application.

F.   Joseph Mifsud's Denials to the FBI

As described in Chapter Three, Priestap and other FBI officials told the OIG that the sole predication for opening the Crossfire Hurricane investigation was the statement George Papadopoulos made to FFG officials that the Trump campaign had received a suggestion or offer of assistance from Russia that involved the anonymous release of disparaging information about then presidential candidate Hillary Clinton. All four Carter Page FISA applications relied upon this information in the probable cause section to help support the FBI's assessment that Russia was attempting to influence the 2016 presidential election and that those efforts were being coordinated by Carter Page and possibly others associated with the Trump campaign.

During an interview with the FBI in late January 2017, Papadopoulos told the FBI that a Maltese citizen, Joseph Mifsud, who was living in London and serving as a university professor, told him that the Russians had "dirt" on Clinton in the form of "thousands of emails." In an interview in February 2017, Papadopoulos told the FBI that Mifsud told him that Clinton had "problems with her emails." In the same interview, Papadopoulos said that the "Russians had her emails" because the Russians told him (Mifsud) they have them. The FBI determined that Mifsud provided this information to Papadopoulos on April 26, 2016, shortly before Papadopoulos's meeting with the FFG.

As part of its investigation, the FBI interviewed Mifsud in February 2017, after Renewal Application No. 1 was filed but before Renewal Application No. 2. According to the FD-302 documenting the interview, Mifsud admitted to having met with Papadopoulos but denied having told him about any suggestion or offer from Russia.[403] Additionally, according to the FD-302, Mifsud told the FBI that "he had no advance knowledge Russia was in possession of emails from the Democratic National Committee (DNC) and, therefore, did not make any offers or proffer any information to Papadopoulos." Renewal Application Nos. 2 and 3 did not include these statements Mifsud made to the FBI.

A written case update indicates that Mifsud's denial was circulated to the Crossfire Hurricane team no later than late April 2017. Case Agent 6 told us that he was not sure he was aware at the time that Mifsud had been interviewed.[404] The OI officials handling Carter Page FISA applications told us that they either had not been advised of the denial or did not recall being advised at the time. Evans told us that he could not say definitively whether OI would have included this information in subsequent renewal applications without discussing the issue with the team (the FBI and OI), but Evans also said that Mifsud's denial as described by the OIG sounded like something "potentially factually similarly situated" to the denials made by Papadopoulos that OI determined should have been included.[405]

G. Carter Page's Alleged Role in Changing the Republican Platform on Russia's Annexation of Ukraine

As described previously, all four FISA applications relied upon information attributed in the Steele reporting to Person 1, including that:

> [A]ccording to [the sub-Source], Candidate #1's [Trump's] team, which the FBI assesses includes at least Page, agreed to sideline Russian intervention in Ukraine as a campaign issue and to raise U.S./NATO defense commitments in the Baltics and Eastern Europe to deflect attention away from Ukraine.

This assessment was based upon information in Steele Report 95 that purportedly came from Person 1 ("Source E" in Report 95), as well as news articles in July and August 2016 reporting that the Trump campaign adopted a milder tone toward

---

[403] According to the Special Counsel's Report, Mifsud made inaccurate statements during this FBI interview about his interactions with Papadopoulos. *See The Special Counsel's Report*, Vol. I at 193.

[404] We did not find any information in the documents we reviewed indicating that Case Agent 6 received the written case update containing the description of Mifsud's interview.

[405] As described in Chapter Seven, Renewal Application Nos. 2 and 3 advised the court in a footnote that, over the course of several interviews with the FBI in early 2017, Papadopoulos confirmed that he met with officials from the FFG but denied that he discussed anything with them relating to the Russian government. However, as described earlier in this chapter, none of the FISA applications advised the court that Papadopoulos denied to FBI CHSs and the FBI that anyone associated with the Trump campaign was involved in the DNC email hack or was collaborating with Russia or with outside groups like WikiLeaks in the release of emails.

Russia's annexation of Crimea and influenced changes to the Republican Party's platform on providing weapons to Ukraine.

We found that, other than this information from Report 95, the FBI's investigation did not reveal any information to demonstrate that Carter Page had any involvement with the Republican Platform Committee. We further found that, even after the FBI identified the individuals who were involved with influencing the Republican Platform change on Ukraine (which did not include Page), the FBI never altered their assessment. The FBI also did not include in any subsequent Carter Page FISA applications information that contradicted the assertion that Carter Page was involved with the Republican Platform Committee's provision on Ukraine, nor did OI provide such information at any time to the FISC.

As discussed in Chapter Ten, in October 2016, Carter Page met with an FBI CHS and, two days later, pertinent statements from that meeting were sent to Case Agent 1, SSA 1, and other agents and analysts on the Crossfire Hurricane team. The excerpts included statements Page made to the CHS about the platform committee during the Republican National Convention. Page told the CHS that he "stayed clear of that—there was a lot of conspiracy theories that I was one of them...[but] totally off the record...members of our team were working on that, and...in retrospect it's way better off that I...remained at arms length."

Case Agent 1 told the OIG that he did not believe Carter Page's statements on the platform issue were "that specific" and said that Page "minimized" and "vacillated on some things." SSA 1 told us he did not recall why Page's denial that he participated in the Republican Platform Committee was not included in the first FISA application. Before FISA Renewal Application No. 1, which was filed in January 2017, the OI Attorney did receive the documents containing Page's October 2016 denials. Yet, the information about the meeting remained unchanged in the renewal applications. The OI Attorney told us that he did not recall the circumstances surrounding this, but he acknowledged that he should have updated the descriptions in the renewal applications to include Page's denials.

Subsequently, an FBI November 30, 2016 Intelligence Memorandum titled "The Trump Campaign and US-Russia-Ukraine Policy—A Quick Overview," stated:

> During a RNC platform sub-committee meeting, Diana Denman, a platform committee member, attempted to insert amendment language calling for the United States to "provide lethal defensive weapons to the Ukrainian government," adding that the Ukraine [sic] was presently "fighting a [Russian–backed] separatist insurrection." In response to Denman's amendment, two Trump campaign members—one of whom was Jeff [JD] Gordon—approached the sub-committee co-chairman and asked for the amendment to be set aside. Denman's amendment was subsequently tabled, and the Trump staffers instead convinced the platform subcommittee to change the language from "lethal defensive weapons" to calling for "appropriate assistance."

The Intelligence Memorandum did not identify or reference Carter Page as the second individual involved, or state that he was involved in any capacity in the platform change. Case Agent 1 said he did not recall reading the November 30 Intelligence Memorandum but said that, at that time, the team was still trying to determine if there was any information connecting Carter Page to the platform change. Case Agent 1 told us that although the FBI did not know who from the Trump campaign approved Carter Page's trip to Moscow prior to the Republican Convention, and the platform change was made shortly after Page returned from his trip to Russia, the belief was that Page was involved in the platform change and the team was hoping to find evidence of that in their review of the FISA collections of Page's email accounts.

Additionally, as described in Chapter Six and earlier in this chapter, in January 2017, Steele's Primary Sub-source provided the FBI with information that was inconsistent with the information Steele reported from Person 1 (Source E in Report 95), including the reporting that Page was involved in the Republican Platform Committee changes on Ukraine. Indeed, the Primary Sub-source made no reference to discussing the Republican Platform Committee or Ukraine provision with Person 1.

Further, on March 16, 2017, Case Agent 1 and Case Agent 6 interviewed Carter Page and asked him about his activities at the 2016 Republican National Convention. Carter Page told them he had no part in the decision by the Platform Committee to omit the reference to "lethal assistance" involving Ukraine, but that he supported the omission of the reference. Page said he learned of the policy change upon receiving an email from Gordon dated July 14, 2016, to himself, Papadopoulos, and four members of the campaign foreign policy team. The email, which Page provided to the FBI during the interview, stated, in part:

> I hope you had a chance to read some of the press coverage over
> Platform [sic]. We are proud to say it is the strongest pro-Israel policy
> statement in the history of the Republican Party. We are also pleased
> to say we defeated red line amendments like providing lethal
> assistance to Ukraine.

That same day, Carter Page replied to this email, "Fantastic, J.D. thanks a lot for the useful insights and context. As for the Ukrainian amendment, excellent work."

Case Agent 6 sent this email to members of the Crossfire Hurricane investigative team, including SSA 2. The OI Unit Chief told us that he did not recall specifically seeing this email but said that if the FBI had any information suggesting Carter Page might not have been involved with the Republican platform, then it should have been discussed with OI.

Renewal Application Nos. 2 and 3 included Carter Page's denials about his involvement in the Republican Platform Committee's changes on assistance to Ukraine from the March 16 interview with the FBI. After including these denials in the applications, the renewal applications stated that,

As the FBI believes that Page also holds pro-Russian views and appears to still have been a member of Candidate #1's [Trump's] campaign in August 2016, the FBI assesses that Page may have been downplaying his role in advocating for the change to Political Party #1's [Republican] platform.

We observed among the NSD's Counterintelligence and Export Control Section (CES) records an April 2017 version of an investigation outline CES prepared and periodically updated reflecting that Carter Page received an email from Gordon in July 2016 about the platform change and that the email "suggests Page was not involved in the decision." Also included in the CES outline were Page's denials to the FBI. Former CES Chief David Laufman told us that, at that time, the FBI was at an "investigative dead end" with respect to Page and the platform issue with no new evidence emerging. During his OIG interview, we provided Laufman with the July 2016 email that Carter Page provided to FBI agents during his March 16 interview. After reviewing the email, Laufman told us that he would reword the reference in the CES outline stating that the email "suggests Page was not involved in the decision to" instead read: "there's no indication in the email that Page was involved."

An FBI March 20, 2017 Intelligence Memorandum titled "Overview of Trump Campaign Advisor Jeff D. [J.D.] Gordon" again attributed the change in the Republican Platform Committee's Ukraine provision to Gordon and an unnamed campaign staffer. The updated memorandum did not include any reference to Carter Page working with Gordon or communicating with the Republican Platform Committee. On May 5, 2017, the Counterintelligence Division updated this Intelligence Memorandum to include open source reporting on the intervention of Trump campaign members during the Republican platform discussions at the Convention to include Gordon's public comments on his role. This memorandum still made no reference to involvement by Carter Page with the Republican Platform Committee or with the provision on Ukraine.

On June 7, 2017, the FBI interviewed a Republican Platform Committee member. This interview occurred three weeks before Renewal Application No. 3 was filed. According to the FBI FD-302 documenting the interview, this individual told the FBI that J.D. Gordon was the Trump campaign official that flagged the Ukrainian amendment, and that another person (not Carter Page) was the second campaign staffer present at the July 11 meeting of the National Security and Defense Platform Subcommittee meeting when the issue was tabled.

Although the FBI did not develop any information that Carter Page was involved in the Republican Platform Committee's change regarding assistance to Ukraine, and the FBI developed evidence that Gordon and another campaign official were responsible for the change, the FBI did not alter its assessment of Page's involvement in the FISA applications. Case Agent 6 told us that when Carter Page denied any involvement with the Republican Platform Committee's provision on Ukraine, Case Agent 6 "did not take that statement at face value." He told us that at the time of the renewals, he did not believe Carter Page's denial and it was the team's "belief" that Carter Page had been involved with the platform change. We

266

asked Case Agent 6 if the FBI had any information to support its continued assessment that Carter Page was involved in the Republican Platform Committee's provision on Ukraine, and he provided no further information.

In the next chapter, we discuss the interactions career Department attorney Bruce Ohr had with the Crossfire Hurricane team, the information he provided to the team regarding his interactions with Steele and Glenn Simpson, and the work Ohr's wife performed for Fusion GPS. We also describe Ohr's actions following the 2016 elections relating to the investigation of Paul Manafort.

CHAPTER NINE
DEPARTMENT ATTORNEY BRUCE OHR'S ACTIVITIES DURING THE CROSSFIRE HURRICANE INVESTIGATION

In this chapter, we describe Department attorney Bruce Ohr's activities during the Crossfire Hurricane investigation, primarily relating to his interactions with Christopher Steele. Ohr was an Associate Deputy Attorney General (ADAG) in the Office of the Deputy Attorney General (ODAG) and the Director of the Organized Crime and Drug Enforcement Task Force (OCDETF) at the time of the Crossfire Hurricane investigation, and was personally acquainted with Steele and Fusion GPS co-founder Glenn Simpson. In addition, Ohr's wife Nellie Ohr was employed as an independent contractor by Fusion GPS. During 2016 and 2017, Ohr received information from Steele and Simpson describing alleged links between the Russian government and the Donald J. Trump campaign and suggesting that the Russian government had leverage over Trump. Ohr provided the information he received from Steele and Simpson to the FBI, which had already received much, but not all, of the same information through its direct contact with Steele. Ohr did not advise any of his supervisors in ODAG about his contacts with Steele and Simpson, about his wife's work for Fusion GPS, or about his acting as a conduit of this information to the FBI, until ODAG leadership confronted Ohr about his activities in late 2017.

We also describe in this chapter Ohr's and several other Department attorneys' activities before and after the November 2016 elections relating to the Department's then ongoing criminal money laundering investigation of Paul Manafort.

I.   Bruce Ohr's Background

A.   Department Positions and Responsibilities

Bruce Ohr joined the Department on January 31, 1991, as an Assistant U.S. Attorney (AUSA) in the U.S. Attorney's Office for the Southern District of New York (SDNY). Ohr remained with SDNY until 1999 when he transferred to the Department's Criminal Division (CRM) in Washington, D.C., as Chief of the Organized Crime and Racketeering Section (OCRS). Ohr told the OIG that as Chief of OCRS, he tried to develop the Department's capacity for fighting transnational organized crime and that this was when he began tracking Russian organized crime.

In 2011, Ohr became Counsel for Transnational Organized Crime and International Affairs to the Assistant Attorney General in CRM and worked primarily for CRM Deputy Assistant Attorney General Bruce Swartz. According to Ohr, in that position he focused on policy issues relating to transnational organized crime and had no prosecutorial responsibilities. He stated that he was often the Department's "public face" at conferences and was sometimes approached by individuals who provided information about transnational organized crime.

In November 2014, Ohr became an ADAG in ODAG and the Director of OCDETF, a Senior Executive Service-level (SES) position. Ohr reported to the Principal Associate Deputy Attorney General (PADAG) and the Deputy Attorney General (DAG) in both of these positions. Ohr stated that as OCDETF Director, he oversaw OCDETF in its "mission...to coordinate organized crime and primarily drug investigations across the different parts of the U.S. government." He said OCDETF is responsible for aspects of the national drug and organized crime policies and provides funding for agents and prosecutors working on drug and organized crime cases. OCDETF is not an operational entity and does not direct prosecutorial actions in any cases. Ohr told us that when he became the OCDETF Director, then DAG Jim Cole expressed his desire for Ohr to expand OCDETF's mission to include transnational organized crime matters. He said that, as a result, he continued working on transnational organized crime policy and, in order to maintain awareness, tracked Russian organized crime issues.

As an ADAG, Ohr also served as Director of the Attorney General's Organized Crime Council, as the Department's Liaison to the Office of National Drug Control Policy, and as a member of the Attorney General's Capital Case Committee. He also assisted with implementing portions of the 2017 Executive Order on Transnational Organized Crime and developing a Transnational Organized Crime initiative.

Throughout his tenure in the Department, Ohr has been a career employee and not a political appointee.

B. Ohr's Relationship with Steele and Glenn Simpson

1. Ohr's Relationship with Steele from 2007 to March 2016

Ohr stated that he met Christopher Steele in late 2007 during meetings with an allied country's government officials.[406] He said that after the meetings, he met Steele for lunch and spoke about the threat of Russian organized crime. Ohr stated that after Steele left government service, Steele set up a private investigations firm and remained in contact with Ohr. Ohr told us that he and Steele spoke "probably less than once a year" and that he would see Steele for social visits, such as breakfast or lunch, if Steele visited Washington, D.C. He described his relationship with Steele as being "primarily professional," but also "friendly" because they shared with each other information about their families. Steele likewise told us that he and Ohr were personal friends and that he would see Ohr whenever he was in Washington, D.C., which was about once or twice a year.

Ohr stated that Steele provided him reports that Steele prepared for his clients, which Steele thought the U.S. government might find interesting. He told

---

[406] Steele told us he recalled meeting Ohr in 2008 while he was visiting a U.S. government agency, and his contact at that agency arranged for him to meet Ohr.

us that he initially did nothing with the information he received from Steele because it was general and not directly useful for an investigation.

Ohr said he introduced Steele to Handling Agent 1 so that Steele could provide information directly to the FBI in approximately spring 2010.[407] He told us that he "pushed" to make Steele an FBI Confidential Human Source (CHS) because Steele's information was valuable. Ohr also said that it was "not efficient" for him to pass Steele's information to the FBI and he preferred having Steele work directly with an FBI agent. According to Steele, Ohr and Handling Agent 1 coordinated over a period of time with Steele to set up his relationship with the FBI.

Ohr's contact with Steele did not end after Steele formalized his relationship with Handling Agent 1 and the FBI.[408] Ohr met or talked with Steele multiple times from 2014 through fall 2016, and on occasion those in-person meetings or video calls included Handling Agent 1. Ohr told us that he viewed meeting with Steele as part of his job because he needed to maintain awareness of Russian organized crime activities and Steele knew Russian organized crime trends better than anyone else. He said he knew Steele was also speaking to Handling Agent 1 at this time because Steele would say that he provided the same information to Handling Agent 1. Handling Agent 1 told us that he knew Steele and Ohr were in contact and talked about issues "at a higher policy level," but stated that he did not know anything further regarding their interactions.

Ohr and Steele also communicated frequently over the years regarding Russian Oligarch 1, including in 2016 during the time period before and after Steele was closed as an FBI CHS.[409] Steele told us his communications with Ohr concerning Russian Oligarch 1 were the result of an outreach effort started in 2014 with Ohr and Handling Agent 1, to approach oligarchs about cooperating with the U.S. government. Ohr confirmed that he and Handling Agent 1 asked Steele to contact Russian oligarchs for this purpose. This effort resulted in Ohr meeting with Russian Oligarch 1 and an FBI agent in September 2015.

2. Ohr's Relationship with Simpson

Ohr told the OIG that he could not recall how he first met Fusion GPS co-founder Glenn Simpson.[410] He estimated that he saw Simpson less than ten times over several years. According to Ohr, Simpson usually reached out to him to

---

[407] Ohr stated that he met Handling Agent 1 when he was with SDNY and remained in contact with him through 2017. As described in Chapter Four, Steele stated he recalled meeting Handling Agent 1 when he was with Ohr at a European seminar on Russian related issues in June 2009.

[408] Ohr stated that he talked to other individuals he met through his job duties over the years and discussed Russian organized crime whenever the opportunity arose. He told us that he spoke with Steele more often than other individuals because Steele contacted him more frequently. Ohr also stated that Steele was the only contact that he introduced to the FBI.

[409] The United States imposed sanctions on Russian Oligarch 1 and his business interests, including his Russian company, for his links to senior Russian government officials, suspected criminal activities, and ties to Russian organized crime.

[410] As noted in Chapter One, Simpson declined our request for an interview.

provide information about Russian organized crime figures. Ohr stated that most of Simpson's past information was not actionable, so he did not do anything with it and did not try to introduce Simpson to the FBI. However, as described below, Ohr told us that when Simpson provided names in 2016 of possible intermediaries between Russia and the Trump campaign, he wanted to introduce Simpson to the FBI, but thought Simpson seemed reluctant and did not do so.

C.   Nellie Ohr's Relationship with Steele and Work for Fusion GPS

Nellie Ohr, Bruce Ohr's wife, told the OIG that she met Steele in 2009 through her husband, and that she recalled meeting him two more times—sometime after 2014 and then at the July 30, 2016 breakfast meeting discussed later in this chapter. She stated that she knew of Steele's interest in Russian oligarchs and understood him to be a Russia analyst. She described his relationship with her husband as a "professional associate" and considered them to be friendly, but not friends.

Nellie Ohr, who has a doctorate in Russian history and is fluent in Russian, told us that she contacted Simpson in October 2015 to ask for a job with Fusion GPS. She stated that she was familiar with Simpson from reading published newspaper articles he wrote relating to Russian criminal activity. She said that she was hired by Fusion GPS as an independent contractor shortly thereafter. According to Nellie Ohr, she worked remotely from home for Fusion GPS, conducting online open source research. Bruce Ohr told us that he did not play any role in Nellie Ohr's hiring by Fusion GPS.

Nellie Ohr stated that while working for Fusion GPS, she initially conducted online, open source research about a Russian company suspected of human trafficking. She told us that, after her first project, Fusion GPS tasked her to research then candidate Trump and his Russian business associates, which involved searching Russian and other foreign language websites and databases and providing periodic reports detailing her findings. Nellie Ohr stated that she was not told who was funding this project and did not know that Steele was also working for Fusion GPS until July 2016. She said that she stopped working for Fusion GPS on September 24, 2016, when she began a full-time job elsewhere.

II.   Ohr's Communications with Steele, Simpson, and the FBI in 2016 and 2017

This section details Ohr's communications in 2016 and 2017 with Steele and Simpson regarding alleged Russian connections with Trump or persons associated with the Trump campaign, Ohr's meetings with FBI personnel concerning the information he received from Steele and Simpson, and the FBI's internal communications regarding Ohr.

A. Ohr's 2016 Contacts with Steele and Simpson Regarding Russian Issues

1. Ohr's July 30, 2016 Meeting with Steele

On Saturday, July 30, 2016, at Steele's invitation, Ohr and Nellie Ohr had breakfast with Steele and an associate in Washington, D.C. Nellie Ohr told us she initially thought it was going to be a social brunch, but came to understand that Steele wanted to share his current Russia reporting with Ohr. According to Steele, he intended the gathering to be a social brunch, but Ohr asked him what he was working on. Steele told us that he told Ohr about his work related to Russian interference with the election. Ohr told us that, among other things, Steele discussed Carter Page's travel to Russia and interactions with Russian officials. He also said that Steele told Ohr that Russian Oligarch 1's attorney was gathering evidence that Paul Manafort stole money from Russian Oligarch 1. Ohr also stated that Steele told him that Russian officials were claiming to have Trump "over a barrel." According to Ohr, Steele mentioned that he provided two reports concerning these topics to Handling Agent 1 and that Simpson, who owned Fusion GPS, had all of Steele's reports relating to the election. Steele did not provide Ohr with copies of any of these reports at this time. Later that evening, Steele wrote to Ohr asking to "keep in touch on the substantive issues" and advised Ohr that Simpson was available to speak with him.[411]

Ohr told the OIG that he did not know before the breakfast that Steele was working with Nellie Ohr's then employer, Fusion GPS, and did not know whether Steele was aware of Nellie Ohr's employment with Fusion GPS. However, Nellie Ohr told us that Steele made a comment during the breakfast indicating to her that he knew about her connection to Fusion GPS and that Simpson was "okay" with Steele talking to her and Ohr. Steele told us he knew Nellie Ohr was working for Fusion GPS, but he did not know she was doing work related to his project—Russian interference with the 2016 U.S. elections.

Ohr stated that because Nellie Ohr was unaware of Steele's information and had never been involved in similar situations, he became uncomfortable during the breakfast and spoke to Steele privately. Ohr said that he did not discuss "the details of the cases that [he was] working on" with Nellie Ohr. He said he explained to Steele that he did not want Nellie Ohr involved and that he made sure that she was not present for any future conversations he had with Steele. Steele told us that Ohr advised him not to discuss his reporting in front of Nellie Ohr.

Ohr said that he knew the information Steele provided to him was opposition research, but did not know who was paying for it. He told us that it was "clear" to him, due to the nature of the research, that Steele and Simpson were hired by a private party "somehow related to the Clinton campaign." He said he also surmised that Steele thought that by giving the information to Ohr, the U.S. government would do "something." Nellie Ohr similarly stated that she understood from the

---

[411] Ohr memorialized each of his meetings with Steele and Simpson with detailed notes about what they told him.

272

meeting that Steele hoped Ohr would speak with the FBI regarding the information concerning then candidate Trump.

Steele later told the FBI that, prior to the 2016 elections, he provided information to Ohr and was "pushing Ohr to do something about the [election] reports."

Following the July 30 breakfast, Ohr reached out to officials in the FBI and the Department about the information Steele had provided, but did not discuss this information with the DAG or anyone in ODAG. On August 3, 2016, Ohr emailed Handling Agent 1 asking to speak to him. Handling Agent 1 told us he talked with Ohr, who asked him if he had seen Steele's election reports and whether the FBI was doing anything with them. Handling Agent 1 stated that he told Ohr that an executive assistant director at FBI Headquarters and executive management in the New York Field Office (NYFO) knew about Steele's reporting and were addressing it.[412]

Ohr told us that because the information provided by Steele on July 30 was "scary" and he was unsure what to do with it, he also reached out to CRM Deputy Assistant Attorney General Bruce Swartz. According to Ohr's calendar, he met with Swartz on August 4, and both Ohr and Swartz told us that Ohr provided Swartz with specific details of what Steele had told Ohr on July 30.

Swartz told us that he did not tell his immediate supervisor, CRM Assistant Attorney General Leslie Caldwell (who was a political appointee), or any other senior Department political appointees that Ohr was meeting with Steele or the FBI because he did not want to politicize Steele's information by providing it to political appointees.

We asked Ohr whether he contemporaneously sought any ethics guidance regarding any of the events connected with Steele, Simpson, and Nellie Ohr. Ohr stated that he did not recall considering at the time whether the connections between Nellie Ohr's employment and his receipt of information from Steele and Simpson presented any ethics issues, nor did he recall contacting an ethics official for advice. Ohr stated it was possible he did not seek ethics advice because he did not want to "spread" the information around the Department before it was evaluated.[413]

---

[412] Chapter Four details Handling Agent 1's actions once he received the election reports from Steele, including how the reports made their way to FBI Headquarters and, eventually, to the Crossfire Hurricane team. Handling Agent 1 also told us that, in October 2016, he advised the members of the Crossfire Hurricane team who came to Europe to interview Steele about his August 2016 conversation with Ohr. Handling Agent 1 stated that they did not appear to be surprised by the information, so he assumed the team knew about Ohr's involvement with Steele. However, when we interviewed the Crossfire Hurricane team members, none of them recalled Handling Agent 1 telling them about Ohr.

[413] Ohr told us that although he did not seek any ethics advice concerning his wife's presence at the July 30, 2016 breakfast, he ensured that Nellie Ohr was not present for any future conversations with Steele.

2. Ohr's August 22, 2016 Meeting with Simpson

On August 22, 2016, Simpson emailed Ohr requesting that Ohr call him. Later that same day, at Simpson's request, Ohr met with Simpson, and Simpson provided Ohr with the names of three individuals who Simpson thought were potential intermediaries between Russia and the Trump campaign.[414] The three names are included in notes that Ohr told us he wrote on the same day as his meeting with Simpson. According to these notes, one of the three names provided by Simpson was one of the sub-sources in Steele's election reports, who we reference as Person 1 in previous chapters. Another of the names was Carter Page's "[b]usiness partner" who was an "[a]lleged" Russian intelligence officer and "the 'brains' behind [Carter] Page's company—Global Energy Capital." Ohr stated that he was uncomfortable receiving this information from Simpson and did not recall Simpson asking him to do anything with it.

Ohr told the OIG that he was troubled by Simpson's information. He stated that he could not remember when or how he provided Simpson's information to the FBI, but would have likely contacted Handling Agent 1 or the FBI's Transnational Organized Crime-East (TOC-East) Section Chief. Emails indicate that Ohr and Handling Agent 1 spoke on August 24, 2016, but neither of them could recall what they discussed.[415]

On September 12, 2016, Ohr and Handling Agent 1 exchanged emails referencing Steele. In one email, Handling Agent 1 informed Ohr that an FBI team was looking into Steele's information. In response, Ohr asked Handling Agent 1 to let him know who to contact with additional information. Handling Agent 1 told us that he did not reply to Ohr's question, and we did not find a response.

3. Ohr's September 23, 2016 Meeting with Steele

On September 23, 2016, at Steele's request, Steele met with Ohr in Washington, D.C. Ohr told us they spoke about various topics related to Russia, including information regarding Russian Oligarch 1's willingness to talk with the U.S. government about Manafort. Ohr said that Steele identified the person who was funding Fusion GPS's opposition research; however, according to Ohr, he did not recognize the name and could not remember it long enough to write it down after the meeting. Ohr also said that he and Steele also discussed allegations that an Alfa Bank server in the United States was a link between Russia and the Trump campaign; that Person 1's Russian/American organization in the United States had

---

[414] On November 14, 2017, Simpson testified before the House Permanent Select Committee on Intelligence. During his testimony, Simpson told the Committee that he did not meet with Ohr prior to the November 2016 presidential election. He stated further that he met with Ohr one time after Thanksgiving 2016. *See Interview of Glenn Simpson Before the Executive Session of the H. Perm. Select Comm. On Intelligence*, 115th Cong. 78 (November 14, 2017) (hereinafter *HPSCI Interview of Glenn Simpson*).

[415] Department emails indicate that Ohr first spoke with the TOC-East Section Chief regarding Steele and Simpson's information in October 2016, which we discuss below.

used the Alfa Bank server earlier in September; and that an individual working with Carter Page was a Russian intelligence officer.

According to Steele, he and Ohr also discussed Steele's concerns that if Trump won the election, Steele's source network may be in jeopardy. Steele said that a new FBI Director and new agency heads appointed by Trump would have a higher degree of loyalty to the new President, and could decide to take action against Steele and his source network. Steele told us that Ohr explained that the FBI Director had a 10-year term and could not be removed from the position by the President, so information about Steele's source network should be protected.[416] According to Steele, he also asked Ohr about why it appeared from the news that the U.S. government was not addressing his election reporting. Steele said that Ohr told him that the Hatch Act made it a criminal offense for a federal official to make a public statement to the detriment or benefit of a candidate within 90 days of an election.[417] When we asked Ohr about this, he told us he did not recall talking to Steele about either of these concerns.

Ohr did not recall whether he provided anyone with the information he received from Steele at this meeting, but stated that he might have spoken to Swartz and Handling Agent 1 about it. Swartz told us that Ohr provided him with specific information at the time regarding Steele's reporting, but he could not recall the specific information when interviewed by the OIG. Handling Agent 1 told us he did not recall discussing these topics with Ohr.

4. Ohr's Early October 2016 Activities Regarding Steele's Information

Sometime prior to October 13, 2016, Ohr talked to the FBI's TOC-East Section Chief about Steele's information, but Ohr could not recall what he told him. The TOC-East Section Chief recalled Ohr mentioning Steele to him starting in mid-2016, but stated that he could not specifically recall the information Ohr relayed concerning Steele's election reporting.[418]

In an October 13, 2016 email, the TOC-East Section Chief told Ohr that counterintelligence agents had traveled to a European city and spoken with Handling Agent 1. Ohr responded that he had additional information to share,

---

[416] This statement concerning the FBI Director's term is incorrect. The President has the authority to remove the FBI Director prior to the expiration of the 10-year term. *See* Pub. L. No. 94-503, § 203, 90 Stat. 2407 (1976); 5 U.S.C. § 532 notes.

[417] The Hatch Act does not address this issue. Rather, among other things, it prohibits federal employees from participating in certain political activities on and off duty. Section 7323(a)(1) provides that "an employee may not use his official authority or influence for the purpose of interfering with or affecting the result of an election." 5 U.S.C. § 7323(a)(1); 5 C.F.R. §§ 734, 734.401(a)(2), 734.407, 734.411.

[418] The TOC-East Section Chief noted that while it was odd to have a high-level Department official in contact with Russian oligarchs, it did not surprise him that Ohr would be approached by individuals, such as Steele, who wanted to talk to the U.S. government. The TOC-East Section Chief said that it would be "outside [of Ohr's] lane" to continue the relationship with these potential sources after their introduction to the FBI.

specifically names of possible intermediaries, and asked if the counterintelligence agents had an interest in receiving this information. We did not find a response to Ohr's email and the TOC-East Section Chief did not recall providing a name to Ohr, but the TOC-East Section Chief said he likely passed the email to a relevant point of contact who could follow up with Ohr.

5. Ohr's October 18-19, 2016 Communications with Steele and Meeting with McCabe and Lisa Page

Early in the morning of October 18, 2016, Steele emailed Ohr, stating "I have something quite urgent I would like to discuss with you, preferably by [video call] (even before work if you can)." Records reflect that Steele and Ohr spoke around 7:00 a.m. Later that morning, Steele wrote Ohr an email referring to U.S. sanctions on the Russian company controlled by Russian Oligarch 1. In the email, Steele referenced their earlier video call and stated that Russian Oligarch 1's attorney wanted Ohr to receive the information. Ohr told us he could not recall what he talked with Steele about that morning, or what the urgent issue was, but based on this email, he said he believed they likely discussed Russian Oligarch 1. Likewise, Steele said he could not recall the topic of the call, but after reviewing the follow-up email, he said he assumed that the conversation included information about Russian Oligarch 1.

Records reflect that shortly after the video call between Ohr and Steele, Ohr called then Deputy Director Andrew McCabe and made a calendar entry indicating a meeting with McCabe for later that day. Ohr told us he set up the meeting to share Steele's and Simpson's information with McCabe. He told us that he contacted McCabe because Ohr had previously worked with McCabe on issues associated with Russian Oligarch 1 and Russian organized crime. Ohr explained that when Ohr was an AUSA in the SDNY, McCabe was leading the Russian organized crime squad at the NYFO. Ohr also stated that he wanted to ensure McCabe knew about Steele's information and assumed McCabe would provide the information to the right people in the FBI.

We asked Ohr if Steele had asked Ohr to meet with the FBI in order to provide the information that Steele had shared with Ohr. Ohr said that he did not think so. We asked Ohr what prompted him to seek a meeting at that time with McCabe, if it was not at Steele's request. He responded that he recalled being concerned sometime between his August conversations with Handling Agent 1 and his later conversation with the TOC-East Section Chief that NYFO was not talking to FBI Headquarters about Steele's reports. Ohr stated that he wanted to meet with McCabe to ensure that McCabe knew about Steele's information and then McCabe could direct it to the right place within the FBI. We asked Ohr why the TOC-East Section Chief's October 13 email advising Ohr that counterintelligence agents were examining Steele's allegations did not alleviate his concern. He responded that he could not recall.

Ohr met with McCabe during the afternoon of October 18, 2016.[419] Ohr told us that he recalled only meeting with McCabe once concerning Steele's information. McCabe's Special Counsel Lisa Page was also present. Ohr told us that he informed McCabe and Lisa Page about his background with Steele and the reporting Steele provided to him. He stated that he told them that Steele and Simpson were hired by a private party to provide opposition research, but said he could not recall whether he specifically mentioned the Clinton campaign. Ohr thought he also shared with them that Steele and Simpson were communicating with others and that their information was generated for a political client and not for the U.S. government. Although Ohr told us that he believed Steele and Simpson were communicating with the media, he said he could not recall whether he specifically mentioned that to McCabe and Lisa Page.

Ohr said that he also told McCabe and Lisa Page that Nellie Ohr had worked for Fusion GPS (by the date of this meeting, Nellie Ohr was no longer working for Fusion GPS). He said he did so because the information he was providing to McCabe and Lisa Page came from Fusion GPS and Steele and that they needed to consider any possible bias. Ohr told us that this was "another reason [for the FBI] to be cautious" when assessing the information's credibility. According to Ohr, he understood from his meeting with McCabe and Lisa Page that he should contact the FBI if Steele contacted him again. Ohr stated that neither McCabe nor Lisa Page discussed the Crossfire Hurricane investigation with him during the meeting.

McCabe told us that he recalled meeting with Ohr in fall 2016. He did not remember Ohr calling him to set up the meeting or how it came to be scheduled.[420] He said that the Crossfire Hurricane team previously told him that Ohr knew Steele and that it was not until the meeting that he better understood Ohr's connection to Steele. McCabe stated that he could not recall specific details from the meeting with Ohr, but believed that the October 18, 2016 notes by Lisa Page and Deputy Assistant Director (DAD) Peter Strzok (as detailed below) accurately captured the meeting's details.

Lisa Page told us she attended the meeting, but did not recall Ohr conveying much substantive information. She stated that in general, Ohr told McCabe that Steele had information he wanted to provide to the FBI. Lisa Page's notes from the meeting show that Ohr discussed Steele, provided Steele's previous employment background, talked about issues concerning Russian Oligarch 1, and indicated that Simpson provided Ohr with names of intermediaries between the Kremlin and the

---

[419] Ohr testified on August 28, 2018, before the House Committees on the Judiciary and on Government Reform and Oversight. He told the committee members that he met with McCabe shortly after his July 30, 2016 meeting with Steele. Based on the documentary evidence, including Ohr's calendar entry and Lisa Page's handwritten notes, along with Ohr's testimony that he met with McCabe a single time, we believe that Ohr met with McCabe on October 18, 2016. We asked Ohr about the date of his meeting with McCabe in light of the documentary evidence. He told us that he did not recall exactly when he contacted McCabe.

[420] McCabe said that he and Ohr first met in 2003, when McCabe was assigned to NYFO's Eurasian Organized Crime Task Force and Ohr was Chief of OCRS. According to McCabe, the two spoke periodically between 2003 and 2016 regarding Russian Oligarch 1.

Trump campaign. Lisa Page also wrote that Ohr met with Russian Oligarch 1 the previous year and "Need report?"

We also reviewed Strzok's notes dated October 18 that detail information concerning Ohr. Strzok told us he believed either Lisa Page or McCabe provided the information to him. In addition to the information contained in Lisa Page's notes, Strzok's notes also stated: "Bruce's wife fluent Russian speaker," "Simpson hired Ohr's wife to find connections," and "She saw no connections [at] first." Additionally, we reviewed Assistant Director E.W. "Bill" Priestap's notes, which reflect an entry dated October 19 that states: "DOJ Bruce [Ohr]—Steele is providing reporting to a variety of people." Priestap told us that he did not recall who told him or how he learned this information.

Steele and Ohr spoke on October 19 at Ohr's request. Ohr and Steele both told us that they could not recall what they spoke about, but Ohr claimed that he did not advise Steele or Simpson that he met with McCabe and Lisa Page.

6. Ohr's November 2016 Communications with the FBI and State Department Regarding Steele

As described in Chapter Six, Handling Agent 1 determined that Steele should be closed as a CHS on November 1, 2016, following the October 31 publication of the *Mother Jones* article.[421] Handling Agent 1 told us that he spoke with Ohr that same day and recommended to Ohr that he read the article. According to Handling Agent 1, as a courtesy, he told Ohr that he was not engaging with Steele anymore, warned Ohr to be careful when dealing with Steele, and said that Steele could not be trusted.

Ohr said that he did not recall whether Handling Agent 1 informed him that Steele was closed as a CHS during the November 1 telephone call, but remembered Handling Agent 1 telling him that he would no longer be working with Steele because Steele spoke to the press. Ohr told the OIG that he was not surprised that Steele talked to the press because he knew that Steele and Simpson were collecting the information for political purposes and that they had previously talked to others about it. According to Ohr, his understanding was that Steele was not collecting the information for the U.S. government, so he was not functioning as an FBI source.

Handling Agent 1 met with Ohr 1 week later in Washington, D.C. According to Handling Agent 1, Ohr apologized for introducing him to Steele and said that he had not realized the impact of the *Mother Jones* article.[422] Ohr told us that he

---

[421] Handling Agent 1 told us that he informed Steele on November 1, 2016, that it was unlikely the FBI would continue a relationship with him and that Steele must cease collecting information for the FBI. Handling Agent 1 completed a Source Closing Communication document on November 17, 2016, stating that Steele had been closed for cause on November 1, 2016.

[422] Handling Agent 1 told us that Ohr also commented to him at this meeting that Nellie Ohr worked at Fusion GPS. Handling Agent 1 stated he never met Nellie Ohr and did not learn her name until the media publicized the Ohrs' involvement.

recalled meeting Handling Agent 1 and discussing the FBI's closure of Steele as a CHS. He also said that Handling Agent 1 told him that the FBI wanted to interview Ohr about his contacts with Steele.[423]

On the morning of November 21, 2016, at the State Department's request, Ohr met with Deputy Assistant Secretary Kathleen Kavalec and several other senior State Department officials regarding State Department efforts to investigate Russian influence in foreign elections and how the Department of Justice might assist those efforts. During a break in this meeting, Ohr and Kavalec discussed together Kavalec's interactions with Steele. Ohr told us that he could not recall how he discovered that Kavalec knew Steele or how he and Kavalec began discussing Steele. Ohr also stated that he recalled meeting with Kavalec on more than one occasion because Ohr was interested in obtaining relevant information about Steele from Kavalec so that he could share it with the FBI's Crossfire Hurricane team.[424] We asked Ohr if he provided Kavalec with any of the information Steele or Simpson shared with him during these conversations. He said that he could not recall.

Kavalec told us that she could not recall the specifics of her conversations with Ohr regarding Steele. She stated that, just before or after the November 21, 2016 meeting, she asked Ohr if he knew Steele. Kavalec said that she generally shared with Ohr the information that Steele had provided, and she said Ohr appeared to be aware of it already. She told us that Ohr responded that Steele's information was "kind of crazy...kind of wild...quite a tale." She told us that she provided this information to Ohr believing that he would pass it along to whoever needed it. Kavalec said that she did not specifically ask Ohr to do anything with the information and did not expect to receive any feedback from Ohr.

Later on November 21, 2016, in a meeting previously arranged by Lisa Page at Strzok's request, Ohr met with Lisa Page, Strzok, SSA 1, the Office of the General Counsel (OGC) Unit Chief, and the Chief of the Counterintelligence Division's (CD) Counterintelligence Analysis Section I (Intel Section Chief). Strzok, the OGC Unit Chief, SSA 1, and the Intel Section Chief told us the purpose of the meeting was to better understand Steele's background and reliability as a source and to identify his source network.

Notes taken by meeting participants indicate that Ohr shared the following information:

- Ohr thought Steele had "great expertise" concerning Russia;

---

[423] Ohr is mentioned in Strzok's notes in connection with a November 9, 2016 Crossfire Hurricane team meeting, but Strzok could not tell us what his handwritten notes said, nor could he recall the conversation.

[424] Ohr stated that obtaining information from Kavalec was not part of his Department responsibilities, and even though he had previously provided her name to individuals who were part of the Crossfire Hurricane team, he actively sought information from her because he thought it could be important to whatever investigation the FBI was conducting about Russian interference in the 2016 U.S. elections.

- Steele wrote well-sourced reports using a variety of sub-sources that he wrote for other purposes and shared with the FBI;

- Steele had participated in past efforts to connect Ohr to Russian oligarchs through intermediaries;

- Simpson hired Steele to research Trump and hired Nellie Ohr to perform open source research on Trump;

- Ohr met with Simpson in August 2016 and Simpson provided Ohr with the names of three "potential conduits" of information between Russia and the Trump campaign;[425]

- Steele's reporting was shared by Simpson with "a lot of people" including the Clinton campaign and the Department of State;[426]

- Steele was "desperate" that Trump not be elected, but was providing reports for ideological reasons, specifically that "Russia [was] bad;"[427] and

- Reporting of Kremlin activities "may be exaggerated or conspiracy theory talk," so Steele cannot know whether all the reporting is true.

According to Ohr, he asked the FBI personnel whether there was a prosecutor assigned to their investigation and was told "no." He also said that no one at the meeting told him about the Crossfire Hurricane investigation, but that he was advised that the FBI was "pushing ahead" on a Manafort case.

SSA 1 memorialized the meeting with Ohr in an FD-302, which largely mirrored the attendees' notes, but also provided additional details.[428] SSA 1 documented in the FD-302 that Ohr told the FBI that:

- Steele was "desperate that Donald Trump not get elected and was passionate about him not being the U.S. President;"

- "Ohr never believed Steele was making up information or shading it;"

- "Simpson and Steele could have met with [Yahoo] or [Yahoo News reporter] jointly, but Ohr [did] not know if they did;" and

---

[425] *See* Section II.A.2 of this chapter regarding the individuals mentioned by Simpson. At the November 21 meeting, Ohr provided SSA 1 with a copy of his notes containing these three names and a short summary of their alleged roles.

[426] Strzok and SSA 1's notes specifically mention then State Department Assistant Secretary Victoria Nuland and then Special Assistant to the Special Envoy to Libya, Jonathan Winer.

[427] When we interviewed Steele, he told us that he did not state that he was "desperate" that Trump not be elected and thought Ohr might have been paraphrasing his sentiments. Steele told us that based on what he learned during his research he was concerned that Trump was a national security risk and he had no particular animus against Trump otherwise.

[428] SSA 1 told us that the FD-302 documenting the meeting with Ohr was incorrectly dated as having occurred on November 22, 2016, instead of November 21, 2016.

- Ohr "knew" that Simpson was "hired by a lawyer who does opposition research" and that Steele's reporting was being distributed to "the Clinton Campaign, Jon Winer at the U.S. State Department and the FBI."[429]

The FD-302 also documented that Ohr provided the FBI with copies of the notes he took about the meetings with Steele on July 30, 2016, and in late September 2016. The FBI did not insert this FD-302 into Steele's closed CHS file.[430]

SSA 1 told us that no one in the meeting directed Ohr to contact Steele or take any action on behalf of the FBI, but added that Ohr likely left the meeting with the impression that he should contact the FBI if Steele contacted him. When asked if the FBI provided him any guidance on what to do if Steele contacted him, Ohr stated that "the general instruction was to let them know...when I got information from Steele," though he could not recall who told him this or whether he was told this at the October 18 or November 21 meeting. Ohr told us that SSA 1 became his initial FBI point of contact when Ohr sought to provide more of Steele's information to the FBI.

7. Ohr's December 2016 Meetings with the FBI and Simpson

On December 5, 2016, Ohr had a follow-up interview with SSA 1 concerning his contacts with Steele and Simpson. During the interview, Ohr told SSA 1 that Simpson directed Steele to speak to the press, which was part of what Simpson was paying Steele to do, but that Ohr did not know whether speaking with *Mother Jones* was Simpson's idea or not. Additionally, according to the FD-302, Ohr gave SSA 1 a document that Nellie Ohr had created, titled "Manafort Chronology" and told SSA 1 that he would provide the FBI with additional research compiled by Nellie Ohr while working for Fusion GPS.

Ohr told us that he did not recall when or why Nellie Ohr provided him with the Manafort Chronology, but pointed to the July 2016 breakfast with Steele as a possible reason she provided it to him. Nellie Ohr told us that she offered Ohr her Fusion GPS research at the end of September 2016, which included the Manafort Chronology, in an effort to supplement what she believed Ohr would tell the FBI after the July 30 meeting with Steele.[431]

On December 7, 2016, Ohr convened an interagency meeting (including representatives from the FBI) regarding strategy in dealing with Russian Oligarch 1. One of Ohr's junior Department colleagues who attended the meeting told us that, after the meeting, she talked with Ohr about why the U.S. government would support trying to work with Russian Oligarch 1. Ohr's colleague said that Ohr told her that Steele provided information that the Trump campaign had been corrupted

---

[429] The FD-302 also stated that Ohr knew "Simpson and others" were talking to Victoria Nuland at the State Department, but did not provide any details.

[430] The FBI drafted a total of 13 FD-302s documenting its meetings with Ohr. None of the FD-302s were added to Steele's closed CHS file.

[431] As discussed above, Nellie Ohr stopped working for Fusion GPS in September 2016.

by the Russians. The colleague told us that she asked Ohr if the allegations went "all the way to the President" and that Ohr responded "yes." She told us that Ohr said to her that this information was "the basis for the [Russian Oligarch 1] discussion." Ohr told us he recalled telling his colleague generally about the information he received from Steele, but said he could not recall when he told her or what prompted him to do so.

According to Ohr's telephone log, Ohr called Simpson on December 8 and arranged a time to meet, but Ohr told us he could not recall why he contacted Simpson. Ohr said that he met with Simpson on December 10, 2016, and that Simpson gave him a thumb drive. Ohr stated that Simpson did not tell him what was on the thumb drive and that Ohr did not ask him, but that Ohr believed it contained Steele's election reports.[432] In testimony to the House Permanent Select Committee on Intelligence, Simpson stated that Ohr requested that he provide information regarding Steele's election reporting.[433]

Ohr stated, and his contemporaneous notes reflect, that Simpson told him during the meeting that Trump's attorney, Michael Cohen, was an intermediary between the Russian government and the Trump campaign and had replaced Manafort and Carter Page as intermediaries. According to Ohr's notes, during the meeting Simpson referenced several other alleged links between the Trump campaign and the Russian government. Ohr's notes show that Simpson told Ohr that Simpson "still thinks [Person 1] is a key figure connecting Trump to Russia." Additionally, Ohr's notes reflect that Simpson told Ohr that it was Simpson who asked Steele to speak with the *Mother Jones* reporter as a "Hail Mary attempt."

On December 11, 2016, Simpson forwarded an article to a personal email account shared by Ohr and his wife (which Nellie Ohr forwarded to Ohr's Department email account) about a Russian senator's possible support of Trump. The next day, December 12, Simpson wrote another email, this time requesting to speak with Ohr on the telephone. According to Ohr's telephone log, he spoke with Simpson that same day, but Ohr could not recall what he and Simpson discussed.

Also on December 12, Ohr met with SSA 1 and told SSA 1 that Simpson had explained to Ohr that it was Simpson who asked Steele to speak with the *Mother Jones* reporter as a "Hail Mary attempt" to stop Trump from being elected. Ohr also gave SSA 1 the thumb drive that he had received from Simpson during their December 10 meeting.

On December 20, 2016, Ohr provided SSA 1 with another thumb drive, this one containing open source research that Nellie Ohr had produced for Fusion GPS.

---

[432] As mentioned in Chapter Six, the thumb drive included 15 election reports and 1 additional document. The FBI had previously received 9 of the 15 election reports from Steele and 4 additional election reports from the *Mother Jones* reporter through then FBI General Counsel James Baker. Two election reports were new to the FBI, but the FBI also received those two reports at about the same time from then Senator McCain through then Director James Comey. The FBI only received one additional document from the thumb drive Ohr provided to the FBI.

[433] *HPSCI Interview of Glenn Simpson*, at 78.

Nellie Ohr stated that after the July 30, 2016 brunch, she understood that Ohr was going to talk to the FBI "on request of Steele" and so she provided her work product to her husband at the end of September 2016 as she finished working for Fusion GPS. Ohr told us he could not recall when Nellie Ohr provided him with her research. According to Nellie Ohr, she removed the Fusion GPS headers from her research because she had not asked Simpson for permission to provide the reports to the FBI and wanted the reports to stand on their own merit.

B. Ohr's Continued Contacts with Steele and Simpson from January to November 2017

In 2017, Ohr's written communications with Steele transitioned from emails using Ohr's Department email account to communications using an encrypted electronic messaging forum. Ohr provided the OIG with a transcript of his encrypted electronic communications with Steele, dating from January 25 to November 27, 2017, and his notes from their conversations. These documents indicate that Ohr and Steele communicated multiple times in 2017 and that Ohr typically informed the FBI of those communications shortly thereafter. The FBI's interviews with Ohr between January and mid-May 2017 were summarized in nine FD-302s, which we discuss below.[434]

During this timeframe, Ohr's FBI point of contact changed. As described in Chapter Three, SSA 1 rotated off the Crossfire Hurricane team in January 2017, and SSA 3 became Ohr's FBI point of contact until April 2017. From approximately May to June 2017, SSA 4 became Ohr's third point of contact. An agent from the Special Counsel's Office became Ohr's final point of contact through November 2017.

In January 2017, Steele expressed concerns to Ohr that the media would identify, and therefore endanger, his employee and the employee's sub-sources. Ohr conveyed Steele's concerns to SSA 3 and SSA 4 several times in the early months of 2017.[435] Steele told us that it was clear to him that Ohr was a conduit to the FBI. He said that Ohr told him that he had talked to the FBI about his concern for his sources' safety, and the FBI had offered to help.

At the end of January 2017 and aware that President Trump had removed Acting Attorney General Sally Yates, Steele asked Ohr for an FBI contact if Ohr were to leave the Department. Ohr provided Steele's concerns to the FBI and, on February 6, 2017, SSA 3 and Case Agent 8 requested Ohr to ask Steele if he would be willing to talk to the FBI again.

On February 14, 2017, Ohr shared with SSA 3 and Case Agent 8 information on topics Steele was working on for different clients, unrelated to Russia or

---

[434] In addition to the information summarized in this section, Ohr also provided information to the FBI from Steele and other individuals on unrelated matters.

[435] Ohr stated that by the end of January 2017, Steele knew that Ohr was talking with the FBI because he informed Steele that the FBI could protect Steele's employee.

Crossfire Hurricane.[436] Ohr also informed the agents that he did not speak to Steele about re-engaging directly with the FBI. Ohr told us that the FBI's offers to talk with Steele in early 2017 were for the purpose of assisting with an emergency with Steele's sub-sources, but when the danger to the sub-sources passed, the need to re-engage disappeared.

On May 8, 2017, Ohr told SSA 4 and Case Agent 5 that Steele was willing to work with the FBI again. Ohr said that Steele had independently raised with Ohr the subject of re-engaging with the FBI. On May 12, 2017, SSA 4 requested that Ohr ask Steele if he was willing to meet with FBI agents in Europe. According to Ohr, he contacted Steele, who agreed to talk with the FBI agents on May 15, 2017. This meeting did not take place, and, as discussed in Chapter Six, the FBI did not have contact with Steele until September 2017 when he was interviewed by agents assigned to the Special Counsel's Office. Ohr told us he continued to communicate with Steele through the end of November 2017 and provided the details of those communications to the FBI, which primarily focused on Steele's interest in being interviewed by the Special Counsel. However, the FBI did not memorialize any meetings its agents had with Ohr after the Crossfire Hurricane investigation was transferred to the Special Counsel's Office in May 2017. Ohr told us that Steele stopped contacting him after Ohr's name appeared in news articles at the end of 2017.

C. Ohr's Lack of Notification to ODAG, NSD, and Others Regarding His Contacts with Steele, Simpson, and the FBI

Ohr stated that it was both his "duty as a citizen" and a Department employee to provide Steele's and Simpson's allegations concerning Russian connections to the Trump campaign to the FBI. Ohr did not inform his supervisors or political leadership in ODAG that he was meeting with Steele, Simpson, or the FBI, and did not seek any ethics advice regarding these activities in light of his wife's employment with Fusion GPS from October 2015 to September 2016.

Ohr told us that while he had the opportunities to do so, he did not advise ODAG's political leadership of his interactions with Steele and Simpson, or of the information they provided and that he shared with the FBI, because he viewed the information as "raw" and "unfinished" Russian source information that the FBI needed to evaluate. Asked whether he instead considered informing a career employee within ODAG of the information, Ohr responded, "I think if I told another ODAG person, then they might have said, well we just got to tell the DAG." Asked whether a factor in his reluctance to tell then DAG Yates was because she may have told him to stop speaking with Steele, Ohr responded, "It may have been, yeah...."

---

[436] Ohr said that he understood Steele was "angling" for Ohr to assist him with his clients' issues. For example, Ohr stated that Steele was hoping that Ohr would intercede on his behalf with the Department attorney handling a matter involving a European company. Ohr denied providing any assistance to Steele in this regard, and we found no evidence that he did. The Department attorney handling the matter involving the European company told us that Ohr never spoke with her about the matter. Steele told us that he asked Ohr about the Department attorney involved in the case because he was considering contacting the attorney about an issue involving his client.

He further stated that he did not want to stop talking to Steele because he was alarmed by the information he was receiving and believed he needed to get it to the FBI.

Ohr told Swartz about his meetings with Steele and Simpson and the information they had provided. Ohr told us that it was possible that he also told then Counsel to the Criminal Division Assistant Attorney General, Zainab Ahmad,[437] and Chief of the Fraud Section, Andrew Weissmann, about his meetings with Steele, Simpson, and McCabe. When asked why he thought he may have told these Department employees as opposed to individuals in ODAG, Ohr stated he wanted "to get the information to career people...to evaluate it and figure out what to do."

Weissmann told us that Ohr told him "nothing" about the allegations Ohr received from Steele. Ahmad told us that Ohr did not provide her with detailed information about what Ohr was hearing from Steele and that Ohr only alluded to the fact that Steele had derogatory information about President-elect Trump.

Former members of ODAG leadership told us they were unaware of Ohr's communications with Steele, Simpson, and the FBI at the time those communications were occurring. Former DAG Yates told the OIG that she was "stunned" to learn through media reports in late 2017 that Ohr had engaged in these activities without telling her, and that she would have expected Ohr to inform her about his communications with Steele because they were outside of his area of responsibility and involved the Russia investigation. Yates added that she "would have hoped that [Ohr and the FBI] would have both told me" of Ohr's meetings with Steele and the FBI. She further stated that Ohr's activities needed to be coordinated with the overall Crossfire Hurricane investigation, which included ensuring that the chain of command at both the Department and FBI were jointly deciding what actions, if any, Ohr might take relating to the Russian interference investigation.

Yates told us that had she learned of Ohr's activities as they were occurring, she would have ensured that all Department and FBI personnel involved in the investigation were informed and consulted. Specifically with respect to Ohr's October 18, 2016 meeting with McCabe, Yates told us she expected Ohr to inform her of any meeting with someone at McCabe's level, regardless of the subject matter, but especially about something "outside of [Ohr's] area" of responsibility.

Then Principal Associate Deputy Attorney General Matthew Axelrod similarly told us that he would have expected to know about Ohr's activities, communicating with Steele and providing information to the FBI, because these were not responsibilities assigned to Ohr and his activities related to a "sensitive" matter. Axelrod said that if had he learned of Ohr's activities as they were occurring, he would have asked questions and sought to determine whether the FBI could stop receiving Steele's information through Ohr. Axelrod told us that he thought ODAG would have been uncomfortable with Ohr continuing to provide Steele's information

---

[437] Ahmad was an Acting Deputy Assistant Attorney General in the Criminal Division from January to April 2017.

to the FBI. Then Associate Deputy Attorney General Scott Schools, who was the highest-ranking career official in the Department, and ODAG's ethics advisor, stated that the FBI had a responsibility to fully report Ohr's involvement to the Department's National Security Division (NSD) and that Ohr had a duty to report his involvement to ODAG's managers.

Dana Boente, who became Acting DAG when Yates was removed from the position on January 30, 2017, told us that he was "really surprised" when he learned that Ohr had multiple conversations with Steele, particularly because Ohr had been a prosecutor and knew that an attorney should never talk to a potential witness without an agent being present. Boente stated that if he had learned about Ohr's contacts with Steele while he was Acting DAG, he may have allowed Ohr to meet with Steele for the limited purpose of putting Steele in direct contact with an FBI agent.

Ohr also told the OIG that he did not approach anyone in NSD because he talked to Swartz, who once oversaw counterintelligence cases for the Department, and thought Swartz was in contact with NSD concerning "Russia stuff."[438] Ohr also said that he did not know whether Swartz passed any of the information to NSD. Ohr said that, in hindsight, he thought he should have told people in ODAG and NSD about his communications with Steele and Simpson so that they could deal with the issues presented and so that Ohr could have guidance about how to proceed when communicating with Steele or Simpson. Swartz told us that he had no recollection of Ohr asking him to do anything with Steele's information. Swartz further stated that he did not think he informed anyone in NSD about Steele's information.

III. The FBI's Understanding of Its Relationship and Communications with Ohr

In this section, we describe the Crossfire Hurricane team's and FBI leadership's knowledge and understanding of Ohr's activities with Steele, and the information Ohr provided to the FBI.

A. The Crossfire Hurricane Team's Understanding of Ohr's Activities Related to the Investigation

As described earlier in this chapter, Ohr met with FBI agents 13 times between November 21, 2016 and May 15, 2017, to discuss his contacts with Steele and Simpson. At two of these meetings, in December 2016 after Nellie Ohr had left Fusion GPS, Ohr provided the FBI with open source research Nellie Ohr compiled while employed by Fusion GPS. All 13 meetings between Ohr and the FBI were memorialized in FBI FD-302s and, except for the first meeting, each meeting was held at Ohr's request. Ohr told us that, other than the FBI's request to inquire about Steele's interest in talking with the FBI again, Ohr did not recall the FBI

---

[438] Swartz's responsibility for overseeing counterintelligence cases for the Department ended when NSD was created in 2006, but he continues to advise NSD's leadership on international matters.

asking him to take any action regarding Steele or Simpson. However, Ohr also stated that "the general instruction was to let [the FBI] know...when I got information from Steele."

The FBI personnel we interviewed generally told us that Ohr did not make any requests of the FBI, nor did he inquire about any ongoing cases or make any recommendations about potential investigative steps. None of the FBI witnesses we interviewed recalled anyone tasking Ohr to gather information from Steele or to act as an intermediary between the FBI and Steele.

However, SSA 1, the first FBI supervisory agent to meet with Ohr in November 2016, told us that after their meetings, Ohr likely knew that the FBI was seeking information regarding Russian interference in the 2016 elections and would subsequently inform SSA 1 about anything relevant he learned from Nellie Ohr, Steele, Simpson, or elsewhere. SSA 1 stated that he was in "receive mode" with respect to Ohr's information and was trying to glean from it as much as he could about Steele's source network. He also said that Ohr was well-versed in Russian organized crime and that, in SSA 1's view, Ohr's motives for coming to the FBI were "pure."

Case Agent 1, the lead agent on the Carter Page investigation, told us he recalled learning about Ohr from SSA 1, likely before the first Carter Page FISA application was filed on October ▮, 2016. Case Agent 1 recalled that contacting Ohr was one of many things on the Crossfire Hurricane team's "to do" list in fall 2016, but it was not as urgent as some of the others. He further stated that the team viewed Ohr as another "stream of reporting" with potentially new information on Steele's election reports. Case Agent 1 told us that ultimately he did not think that Ohr's information presented anything new and said it did not impact the FBI's work on the Carter Page investigation. He also said that once Steele was closed as a CHS, Case Agent 1 did not believe there were any issues with Ohr being a "conduit" to Steele, but the team never discussed specifically tasking Ohr. Case Agent 1 told us that he thought it was "a patriotic thing" for Ohr to provide information to the FBI. Case Agent 1 also stated that Nellie Ohr's former employment with Fusion GPS did not cause him any concern in November and December 2016 because the team was still trying to understand Fusion GPS's role, and the team trusted that Ohr was a professional, career Department official.

SSA 3, one of the supervisory agents who replaced SSA 1, stated that in January 2017, SSA 1 briefed him on the case during their changeover and identified Ohr only as a "DOJ official" and Nellie Ohr as working for Fusion GPS. He recalled SSA 1 informing him that Ohr provided a version of Steele's election reports to the FBI. SSA 3 also told us that Ohr forwarded other information to the team regarding Russian oligarchs and other issues unrelated to the Crossfire Hurricane investigation. SSA 3 stated that he received the information but took no action and did not provide feedback to Ohr because he did not want Ohr to perceive anything as a tasking or discern the focus of the investigation. SSA 3 also stated that he did not task Ohr because of the appearance of using Ohr to obtain information from a closed source. According to SSA 3, he had two main concerns: 1) Ohr's and Nellie Ohr's connections to Steele and Fusion GPS, the latter of which appeared to have political connections, and 2) the FBI's continual contact with Steele through Ohr about such a sensitive matter, particularly because such contact with a closed source was "out of the norm." He told us that the members of his team shared these concerns, and he expressed them to his supervisor, DAD Jennifer Boone. SSA 3 stated that each time Ohr asked to meet with him, he consulted Boone and was directed to attend the meeting. He told us he fully informed Boone about the information Ohr provided after each interview and provided her with the FD-302s.[439] SSA 3 stated that it was his understanding that Boone would then determine what information to share at the executive level meetings.

SSA 4, who became the third SSA to meet with Ohr after SSA 3 rotated off the investigation in May 2017, said that SSA 3 told him that Ohr would come in and talk about "stuff" related to Steele and the agents would listen to Ohr's information, but that they did not consider the information important. According to SSA 4, SSA 3 stated that Ohr was "just some [person] you [had] to talk to when [he] call[ed]." SSA 4 was working from the FBI's Washington Field Office (WFO) and said that he provided updates regarding his communications with Ohr through WFO's chain of command to FBI Headquarters. SSA 4 also said he updated SSA 2 at FBI Headquarters.[440] SSA 2 told us he talked with SSA 4 about it being a "bad idea" to continue engaging with Ohr regarding his contacts with Steele. SSA 2 also said that by May 2017 he was "completely tired" of dealing with Ohr as an intermediary and thought the team should cease doing so.

The Supervisory Intelligence Analyst (Supervisory Intel Analyst) who was assigned to the Crossfire Hurricane investigation from its opening in July 2016 and participated in an interview with Ohr in January 2017, told the OIG that the Crossfire Hurricane team was initially receptive to Ohr's information and cited the Simpson thumb drive containing some of Steele's reports the FBI did not already possess as an example of useful information from Ohr. However, the Supervisory Intel Analyst also said that when Ohr began relaying Steele's concerns about the sub-sources and talking about topics unrelated to Crossfire Hurricane, he believed that Ohr was "acting or trying to act more as a conduit."

B.   FBI Management's Knowledge of Ohr's Activities

Strzok told the OIG that he did not know whether Ohr continued to meet with Steele after Steele was closed. Strzok said that, if Ohr had continued to meet with Steele, he hoped Ohr would not have talked about anything work related. Strzok also said that he did not recall having any indication or concern that Ohr was meeting with Steele and did not recall anyone having such concerns. However, Strzok's handwritten notes indicate that he received updates from SSA 1 and others on December 12, 2016, December 20, 2016, December 22, 2016, and January 23,

---

[439] SSA 3's notes also reflect he briefed Boone and several others regarding Ohr or the information Ohr provided.

[440] As mentioned in Chapter Seven, SSA 2 was the Headquarters Program Manager assigned to the Crossfire Hurricane investigation and the affiant for the three Carter Page FISA renewal applications.

2017, regarding Ohr's ongoing communications with Steele and Simpson about Steele's election reporting and Steele's concerns about his sub-sources.

In January 2017, Boone and the new team of agents assigned to Crossfire Hurricane assumed responsibility for communicating with Ohr. Boone stated that she knew SSA 3 had spoken with Ohr regarding his contacts with Steele and was documenting the communications in FD-302s, but she did not recall receiving or reviewing them, but said it was possible that she did. She told us that she recalled advising Priestap about the team's contacts with Ohr and the information they received from him, including how to respond to Steele's interest in re-establishing contact with the FBI. Priestap told us that Boone may have briefed him on the team's interviews of Ohr, but he did not remember her doing so.[441]

Priestap told us he knew that the Crossfire Hurricane team met with Ohr, but was unaware of how often the meetings occurred and did not know the full extent of Ohr's involvement with Steele until mid-to-late 2017. Priestap stated that the FBI's engagement with Ohr to learn what Steele had shared with Ohr was potentially useful in understanding Steele and verifying his reporting. Priestap said that he believed Ohr was not a "major factor" in the investigation, but instead saw Ohr as a liaison due to his relationship with Steele.

Priestap said he told the team to document what they learned from Ohr to compare it to the other information gathered. Priestap said he was surprised to later learn that the FBI treated Ohr more like a witness or a source. Priestap also stated that he was not told about Ohr's meetings with Simpson, Nellie Ohr's employment with Fusion GPS, or that Ohr provided Simpson's and Nellie Ohr's thumb drives to the FBI—information that was provided by Ohr to the FBI between November 21 and December 20, 2016. He told us that he did not inform Comey or McCabe about Ohr's involvement in the Crossfire Hurricane investigation, because he was unaware of the full extent of it.

Priestap stated that knowing the full extent of Ohr's activities would have raised "red flags" for him because the situation would have been different than Ohr merely having a pre-existing relationship with Steele. He told us that had he been fully aware of the extent of Ohr's activities, he would have inquired about Ohr's motivations and involvement with Steele, Simpson, and the Crossfire Hurricane investigation.

General Counsel Baker stated that he understood from Crossfire Hurricane leadership briefings he attended in fall 2016 that Ohr had a pre-existing relationship with Steele and that Steele may have had conversations with Ohr about Steele's election reporting. He told us that he did not understand Ohr to be acting as a conduit between Steele and the FBI at this time. According to Baker, he was concerned that if the FBI took an action with which Steele disagreed, Steele would

---

[441] We reviewed notes taken by a Counterintelligence Division DAD. Her notes from January 23, 2017, contain a reference to Ohr's interview that day and specific information provided by Ohr concerning Steele's sub-sources. Although the notes do not list the attendees of this meeting, they appear to be from a Crossfire Hurricane update meeting.

complain to Ohr, whom Baker viewed as being a prominent Department official. He explained that if Steele complained, Ohr would feel compelled to intervene on Steele's behalf.

Baker told us that he obtained more information regarding Ohr's interactions with Steele during a Crossfire Hurricane leadership meeting with Comey and McCabe in spring 2017. He stated that he did not recall Ohr being critical of how the FBI was handling Steele, but that Ohr had become involved to a greater degree than he had in the past. Baker told us that he learned that Ohr was providing to the FBI information that Ohr had received from Steele, and it was Baker's view that "this [was] not good." He said that he could not recall who was discussing this, but he believed it was McCabe and maybe Priestap and then Executive Assistant Director Michael Steinbach.[442] He also stated that he thought it was "imprudent" to have Ohr involved and "a bit of a mess," but that he believed that McCabe, Steinbach, and Priestap were "on top of it." Baker told us he "may have mentioned" the issue to OGC Principal Deputy General Counsel Trisha Anderson, and asked her to look into it. Anderson told us that she had limited contemporaneous knowledge about Ohr's interactions with Steele and the FBI. In particular, she told us that she did not know at the time that Ohr had repeatedly provided information from Steele to the investigative team or that Ohr's interviews with the FBI were documented in FD-302s. McCabe told us he did not recall the discussion Baker described.

We asked Baker if he had concerns about Ohr receiving information from Steele. He told us that Ohr was "arguably a source," and the situation needed to be handled carefully to protect Ohr and the Department. Baker further stated that accepting information from a closed source through Ohr was "not the right way to run a railroad" and either the FBI needed to reopen Steele or tell Ohr to stop taking information from him. According to Baker, the decision about whether to utilize Ohr, a senior Department official, as an ongoing, frequent conduit with Steele was not a decision for the investigative team to make, but for the Director. He also said the FBI's use of Ohr in this fashion should have been shared with the Department, but he did not recall anyone doing so.

McCabe told us that he knew Ohr was meeting with the investigative team concerning his contacts with Steele, but did not know how often the team met with Ohr until it was reported in the news media. He said he did not recall knowing that Ohr provided the investigative team with a thumb drive from Simpson or from Nellie Ohr. McCabe told us that Ohr was doing the "responsible thing" by informing the investigative team about his conversations with Steele and that he did not tell the Department about Ohr's involvement because he viewed doing so as Ohr's responsibility. Lisa Page stated that she met with Ohr twice in fall 2016 and had no knowledge of Ohr providing information from Steele and Simpson to the FBI.

Comey told us he had no knowledge of Ohr's communications with members of the Crossfire Hurricane investigative team and only discovered Ohr's association

---

[442] Steinbach told us he did not recall ever knowing about Ohr's involvement with Steele. Steinbach retired from the FBI on February 24, 2017.

with Steele and the Crossfire Hurricane investigation when the media reported on it. However, notes taken by Strzok during a November 23, 2016 Crossfire Hurricane update meeting attended by Comey, McCabe, Baker, Lisa Page, Anderson, the OGC Unit Chief, the FBI Chief of Staff, and Priestap, reference a discussion at the meeting concerning "strategy for engagement [with Handling Agent 1] and Ohr" regarding Steele's reporting. Strzok stated that, based on his notes, he believed he informed FBI leadership that Ohr approached the FBI concerning his relationship with Steele and that Ohr relayed Steele's information regarding Russia to the team. Although the OGC Unit Chief could not recall when it occurred, she recalled discussing with executive leadership that the FBI should not use Ohr to direct Steele's actions. Because Strzok's notes of the meeting were classified at the time we interviewed Comey, and Comey chose not to have his security clearances reinstated for his OIG interview, we were unable to show him the notes and ask about the reference in them to Steele and Ohr.

IV. Ohr's Activities Relating to the Criminal Division's Manafort Investigation

In addition to Ohr's interactions with the FBI and Steele in connection with the Crossfire Hurricane investigation, Ohr also participated in discussions about a separate money laundering investigation of Paul Manafort that was then being led by prosecutors from the Money Laundering and Asset Recovery Section (MLARS), which is located in the Criminal Division at the Department's headquarters. That criminal investigation was opened by the FBI's Criminal Investigation Division in January 2016, approximately 2 months before Manafort joined the Trump campaign as an advisor, and concerned allegations that Manafort had engaged in money laundering and tax evasion while acting as a political consultant to members of the Ukrainian government and Ukrainian politicians.

Shortly after the 2016 elections, Ohr participated in several meetings with three senior attorneys from the Department's Criminal Division during which they discussed ways to move the Manafort investigation forward more quickly. Ohr and the three senior Criminal Division attorneys were not assigned to the MLARS Manafort investigation and did not advise MLARS or anyone in their respective chain of command of their discussions. In this section, we describe these meetings regarding the MLARS money laundering case.

A. November 2016 to December 2016

Between November 16, 2016 and December 15, 2016, Ohr attended four meetings to discuss the MLARS investigation. These meetings were attended, at various times, by some or all of the following individuals: Bruce Swartz, Criminal Division Deputy Assistant Attorney General (Deputy AAG); Zainab Ahmad, then Counsel to the Criminal Division's Assistant Attorney General; Andrew Weissmann, then Section Chief of the Criminal Division's Fraud Section; Strzok; and Lisa Page. MLARS was not represented at any of these meetings or told about them.[443]

The meetings involving Ohr, Swartz, Ahmad, and Weissmann focused on their shared concern that MLARS was not moving quickly enough on the Manafort investigation and whether there were steps they could take to move the investigation forward. The meetings with Strzok and Page focused primarily on whether the FBI was aware of the Manafort investigation so that it could assess the case's relevance, if any, to the FBI's Russian interference investigation.

Then Section Chief of MLARS, Kendall Day, told us that Ohr, Ahmad, and Weissmann did not have any role in the MLARS Manafort investigation. Day told us that Swartz provided assistance to the investigation because it involved gathering foreign evidence and working with foreign governments, but that his assistance was limited to consulting on those specific issues. According to Swartz, he had a long standing interest in the investigation and prosecution of Manafort, dating to at least 2014, and it was therefore appropriate for him to "strategize" with others about how best to move the MLARS Manafort investigation forward. However, Day and Swartz told us that Swartz could not direct the manner in which such investigations progressed. Swartz also told us that as the Deputy AAG responsible for, among other things, the Office of International Affairs, he could not make prosecutorial decisions relating to cases, but "might weigh in on" case-related decisions such as the timing or sensitivities of charges.[444]

Ohr told the OIG that during a meeting with Swartz and Ahmad on November 16, 2016, he advised them of information "about [Paul] Manafort and Trump and possible Russian influence that [Ohr] was getting from Steele and Glenn Simpson," and that he recalled their response was that they should look into the MLARS Manafort investigation.[445] Ohr and Swartz both told us that they felt an urgency to move the Manafort investigation forward because of Trump's election and a concern that the new administration would shut the investigation down. Ahmad said that her concerns regarding the Manafort investigation, which were based upon her conversations with Swartz and Ohr, were focused on the line prosecutors not adequately working the investigation. Weissmann stated that Ahmad expressed to him that there was a concern, with which he later agreed, that MLARS was not

---

[443] Swartz, Ohr, and Weissmann were members of the Senior Executive Service (SES). Ahmad was on detail to the Criminal Division from the U.S. Attorney's Office for the Eastern District of New York and was not a member of the SES.

[444] As a Deputy Assistant Attorney General, Swartz supervised three sections in the Department's Criminal Division: the Office of International Affairs (OIA), the Overseas Prosecutorial Development Office (OPDAT), and the Department's police training organization. He also acted as an advisor to the Attorney General, the DAG, and the Assistant Attorney General for the Criminal Division on international affairs issues.

[445] Swartz told us that he became aware of allegations that Manafort may have engaged in criminal conduct through the media when former Ukrainian President Victor Yanukovych was ousted from office in February 2014. Swartz said that because he was aware of Manafort's connection to the Russian-backed Yanukovych and other alleged misconduct through MLARS's Manafort investigation, he was concerned when the Trump Campaign named Manafort as its manager in May 2016.

moving quickly enough on its Manafort investigation and that he accepted an invitation from Ahmad to attend a meeting with Ohr and Swartz.

The Fraud Section that Weissmann supervised at the time was part of the Department team that had indicted a foreign national whom Ohr, Swartz, Ahmad, and Weissmann came to believe had information relating to Manafort's alleged criminal conduct. Swartz said that because MLARS had not moved the Manafort investigation forward, he thought it appropriate to meet with Weissmann and discuss the possibility of seeking to obtain information from this foreign national regarding Manafort. In December 2016, the four of them discussed a plan for the Department to approach this foreign national and seek his cooperation against Manafort. Because the extradition of this foreign national was being handled by OIA, Swartz had supervisory responsibility for the extradition aspect of that matter.

Ohr told us that after his November 21, 2016 meeting with FBI officials concerning Steele's information, discussed above, Ohr was advised that the FBI was "pushing ahead" on its Manafort case. Ohr said that he probably shared this information with Swartz. According to Ohr, because "we [had] information that Manafort [was]...somehow...a possible connection between the Russian government and the Trump campaign" it was important to get "national security people" involved in that investigation. Ohr said that because Swartz, Strzok, and Lisa Page were all working on matters involving Manafort, he wanted them to meet and get on the "same page." Consequently, at Ohr's suggestion, Ohr, Swartz, and Ahmad met with Strzok and Lisa Page on December 15, 2016.

Strzok told us that the December 15 meeting consisted mainly of Ohr, Swartz, and Ahmad describing information they had regarding Manafort, and inquiring if they could assist the FBI's investigation. He stated that Swartz discussed the MLARS Manafort investigation and stated that the investigation had stalled. Strzok told us that Swartz wanted him to "kick that [investigation] in the ass and get it moving." We asked Strzok if he understood that Swartz was speaking on behalf of the Department about the Manafort investigation. He responded that his "assumption and belief was that [Swartz] and Bruce Ohr were speaking about topics for which they had relevant supervision and authority over."

Swartz stated that the reason he wanted to talk to Strzok about Manafort was to see if Strzok had any counterintelligence information that would be relevant to what Manafort may have been doing and to push the MLARS Manafort investigation forward. Strzok later sent an email to Boone and others, including the OGC Unit Chief, stating that Boone and he needed to speak with the FBI's Criminal Investigation Division regarding its Manafort investigation to get a better understanding its investigative efforts. The OGC Unit Chief responded: "we have got to get our arms around what CID investigated and what it means for [Manafort]...figure what resources, if any, we can bring to bear to get a better understanding of [Manafort's] foreign power connections and the money that passed hands (if any)."

Ohr, Swartz, Ahmad, and Weissmann all told us that they did not inform anyone in their chain of command, such as the leadership of the Criminal Division or ODAG, about these meetings.[446] Ohr stated that he should have advised ODAG leadership that he was participating in meetings about the MLARS Manafort investigation because it was a sensitive matter. Swartz told us that the political appointees leading the Criminal Division knew the Manafort investigation existed, and therefore they should only be briefed if "steps were going to be taken" to move the case forward. Swartz added that he did not advise them of his meetings with Ohr, Ahmad, and Weissmann, as well as those with Strzok and Lisa Page, because he was keeping the Manafort investigation from being "politicized" and protecting the Department from allegations that its investigation of Manafort was politically motivated.

Weissmann told us that at around the time of these meetings, he and Ahmad had a conversation in which Ahmad told him that she and Swartz were not going to tell the Department's political leadership about their efforts to move the Manafort investigation forward. Weissmann said that he remembered thinking, at the time, that this was because Swartz and Ahmad wanted to insulate the political leadership from an allegation of politically targeting Manafort. He stated further that he thought it was "an incorrect judgment call," but could not recall if he told that to Ahmad and said he satisfied himself that it was appropriate because the Criminal Division's front office was aware of the fact MLARS had an open investigation of Manafort. Ahmad told us that she did not recall telling Weissmann that political appointees would not be advised of the meetings and that being the "junior person" in the meetings, she would not have made such a decision, but that Swartz may have done so.

The then Section Chief of MLARS, Kendall Day, a career Department official, told us that he was unaware of the meetings discussed above.[447] He stated that, given that he was supervising MLARS's Manafort investigation, he should have been invited to these meetings because none of those involved knew the strength of the evidence amassed by MLARS against Manafort or the investigation's status. Day also stated that, because the Manafort investigation was a "sensitive matter," it was imperative to keep the Criminal Division's leadership aware of relevant events to ensure that there were no surprises. He stated further that he was providing briefings regarding MLARS's investigation to his political supervisors, including then Criminal Division Assistant Attorney General Leslie Caldwell.

Caldwell told us that she was unaware of any meetings involving Ohr, Swartz, Ahmad, and Weissmann in which they discussed the MLARS investigation of Manafort. She stated further that she thought that not advising political supervisors about the meetings "suggest[ed] a lack of trust or a lack of confidence in the political appointee...and that seem[ed] a little bit paranoid to [her]." She stated further that a rationale that not advising political appointees of the meetings

---

[446] Ahmad told us that she did not advise her chain of command of work she did with Swartz. She said that Swartz was a higher-level supervisor within the Criminal Division and, to her knowledge, was reporting on those activities.

[447] Day, who had been Chief of MLARS, became an Acting Deputy Assistant Attorney General in the Criminal Division in January 2017.

protected them from an allegation of engaging in a political prosecution was "inappropriate," showed "poor judgment" and was "in itself political."

Yates told us that she too was unaware of the meetings involving Ohr, Swartz, Ahmad, and Weissmann. She said that not telling political appointees about these activities "trouble[d]" her because the Department of Justice does not "operate that way." Yates then stated that there is not "a career Department of Justice and a political appointees' Department of Justice. It's all one DOJ."

B.   January 31 and February 1, 2017 Meetings

There were no meetings about the Manafort case involving Ohr, Swartz, Ahmad, and Weissmann from December 16, 2016 to January 30, 2017. On the morning of January 31, 2017, the day after Yates was removed as Acting Attorney General, Ahmad, then an Acting Deputy AAG, sent an email to Ohr, copying Swartz, stating that Weissmann "had something he wanted to discuss with us" and asking Ohr if he was free to meet with Weissmann that morning. Due to scheduling conflicts, Ohr could not attend the meeting, which went forward with Weissmann, Swartz, and Ahmad. Neither Swartz, Weissmann, nor Ahmad could remember what occurred at this meeting. However, each of them speculated that they may have discussed the case involving the indicted foreign national pending extradition, referenced above, who they believed might have evidence detrimental to Manafort.

After the meeting, Ahmad sent an email to Lisa Page, copying Weissmann, Swartz, and Ohr, requesting a meeting the next day, February 1. Ahmad wrote:

> Do you by chance have time to meet around 11 tomorrow to follow up on our last discussion? There have been a few Criminal Division related developments that we wanted to discuss. Bruce Swartz is leaving for Mexico tomorrow afternoon, so we were hoping we could squeeze this in before he leaves....

On February 1, 2017, Swartz, Ohr, Ahmad, and Weissmann met with Strzok, Lisa Page, and Acting Section Chief 1 of the FBI.[448] Strzok told us that the meeting was "largely a discussion about [the Criminal] Division's work on Manafort" and that he did not find the meeting "notable." According to contemporaneous notes taken by Strzok and Lisa Page, they discussed efforts that the Department could undertake to investigate attempts by Russia to influence the 2016 elections. Specifically, the FBI was advised that, with regard to Manafort, the Department was "looking just at [Money Laundering]/Kleptocracy" violations and wanted to bring financial analysis experts into the investigation. The notes also show that Swartz inquired whether there were other types of offenses relating to Manafort that could be investigated, such as Foreign Corrupt Practices Act violations. MLARS was not represented at the meeting and was not notified of it. None of the attendees recalled any discussion of new "Criminal Division related developments," and

---

[448] Acting Section Chief 1 attended the meeting because his section was handling the Manafort counterintelligence investigation. As discussed in Chapter Four, Acting Section Chief 1 attended the FBI's meeting with Steele in early October 2016.

neither Ahmad nor Weissmann could recall what the reference in Ahmad's email concerned.

We asked Weissmann, Ahmad, Ohr, and Swartz whether there was a connection between the removal of Yates and these meeting requests. Weissmann and Ahmad denied that this was the case. Ohr, on the other hand, told us that it made sense that Yates's firing influenced the decision to have a meeting with Strzok and Lisa Page. Ohr stated further that he could not specifically recall the discussion, but Yates's name may have been mentioned in connection with this meeting. Swartz stated that Yates's departure obviously could have come up, and he was sure they discussed how to proceed with the Manafort investigation in light of her removal.

Ohr stated that Swartz and Ahmad were worried that the Trump Administration would shut down the Manafort investigation after Yates's departure from the Department. Swartz told us that he may have speculated that the Trump Administration would shut down the MLARS Manafort investigation. Weissmann told us that he was not concerned by Yates's removal and did not recall anyone discussing the impact her removal might have on the Manafort investigation. Ahmad similarly told us that she did not recall anyone expressing concerns to her about political appointees interfering with the Manafort investigation.

No one in MLARS, or the Criminal Division's or ODAG's leadership were made aware of this meeting. Then Principal Associate Deputy Attorney General James Crowell told us that career employees do not get to brief the FBI on a very important case without going through Department leadership. He told us that the Manafort case was important with "potentially...national implications" and that not briefing the AG or the AG's staff was not "okay." Crowell further stated that it was "unbelievable" that Ohr was involved in these meetings because as OCDETF Director it was not his job to involve himself in the Manafort investigation.

When we told then Acting DAG Boente that political appointees may not have been advised of these meetings for the purpose of insulating them from allegations of engaging in a political prosecution of Manafort, Boente responded that that was a "less than satisfying answer." He stated that "political appointees make tough calls on political cases every day," and "[that is] not a reason not to tell [political appointees] about [the case]." He stated further that career officials, such as Swartz, Ohr, Ahmad, and Weissmann, have to depend on the Department's political appointees to do the "right thing."

Boente also told us that the Manafort investigation was an MLARS case and that MLARS ought to be prosecuting it. He added that if Swartz, Weissmann, or Ahmad were unhappy with MLARS's prosecution of the matter, they could have spoken with the then Acting Assistant Attorney General, who was a career Department employee, to see if one of them could take over the investigation.

On February 23, 2017, Swartz sent an email to Ohr, Ahmad, and Weissmann proposing a "check-in meeting" and suggested that they invite Lisa Page to attend. Weissmann responded that Lisa Page should not be invited to the meeting, but that the new Acting Chief of MLARS should be.[449] Weissmann told us that he wanted the Acting Chief included in the meeting because she had "equity" in the Manafort investigation. He stated further that he had spoken with the Acting Chief about the Manafort case, but had no recollection if he had told her about his prior meetings with Swartz, Ohr, and Ahmad.

The then Acting Chief of MLARS told us that she only learned about the November 2016 to early February 2017 meetings involving Ohr, Swartz, Weissmann, and Ahmad as a result of her OIG interview. Day, the Acting Deputy AAG overseeing MLARS, told us that he discovered in late March or early April 2017 that Weissmann was planning a meeting with reporters to obtain evidence associated with MLARS's Manafort investigation and that Swartz, Ohr, Weissmann and Ahmad were "collectively interested" in the investigation.[450] He stated further that he met with Swartz and Ahmad in his office and inquired about Weissmann's meeting and their interest in the Manafort investigation. Day recalled telling Swartz and Ahmad that, given their high-ranking positions in the Department, their "unusual level of interest" in the Manafort investigation could create a perception that the Department was investigating Manafort for inappropriate reasons. According to Day, Swartz expressed concern that "because of the change in the administration" the Manafort investigation "might not be allowed to progress." Day said he told Swartz and Ahmad that the investigation would be handled "just like any other" and that Swartz even asking the question suggested that it was going to be treated differently, which was not going to happen. He also told us that he was "comfortable that no decisions were made for any improper reasons" because he "owned" the Manafort investigation and supervised the attorneys working on it. Swartz told us that he did not recall this conversation with Day.[451]

The Manafort money laundering investigation remained with MLARS until it was transferred to the Special Counsel's Office in May 2017. Manafort was subsequently indicted on a series of criminal charges. On August 21, 2018, a jury in the United States District Court for the Eastern District of Virginia found Manafort guilty of five counts of filing false tax returns, failing to report foreign bank accounts, and two counts of bank fraud. He was sentenced to 47 months in federal prison. On September 14, 2018, Manafort pled guilty in the United States District Court for the District of Columbia to one count of conspiracy to launder money, tax fraud, failing to file foreign bank account reports, violating the Foreign Agents Registration Act, and making false statements to the Department of Justice. He was sentenced to 43 months in federal prison.

---

[449] In early 2017, after Day had been appointed an Acting Criminal Division Deputy AAG, a new Acting Chief was appointed to lead MLARS.

[450] Weissmann told us that on or about March 31, 2017, an Associated Press (AP) reporter contacted him and stated that he had information regarding Manafort having a storage locker in Virginia. Weissmann said that he believed the information was worth obtaining and set up a meeting with the AP reporter.

[451] After reviewing a draft copy of this report, Ahmad told us that she did not recall having this conversation with Day.

V. Ohr's Removal from ODAG and OCDETF

Prior to fall 2017, ODAG management had no knowledge of Ohr's ongoing relationship with Steele, Ohr's meetings with the FBI, or Fusion GPS's employment of Nellie Ohr. In November 2017, shortly after the Department received a Congressional request to interview Ohr, ODAG received from the FBI the FD-302s detailing Ohr's relationship with Steele and Ohr's subsequent meetings with the FBI. Shortly after receiving the FD-302s, then DAG Rod Rosenstein directed Ohr's removal from his ADAG position. In January 2018, Ohr was removed as Director of OCDETF. This section discusses ODAG's communication expectations, lack of knowledge regarding Ohr's activities with Steele and Simpson, the limited information Ohr provided to Rosenstein in October 2017 about his connection to Steele and Fusion GPS, the eventual full accounting of Ohr's activities provided to ODAG, and ODAG leadership's decisions to remove Ohr from ODAG and OCDETF.

A. ODAG's Communication Expectations and Lack of Knowledge of Ohr's Activities

Several leaders and managers in ODAG during the time period of our review told us that communication within ODAG is imperative.[452] As explained below, the DAG relies upon assistance from the career Associate Deputy Attorneys General (ADAGs), such as Ohr, to ensure the Department's effective operation. Among other things, the ADAGs contribute to that effort by keeping ODAG leadership aware of pertinent information and issues affecting the Department.

Then PADAG Axelrod explained that, as the PADAG, he was the day-to-day manager of ODAG, and Ohr reported to Yates through him. Axelrod told us that when he started in ODAG, he told everyone in that office to be "canaries in the coal mine" and advise ODAG management of any issues affecting the Department. Axelrod explained that to properly manage ODAG, he needed to be aware of the issues that ODAG personnel were addressing to ensure that work was not being duplicated, nothing "[fell] through the cracks," and Department components knew who to speak with if questions arose. Yates also stressed that raising significant issues to her enabled her decision making process and prevented her from being surprised.

New ODAG leadership reiterated this theme on January 23, 2017, when Crowell sent an email to the Department's top leadership, including Ohr, directing "timely and complete communication" including the details of "any sensitive or

---

[452] From summer 2016 through December 2017, ODAG leadership and management changed several times, with three separate DAGs and several iterations of their staff. Yates was DAG until President Trump removed her on January 30, 2017, at which time Boente was appointed Acting DAG. On April 26, 2017, Rosenstein was sworn in as the DAG. Matt Axelrod was Yates's PADAG until he left the Department on January 30, 2017. Crowell joined ODAG in January 2017 and served as Acting PADAG until June 28, 2017, when Robert Hur arrived, at which point Crowell served as Rosenstein's Chief of Staff until December 9, 2017. Tashina Gauhar was the Associate Deputy Attorney General (ADAG) responsible for ODAG's national security portfolio at this time. Scott Schools, who had served in ODAG during a prior tenure in the Department, rejoined ODAG on October 31, 2016, and served as an ADAG until his departure from the Department on July 6, 2018.

high-profile matters" or issues "[l]ikely to generate significant press attention." Additionally, Crowell requested that "unexpected and/or urgent matters" be raised with ODAG to allow for proper collaboration and response.

When asked why he did not alert anyone in ODAG about his contacts with Steele and Simpson after Crowell's January 24, 2017 email, Ohr stated that his contacts with Simpson and Steele were not part of any of his OCDETF cases, so he provided the information to the FBI and career people instead. Ohr told us he felt that he should talk to career people with experience in dealing with Russian information instead of talking to a supervisor within ODAG. According to Ohr, he did not view the fact that he, as a member of ODAG, was receiving information from Steele as significant or problematic, but rather he viewed the information itself as significant and thought it needed to be provided to the FBI.

Crowell stated that he was "flabbergasted" when he learned about Ohr's involvement with Steele and the FBI. He stated that Ohr should have informed ODAG officials of his relationships with Steele and Simpson and his provision of information from them to the FBI, especially when Rosenstein appointed the Special Counsel and began supervising the investigation, because "a potential fact witness" was on Rosenstein's staff.

Crowell told us that if he had known about Nellie Ohr's connection to Fusion GPS or Ohr's involvement with the Russia investigation, he would have moved Ohr away from the DAG to eliminate any appearance that Ohr was involved in the DAG's oversight of the investigation. Crowell also opined that knowing this information about Nellie Ohr or about Ohr's relationship with Steele earlier would have given Department leadership the time and opportunity to determine how to handle the situation as "the American public need[ed] to have confidence that [the investigation was] done the right way...."

Rosenstein stated that, like his predecessor, his Chief of Staff or PADAG ran weekly staff meetings with the ADAGs. He told us that if Ohr or other members of ODAG had any issues or problems, he expected them to talk to his Chief of Staff, the PADAG, or Scott Schools, who was the ODAG ethics advisor and a career Department employee. According to Rosenstein, "everybody understood that if you had...an ethical issue or just a difficult process issue, that's what [Schools was] there for" and that he expected anyone with a sensitive issue to bring it to Schools.

In his position as ADAG, Ohr was not briefed on the existence of the Crossfire Hurricane investigation and the naming of U.S. persons as subjects. This information was known by ODAG leadership and those ADAGs with national security portfolios, which did not include Ohr. However, as detailed in earlier chapters, by fall 2016, rumors about the investigation were in the press; by January 2017, Steele's election reports were published online; and by March 2017, Comey publicly acknowledged the investigation to Congress in a public hearing. Yates told us that the Russian interference investigation in general was well known within ODAG by the time Ohr met with McCabe in October 2016, and that Ohr knew to speak with Tashina Gauhar, the ADAG responsible for ODAG's national security portfolio, about his involvement with Steele and the FBI. Ohr told us he knew from his November

21, 2016 meeting with members of the Crossfire Hurricane investigative team, Strzok, and Lisa Page that the FBI was doing something regarding the allegations, but he did not know prior to that that the FBI had opened a "specific" investigation. During this period, Ohr never disclosed to anyone in ODAG his contacts with Steele regarding Steele's election reporting. Ohr told us that he could have gone to Gauhar as the national security ADAG, but he decided to speak with Swartz instead. Boente told us that at least after the release of the Intelligence Community Assessment (ICA) on Russian interference with the 2016 presidential elections in January 2017, Boente thought Ohr would have appreciated the potential for an investigation into Russia's activities even if nobody in ODAG mentioned it specifically to Ohr.

As discussed above, Ohr also told us that he did not tell any career attorneys within ODAG about his contacts with Steele and Simpson because he thought that if he told another "ODAG person...they might have said, well we just got to tell the DAG." He said another factor may have been concern that the DAG may tell him to stop speaking with Steele.

The OIG identified notes taken during three FBI Russia briefings to Department personnel that mention Ohr.[453] In connection with a Department meeting with FBI representatives (including Strzok) on February 16, 2017, notes by Boente, Gauhar, and Schools indicate that someone likely from the FBI mentioned that Nellie Ohr was employed by Simpson and that Ohr and Steele were in contact.[454] Additionally, notes from an FBI briefing for Boente on March 6, 2017, indicate that someone in the meeting stated that Ohr and Swartz had a "discussion of kleptocracy + Russian org. crime" in relation to the Manafort criminal case in an effort to "re-energize [the] CRM case." Finally, a section of Boente's notes from a March 22, 2017 meeting include the names Weismann, Swartz, and Ohr next to a section of notes regarding Manafort.

After reviewing these notes, none of the ODAG personnel at these meetings could remember Ohr being mentioned, or recall any additional information provided during these briefings beyond what was stated in these notes. Boente, Gauhar, and Schools did not remember the references to Ohr until they reviewed their notes. Gauhar and Schools stated that without more of the salient information now known concerning Ohr's involvement, the remarks about Ohr did not make an impression on them or indicate to them that Ohr was substantially involved in the investigation. Gauhar told us that had the FBI provided any additional information regarding Ohr's involvement at the February 16, 2017 meeting, she would have included that in her notes.[455] Gauhar further stated that, given the information now available regarding the extent of Ohr's contributions to the FBI's investigation, the

---

[453] See Chapter Three for further information regarding these briefings.

[454] Schools stated that he also recalled that sometime after the February 16, 2017 meeting, the FBI OGC Unit Chief made a passing reference to Ohr knowing Simpson and Steele.

[455] Gauhar took extensive notes during Crossfire Hurricane meetings. For example, her notes for the February 16, 2017 meeting are eight pages long.

FBI should have alerted somebody at the Department about Ohr's activities, or Ohr should have alerted ODAG leadership about what he was doing.[456]

B. Ohr Provides Rosenstein with Limited Information about His Connection with Steele and Fusion GPS

Ohr told the OIG that in October 2017, Nellie Ohr received a call from someone at Fusion GPS who told her that the company was providing documents to Congress that identified her as a Fusion GPS contractor and that he realized that then DAG Rosenstein may need to know about this, so he asked to speak with him. He stated that he informed Rosenstein that his wife, Nellie Ohr, worked for Fusion GPS, and that it may become public that Ohr knew Steele and introduced him to the FBI. Ohr told the OIG that he was "prepared to go into more detail [with Rosenstein], but there really wasn't time."

Rosenstein recalled having this conversation in Ohr's office and told us he remembered Ohr stating he knew Steele and that Nellie Ohr worked for Fusion GPS. Rosenstein told us that during this conversation, Ohr may have also said that he introduced Steele to the FBI and that all this information may become public. Rosenstein described the meeting with Ohr as casual and noted that he was in Ohr's office for another reason, which indicated to him that Ohr did not make a special effort to notify him. Rosenstein stated that he left the conversation under the impression that it was only a "strange coincidence" that Ohr knew Steele.

Schools recalled that Ohr, at some point, "stuck his head in the door and said, hey I just wanted to make sure there's nothing I need to do. My wife works at Fusion GPS. I don't know if there's anything, like, a recusal, or anything I need to deal with." Schools stated that he responded to Ohr by saying that "you don't have anything to do with that case. We don't typically in the Department recuse individuals who aren't responsible for the matter giving rise to a potential conflict." Schools believed this conversation occurred a couple months before Ohr's conduct became public and may have coincided with Ohr's October 2017 conversation with Rosenstein.

Ohr told us that a few weeks after his first conversation with Rosenstein on this issue, he spoke with Rosenstein again and told him that he still talked to Steele from time to time and provided information to the FBI when Steele called him. Rosenstein told us that he recalled a second conversation with Ohr concerning Steele, which he believed occurred in early December 2017. According to Rosenstein, Ohr told him that he delivered a thumb drive containing Steele's election reports to the FBI. Rosenstein said this information changed his perspective of the situation. Rosenstein told us the fact that Ohr

---

[456] As explained in previous chapters, no one in NSD had knowledge of Ohr's substantive contacts with Steele. Nor were they aware of his delivery to the FBI of Simpson's and Nellie Ohr's thumb drives. NSD attorneys only learned of Ohr's participation in Crossfire Hurricane in late 2017 or early 2018. NSD witnesses told the OIG that they would have expected the FBI or Ohr to have informed them of Ohr's involvement in the investigation as it occurred.

knew Steele was kind of just an unusual coincidence, but the idea that he had actually had some role in this Russia investigation was shocking to me.... [W]e had been fending off these Congressional inquiries. And they were asking for all sorts of stuff, [FD-]302s and things, and...I had no idea that somebody on my staff had actually been involved in...an operational way in the investigation.

According to Rosenstein, he learned that day or the next day that there were several FD-302s from Ohr's interviews with the FBI. He said that Ohr appeared to be serving as an "intermediary" with Steele.

C. ODAG Learns of Ohr's Activities in Connection to the Russian Investigation and Transfers Ohr

On November 28, 2017, the Department received a letter from the Senate Select Committee on Intelligence (SSCI) requesting a closed interview of Ohr as part of its inquiry into Russian interference with the 2016 presidential election. SSCI's request was forwarded to Ohr and Crowell the next day, and the FBI subsequently provided ODAG with the Ohr FD-302s, which Crowell and Schools reviewed. Schools told us he was shocked by the number of FD-302s concerning Ohr because no one from the FBI had mentioned meeting with Ohr as part of the FBI's efforts to corroborate Steele's reporting.

Following ODAG receiving this information, there were a series of meetings within ODAG involving Rosenstein, Crowell, then PADAG Robert Hur, and Schools. These meetings concerned Ohr's involvement in the investigation and what Ohr had previously described as his limited connection to Steele in his conversations with Rosenstein and Schools. Rosenstein stated he was uncomfortable with Ohr's failure to fully inform anyone in ODAG about his communications with Steele and Simpson. Crowell told us that, after reading the FD-302s, he thought Ohr essentially functioned as a source for the FBI on a sensitive investigation without informing his leadership and was surprised that Ohr provided a version of Steele's election reporting to the FBI. Likewise, Schools told us:

> [I]t's just inconceivable to me that somebody in the DAG's office would be having those communications [with Steele], and not report them to the DAG and the PADAG. Just because [the DAG and PADAG] have a right to know.

On December 5, 2017, Crowell and Schools met with Ohr to discuss Ohr's contacts with Steele. Crowell stated that they informed Ohr that they reviewed the FD-302s of his meetings with the FBI and asked Ohr why he did not inform anyone in ODAG about his activities. Schools stated that Ohr told them that he thought Steele's information needed to go to the FBI and not to ODAG political leadership because it was a political matter. According to Crowell and Schools, Ohr also stated that he should have let someone know and apologized.

Rosenstein told us Crowell and Schools reported back to him with their findings, and at that point, he realized Congress likely knew more about Ohr's activities with Steele and the FBI than anyone in ODAG did. Rosenstein told us:

[It] was really disappointing to me that he had made the decision originally not to brief anybody [on] our staff and then even after it was clear it was going to be...of national interest...he chose not to disclose, at least to [Schools], that he had actually had an active role....I felt like, if you're in the DAG's office, and the DAG is getting criticized by Congress for the handling of the Russia investigation, you ought to tell him that you had some role in it.

Rosenstein told us he focused on Ohr's role as essentially the equivalent of an FBI agent when dealing with Steele, over the substance of the information Ohr provided to the FBI. According to Rosenstein, the fact that Ohr had extensive conversations with Steele regarding the allegations of Russian interference and transmitted this information from Steele to the FBI—essentially acting as an intermediary, which was not a normal attorney role—formed the basis for Rosenstein's decision to remove Ohr from ODAG. According to Rosenstein, he viewed what Ohr did as collateral to his primary Department responsibilities, and that Ohr should have informed his supervisors about his involvement or sought ethics advice before taking these actions. Rosenstein said he expected an ADAG in these situations to err on the side of disclosure.

Crowell stated his recommendation, as Chief of Staff, was to remove Ohr as an ADAG and alert the appropriate investigative entities for further determination of the extent of Ohr's activities. According to Rosenstein, Crowell, and Schools, Rosenstein decided to use his discretion to move Senior Executive Service-level (SES) employees. He removed Ohr as an ADAG and reassigned him to the Criminal Division.

Crowell and Schools talked to Ohr again on December 6, 2017. They informed him that he was no longer an ADAG, but would remain Director of OCDETF. Crowell stated that he led Ohr through his options to dispute the decision or accept his removal as an ADAG, and that Ohr agreed to the reassignment.

According to Schools, on December 20, 2017, he met with Ohr to inform him that he also was being removed from his position as Director of OCDETF. Ohr stated that Schools told him that then Attorney General Jefferson Sessions and DAG Rosenstein decided to remove him as Director of OCDETF because the position required coordination with the White House, which was something they no longer wanted Ohr to do. During his OIG interview, Schools told us he could not recall what he told Ohr about the reason for his removal; however, after reviewing a draft of this report, Schools stated that Ohr was correct in his recollection of the reason Schools had provided to him for his removal as OCDETF Director.

Rosenstein told the OIG that he and Sessions were both involved in the decision to move Ohr from OCDETF to the Criminal Division. Rosenstein said that Sessions did not want Ohr running the transnational organized crime program and wanted to replace Ohr as a member of the associated threat management working group at the White House. He said that, independently from Sessions, he wanted to take OCDETF in a different direction with a more proactive OCDETF Director. Rosenstein stated that neither of Ohr's moves were disciplinary actions.

303

In the next chapter, we discuss the FBI's use of CHSs other than Steele and its use of Undercover Employees as part of the Crossfire Hurricane investigation. We also describe several individuals we identified who had either a connection to candidate Trump or a role in the Trump campaign, and were also FBI CHSs, and explain why such individuals were not tasked as part of the Crossfire Hurricane investigation. Finally, we describe the participation of the SSA supervising Crossfire Hurricane at ODNI strategic intelligence briefings given to the presidential candidates and certain campaign advisors.

CHAPTER TEN
THE USE OF OTHER CONFIDENTIAL HUMAN SOURCES AND UNDERCOVER EMPLOYEES IN CROSSFIRE HURRICANE

In this chapter, we examine the FBI's use of Confidential Human Sources (CHSs) other than Steele and its use of Undercover Employees (UCEs) in the Crossfire Hurricane investigation to determine whether the FBI had placed any CHSs within the Donald J. Trump for President Campaign or tasked any CHSs to report on the Trump campaign. We found no evidence that the FBI placed any CHSs or UCEs within the Trump campaign or tasked any CHSs or UCEs to report on the Trump campaign. However, we found that the Crossfire Hurricane team did task several CHSs and UCEs during the 2016 presidential campaign, which resulted in interactions with Carter Page, George Papadopoulos, and a high-level Trump campaign official who was not a subject of the investigation. All of the CHS interactions were consensually monitored by the FBI. We found that the Crossfire Hurricane team tasked CHSs to interact with Page and Papadopoulos both during the time Page and Papadopoulos were advisors to the Trump campaign, and after Page and Papadopoulos were no longer affiliated with the Trump campaign. We describe the types of information the CHSs sought to elicit from Page, Papadopoulos, and the high-level campaign official, as well as the information the CHSs obtained and the use, if any, that the Crossfire Hurricane team made of that information.

We also determined that additional CHSs were tasked by the FBI to attempt to contact Papadopoulos, but that those attempted contacts did not lead to any operational activity. In addition, we identified several individuals who had either a connection to candidate Trump or a role in the Trump campaign, and were also FBI CHSs, but who were not tasked as part of the Crossfire Hurricane investigation. One such CHS did provide the Crossfire Hurricane team with general information about Crossfire Hurricane subjects Carter Page and Paul Manafort, but we found that this CHS had no further involvement in the investigation. We identified another CHS that the Crossfire Hurricane team first learned about in 2017, when the CHS voluntarily provided his/her Handling Agent with ███████████ ██████████████. These ████████ were placed into the FBI's files and provided to the Crossfire Hurricane team for review, which determined there was not "anything significant" in the ████████████████. Below, we provide additional information about the individuals who had either a connection to candidate Trump or a role in the Trump campaign, and who were also FBI CHSs, and explain why they were not tasked in the Crossfire Hurricane Investigation.

Finally, we learned during the course of our review that, in August 2016, the supervisor of the Crossfire Hurricane investigation, SSA 1, participated on behalf of the FBI in a strategic intelligence briefing given by the Office of the Director of National Intelligence (ODNI) to candidate Trump and his national security advisors, including Michael Flynn, and in a separate strategic intelligence briefing given to candidate Clinton and her national security advisors. Although the briefing of candidate Trump and his advisors was not an undercover operation, because SSA 1 was introduced to the briefing participants as an FBI agent, we discuss this briefing in this chapter, including the reason why SSA 1 was in attendance, and the observations that SSA 1 made as a result of his participation.

I.   Methodology

To review the FBI's use of CHSs and UCEs in the Crossfire Hurricane investigation, the OIG was given broad access to highly classified information. In July 2018, the FBI's then Assistant Director (AD) for the Counterintelligence Division (CD), E.W. "Bill" Priestap, briefed the OIG regarding the FBI CHSs and UCEs who provided information for the Crossfire Hurricane investigation. This briefing was based on CD's knowledge of the Crossfire Hurricane investigation as well as searches of the FBI's Sentinel and Delta databases.[457] In this briefing, Priestap described the FBI's operational use of CHSs other than Steele and his sub-sources, and use of UCEs in the Crossfire Hurricane investigation.

Separately, the OIG reviewed emails, text messages, and instant messages of the FBI agents, analysts, and supervisors working on the Crossfire Hurricane investigation, as well as contemporaneous handwritten notes, to identify references to CHSs and UCEs. Through our Delta searches and review of documents, we learned of additional CHSs who were discussed for potential use in Crossfire Hurricane, but ultimately were not tasked by the FBI. We describe these CHSs in greater detail below.

We also obtained and analyzed the FBI's index for the Crossfire Hurricane case file, as well as the indices of the Crossfire Hurricane sub-files for Papadopoulos, Carter Page, Manafort, and Flynn, who were named subjects of the Crossfire Hurricane investigation. These indices reference activities undertaken by the Crossfire Hurricane team involving CHSs by listing the CHS ██████████ ██████████ in each line item that pertains to CHS activity. We then analyzed the underlying documents from the Crossfire Hurricane case file and sub-files that further described any activities involving CHSs.

The OIG was also given access to the FBI's classified Delta database, which is the FBI's automated case management system for all CHS records. We were able to review ███████████████████████████ the files of CHSs who were used, as well as those who were considered for use, in the Crossfire Hurricane investigation. The Delta files for these CHSs contained historical information, including when the FBI opened each CHS; the issues on which the CHS had reported; contact reports for all interactions with the FBI; quarterly (QSSR) reports and annual (FOASR) reviews of each CHS; and, where one had been performed, a human source

---

[457] As described in Chapter Two, the FBI maintains an automated case management system for all CHS records, which the FBI refers to as "Delta." The Delta file for each CHS contains all of the personal and administrative information about the CHS, as well as sub-files for unclassified reporting, classified reporting, validation documentation, and payment records.

validation report. For any CHS that had been closed by the FBI, the Delta file also described the events that led to the closure, and the basis for the FBI's decision.

We also conducted word searches within the FBI's Delta database for a number of terms, including "Trump" and "campaign," as well as the names of individuals who held leadership positions within the Trump campaign. We analyzed each of the Delta documents containing the search terms related to the Trump campaign and its members. In addition, for any CHS identified through these word searches, we reviewed that CHS's Delta file index for at least the 2016-2017 time period, as well as CHS reports within that file, as appropriate, to determine whether the CHS contributed to Crossfire Hurricane, and, if so, how. We also interviewed numerous former and current Department and FBI officials concerning the FBI's use of CHSs and UCEs during the Crossfire Hurricane investigation.

II.   Background

CHSs play an important role in the FBI's efforts to combat crime and protect national security, by allowing law enforcement direct access to information that is often not available through other investigative means. At any one time, the FBI has thousands of active CHSs from diverse backgrounds who report on a wide variety of threats. We were told by the FBI that the relationship between a CHS and the FBI may continue for many years, during which time a source may become inactive, and then become active again. We also were advised that it is commonplace for CHSs to bring information to the FBI that is outside of his or her typical focus, because that individual believes the information may be of interest or value to the FBI.

According to the FBI, its use of CHSs in counterintelligence investigations is common. Priestap told the OIG that CHSs are an "ordinary investigative tool" that are "part and parcel of what [FBI] agents do in an investigative sense every day." Priestap added that the upper levels of FBI management, including the Assistant Director and the Deputy Director, are not usually advised when an investigative team wants to use a CHS for a particular investigation. Indeed, the FBI Confidential Human Source Policy Guide (CHSPG) specifies that "daily oversight responsibility for...CHSs resides with the [Supervisory Special Agent (SSA)], who must review all communications regarding the CHSs on his or her squad and supervise the special agents (SAs) operating those CHSs."

With respect to the involvement of CHSs in political campaign activities, as described in Chapter Two, FBI policies allow for the use of "sensitive" sources (a category which includes individuals who are "prominent within domestic political organizations"), the use of CHSs in sensitive monitoring circumstances, and the undisclosed participation of CHSs in organizations exercising First Amendment rights. The use of CHSs in these circumstances requires heightened levels of supervisory approval to safeguard Constitutional rights and protect civil liberties. In our analysis in Chapter Eleven, we explain why those requirements did not apply to any of the CHS or UCE activities undertaken in the Crossfire Hurricane investigation, from its inception through the November 8, 2016 elections.

III. Strategy and Planning for Use of CHSs and UCEs in the Crossfire Hurricane Investigation

A. Strategy for Use of CHSs and UCEs in Crossfire Hurricane

The agents, analysts, and supervisors who worked on Crossfire Hurricane told the OIG that CHSs played an important role in the investigation. The Section Chief of CD's Counterintelligence Analysis Section I (Intel Section Chief) told the OIG that the use of CHSs was

> viewed as...one of the best avenues to potentially get some meat on the bones of the allegation that came through that started the case, to get somebody talking about what that reality was, even if the reality was, this guy Papadopoulos knows nothing or...this is what happened that actually explains that predication.... [I]t was one of those few avenues...available to us in that moment, where you could start to get some clarity around...that initial predicating allegation.... [The idea] was to get...[a] source...to develop enough of a relationship to be able to ask some relatively pointed questions around the Russia issue to try to get clarity on that predicating information.

Case Agent 2 agreed that the best way to find the truth was to get a human source to gather information "to tell [us] where the problem is, period. Period."

The witnesses we interviewed gave the OIG three practical reasons for focusing on operations using CHSs in the investigation. First, the case agents said they were conscious that they were working on a compressed time frame, and told us that CHSs can be an effective tool for quickly obtaining information, such as the telephone numbers and email addresses of the named subjects.

Second, early in the investigation, the Crossfire Hurricane team discovered that it had an existing FBI CHS who had previously interacted with named subjects of the investigation. Then Deputy General Counsel Trisha Anderson told the OIG that using such a source operationally in a counterintelligence investigation is "an obvious selection because of those preexisting relationships." SSA 1 told the OIG that "if we have a source...who has direct contact with...predicated subjects, we can run potential consensual monitoring operations and us[e]...undercovers, and...that was a better use of our limited time and resources." Case Agent 2 added that in thinking about which CHSs to use, the Crossfire Hurricane team "didn't have resources to start going out to every Field Office and sensitizing sources," so using an existing CHS to conduct operations against the Crossfire Hurricane subjects made sense.

Third, multiple witnesses told the OIG that they were very concerned about preventing leaks regarding the nature and existence of the Crossfire Hurricane investigation. SSA 1 told the OIG that one of the overriding concerns was keeping information about the investigation out of the public realm, because the team did not want to impact the presidential election in any way. Priestap said that, in an effort to prevent leaks, the investigative team was kept to a "small group...to try to control the information from getting out."

B.   Planning for Operations Involving CHSs and UCEs

SSA 1 told the OIG that he and the case agents were responsible for planning how to use CHSs in the Crossfire Hurricane investigation.[458] Case Agent 1, Case Agent 2, and Case Agent 3 likewise told us that plans for the operational activities using CHSs and UCEs were driven by the agents and SSA 1. Case Agent 1 said that the investigative team was not "told to do anything specifically. It usually emanated from us coming up with our plans and operations." The Intel Section Chief told the OIG the same thing—that the decisions about the use of CHSs and UCEs for Crossfire Hurricane were made by the case agents and SSA 1, and then approved through the chain of command.

SSA 1 told the OIG he did not remember any instances of then Section Chief Peter Strzok expressing opinions about how CHSs should be used or not used, or instructing the team on how to task the CHSs.[459] Case Agent 1 told the OIG that he did not recall Strzok "telling us to do anything or directing us to do anything" and did not remember "anything [Strzok] did on his own."[460] Similarly, Case Agent 2 told the OIG that he had no memory of Strzok ever "com[ing] in and say[ing], nope, I don't want this; I want this." Case Agent 3 told us he remembered talking to Strzok on "a couple of occasions" but Case Agent 3 said he could not "remember engaging him in a whole lot." Priestap told the OIG that there were no operational decisions involving CHSs for which Strzok was the sole decision maker.

Strzok's description of his role matched the information provided by the case agents, SSA 1, and Priestap. Strzok told the OIG that there were no investigative steps or operational decisions that he made on his own, independent of the team. With respect to CHS operations, Strzok told the OIG that his role was not exercising decision making authority, but rather "awareness and oversight." Strzok told the OIG he received briefings on the use of CHSs, but that "by and large, the kind of day-to-day operational use of sources was at a lower level than me." Strzok said that decisions on operations involving CHSs were made at the team level, and FBI managers were told by the team "[w]e've got these operations coming up. This is how we're going to use" each CHS.

---

[458] The FBI's CHSPG allowed an SSA to approve the operation of CHSs for all of the circumstances involved in the Crossfire Hurricane investigation, except for a heightened approval requirement for extraterritorial operation of a CHS, which applied to one of the Crossfire Hurricane CHS operations addressed in this chapter. We determined that the heightened approval requirement was met in the applicable circumstance. See CHSPG §§ 19.2 & n.12.

[459] Strzok was promoted to CD Section Chief in February 2016, and later to Deputy Assistant Director (DAD) of CD's Operations Branch I on September 4, 2016.

[460] The one issue Case Agent 1 remembered Strzok weighing in on was how aggressively to task one of the CHSs. Case Agent 1 told the OIG he remembered Strzok voicing concern that the investigative team was using the CHS "too often" and that repeated use of a CHS could possibly raise suspicions. Case Agent 1 told the OIG he disagreed and thought the team should be more aggressive "given the compressed time frame in which we had to operate" but characterized the discussion as "just a normal kind of give and take" that occurs in planning CHS operations.

The FBI's Office of the General Counsel (OGC) Unit Chief told the OIG that, following a briefing in August 2016, then Deputy Director Andrew McCabe was "on board with using the sources and using them quickly given the timing issue." However, the OGC Unit Chief added that McCabe did not give direction about what sources to use and how.[461] The OGC Unit Chief also did not remember any position that Lisa Page ever took about whether to use any of the CHSs, and said that Lisa Page had no final say over decisions on operations involving CHSs.[462] Priestap told the OIG that, in the updates that the Director, Deputy Director, and EAD received, they were not provided with the "detail[s] of how...[each] confidential human source was going to be used going forward." During his OIG interview, McCabe said that he did not expect the Crossfire Hurricane team to brief him on every CHS, and that he did not direct the Crossfire Hurricane team to use any specific CHSs. Rather, he said that it was the responsibility of the investigative team "to make [the] assessments" of which CHSs to use and how to use them. He added that FBI policies contain no requirement for a case agent to "get[] the Deputy Director's opinion on whether [a] source operation is a good idea or not or what the limitations should be."

The OGC Unit Chief also told us that members of the investigative team identified the CHSs and UCEs they wanted to use, and proposed the operational activities, as "the best way to try to get [the] answer quickly and covertly." She said that, under FBI policy, SSA 1 had the authority to approve the types of CHS operations used in the Crossfire Hurricane investigation. The Department was not part of the discussions regarding how to use FBI CHSs and UCEs to further the investigation. Department approval was not required to conduct operations using CHSs and UCEs, and the OGC Unit Chief told the OIG that the FBI does not "generally loop in DOJ...to discuss source operations" in counterintelligence investigations because the FBI is very protective of its source base and the identity of its CHSs.

In determining how to use CHSs in the Crossfire Hurricane investigation, SSA 1 and the case agents told the OIG that they focused their CHS operations on the predicating information and the four named subjects. Case Agent 1 told the OIG

---

[461] The only express direction we found that McCabe gave regarding the use of a CHS concerned a former FBI CHS, who contacted an FBI agent in an FBI field office in late July 2016 to report information from "a colleague who runs an investigative firm...hired by two entities (the Democratic National Committee [DNC] as well as another individual...[who was] not name[d]) to explore Donald Trump's longstanding ties to Russian entities." The former CHS also gave the FBI agent a list of "individuals and entities who have surfaced in [the investigative firm's] examination," which the former CHS described as "mostly public source material." In mid-September 2016, McCabe told SSA 1 to instruct the FBI agent from the field office not to have any further contact with the former CHS, and not to accept any information regarding the Crossfire Hurricane investigation. McCabe told the OIG he did not remember giving those instructions, and could not tell us why he might have done so. We found no evidence that the FBI reopened the former CHS for the Crossfire Hurricane investigation, or tasked the former CHS in connection with the Crossfire Hurricane investigation.

[462] Case Agent 1, Case Agent 2, and Case Agent 3 each told us that they were not aware of any decision making by Lisa Page in the investigation and that they had little to no interaction with her.

that the team "had a very narrow mandate" and that was "a mandate to look at these four individuals...and see if there's any potential cooperation between themselves and the Russian government...that was our goal in that investigation." He added that they were focused on the information from the Friendly Foreign Government (FFG) "and wanted to prove or disprove it, [as] best we could" but also "wanted to make sure that it didn't get broadcast out and we didn't harm the electoral process." Case Agent 2 told the OIG that the Crossfire Hurricane team was "focused on four predicated subjects." He stated that the core of the investigation was "literally looking at the predication and saying, okay, who reasonably could have had been in a position to receive suggestions from the Russians?" Case Agent 2 also said that in his "experience over twenty years [in the FBI]...a human source every time is going to answer that question" and so the team had "to start thinking about what human sources we can use."

SSA 1 also told the OIG that he did not have any information that the use of the CHSs was motivated in any way by political objectives rather than investigative objectives. He said that there was "no inkling of that. I never detected that, or had any indication of that." Priestap likewise told the OIG he was not aware of anyone's political preferences playing any role in the tasking of the CHSs. Priestap said that if he had seen any indication that Strzok was taking investigative actions for political reasons, Priestap would have removed Strzok from the Crossfire Hurricane team. Priestap said that he "absolutely would not have tolerated" politicization of the investigation, and that he never saw anything to indicate that type of activity was occurring.

C. Absence of FBI CHSs Inside the Trump Campaign

All of the witnesses we interviewed told the OIG that the FBI did not try to recruit members of the Trump campaign as CHSs, did not send CHSs to collect information in Trump campaign headquarters or Trump campaign spaces, and did not ask CHSs to join the Trump campaign or otherwise attend campaign related events as part of the investigation. Using the methodology described above, we found no information indicating otherwise.

Priestap told the OIG he knew of no effort by the FBI to infiltrate the Trump campaign. He said the Investigation

> was about a foreign adversary trying to mess with our free and fair election system. We wanted to know if any U.S. persons assisted in any way. In no way was it an investigation into...the political process.... [I]t's not the FBI's role in any way to try to monitor or...investigate campaigns.

Priestap added that the FBI wasn't

> after policy and plans. We were after some specific information about possible collusion with the Russians.... We never tried to develop somebody and insert them into the campaign. I'm actually pretty darn confident we could have been able to do that...if that was the objective. The FBI is pretty good at developing sources and inserting

them into situations to advance our investigations. I know of no conversation in which that was a plan on the part of the FBI's.

McCabe told the OIG that he was never involved in any discussions about placing an FBI CHS into the Trump campaign to further the Crossfire Hurricane investigation, or for any other purpose. Former Director James Comey told the OIG that, if there had been an effort to place a CHS within the Trump campaign, he would have expected to have been notified of that. He also said he had no knowledge of any FBI CHSs that had been asked by the FBI to join the Trump campaign in any capacity, and no information that would support an allegation that the FBI had been spying on the Trump campaign.

IV.   Use of CHSs and UCEs in the Crossfire Hurricane Investigation

A.   No CHSs and UCEs Used Prior to the Opening of the Crossfire Hurricane Investigation

In our review, we did not find any evidence that the FBI used CHSs or UCEs to interact with members of the Trump campaign prior to the opening of the Crossfire Hurricane investigation. All of the members of the Crossfire Hurricane team told the OIG that no investigative steps of any type were taken prior to receipt of the predicating information for the Crossfire Hurricane investigation on July 28, 2016, and we found no evidence to the contrary.

We investigated allegations that the FBI used specific individuals to undertake CHS activities prior to the predication of Crossfire Hurricane. For example, we investigated an allegation that the FBI sent a CHS (known as "Henry Greenberg" by other aliases) to meet with Trump advisors Roger Stone and Michael Caputo in March 2016, to offer to sell derogatory information about Hillary Clinton for $2 million. We found no evidence in the FBI's Delta files or from witness testimony that this individual was acting as an FBI CHS for any purpose in 2016.

We also investigated an allegation, raised by Papadopoulos, that the FBI used Joseph Mifsud, a Maltese citizen who was living in London and serving as a university professor, to pass information to Papadopoulos in April 2016 as a set up, so that the FBI could predicate the Crossfire Hurricane investigation. Papadopoulos raised this possibility during his October 25, 2018 testimony before the House Judiciary Committee and House Committee on Government Reform and Oversight, by stating that Mifsud might have been "working with the FBI and this was some sort of operation" to entrap Papadopoulos. The FBI's Delta files contain no evidence that Mifsud has ever acted as an FBI CHS,[463] and none of the witnesses

---

[463] As previously noted, we searched the FBI's Delta database for evidence of FBI CHSs interacting with Papadopoulos and other targets of the Crossfire Hurricane investigation, and found no evidence of such interactions, other than the CHSs specifically described in this chapter.

312

we interviewed or documents we reviewed had any information to support such an allegation.[464]

In addition, we investigated whether the FBI tasked any CHSs to meet with Carter Page prior to the opening of Crossfire Hurricane. We found no evidence that the FBI had. Case Agent 1, SSA 1, and the Supervisory Intelligence Analyst (Supervisory Intel Analyst) each told the OIG that the FBI did not have anything to do with any operational activities against Carter Page prior to the start of the Crossfire Hurricane investigation on July 31, 2016.[465]

B.   CHS and UCE Involvement in Crossfire Hurricane

We found no evidence that the FBI placed any CHSs or UCEs within the Trump campaign or tasked any CHSs or UCEs to report on the Trump campaign. However, through our review, we determined that, during the 2016 presidential campaign, the Crossfire Hurricane team tasked four CHSs and a few UCEs, which resulted in interactions with Carter Page, George Papadopoulos, and a high-level Trump campaign official who was not a subject of the investigation. We found that the Crossfire Hurricane team tasked CHSs to interact with Page and Papadopoulos both during the time Page and Papadopoulos were advisors for the Trump campaign, and after Page and Papadopoulos were no longer affiliated with the Trump campaign. All of the CHS interactions were consensually monitored by the FBI. Two of the CHSs tasked by the FBI are referred to below as Source 2 and Source 3. Below we discuss the types of information these CHSs sought to elicit from Page, Papadopoulos, and the high-level campaign official, the information that the CHSs obtained, and the use, if any, that the Crossfire Hurricane team made of that information.

We also determined that two additional CHSs were tasked by the FBI to attempt to contact Papadopoulos, but that those attempted contacts did not lead to any operational activity, and those CHSs are not discussed further in this report.

1.   Source 2

Source 2 was closed by the FBI in 2011 for "aggressiveness toward handling agents as a result of what [Source 2] perceived as not enough compensation" and "questionable allegiance to the [intelligence] targets" with which Source 2 maintained contact. However, Source 2 was re-opened 2 months later by Case Agent 1, and was handled by Case Agent 1 from 2011 through 2016 as part of Case Agent 1's regular investigative activities at an FBI field office. The FBI conducted human source validation reviews on Source 2 in 2011, 2013, and 2017.

---

[464] The FBI also requested information on ██████████████████████████████

[465] As noted in Chapter Three, a New York Field Office (NYFO) Counterintelligence (CI) Agent also told us that the FBI did not use any CHSs to target Carter Page during the NYFO counterintelligence investigation of Page, which was opened on April 6, 2016, and transferred to the Crossfire Hurricane team on August 10, 2016.

Case Agent 1 told the OIG that Source 2 can be "mercurial" and explained that Source 2 was closed for cause in 2011 because the former FBI handler, although very skilled, was "not the right match" for Source 2, which resulted in interpersonal conflict. Case Agent 1 said that when he reopened Source 2, he told Source 2 that this was the "last opportunity" and that the FBI would not tolerate the issues that had arisen in the past. According to Case Agent 1, since that time Case Agent 1 has not experienced any aggressiveness, and has not seen any indication that Source 2 has questionable allegiances to intelligence targets. Instead, Case Agent 1 described Source 2 as willing to assist the FBI "without any hesitation." He added that Source 2 has never given Case Agent 1 any reason to doubt the veracity of Source 2's reporting. Case Agent 1 and SSA 1 both told the OIG that nothing happened in the Crossfire Hurricane investigation to suggest that the concerns leading to Source 2's closure for cause in 2011 had any impact on Crossfire Hurricane.

a. Crossfire Hurricane Team's Initial Meeting with Source 2 on August 11, 2016

Source 2's involvement in the Crossfire Hurricane investigation arose out of Case Agent 1's pre-existing relationship with Source 2. Case Agent 1 told the OIG that when he arrived in Washington, D.C. in early August 2016 to join the Crossfire Hurricane team, he had never previously dealt with the "realm" of political campaigns. He said he lacked a basic understanding of simple issues, for example what the role of a "foreign policy advisor" entails, and how that person interacts with the rest of the campaign. Case Agent 1 said he proposed meeting with Source 2 to ask these questions because Case Agent 1 knew that Source 2 had been affiliated with national political campaigns since the early 1970s. Case Agent 1 also believed Source 2 might have information about, and potentially may have met, one or more of the Crossfire Hurricane subjects. Case Agent 1 told the OIG that he did not know at the time he proposed the meeting that Source 2 had been invited to join the Trump campaign. SSA 1 told the OIG that he did not know about Source 2, or know that Case Agent 1 was Source 2's handler, prior to Case Agent 1 proposing the meeting, which SSA 1 approved.

On August 11, 2016, Case Agent 1, Case Agent 2, and a Staff Operations Specialist (SOS) met with Source 2. Case Agent 1 told the OIG that the plan going into the meeting was to talk generally with Source 2 about Russian "interference in the election, what [Source 2] may know, and...to bring up Papadopoulos." Case Agent 1 added that the team used media reports concerning the release of emails and allegations of Russian hacking to frame the discussion. The Electronic Communication (EC) documenting the meeting states that the investigative team told Source 2 they were "assigned to a project" concerning Russian interference in the Presidential campaign. Case Agent 1 said they did not tell Source 2 that there was an open investigation or who the subjects were. Case Agent 1 also said they did not tell Source 2 about any specifics, including the information the FBI had received from the Friendly Foreign Government (FFG) that led to the opening of the investigation.

Case Agent 1 told the OIG that the team asked Source 2 about Papadopoulos, but Source 2 said he had never heard of him. The EC documenting the meeting reflects that Source 2 agreed to work with the Crossfire Hurricane team by reaching out to Papadopoulos which would allow the Crossfire Hurricane team to collect assessment information on Papadopoulos and potentially conduct an operation.

Case Agent 1 told the OIG that Source 2 then asked whether the team had any interest in an individual named Carter Page. Case Agent 1 said that the members of the investigative team "didn't react because at that point we didn't know where we were going to go with it" but asked some questions about how Source 2 knew Carter Page. Source 2 explained that, in mid-July 2016, Carter Page attended a three-day conference, during which Page had approached Source 2 and asked Source 2 to be a foreign policy advisor for the Trump campaign. According to the EC summarizing the August 11, 2016 meeting, Source 2 said he/she had been "non-committal" about joining the campaign when discussing it with Carter Page in mid-July, but during the August 11, 2016 meeting with the Crossfire Hurricane team, Source 2 "stated that [he/she] had no intention of joining the campaign, but [Source 2] had not conveyed that to anyone related to the Trump campaign." Source 2 further stated he/she "was willing to assist with the ongoing investigation and to not notify the Trump campaign about [Source 2's] decision not to join." Source 2 also told the Crossfire Hurricane team that Source 2 was expecting to be contacted in the near future by one of the senior leaders of the Trump campaign about joining the campaign.

In addition, Source 2 told the Crossfire Hurricane team that Source 2 had known Trump's then campaign manager, Manafort, for a number of years and that he had been previously acquainted with Michael Flynn. Case Agent 1 told the OIG that "quite honestly...we kind of stumbled upon [Source 2] knowing these folks." He said that it was "serendipitous" and that the Crossfire Hurricane team "couldn't believe [their] luck" that Source 2 had contacts with three of their four subjects, including Carter Page.

b. Internal FBI Discussions Concerning Source 2 and the Trump Campaign

Case Agent 1 told the OIG that, after meeting with Source 2 on August 11, 2016, he drove back to FBI Headquarters with Case Agent 2 and the SOS, and met with other members of the Crossfire Hurricane team to discuss how to proceed. During that meeting, the OGC Unit Chief, SSA 1, Strzok, and Priestap learned that Source 2 had been invited to join the Trump campaign by Carter Page and that Source 2 was going to turn down the invitation. All of the FBI witnesses we interviewed said that they would not have used Source 2 for the Crossfire Hurricane investigation if Source 2 had actually wanted to join the Trump campaign. SSA 1 said he did not remember anyone on the Crossfire Hurricane team advocating for Source 2 to actually join the Trump campaign and told the OIG he was relieved that Source 2 did not want to join the campaign "at all." Strzok told the OIG his reaction was "no, no, no, no, no, no.... [O]h god no. Absolutely not" when he learned that Source 2 had been invited to join the Trump campaign. Case Agent 1 told the OIG that if Source 2 had joined the campaign, the Crossfire Hurricane team would not have used Source 2 "because that's not what we were after." He added that having Source 2 in the campaign would have been difficult because "then [Source 2] actually has a job to do and [Source 2 is] going to actually have to do that job." Case Agent 2 told us that the reaction of the OGC attorneys advising the Crossfire Hurricane team was "no freaking way" and that the team was not "pushing for that...[because they were] not trying to get into the campaign." Case Agent 2 said that by using Source 2 outside of the campaign, the Crossfire Hurricane team could find "smart ways, and quiet ways to get information that we can corroborate, that helps us understand what the heck Mr. Papadopoulos meant by...the Trump team received a suggestion from the Russians." Priestap said that his first question was "what was Source 2's answer?" and that the response was Source 2 did not want to join the campaign.

The OGC Unit Chief said that she remembered the team seeking her advice, and said she told them they should not direct Source 2 to join the campaign, but they also should not tell Source 2 not to join the campaign. She told the OIG her advice was that Source 2 "should do what [Source 2] would normally do" and that the Crossfire Hurricane team should "follow [Source 2's] lead." She added that she was "grateful" when she learned that Source 2 did not want to join the Trump campaign, because she said that if the Crossfire Hurricane team had wanted to operate a CHS within the campaign (which she said none of the team members ever proposed to her), that would have raised a host of complicated issues under the FBI's Domestic Investigations and Operations Guide (DIOG), including undisclosed participation in political activities, appearance issues if it became publicly known an FBI source was in the Trump campaign, and the potential that the source could influence campaign policy or strategy.

c. Follow-up Crossfire Hurricane Team Meeting with Source 2 on August 12, 2016

The next day, August 12, 2016, Case Agent 1, Case Agent 2, and the SOS met with Source 2 again. During the August 12, 2016 meeting, Source 2 provided additional information about the role of a foreign policy advisor in a presidential campaign. Case Agent 1 described this portion of their conversation as "more of a generic question, like what is the foreign policy advisor doing" and who does that person report to? Case Agent 1 said that the Crossfire Hurricane team was not interested in the Trump campaign's "policies or any of their positions," but more generally just needed to understand the role of a foreign policy advisor.

During the August 12, 2016 meeting, Case Agent 1, Case Agent 2, and the SOS also told Source 2 that the FBI was interested in Carter Page, and asked whether Source 2 would be willing to contact Carter Page for a private meeting, as a follow-up to their meeting in July 2016. The investigative team told Source 2 that, because the Trump campaign appeared interested in recruiting Source 2, Source 2 was in a perfect position to directly ask Carter Page about media reports regarding links between the campaign and Russia. The team also discussed with Source 2 plans regarding Papadopoulos. As discussed below, Source 2 ultimately met with three members of the Trump campaign on behalf of the FBI—Carter Page,

George Papadopoulos, and a high-level campaign official who was not a subject of the investigation—and the FBI consensually monitored Source 2's conversations with each of these individuals.

d.   Source 2's Meetings with Carter Page

(1)   August 20, 2016

The first consensually monitored meeting between Source 2 and Carter Page took place on August 20, 2016. As described in Chapter Seven, some of the information obtained from this meeting was referenced in the Carter Page FISA Renewal Application No. 3. Case Agent 1 said that he instructed Source 2 to use the information in the media regarding Russia and Hillary Clinton's emails, and to ask questions Source 2 would normally ask if Source 2 was talking to a foreign policy advisor to a campaign. Members of the Crossfire Hurricane team told the OIG that they expected Source 2 to ask whether the campaign was planning an "October Surprise," as had been reported in the media, in addition to asking Carter Page if he maintained contacts with Russians or knew whether the Russians had been releasing emails to benefit the campaign.

We reviewed the transcript of Source 2's August 20, 2016 meeting with Carter Page. Through their conversations, Source 2 learned where Page was staying while in Washington for campaign meetings. Page also claimed to "personally...have no ambition" to seek a position in the administration if Trump won the election. Page also stated that he had "literally never met" Manafort, had "never said one word to him," and that Manafort had not responded to any of Carter Page's emails. Source 2 (who had known Manafort for decades) told Carter Page not to "feel bad" because everybody who has ever sent emails to Manafort "never got a response."[466]

During their conversation, Page told Source 2 that his July 2016 trip to Moscow "was the most incredible experience of my life." However, Page repeatedly complained about the negative, and highly personal, media attention he was receiving. For example, Page described an article from *The Washington Post* and how "95% of it was complete garbage." Page also complained that, next to Manafort (who he called "public enemy number one") Page was being treated as "public enemy number two." Page said that as a result of a "hit job" in Bloomberg News he had been branded as "Trump's Russia Advisor" with "close ties with the Russian government," and that idea had become "the consistent narrative ever since." Page told Source 2 that he was "just a shareholder" in the Russian energy company Gazprom, but that the media's approach was to highlight "anything that they can kind of spin in a...negative way." As a result of the negative media coverage, Page said that others working for the campaign were joking with him

---

[466] As described in Chapters Five and Seven, the FBI did not advise NSD's Office of Intelligence or the Foreign Intelligence Surveillance Court (FISC) of Carter Page's statements concerning Manafort, which contradicted information from Steele's election reporting that was relied upon in the Carter Page FISA applications.

about "attract[ing] all the attention" and keeping the rest of them "off the radar screen."

When Source 2 raised the issue of an "October Surprise," Carter Page said "there's a different October Surprise...[a]lthough maybe some similarities" to the October Surprise in the 1980 Presidential Campaign. Page did not elaborate. Source 2 raised the issue again later in the meeting, and asked if the Trump campaign could access information that might have been obtained by the Russians from the DNC files. Source 2 added that in past campaigns "we would have used [it] in a heartbeat." Page's response was that, because he had been attacked by the media for his connections to Russia, he was "perhaps...[being] overly cautious." When the October Surprise issue came up again, Page alluded to "the conspiracy theory about...the next email dump with...33 thousand" additional emails, but did not further explain what he meant. Source 2 asked "[w]ell the Russians have all that don't they?" to which Page responded "I don't, I-I don't know."

Page also said that "we were not on the front lines of this DNC thing" during the Philadelphia convention and wondered aloud "who's better to do this?" Page asked Source 2 whether the Trump campaign should just leave it to the "other forces that be" and just let it "run its course," with the Trump campaign "egg[ing] it a long a little bit" but without being "seen as the one advancing this in concert with the Russians." Source 2 responded "it needs to be done very delicately and with no fingerprints" to which Page said "[o]kay." Page asked Source 2 if "picking out a couple trusted journalists" and giving them "some ideas of...potential big stories" would be the right way to handle it. Page also suggested that "there may be people that kind of work this angle" but that Page was being "very cautious, you know, right now."

Source 2 also asked Page for information about Papadopoulos. Page said that Papadopoulos was the youngest guy on the campaign, that he used to live in London, and that he had not been to the last campaign meeting. Page also said he had "no comment" on whether Papadopoulos was easily triggered emotionally.

At one point, Source 2 steered the conversation toward Source 2's contacts in the Russian ███████████████████, and described how Source 2 arranged fully paid trips for the ██████████ and other Russians to speak ███████ ███████████████. Source 2 asked if Page knew anyone of that type that might be interested in coming to speak ███████, and Page responded that he "know[s] a couple of people in London" but that he wanted to be "doubly cautious...to limit conspiracy theories" and that his preference would be to "pass along names discreetly." Page added that he would need to "think about the easiest[,] most efficient[,] frankly safest way to...navigate this."

Throughout the meeting, Page asked Source 2 to assist the Trump campaign by writing op-eds. Source 2 stated a willingness "to be helpful to the campaign" but also said that Source 2 would like to know "what the plan is" before committing. Page responded that it was "unfortunate" that Source 2 had not yet gotten to meet a high-level campaign official who was not a subject of the investigation, and Source 2 responded that Source 2 was available whenever that high-level campaign official "wants to chat." Later in the meeting, Source 2 told Page that Source 2 would like to meet with the high-level campaign official to discuss "what I'm getting in to" because Source 2 said there are "some things that have to be done at this part of...the campaign.... And if you don't do them you're going to lose."

Case Agent 1 told the OIG that Page's comment about the "October Surprise" was meaningful to the Crossfire Hurricane team. He said that when Page was asked the question, Page

> kind of trailed off and it...piqued our interest because it seemed like that he knew of something, but he wasn't 100 percent sure and was just kind of alluding to something, but he didn't really give much more information to it. So that kind of pique[d] our interest.

Case Agent 1 said that within the investigative team "there was a discussion whether or not [Carter Page] knew more than he was [letting] on." SSA 1 told the OIG that the Crossfire Hurricane team viewed Page's responses to questions as "less than forthright" and Case Agent 3 described Page as not "as forthcoming as he could have been." As described previously in Chapters Five and Seven, however, the FBI did not include any of the information from the August 20, 2016 meeting between Source 2 and Carter Page in the first FISA application, or Renewal Application Nos. 1 and 2, but did include some of Page's comments to Source 2 about the "October Surprise" in Renewal Application No. 3.

SSA 1 and Case Agent 1 told the OIG that this meeting between Source 2 and Carter Page was important for the investigation in other ways. SSA 1 told the OIG that it was important for the team to determine "where [Carter Page] was living, [and] what he was up to." Case Agent 1 said that, as a result of this operation, "we now had a successful contact between the established FBI source and one of our targets" which gave the Crossfire Hurricane team confidence that they could "find out investigatively what we've been charged to do." Case Agent 1 also said that, because "there were several emails sent back and forth thanking [Source 2]," the FBI obtained Carter Page's email address and telephone number, which could be used in the first FISA application.

Consensual monitoring of the August 20 meeting between Source 2 and Carter Page was presented to McCabe, Priestap, then FBI General Counsel James Baker, Strzok, Anderson and other FBI personnel during briefings on August 25, 2016. Baker told the OIG that what he remembered about the briefing

> was feeling comfortable that the focus was on the Russians, the focus was on trying to get foreign-intelligence information, [and] that this other stuff [regarding the campaign] was part of the cover story and not what we were interested in, and something that we...just weren't going to make any use of.

He added that "even though the FBI was collecting some type of political information" through Source 2's conversation with Carter Page, the political information "was not the focus of what we were after...[and] it was being minimized in the sense that it was just extra crap that we got that we didn't really want." He also said that at the time he felt the people presented the monitoring were appropriately focused on the fact that Source 2 "couldn't get Carter Page to say anything about the Russians." Anderson told the OIG that her impression of the consensual monitoring was that Carter Page was "pretty guarded" in talking to Source 2. McCabe told the OIG he remembered that "there weren't any...smoking guns from the conversation" but that "Page seemed kind of evasive." McCabe did not remember being told about any portions of the conversation other than what was contained on the consensual monitoring that the Crossfire Hurricane team provided to him for review. McCabe also said he remembered having an "expectation that [the Crossfire Hurricane team] would continue to use [Source 2, who] obviously had access to" Carter Page, but McCabe could not remember any follow-up discussions or what the investigative team planned to do next.As described previously in Chapters Five and Seven, the FBI did not inform the National Security Division (NSD) attorney in the Office of Intelligence (OI) who was working on the Carter Page FISA applications about Page's August 2016 interaction with Source 2 until 10 months later, in June 2017. As a result, none of the information from this interaction was considered by OI for inclusion in the first FISA application, or Renewal Application Nos. 1 and 2. Page's comments about the "October Surprise" were included in Renewal Application No. 3, which was filed in June 2017, after Case Agent 6 sent the OI Attorney a 163-page document for the purpose of showing him Page's statements about the "October Surprise." The OI Attorney told the OIG that he used the 163-page document to accurately quote Page's statements concerning the "October Surprise" in Renewal Application No. 3, but that he did not read the other aspects of the 163-page document and that Case Agent 6 did not flag for him Page's statements about Manafort. The OI Attorney told us that these statements, which were available to the FBI before the first application, should have been flagged by the FBI for inclusion in the FISA applications at the time the statements were made because they were relevant to the court's assessment of the allegations concerning Manafort using Page as an intermediary with Russia. Case Agent 6 told the OIG that he did not know that Page made the statement about Manafort because the August 2016 meeting between Source 2 and Page took place before Case Agent 6 was assigned to the investigation. He said that the reason he knew about the "October Surprise" statements in the document was that he had heard about them from Case Agent 1 and did a word search to find the specific discussion on that topic.

(2)   October 17, 2016

The second consensually monitored meeting between Source 2 and Carter Page took place on October 17, 2016, 4 days before the FBI obtained the first FISA targeting Page, and after Page had left the Trump campaign. As described in Chapter Five, Page made statements to Source 2 that led the FBI to believe that Page was continuing to be closely tied to Russian officials, including Page's suggestion (described below) that "the Russians" may be giving him an "open checkbook" to fund a foreign policy think tank.

Case Agent 1 told the OIG that the Crossfire Hurricane team had learned through travel records that Page was planning a trip. Case Agent 1 said that the Crossfire Hurricane team

> wanted to find out what he was going to do...because at that point he was no longer affiliated with the campaign. He was out. As far as we could tell he was no longer a part of the campaign. We still didn't have the FISA up, but we wanted to see who he was going to be in contact with..., and why he was going...because it just seemed very odd.

Case Agent 1 told the OIG that the investigative team believed that Page may be going to meet an individual with ties to Russian Intelligence. The investigative team was also aware of a Russian responsible for "recruiting U.S. government employees and handling U.S. government employees." Case Agent 1 said that the plan was for Source 2 to help determine where Page was planning to stay and what he was planning to do during his trip.

Case Agent 1 told the OIG that the Crossfire Hurricane team did not get a complete transcript of the meeting, which was consensually monitored, but instead "wrote up only the pertinent parts of whatever meetings occurred just because...doing a full transcript would have taken too long and it was just not pertinent." We reviewed the Crossfire Hurricane team's partial transcript of Source 2's October 17, 2016 meeting with Carter Page.

During the meeting, Page told Source 2 that Page "never had any ambitions to go into government regardless of who won" the upcoming presidential election, and instead called himself the "equivalent" of influential diplomat and academic George Kennan. Page said that, like Kennan who "found[ed] his Institute of Advanced Study," Page would like to develop a research institute to be "a rare voice that talks against this consensus" of Russian containment, which Page believes is too "hawkish and aggressive in a lot of ways against the Russians." In talking about how he would fund this institute, Page told Source 2 "I don't want to say there'd be an open checkbook, but the Russians would definitely..." then, according to the partial transcript, the sentence trailed off as Page laughed. Source 2 asked "they would fund it—yeah you could do alright there" and Page responded "Yeah, but that has its pros and cons, right?"

At other points in the conversation, Page stated that he had "a longstanding constructive relationship with the Russians going back throughout" his life, and that he "could talk for the next 5 hours about all these sneaky little approaches that the [U.S. government] has been taking against Russia—going back...a couple decades." Page also stated his belief that "if these ridiculous approaches and these failed policies continue next January, you know...we're on the brink of war."

When asked about the link between the Russians and WikiLeaks, Page said that, as he has

> made clear in a lot of...subsequent discussions/interviews...I know nothing about that—on a personal level, you know no one's ever said

one word to me. But it's interesting, you know, off the record between us—if the only source of transparency and the truth is an external source, you know, c'est la vie right?

Page also mentioned to Source 2 "very deep off the record" that the Clinton campaign had "hired investigators to come after me, including some in London," and that Page had "very good sources...[and knew] the names of the investigators as well."

As for the platform committee during the Republican National Convention, Page told Source 2 that he "stayed clear of that—there was a lot of conspiracy theories that I was one of them.... [But] totally off the record...members of our team were working on that, and...in retrospect it's way better off that I...remained at arms' length. But again, our team was working on that."

Page also told Source 2 that the "core lie" against Page in the media "is that [Page] met with these sanctioned Russian officials, several of which I've never even met in my entire life." Page said that the lies concern "Sechin [who] is the main guy, the head of Rosneft...[and] there's another guy I had never even heard of, you know he's like in the inner circle." When Source 2 asked Page about that person's name, Page said "I can't even remember, it's just so outrageous."[467] Page stated that he did meet a number of people when he was the commencement speaker at the July 2016 New Economic School graduation in Moscow, and told Source 2 that "the irony of it [was]...there's no law against meeting with sanctioned officials" and that his lawyer said everything would be fine "as long as you don't take gifts or have any sort of business dealings...the lawyer quote was 'don't even take a pen.'"

When Source 2 asked whether Page could introduce Source 2 to Russians who might be interested in speaking ████████████████, Page laughed and said "[m]y lawyers would probably advise me to..." then laughed again and mentioned Harry Reid's letter to FBI Director Comey asking the FBI to "please look into Carter Page's connections to these people." When asked again, Carter Page reiterated that "lawyers are always cautious...and... this would be setting off such big alarm bells." Page also told Source 2 that Page did not have their "contact details."

Members of the Crossfire Hurricane team and FBI OGC told the OIG they considered Page's discussion of having a potentially "open checkbook" as the most useful and concerning piece of information from the October 17, 2016 meeting between Source 2 and Page. Case Agent 1 told the OIG that, as a result of that comment, the Crossfire Hurricane team was "trying to figure out at the time if that was part of a quid pro quo." SSA 1 told the OIG that Page's comment on funding a research institute using "an open checkbook" from Russia brought SSA 1 closer to believing that Carter Page may actually be acting as an agent of a foreign power. The OGC Attorney told us that he viewed the remark as an indication that Page had "connections that he expected to be able to use to his advantage as a result of the

---

[467] As described in Chapters Five and Seven, the FBI did not include Carter Page's denials of these meetings with Russian officials in its description of this CHS operation in the FISA applications.

potential election of Donald Trump." The OGC Unit Chief told the OIG she viewed this as a suggestion "that the Russians would pay for [Page] to operate a think tank in the United States...basically as a propaganda machine."

As discussed in Chapters Five and Seven, these statements about "an open checkbook" from Page's interaction with Source 2 were included in the FISA applications, but Page's statements denying knowing about a WikiLeaks connection to Russia, having involvement in the platform committee, or having met with the sanctioned Russian officials, or even knowing who one of them was, were not included in any of the FISA applications.

(3)   December 15, 2016

The third consensually monitored meeting between Source 2 and Carter Page took place on December 15, 2016, which was several days after Page returned from giving a lecture at the New Economic School in Moscow. The New Economic School was the university in Moscow where Page had spoken in July 2016. During their lunch meeting, Page described his recent trip to Moscow as involving "18 hour days for a...week." Page also told Source 2 that Page would be traveling back to Moscow "after the New Year" and that Page had been invited to Christmas parties at Gazprom and Rosneft, but declined those invitations because of recent media reports suggesting that Page was being investigated by the FBI. Page also complained that media outlets had been "bad mouthing" him earlier that day, and told Source 2 that one of the issues Page wanted to discuss was "damage control."

During the meeting, Page and Source 2 discussed some of the individuals who were under consideration for prominent positions in the Trump Administration. With respect to President-elect Trump's announcement that he would nominate Rex Tillerson to be Secretary of State, Page stated that one of the things Tillerson will "get[] hit the worst on" by critics is his relationship with Igor Sechin. However, Page added "[t]hey tried it on me...[and] [t]hey've already played that card so they['ve] got to come up with something new." When Source 2 asked Page how the Russians viewed Tillerson, Page stated that the Russians are "almost in awe" of him, and that they view him as "[s]omeone who has real knowledge as opposed to just standard rhetoric that's been in place for 70-some years."

When asked by Source 2 about where the Russians might take the relationship with the United States, Page said that the Russians are "[e]xcited but cautious" because the Russians had "been...burned a lot in the past." Page also told Source 2 that he thought the question with respect to the relationship between the United States and Russia was whether the United States was going to be "scolding or nasty or [have an] actual friendship."

Source 2 also asked Page about Congressional inquiries into whether the Russians had been leaking Hillary Clinton's emails to try to alter the results of the presidential election. Page responded by saying that, even if they were to "assume [the allegations] are correct," Page believed the real impact was "giving some transparency to the actual corruption of...the people that [the Russians] were exposing," and that was important to the functioning of the democratic process

323

because "democracy is based on information." Page told Source 2 that the difference between Hillary Clinton's "public versus private positions...never would have come to the forefront" otherwise, and that without such transparency, the American people would have been left with "lies and false information." Page stated that democracy had been "actually made more pure by this exposure, public versus private" of Hillary Clinton's positions, such that the disclosure of her emails "actually served a positive role." When Source 2 suggested that information in U.S. government elections should not be provided by "actors outside the process," Page asked Source 2 "how many times have parties within this town...the U.S. government, interfered in the direction of governments around the world?" Page then stated that he had "an even more controversial statement" which was that the Russian media organizations RT and Sputnik "may...warrant a Nobel Peace Prize" for "providing this transparency and helping to facilitate a pure democracy."

Source 2 also asked Page about the think tank they had discussed in their October 17, 2016 meeting. Page told Source 2 that he had been talking with the New Economic School "a little bit," that "they were actually quite...positive" about the idea, they were thinking about "doing something jointly or...actually based there," and that the New Economic School was "possibly" going to help with the financing. Page added that the New Economic School had a "lot of support internally...[f]rom the government.... High level." When Source 2 asked about Page's statement, during their October 17, 2016 meeting, about Russians giving Page a "blank check" for the think tank, Page stated that he didn't "know that [he] went that far" but that "there was some support...[and] this trip proved it." According to Page, the New Economic School told him to "come back to us with a proposal" and that "very high-level people were quite supportive." Page added that he was weighing the "pros and cons" and that "some people have warned [him to] be careful with having too much Russia connection for obvious reasons."

During their meeting, Page used his personal laptop to show Source 2 the PowerPoint presentation from his most recent lecture, and then gave Source 2 a thumb drive containing a copy of the PowerPoint presentation. Page told Source 2 that one of Page's comments during the Moscow lecture was a play on Trump's phrase "[d]rain the swamp." According to Page, in his lecture he said the "reference for U.S.–Russia relations is, '[d]rain the septic tank,'" by which Page meant that prior dealings with Moscow could be characterized as "deep misunderstandings and...huge missed opportunities." Page pointed out one of the slides from the presentation, which was a "score card" Page had put together concerning previous administrations' positions on Russia. In discussing the "score card," Page told Source 2 that when Hillary Clinton was Secretary of State in 2011, she was interfering with other governments in the same way "that people...are accusing Russia of doing" in the 2016 elections.

As described in Chapter Seven, the Crossfire Hurricane team incorporated some of the information from this December 15, 2016 meeting between Carter Page and Source 2 into Renewal Application No. 1.

(4)   January 25, 2017

The final consensually monitored meeting between Source 2 and Carter Page took place on January 25, 2017. None of the information from this meeting was included in any of the Carter Page FISA applications.

During the January 25, 2017 meeting between Page and Source 2, Page asked whether Source 2 had ever "come across that [Steele] guy." Source 2 told Page that he did not know Steele. Page then stated that the reports were "just so false." Page said that he wished the reports "had come out...three [or] four months earlier because...all the stuff...against [Page was] based...directly upon that." Page stated that the reporting, which included "some sort of sex escapade...discredits itself so much" and contains "a lot of factual errors," although Page did not specify which part of the reporting he viewed as erroneous. Page characterized the reporting as "a bigger fraud" than the allegations of voter fraud made by President Trump reported by the media that morning, because Hillary Clinton "was playing against [Page] and...everyone around [Trump] and this [reporting] is the basis of it," which Page described as "complete lies and spin." Page added that, in his view, the lies in the reporting were comparable to the obstruction of justice at issue in Watergate, because "[o]ne of the key elements of obstruction of justice is false evidence" and this "false evidence is directly traceable back to [Hillary Clinton]...sending this over to...the authorities at the J. Edgar Hoover building." In addition, Page told Source 2 that, according to "the front page of the Wall Street Journal," Page was "under surveillance." Page said he thought there was an analogy to Dr. Martin Luther King Jr., "[w]here J. Edgar Hoover was all over this guy," and that Page felt he was being targeted by those in "positions of power, [using] government resources to come after someone [for exercising] freedom of speech" because Page had spoken out on his views regarding Russia. Page told Source 2 he thought it was "completely outrageous" but that he would have to talk to Source 2 "about this offline...[because Page was] not going to put this in email or [discuss it] on a phone call."

Page also told Source 2 that Page was scheduled to meet with Steve Bannon later that afternoon. At the time, Bannon was President Trump's Chief Strategist. Page said he would be "curious to hear" any ideas Source 2 had about ways Page could be "helpful" to the Trump Administration. Page asked for Source 2's advice on whether Page should "take this [fraud] on aggressively and...go on the offensive and fight back" because the allegations against him are "not going away." Page also suggested that if he were offered a position in the Trump Administration and went through a Senate confirmation hearing, he could use the opportunity as "a way of getting it all out there...what a complete lie and what a complete sham...this is" and that it was all done "using government resources based on completely false evidence." Page said that he wanted to show how "this all started based on complete utter lies." Page told Source 2 that he thought Bannon might be receptive to this "forward leaning approach" through which the "lies are exposed and everyone[] kind of understands how this all came about and the impact." In response, Source 2 suggested that the Trump Administration was unlikely to put Page "through a Senate confirmation, [because] everybody who objects to [Page's] viewpoint on [Russia] will be rounded up and trotted through in front of the cameras" and it would be politically impossible to get the votes needed for confirmation.

Source 2 asked Page whether he had made any more progress on the think tank, which Source 2 said could be helpful by undertaking projects "exploring how...international business leads to international political cooperation," for example. Source 2 stated that he thought Page "might be able to create something useful in London," and added that if Page "could bring some Russian money to the table...[Source 2] might be able to help...get some US money." Page told Source 2 that he was concerned about "anything that's sort of balanced, getting that weight correct." Page said he was trying to take his time and weigh the pros and cons, but also was "kind of anxious...[based on] conversations last month in Moscow...[that the] momentum is building" toward another potential Cold War. Page said that, based on his conversations with Deputy Prime Minister Arkady Dvorkovich, who Page described as the "de facto chairman" of the New Economic School, the Russians are "fully on board" and want to "get started." But Page said that he was concerned that doing this "on that side that can be a black mark for people like McCain" who might view it as "[t]oo un-American." When Source 2 asked Page if Page could "tie him down to...a dollar amount...that then [Source 2] can try to match" Page responded "a million and a million?" but Source 2 expressed doubt about whether Source 2 could raise a million dollars to contribute to the think tank.

The only other subject of the Crossfire Hurricane investigation that was mentioned during the January 25, 2017 conversation was Michael Flynn. Source 2 asked Page if he knew Flynn "pretty well," and Page responded that he "kind of" knew Flynn's "number two."

As with other denials made by Page to an FBI CHS, these statements about the Steele reports were not included in FISA Renewal Application No. 2 or FISA Renewal Application No. 3.

e. Source 2's Meeting on September 1, 2016 with a High-Level Trump Campaign Official Who Was Not a Subject of the Crossfire Hurricane Investigation

At the request of the Crossfire Hurricane team, Source 2 also reached out to a high-level official of the Trump campaign, who was not a subject of the investigation. Source 2 succeeded in arranging a meeting with the high-level Trump campaign official on September 1, 2016, and their meeting was consensually monitored by the Crossfire Hurricane team. Case Agent 1 told the OIG that this meeting occurred after Case Agent 1 got approval from the OGC Unit Chief to consensually monitor the conversation, as required by the DIOG. Priestap told the OIG that from an operational standpoint, he personally reviewed and approved the operation even though review at his level was not required by the DIOG. McCabe's handwritten notes reflect that he was told ahead of time that Source 2 was going to be meeting with the high-level Trump campaign official, but McCabe told the OIG he did not remember anything specific about that discussion. He added that his approval was not required for such an operation, and if he was told ahead of time, it was "likely that [he] asked...who [that] was because that [name] would not have...stood out to [him] independently." FBI and Department policy did not require that the FBI obtain Department approval to consensually monitor this conversation. Then Chief of NSD's Counterintelligence and Export Control Section (CES) David Laufman told the OIG that he had no recollection of being informed that the FBI was planning to consensually monitor a conversation between a CHS and a high-level official of the Trump campaign, and we are not aware of any Department official having been informed in advance by the FBI.

Case Agent 1 told the OIG that the plan for this meeting was for Source 2 to ask the high-level campaign official about Papadopoulos and Carter Page "because they were...unknowns" and the Crossfire Hurricane team was trying to find out how "these two individuals who are not known in political circles...[got] introduced to the campaign," including whether the person responsible for those introductions had ties to Russian Intelligence Services (RIS). SSA 1 told the OIG that he did not remember having a plan in place in case the FBI monitored information that was politically sensitive. He told the OIG that "if we received that information and recognized it for what it was, our first call would be to our general counsel to talk to them about how we need to ingest that." SSA 1 also told the OIG that he did not think the Crossfire Hurricane team gathered any of that type of information through Source 2's meeting with the high-level campaign official.

The OGC Unit Chief remembered discussing with the team, with respect to the use of Source 2, the need to be careful about First Amendment-protected activities. However, she said that her concern about a CHS collecting that type of information arises if the operation seeks information falling outside the authorized purpose of the investigation or if the FBI is "broadly disseminating that information and/or using it in a way that would undermine or promote" one candidate or the other. The OGC Unit Chief said the Crossfire Hurricane investigation did not really raise that concern, because the FBI did not seek information outside the authorized purpose of the investigation and was not disseminating the information it gathered from the CHSs or using it "in a way that would expose it to people that didn't need to know it." The OGC Unit Chief also said that her main concern about CHSs interacting with members of the Trump campaign was ensuring that CHSs were not "influencing steps the campaign was going to take."

Priestap told the OIG he remembered multiple meetings where the team discussed the objectives of having Source 2 engage with members of the Trump campaign and former members of the Trump campaign, and the "need to steer clear" of collecting campaign information "deal[ing] with policies, plans, staffing decisions, [or] anything related." Priestap also said that "it's not always possible...[o]nce people start talking" to a source to stay on point, because the target of the operation may tell a source about the topic that interests the FBI, as well as a lot of additional information. He added that "the FBI tries really hard to take the information we're authorized to collect and to disregard the information it [isn't], no matter how embarrassing, scintillating, or whatever else that information might be to others."

Case Agent 1 told the OIG that none of the information collected from monitoring Source 2's conversation with the high-level Trump campaign official was ever used in the Crossfire Hurricane investigation. He said that the team determined that "the conversation wasn't germane to any of the investigative activity we were taking, so we didn't do anything with that." We found that the Crossfire Hurricane team did not transcribe the meeting. Instead, Case Agent 1 said that the consensual monitoring was "check[ed]...into evidence and that was about it. We didn't do anything with that conversation."

We reviewed the consensual monitoring of the September 1, 2016 meeting between Source 2 and the high-level Trump campaign official who was not a subject of the investigation.[468] In the consensual monitoring, Source 2 raised a number of issues that were pertinent to the investigation, but received little information in response. For example, Source 2 asked whether the Trump campaign was planning an "October Surprise." The high-level Trump campaign official responded that the real issue was that the Trump campaign needed to "give people a reason to vote for him, not just vote against Hillary." When asked about the allegations of Russian interference in the 2016 elections, the high-level Trump campaign official told Source 2:

> Honestly, I think for the average voter it's a non-starter. I think in this city [Washington, D.C.] it's a big deal. I think in New York it's a big deal, but I think from the perspective of the average voter, I just don't think they make the connection.

The high-level Trump campaign official added that in his view, the key for the Trump campaign "is to say what we have said all along—we need to raise the level of abstraction, we need to talk about the security of the election system, which includes things like voter IDs."

Source 2 also asked about George Papadopoulos, who the high-level Trump campaign official described as "very eager" and "a climber." The high-level campaign official added that he was "always suspicious of people like that." The high-level campaign official described Carter Page as a "treasure," but agreed with Source 2 that Carter Page is "ambiguous" in his thinking, and that it can be hard to get a clear answer out of him. When Source 2 asked whether the Trump campaign needed to do something to put the ideas raised by Carter Page's Moscow speech in perspective, the high-level campaign official told Source 2 that "it's not that it's not important," but that the campaign official was "not sure it was something that in the grand scheme of things rises to the level of the campaign making an open effort" to do "other than to say we should never have any interference in our electoral process." As for the relationship between candidate Trump and Manafort, Source 2 was told that the high-level campaign official thought Trump and Manafort did not "ever hit it off" and that Manafort "was trying to do a traditional campaign, and Mr. Trump wasn't buying it." The high-level campaign official made a few additional comments about the internal structure, organization, and functioning of

---

[468] At the beginning of this consensual monitoring, Source 2 has a brief conversation with the FBI agent. The FBI agent clearly instructs Source 2 that, in meeting with the high-level campaign official, "consistent with our theme...listen to him, talk to him with your points, we are not directing you to join the campaign."

the Trump campaign. During the conversation, Source 2 and the high-level campaign official also discussed issues unrelated to the Crossfire Hurricane investigation, such as an internal campaign debate about Trump's immigration strategy, efforts to reach out to minority groups and the impact of those efforts, and the campaign's strategies for responding to questions about Trump's decision not to release his tax returns. We found no evidence that any information contained on the consensual monitoring was put to any use by the Crossfire Hurricane team.

f.   Source 2's Meetings with George Papadopoulos

At the direction of the Crossfire Hurricane team, Source 2 invited Papadopoulos to meet with Source 2 in September 2016, to discuss a project. Case Agent 1 said that the Crossfire Hurricane team thought it would play to "Papadopoulos's ego to help take part in a project." The project was based on Papadopoulos's past writings about the Leviathan oil fields off the coast of Israel and Turkey, and was not related to Papadopoulos's role in the Trump campaign. The FBI, through Source 2, covered the costs of Papadopoulos's travel, and paid Papadopoulos $3,000 for the project.

The Crossfire Hurricane case agents told the OIG that they were trying to recreate the conditions that resulted in Papadopoulos's comments to the FFG officials about the suggestion from Russia that it could assist the Trump campaign by anonymously releasing derogatory information about presidential candidate Hillary Clinton, which we described in Chapter Three. Case Agent 1 said that by taking Papadopoulos to another country, Papadopoulos might "feel a little freer to talk outside the confines of the United States and...repeat that conversation" he had with the FFG officials. Case Agent 3 said that it made sense to take him there, "have a political discussion over a couple drinks and reproduce" Papadopoulos's statements to the representative of the FFG if possible.

The members of the Crossfire Hurricane team who traveled for the operation were Case Agent 1, Case Agent 2, and the SOS. The written plan for the operation stated that Papadopoulos would meet with Source 2 to discuss the project. The written plan stated that during that time "there will be ample opportunity and various angles to have [Papadopoulos] expound on the initial comments made in May 2016" to the FFG regarding the anonymous release of emails by the Russians that would damage the Clinton presidential campaign.

SSA 1 told the OIG that it was his understanding that FBI executive managers were "briefed consistently" during the planning for this operation, and orally approved the operation before it took place.[469] Case Agent 1 said that he did not remember any FBI managers voicing concerns about this operation. Priestap

---

[469] There is no requirement in the CHSPG for the FBI to inform the Department of extraterritorial CHS operations in support of national security investigations. In fact, the CHSPG states: "Pursuant to the AG memo dated May 5, 2006, the AG delegated to the FBI Director the authority to approve national security [extraterritorial] operations," which the Director then delegated to the Assistant Director.

329

told the OIG that he recalled being aware of the operation and approving it. McCabe told the OIG that he did not remember knowing ahead of time that the FBI was going to be consensually monitoring Source 2's meetings, but that approval for such an operation by the Deputy Director was not required.

The OGC Unit Chief told the OIG that because the operation targeted Papadopoulos individually and wasn't directed at anything related to the campaign, she thought that it was appropriate. She said that her main concern about using Source 2 to interact with members of the Trump campaign was ensuring that Source 2 was not "influencing steps the campaign was going to take" and that "asking questions of Papadopoulos to collect information did not raise those kinds of concerns." Priestap signed the formal authorization for the operation on September 15, 2016, the day the operation concluded. SSA 1 told the OIG that it was "just standard practice...[to] get verbal authority" before such an operation and to have the paperwork "signed after the fact."

(1) September 15, 2016 Brunch Meeting with Source 2 and Papadopoulos

On September 15, 2016, Papadopoulos met for brunch with Source 2 and to discuss the project. The meeting was consensually monitored by the FBI, and later transcribed. Much of the conversation between Source 2 and Papadopoulos concerned Papadopoulos's academic pursuits, his work with the Hudson Institute, and his research on the Arab Spring, Greek energy production, and the strategic importance of Cyprus. During the meeting, Source 2 told Papadopoulos that the paper Papadopoulos was writing should focus on geopolitical dimensions in the eastern Mediterranean, including the energy sector and Russia's engagement with the Israelis. Source 2 offered Papadopoulos $3,000 for the paper, and asked for Papadopoulos to complete it within three weeks.

During the meeting, Source 2 told Papadopoulos that Carter Page "always says nice things about you." Papadopoulos told Source 2 that although Carter Page was one of the campaign's "Russian people," Page "has never actually met Trump...[and] hasn't actually advised him on Russia...[but] [h]e might be advising him indirectly through [another campaign official]." Papadopoulos also told Source 2 that General Flynn "does want to cooperate with the Russians and the Russians are willing to...embrace adult issues." As for Papadopoulos's own connections with Russia, Papadopoulos told Source 2 he thought that "we have to be wary of the Russians" and mentioned that "they actually invited me to their...faith talk. I didn't go though." Papadopoulos explained to Source 2 that he made the decision not to go because it is "just too sensitive...[as an] advisor on the campaign trail...especially with what is going [on] with Paul Manafort." Source 2 also asked Papadopoulos about the possibility of the public release of additional information that would be harmful to Hillary Clinton's campaign. Papadopoulos responded that Julian Assange of WikiLeaks had said in public statements to "get ready for October...[but] [w]hatever that means no one knows."

As a result of this brunch meeting, the Crossfire Hurricane team assessed that Papadopoulos was "responding in a deferential mode" to Source 2, and decided that Source 2 would set a follow-up meeting for drinks with Papadopoulos later that afternoon "to ask direct questions...pertaining to the Crossfire Hurricane predicating material."

(2)   September 15, 2016 Evening Meeting with Source 2 and Papadopoulos

On the evening of September 15, 2016, Source 2 and Papadopoulos met for pre-dinner drinks and further discussion. The meeting was consensually monitored by the FBI, and later transcribed. According to the executive summary written by Case Agent 2 after the operation, the goal of this meeting was for Source 2 to ask Papadopoulos direct questions about whether the Trump campaign benefitted from, or anyone in the Trump campaign had knowledge of, Russian assistance or the WikiLeaks release of information that was damaging to the Clinton campaign.

When Source 2 initially asked about WikiLeaks, Papadopoulos commented that with respect to Assange "no one knows what he's going to release" and that he could release information on Trump as a "ploy to basically dismantle... [or] undercut the...next President of the United States regardless of who it's going to be." Papadopoulos also stated that "no one has proven that the Russians actually did the hacking," then continued to discuss hacking by pointing out that he had "actually had a few...Israelis trying to hack" his cell phone, which Papadopoulos said "shocked" him because he had "done some sensitive work for that government," and he said the Israelis had "allowed [him] quite a high level of access." Papadopoulos also stated that "no one else" did the work that he did for the Israelis, and that it had led "some folks [to] joke...[that Papadopoulos] should go into the CIA after this if [Trump] ends up losing."

Later in the conversation, Source 2 asked Papadopoulos directly whether help "from a third party like WikiLeaks for example or some other third party like the Russians, could be incredibly helpful" in securing a campaign victory. Papadopoulos responded:

> Well as a campaign, of course, we don't advocate for this type of activity because at the end of the day it's, ah, illegal. First and foremost it compromises the US national security and third it sets a very bad precedence [sic].... So the campaign does not advocate for this, does not support what is happening. The indirect consequences are out of our hands.... [F]or example, our campaign is not...engag[ing] or reaching out to wiki leaks or to the whoever it is to tell them please work with us, collaborate because we don't, no one does that.... Unless there's something going on that I don't know which I don't because I don't think anybody would risk their, their life, ah, potentially going to prison over doing something like that. Um...because at the end of the day, you know, it's an illegal, it's an illegal activity. Espionage is, ah, treason. This is a form of treason.... I mean that's why, you know, it became a very big issue when Mr. Trump said, "Russia if you're listening...." Do you remember?... And you know we had to retract it because, of course, he didn't mean for

them to actively engage in espionage but the media then took and ran with it.

When Source 2 raised the issue again, Papadopoulos added:

> to run a shop like that...of course it's illegal. No one's looking to...obviously get into trouble like that and, you know, as far as I understand that's, no one's collaborating, there's been no collusion and it's going to remain that way. But the media, of course, wants to take a statement that Trump made, an off-the-cuff statement, about [how] Russia helped find the 30,000 emails and use that as a tool to advance their [story]...that Trump is...a stooge and if he's elected he'll permit the Russians to have carte blanche throughout Eastern Europe and the Middle East while the Americans sit back and twiddle their thumbs. And that's not correct.[470]

The meeting ended with Papadopoulos offering to introduce Source 2 to more members of the Trump campaign team, and offering to set up a follow-up meeting the next time Source 2 is in Washington, D.C. Source 2 advised Papadopoulos that Source 2 did not "really want to be in government again" but was "wanting to help on China" and willing to provide Papadopoulos with written materials, such as speeches and pre-position papers, which might be helpful on foreign policy issues involving China.

Case Agent 1 told the OIG that Papadopoulos's "response to the direct questions seemed weird" to the Crossfire Hurricane team because it "seemed rehearsed and almost rote." Case Agent 1 added that at these points in the conversation, Papadopoulos "went from a free-flowing conversation with [Source 2] to almost a canned response. You could tell in the demeanor of how [Papadopoulos] changed his tone, and to [the Crossfire Hurricane team] it seemed almost rehearsed." Case Agent 1 emailed SSA 1 and others to report that Papadopoulos "gave...a canned answer, which he was probably prepped to say when asked." According to Case Agent 1, it remained a topic of conversation on the Crossfire Hurricane team for days afterward whether Papadopoulos had "been coached by a legal team to deny" any involvement because of the "noticeable change" in "the tenor of the conversation."

Case Agent 2 told the OIG that his concern after Papadopoulos's meetings with Source 2 was that the team was not "any closer to answering the question of whether...any of these guys have information on penetration" of the Trump campaign. Case Agent 3 added that because Papadopoulos "made statements about doing sensitive work for [a foreign] government" that opened a new area of inquiry with respect to Papadopoulos's foreign contacts.

SSA 1 told the OIG that his main observation was that when Papadopoulos was pushed for answers, he seemed to have a "prepared statement. It sounded

---

470 As described in Chapters Five and Seven, none of the Carter Page FISA applications advised the FISC of Papadopoulos's denials to Source 2 that the Trump campaign had any involvement in the release of DNC emails by WikiLeaks.

like a lawyer wrote it." OGC Deputy General Counsel Trisha Anderson similarly said that, when she learned of Papadopoulos's responses in 2018 while working on the Rule 13 Letter to the FISC (described in Chapter Eight), she viewed them as "self-serving" and "sound[ing] like a lawyered statement." SSA 1 said that, as a result of Source 2's meetings with Papadopoulos, SSA 1 did not have any concerns that the information gathered intruded upon planning or strategy of the Trump campaign.

2.   Source 3

Case Agent 3 and an Intelligence Analyst identified Source 3 as an individual with a connection to Papadopoulos who may be willing to act as a CHS, based on statements Source 3 had made to the FBI several years prior, during an interview in an unrelated investigation. Source 3 had never previously worked for the FBI as a CHS, and the Delta records for Source 3 state that the opening of this CHS "was accelerated due to operational necessity."

Case Agent 3 said that he considered Source 3 to be a reliable CHS because Source 3 was always available when the FBI needed Source 3, provided good descriptions of the conversations with Papadopoulos, and the summaries that Source 3 provided to the FBI were corroborated by the consensual monitoring. The FBI performed a human source validation review on Source 3 in 2017, and recommended Source 3 for continued operation.

Papadopoulos and Source 3 met multiple times between October 2016 and June 2017, all of which occurred after the FBI understood that Papadopoulos had ceased working on the Trump campaign.[471] All but one of their meetings were consensually monitored by the FBI; however, not all of them were transcribed by the FBI. Instead, Case Agent 3 said that he and the Intelligence Analyst would review the recordings to find portions that were of investigative interest, and those portions were written up or reviewed.

Case Agent 3 told the OIG that, with respect to Source 3, the topics that Case Agent 3 "was interested in didn't pertain to the [Trump] campaign. They

---

[471] The precise date that Papadopoulos left the Trump campaign is unclear. Case Agent 3 told the OIG that it was his understanding that Papadopoulos left the Trump campaign on October 4, 2016. We noted that, on October 10, 2016, Papadopoulos sent a text message stating that he was "no longer with the campaign." However, we also reviewed a text message that Papadopoulos sent to a different contact on October 17, 2016, stating that he was still working for the Trump campaign, but that he was "laying low" after getting in trouble for comments during an "interview on Russia." The Special Counsel's Report stated that Papadopoulos was dismissed from the Trump campaign in early October 2016, after the September 30, 2016 publication of an interview he gave to a Russian news agency created negative publicity. *See The Special Counsel's Report*, Vol. I at 93 & n. 492. In his interview with the House Judiciary Committee and House Committee on Government Reform and Oversight on October 25, 2018, Papadopoulos said that the date he was removed from the campaign was unclear, and that he did not think he "ever really left the campaign." *See Transcript of Interview of George Papadopoulos before the House Judiciary Committee and House Committee on Government Reform and Oversight*, October 25, 2018, 133. For the purpose of this report, we have used early October as the approximate date of Papadopoulos's separation from the Trump campaign, as that is the date that the FBI believed such separation occurred.

pertained to Russia and [another foreign country], with regard to whatever Papadopoulos was doing." Case Agent 3 said the guidance he gave to Source 3 was that the FBI was "interested in these foreign activities, and we're not interested in the campaign stuff."

Case Agent 3 told the OIG that Source 3 collected information about Papadopoulos's contacts with Russians through their monitored conversations. However, Case Agent 3 said that the consensual monitoring revealed that Papadopoulos had contacts with, and an interest in selling access to the United States government, which Case Agent 3 said he pursued as a separate "prong" of the Crossfire Hurricane investigation. Case Agent 3 said that, as a result, he "pivoted with the source to try to passively collect the Russia stuff and bring that up subtly during conversation" while collecting information about Papadopoulos's contacts with the other foreign government. Case Agent 3 also said that the monitored conversations between Source 3 and Papadopoulos gave the FBI information about how Papadopoulos "reacts to different topics...[which] was incredibly useful" in the FBI's preparation to interview Papadopoulos.

We reviewed the transcripts of two conversations between Source 3 and Papadopoulos that were monitored prior to the November 8, 2016 elections. In the first consensually monitored conversation, during the third week of October 2016, Papadopoulos described how he had worked for the presidential campaign of Ben Carson before joining the Trump campaign, and that when he was with the Trump campaign, he "set up a meeting with...[t]he President of Egypt and Trump." Papadopoulos also told Source 3 that, since leaving the Trump campaign, Papadopoulos had "transitioned into like my own private brand." Papadopoulos later stated he was "still with...the campaign indirectly" and that he had made "a lot of cool [connections] and I'm going to see what's going to happen after the election." He added that he had learned "[i]t's all about connections now days, man." Papadopoulos did not say much about Russia during the first conversation with Source 3, other than to mention a "friend Sergey...[who] lives in...Brooklyn," and invite Source 3 to travel with Papadopoulos to Russia in the summertime.

In the second consensually monitored conversation, at the end of October 2016, Papadopoulos told Source 3 that Papadopoulos had been "on the front page of Russia's biggest newspaper" for an interview he had given 2 to 3 weeks earlier. Papadopoulos said that he was asked "[w]hat's Mr. Trump going to do about Russia if he wins, what are your thoughts on ISIS, what are your thoughts on this?" and stated that he did not "understand why the U.S. has such a problem with Russia." Papadopoulos also said that he thinks Putin "exudes power, confidence." When Source 3 asked Papadopoulos if he had ever met Putin, Papadopoulos said that he was invited "to go and thank God I didn't go though." Papadopoulos said that it was a "weird story" from when he "was working at...this law firm in London" that involved a guy who was "well connected to the Russian government." Papadopoulos also said that he was introduced to "Putin's niece" and the Russian

334

Ambassador in London.[472] Papadopoulos did not elaborate on the story, but he added that he needed to figure out

> how I'm going monetize it, but I have to be an idiot not to monetize it, get it? Even if [Trump] loses. If anything, I feel like if he loses probably could be better for my personal business because if he wins I'm going to be in some bureaucracy I can't do jack..., you know?

Papadopoulos added that there are plenty of people who aren't even smart who are cashing in, and asked Source 3 "Do you know how many Members of Congress I've met that know jack...about anything? Except what their advisors tell them?... They can barely put a sentence together.... I'm talking about Members of Congress dude." In other portions of the conversation with Source 3, Papadopoulos repeated that what he really wanted to figure out was how to "monetize...[his] connections" because Papadopoulos felt like he knew "a lot of Ambassadors...[and] a lot of Presidents." Papadopoulos said that once the election was over, Papadopoulos was going

> to sit down and systematically write who I know, what they want, and how I can leverage that because if you know like government guys and ambassadors you should be making money, that's all I know because there's not one person I know who has those connections that isn't making...money.

He observed that what he had to "sell is access," and "[t]hat's what people pay millions of dollars for every year. It's the cleanest job."

However, when Source 3 asked Papadopoulos whether Papadopoulos thought "Russia's playing a big game in this election," Papadopoulos said he believed "That's all bull[]." Papadopoulos said "[n]o one knows who's hacking [the DNC].... Could be the Chinese, could be the Iranians, it could be some Bernie...supporters." Papadopoulos added that arguments about the Russians are "all...conspiracy theories." He said that he knew "for a fact" that no one from the Trump campaign had anything to do with releasing emails from the DNC, because Papadopoulos said he had "been working with them for the last nine months.... And all of this stuff has been happening, what, the last four months?" Papadopoulos added that he had been asked the same question by Source 2. Papadopoulos said he believed Source 2 was going to go

> and tell the CIA or something if I'd have told him something else. I assume that's why he was asking. And I told him, absolutely not....it's illegal, you know, to do that....

The FBI did not inform OI of these conversations at the time they occurred and, as described in Chapters Seven and Eight, the subsequent FISA renewal applications

---

[472] As described in The Special Counsel's Report, Papadopoulos later learned that the woman he had met was not actually Putin's niece. *See The Special Counsel's Report*, Vol. I at 84 & n.424.

on Carter Page did not include these statements. In its July 12, 2018 Rule 13 Letter to the FISC, NSD advised the court of this information.

B. Other CHSs Who Were Not Tasked As Part of Crossfire Hurricane

In our review, we also learned that, in 2016, the FBI had several other CHSs with either a connection to candidate Trump or a role in the Trump campaign. Some of these sources were known to and available for use by the Crossfire Hurricane team during the 2016 presidential campaign, while others were not.

As one example, the Crossfire Hurricane team received general information about Page and Manafort in August 2016 from one such CHS. This CHS was not involved in the presidential campaign but, according to the Handling Agent, knew candidate Trump and had been in contact with the candidate. The Handling Agent for this CHS told the OIG that he was given "zero context" about the Crossfire Hurricane investigation, "told absolutely nothing." According to the Handling Agent, the information the CHS provided about Page was "open-source information" that was "[a]ll over the Internet." The Handling Agent also said that, once FBI Headquarters received this general information, the "matter was dropped." We found no evidence that any members of the Crossfire Hurricane team ever suggested inserting this CHS into the Trump campaign to gather investigative information. SSA 1 told the OIG "that was not what we were looking to do." SSA 1 added that the Crossfire Hurricane team was "looking for information about the predicate, and didn't want it to be construed later...as something other than what we were really after."[473]

---

[473] SSA 1 did contact the Handling Agent for this CHS after the November 8, 2016 election, and asked for "a read-out from your CHS regarding possible positions in administration." SSA 1 told the OIG that he sent this email because he thought that the CHS might receive "a position somewhere in the administration" which would become a "sensitive matter that we would need to handle differently." In late November 2016, the Handling Agent met with the CHS. The Handling Agent later wrote a document stating one purpose of the meeting was "to obtain insight regarding the upcoming Trump Administration following the recent U.S. Presidential elections." We asked the members of the Crossfire Hurricane team about this statement in the document. SSA 1 told the OIG that he had never seen this document before and that this was not what he intended the Handling Agent to discuss with the CHS. Priestap told the OIG that this statement "absolutely" would have raised concerns if he had learned of it in real time. He said he was not aware that this type of information was being collected from a CHS and that he "hope[d] it was misstated [in the document], because we don't, well, it's not what we should be doing." The Handling Agent told the OIG that, to him, the phrase "obtain insight" was a synonym for asking a "[p]ersonal opinion," and that he was just making "small talk" with the CHS, the way you would expect to converse with those "tied to political circles" immediately following an election. The Handling Agent added that this information was "not investigative in nature" and was not placed into any case file. The Handling Agent's SSA said that "because the Trump Administration...was not under any kind of investigation" by her squad, she was not concerned about this sentence when she saw it, and she understood it to be written in the general context of preparation for the CHS's meeting with a foreign intelligence officer unrelated to the Crossfire Hurricane investigation. The Handling Agent added that he was not aware of this document being shared with or accessible to the Crossfire Hurricane team, and we found no evidence that members of the Crossfire Hurricane team ever received this document.

We also learned about a different CHS who at one point held a position in the Trump campaign. However, by the time that the CHS told his/her Handling Agent about this involvement, the CHS was no longer part of the Trump campaign. After Crossfire Hurricane team members learned about this CHS, they reviewed the CHS's file, but did not task the CHS as part of the investigation. The OGC Attorney told the OIG that he distinctly remembered the OGC Unit Chief "strongly advising [the Crossfire Hurricane agents] to be cautious with this particular CHS." Case Agent 1 recalled that, because this CHS was "at one point...part of the campaign...we just said, hey, hands off." Documents in the CHS's Delta file reflect that the Handling Agent minimized contact with the CHS because of the CHS's campaign activities, even though the CHS was no longer involved in the Trump campaign.[474]

As part of our review, we also discovered an October 2016 email written to SSA 1 by an Intelligence Analyst on the Crossfire Hurricane team. The email copied information out of a CHS's Delta file stating that the CHS is "scheduled to attend a 'private' national security forum with Donald Trump" in October 2016, after which the CHS will provide "an update on the Trump meeting." However, none of the Crossfire Hurricane case agents remembered knowing that any FBI CHS had been scheduled to attend a private forum with candidate Trump. SSA 1 told the OIG he did not remember this CHS "at all" and had no information about whether the CHS actually attended such a meeting. The Handling Agent for this CHS told the OIG that what was described in the document was a gathering at a hotel that was "more of a...campaign speech or campaign discussion" and "more like a campaign stop than a meeting." The Handling Agent told the OIG he could not remember if the CHS ended up attending or not, and added that he "would certainly not be tasking a source to go attend some private meeting with a candidate, any candidate, for president or for other office, to collect the information on what that candidate is saying." We found no evidence that this CHS ever reported any information collected from a meeting with Trump or a Trump campaign event.

Although the Crossfire Hurricane team was aware of these CHSs during the 2016 presidential campaign, we were told that operational use of these CHSs would

---

[474] The email stating that the CHS would not be used in Crossfire Hurricane said:

> After careful consideration, the CROSSFIRE HURRICANE team has decided, at this time, it is best to utilize your CHS as a passive listening post regarding any observations [he/she] has of the campaign so far. Base[d] on current, on-going operations/developments in the CROSSFIRE HURRICANE investigation, we are not going to directly task or sensitize the CHS at this point in time. We appreciate [your] assistance in this matter and remain interested in any campaign related reporting that you guys may receive from the CHS during normal debriefs.

Case Agent 2, who wrote the email, told the OIG that the email was "incorrect" and what he was asking for was any information about attempts by Russia "to screw around with the campaign or the elections." He also acknowledged that it was "a mistake" not to make that clear in the email. The Handling Agent for this CHS told the OIG he "dismissed the e-mail...outright" because the CHS was "not even in the campaign" by that time. He added that within the field office, they had "made the decision...that we weren't touching this...right prior to a Presidential election." We found no evidence that the Crossfire Hurricane team received any information from this CHS in response to Case Agent 2's email.

not have furthered the investigation, and so these CHSs were not tasked with any investigative activities. Moreover, SSA 1 told the OIG that the members of the Crossfire Hurricane team "never [had] any intent, never any desire...to collect...campaign or privileged information with regard to the presidential election."

We also learned of two other FBI CHSs, one of whom held a position █████ █████████████ and the other of whom ██████████████████████████ ████████████████████ We found no evidence that the Crossfire Hurricane team ever knew about the CHS who held a position ██████████████████ and, accordingly, no evidence that the CHS was tasked to do anything as part of the Crossfire Hurricane investigation.

With respect to the CHS with connections to ████████████████████ ████████████, the Handling Agent told the OIG that this CHS regularly provides "a ton of information on all sorts of things" to the FBI without being tasked and brings "reams of information" to their meetings. In March 2017, after the campaign had ended, the CHS voluntarily provided his/her Handling Agent with five sets of documents on multiple topics ███████████████████████████ ████████████████████████████████. According to the Handling Agent, this was not information that he had asked the CHS to obtain or provide to the FBI. The Handling Agent told the OIG that the CHS gave the ████████████████████ to the FBI because the CHS "thought it was of interest to the U.S. government." The Handling Agent placed the materials into the FBI's files.[475] Also in March 2017, the Handling Agent forwarded the ████████████ ████ to his supervisor, who sent it to FBI Headquarters, after which it was provided to the Crossfire Hurricane team for review.[476] Later, the Handling Agent learned from the CHS ███ ████. An Intelligence Analyst assigned to the Crossfire Hurricane team asked the Handling Agent ████████████████████████ from the CHS, which the Handling Agent placed in the FBI's files and sent to the Crossfire Hurricane team. The Crossfire Hurricane Intelligence Analyst who reviewed █████████ advised Crossfire Hurricane supervisors and case agents that there was not "anything significant" in ███████████████████████. Moreover, the Crossfire Hurricane team ████████ ██████████████████████████████████

The OGC Unit Chief told the OIG she had no concerns about the Crossfire Hurricane team receiving ████████████████████████████████ ████████ was over and that, because the focus of the Crossfire Hurricane

---

[475] We notified the FBI upon learning during our review that ████████████████ materials that the CHS had provided to the FBI were still maintained in FBI files.

[476] The Handling Agent for this CHS and the Handling Agent's SSA were aware that FBI Headquarters was conducting a "special" investigation because the Handling Agent assisted the Crossfire Hurricane team by serving a court order in October 2016 related to the investigation. However, neither the Handling Agent nor his SSA was provided any information about the nature or scope of the Crossfire Hurricane investigation.

investigation was "trying to identify whether or not the Russians had infiltrated or were working with U.S. persons associated with the Trump campaign,...[it] would have been fine to collect it either during the campaign or afterwards" because it went to "the heart of the question of whether or not there was any sort of conspiracy."

The Handling Agent for this CHS told the OIG that he did not recall asking this CHS any questions ██ ██ The Handling Agent said he was aware that the CHS "may have had some political meanderings toward...████████████████, and was trying to be associated with that," but the Handling Agent did not understand, or inquire about, the full extent of the CHS's involvement. The SSA in the field office who supervised the Handling Agent told the OIG that he had no memory of knowing ████████████████ ████████████████████████. He characterized the CHS's involvement as the source's "hobby" or "outside interests." He said:

> the FBI did not have a source in the campaign, ████████████████ ████████████████████████, that we didn't even know about at the time or didn't care about at the time.

He said that, in his view, any ████████████████ "was totally separate from [the CHS's] work with the FBI." He added that, because the CHS was a Trump supporter, he was "not worried about [the source] trying to provide information or getting dirty information on Trump." He said any suggestion this CHS "was directed to damage or investigate the Trump Administration is just absurd."[477]

---

[477] We reviewed the text and instant messages sent and received by the Handling Agent, the co-case Handling Agent, and the SSA for this CHS, which reflect their support for Trump in the 2016 elections. On November 9, the day after the election, the SSA contacted another FBI employee via an instant messaging program to discuss some recent CHS reporting regarding the Clinton Foundation and offered that "if you hear talk of a special prosecutor...I will volunteer to work [on] the Clinton Foundation." The SSA's November 9, 2016 instant messages also stated that he "was so elated with the election" and compared the election coverage to "watching a Superbowl comeback." The SSA explained this comment to the OIG by saying that he "fully expected Hillary Clinton to walk away with the election. But as the returns [came] in...it was just energizing to me to see....[because] I didn't want a criminal to be in the White House."

On November 9, 2016, the Handling Agent and co-case Handling Agent for this CHS also discussed the results of the election in an instant message exchange that reads:

Handling Agent: "Trump!"

Co-Case Handling Agent: "Hahaha. Shit just got real."

Handling Agent: "Yes it did."

Co-Case Handling Agent: "I saw a lot of scared MFers on...[my way to work] this morning. Start looking for new jobs fellas. Haha."

Handling Agent: "LOL"

No one involved with the Crossfire Hurricane investigation, including Strzok, Priestap and Comey, knew about this CHS during the campaign, or when the CHS was ███████████████████████████████, or when the CHS met with ███████ ████████████████████████. Priestap told the OIG he "did not know it was happening," and that, as the AD of the Counterintelligence Division, he "absolutely" should have been told that there was an active FBI CHS with access to ████████ █████████████████████████████████. He said that, no matter what level of approval was required to continue operating such a CHS, that as a matter of "common sense" this was a situation where "[t]he bosses need to know." We make a recommendation in Chapter Eleven to address this issue. We found no evidence that this CHS was tasked by the FBI to interact with any members of the Trump campaign, transition team, or Administration.

V.   ODNI Strategic Intelligence Briefing Provided to Candidate Trump, Flynn, and Another Trump Campaign Advisor

As we described in Chapter Three, the FBI decided not to conduct defensive briefings for any members of the Trump campaign about the information the FFG provided to the U.S. government that served as the predicate for opening Crossfire Hurricane. However, we learned during the course of our review that, during the presidential election campaign, the FBI was invited by ODNI to provide a baseline counterintelligence and security briefing (security briefing) as part of ODNI's strategic intelligence briefing given to members of both the Trump campaign and the Clinton campaign, consistent with ODNI's and the FBI's practice in prior presidential election cycles. We also learned that, because Flynn was expected to attend the first such briefing for members of the Trump campaign on August 17, 2016, the FBI viewed that briefing as a possible opportunity to collect information potentially relevant to the Crossfire Hurricane and Flynn investigations. We found no evidence that the FBI consulted with Department leadership or ODNI officials about this plan.

In the first week of August 2016, the FBI's Presidential Transition Team requested that CD begin preparations for providing unclassified "counterintelligence awareness" briefings to the transition teams for the Trump and Clinton campaigns. The FBI participated in strategic intelligence briefings conducted by ODNI on August 17, 2016, for Trump and his selected advisors, including Flynn; and on August 27, 2016, for Clinton and her selected advisors. The FBI also participated in ODNI strategic intelligence briefings for members of each campaign: on August 31, 2016, to Trump campaign staff; on August 31, 2016, to Clinton campaign staff; on September 8, 2016, to Vice Presidential candidate Tim Kaine; and on September 9, 2016, to Vice Presidential candidate Michael Pence.

Co-Case Handling Agent: "Come January I'm going to just get a big bowl of popcorn and sit back and watch."

Handling Agent: "That's hilarious!"

The FBI selected SSA 1, the supervisor for the Crossfire Hurricane investigation, to provide the FBI security briefings for Trump and Clinton.[478] SSA 1 told us that one of the reasons for his selection was that ODNI had informed the FBI that one of the two Trump campaign advisors attending the August 17 briefing would be Flynn. He further stated that the briefing provided him "the opportunity to gain assessment and possibly have some level of familiarity with [Flynn]. So, should we get to the point where we need to do a subject interview...I would have that to fall back on." Asked to explain what he meant by "assessment," the SSA 1 continued,

> [Flynn's] overall mannerisms. That overall mannerisms and then also if there was anything specific to Russia, or anything specific to our investigation that was mentioned by him, or quite frankly we had an...investigation, right. And any of the other two individuals in the room, if they, any kind of admission, or overhear, whatever it was, I was there to record that.

SSA 1 told us that he did not recall specific internal FBI discussions about having him provide the FBI security briefings for Trump and Clinton, but believes that the group who likely would have been part of any such discussions—Strzok, the Intel Section Chief, and possibly Lisa Page—shared a general understanding of the reasons for doing so. SSA 1 also told us that using an opportunity to interact with the subject of an investigation is not unusual for the FBI, and that in this instance, it actually proved useful because SSA 1 was able to compare Flynn's "norms" from the briefing with Flynn's conduct at the interview that SSA 1 conducted on January 24, 2017, in connection with the FBI's investigation of Flynn.

We asked SSA 1 whether he was aware of any discussions within the FBI about the appropriateness of the FBI using an ODNI strategic intelligence briefing for a presidential candidate, organized by ODNI as part of the presidential transition process, as an opportunity to gather potentially relevant investigative information about or from a staff member who is the subject of an FBI investigation. SSA 1 responded that he did not recall if there were any such discussions, but that if there were, they would have occurred at levels above him. He also told us that he did not personally have any concerns with the plan.

According to Baker, discussions about using SSA 1 as the FBI briefer did occur at higher levels. Baker told us that he recalled these discussions included himself, McCabe, Priestap, Strzok, possibly Lisa Page, and the FBI's then Executive Assistant Director of the National Security Branch. Baker said the decision to use SSA 1 for the briefing was reached by consensus within this group. Baker told us that he did not raise any concerns about using SSA 1 as the briefer because "[h]e was not there to induce anybody to say anything.... He was not there to do an undercover operation or...elicit some type of statement or testimony.... He was there on the off chance that somebody said something that might be useful." From Baker's perspective, the benefit of having SSA 1 at the briefing was to pick up on

---

[478] SSA 1 also provided the FBI security briefings on behalf of the FBI to Kaine and Pence, but not to the campaigns' staffs.

any statements by the attendees that might have relevance to the Crossfire Hurricane investigation:

> [I]f somebody said something, you want someone in the room who knew enough about the investigation that they would be able to understand the significance of something, or some type of statement, whereas...a regular briefer who didn't know anything about that might just let it go, and it might not even register with them. And so...that was the reason to have [SSA 1] there.

We asked Baker whether he recalled any discussion about the potential chilling effect on, and the FBI's participation in, future presidential transition briefings if the FBI's use of SSA 1 in this manner became known. Baker told us that he did not recall that issue being discussed, and added that the use of SSA 1 was focused on the FBI's counterintelligence investigation and Russian activities, including any directed at the Trump campaign; it was not the intention to collect any "political intelligence about campaign strategy, about campaign personalities, or anything that could be used in any political way."

We asked McCabe about his knowledge of the ODNI strategic intelligence briefings of the presidential campaigns and the decision to use SSA 1 as the FBI briefer because of SSA 1's role in the Crossfire Hurricane investigation. McCabe told us that ODNI was primarily responsible for providing national security threat briefings, and that the FBI was given a limited period of time in this instance to cover what it needed to address. He told us that he could not recall if he was aware in advance of the briefing that SSA 1 would attend for the FBI, or why SSA 1 was selected. McCabe acknowledged that it was possible he was part of a conversation about whether SSA 1 should handle the briefing because of his involvement with Crossfire Hurricane, but said he could not recall any such conversation. Asked whether he was aware there was an investigative purpose for SSA 1 handling the briefing, McCabe told us that he did not recall such a conversation and was not aware there was an investigative purpose for SSA 1 attending.

SSA 1 told us that he recalled Strzok being primarily responsible for providing SSA 1 with instruction on how to handle the FBI's portion of the ODNI strategic intelligence briefings, but that others also assisted, including the Intel Section Chief and possibly Lisa Page. SSA 1 did not recall Priestap having any role. SSA 1 told us that he believed he and Strzok created the briefing outline together, and that he prepared himself through mock briefings attended by Strzok, Lisa Page, the Intel Section Chief, and possibly the OGC Unit Chief. According to SSA 1, the briefing outline was not tailored to serve the investigative interests of Crossfire Hurricane and there was nothing he did differently for the Trump briefing as compared to the Clinton briefing: "that was one of the things that was very key. [The briefings] needed to be consistent."

The OIG reviewed the briefing outline prepared by SSA 1 and Strzok. According to the outline, the purpose of the briefing was to "give [the recipients] a baseline on the presence and threat posed by Foreign Intelligence Services to the

National Security of the U.S." The outline described the type of information that Foreign Intelligence Services (FIS) seek to obtain, the presence of FIS intelligence officers in the United States, and the primary methodologies FIS intelligence officers use to collect information. The outline also identified the Russian FIS and the Chinese as posing the greatest threat to the United States and described generally the difference in how the two countries conduct intelligence operations.

SSA 1 told us that he was the only FBI representative at the ODNI briefing on August 17, 2016, which was attended by Trump, Flynn, and another Trump campaign advisor. According to SSA 1, he understood the ODNI briefing would take about 2 hours to complete and that SSA 1 would have about 10 minutes to conduct the FBI's security briefing. After completing his briefing, SSA 1 said he remained for the duration of the ODNI briefing. About a week after the briefing, SSA 1 communicated separately with the OGC Attorney and Strzok about whether to formally document the briefing. There was agreement that he should. SSA 1 told us that given the "[b]ig stakes" involved, it was important to document the interaction with the subject of an FBI investigation so that there was a clear record of what was said. There was also agreement that an Electronic Communication (EC) instead of an FD-302 was the better document form to use because the briefing was not an interview and there was nothing testimonial to memorialize.

The August 30, 2016 EC was drafted by SSA 1 and approved by Strzok and the OGC Attorney. The 3-page document describes the purpose, location, and attendees of the briefing. It states that the FBI security briefing lasted approximately 13 minutes, and describes how one of the ODNI briefers initiated the briefing, explained the ground rules, and introduced SSA 1. The EC then recounts in summary fashion the briefing SSA 1 provided. In this regard, the EC is consistent with the outline of the briefing described above. Woven into the briefing summary are questions posed to SSA 1 by Trump and Flynn, and SSA 1's responses, as well as comments made by Trump and Flynn.

Other than identifying the ODNI briefers and the length of the ODNI strategic intelligence briefing, the EC does not contain any details about the information that was provided by ODNI. With regard to comments made by Trump or Flynn during the ODNI briefing, the EC describes two questions asked by Trump. SSA 1 told us that Flynn made comments during exchanges with the ODNI briefers on many subjects unrelated to Russia that SSA 1 did not document because the information was not pertinent to any FBI interests. SSA 1 told us that he documented those instances where he was engaged by the attendees, as well as anything related to the FBI or pertinent to the FBI Crossfire Hurricane investigation, such as comments about the Russian Federation. SSA 1 said that he also documented information that may not have been relevant at the time he recorded it, but might prove relevant in the future. After completing the EC, SSA 1 added it to the Crossfire Hurricane case file.[479]

---

[479] FBI records indicate the EC was uploaded to the FBI's Sentinel case management system on August 30, 2016.

With respect to the FBI security briefings SSA 1 provided to Clinton, Kaine, and Pence, SSA 1 told us that he did not memorialize those briefings in writing because the attendees did not include a subject of an FBI investigation.[480] He also told us that there was nothing from the other briefings that was of investigative value to the Crossfire Hurricane team; had there been, he said he would have documented it. We also asked SSA 1 whether he participated in any post-presidential election transition briefings.[481] He told us that he did not and that he would be surprised if the FBI provided any such briefings that included Flynn without SSA 1's knowledge.

We identified no Department or FBI policies or procedures regarding the handling of presidential transition briefings, and no requirement that Department leadership be consulted before using a presidential transition briefing, or a defensive briefing, for possible investigative purposes. Because we believe doing so presents important policy issues, we make a recommendation in Chapter Eleven that addresses this issue.

---

[480] We identified text messages between Strzok and Lisa Page from November 2016 suggesting the FBI may have considered using a connection between a then member of Pence's staff and an FBI employee in some manner to further the Crossfire Hurricane investigation. We asked SSA 1 about this. He said that he had been told of the connection but did not personally know the FBI employee, and that he did not change his approach to Pence's FBI security briefing because of the connection. He also said he could not recall any discussions about using the connection to further the Crossfire Hurricane investigation, and we did not find any evidence that it was used.

[481] On September 2, 2016, ODNI provided a second strategic intelligence briefing to Trump, Flynn, and another Trump campaign advisor. We found no evidence that SSA 1 or anyone from the FBI attended this briefing, although instant messages indicate that the FBI had contacted ODNI about including SSA 1 at the briefing.

CHAPTER ELEVEN
ANALYSIS

In this chapter, we provide the OIG's analysis of the events described in Chapter Three through Chapter Ten. We divide our analysis into five sections. In Section I, we discuss whether the opening of the Crossfire Hurricane investigation and four related investigations, and whether certain early investigative techniques used by the FBI, complied with the requirements of the Attorney General's Guidelines for Domestic FBI Operations (AG Guidelines) and the FBI's Domestic Investigations and Operations Guide (DIOG).

In Section II, we analyze the role of Christopher Steele's election reporting in the four Carter Page Foreign Intelligence Surveillance Act (FISA) applications and the numerous instances in which factual representations in those applications were inaccurate, incomplete, or unsupported by appropriate documentation, based upon information the FBI had in its possession at the time the applications were filed. In Section III, we analyze the FBI's handling of Christopher Steele and his election reporting, and whether the FBI's receipt and use of his reporting during the Crossfire Hurricane investigation complied with FBI Confidential Human Source (CHS) policies and procedures.

Section IV examines issues relating to Department attorney Bruce Ohr's interactions with Steele, Glenn Simpson, the FBI, and the State Department during the Crossfire Hurricane investigation, as well as whether the work Ohr's spouse performed for Simpson's firm implicated any ethical rules applicable to Ohr. We also analyze Ohr's interactions with Department attorneys and FBI officials concerning the Department's criminal investigation of Paul Manafort.

Lastly, in Section V, we focus on the FBI's use of CHSs, other than Steele, and Undercover Employees (UCEs) in the Crossfire Hurricane investigation and analyze whether the Crossfire Hurricane team's use of such individuals complied with Department and FBI policies. We also analyze the attendance of an FBI Supervisory Special Agent (SSA) assigned to the Crossfire Hurricane investigation at counterintelligence briefings given to the 2016 presidential candidates and certain campaign advisors.

As we explained in Chapter One, we did not analyze all of the decisions in the Crossfire Hurricane investigation. Rather, we reviewed the topics described above. Moreover, our role in this review was not to second-guess discretionary judgments by Department personnel about whether to open an investigation, or specific judgment calls made during the course of an investigation, where those decisions complied with or were authorized by Department rules, policies, or procedures. We do not criticize particular decisions merely because we might have recommended a different investigative strategy or tactic based on the facts learned during our investigation. The question we considered was not whether a particular investigative decision was ideal or could have been handled more effectively, but rather whether the Department and the FBI complied with applicable legal requirements, policies, and procedures in taking the actions we reviewed, or, alternatively, whether the circumstances surrounding a decision indicated that it was based on inaccurate or incomplete information, or considerations other than the merits of the investigation. If the explanations we were given for a particular decision were consistent with legal requirements, policies, and procedures, and were not unreasonable, we did not conclude that the decision was based on improper considerations in the absence of documentary or testimonial evidence to the contrary.

I.   The Opening of Crossfire Hurricane and Four Related Counterintelligence Investigations

In this section, we examine the opening of Crossfire Hurricane and four related counterintelligence investigations of individuals associated with the Donald J. Trump for President Campaign. Specifically, we analyze whether, in opening these investigations, the FBI complied with the requirements set forth in the AG Guidelines and the DIOG.

The applicable provisions of the AG Guidelines and the DIOG require that FBI investigations be undertaken for an "authorized purpose"—that is, "to detect, obtain information about, or prevent or protect against federal crimes or threats to the national security or to collect foreign intelligence." The AG Guidelines also require that FBI investigations have adequate factual predication—that is, allegations, reports, facts, or circumstances indicative of possible criminal activity or a national security threat. In addition, for investigations designated as Sensitive Investigative Matters (SIMs), such as Crossfire Hurricane, the DIOG imposes special approval and notification requirements when opening such a matter. The DIOG also emphasizes that investigators take particular care to consider whether a planned investigative activity is the least intrusive method and is reasonably based upon the needs of the investigation.

As described in Chapter Three, on July 31, 2016, the FBI's Counterintelligence Division (CD) opened a Full Investigation titled "Crossfire Hurricane" to determine whether individual(s) associated with the Trump campaign were "witting of and/or coordinating activities with the Government of Russia." The opening of the investigation occurred days after WikiLeaks publicly released hacked emails from the Democratic National Committee (DNC). According to the FBI Electronic Communication (EC) documenting the decision, the investigation was opened in response to information CD officials received on July 28, 2016, from a Friendly Foreign Government (FFG) indicating that in a May 2016 meeting with the FFG, George Papadopoulos, an advisor to the Trump campaign, "suggested the Trump team had received some kind of a suggestion" from Russia that it could assist in the election process with the anonymous release of information during the campaign that would be damaging to candidate Clinton and President Obama. We did not find information in FBI or Department emails, or other documents, or through witness testimony, indicating that any information other than the FFG information was relied upon to predicate the opening of the Crossfire Hurricane investigation. However, as noted below, the FBI received the FFG information at a time when it had reason to believe that Russia may have been connected to the

WikiLeaks disclosures that occurred earlier in July 2016, and when the U.S. Intelligence Community (USIC), including the FBI, was aware of Russia's efforts to interfere with 2016 U.S. elections.

In the following weeks, the FBI also opened related counterintelligence investigations into four individuals associated with the Trump campaign—Papadopoulos, Carter Page, Michael Flynn, and Paul Manafort—because the FBI identified these individuals as having alleged ties to Russia or a history of travel to Russia.

We concluded that the FBI's decision to open Crossfire Hurricane and the four related individual investigations was, under Department and FBI policy, a discretionary judgment call and that the FBI's exercise of discretion was in compliance with those policies. For the reasons described below, we found that each investigation was opened for an authorized purpose and, in light of the low threshold established by Department and FBI predication policy, with adequate factual predication. We also found that the FBI satisfied the DIOG's notification and approval requirements for designating Crossfire Hurricane and the four related individual investigations as SIMs. Nevertheless, we were concerned about the limited notice requirements under Department and FBI policy before opening investigations such as these, relating to constitutionally protected activity occurring during a national presidential campaign. We were also concerned about the limited notice requirements before using more intrusive investigative techniques that could impact constitutionally protected activity. Accordingly, we make several recommendations below to address these concerns.

A. Authorized Purpose

The AG Guidelines and the DIOG both require that FBI investigations be undertaken for an "authorized purpose"—that is, "to detect, obtain information about, or prevent or protect against federal crimes or threats to the national security or to collect foreign intelligence." Under both the AG Guidelines and the DIOG, the FBI may not undertake an investigation for the sole purpose of monitoring activities protected by the First Amendment or to interfere with the lawful exercise of other rights secured by the Constitution or laws of the United States. However, both the AG Guidelines and the DIOG permit the FBI to conduct an investigation, even if it might impact First Amendment or other constitutionally protected activity, so long as there is a legitimate law enforcement purpose associated with the investigation.

We concluded that, under the AG Guidelines and the DIOG, the FBI had an authorized purpose when it opened Crossfire Hurricane to obtain information about, or to protect against, a national security threat or federal crime, even though the investigation also had the potential to impact constitutionally protected activity. The FBI's opening EC referenced the Foreign Agents Registration Act (FARA) and stated, "[b]ased on the information provided by [the FBI Legal Attaché], this investigation is being opened to determine whether individual(s) associated with the Trump campaign are witting of and/or coordinating activities with the Government of Russia." We found that the FBI opened the Crossfire Hurricane investigation shortly after officials in CD received the FFG information on July 28. The opening EC documented the pertinent FFG information verbatim and described relevant background information. All of the senior FBI officials who participated in the discussions about whether to open a case told us the information from the FFG warranted investigation. For example, the FBI's then Deputy General Counsel told us that the FBI "would have been derelict in our responsibilities had we not opened the case," because a foreign power allegedly colluding with a presidential candidate or his campaign was a threat to our nation that the FBI was obligated to investigate under its counterintelligence mission.

Then CD Assistant Director E.W. "Bill" Priestap, who approved opening the case, told us that the combination of the FFG information and the FBI's ongoing cyber intrusion investigation into the July 2016 hacks of the DNC's emails created a counterintelligence concern that the FBI was "obligated" to investigate. Priestap also told us that, prior to making the final decision to approve the opening of Crossfire Hurricane, he considered whether the FBI should conduct defensive briefings for the Trump campaign about the information from the FFG. However, Priestap ultimately decided that providing such briefings created the risk that "if someone on the campaign was engaged with the Russians, he/she would very likely change his/her tactics and/or otherwise seek to cover-up his/her activities, thereby preventing us from finding the truth." We did not identify any Department or FBI policy that applied to this decision and therefore determined that the decision whether to conduct defensive briefings in lieu of opening an investigation, or at any time during an investigation, was a judgment call that is left to the discretion of FBI officials.[482]

As part of our review, we sought to determine whether there was evidence that political bias or other improper considerations affected decision making in Crossfire Hurricane, including the decision to open the investigation. Such evidence would raise questions as to whether Crossfire Hurricane was opened for an authorized purpose, and serious concerns about whether the decision compromised the constitutional rights of any U.S. persons. We discussed the issue of political bias in a prior OIG report, *Review of Various Actions in Advance of the 2016 Election*, where we described text messages between then Special Counsel to the Deputy Director Lisa Page and then Section Chief Peter Strzok, among others. These text messages included statements of hostility toward then candidate Trump and statements of support for then candidate Hillary Clinton. These messages, most of which pertained to the Russia investigation, potentially indicated or created the appearance that investigative decisions were impacted by bias or improper considerations. Our prior review stated that the text messages were "not only

---

[482] Later in this chapter, we recommend that the Department and FBI evaluate which types of sensitive investigative matters should require advance notification to a senior Department official, such as the Deputy Attorney General, in addition to the notifications currently required for such matters, especially for opening investigations that implicate core First Amendment activity and raise policy considerations or heighten enterprise risk. Such a requirement would not only give senior Department leadership the opportunity to consider the constitutional and prudential issues associated with opening certain investigations but also the opportunity to consult with the FBI about whether to conduct a defensive briefing in a circumstance such as this one.

indicative of a biased state of mind but, even more seriously, impl[y] a willingness to take official action to impact [Trump's] electoral prospects." For example, on July 31, 2016, in connection with the formal opening of Crossfire Hurricane, Strzok texted Page: "And damn this feels momentous. Because this matters. The [Clinton email investigation] did, too, but that was to ensure we didn't F something up. This matters because this MATTERS. So super glad to be on this voyage with you." Additionally, on August 8, 2016, Page sent a text message to Strzok that stated, "[Trump's] not ever going to become president, right? Right?!" Strzok responded, "No. No he's not. We'll stop it." Although we did not find in our prior report any documentary or testimonial evidence directly connecting the political views stated in the text messages to the specific investigative actions in Midyear that we reviewed, we concluded that Strzok's text messages with Page indicated or created the appearance of bias against Trump. We further concluded that the messages raised serious questions about the propriety of any investigative decisions in which Strzok and Lisa Page played a role. Because several of these inappropriate and troubling messages occurred at or near the time of the opening of Crossfire Hurricane, we closely reviewed the roles of Strzok and Lisa Page in the investigation's opening and whether there was any documentary or testimonial evidence that their views impacted the decision to open the investigation.

We found that while she attended some of the discussions, Lisa Page did not play a role in the decision to open Crossfire Hurricane or the four individual cases. Strzok was directly involved in the decisions to open Crossfire Hurricane and the four individual cases, but we found that he was not the sole, or even the highest level decision maker as to any of those matters. Priestap, Strzok's supervisor, told us that ultimately he was the official who made the decision to open the Crossfire Hurricane investigation, and Strzok then prepared and approved the formal documentation, as required by the DIOG. Evidence reflected that this decision by Priestap was reached by consensus after multiple days of discussions and meetings that included Strzok and other leadership in CD, the FBI Deputy Director, the FBI General Counsel, and the FBI Deputy General Counsel. We similarly found that the decisions to open the four individual cases were reached by consensus of Crossfire Hurricane agents and analysts who identified individuals associated with the Trump campaign who had recently travelled to Russia or had other alleged ties to Russia, and that Priestap was involved in those decisions. The formal documentation opening each of these four investigations was approved by Strzok, as required by the DIOG.

We did not find documentary or testimonial evidence that political bias or improper motivation influenced Priestap's decision to open Crossfire Hurricane. The evidence also showed that FBI officials responsible for and involved in the case opening decisions were unanimous in their belief that, together with the July 2016 release by WikiLeaks of hacked DNC emails, the Papadopoulos statement described in the FFG information reflected the Russian government's potential next step to interfere with the 2016 U.S. elections. These FBI officials were similarly unanimous in their belief that the FFG information represented a threat to national security that warranted further investigation by the FBI. Witnesses told us that they did not recall observing during these discussions any instances or indications of improper motivations or political bias on the part of the participants, including Strzok.

We also reviewed the text messages and emails of each of the FBI officials, in addition to Strzok, who participated in the decision to open Crossfire Hurricane and the four individual cases, and did not identify any statements in those communications that indicated or suggested the decision could have been affected by political bias or other improper considerations. We also reviewed other contemporaneous documents, such as meeting notes, and asked witnesses who were not involved in the decision to open Crossfire Hurricane but who were familiar with the predication for the case for any evidence of political bias or improper motivation in the FBI's decision making. Again, we found no such evidence, including from Department officials briefed about Crossfire Hurricane subsequent to it being opened. These officials also did not express any concerns about the FBI's decision to open the investigation. By way of example, David Laufman, then Chief of the National Security Division's (NSD) Counterintelligence and Export Control Section (CES), told us that it would have been "a dereliction of duty and responsibility of the highest order not to commit the appropriate resources as urgently as possible to run these facts to the ground, and find out what was going on."

We therefore concluded the FBI met the requirement in the AG Guidelines and the DIOG that Crossfire Hurricane be opened for an "authorized purpose," namely "to detect, obtain information about, or prevent or protect against federal crimes or threats to the national security or to collect foreign intelligence." We also determined that, although the investigation had the potential to impact constitutionally protected activity, the FBI's decision to open the investigation was permissible under both Department and FBI policies because there was a legitimate law enforcement purpose associated with the investigation. Nevertheless, we believe that investigations affecting core First Amendment activity and national political campaigns raise significant constitutional and prudential issues and therefore we recommend below that Department policy require advance notification to a senior Department official, such as the Deputy Attorney General (DAG), before a Department component opens such an investigation so that Department leadership can consider these issues from the outset.

B.   Factual Predication

In addition to requiring an authorized purpose, Department and FBI policy also mandate that each case have adequate factual predication before being initiated. The predication requirement is not a legal requirement but rather a prudential one imposed by Department and FBI policy. For example, the Supreme Court has held that the Department and FBI can lawfully open a federal criminal grand jury investigation even in the absence of predication. *See United States* v. *Morton Salt*, 338 U.S. 632, 642-43 (1950) (a grand jury "can investigate merely on suspicion that the law is being violated, or even just because it wants assurance that it is not"); *see also United States* v. *R. Enterprises*, 498 U.S. 292, 297 (1991).

The AG Guidelines generally describe predication as allegations, reports, facts, or circumstances indicative of possible criminal activity or a national security threat, or the potential for acquiring information responsive to foreign intelligence collection requirements. For full counterintelligence investigations such as Crossfire Hurricane and the four related individual investigations, Section II.B.4 of the AG Guidelines and Section 7 of the DIOG state that the required level of predication is an "articulable factual basis" that "reasonably indicates" that any one of three defined circumstances exists, including:

> An activity constituting a federal crime or a threat to the national security has or may have occurred, is or may be occurring, or will or may occur and the investigation may obtain information relating to the activity or the involvement or role of an individual, group, or organization in such activity.[483]

The AG Guidelines and the DIOG do not provide heightened predication standards for sensitive matters, or for allegations potentially impacting constitutionally protected activity, such as First Amendment rights. Rather, as we discuss below, the approval and notification requirements contained in the AG Guidelines and DIOG are, in part, intended to provide the means by which such concerns can be considered by senior officials.

In Crossfire Hurricane, the "articulable factual basis" set forth in the opening EC was the FFG information received from an FBI Legal Attaché stating that Papadopoulos had suggested during a meeting in May 2016 with officials from a "trusted foreign partner" that the Trump team had received some kind of suggestion from Russia that it could assist by releasing information damaging to candidate Clinton and President Obama.[484] Additionally, by July 31, 2016, although not specifically mentioned in the EC, the FBI had reason to believe that Russia may have been connected to the WikiLeaks disclosures that occurred earlier in July 2016. Further, as we note in Chapter Three, the FBI received the FFG information at a time when the USIC, including the FBI, was aware of Russia's efforts to interfere with the 2016 U.S. elections. Given the low threshold for predication in

---

[483] As detailed in Chapter Two, the DIOG separately provides that a Preliminary Investigation may be opened based upon "any allegation or information" indicative of possible criminal activity or threats to the national security. In cases opened as Preliminary Investigations, the DIOG provides that all lawful investigative methods (including CHS and UCE operations) may be used except for mail opening, physical searches requiring a search warrant, electronic surveillance requiring a judicial order or warrant (Title III wiretap or a FISA order), or requests under Title VII of FISA. A Preliminary Investigation may be converted to a Full Investigation if the available information provides predication for a Full Investigation.

[484] Papadopoulos has stated that the source of the information he shared with the FFG was a professor from London, Joseph Mifsud, and has raised the possibility that Mifsud may have been working with the FBI. As described in Chapter Ten of this report, the OIG searched the FBI's database of Confidential Human Sources (CHSs) and did not find any records indicating that Mifsud was an FBI CHS, or that Mifsud's discussions with Papadopoulos were part of any FBI operation. The FBI also requested information on ██

the AG Guidelines and the DIOG, we concluded that the FFG information, provided by a government the USIC deems trustworthy, and describing a first-hand account from an FFG employee of the content of a conversation with Papadopoulos, was sufficient to predicate the full counterintelligence investigation because it provided the FBI an articulable factual basis that, if true, reasonably indicated activity constituting either a federal crime or a threat to national security may have occurred or may be occurring.[485]

We similarly concluded that the FBI had sufficient predication to open full counterintelligence investigations of Papadopoulos, Page, Flynn, and Manafort in August 2016. The investigation of Papadopoulos was predicated upon his alleged statements in May 2016 to an employee of the FFG. According to the opening EC, Papadopoulos was "identical to the individual who made statements indicating that he is knowledgeable that the Russians made a suggestion to the Trump team that they could assist the Trump campaign with an anonymous release of information during the campaign that would be damaging to the Clinton campaign." The three other cases were predicated on information developed by the Crossfire Hurricane team through law enforcement database and open source searches, conducted to determine which individuals associated with the Trump campaign may have been in a position to have received the alleged offer of assistance from Russia. As described in Chapter Three, through these efforts, the Crossfire Hurricane team identified three individuals—Page, Manafort, and Flynn—associated with the Trump campaign with either ties to Russia or a history of travel to Russia, two of whom (Page and Manafort) were already the subjects of open FBI investigations pertaining to, in part, their Russia-related activities. The FBI determined that this information, taken together with the information from the FFG indicating Russia had made a suggestion to the Trump team that it could assist by releasing information damaging to candidate Clinton, stated an articulable factual basis reasonably indicating activity may be occurring that may constitute a federal crime or a threat to national security. As with the opening of Crossfire Hurricane, we concluded that the quantum of information articulated by the FBI to open these individual investigations was sufficient to satisfy the low threshold established by Department and FBI predication policy, particularly in the context of the FBI's separate and ongoing investigative efforts to address Russian interference in 2016 U.S. elections.

C.   Sensitive Investigative Matters (SIMs)

We concluded that the FBI appropriately designated Crossfire Hurricane and each of the four individual counterintelligence investigations as SIMs, or Sensitive

---

[485] We determined that the election reporting from Christopher Steele played no role in the opening of Crossfire Hurricane. As described in Chapter Four, while some individuals in the FBI, including Steele's handling agent, had received Steele's election reporting as early as July 2016, the CD officials at FBI Headquarters and the members of the Crossfire Hurricane team did not receive the first Steele reports until September 19—weeks after the Crossfire Hurricane investigation was opened—and were not aware of any of the information in the reports prior to that date. We also found no evidence that the FBI undertook any investigative activities directed at the Trump campaign or members of the Trump campaign before opening Crossfire Hurricane on July 31, 2016. As described in Chapters Three and Nine, the FBI had ongoing investigations of Paul Manafort and Carter Page at that time, which were unrelated to the information that predicated Crossfire Hurricane.

Investigative Matters. As described in Chapter Two, a SIM is an investigative matter that must be approved for opening by FBI management and brought to the attention of Department officials because of the possibility of public notoriety and sensitivity. The categories of matters designated as SIMs include investigations involving the activities of a domestic political organization or an individual prominent in such an organization. Under the DIOG's definition, the term "domestic political organization" includes a committee or group formed to elect an individual to public office. Moreover, if an assessment or predicated investigation concerns a person prominent in a "domestic political organization" but not the political organization itself, it nonetheless must be treated as a SIM.

For Crossfire Hurricane, the FBI believed that any potential subjects of the investigation would be "prominent" members of a political campaign. With the four individual cases, the FBI determined that the individuals identified as subjects—foreign policy advisors Page, Papadopoulos, and Flynn; and campaign manager Manafort—were "prominent" in the Trump political campaign. We found the decision to designate the cases as SIMs to be appropriate. However, as discussed later in this chapter, our interviews with certain FBI agents revealed significant confusion over the meaning of the phrase "prominent within a domestic political organization" in the context of the policies applicable to CHSs, with some agents interpreting that phrase as limited to a person "running for office," and other agents questioning whether a presidential campaign was a "domestic political organization." We recommend later in this chapter that the FBI establish guidance to better define this phrase with respect to CHS use. Because the phrase is also used in FBI policies applicable to SIMs, we recommend that any additional guidance also take into account and be applied to the SIM requirements.

We also determined that the FBI satisfied the DIOG's approval and notification requirements for SIMs. At the FBI, these requirements included review of the opening by the FBI Office of the General Counsel (OGC), which in this case was conducted by the OGC Unit Chief; and approval by the FBI Headquarters operational Section Chief, which was provided here by then Section Chief Strzok. The DIOG also requires that NSD be notified of the opening of a SIM. The FBI satisfied this requirement by briefing NSD officials in the Counterintelligence and Export Control Section—orally, due to the sensitivity of the cases—about the openings within days of the investigations being initiated.[486]

Although the FBI satisfied the approval and notification requirements for SIMs, we believe such sensitive cases should also include advance notice to Department senior management officials, especially for case openings such as this one that implicated core First Amendment activity and a national political campaign. The FBI did not formally brief anyone in Department leadership at the time that Crossfire Hurricane was opened. While the then FBI Deputy Director was aware of

---

[486] Technically, the DIOG's notice requirement for cases designated as a SIM provides that notice be emailed to a NSD email account within 30 days of the case opening. As described in Chapter Three, the Crossfire Hurricane team orally briefed NSD and Department officials on two occasions within days of the case opening rather than email notice to a general email account due to the sensitivity of the cases.

and gave his approval for the investigation prior to its opening, the investigation—concerning the actions of individuals associated with a presidential campaign—could have been opened, consistent with FBI and Department policy, without any notice to FBI or Department leadership and based solely on the decision of an FBI Headquarters Section Chief, with review by FBI OGC and notice to an "appropriate NSD official." As noted in Chapter Two, current Department and FBI policies require high-level notice and approval in other circumstances where investigative activity could substantially impact certain civil liberties. The purpose of such notice and approval is to allow senior Department officials to consider the potential constitutional and prudential implications of opening certain investigations, even where there is sufficient predication to do so. Accordingly, we recommend that the Department and FBI evaluate which types of SIMs should require advance notification to a senior Department official, such as the DAG, in addition to the notifications currently required for SIMs, especially for cases that implicate core First Amendment activity and a national political campaign, and establish, as necessary, implementing policies and guidance.

D. Staffing of Investigation

Due to the sensitivity of the investigation, FBI leadership initially ran the investigation out of FBI Headquarters, rather than out of one or more field offices as is typically done in FBI investigations. We found that the decision to run the investigation out of FBI Headquarters created challenges for the team, which we were told were known risks consciously taken by CD officials, including Priestap, in order to minimize the potential of an unauthorized public disclosure of the investigation and allow for better coordination with Headquarters and interagency partners. These challenges included difficulties in obtaining needed investigative resources, such as surveillance teams, electronic evidence storage, technically trained agents, and other investigative assets standard in field offices to support investigations. Additionally, the FBI had to detail agents to FBI Headquarters from field offices for 90-day temporary duty assignments (TDYs). Then, when these 90-day TDY assignments expired, new agents were detailed to FBI Headquarters, resulting in three iterations of Crossfire Hurricane teams and supervisors from July 31, 2016, to the transfer of the case to the Special Counsel's Office in May 2017.

We found that this ad hoc staffing presented challenges compared to the established chain of command structure that exists in FBI field offices. The turnover of agents and supervisors resulted in a loss of institutional knowledge and a lack of communication among agents, analysts, and supervisors. While we did not find that conducting the investigation from FBI Headquarters was the cause of the problematic issues we identify in this report, witnesses we interviewed told us that investigating Crossfire Hurricane from FBI Headquarters created significant challenges. We therefore recommend that the FBI develop specific protocols and guidelines for staffing and running any future sensitive investigations from FBI Headquarters.

E.   Least Intrusive Investigative Techniques

The AG Guidelines and the DIOG require that the "least intrusive" means or method be "considered" when selecting investigative techniques and, "if reasonable based upon the circumstances of the investigation," be used to obtain information instead of a more intrusive method. The least intrusive method principle reflects an attempt to balance the FBI's ability to effectively conduct investigations with the potential negative impact an investigation can have on the privacy and civil liberties of individuals encompassed within an investigation. The DIOG emphasizes that in the context of cases designated as SIMs, particular care should be taken when considering whether the planned course of action is the least intrusive method if reasonable based upon the circumstances of the investigation. However, DIOG § 4.1.1 states that investigators "must not hesitate to use any lawful method consistent with the [AG Guidelines] when the degree of intrusiveness is warranted in light of the seriousness of the matter concerned." According to DIOG § 4.4.5, "[i]n the final analysis, choosing the method that [most] appropriately balances the impact on privacy and civil liberties with operational needs, is a matter of judgment, based on training and experience."

As described in Chapter Three, immediately after opening the investigation, the Crossfire Hurricane team submitted name trace requests to other U.S. government agencies and a foreign intelligence agency, and conducted law enforcement database and open source searches, to identify individuals associated with the Trump campaign in a position to have received the alleged offer of assistance from Russia. Members of the Crossfire Hurricane team told us that they avoided the use of compulsory legal process to obtain information at this time in order to prevent any public disclosure of the investigation's existence and to avoid any potential impact on the election. The FBI also sent Strzok and an SSA to a European city to interview the source of the information the FBI received from the FFG, and also searched the FBI's CHS database to identify sources who potentially could provide information about connections between individuals associated with the Trump campaign and Russia. Each of these early steps is authorized under the DIOG and was a less intrusive investigative technique.

After the FBI opened the four individual cases based on information obtained through the above-described efforts, the Crossfire Hurricane team used CHSs to interact and consensually record conversations with two of the investigative subjects—Page and Papadopoulos—on multiple occasions in an effort to obtain specific information relevant to the allegations. The FBI also used a CHS to consensually record a conversation with a high-level Trump campaign official who was not a subject of the Crossfire Hurricane investigation. Use of a CHS to conduct consensual monitoring is a more intrusive investigative technique than the ones used immediately after Crossfire Hurricane was opened, but is also one that FBI witnesses told us is commonly used in FBI counterintelligence investigations. For example, Priestap told the OIG that CHSs are an "ordinary investigative tool" that are "part and parcel of what [FBI] agents do in an investigative sense every day."[487]

As noted above, FBI policy provides that these decisions are matters of judgment to be made based on an investigator's training and experience. We found that, in making these judgments about using CHSs to interact with investigative subjects, the Crossfire Hurricane team complied with applicable Department and FBI policies for these operations, and obtained all requisite approvals. Although the CHS operations implicated constitutionally protected activity, we found no evidence that they were undertaken solely for the purpose of monitoring constitutionally protected activity, which is prohibited by the DIOG. We also found no testimonial or documentary evidence that these operations resulted from political bias or other improper considerations. We therefore concluded that these early investigative activities undertaken by the Crossfire Hurricane team were matters of judgment that were permitted by the AG Guidelines and the DIOG. However, as discussed later in this chapter, we are concerned that current Department and FBI policies do not require, at a minimum, consultation with the Department before using a CHS to monitor conversations with members of a major party candidate's presidential campaign, including a high-level campaign official who was not a subject of the investigation. Further, we are concerned that the FBI did not have a plan or process in place to address what the team should have done in the event a CHS operation resulted in the FBI's incidental receipt of sensitive campaign information. Accordingly, we make a recommendation below to ensure additional oversight, accountability, and consideration of the constitutional interests at stake in such operations.

In addition to these CHS operations, the FBI also discussed in August 2016, within days of opening the Carter Page investigation, the possible use of a separate, highly intrusive technique to obtain information: FISA-authorized electronic surveillance ███████████████ targeting Carter Page. According to Case Agent 1, the Crossfire Hurricane team had hoped that emails and other communications obtained through surveillance would help provide valuable information about what Page did while in Moscow in the previous month and the Russian officials with whom he may have spoken. As detailed in Chapter Five, the FBI ultimately did not seek a FISA order in August 2016 because OGC, NSD's Office of Intelligence (OI), or both determined that more evidence was needed to support a probable cause determination that Page was an agent of a foreign power.

As discussed below, after the Crossfire Hurricane team received the election reporting from Christopher Steele on September 19, they reinitiated discussions with OI and efforts to obtain authority for FISA surveillance ███████████████ targeting Page, which they received from the Foreign Intelligence Surveillance Court (FISC) on October ██. Because of the reviews and approvals required before submitting a FISA application to the FISC, the decision to seek to use this highly

---

[487] As we summarize in Chapter Ten, the consensual recordings done by the CHSs did not generate information tending to support the allegation that Page and Papadopoulos were, wittingly or unwittingly, providing assistance to Russia. Members of the Crossfire Hurricane team told us that the recordings nevertheless provided important background information about the subjects.

intrusive investigative technique was reviewed and approved at multiple levels of the Department, including by then DAG Sally Yates for the initial FISA application and first renewal and by then Acting Attorney General Dana Boente and then DAG Rod Rosenstein for the second and third renewals. However, as we explain in the next section, the Crossfire Hurricane team failed to inform the Department of significant information that was available to the team at the time that the FISA applications, including the first application, were drafted and filed. Much of that information was inconsistent with, or undercut, the allegations contained in the FISA applications to support probable cause and, in some instances, resulted in inaccurate information being included in the applications. Accordingly, we questioned the judgment and performance of members of the Crossfire Hurricane team involved in the FISA applications, and determined that, as a result of their actions, senior Department officials authorized the FBI to seek to use this highly intrusive investigative technique targeting Carter Page based on significant omissions and inaccurate information in the initial and renewal FISA applications. While we do not speculate whether senior Department officials would have authorized the FBI to seek to use FISA authority had they been made aware of all relevant information, it was clearly the responsibility of Crossfire Hurricane team members to advise Department officials of such critical information so that they could have made a fully informed decision.

II.   The FISA Applications

In this section, we analyze the role of Christopher Steele's election reporting in the four Carter Page FISA applications filed with the FISC. Additionally, we detail and analyze the numerous instances in which factual representations in the applications were inaccurate, incomplete, or unsupported by appropriate documentation, based upon information the FBI had in its possession at the time the applications were filed.

As described in Chapter Five, within days of opening the Carter Page and George Papadopoulos cases on August 10, 2016, the FBI first considered the possibility of seeking to obtain a FISA order authorizing electronic surveillance ████ ████████████ targeting Carter Page and George Papadopoulos. We found that the Crossfire Hurricane team initially focused its efforts on obtaining FISA authority targeting Page, more than on efforts to surveil Papadopoulos or other members of the Trump campaign, because of Page's prior contacts with known Russian intelligence officers, which the Crossfire Hurricane team believed would have made Page most susceptible, and most likely, to have received, the suggestion or offer of assistance reported in the FFG information.[488]

---

[488] As described in Chapter Five, although the Crossfire Hurricane team was also interested in seeking FISA surveillance targeting Papadopoulos, the FBI OGC attorneys were not supportive because the FBI had no information that Papadopoulos was being directed by the Russians. FBI and NSD officials told us that the Crossfire Hurricane team ultimately did not seek FISA surveillance of Papadopoulos. We were also told that the team also did not seek FISA surveillance of Manafort or Flynn, and we are aware of no information indicating that the Crossfire Hurricane team requested or seriously considered FISA surveillance of Manafort or Flynn.

We determined that, on August 15, 2016, Case Agent 1 sent a written summary by email to the OGC Unit Chief describing Page's Russian business and financial ties, his prior contacts with known Russian intelligence officers, and his recent travel to Russia. In this email, Case Agent 1 stated his belief that the information provided "a pretty solid basis" for requesting authority under FISA to conduct surveillance targeting Page. The next day, August 16, the OGC Unit Chief emailed Stuart Evans, then NSD's Deputy Assistant Attorney General with oversight responsibility over OI, to advise him of the possible FBI request for a FISA order to surveil Page. The email from the OGC Unit Chief stated that "I don't think we are quite there yet, but given the sensitivity and urgency of this matter, I would like to get OI involved as early as possible."

On or about August 17, 2016, in response to the Crossfire Hurricane team's prior Carter Page name trace request, the Crossfire Hurricane team received a memorandum from another U.S. government agency detailing its prior interactions with Page, including that Page had been approved as an "operational contact" for the other agency from 2008 to 2013.[489] The memorandum also detailed the information that Page had provided to the other agency concerning his prior contacts with certain Russian intelligence officers. As detailed in Chapters Five and Eight, the Crossfire Hurricane team did not accurately describe to OI the nature and extent of the information that the FBI received from the other agency, which we found was highly relevant to an evaluation of the FISA request.

Additionally, in August 2016, Page made statements to an FBI CHS that, if true, were in tension with the reporting the FBI received subsequently from Steele, alleging that Page was being used as an intermediary by Manafort to conspire with Russia. The FBI did not inform OI of Page's statements before any of the four FISA applications were filed, and did not inform OI of the CHS operation until June 2017, shortly before filing the last FISA application.

On or about August 22, 2016, a decision was made by the FBI OGC, OI, or both that more evidence was needed to support probable cause that Carter Page was an agent of a foreign power. The OGC ceased its discussions with OI about seeking a FISA order targeting Page. However, on September 19, 2016, the same day that the Crossfire Hurricane team first received Steele's election reporting, the team reinitiated discussions with OGC about seeking a FISA order authorizing surveillance targeting Page and specifically focused on Steele's reporting in drafting the FISA request. Two days later, on September 21, the OGC Unit Chief contacted the NSD OI Unit Chief to advise him that the FBI believed it was ready to submit a formal FISA request to OI relating to Page.

---

[489] As described in Chapter Five, according to the U.S. government agency, "operational contact," as that term is used in the memorandum about Page, provides "Contact Approval," which allows the agency to contact and discuss sensitive information with a U.S. Person and to collect information from that person via "passive debriefing," or debriefing a person of information that is within the knowledge of an individual and has been acquired through the normal course of that individual's activities. According to the U.S. government agency, a "Contact Approval" does not allow for operational use of a U.S. Person or tasking of that person.

Over the next several weeks, the FBI and OI prepared the FISA application targeting Carter Page, which was filed with the FISC on October █, 2016. The FISC granted the first FISA warrant the same day, authorizing electronic surveillance ███████████████ targeting Page for 90 days. As the Crossfire Hurricane investigation proceeded, the Department submitted three renewal applications with the FISC on January █, April █, and June █, 2017, seeking authority to continue electronic surveillance ████████████ targeting Carter Page. A different FISC judge considered each application before issuing the requested orders, which collectively resulted in approximately 11 months of FISA coverage from October █, 2016, until September █, 2017.

As noted above, in the OIG's June 2018 report, *Review of Various Actions in Advance of the 2016 Election*, we described text messages between Peter Strzok and Lisa Page discussing statements of hostility toward then candidate Trump and statements of support for candidate Clinton. Several of these text messages appeared to mix political opinions with discussions about the investigation into candidate Clinton's email use and refer to the Crossfire Hurricane investigation. As part of our review of the Carter Page FISA applications, we sought to determine whether there was evidence that Strzok or Page affected the preparation of or decision to file any of the applications. As described in Chapter Five, Strzok approved the request to expedite the FISA application proposed by the Crossfire Hurricane team, and he and Lisa Page communicated with Department officials, as did other FBI officials, in an effort to move the first application forward. This included conversations with NSD officials during which Strzok expressed frustration that the FISA process was not moving forward at the pace desired by the FBI. However, testimonial and documentary evidence we reviewed established that Strzok and Lisa Page played no role in the substantive preparation or approval of any of the four FISA applications, including the Woods process. We did not find documentary or testimonial evidence that political bias or improper motivation influenced the FBI's decision to seek FISA authority on Carter Page.

A.   The Role of the Steele Election Reporting in the Applications

We concluded that the Crossfire Hurricane team's receipt of Steele's election reporting on September 19, 2016, played a central and essential role in the decision by FBI OGC to support the request for FISA surveillance targeting Carter Page, as well as the Department's ultimate decision to seek the FISA order. In particular, the OGC Unit Chief told us that she thought probable cause was a "close call" when the team first proposed seeking a FISA in mid-August and separately when she discussed the idea with OI around the same time. She said that it was the Steele reporting received in September, concerning Page's alleged activities with Russian officials in the summer of 2016, that "pushed it over" the line in terms of establishing probable cause that Page was acting in concert with Russian officials. The OGC Unit Chief's testimony was consistent with the testimony of the OI Unit Chief who told us that the Steele reporting was "what kind of pushed it over the line" in terms of the FBI being ready to pursue FISA authority targeting Page. Contemporaneous handwritten notes from Case Agent 1 and the then Chief of NSD's Counterintelligence and Export Control Section similarly indicated that in late

August 2016 an assessment had been made, by FBI OGC, OI, or both, that the information known at that time did not establish probable cause.

In addition, we found no evidence of further discussions between the FBI and OI between late August and September 19 concerning the possibility of obtaining a FISA order targeting Page. We determined those discussions were effectively reinitiated on September 21, two days after the Crossfire Hurricane team's receipt of the Steele election reporting. At that time, FBI OGC attorneys advised OI of the reporting from Steele and said for the first time that the FBI was ready to move forward with a FISA application targeting Page. Further, we found that the first FISA application drew heavily, although not entirely, upon the Steele reporting to support the government's position that Page was an agent of a foreign power.

We found that the FBI's decision to rely upon Steele's election reporting to help establish probable cause that Page was an agent of Russia was a judgment reached initially by the case agents on the Crossfire Hurricane team. We further found that FBI officials at every level concurred with this judgment, from the OGC attorneys assigned to the investigation to senior CD officials, then FBI General Counsel James Baker, then Deputy Director Andrew McCabe, and then Director James Comey. FBI leadership supported relying on Steele's reporting to seek a FISA order authorizing surveillance targeting Page after being advised of, and giving consideration to, the concerns expressed by Evans that Steele may have been hired by someone associated with presidential candidate Clinton or the DNC, and that the foreign intelligence to be collected through the FISA order would probably not be worth the "risk" of being criticized later for collecting communications of someone (Carter Page) who was "politically sensitive." According to McCabe, the FBI "felt strongly" that the FISA application should move forward because the team believed they had to get to the bottom of what they considered to be a potentially serious threat to national security, even if the FBI would later be criticized for taking such action. As described in Chapter Five, McCabe and others discussed the FBI's position with NSD and ODAG officials, and these officials accepted the FBI's decision to move forward with the application, based substantially on the Steele information.

The FISA statute and FISC Rules of Procedure (FISC Rules) do not establish requirements specific to the use of CHS information, such as Steele's, to support probable cause in a FISA application. The FBI OGC's FISA guidance (described in Chapter Two) specifies that agents should take into account the reliability of any "informant," the circumstances of the informant's knowledge, and the age of the information relied upon when judging the evidence to support probable cause in any given case. As described in earlier chapters, we found that the FBI did not have information corroborating the specific allegations against Carter Page in Steele's reports when it relied upon them in the FISA applications. FBI OGC and NSD officials told us that the verification process set forth in the FBI's Woods Procedures does not require that the FBI have corroboration for the CHS information presented in an application. According to these officials, when information in a FISA application is attributed to a CHS, the Woods Procedures require only that the agent verify, with supporting documentation, that the application accurately reflects what the CHS told the FBI. The procedures do not require that the agent verify, through a second, independent source, that what the CHS told the FBI is true. We did not identify anything in the Woods Procedures that is inconsistent with these officials' description of the procedures. According to Evans, the FISC is aware of how the FBI "verifies" information in a FISA application under the Woods Procedures, including information attributed to a CHS.

However, without corroboration, it was particularly important for the FISA applications to articulate to the court the FBI's knowledge of Steele's background and its assessment of his reliability. On these points, the applications advised the court that Steele was believed to be a reliable source for three reasons: his professional background, his history of work as an FBI CHS since 2013, and his prior reporting, which the FBI described as "corroborated and used in criminal proceedings." As described below, the representations about Steele's prior reporting were overstated and not approved by Steele's handling agent, as required by the Woods Procedures. Our analysis of the FBI's assessment of the Steele reporting is described later in this chapter.

Following the FBI's decision to proceed with seeking a FISA order after consideration of the risks identified by Evans, OI developed a footnote, based on information provided by the Crossfire Hurricane team, to address Evans's concern about the potential political bias of Steele's research. The footnote stated that Steele was hired by an identified U.S. person (Glenn Simpson) to conduct research regarding "Candidate #1's" (Donald Trump) ties to Russia and that the FBI "speculates" that this U.S. person was likely looking for information that could be used to discredit the Trump campaign. Evans told us that this additional information made him comfortable with the way Steele was described in the application, based upon the information the FBI provided to OI at that time. However, Evans also expressed frustration to the FBI at the time, and later to the OIG, that the FBI had not advised OI of the political origins of Steele's election reporting until late in the drafting process on the first FISA application, and only after OI asked the team three times for information about Steele's possible political connections.

B. Inaccurate, Incomplete, or Undocumented Information in the FISA Applications

The FBI's FISA and Standard Minimization Procedures Policy Guide (FISA SMP PG) states that the U.S. government's "ability to obtain FISA authority depends on the accuracy of applications submitted to the FISC. Because FISA proceedings are *ex parte*, the FISC relies on the [U.S. government's] full and accurate presentation of the facts to make its probable cause determinations." It further states that it is the case agent's responsibility to ensure that statements contained in applications submitted to the FISC are "scrupulously accurate." As we discuss below, we found that the FBI failed to fulfill this obligation to the court. This failure falls most immediately on the shoulders of the case agents and supervisors who were responsible for assisting OI in the preparation of the FISA applications and performing the factual accuracy review during the Woods process. However, as we discuss below, we identified (1) numerous serious factual errors and omissions in the applications, (2) a failure across three investigative teams to advise NSD attorneys of significant information that undercut certain allegations in the FISA applications, (3) a lack of satisfactory explanations for these failures, and (4) a continuous failure to reassess the factual assertions supporting probable cause in the FISA applications as the investigation proceeded and information was obtained raising significant questions about the Steele reporting. We concluded that these facts demonstrated a failure on the part of the managers and supervisors in the Crossfire Hurricane chain of command, including FBI senior officials.

As described in Chapter Five, NSD officials told us that the nature of FISA practice requires that OI rely on the FBI agents who are familiar with the investigation to provide accurate and complete information. Unlike federal prosecutors, OI attorneys are usually not involved in an investigation, or even aware of a case's existence, unless and until OI receives a request to initiate a FISA application. Once OI receives a FISA request, OI attorneys generally interact with field offices remotely and do not have broad access to FBI case files or sensitive source files. NSD officials cautioned that even if OI received broader access to FBI case and source files, they still believe that the case agents and source handling agents are better positioned to identify all relevant information in the files. In addition, NSD officials told us that OI attorneys often do not have enough time to go through the files themselves, as it is not unusual for OI to receive requests for emergency authorizations with only a few hours to evaluate the request.

Despite the necessity that OI receive complete and accurate information from the FBI, our review identified numerous instances in which the FBI did not provide information relevant to the probable cause determination to OI and, therefore, that information was not shared with either the decision makers in the Department who ultimately approved the applications, or with the court, which ultimately found probable cause to believe that Carter Page was an agent of a foreign power and authorized FISA surveillance of him on four separate occasions. We found this failure by the FBI particularly concerning given the critical gatekeeper role that OI attorneys have in ensuring that FISA applications (a) contain sufficient evidence, in NSD's view, to support a probable cause finding, and (b) include information that is inconsistent with or contrary to the information presented in support of establishing probable cause. We concluded that OI attorneys were unable to fulfill this responsibility because members of the Crossfire Hurricane team repeatedly failed to provide OI with all relevant information. As a consequence, the factual representations in the initial and renewal FISA applications filed with the FISC contained information that was inaccurate, incomplete, or unsupported by appropriate documentation, based upon information the FBI had in its possession at the time the applications were filed.

In addition, we identified significant errors with the Crossfire Hurricane team's compliance with the FBI's Woods Procedures, which were adopted by the FBI in 2001 after errors were identified in numerous FISA applications in FBI counterterrorism investigations. The Woods Procedures are intended to ensure the accuracy of every piece of information asserted in a FISA application by requiring that both an agent and a supervisory agent verify, with supporting documentation that must be maintained in the Woods File, that each factual assertion is accurately stated. We determined that these requirements were not met with regard to any of the four Carter Page FISA applications.

Below we highlight the significant instances of inaccurate, incomplete, or undocumented information identified during our review, beginning with the first application. After the first application, we highlight significant additional errors and omissions in the renewal applications, including the agents' failures to update factual assertions repeated in the renewal applications, disclose new relevant information, and reassess the evidence supporting probable cause as the investigation progressed. Finally, we describe the failures in the performance of the Woods Procedures that could have prevented some, but not all, of the errors and omissions we identified.[490]

1.   The First FISA Application

As with all applications, the FISC Rules and FBI procedures required that the Carter Page FISA applications contain all material facts. Although the FISC Rules do not define or otherwise explain what constitutes a "material" fact, the FISA SMP PG states that a fact is "material" if it is relevant to the court's probable cause determination.

In all four applications, the factual basis supporting probable cause relied upon Page's historical (pre-2016) contacts with known Russian intelligence officers, as well as information from four Steele reports (Reports 80, 94, 95, and 102). The most prominent of the Steele reports were Report 94 concerning alleged secret meetings between Carter Page and two Russian nationals (Igor Sechin and Igor Divyekin) in July 2016, and Report 95 concerning the alleged role of Page as an intermediary between the Trump campaign and Russia. According to Report 95, Paul Manafort was using Page as an intermediary between the Trump campaign and Russia in a "well-developed conspiracy" that involved Russia's agreement to disclose hacked DNC emails to WikiLeaks in exchange for the Trump campaign's agreement, to include at least Page, to sideline Russian intervention in Ukraine as a campaign issue. Steele told us that the allegations in Report 95 came from one person (Person 1) and were provided to Steele by Steele's Primary Sub-source. The allegation in Report 102 that Russia released the DNC emails to WikiLeaks in an attempt to swing voters to Trump, an objective allegedly conceived and promoted by Page and others, also came from Person 1 and was provided to Steele by Steele's Primary Sub-source.[491]

However, as more fully described in Chapter Five, based upon the information known to the FBI in October 2016, the first application:

---

[490] Chapters Five and Eight more fully describe the most significant instances of inaccurate, incomplete, and undocumented information we identified during our review, and Appendix One provides a complete list of the failures we identified in the Woods Procedures.

[491] Person 1 was also one of two sources for the allegation in Report 80 that derogatory information about Hillary Clinton had been compiled for many years, was controlled by the Kremlin, and had been fed by the Kremlin to the Trump campaign for an extended period of time.

1. Omitted information from another U.S. government agency detailing its prior relationship with Page, including that Page had been approved as an operational contact for the other agency from 2008 to 2013, and that Page had provided information to the other agency concerning his prior contacts with certain Russian intelligence officers, one of which overlapped with facts asserted in the FISA application;

2. Included a source characterization statement asserting that Steele's prior reporting had been "corroborated and used in criminal proceedings," which overstated the significance of Steele's past reporting and was not approved by Steele's FBI handling agent, as required by the Woods Procedures;

3. Omitted information relevant to the reliability of Person 1, a key Steele sub-source (who, as previously noted, was attributed with providing the information in Report 95 and some of the information in Reports 80 and 102 relied upon in the application), namely that (1) Steele himself told members of the Crossfire Hurricane team that Person 1 was a "boaster" and an "egoist" and "may engage in some embellishment" and (2) █████████████████████████████ ███████████████ ;

4. Asserted that the FBI had assessed that Steele did not directly provide to the press information in the September 23 *Yahoo News* article, based on the premise that Steele had told the FBI that he only shared his election-related research with the FBI and Simpson; this premise was factually incorrect (Steele had provided direct information to *Yahoo News*) and also contradicted by documentation in the Woods File—Steele had told the FBI that he also gave his information to the State Department;

5. Omitted Papadopoulos's statements to an FBI CHS in September 2016 denying that anyone associated with the Trump campaign was collaborating with Russia or with outside groups like WikiLeaks in the release of emails;

6. Omitted Page's statements to an FBI CHS in August 2016 that Page had "literally never met" or "said one word to" Paul Manafort and that Manafort had not responded to any of Page's emails; if true, those statements were in tension with claims in Steele's Report 95 that Page was participating in a "conspiracy" with Russia by acting as an intermediary for Manafort on behalf of the Trump campaign; and

7. Selectively included Page's statements to an FBI CHS in October 2016 that the FBI believed supported its theory that Page was an agent of Russia but omitted other statements Page made, including denying having met with Sechin and Divyekin, or even knowing who Divyekin was; if true, those statements contradicted the claims in Steele's Report 94 that Page had met secretly with Sechin and Divyekin about

future cooperation with Russia and shared derogatory information about candidate Clinton.

We found no indication that NSD officials were aware of these issues at the time they prepared or reviewed the first FISA application. Regarding the third listed item above, the OI Attorney who drafted the application had received an email from Case Agent 1 before the first application was filed containing the information about Steele's "boaster" and "embellishment" characterization of Person 1, whom the FBI believed to be Source E in Report 95 and the source of other allegations in the application derived from Reports 80 and 102. This information was part of a lengthy email that included descriptions of various individuals in Steele's source network and other information Steele provided to the Crossfire Hurricane team in early October 2016. The OI Attorney told us that he did not recall the Crossfire Hurricane team flagging this issue for him or that he independently made the connection between this sub-source and Steele's characterization of Person 1 as an embellisher. We believe Case Agent 1 should have specifically discussed with the OI Attorney the FBI's assessment that this sub-source was Person 1, that Steele had provided derogatory information regarding Person 1, and that ██ ██, so that OI could have assessed how these facts might impact the FISA application. As described in Chapter Five, Evans and the OI Attorney told us that they would have wanted to discuss this information internally within NSD and with the FBI and likely would have, at a minimum, disclosed the information to the court.

We were particularly concerned by Case Agent 1's failure to provide accurate and complete information to the OI Attorney concerning Page's relationship status with the other U.S. government agency and Page's communications with the other agency about his contacts with Russian intelligence officers. As described in Chapter Five, in response to a question from the OI Attorney in late September 2016 as to whether Carter Page had a current or prior relationship with the other agency, Case Agent 1 stated that Page's relationship was "dated" (when Page lived in Moscow in 2004-2007) and "outside scope." This representation was contrary to the information that the other agency provided in its August 17, 2016 Memorandum to the FBI, which stated that Page was approved as an operational contact of the other agency from 2008 to 2013 (after Page had left Moscow); it also was contrary to information in the FBI's own case files regarding Page's claims of interactions with the other agency. Moreover, rather than being outside the scope of the FISA application, Page's status with the other agency overlapped in time with some of the interactions between Page and known Russian intelligence officers alleged in the FISA applications. Further, Page provided information to the other agency about his past contacts with a Russian intelligence officer (Intelligence Officer 1), which were among the historical connections to Russian intelligence officers that the FBI relied upon in the first FISA application (and subsequent renewal applications) to help support probable cause.[492] According to the August 17 Memorandum, an employee of the other agency assessed that Page "candidly described his contact with" Intelligence Officer 1 to the other agency. Thus, the FBI relied upon Page's contacts with Intelligence Officer 1, among others, in support of its probable cause statement, while failing to disclose to OI or the FISC that (1) Page had been approved as an operational contact by the other agency during a five-year period that overlapped with allegations in the FISA application, (2) Page had disclosed to the other agency contacts that he had with Intelligence Officer 1 and certain other individuals, and (3) the other agency's employee had given a positive assessment of Page's candor. The FBI also did not engage with the other U.S. government agency to understand what it meant for Page to have been approved as an operational contact, whether Page interacted with Russian intelligence officers at the behest of the other agency or with the intent to assist the U.S. government, and the breadth of the other agency's information concerning Page's interactions with Intelligence Officer 1, all information that would have been highly relevant to the FISC's probable cause determination.[493]

Case Agent 1 was unable to reconcile for us the information he provided to the OI Attorney with the information in the August 17 Memorandum or FBI case files, explaining to the OIG that he did not recall his state of knowledge in 2016 regarding Page's history with the other U.S. government agency. We concluded that Case Agent 1 failed to provide accurate and complete information to the OI Attorney concerning Page's relationship and cooperation with the other agency. Further, we believe Case Agent 1 or his supervisor, SSA 1, should have ensured that someone on the team contacted the other agency after receiving the August 17 Memorandum to determine what it meant for Page to have been approved as an operational contact, whether Page interacted with Russian intelligence officers at the behest of the other agency or with the intent to assist the U.S. government, and to seek additional information concerning Page's interactions with Intelligence Officer 1.

We also found troubling the Crossfire Hurricane team's failure to advise OI of statements Page made, as noted in the sixth item above, to an FBI CHS in August 2016 during a consensually monitored meeting through which the Crossfire Hurricane team had sought to obtain information from Page about possible links between the Trump campaign and Russia. This CHS operation was one of the first investigative steps in the Carter Page investigation and took place before the media had publicly reported the allegations in the Steele reports. During the operation, Page made statements that, if true, undercut the allegation in Steele's Report 95 (received by the team in September) that Manafort was using Page as an intermediary with Russia. According to the transcript of the operation, Page told the CHS that he had "literally never met" or "said one word to" Manafort, and that

---

[492] The other agency did not provide the FBI with information indicating it had knowledge of Page's reported contacts with another particular intelligence officer. The FBI also relied on Page's contacts with this intelligence officer in the FISA application.

[493] As noted earlier in this chapter, according to the U.S. government agency that approved Page as an operational contact, the approval did not allow for the operational use or tasking of Page.

Manafort had not responded to any of Page's emails. Page's statements concerning Manafort, which Page made before he had reason to know about Steele's reporting connecting him to Manafort in a conspiracy with Russia, were not provided to OI prior to the filing of the first FISA application. We agree with the OI Attorney who told us that the FBI should have flagged these statements for inclusion in the FISA application because they were relevant to the court's assessment of the allegations in Report 95 concerning Manafort using Page as an intermediary with Russia. We also believe that as the case proceeded and the FBI gathered substantial evidence of Page's past electronic communications, the lack of evidence showing substantive communications between Page and Manafort bolstered the need to, at a minimum, include Page's statements regarding Manafort in the renewal applications.

Further, we were concerned by the Crossfire Hurricane team's assertion, without approval from Steele's handling agent (Handling Agent 1), that Steele's prior reporting had been "corroborated and used in criminal proceedings" (second item noted above), which we were told was primarily a reference to Steele's role in the International Federation of Association Football (FIFA) corruption investigation. According to Handling Agent 1, he would not have approved the representation in the application because only "some" of Steele's prior reporting had been corroborated—most of it had not—and because Steele's information was never used in a criminal proceeding. The Supervisory Intelligence Analyst (Supervisory Intel Analyst), who told us he originally provided this language for an intelligence product prepared by his analytical team, told us that he did not review the FIFA case file or "dig into" exactly how Steele's information was used in the FIFA case. SSA 1 told us that the team had "speculated" that Steele's prior reporting had been corroborated and used in criminal proceedings because they knew Steele had been "a part of, if not predicated, the FIFA investigation" and was known to have an extensive source network into Russian organized crime.

The source characterization statement in all four FISA applications stated that Steele's prior reporting had been corroborated and used in criminal proceedings, and the renewal applications further relied upon this assertion as the basis for the FBI's assessment that Steele was still reliable despite his disclosure of the FBI's investigation to media outlet *Mother Jones* in late October 2016. Given the importance of a source's bona fides to a court's determination of reliability—particularly in cases where, as here, the source information supporting probable cause is uncorroborated—we concluded that the repeated failure in all four applications by the agents and the SSAs involved to comply with FBI policy requiring that the handling agent review and approve the language was significant. This created the impression that at least some of Steele's past reporting had been deemed sufficiently reliable by prosecutors to use in court, and that more of his information had been corroborated than was actually the case.

None of the inaccuracies and omissions we identified in the first application were brought to the attention of OI before the last FISA application was filed in June 2017. Consequently, these failures were repeated in all three renewal applications. As a result, the Department officials who reviewed one or more of the applications, including DAG Yates, Acting Attorney General Boente, and DAG Rosenstein, did not have accurate and complete information at the time they

367

approved the applications. We do not speculate as to whether or how this additional information might have influenced the decisions of senior leaders who supported the applications, if they had known all of the relevant information. Nevertheless, we believe it was the obligation of the agents who were aware of the information to ensure that OI and the decision makers had the opportunity to consider it, both to decide whether to proceed with the applications and, if so, how to present this information to the court. We also do not speculate as to whether this additional information would have influenced the court's decision on probable cause if the court had accurate and complete information at the time of the first application. However, it was the Department's and FBI's obligation to ensure that the applications were "scrupulously accurate" and that the court was provided with a complete and accurate recitation of the relevant facts, which we found did not occur.

2.   The Three Renewal Applications

In addition to repeating the errors contained in the first FISA application, we identified other, similarly significant errors in the three renewal applications, based upon information known to the FBI after the first application was filed and before one or more of the renewals was filed. As more fully described in Chapter Eight, the renewal applications:

8.   Omitted the fact that Steele's Primary Sub-source, who the FBI found credible, had made statements in January 2017 raising significant questions about the reliability of allegations included in the FISA applications, including, for example, that he/she had no discussion with Person 1 concerning WikiLeaks and there was "nothing bad" about the communications between the Kremlin and the Trump team, and that he/she did not report to Steele in July 2016 that Page had met with Sechin;

9.   Omitted Page's prior relationship with another U.S. government agency, despite being reminded by the other agency in June 2017, prior to the filing of the final renewal application, about Page's past status with that other agency; instead of including this information in the final renewal application, the FBI OGC Attorney altered an email from the other agency so that the email stated that Page was "not a source" for the other agency, which the FBI affiant relied upon in signing the final renewal application;

10.   Omitted information provided by persons with direct knowledge of Steele's work-related performance in a prior position about Steele's professional judgment, including statements that Steele had held a "moderately senior" position (not "high-ranking" as noted in the applications), had no history of reporting in bad faith but demonstrated "poor judgment," "pursued people with political risk but no intelligence value," "didn't always exercise great judgment," and it was "not clear what he would have done to validate" his reporting;

11. Omitted information from Department attorney Bruce Ohr about Steele and his election reporting, including that (1) Steele's reporting was going to Clinton's presidential campaign and others, (2) Simpson was paying Steele to discuss his reporting with the media, and (3) Steele was "desperate that Donald Trump not get elected and was passionate about him not being the U.S. President";

12. Failed to update the description of Steele after information became known to the Crossfire Hurricane team, not only from Ohr but from others, that provided greater clarity on the political origins and connections of Steele's reporting, including that Simpson was hired by someone associated with the Democratic Party and/or the DNC;

13. Failed to correct the assertion in the first FISA application that the FBI did not believe that Steele directly provided information to the reporter who wrote the September 23 *Yahoo News* article, even though there was no information in the Woods File to support this claim and even after certain FBI officials involved in Crossfire Hurricane learned in 2017, before the third renewal application, of an admission that Steele made in a court filing about his interactions with the news media in the late summer and early fall of 2016;

14. Omitted the finding from a formal FBI source validation report that Steele was suitable for continued operation but that his past contributions to the FBI's criminal program had been "minimally corroborated," and instead continued to assert in the source characterization statement that Steele's prior reporting had been "corroborated and used in criminal proceedings";

15. Omitted Papadopoulos's statements to an FBI CHS in late October 2016 (after the first application was filed) denying that the Trump campaign was involved in the circumstances of the DNC email hack;

16. Omitted Joseph Mifsud's denials to the FBI that he supplied Papadopoulos with the information Papadopoulos shared with the FFG (suggesting that the campaign received an offer or suggestion of assistance from Russia);[494] and

17. Omitted evidence indicating that Page played no role in the Republican platform change on Russia's annexation of Ukraine as alleged in Steele Report 95, which was inconsistent with a factual assertion relied upon to support probable cause in all four FISA applications.

We found the FBI's failure, noted in the eighth listed item above, to advise OI or the court of the inconsistences between Steele and his Primary Sub-source to be among the most serious omissions of information. As described in Chapter Four,

---

[494] According to The Special Counsel's Report, Mifsud made inaccurate statements during this FBI interview about his interactions with Papadopoulos. *See The Special Counsel's Report*, Vol. I at 193. Nevertheless, Evans told us that Mifsud's denials during his FBI interview sounded like something "potentially factually similarly situated" to the denials made by Papadopoulos that OI determined should have been included in the applications.

Steele himself was not the originating source of any of the factual information in his reporting; Steele instead relied on his Primary Sub-source for information, who used his/her network of sub-sources to gather information that was then passed to Steele. As described in Chapters Six and Eight, during his/her January 2017 interview with the FBI, the Primary Sub-source made statements that were inconsistent with multiple sections of the Steele reports, including the allegations relied upon in the FISA applications. These inconsistencies should have resulted in serious discussions about the reliability of Steele's reporting—particularly to support a probable cause showing in a court filing—but did not. For example, regarding the allegations in Report 95 that came from Person 1 (Source E), the Primary Sub-source said, among other things, that he/she had only one, 10- to 15-minute telephone call with someone he/she believed was Person 1 and that during this call they had no discussion at all regarding WikiLeaks. Further, the Primary Sub-source told the FBI that there was "nothing bad" about communications between the Kremlin and the Trump team. The Primary Sub-source's account of these communications, if true, was not consistent with the allegations of a "well-developed conspiracy" in Reports 95 and 102 attributed to Source E (Person 1). Further, his/her assertion that he/she and Person 1 had no discussion at all regarding WikiLeaks directly contradicted those allegations. However, the FBI did not share this information with OI. The FBI also failed to share other inconsistencies with OI, including the Primary Sub-source's account of the alleged meeting between Page and Sechin in Steele's Report 94 and his/her descriptions of the source network.[495]

The fact that the Primary Sub-source's account was inconsistent with key assertions attributed to his/her own sub-sources in Reports 94, 95, and 102 should have generated significant discussions between the Crossfire Hurricane team and OI prior to submitting the next FISA renewal application. According to Evans, had OI been made aware of the information, such discussions might have included the possibility of foregoing the renewal request altogether, at least until the FBI reconciled the differences between Steele's account and the Primary Sub-source's account to the satisfaction of OI. However, we found no evidence that the Crossfire Hurricane team ever considered whether any of the inconsistencies warranted reconsideration of the FBI's previous assessment of the reliability of the Steele reports or notice to OI before the subsequent renewal applications were filed.

As a result, the second and third renewal applications provided no substantive information concerning the Primary Sub-source's interview, and instead offered a brief conclusory statement that the FBI met with the Primary Sub-source

---

[495] As more fully described in Chapter Eight, according to the Primary Sub-source, he/she was not told until October 2016 that the Page-Sechin meeting had taken place the previous July. According to the Primary Sub-source, he/she had only told Steele in July 2016 that he/she had heard that the meeting would be taking place. However, Steele authored Report 94 in July 2016 alleging that the Page-Sechin meeting had taken place that month and describing the topics that were discussed at the meeting. As noted previously, Page denied to an FBI CHS that he had met with Sechin in July 2016, and, as of the date of the last FISA application, the FBI had not determined whether a meeting between Sechin and Page took place. In addition, the Primary Sub-source's description of each of his/her sources indicated that their positions and access to the information they were reporting were more attenuated than represented by Steele and described in the FISA applications.

"[i]n an effort to further corroborate Steele's reporting" and found the Primary Sub-source to be "truthful and cooperative." We believe that including this statement, without also informing the court that the Primary Sub-source gave an account of the events that was inconsistent with key assertions in Steele's reporting, left a misimpression that the Primary Sub-source had corroborated the Steele reporting. Indeed, as we describe in Chapter Eight, in its July 2018 Rule 13 letter to the court, the Department—which was continuing to rely on the FBI's representations regarding the Primary Sub-source's interview—defended the reliability of Steele's reporting and the FISA applications by citing, in part, to the Primary Sub-source's interview as "additional information corroborating [Steele's] reporting" and noting the FBI's determination that he/she was "truthful and cooperative."

When we asked the case agents and supervisory agents who participated in the preparation or Woods review of the second and third renewal applications, they either told us that they were not aware of the inconsistences or, if they were aware, they did not make the connection that the inconsistencies affected aspects of the FISA applications. For example, Case Agent 1 told us that he believed that someone else should have highlighted the issue for the agents working on the second renewal application because he did not know some of the details concerning Person 1 that would have helped him make the necessary connections. He told us that he did not know whether Steele had his own relationship with Person 1 such that Steele could have had another basis for attributing all the information in Report 95 to Person 1. However, given Case Agent 1's central role in the Page investigation, the Primary Sub-source interview, and the preparation of the first two FISA applications and factual accuracy review on the third, we believe he should have been one of the first to notice, and advise others about, the problems the Primary Sub-source's accounts created for the FISA applications. Similarly, we believe the Supervisory Intel Analyst also should have noticed and advised others about the conflicting information, given he participated in the January 2017 Primary Sub-source interview, helped supervise the team's evaluation of the Steele reporting, and played a supportive role in the preparation of the prior FISA applications. Instead, as discussed in Chapter Eight, the Supervisory Intel Analyst circulated a 2-page intelligence memorandum to senior FBI officials highlighting aspects of the Primary Sub-source's account but failed to advise them of the inconsistencies between Steele and his Primary Sub-source on, among other things, the key allegations against Page in Reports 94 and 95.

In addition to the Primary Sub-source's interview, we found other information in the FBI's possession that raised questions about the accuracy of the Steele reporting regarding Carter Page, but that was not included in the renewal applications. As described in Chapter Five, to support the allegations in Report 95 that Page worked to sideline Ukraine as a campaign issue, the first FISA application described two news articles from July and August 2016 reporting that the Trump campaign had worked behind the scenes to change the Republican Party's platform on providing weapons to Ukraine. As more fully described in Chapter Eight, after the first application, the Crossfire Hurricane team did not learn of any information that Page was involved in the platform change and instead developed evidence tending to show that two other Trump campaign officials were responsible for the change. Despite this, as noted in the seventeenth item above, the FBI did not include this information in any of the renewal applications or alter its assessment that Page was involved in the platform change. Instead, the renewal applications stated that Page had denied any role in the platform change to the FBI in March 2017 but that the FBI assessed Page may have been downplaying his role.

The renewal applications also continued to fail to include information regarding Carter Page's relationship with another U.S. government agency and information Page had shared with the other agency about his contacts with Russian intelligence officers, even after the Crossfire Hurricane team re-engaged with the other U.S. government agency in June 2017 (item nine above). As described in Chapter Eight, following interviews that Page gave to news outlets in April and May 2017 stating that he had assisted the U.S. intelligence community in the past, one of the SSAs supervising Crossfire Hurricane sought additional information about the issue. SSA 2, who was to be the affiant for Renewal Application No. 3 and had been the affiant for the first two renewals, told us that he wanted a definitive answer to whether Page had ever been a source for another U.S. government agency before he signed the final renewal application, because he was concerned that Page could claim that he had been acting on behalf of the U.S. government when engaging with certain Russians. This led to interactions between the OGC Attorney assigned to Crossfire Hurricane and a liaison from the other U.S. government agency. In an email from the liaison to the OGC Attorney, the liaison provided written guidance, including that it was the liaison's recollection that Page had a relationship with the other agency, and directed the OGC Attorney to review the information that the other agency had provided to the FBI in August 2016. As noted above, that August 2016 information stated that Page did, in fact, have a prior relationship with that other agency. However, the OGC Attorney altered the liaison's email by inserting the words "not a source" into it, thus making it appear that the liaison had said that Page was "not a source"; the OGC Attorney then sent the altered email to SSA 2. Relying upon this altered email, SSA 2 signed the third renewal application (that again failed to disclose Page's past relationship with the other agency). Consistent with the Inspector General Act of 1978, following the OIG's discovery that the OGC Attorney had altered and sent the email to SSA 2, who thereafter relied on it to swear out the final FISA application, the OIG promptly informed the Attorney General and the FBI Director and provided them with the relevant information about the OGC Attorney's actions.

None of these inaccuracies and omissions that we identified in the renewal applications were brought to the attention of OI before the applications were filed. As a result, similar to the first application, the Department officials who reviewed one or more of the renewal applications, including Yates, Boente, and Rosenstein, did not have accurate and complete information at the time they approved them. An exception with respect to Boente concerned information regarding the ties between Steele's reporting and the Democratic Party, which documents indicate were broadly known among relevant Department officials by February and March 2017. Boente recalled knowing the information at the time he approved the second renewal. Rosenstein told us he believes he learned that information from news media accounts, but did not recall whether he knew at the time he approved the third renewal. As with the first FISA application, we do not speculate whether or how having accurate and complete information might have influenced the decisions of senior Department leaders who supported the renewal applications, or the court, if they had known all of the relevant information. Nevertheless, it was the obligation of the FBI agents and supervisors who were aware of the information to ensure that the FISA applications were "scrupulously accurate" and that OI, the Department's decision makers, and ultimately, the court had the opportunity to consider the additional information and the information omitted from the first application. The individuals involved did not meet this obligation.

Multiple factors made it difficult for us to assess the extent of FBI leadership's knowledge as to each fact stated incorrectly or omitted from the FISA applications. As described in prior chapters, Comey certified the first three applications as the FBI Director, and McCabe certified the final renewal application as the Acting FBI Director. As the FBI's senior leaders, Comey and McCabe would have had greater access to case information than Department leadership and also more interaction with senior CD officials and the investigation team. Further, as described in Chapter Three, CD officials orally briefed the Crossfire Hurricane cases to FBI senior leadership throughout the investigation. McCabe received more briefings than Comey, but both received oral briefings of the team's investigative activities. During one such briefing, McCabe listened to parts of the recording of the conversation between Carter Page and an FBI CHS in August 2016. In addition, in her capacity as the Deputy Director's counsel, Lisa Page attended meetings with Strzok and the Crossfire Hurricane team and reported information back to McCabe. However, limited recollections and the absence of detailed documentation of meetings made it impracticable for us to determine, beyond the more general investigative updates that we know were provided, what specific information was described during these leadership briefings and the precise nature of FBI leadership awareness of critical facts.[496] Moreover, we identified instances in which senior FBI officials were not provided with complete information. For example, although we found that Comey and McCabe had been informed that the FBI had interviewed Steele's Primary Sub-source, the 2-page intelligence memorandum that they were sent highlighting aspects of the Primary Sub-source's account failed to advise them of inconsistencies between Steele's reporting and the Primary Sub-source on key allegations. Thus, while we believe the opportunities for learning investigative details were greater for FBI leadership than for Department leadership, we were unable to conclusively determine whether FBI leadership was provided with sufficient information, or sufficiently probed the investigative team, to enable them to effectively assess the evidence as the case progressed.

3. Failures in the Woods Process

As more fully described in Chapter Two, the FBI's Woods Procedures seek to ensure the accuracy of every factual assertion in a FISA application by requiring that an agent and his or her supervisor verify, with supporting documentation, that

---

[496] In addition, Comey's decision not to reinstate his security clearance for his OIG interview made the OIG unable to question him or refresh his recollection with relevant, classified documentation.

the assertion is correct and maintain the supporting document in the Woods File. In the case of renewal applications, this process involves re-verifying the accuracy of "old facts" from prior applications that are repeated and verifying and obtaining supporting documentation for any "new facts" that are added.

We examined the FBI's compliance with the Woods Procedures by comparing the facts asserted in the probable cause sections of the FISA applications to the documents maintained in each application's Woods File. Our comparison identified numerous instances in which a fact asserted in the application was not supported by appropriate documentation in the Woods File. The Woods errors we identified generally fell into three categories: (1) a fact asserted in the FISA application that had no supporting documentation in the Woods File, (2) a factual assertion had a corresponding document in the Woods File, but the document did not state the fact asserted in the FISA application, or (3) the corresponding document in the Woods File indicated that the fact asserted in the FISA application was inaccurate.

Among the most significant Woods errors we identified in this review were: (1) the failure to obtain the handling agent's approval of the source characterization statements for Steele and another FBI CHS whose information was relied upon in the applications; (2) documentation in the Woods File used to support the FBI's statement that Steele only shared his election related research with Simpson actually stated that Steele also shared the information with the State Department; and (3) documentation in the Woods File to support the FBI's assertion that Page did not refute his alleged contacts with Sechin and Divyekin to an FBI CHS actually stated that Page specifically denied meeting with Sechin and Divyekin to the CHS. Appendix One describes additional Woods errors that our review identified.

Some of the Woods errors, including the ones highlighted above, were repeated in all four applications, demonstrating that the agents and supervisors performing the Woods Procedures did not attempt to re-verify the accuracy of factual assertions repeated from prior applications—or if they did, they did not read the documents completely but only confirmed that a corresponding document appeared in the Woods File.

As described in Chapter Two, the Woods Procedures were adopted in 2001 following errors in numerous FISA applications in counterterrorism investigations. When properly followed, the Woods Procedures help reduce errors in the information supporting a FISA application by requiring an agent to identify and maintain a source document for every fact asserted in the application and complete a list of database searches on the FISA target and any CHSs relied upon in the application. We observed that the Woods process focuses on the facts actually asserted in an application and will not necessarily identify relevant facts that are missing from an application. For this reason, performance of the Woods Procedures, alone, would have caught some but not all of the many problems we identified. We believe these problems nevertheless would have been caught, or never would have existed in the first place, had the Crossfire Hurricane team adequately performed its duty of sharing all relevant information with OI.

C. Conclusions Regarding the FISA Applications

1. The Failure to Share Relevant Factual Information with OI, the Department's Decision Makers, and the Court, and Other FISA Related Errors

As described in Chapters Five and Seven, all four FISA applications received the necessary Department approvals and certifications—in each instance the approval required for submission of the proposed application (read copy) was appropriately executed by the OI Unit Chief, and the final application was certified by the FBI Director or Acting Director and approved by the DAG or, in the case of the second renewal application, the Acting Attorney General. Further, we found that all four applications received more attention and scrutiny than a typical FISA application in terms of the additional layers of review and number of high-level officials who read the application. This was particularly true of the first application, which underwent a lengthy review and editing process within NSD, the FBI OGC, and ODAG.

However, as discussed above, relevant information was not shared with, and consequently not considered by, the decision makers who ultimately decided to support the applications. The failure to update OI with accurate and complete information resulted in FISA applications that made it appear that the evidence supporting probable cause was stronger than was actually the case. Based upon the information in the application, Yates told us that when she approved and signed the first application, she did not believe it presented a close call from a legal sufficiency standpoint, and she was comfortable that the request for FISA authority sought by the FBI was an appropriate investigative step to take. Similarly, Rosenstein told us that by the time he signed Renewal Application No. 3 probable cause was not "a great stretch" and seemed obvious to him, given that the prior applications relied upon the same information that had been approved and granted three times by federal judges. As detailed in this report, these assessments by these decision makers were not based on a complete understanding of all relevant information that was available to the FBI at the time the applications were submitted. Indeed, by the time Rosenstein signed the final application, among other things, the following information had not been provided to the decision makers: (1) Steele's Primary Sub-source had not confirmed the allegations regarding Carter Page to the FBI and instead gave an account that was inconsistent with and contradicted them, and (2) testimonial and documentary evidence obtained by the FBI tended to show that other Trump campaign officials, not Page, were responsible for influencing the Republican platform change.

Some factual misstatements and omissions were arguably more significant than others, but we concluded that the case agents' failures to share all relevant information with OI made OI unable to perform its gatekeeper function and deprived the decision makers the opportunity to make fully informed decisions. While we found isolated instances where a case agent forwarded documentation to the OI Attorney that included, among other things, information omitted from the FISA applications, we noted that, in those instances, the Crossfire Hurricane team did not alert the OI Attorney to the information. For example, when Case Agent 6 provided the OI Attorney in June 2017 with the 163-page document detailing Page's meeting with the FBI CHS in August 2016, he directed the OI Attorney's attention to statements that Page made that the FBI believed furthered the FISA application but did not identify for the OI Attorney relevant information that tended to undercut the probable cause analysis.[497] Although we agreed with the OI Attorney that he should have examined material that the FBI provided to him more carefully, we concluded that the responsibility to raise relevant issues for OI fell squarely on the case agents who were most familiar with the case information. Further, we found instances when the OI Attorney asked the Crossfire Hurricane team the right questions, such as in September 2016 when he asked the case agent about Page's relationship with the other U.S. government agency, yet was provided with inaccurate or incomplete information. As noted previously, we do not speculate whether the correction of any particular misstatement or omission, or some combination thereof, would have resulted in a different outcome. Nevertheless, the decision makers should have been given complete and accurate information so that they could have meaningfully performed their duty to evaluate probable cause.

The failure to update OI on all significant case developments relevant to the FISA applications led us to conclude that the agents did not give equal attention or treatment to the relevant facts that did not support probable cause, or reassess the evidence supporting probable cause as the investigation progressed. The FISA Request Form does not specifically ask the case agent to share with OI information that, if accurate, would tend to undermine or would be inconsistent with the information being relied upon to support the government's theory, in whole or in part, that the target is a foreign power or an agent of a foreign power. We believe sworn law enforcement officers should already understand this basic obligation based on their training and experience. Nevertheless, we recommend that the FBI and the Department take additional steps to re-emphasize this obligation in the FISA context and help ensure that agents focus their attention equally on their obligation to share information with OI that might detract from a probable cause finding, regardless of whether they believe it to be true. FBI procedures should also ensure that OI receives all information that bears on the reliability of every CHS whose information the FBI intends to rely upon in the FISA application. This should include all information from the derogatory information sub-file, recommended later in our analysis of the FBI's relationship with Steele and its assessment of Steele's election reporting. A more robust questionnaire in the FISA Request Form could also help ensure that all relevant information is shared with OI so that its attorneys can do their job, and that case agents are not leaving to themselves the determination that is also properly OI's of what information might be significant or relevant to probable cause, or should be disclosed to the court.

We also found the quantity of omissions and inaccuracies in the applications and the obvious errors in the Woods Procedures deeply concerning. Although we

---

[497] As described in Chapter Five, Case Agent 6 told us that he did not know that Page made the statement about Manafort because the August 2016 meeting took place before he was assigned to the investigation. He said that the reason he knew about the "October Surprise" statements in the 163-page document was that he had heard about them from Case Agent 1 and did a word search to find the specific discussion of that topic.

did not find documentary or testimonial evidence of intentional misconduct on the part of the case agents who assisted OI in preparing the applications, or the agents and supervisors who performed the Woods Procedures, we also did not receive satisfactory explanations for the errors or missing information. In most instances, witnesses told us that they either did not know or recall why the information was not shared with OI, that the failure to do so may have been an oversight, that they did not recognize at the time the relevance of the information to the FISA application, or that they did not believe the missing information to be significant. On this last point, we believe that case agents may have improperly substituted their own judgments in place of the judgment of OI to consider the potential materiality of the information, or in place of the court to weigh the probative value of the information. As described above, given that certain factual misstatements were repeated in all four applications, across three different investigative teams, we also concluded that agents and supervisors failed to appropriately perform the Woods Procedures on the renewal applications by not giving much, if any, attention to re-verifying "old facts." We recommend that the Woods Form be revised to emphasize to agents and their supervisors this obligation and to have them certify that they re-verified factual assertions repeated from prior applications.

As noted throughout this report, Case Agent 1 was primarily responsible for some of the most significant errors and omissions in the FISA applications, including (1) the mischaracterization of Steele's prior reporting resulting from his failure to seek review and approval of the statement from the handling agent, as the Woods Procedures required, (2) the failure to advise OI of Papadopoulos's statements to FBI CHSs that were inconsistent with the Steele reporting relied upon in the FISA applications that there was a "well-developed conspiracy of co-operation" between individuals associated with the Trump campaign and Russia, (3) the failure to advise OI of Page's statements to an FBI CHS regarding him having no communications with Manafort and denying the alleged meetings with Sechin and Divyekin, (4) providing inaccurate and incomplete information to OI about information provided by another U.S. government agency regarding its past relationship with Page that was highly relevant to the applications, (5) the failure to advise OI of the information from Bruce Ohr about Steele and his election reporting, and (6) the failure to advise OI of the inconsistences between Steele and his Primary Sub-source. The explanations that Case Agent 1 provided for these errors and omissions are summarized in Chapter Five and Chapter Eight of this report. While we found no documentary or testimonial evidence that this pattern of errors by Case Agent 1 was intentional, we also did not find his explanations for so many significant and repeated failures to be satisfactory. We therefore concluded that these explanations did not excuse his failure to meet his responsibility to ensure that the initial FISA application, the first renewal application, and the third renewal application were "scrupulously accurate."

We similarly found errors by supervisory FBI employees with responsibility for the accuracy of the FBI applications. For example, SSA 1 performed the supervisory accuracy review for the first application required under the Woods Procedures and did not correct the errors we identified before the application was filed. We found that the team "speculated" that Steele's prior reporting had been corroborated and used in criminal proceedings, but did not take reasonable steps to ensure the accuracy of this statement and did not confirm that Handling Agent 1 had reviewed and approved its content, as required by the Woods Procedures. Separately, SSA 3 and SSA 5 failed to correct all of the errors we identified in the renewal applications, as did Case Agent 1 and Case Agent 7, when they performed the accuracy review under the Woods Procedures for one or more of the renewals.[498]

These failures by supervisory and non-supervisory agents represent serious performance failures.[499] However, as we next discuss, the breadth and significance of these and other errors raised broader concerns as well.

2. Failure of Managers and Supervisors, including Senior Officials, in the Chain of Command

As this chapter summarizes, we identified at least 17 significant errors and omissions in the Carter Page FISA applications, and many additional Woods related errors. These errors and omissions resulted from case agents providing wrong or incomplete information to OI and failing to flag important issues for discussion, without any satisfactory explanations. Moreover, case agents and SSAs did not give equal attention or treatment to the relevant facts that did not support probable cause, or reassess the evidence supporting probable cause as the investigation progressed and the information gathered undercut the assertions in the FISA applications. Further, the agents and SSAs did not follow, or appear to even know, the requirements in the Woods Procedures to re-verify the factual assertions from previous applications that are repeated in renewal applications and verify source characterization statements with the CHS handling agent and document the verification in the Woods File. That so many basic and fundamental errors were made on four FISA applications by three separate, hand-picked teams, on one of the most sensitive FBI investigations that was briefed to the highest levels within the FBI and that FBI officials expected would eventually be subjected to close scrutiny, raised significant questions regarding the FBI chain of command's management and supervision of the FISA process.

As described in prior chapters, FBI Headquarters established a chain of command for Crossfire Hurricane that included close supervision by senior CD managers, who then briefed FBI leadership throughout the investigation. Although we do not expect managers and supervisors to know every fact about an

---

[498] Case Agent 7 was a relatively new FBI special agent who was recently assigned to assist Case Agent 6 with the Carter Page investigation when he conducted the Woods Procedures on Renewal Application No. 3. During the Woods process, Case Agent 7 and Case Agent 6 identified and added some documents missing from the Woods File to provide support for the factual assertions in Renewal Application No. 3. In addition, SSA 5 said that on numerous occasions, Case Agent 1 and Case Agent 6 told him that the OI Attorney preparing the Carter Page FISA applications had "already seen all of the supporting documentation."

[499] After reading a draft of our report, SSA 1 and other members of the Crossfire Hurricane team told us that their performance should be assessed in light of the full scope of responsibilities they had in 2016, in connection with the FBI's Russian counterintelligence investigation, and that the Carter Page FISA was a narrow aspect of their overall responsibilities.

investigation, or senior leaders to know all the details of cases they are briefed on, in a sensitive, high-priority matter like this one, it is reasonable to expect that they will take the necessary steps to ensure that they are sufficiently familiar with the facts and circumstances supporting and potentially undermining a FISA application in order to provide effective oversight consistent with their level of supervisory responsibility. We did not find that this was the case with the Carter Page FISA applications. Time and again, when we questioned managers, supervisors, and senior officials during their OIG interviews about the breadth of issues we identified during the review, the answers we received reflected a lack of understanding or awareness of important information that related to many of the problems we identified.

Nevertheless, we found that managers, supervisors, and senior officials in the chain of command were aware of sufficient information that should have resulted in questions being raised regarding the reliability of the Steele reporting and the probable cause supporting the FISA applications. For example, after months of effort, the Crossfire Hurricane team had not corroborated any of the specific substantive allegations against Carter Page contained in the election reporting and relied on in the FISA applications (confirming only limited factual details such as Page's dates of travel), or any other evidence implicating Page. In fact, as discussed in Chapter Seven, before Renewal Application No. 2 was submitted to the court in April 2017, the Deputy Assistant Director and SSAs at FBI Headquarters supervising the Carter Page case had actually discussed, based upon the information gathered by that time, whether Page was a significant subject in the FBI's investigation by that time, let alone be the target of a FISA order.[500] In addition, senior FBI officials were aware of Steele's political ties, and his disclosures of information to *Mother Jones* and other third parties. The Crossfire Hurricane team had also received information directly from persons with direct knowledge of Steele's work-related performance in a prior position that he had a history of demonstrating poor judgment, and they were aware of the information from Ohr concerning Steele's motivations and potential bias. Additionally, before the final FISA renewal application, the team had received the results of the FBI's source validation review of Steele, including the finding that Steele's past assistance to the FBI's criminal program had been "minimally corroborated," and Strzok and other supervisors had received information that Steele had been a source for the *Yahoo News* article. We recognize that FBI managers, supervisors, and senior officials in the chain of command were not made aware of all of the significant information undermining the Steele reporting, such as the inconsistencies between the reporting relied upon in the FISA applications and the Primary Sub-source's accounts of this information. Nevertheless, we concluded that the information that was known to them should have resulted in greater vigilance in overseeing the use of a highly intrusive technique in such a sensitive case, but did not. In our view,

---

[500] Under existing FBI policy the CD Assistant Director has no role in the review or approval of FISA applications. Priestap told us that, in comparison to the FBI Director, Deputy Director, and their staffs, the Assistant Director is in a better position to understand the facts supporting FISA applications, though he cautioned that review and approval of FISA applications by an Assistant Director should be limited to the only the most significant cases, if FBI policy is changed in this way.

this was a failure of not only the operational team, but also the managers and supervisors, including senior officials, in the chain of command.

For these reasons, we recommend that the FBI review the performance of the employees who had responsibility for the preparation, Woods review, or approval of the FISA applications, as well as the managers, supervisors, and senior officials in the chain of command of the Carter Page investigation, and take any action deemed appropriate. In addition, given the extensive compliance failures we identified in this review, we believe that additional OIG oversight work is required to assess the FBI's compliance with Department and FBI FISA-related policies that seek to protect the civil liberties of U.S. persons. Accordingly, we have initiated an OIG audit that will further examine the FBI's compliance with the Woods Procedures in FISA applications that target U.S. persons in both counterintelligence and counterterrorism investigations. This audit will be informed by the findings in this review, as well as by our prior work over the past 15 years on the Department's and FBI's use of national security and surveillance authorities, including authorities under FISA, as detailed in Chapter One.

3. Clarification Regarding OGC Legal Review During the Woods Process

As described in Chapter Two, the Woods Procedures do not currently explain the steps that should be taken during OGC's final legal review of a FISA application or require that documentation of the final legal review be maintained in an appropriate FBI file. And, as described in Chapter Seven, the FBI was unable to provide the OIG with documentation of the OGC legal review of Renewal Application Nos. 1 and 2. We therefore recommend that the FBI revise the Woods Procedures to specify what steps must be taken and documented during the legal review performed by an OGC line attorney and SES-level supervisor before submitting the FISA application package to the FBI Director for certification. Because we were advised that the SES-level review is sometimes delegated to a non-SES-level supervisor, we also recommend that the FBI revise the Woods Procedures to clarify which positions may serve as the supervisory reviewer for OGC.

III. The FBI's Relationship with Christopher Steele and Its Receipt and Use of His Election Reporting

In this section, we analyze the FBI's handling of Christopher Steele and its use of his election reporting in Crossfire Hurricane, and whether the FBI's receipt and use of his reporting during that investigation complied with FBI CHS policies and procedures. As described in Chapter Four, Steele is a former intelligence officer ██ who in 2009 formed a consulting firm specializing in corporate intelligence and investigative services. In 2010, Steele was introduced by Department attorney Bruce Ohr to an FBI agent, and for several years provided information to the FBI about various matters, such as corruption in the International Federation of Association Football (FIFA). In October 2013, the FBI agent, referred to in our report as Handling Agent 1, completed the paperwork to make Steele an FBI CHS. Handling Agent 1 took this step because the volume of Steele's reporting had increased and involved persons of interest to the FBI, and he wanted to task Steele to collect additional information and compensate him for this work. Over the next 3 years, Steele provided the FBI with reporting primarily about Russian oligarchs.

In June 2016, Steele and his consulting firm were hired by Fusion GPS, a Washington, D.C. investigative firm, to obtain information about whether Russia was trying to achieve a particular outcome in the 2016 U.S. elections, what personal and business ties then candidate Trump had in Russia, and whether there were any ties between the Russian government and Trump or his campaign. Steele's work for Fusion GPS resulted in at least ██ reports related to the election and, with Fusion GPS's authorization, Steele provided ██ of the reports to the FBI between July and October 2016, and ██ others to the FBI through Ohr and other third parties (as we described in Chapters Six and Nine).[501] As noted earlier, we determined that Steele's election reporting played a central and essential role in the Department's decision in connection with the Crossfire Hurricane investigation to seek a FISA order in October 2016 authorizing electronic surveillance ████████████ ████████ targeting Carter Page.

We found that FBI policy permitted the receipt and use of Steele's election reporting in the Crossfire Hurricane investigation, and we did not find documentary or testimonial evidence that this decision was the result of political bias or other improper considerations. We further found that the FBI was aware of the potential for political influences on Steele's reporting from the outset of receiving it in July 2016 and, in part to account for those potential influences, the Crossfire Hurricane team undertook substantial efforts to evaluate the accuracy of the reporting and the reliability of the sources of Steele's information. We determined that these investigative efforts raised significant questions about the accuracy and reliability of Steele's election reporting. However, as described in Chapters Seven and Eight and earlier in this chapter, we concluded that the FBI did not share these questions about the reporting with Department attorneys working on the Carter Page FISA applications and failed to reassess its reliance on Steele's reporting in the Crossfire Hurricane investigation.

We also found the FBI and Steele held differing views about the nature of their relationship during this time period. Steele had signed CHS paperwork with the FBI following his opening as a CHS in 2013. Accordingly, the FBI considered

---

[501] Following his attorney's review of a draft of this report, Steele advised us through his attorney that it was important to note that his election reporting consisted of information transmitted by word of mouth by a number of individual sources. According to Steele, this is a necessary practice to obtain information in a closed society like Russia and the election reports are descriptions of what certain individual sources, deemed to be reliable by Steele's consulting firm (Orbis), stated. Further, in Steele's view, his election reports should not have been treated as facts or allegations but as the starting point for further investigation, which he said was the intended use of the reports furnished to Fusion GPS. Steele advised us through his attorney that "it is with that lens that the accuracy and value of Steele's reporting should be assessed." Steele told us that it was his hope and expectation that the FBI would have used its resources to investigate the report information. We found no evidence that Steele communicated this view of his reporting to Handling Agent 1 or members of the Crossfire Hurricane team.

Steele a CHS bound by certain obligations. Steele, however, considered himself a businessperson whose firm (not Steele) had a contractual CHS agreement with the FBI and whose election related work was not undertaken pursuant to that agreement, but instead was conducted solely on behalf of his firm's client (Fusion GPS), not the FBI. This disagreement led to divergent expectations about Steele's conduct, affected the FBI's control over Steele during the Crossfire Hurricane investigation, and ultimately resulted in the FBI formally closing Steele as a CHS (although, as we discuss later in this chapter, we found the FBI continued its relationship with Steele through Ohr).

A.   The FBI's Receipt, Use, and Assessment of Steele's Reporting

As described in Chapter Four, the Crossfire Hurricane team first learned of Steele's reports when they received six of them from Handling Agent 1 in September 2016.[502] The reporting was not the result of any proactive FBI investigative action, or any FBI tasking or direction to Steele. Rather, Steele's election reporting was developed at the request of his consulting firm's client, Fusion GPS, and was provided to the FBI with his client's consent. We found that the FBI was aware of the potential for political bias in the Steele election reporting from the outset of obtaining it. Handling Agent 1 told us that when Steele provided him with Report 80 in July 2016 and described his engagement with Fusion GPS, it was obvious to Handling Agent 1 that the request for the research was politically motivated.[503] The Supervisory Intel Analyst explained that he also was aware of the potential for political influence on the Steele election reporting when it became available to the Crossfire Hurricane team in September 2016.

We determined that the FBI's decisions to use Steele's information in Crossfire Hurricane and to task him in October 2016 were based on multiple factors unrelated to political considerations, including: (1) Steele's prior work as an intelligence professional for a ███████████████████████████ ███████; (2) his expertise on Russia; (3) his past record as an FBI CHS, which included furnishing information concerning the activities of Russian oligarchs and investigative leads involving corruption in FIFA; (4) the assessment of Handling Agent 1 that Steele was reliable and had provided information to the FBI in the past

---

[502] Steele first gave Handling Agent 1 two of these six reports in July 2016, approximately 2 months before the Crossfire Hurricane team received them on September 19. We describe in Chapter Four the various explanations we received for this delay in transmitting the reports to the team, none of which we found to be satisfactory.

[503] As described in Chapter Four, Handling Agent 1 told us that Steele informed him at their July 2016 meeting that Fusion GPS had been hired by a law firm to conduct research, though, according to Handling Agent 1, Steele stated that he did not know the law firm's name or its political affiliation. Notes that Steele allowed us to review and that he represented were written contemporaneously with the meeting state that Steele told Handling Agent 1 that "Democratic Party associates" were paying for Fusion GPS's research, the "ultimate client" was the leadership of the Clinton presidential campaign, and "the candidate" was aware of Steele's reporting. We also reviewed notes made by an Assistant Special Agent in Charge (ASAC) in the FBI's New York Field Office (NYFO) of a July 13 call the ASAC had with Handling Agent 1 about Report 80. Among other things, the notes identify Simpson as a client of a law firm and that the "law firm works for the Republican party or Hillary and will use [the information described in Report 80] at some point."

that had been corroborated; and (5) that Steele's reporting was consistent with the FBI's knowledge at the time of alleged Russian efforts to interfere in the 2016 U.S. elections.

The fact that Steele had been retained to conduct political opposition research did not require the FBI, under either Department or FBI policies, to ignore the information. The FBI and federal law enforcement regularly receive information from individuals with potentially significant biases and motivations, including drug traffickers, convicted felons, and even terrorists. The FBI is not required to set aside such information; rather, under CHS policy, the FBI is required to critically assess the information in light of any potentially significant biases and motivations. The "FBI must, to the extent practicable, ensure that the information collected from every CHS is accurate and current, and not given to the FBI in an effort to distract, mislead, or misdirect FBI organizational or governmental efforts."[504] Past OIG reviews of the Department's law enforcement components have found that the use of information from such individuals presents significant risks.[505]

In the Crossfire Hurricane investigation, as described in detail in Chapters Four and Six of this report, the team undertook substantial efforts to verify Steele's election reporting, including interviewing Steele; identifying and interviewing certain of Steele's sub-sources; undertaking CHS and Under Cover Employee (UCE) meetings with Papadopoulos, Page, and a high-level Trump campaign official; conducting database inquiries; open source research; and seeking information from other U.S. government intelligence agencies.[506] However, we found that corroboration for the election reporting proved to be elusive for the FBI to identify. FBI officials told us that the singular nature of the reporting (e.g., its recounting of conversations between a small number of persons) made it extremely difficult to verify. We determined that prior to and during the pendency of the FISAs the FBI was unable to corroborate any of the specific substantive allegations against Carter Page contained in the election reporting and relied on in the FISA applications, and was only able to confirm the accuracy of a limited number of circumstantial facts, most of which were in the public domain, such as the dates that Page traveled to Russia, the timing of events, and the occupational positions of individuals referenced in the reports.

---

[504] Confidential Human Source Validation Standards Manual ("VSM"), 0258PG (March 26, 2010), § 1.0.

[505] U.S. Department of Justice (DOJ) Office of the Inspector General (OIG), Audit of the Bureau of Alcohol, Tobacco, Firearms, and Explosives' Management and Oversight of Confidential Informants, Audit Report 17-17 (March 2017); DOJ OIG, Audit of the Drug Enforcement Administration's Confidential Source Policies and Oversight of Higher-Risk Confidential Sources, Audit Report 15-28 (July 2015); DOJ OIG, A Review of ATF's Operation Fast and Furious and Related Matters (September 2012); and DOJ OIG, The FBI's Compliance with the Attorney General's Investigative Guidelines (September 2005).

[506] FBI staff told us that because they knew of the potential for political influences on the election reporting, they did not devote resources to determine precisely which organization or persons were sponsoring Steele's reporting. Consistent with what we were told, we found that the FBI did not focus much attention on seeking to identify the client of Fusion GPS that was funding Steele's research.

In addition to the lack of corroboration, we found that the FBI's interviews of Steele, the Primary Sub-source, and a second sub-source, and other investigative activity, revealed potentially serious problems with Steele's description of information in his election reports. For example, as noted above, the Primary Sub-source's accounting of events during his/her January 2017 interview with the FBI (after the filing of the first FISA application and Renewal Application No. 1, but before the filing of Renewal Application No. 2) was not consistent with and, in fact, contradicted the allegations in Reports 95 and 102 attributed to Person 1, as well as those in Report 94 concerning the meeting between Page and Sechin. In addition, another sub-source told the FBI in August 2017 (after the filing of Renewal Application No. 3) that information in Steele's election reporting attributable to him/her had been "exaggerated." Because the sub-sources themselves could have furnished exaggerated or false information to Steele, as well as to the FBI during their interviews, the cause of these inconsistencies remains unknown. According to the Supervisory Intel Analyst, the FBI ultimately determined that some of the allegations contained in Steele's election reporting were inaccurate, such as the allegation that Manafort used Page as an intermediary (Report 95) and that Michael Cohen had travelled to Prague for meetings with representatives of the Kremlin (Reports 134, 135, 136, and 166). Although the Supervisory Intel Analyst also stated that some of the broader themes in Steele's election reporting were consistent with USIC assessments, such as Russia's desire to sow discord in the Western Alliance, he further told us that, as of September 2017, the FBI had corroborated limited information in the Steele election reporting, and much of that information was publicly available.[507]

As we described earlier in our analysis, the FBI failed to notify OI, which was working on the Carter Page FISA applications, of the potentially serious problems identified with Steele's election reporting that arose as early as January 2017 through the efforts described above. As previously stated, we believe it was the obligation of the agents who were aware of this information to ensure that OI and the decision makers had the opportunity to consider it, both for their own assessment of probable cause and for consideration of whether to include the information in the applications so that the FISC received a complete and accurate recitation of the relevant facts. Moreover, even as the FBI developed this

---

[507] As discussed in detail in Chapter Six, FBI leadership, including Comey and McCabe, advocated for the Steele election reporting to be included in the Intelligence Community Assessment (ICA) on Russian election interference that was being prepared in December 2016. For example, in a December 17 telephone call with the Director of National Intelligence (DNI), Comey stated that the FBI was "proceeding cautiously to understand and attempt to verify the reporting as best we can, but we thought it important to bring it forward to the IC effort." However, according to the Intel Section Chief and Supervisory Intel Analyst, as the interagency editing process for the ICA progressed, the CIA expressed concern about using the Steele election reporting in the body of the ICA, and recommended that it be moved to an appendix. In a December 28, 2016 email to the Office of the Director of National Intelligence (ODNI) Principal Deputy Director, McCabe objected to this recommendation, stating, "We oppose CIA's current plan to include [the election reporting] as an appendix." However, the FBI Intel Section Chief told us that the CIA viewed the Steele reporting as "internet rumor." The FBI's view did not prevail, and the final ICA report included a short summary of the Steele election reporting in an appendix.

information, we found no evidence that the Crossfire Hurricane team reconsidered its reliance on the Steele reporting in the FISA renewal applications.

In addition to these investigative efforts by the Crossfire Hurricane team to evaluate Steele as a source, the FBI's Validation Management Unit (VMU) completed a human source validation review of Steele in March 2017. We examined VMU's assessment, and in doing so, identified two procedural problems that affected the usefulness of its work product that, if not addressed by the FBI, could negatively affect VMU's future CHS assessments.[508] First, we found instances where information we deemed significant about Steele was not included in his Delta file, and therefore was not available to VMU so that it could be taken into account during VMU's validation review. The information omitted from Steele's Delta file included facts that the Crossfire Hurricane team learned in December 2016 about Steele relating to his work-related performance in a prior position, and the FBI Transnational Organized Crime Intelligence Unit's concerns about the number of contacts that Steele purportedly had with Russian oligarchs. We have raised issues in prior OIG reviews about the FBI's handling of derogatory CHS information.[509] We believe the FBI needs to assess how to better ensure that derogatory information about its CHSs is included in Delta and is readily identifiable once added. The FBI should establish enhanced procedures to ensure the completeness of its Delta files, including for investigations that are operated from FBI Headquarters.

Second, we determined that it was an error for VMU to omit from the Steele validation report its finding that its assessment of Steele's work for the FBI failed to reveal corroboration for the election reporting from the FBI and other U.S. government holdings that VMU examined. The supervising Unit Chief told us that the reason for the omission was VMU's practice of reporting on "what we positively find" and not on what is lacking. As a result, the VMU report acknowledged Steele's contribution to the FBI criminal program but did not elaborate on his contributions, or lack thereof, to the counterintelligence program. In Steele's case, VMU's approach misapprehended the reason for CD's request for the validation review. CD's interest in Steele resulted from his election reporting so any conclusions that VMU reached about it would be of intense interest to CD. According to Priestap, who had previously overseen the work of VMU in his capacity as Deputy Assistant Director in the Directorate of Intelligence, VMU's decision to omit its conclusion that Steele's election reporting was uncorroborated "defeats the whole purpose of us asking [VMU] to do the validation reporting." We believe the FBI should evaluate the reporting practices of VMU.

Finally, we found that the FBI was aware of the potential for disinformation in the Steele election reporting and, in part to address that issue, made some effort to

---

[508] We note that, by the date of the VMU human source validation review in March 2017, the Crossfire Hurricane team had identified potentially significant issues with Steele's reporting and the VMU validation review did not make any findings that would have altered that judgment.

[509] U.S. Department of Justice (DOJ) Office of the Inspector General (OIG), *Audit of the Federal Bureau of Investigation's Management of its Confidential Human Source Validation Process*, Audit Report 20-009 (November 2019); DOJ OIG, *A Review of the FBI's Handling and Oversight of FBI Asset Katrina Leung* (May 2006).

assess that possibility. However, in view of information we found in FBI files we reviewed, and that was available to the Crossfire Hurricane team during the relevant time period, we believe that more should have been done to examine Steele's contacts with intermediaries of Russian oligarchs in order to assess those contacts as potential sources of disinformation that could have influenced Steele's reporting or, at a minimum, influenced Steele's understanding of events in Russia that furnished context for the analytical judgments he used to evaluate the reporting. We agree with the assessment of Priestap and Evans that this issue warranted more scrutiny than it was afforded.

B. The Lack of Agreement on Steele's Status as an FBI CHS and its Effect on the Crossfire Hurricane Team's Relationship with Steele

We determined that, from the outset of the FBI's formal relationship with Steele in 2013 (when Steele first received FBI CHS admonishments), the FBI and Steele had differing views on the nature of Steele's relationship with the FBI. The FBI considered Steele to be an FBI CHS following his enrollment as a CHS, which was reinforced by Steele's later signing of CHS payment and admonishment paperwork, while Steele considered the CHS documentation to be a business arrangement between him, on behalf of his consulting firm, and the FBI. As detailed in Chapter Four, we found evidence during our review that supported both the FBI's view and Steele's position.

The paperwork enrolling Steele as a CHS in 2013 was the FBI's standard CHS opening documentation; the FBI documented Steele's receipt of CHS admonishments; and the documentation did not reference in any way a relationship between the FBI and Steele's consulting firm. Similarly, on multiple occasions thereafter, Steele signed, using his FBI assigned code name, FBI payment forms that were plainly denominated as CHS documentation and that did not reference his consulting firm. However, we also identified material indicating that Steele made known to Handling Agent 1 from the outset of their discussions in 2010 that he could not be a CHS for the FBI due to his prior work as a foreign intelligence professional. We also identified a memorandum that the FBI sent to Steele's ███████████████████████████████████, prior to opening Steele as a CHS in 2013, explaining that "Mr. Steele is providing the FBI with information," while also stating that the information that the FBI was to obtain would be furnished "primarily through Mr. Steele's privately owned company" and that the FBI would "treat any material provided as information obtained through a Confidential Human Source." Similarly, Steele's letter to his ████████████, dated at around the same time as the FBI memorandum, informed the ████████████ that Steele's consulting firm (rather than Steele) was planning to enter into a commercial relationship with the FBI. Given the similarities between the FBI and Steele memoranda to Steele's ████████████, the FBI's description of Steele appears crafted to satisfy Steele's concerns and, in our view, is indicative of the understanding reached between Steele and the FBI concerning his status—that both sides would leave unresolved their differing perspectives on the nature of their relationship in order to keep information flowing to the FBI and to ensure that Steele could be paid for any work he performed on behalf of the FBI.

This uncertainty about the nature of the relationship had an impact on each side's understanding of Steele's obligations to the FBI in the Crossfire Hurricane investigation, particularly after the meeting between the FBI and Steele in early October 2016 about Steele's election reporting. Steele told us that he never viewed himself or his firm as performing election-related work on behalf of the FBI; rather, Steele considered himself to be functioning as a consultant to a paying client of his firm, which was seeking information about Russian interference in the 2016 U.S. elections from Steele's source network. Steele reported the information to his client, Fusion GPS, as he acquired it and followed his client's instructions. In contrast, we found that the FBI agents viewed Steele as a former intelligence officer colleague who was an FBI CHS with obligations to the FBI, and that the agents displayed insufficient awareness of the priority Steele placed on his business commitments.[510]

We concluded that, at the outset of Steele's interactions with the FBI in July 2016 regarding his election reporting work, it was clear that Steele was operating as a businessperson working on behalf of a client of his firm, rather than as a CHS for the FBI. Indeed, as detailed in Chapter Four, when Steele met Handling Agent 1 on July 5, 2016, Steele told him about his consulting firm having been retained by Fusion GPS, and provided Handling Agent 1 with Report 80. Handling Agent 1 made clear to Steele that he was not working for the FBI on his election assignment and was not being tasked to collect election related information. We found that Handling Agent 1's caution to Steele was unnecessary from Steele's perspective, as he did not view himself as working on behalf of the FBI to gather election related information, and he and his client were taking steps to disseminate the election reporting to other parties. Handling Agent 1 told us, however, that from his perspective he believed his caution to Steele was necessary because he believed Steele was a CHS and his election related activity would be harmful to Steele's relationship with the FBI.

As detailed in Chapter Nine and discussed later in this chapter, beginning in July 2016, Steele had multiple contacts with Department attorney Bruce Ohr about his reports. That same month, Steele first provided his election reporting to the State Department. In August 2016, the FBI received correspondence from Members of Congress that described information included in the Steele reports, and in September 2016, Steele met with journalists from The *New York Times*, The *Washington Post*, *Yahoo News*, *The New Yorker*, and CNN about his work. Steele in fact was the "Western intelligence source" referenced in the September 23, *Yahoo News* article entitled, "*U.S. Intel Officials Probe Ties Between Trump Advisor and Kremlin*," that described efforts by U.S. intelligence to determine whether Carter Page had opened communication channels with Kremlin officials. The FBI did not ask Steele whether he was a source for the article, nor did it question Steele about the apparent dissemination of his election reporting to other parties.

---

[510] In comments on this report, Handling Agent 1 told us that he was well aware of Steele's business priorities, but that he was not aware that Steele would be a "front man" in dealings with the press and that Steele would fail to inform him of these and other contacts that violated the FBI's instructions at the early October meeting.

However, the caution provided by Handling Agent 1 to Steele at their July 2016 meeting—that Steele was not being tasked to collect election related information—changed in early October 2016 when Crossfire Hurricane investigators met with Steele and attempted to task him as a CHS. During that meeting, the FBI requested that Steele collect "3 buckets" of information, which was a small subset of information related to the FBI's investigation into Russian interference in the 2016 U.S. elections.[511] The FBI told Steele that the FBI was willing to compensate him "significantly" for this information, and that he would be paid $15,000 just for attending the October meeting.[512] Additionally, investigators told us that they orally instructed Steele to report information he gathered in response to these taskings exclusively to the FBI. These taskings and instructions were consistent with the FBI considering Steele to be a CHS going forward.[513]

Based on the testimony we obtained from participants in the early October meeting and the documents we reviewed that memorialized it, Steele appears to have made no commitments in response to this FBI request for exclusivity, though we found that he did not expressly reject it either. From the surrounding circumstances, we concluded it was unlikely that Steele agreed to the FBI's request. Steele was a businessperson with a paying client for whom he had worked on other projects and had committed to assist the client on the election project. Steele told us that any attempt by the FBI to interfere in his assignment from Fusion GPS would have been a "showstopper." Case Agent 2 could not recall Steele agreeing to anything during the meeting in early October, and acknowledged to OI following the meeting that they needed to be "realistic" about the prospects of Steele limiting the dissemination of his reporting to the FBI.[514]

---

[511] The 3 buckets concerned (1) information on the Crossfire Hurricane subjects; (2) physical evidence; and (3) leads for sources.

[512] Although the FBI did not condition this payment on Steele's future performance, the FBI cancelled the payment after it decided to close Steele as a CHS in November 2016.

[513] We also examined whether the FBI disclosed classified information to Steele during the early October meeting. We determined that Case Agent 2 did when he discussed information with Steele that the FBI received from the FFG, and that he did not have prior authorization to make the disclosure. However, we found that: (1) Case Agent 2 was given significant latitude from his supervisors to frame his discussions with Steele; (2) Case Agent 2 believed he had authorization to discuss classified information with Steele based on prior discussions with his supervisors; (3) a CD Section Chief was present when Case Agent 2 made the disclosure, and the CD Section Chief did not voice objection to it at the time or afterward; and (4) Case Agent 2 included the disclosure in a written summary he prepared of the early October meeting that was uploaded to the Crossfire Hurricane case file. We also found that the CHS Policy Guide (CHSPG) does not address the disclosure of sensitive or classified information to CHSs and that the FBI has not otherwise developed guidance on the issue. We found no evidence that Case Agent 2 attempted to conceal his disclosure or that it was for any purpose other than advancing the objectives of the Crossfire Hurricane investigation. Case Agent 2 is retired from the FBI. We make a recommendation in this report that the FBI establish guidance for sharing sensitive information with CHSs.

[514] As we described in Chapter Four, Handling Agent 1 believed that Steele failed to abide by FBI instructions when he continued to meet with the media and the State Department about issues over which the FBI had sought to establish an exclusive reporting relationship at the early October meeting. Case Agent 2 told the OIG that he thought it was "terrible" for Steele to complain to the FBI about leaks during the meeting given that he had been meeting with media outlets in September and

Nevertheless, we found that, following this October meeting, the FBI viewed Steele as a CHS with respect to these taskings and considered him bound by the standard "CHS admonishments" that he had received initially in 2013 and renewed most recently in January 2016, which committed him to "abide by the instructions of the FBI" and to "provide truthful information to the FBI."[515] Handling Agent 1 told us that he previously had provided oral instructions to Steele that included not divulging the existence of his relationship with the FBI to others, and not sharing with third parties the information he was providing to the FBI aside from his client paying for the research. However, these oral instructions were not documented in Steele's Delta file, and Steele told us that he did not recall receiving them, but understood that the FBI did not want him to reveal their relationship to others. We also found that the FBI's standard admonishment form does not include an instruction to the CHS not to disclose the existence of the CHS's relationship with the FBI to others absent the FBI's permission.[516]

In contrast, Steele told us that, from the outset of his relationship with the FBI, the FBI acquiesced in practice to an arrangement that recognized the existence of the "two pipelines" of information that Steele described to us and which we discussed more fully in Chapter Four. In Steele's view, any FBI admonishments and instructions were relevant only to his FBI assignments (*i.e.* Pipeline 2 work), but not to his work for his firm's clients that Steele chose to share with the FBI (*i.e.* Pipeline 1 work). Steele stated that he was free to discuss Pipeline 1 work with his clients and with third parties, as necessary, without gaining permission from the FBI. Steele told us that the FBI indicated at the meeting in early October that it sought to convert his Pipeline 1 election project for Fusion GPS into a Pipeline 2 project for the FBI, and take control of it. Steele also told us that he made it clear during the meeting that was not going to happen because he was obligated to his client and was "not dumping the client" in favor of the FBI, but that he also wanted to be as helpful to the FBI as he could. According to Steele, the FBI accepted his position, though they requested that he not share his election reporting with other U.S. government entities or with third-party clients other than Fusion GPS. Steele said he could not recall if he agreed to this FBI request but believed that the request was not resolved at the meeting. FBI attendees at the early October meeting told us they had no recollection of Steele rejecting their request that he provide information on the "3 buckets" exclusively to the FBI, and if he had rejected their request it would have been documented.

Consistent with their inability in 2013 to reach a shared understanding on Steele's status with the FBI, we concluded that the FBI and Steele in October 2016

had provided information that was used in the *Yahoo News* article. According to Case Agent 2, in hindsight "[c]learly [Steele] wasn't truthful with us. Clearly." Steele denied to us that he ever lied or purposely misled the FBI.

[515] The FBI form memorializing Steele's receipt of admonishments in 2016 states that Handling Agent 1 "verbally admonished the CHS with CHS admonishments, which the CHS fully acknowledged, signed and dated." The FBI could not locate the signed admonishment form, however.

[516] For safety and security reasons, among others, we believe such an instruction should be a part of the standard admonishments provided by the Department's law enforcement components to its CHSs, and we therefore include a recommendation to that effect in this report.

appeared to reach a similarly imperfect arrangement that reflected the competing needs and interests of each party. The FBI provided instructions to Steele, but Steele did not make any express commitment to abide by specific terms. The FBI also sought exclusivity for information Steele developed in response to the tasking, but we found that Steele did not make an express commitment to the FBI to honor this request.

As described in Chapter Six, the FBI closed Steele as a CHS for cause in November 2016, after determining that Steele breached an obligation when he divulged his FBI relationship to a journalist for *Mother Jones* the month before. This obligation was based upon the oral admonishment the FBI said it previously provided to Steele, an admonishment Steele said he did not recall receiving or agreeing to, but one that he said reflected an expectation he understood. Steele also told us, in explaining his disclosure to *Mother Jones*, that he believed the FBI had misled him when Comey notified Congress in late October 2016 that the FBI was reopening the Clinton email investigation while at the same time an FBI official was quoted in *The New York Times* as saying that there was no investigation of Trump or the Trump campaign.

We believe that the FBI's decision to close Steele, as well as its failure to press him about his role in the September 2016 *Yahoo News* story and his October 2016 visit to the State Department, were consequences of the FBI's and Steele's inability to come to a shared understanding on the terms of their relationship. We also believe that the FBI allowed the arrangement with Steele to exist because its expectations about Steele's behavior were heavily influenced by his background as a former intelligence officer and his past assistance to the FBI in that capacity, with insufficient focus on Steele's current business interests and obligations, even though Steele disclosed them to the FBI. Indeed, as we describe in the next section, we found that even after the FBI closed Steele as a CHS in November 2016 for cause, and as a result, under FBI policy should have ceased its contact with Steele absent exceptional circumstances or reopening him as a CHS, the FBI continued its relationship with Steele by allowing Steele to regularly provide information to the FBI through a senior Department attorney, Bruce Ohr, with whom Steele was friendly.

IV. Issues Relating to Department Attorney Bruce Ohr

In this section, we analyze the interactions Department attorney Bruce Ohr had with Christopher Steele, Simpson, the FBI, and the State Department during the Crossfire Hurricane investigation. We also analyze Ohr's interactions with Department attorneys and FBI officials concerning the Department's criminal investigation of Paul Manafort. At the time of these activities, Ohr was an Associate Deputy Attorney General in ODAG and the Director of the Organized Crime and Drug Enforcement Task Force (OCDETF).

As described more fully in Chapter Nine, at about the same time that Steele was engaging with the FBI on his election reporting, Steele was also sharing his reporting with Ohr, with whom he had a pre-existing professional and "friendly" relationship since at least 2007. Beginning in July 2016, Steele had contacted Ohr on multiple occasions to discuss information from Steele's election reports. At Steele's suggestion, Ohr also met in August 2016 with Simpson, the owner of Fusion GPS, to discuss Steele's reports. At the time, Ohr's wife, Nellie Ohr, worked at Fusion GPS as an independent contractor. Ohr had a second meeting with Simpson in December 2016, at which time Simpson gave Ohr a thumb drive containing numerous Steele election reports.

On October 18, 2016, three days before the first FISA application was submitted to the FISC, and after speaking with Steele that morning, Ohr requested a meeting with, and that same day met with McCabe to share Steele's and Simpson's information with him. Thereafter, Ohr met with members of the Crossfire Hurricane team 13 times between November 21, 2016, and May 15, 2017, concerning his contacts with Steele and Simpson. All 13 meetings occurred after the FBI had closed Steele as a CHS for disclosing information to *Mother Jones* and, except for the November 21 meeting, each meeting was initiated at Ohr's request. Ohr told us he did not recall the FBI asking him to take any action regarding Steele or Simpson, but Ohr also stated that "the general instruction was to let [the FBI] know…when I got information from Steele." At two of these meetings, both in December 2016, after Nellie Ohr had left Fusion GPS, Ohr provided the FBI with open source research Nellie Ohr conducted on Manafort while working at Fusion GPS. The Crossfire Hurricane team memorialized each meeting with Ohr as an "interview" using an FBI FD-302 form.

In addition to the FBI, Ohr met with senior State Department officials in November 2016 to discuss State Department efforts to investigate Russian influence in foreign elections. On this and several other days Ohr had separate discussions with State Department Deputy Assistant Secretary Kathleen Kavalec about Steele and his election information specifically to obtain relevant information that he could share with the FBI.

Department leadership, including Ohr's supervisors in ODAG and ODAG officials who reviewed and approved the Carter Page FISA applications, were unaware of Ohr's meetings with FBI officials, Steele, Simpson, and the State Department until after Congress requested information from the Department regarding Ohr's activities in late November 2017.

In addition, shortly after the U.S. elections in November 2016, Ohr participated in several meetings with Deputy Assistant Attorney General (Deputy AAG) Bruce Swartz, Chief of the Fraud Section Andrew Weissmann, and Counsel to the Criminal Division Assistant Attorney General Zainab Ahmad regarding the Department's money laundering investigation of Manafort. Two of these meetings included FBI officials Peter Strzok and Lisa Page.[517] The FBI opened the Manafort money laundering investigation in January 2016, before the opening of Crossfire Hurricane and before Manafort joined the Trump campaign, and the case was being led in 2016 by prosecutors from the Criminal Division's (CRM) Money Laundering

---

[517] One of the two meetings attended by Strzok and Page was also attended by Acting Section Chief 1 of the FBI.

and Asset Recovery Section (MLARS). Ohr and the three CRM officials he met with did not have supervisory authority over the MLARS criminal investigation, and they did not advise their supervisors in ODAG and CRM MLARS prosecutors of the meetings. However, we did not find evidence that these meetings progressed beyond discussion into any specific actions that interfered with the MLARS investigation or Department leadership's oversight of that matter.

In light of these activities, we considered the following issues addressed below: (1) whether Ohr's interactions with Steele, Simpson, the FBI, and State Department violated Department policy or resulted in any specific performance failures, (2) whether the FBI's interactions with Ohr concerning Steele and Simpson after Steele was closed as an FBI CHS violated Department or FBI policy, (3) whether Nellie Ohr's work for Fusion GPS implicated any ethical rules applicable to Ohr, and (4) whether the meetings between Ohr, CRM officials, and the FBI regarding the MLARS investigation violated Department policy or resulted in any specific performance failures.

A.   Bruce Ohr's Interactions with Steele, Simpson, the State Department, and the FBI

We did not identify a specific Department policy prohibiting Ohr from meeting with Steele, Simpson, or the State Department and providing the information he learned from those meetings to the FBI. Further, we found no evidence that the FBI expressly requested that Ohr obtain information from Steele, or anyone else, on the FBI's behalf. However, as described in Chapter Nine, Ohr told us that "the general instruction [he received from the FBI] was to let them know...when I got information from Steele." Similarly, SSA 1 told us that Ohr likely left their initial November 21, 2016 meeting with the impression that he should contact the FBI if Steele contacted him, which is what Ohr did.

In this regard, we concluded that Ohr committed consequential errors in judgment by (1) failing to advise his direct supervisors or the DAG that he was communicating with Steele and Simpson and then requesting meetings with the FBI's Deputy Director and Crossfire Hurricane team on matters that were outside his areas of responsibility, and (2) making himself a witness in the investigation by having direct communications with Steele about his reporting and activities and providing Steele's information to the FBI.[518]

We found that Ohr's failure to advise his supervisors resulted in Ohr being aware of relevant information that was not made known to Department officials, thereby interfering with those officials' supervisory responsibility for the Crossfire Hurricane investigation and the Carter Page FISA applications. As described in Chapter Eight, Yates, Boente, and Rosenstein told us that they had no knowledge at the time they reviewed and approved the Page FISA applications that Ohr had provided the FBI with information related to the Crossfire Hurricane investigation and that was relevant to the FISA applications. Other ODAG officials who reviewed one or more of the applications told us that they were also unaware of Ohr's

---

[518] We did not find evidence that Ohr shared non-public information with Steele or Simpson.

activities at the time, including the Associate Deputy Attorney General responsible for ODAG's national security portfolio who interacted with NSD and OI officials on the FISA applications and was aware of their efforts described in Chapter Five to evaluate the Steele information being relied upon to support probable cause. Although we found no information suggesting that Ohr knew about any of the FISA applications before they were filed, by failing to advise his supervisors of his interactions with Steele, Simpson, and the FBI, Ohr deprived those supervisors of the ability to ensure that the ODAG officials working on the applications were made aware of information relevant to evaluating the Steele reporting in the applications. It also deprived ODAG officials of the opportunity to ensure that NSD and OI were made aware of the information that Ohr knew from his Steele interactions so that NSD and OI could consider whether to include the information in the next FISA application, though we believe that the FBI case agent should have been the first to advise NSD and OI of Ohr's activities. As described in Chapter Eight, the late discovery of Ohr's interviews with the FBI prompted NSD to submit a Rule 13 letter to the court, over a year after the final FISA orders were issued, to inform the court, among other things, of information that Ohr had provided to the FBI but that the FBI had failed to inform NSD and OI about, including that Steele was "desperate that Donald Trump not get elected and was passionate about him not being the U.S. President."

Additionally, as described in earlier chapters, beginning in early 2017, Boente and later Rosenstein requested multiple briefings on the Crossfire Hurricane investigation, which included, among many topics, updates on the FBI's continued efforts to assess Steele and his information. Because Ohr did not advise anyone in ODAG about his activities, Boente, Rosenstein, and the other ODAG officials briefed into Crossfire Hurricane had no idea that one of the senior attorneys on their staff, with no responsibility over counterintelligence investigations, had made himself a witness in the investigation by having direct communications with Steele about his reporting and activities and initiating contact with the Crossfire Hurricane team to provide the FBI with information he received from Steele, as well as information he received separately from Simpson, Kavalec, and Nellie Ohr.

Further, we found that Ohr's failure to advise his supervisors of his activities deprived the DAG and senior ODAG officials of the ability to decide for themselves the prudential question of whether to have an ODAG attorney act as a conduit between a closed FBI CHS and the FBI on matters relating to an open investigation. The opportunity to consider that question for themselves was particularly important here, given the connections to a high priority, politically sensitive investigation and the involvement of a closed CHS with ties to a political party and candidate for President, and indirect connections to the ODAG attorney's spouse. Former Principal Associate Deputy Attorney General (PADAG) Matthew Axelrod, Ohr's direct supervisor in 2016, told us that he would have expected to know about Ohr's communications with Steele and the FBI. Axelrod stated that if ODAG officials had known, they would have questioned Ohr's involvement and determined whether the FBI had the ability to "pull him out" of acting as a conduit between Steele and the FBI. He said that he thought it "unlikely that we would have been comfortable with [Ohr] continuing to play that role." Axelrod's immediate successor, former Acting

PADAG James Crowell, who supervised Ohr in 2017, told us that he was "flabbergasted" when he learned of Ohr's interactions with the FBI regarding Steele. According to Crowell, Ohr should have informed ODAG officials of his relationship with Steele and Simpson and his interactions with the FBI, especially after Rosenstein appointed the Special Counsel and began directly supervising the investigation, because "a potential fact witness" was on Rosenstein's staff. Crowell told us that he would have taken steps to eliminate any appearance that Ohr was involved in ODAG's oversight of the investigation.

We found that, while no Department or ODAG policy specifically prohibited Ohr's activities, Ohr was clearly cognizant of his responsibility to inform his supervisors of his interactions with Steele, the FBI, and State Department. Indeed, Ohr acknowledged to the OIG that the possibility that he would have been told by his supervisors to stop having such contact may have factored into his decision not to tell them about it. Precisely because of this possibility, and the reasons more fully described above, we concluded that Ohr committed consequential errors in judgment by failing to advise his direct supervisors or the DAG that he was communicating with Steele, Simpson, and the FBI on matters related to the Crossfire Hurricane investigation, and that this performance failure had a negative impact on the investigation and ODAG's fulfillment of its own management responsibilities. We are referring our finding to the Department's Office of Professional Responsibility for any action it deems appropriate. We are also providing our finding to Ohr's current supervisors in CRM for any action they deem appropriate.

B.   FBI Interactions with Ohr Concerning Steele and Simpson

As described in Chapter Two, the FBI's CHS Policy Guide (CHSPG) provides guidance to agents concerning contacts with CHSs after they have been closed for cause, as was the case with Steele as of November 1, 2016. According to the CHSPG, a handling agent must not initiate contact with or respond to contacts from a former CHS who has been closed for cause absent exceptional circumstances that are approved (in advance, whenever possible) by an SSA. Where there is contact with a CHS following closure (whether or not for cause), new information "may be documented" to a closed CHS file. However, the CHSPG requires the reopening of the CHS if the relationship between the FBI and the CHS is expected to continue beyond the initial contact or debriefing. Reopening requires high levels of supervisory approval, including a finding that the benefits of reopening the CHS outweigh the risks.

In this instance, we found that the FBI did not initiate direct contact with Steele after his closure on November 1, 2016. However, the FBI did respond to numerous contacts made by Steele to the FBI through Ohr. Ohr himself was not a direct witness to the facts and circumstances that were the focus of the Crossfire Hurricane investigation; rather, his purpose in communicating with the FBI was to pass along information from Steele. Further, although Ohr initiated his meetings with the Crossfire Hurricane team, as noted above, the team gave Ohr the impression that he should contact them in the event he had additional contact with Steele. While the FBI's CHS policy does not explicitly address indirect contact between an FBI agent and a closed CHS, we concluded that the FBI's repeated acceptance of information from Steele through a conduit (Ohr) was equivalent to responding to a contact from Steele and therefore should have triggered the CHS policy requiring that such contact occur only after an SSA determines that exceptional circumstances exist. Here, the SSAs on the Crossfire Hurricane team attended the meetings with Ohr and served as Ohr's points of contact, and in this manner approved the contact. However, we found no evidence that the SSAs made a considered judgment that exceptional circumstances existed for the repeated contact; in the absence of such a circumstance, the FBI's re-engagement of Steele did not fully comply with the FBI's CHS policy.

In addition, the Crossfire Hurricane team memorialized the meetings with Ohr and the information Ohr provided in FD-302 forms serialized to the case file. Although the information was not separately documented in Steele's closed CHS file, the guidance regarding documentation is discretionary (new information "may be documented" to a closed CHS file). We believe the FBI should make such documentation mandatory so that the CHS file contains all relevant information about the CHS.

As noted above, the CHSPG contemplates the reopening of the CHS if the relationship between the FBI and the CHS is expected to continue beyond the initial contact or debriefing, which helps to ensure that high level supervisors weigh the risks presented by reengagement with the CHS and that operational assessments of the CHS are undertaken. Although the FBI met with Ohr on 13 occasions and accepted information that Ohr received from Steele, the FBI never assessed whether to re-open Steele as a CHS. As described in Chapter Nine, there were differing views about whether the information Ohr was providing had any investigative value. SSAs on the investigation also told us that they had some concern at the time that continuing to engage with Ohr regarding his interactions with Steele was "out of the norm" and a "bad idea." Although the FBI did not have a direct "relationship" with Steele after November 1, 2016, we believe the use of Ohr as a conduit between the two created a relationship by proxy that should have triggered a supervisory decision early in the process about whether to reopen Steele as a CHS or discontinue accepting information indirectly through Ohr. We concluded that not obtaining supervisory review was inconsistent with the CHS policy's intent to have a higher level official determine whether the "exceptional circumstances" that an SSA believes are present to authorize an initial contact with a closed CHS warrant reopening of the CHS.[519]

We found that the Crossfire Hurricane team did not consider Ohr providing the FBI with information from Steele to be a re-engagement of their relationship with Steele. Rather, the team viewed Ohr as just another "stream of reporting." On the other hand, Priestap told us that he was not aware of the full extent of Ohr's communications with Steele and the Crossfire Hurricane team and that the number

---

[519] Even if the SSAs had determined that exigent circumstances existed for the initial re-engagement with Steele, once it was clear the contact between FBI and Ohr was expected to continue beyond the initial contact, we believe FBI policy required the SSAs to either reopen Steele at that time or discontinue accepting his information indirectly through Ohr.

of times Ohr provided the FBI with information from Steele would have raised "red flags" for him. We believe that additional policy guidance would be helpful to clarify the considerations and requirements that apply in the third-party context. Accordingly, we recommend that the FBI revise its CHS policy to explicitly address the situation that occurred here, namely the steps that should be followed before and after accepting information from a closed CHS indirectly through a third party, and the considerations that should be taken into account before doing so. Further, we recommend that the CHS policy be clarified to require that contact with a closed CHS be documented in the CHS file.

C. Ethics Issues Raised by Nellie Ohr's Former Employment with Fusion GPS

Fusion GPS employed Nellie Ohr as an independent contractor from October 2015 to September 2016. We considered whether Bruce Ohr complied with his financial disclosure reporting obligations under 5 C.F.R. part 2634 related to Nellie Ohr's employment. On his annual financial disclosure forms covering calendar years 2015 and 2016, Ohr listed Nellie Ohr as an "independent contractor" and reported her income from that work on the form. We determined that 5 C.F.R. part 2634, which sets forth the financial disclosure rules for executive branch employees, and the supplemental guidance from the Office of Government Ethics (OGE), did not require Ohr to list on the form the specific organizations, such as Fusion GPS, that retained and paid Nellie Ohr as an independent contractor during the reporting period. We further noted that, consistent with OGE practice, Ohr's financial disclosure form, which listed Nellie Ohr as an "independent contractor" and reported her total income but not the specific source(s) of the income, was reviewed and approved for filing by the ODAG and Department ethics officers before being submitted to OGE. Accordingly, we determined that Ohr complied with his financial disclosure reporting obligations.

We separately considered whether the Standards of Ethical Conduct for Employees of the Executive Branch required Ohr to recuse himself from participating in activity related to the Crossfire Hurricane investigation because of Nellie Ohr's prior work for Fusion GPS as an independent contractor. Specifically, 5 C.F.R. § 2635.502(a) provides that an employee should not participate in a matter, unless agency ethics counsel authorizes participation, "[w]here an employee knows that a particular matter involving specific parties is likely to have a direct and predictable effect on the financial interest of a member of his household...and where the employee determines that the circumstances would cause a reasonable person with knowledge of the relevant facts to question his impartiality in the matter...." Section 402(b)(1) defines "direct and predictable effect" as "a close causal link between any decision or action to be taken in the matter and any expected effect of the matter on the financial interest." We found that Nellie Ohr's relationship with Fusion GPS ceased on September 24, 2016, which was prior to Ohr's meeting with McCabe on October 18, 2016, as well as all 13 of his meetings with the Crossfire Hurricane team, the first of which was on November 21, 2016. Accordingly, by those dates, Ohr's activities could not have had a direct and predictable effect on his or his wife's financial interests, and federal ethics rules did

396

not require that Ohr obtain Department ethics counsel approval before engaging with the FBI in connection with the Crossfire Hurricane matter.

The federal ethics rules further provide in Section 502(a)(2) that an employee "who is concerned that circumstances other than those specifically described in this section would raise a question regarding his impartiality should use the process described in this section [namely, to consult with Department ethics officials] to determine whether he should or should not participate in a particular matter." However, while OGE has made clear that employees are "encouraged" to use this process, it also has stated that "[t]he election not to use that process should not be characterized...as an 'ethical lapse.'" OGE 94 x 10(1), Letter to a Department Acting Secretary, March 30, 1994; *see also*, OGE 01 x 8 Letter to a Designated Agency Ethics Official, August 23, 2001. While OGE guidance establishes that Ohr did not commit a formal ethical violation, we nevertheless concluded that Ohr, an experienced Department attorney and a member of the SES, should have been more cognizant of the appearance concerns created by Nellie Ohr's employment with Fusion GPS and availed himself of the process described in Section 502(a). We found that his failure to take this step displayed a lapse in judgment.

D.   Meetings Involving Ohr, CRM officials, and the FBI Regarding the MLARS Investigation

As described in more detail in Chapter Nine, on November 16, 2016, Ohr advised CRM officials Bruce Swartz and Zainab Ahmad of information "about [Paul] Manafort and Trump and possible Russian influence that [Ohr] was getting from Steele and Glenn Simpson." This discussion led to subsequent meetings with them and Andrew Weissmann about the pre-existing MLARS investigation of Manafort and whether the Fraud Section could move the investigation forward. At the time of these meetings, Swartz was a CRM Deputy AAG and Weissmann was the Chief of the Fraud Section. During this period, Ahmad was initially Counsel to the Criminal Division AAG and then became an Acting CRM Deputy AAG.[520] None of these CRM officials had supervisory responsibility over the MLARS investigation. Ahmad and Weissmann did not have prior direct involvement in the investigation. Swartz had assisted MLARS with gathering evidence from abroad, and therefore, had extensive prior knowledge and involvement with the investigation, but was not responsible for investigative decisions. The MLARS Manafort investigation was outside Ohr's areas of responsibility. At Ohr's suggestion, Ohr, Swartz, and Ahmad also met with FBI officials Peter Strzok and Lisa Page in December 2016 to discuss the MLARS investigation because Ohr knew by that time that the FBI's CD was working on a separate matter involving Manafort. On January 31, 2017, one day after Yates was removed as Deputy Attorney General, Ahmad, after consulting with Swartz and Weissmann, called a second meeting, citing to "a few Criminal Division related developments." None of the attendees of the meeting could explain to us what the "Criminal Division related developments" were, and we did not find any. However,

---

[520] Swartz, Ohr, and Weissmann were members of the Senior Executive Service (SES). Ahmad was on detail to the Criminal Division from the U.S. Attorney's Office for the Eastern District of New York and was not a member of the SES.

we are not aware of any information indicating that these discussions resulted in any actions taken or not taken in the MLARS investigation and ultimately the investigation remained in MLARS until it was transferred to The Special Counsel's Office in May 2017.

MLARS officials were not invited to these meetings or informed of them. The then Chief of MLARS, Kendall Day and the acting Chief who replaced him in January 2017, both told us that they were unaware at the time that these CRM officials and Ohr were discussing the MLARS investigation and engaging with the FBI Day told us that when he learned in March or April 2017 that Swartz, Ohr, Ahmad, and Weissmann were "collectively interested" in the Manafort investigation, he met with Swartz and Ahmad and told them that their "unusual level of interest" could create a perception that the Department was investigating Manafort for inappropriate reasons.[521]

In addition, Ohr, Swartz, Ahmad, and Weissmann told us that they did not advise their supervisors of their meetings, and senior CRM and ODAG officials told us that they were unaware of them. Further, Swartz told us that he specifically did not advise political appointees leading the Criminal Division of the meetings. According to Swartz, he did not believe at the time that he needed to advise political appointees because the meetings had not resulted in any steps being taken in the MLARS investigation, and by not informing them he was keeping the MLARS investigation from being "politicized" and protecting the Department from allegations that its MLARS investigation of Manafort was politically motivated. Swartz stated that he would have informed his political superiors if any decision to take action had been made as a consequence of the meetings. Weissmann told us that he thought not telling Department leadership was an "incorrect judgment call," but could not recall if he expressed this view to Swartz or Ahmad.

The former senior Department leaders we interviewed expressed serious concern about Swartz's assertion that not informing Department leadership about case related investigative activities somehow protected the Department. For example, after Yates learned during her OIG interview of the meetings involving Ohr, Swartz, Ahmad, and Weissmann, she told us that a decision not to advise political appointees "trouble[d]" her because the Department does not "operate that way." Yates said that there is not "a career Department of Justice and a political appointees' Department of Justice. It's all one DOJ." Former CRM Assistant

---

[521] After reviewing a draft of this report, Swartz told us that he had provided information to the OIG demonstrating his long standing interest and official involvement in reviewing Manafort's conduct, dating back to at least 2014, and that he was concerned by what he perceived as the "languishing" pace at which the MLARS investigation was progressing, and that it was his "duty" to attempt to move it forward. He therefore believed it was appropriate for him to meet with Weissmann to discuss potential avenues for doing this, and to meet with FBI officials to ensure that the FBI was aware of MLARS' investigation. Although we acknowledge Swartz's long-standing interest and official involvement in Manafort-related inquiries, we believe that Swartz could have raised his concerns directly with MLARS, Day, or others in MLARS' direct supervisory chain. Indeed, when asked about Swartz's concerns, then Acting DAG Boente told us that the Manafort investigation was an MLARS case, and Swartz could have taken his concerns to the then Acting Assistant Attorney General, who was a career Department employee, to attempt to address his concerns.

Attorney General (AAG) Leslie Caldwell told us that a decision to not advise political appointees of meetings they were having relating to the MLARS investigation to avoid "politicizing" it was "inappropriate" and showed "poor judgment" because it "suggest[ed] a lack of trust or a lack of confidence in the political appointee . . . and that seem[ed] a little bit paranoid to [her]."

We did not identify any Department policies prohibiting internal discussions about a pending investigation among officials not assigned to a matter, or between those officials and senior officials from the FBI. However, we were troubled by the testimony more fully described in Chapter Nine that there was a deliberate decision not to inform the political appointees, or the Acting AAG of CRM after the change in presidential administrations – who was a career Department employee – of these discussions in order to insulate the MLARS investigation from becoming "politicized." We concluded that the decision to intentionally withhold information from the Department's leadership in both the prior and current administrations, in the absence of concerns of potential wrongdoing or misconduct fundamentally misconstrued who is ultimately responsible and accountable for the Department's work.[522] We agree with the concerns expressed to us by Yates and Caldwell. Department leaders cannot fulfill their management responsibilities, and be held accountable for the Department's actions, if subordinates intentionally withhold information from them in such circumstances. The Department's leadership, which is nominated by the President and confirmed by the Senate, is ultimately answerable within the Executive Branch, to Congress, and in the courts for the investigations, prosecutions, and other activities of the Department, whether politically sensitive or routine. Ultimately, however, we did not find evidence that the meetings between Ohr and CRM officials Swartz, Ahmad, and Weissmann, amongst themselves and with FBI officials Strzok, Lisa Page, and Acting Section Chief 1, progressed beyond discussion to any specific actions that interfered with the MLARS investigation or Department leadership's oversight of that matter.

V. The Use of Other Confidential Human Sources and Undercover Employees and Compliance with Applicable Policies

In this section, we analyze the FBI's use of CHSs, other than Steele, and Under Cover Employees (UCEs) in the Crossfire Hurricane investigation, and discuss whether the FBI placed any CHSs or UCEs within the Trump campaign or tasked any CHSs or UCEs to report on the Trump campaign. Additionally, we analyze whether the Crossfire Hurricane team's use of such individuals complied with Department and FBI policies. We also discuss SSA 1's participation on behalf of the FBI in a strategic intelligence briefing given by the Office of the Director of National Intelligence (ODNI) to candidate Trump and his national security advisors, including Michael Flynn, and a separate strategic intelligence briefing given to candidate

---

[522] Had Ohr and the CRM officials believed that the circumstances involved potential wrongdoing or misconduct, they should have reported their concerns to the OIG or the Department's Office of Professional Responsibility; they also could have reported their concerns to Congress.

Clinton and her national security advisors, and the observations that SSA 1 made of Flynn and others as a result of his participation in those briefings.

Overall, we determined that the Crossfire Hurricane team tasked several CHSs and UCEs during the 2016 presidential campaign, which resulted in multiple interactions with Carter Page and Papadopoulos, before and after they were affiliated with the Trump campaign, and an interaction with a high-level Trump campaign official who was not a subject of the investigation. The Crossfire Hurricane team also attempted to contact Papadopoulos through additional CHSs, but those efforts were unsuccessful. We further determined that the Crossfire Hurricane team received general information about Page and Manafort from another FBI CHS, but that this CHS had no further role in the Crossfire Hurricane investigation. Additionally, we identified several individuals who had either a connection to candidate Trump or a role in the Trump campaign, and were also FBI CHSs, who the Crossfire Hurricane team could have tasked, but did not. We found no evidence that the FBI placed any CHSs or UCEs within the Trump campaign or tasked any CHSs or UCEs to report on the Trump campaign. We also did not find documentary or testimonial evidence that political bias or improper motivation influenced the FBI's decision to use CHSs to interact with Page, Papadopoulos, and the high-level Trump campaign official in the Crossfire Hurricane investigation.

We concluded that the investigative activities undertaken by the Crossfire Hurricane team involving CHSs and UCEs received the necessary FBI approvals and complied with applicable Department and FBI policies. However, we also determined that neither the Department's nor the FBI's policies required the FBI to notify the Department of these investigative activities, and we are unaware of any Department official having had advance knowledge of the FBI's plans to consensually monitor conversations between FBI CHSs and Page, Papadopoulos, and a high-level official of the Trump campaign. We concluded that Department and FBI policies do not, in these circumstances, provide sufficient oversight and accountability for investigative activity that has the potential to gather sensitive information involving protected First Amendment activity. For example, prior to the operation involving the high-level campaign official, SSA 1 told the OIG that he did not remember having a plan in place in case the FBI recorded information that was politically sensitive. We believe that notification to Department officials in such situations would help to ensure that the FBI has planned sufficiently to address the incidental collection of political information, and make an assessment prior to that collection of whether the potential impact on constitutionally protected activity outweighs any potential investigative benefit.

We therefore make several recommendations to strengthen Department and FBI CHS policies to require Department consultation, at a minimum, when tasking a CHS to interact with officials in national political campaigns; to provide additional guidance to FBI handling agents about how to document the affiliations of CHSs who, on their own, participate in political organizations or activities and then voluntarily provide information to the FBI; and to provide FBI supervisors with the information necessary to assess whether to close a CHS, or designate that individual as a "sensitive source," depending on the level of CHS participation in political organizations or activities.

E.   Use of CHSs and UCEs

The agents, analysts, and supervisors assigned to the Crossfire Hurricane investigation told us that CHSs are routinely used in FBI counterintelligence investigations, and that they viewed CHS operations as one of the best methods available to quickly obtain information about the predicating allegations in the Crossfire Hurricane investigation, while preventing information about the nature and existence of the investigation from becoming public, and potentially impacting the presidential election. In Chapter Ten we described multiple CHS operations undertaken by the Crossfire Hurricane team, including the tasking of CHSs and UCEs during the 2016 presidential campaign. These investigative activities included numerous CHS interactions with Page and Papadopoulos to collect information about the predicating allegations while both were Trump campaign advisors and after they were no longer affiliated with the Trump campaign. In addition, an FBI CHS was tasked to interact with a high-level Trump campaign official who was not a subject of the Crossfire Hurricane investigation in an effort to gather information potentially relevant to the predicating allegations. We also determined that the FBI attempted to contact Papadopoulos through additional CHSs, but those attempted contacts did not lead to any operational activity.

In our review, we also learned that, in 2016, there were several other individuals who had either a connection to candidate Trump or a role in the Trump campaign, and were also FBI CHSs. Some of these sources were known to and available for use by the Crossfire Hurricane team during the 2016 presidential campaign. The Crossfire Hurricane team received general information about Page and Manafort from one such CHS, but that CHS did not further assist the Crossfire Hurricane team in any way. We found no evidence that any members of the Crossfire Hurricane team ever suggested inserting this CHS into the Trump campaign to gather investigative information. SSA 1 told the OIG, "that was not what we were looking to do." For a different CHS who held a position in the Trump campaign, we learned that the Crossfire Hurricane team decided not to task the CHS, and the FBI Handling Agent minimized contact with the CHS, because of the CHS's campaign involvement. The Crossfire Hurricane team also made no use of an FBI CHS who had a potential opportunity for a private meeting with candidate Trump. That CHS's Handling Agent told the OIG that he "would certainly not be tasking a source to go attend some private meeting with a candidate, any candidate, for president or for other office, to collect the information on what that candidate is saying." Although the Crossfire Hurricane team was aware of these CHSs during the 2016 presidential campaign, we were told that operational use of these CHSs would not have furthered the investigation, and so these CHSs were not tasked with any investigative activities.[523] Moreover, SSA 1 told the OIG that the members of the Crossfire Hurricane team "never [had] any intent, never any

---

[523] We were troubled by some of the language contained in certain documents we reviewed regarding the use and possible use of some of the CHSs, as we detail in Chapter 10. However, we saw no evidence that the FBI, or specifically the Crossfire Hurricane team, actually used any CHSs as a "passive listening post" for the Trump campaign or to "obtain insight" regarding the incoming Trump Administration.

desire...to collect...campaign or privileged information with regard to the presidential election."

We also learned of two other FBI CHSs, one of whom held a position ███████ ███████████████ and the other of whom ███████████████████████ ███████████████████████████ We found no evidence that the Crossfire Hurricane team ever knew about the first CHS, who held a position ██████████████████ and, accordingly, no evidence that the first CHS was tasked to do anything as part of the Crossfire Hurricane investigation.

We found that the Crossfire Hurricane team did not learn about the second CHS until months after the election. In 2017, the Crossfire Hurricane team learned about the second CHS after the CHS voluntarily provided to the CHS's Handling Agent, after the campaign was over and prompted by events reported in the media, ██ ██ and the Handling Agent forwarded the material, through his supervisor and FBI Headquarters, to the Crossfire Hurricane team. The team determined that ████ ██. The Handling Agent told us that, when he subsequently informed the Crossfire Hurricane team that the CHS had ██████████████████████████ ████████████████████████████████████ an Intelligence Analyst assigned to the Crossfire Hurricane team asked the Handling Agent to collect ████████ from the CHS, which the Handling Agent did. We learned that the Crossfire Hurricane team determined that there was not "anything significant" in this ████████████, and never tasked the CHS to interact with anyone ██████████████████████████ ████████████

While we found that no action was taken by the Crossfire Hurricane team in response to receiving ████████████, we nevertheless were concerned to learn that the Handling Agent for the second CHS ██████████████████████████████ ████ that the CHS had voluntarily provided into the FBI's files, and we promptly notified the FBI upon learning that they were still being maintained in the FBI's files. We further concluded that because the second CHS's Handling Agent did not understand the CHS's political involvement, no assessment was performed by the source's Handling Agent or his supervisors (none of whom were members of the Crossfire Hurricane team) to determine whether the CHS required re-designation as a "sensitive source" or should have been closed during the pendency of the campaign. To address this issue, we recommend the FBI provide additional guidance to handling agents concerning their responsibility to inquire whether their CHS participates in the types of groups or activities that would bring their CHS within the definition of a "sensitive source." Handling agents should document (and update as needed) those affiliations, and any others voluntarily provided to them by the CHS, in the Source Opening Communication, the "Sensitive Categories" portion of each CHS's Quarterly Supervisory Source Report, the "Life Changes" portion of CHS Contact Reports, or as otherwise directed by the FBI, so that the FBI can assess the appropriateness of continuing to use a CHS, particularly where the CHS is participating in political organizations or activities and then voluntarily providing information to the FBI.

Finally, we found no evidence that the Crossfire Hurricane team tasked any CHSs or UCEs to join the Trump campaign, sent any CHSs or UCEs to campaign offices or to campaign events to collect information for the Crossfire Hurricane investigation, or tasked any CHSs or UCEs to report on the Trump campaign.

F.   Compliance with FBI Policies

We determined that the Crossfire Hurricane investigation was opened before any CHSs or UCEs were tasked to interact with any members of the Trump campaign. Once the Crossfire Hurricane investigation was opened, the use of CHSs and UCEs was authorized under the AG Guidelines and the DIOG, which permit use of "all lawful investigative methods in the conduct of a Full Investigation" including specifically "CHS use and recruitment," "consensual monitoring of communications," and "Undercover Operations."[524]

As noted previously, the Crossfire Hurricane investigation was designated a SIM under DIOG § 10.1.2, because the FBI determined that any potential subjects of the investigation would be "prominent" members of a political campaign. The same designation was assigned to the four individual cases because the FBI determined that the individuals identified as subjects were "prominent" in the Trump campaign. However, the CHS operations undertaken in Crossfire Hurricane did not require heightened review by FBI supervisors or Department approval because, under the DIOG, the operations did not involve the use of "sensitive" sources, "Undisclosed Participation" (UDP) in political organizations, or "sensitive monitoring circumstances." As discussed in Chapter Two, the DIOG requires SAC approval to open a "sensitive" source; SAC approval with notice to the Sensitive Operations Review Committee (a panel that includes Department AAGs or their designees) for UDP in a political organization or other organization exercising First Amendment rights; and Department approval for a CHS to record conversations in a "sensitive monitoring circumstance." We determined that none of these approval requirements applied to the investigative activities undertaken by the Crossfire Hurricane team.

FBI policy defines "sensitive" sources to include CHSs who are political candidates or who are "prominent within a domestic political organization." None of the CHSs tasked in the Crossfire Hurricane investigation fell within these categories, because none of the CHSs were themselves candidates or prominent members of a campaign. The agents, analysts, and supervisors on the Crossfire Hurricane team told the OIG that they did not attempt to recruit or use members of the Trump campaign as CHSs, and we found no evidence suggesting otherwise. However, our interviews with FBI handling agents revealed significant confusion over the meaning

---

[524] AG Guidelines § II.B.4(b)(ii); DIOG §§ 7.3, 7.9(E), 7.9(I), 7.9(U). As noted in Chapter Two, had the investigation been opened as a Preliminary Investigation, rather than a Full Investigation, the use of CHSs and UCEs would similarly have been authorized under the AG Guidelines and the DIOG.

of the phrase "prominent within a domestic political organization," with some agents interpreting that phrase as limited to a person "running for office," and other agents questioning whether a presidential primary campaign was a "domestic political organization." Accordingly, we recommend that the FBI establish guidance to better define this phrase, so that agents understand the meaning of this phrase as it is used in FBI policy.

FBI policies concerning "Undisclosed Participation" (UDP) apply when anyone acting on behalf of the FBI, to include CHSs and UCEs, becomes a member of, or participates in, the activity of an organization without disclosing to the organization their FBI affiliation. These policies likewise did not apply to the Crossfire Hurricane case because we found no evidence that any of the FBI CHSs or UCEs used in Crossfire Hurricane joined or participated in the Trump campaign at all, and certainly not at the direction of, or otherwise on behalf of, the FBI. During our review, this issue briefly arose because we learned that one of the subjects of the Crossfire Hurricane investigation had invited an FBI CHS to join the Trump campaign, prior to the opening of the investigation. However, we found that when the Crossfire Hurricane team learned about this invitation following the investigation's opening, the team did not consider using this opportunity to engage in UDP. Rather, every FBI witness we interviewed said they would not have done so even if the FBI CHS had actually wanted to join the campaign. Strzok's reaction to the possibility—"[O]h god no. Absolutely not"—and the reaction Case Agent 2 attributed to the OGC attorneys—"no freaking way"—were indicative of the reactions we heard from all members of the Crossfire Hurricane team when we questioned them about whether they considered the possibility of inserting an FBI CHS into the Trump campaign to collect investigative information. None of the documents we reviewed indicated that any member of the Crossfire Hurricane team ever advocated for that type of investigative activity.

The use of CHSs and UCEs by the Crossfire Hurricane team also did not present a "sensitive monitoring circumstance," as defined by the AG Guidelines and the DIOG. As described in these policies, a "sensitive monitoring circumstance" arises when the FBI seeks to record communications with officials who have already been elected or appointed, such as Members of Congress, federal judges, or high ranking members of the executive branch. The AG Guidelines and the DIOG do not require prior notice to, or approval by, the Department when the FBI uses a CHS to consensually monitor communications with candidates for political office or prominent officials within their campaigns.

Because the CHS operations conducted during the Crossfire Hurricane investigation did not implicate the FBI's policies regarding sensitive sources, UDP, or sensitive monitoring circumstances, Department or higher level FBI notice or approval was not required for such operations. Under the CHSPG, which vests SSAs with daily oversight responsibility for CHSs in routine investigations, approval at the SSA level was sufficient.[525] The only relevant exception for the Crossfire

---

[525] CHSPG § 2.1.1.

Hurricane investigation were counterintelligence CHS extraterritorial operations, which required approval by an FBI Assistant Director, and which we found received approval by Priestap.[526] We determined that the day-to-day decisions concerning whether and how to use CHSs and UCEs in the Crossfire Hurricane investigation were made by the investigative team, with the approval of SSA 1 as required by FBI policy. We further found that SSA 1 briefed the FBI supervisors in his chain of command—Strzok, Priestap, and on one occasion McCabe—about the CHS operations planned by the investigative team. Priestap told the OIG that he remembered knowing about, and approving of, all of the CHS operations in Crossfire Hurricane, even though review and approval at his level was not required by the DIOG for operations conducted within the United States.

We further concluded that the use of CHSs and UCEs in the Crossfire Hurricane investigation complied with the DIOG's requirement that "investigative activities be conducted for an authorized purpose."[527] As discussed previously, the Crossfire Hurricane investigation was opened for an authorized purpose—which means "to detect, obtain information about, or prevent or protect against federal crimes or threats to the national security or to collect foreign intelligence."[528] The DIOG also provides that the underlying purpose of the investigative activity "may not be solely to monitor the exercise of constitutional rights…."[529] While the investigative activity in this case clearly implicated First Amendment protected activity, we did not find evidence that members of Crossfire Hurricane team attempted to use CHSs or UCEs for the sole purpose of monitoring activities protected by the First Amendment. Rather, we determined that these investigative activities were focused on obtaining information that would enable investigators to better assess the predicating information. Indeed, a significant amount of the information gathered during these operations was inconsistent with the Steele election reporting and should have been provided to Department attorneys, but was not.

For example, our review of CHS interactions with Page indicated that they were initiated to obtain information relevant to the allegations under investigation. Page was asked about his ongoing ties to Russia, contacts with Russian intelligence officials, views on media reports linking the Trump campaign and Russia, involvement in the committee responsible for the Republican platform language concerning aiding Ukraine, and views on the possibility of an "October Surprise" if the Trump campaign could access information obtained by the Russians from the

---

[526] As described in Chapter Two, the ████████████████████████████████████ ██ Because the Crossfire Hurricane investigation at the outset was a national security investigation, the ████ ████████████████████████████████.

[527] DIOG § 4.1.2.

[528] DIOG § 7.2.

[529] DIOG § 4.1.2.

DNC emails. Similarly, CHS operations aimed at Papadopoulos were linked to the allegations under investigation in Crossfire Hurricane. For example, when Papadopoulos was asked about the Trump campaign, the questions were focused on obtaining information about other Crossfire Hurricane subjects (Page and Flynn) or determining whether the Trump campaign benefitted from, or anyone in the Trump campaign had knowledge of, Russian assistance or the WikiLeaks release of information that was damaging to the Clinton campaign. Papadopoulos's response—that the Trump campaign was not "advocat[ing] for this type of activity because at the end of the day it's...illegal"—clearly pertained to the issues under investigation and, as discussed elsewhere in this report, should have been provided to the Department's attorneys for evaluation as part of the FISA applications. Likewise, the high-level Trump campaign official was asked about the role of three Crossfire Hurricane subjects—Page, Papadopoulos, and Manafort—in the Trump campaign, and also asked about allegations in public reports concerning Russian interference in the 2016 U.S. elections, the campaign's response to ideas featured in Page's Moscow speech, and the possibility of an "October Surprise." These areas of inquiry were focused on the allegations under investigation in an effort to elicit pertinent information.

However, the CHS and the high-level campaign official ▮▮▮. We found that the Crossfire Hurricane team made no use of any information collected from the high-level Trump campaign official, because the team determined that none of the information gathered was "germane" to the allegations under investigation. However, as noted above, we were concerned that the Crossfire Hurricane team did not recall having in place a plan, prior to the operation involving the high-level campaign official, to address the possible collection of politically sensitive information.

We also looked for, but did not find, documentary evidence that investigative activities involving CHSs and UCEs during Crossfire Hurricane were undertaken for political purposes, rather than investigative objectives. Similarly, none of the witnesses provided any such information to us. In addition, we evaluated the roles of Lisa Page and Strzok in decision making about how to use CHSs and UCEs in the Crossfire Hurricane investigation. We learned that the Crossfire Hurricane case agents had limited and, in some cases, no interaction with Lisa Page, and that she had no authority over, or even involvement in, decision making concerning the use of CHSs or UCEs. Although we found that Strzok oversaw aspects of Crossfire Hurricane, and was briefed regarding the plans for the use of CHSs and UCEs, we found no evidence that Strzok gave specific directions as to which CHSs to task and how to task them, or acted as the sole decision maker for any of the CHS or UCE operations. In addition, none of the Crossfire Hurricane team members stated that they believed Strzok's political views impacted the use of CHSs or UCEs, and we did not find any documentary evidence suggesting such an impact.

Although we found that the Crossfire Hurricane team complied with all applicable Department and FBI policies regarding the use of CHSs, we are concerned that current FBI and Department policies are not sufficient to ensure appropriate oversight and accountability when such operations potentially implicate sensitive, constitutionally protected activity. During Crossfire Hurricane, the FBI conducted multiple CHS operations that involved interactions with members of a major party candidate's presidential campaign, including a high-level campaign official who was not an investigative subject. Under current Department guidelines and FBI policy, those operations only required the approval of an FBI SSA, a first-level supervisor (although here, as noted above, an FBI Assistant Director approved of all of the CHS operations). The FBI was not required to notify the Department of those investigative activities and we are unaware of any Department official having had advance knowledge of the FBI's plan to consensually monitor conversations between CHSs and Page and Papadopoulos, both before and after they were affiliated with the Trump campaign, and a conversation with a high-level Trump campaign official. The then Chief of NSD's Counterintelligence and Export Control Section David Laufman told the OIG that he believed such activity should require Department authorization. We agree.

We recommend that the Department and FBI assess the definition of a "sensitive monitoring circumstance" contained in the AG Guidelines and the DIOG to determine whether to expand its scope to include consensual monitoring of major party domestic political candidates for federal office or individuals prominent within those domestic political organizations, so that at a minimum, Department consultation is required when tasking a CHS to interact with officials in national political campaigns. Such a change would be consistent with other currently-existing FBI and Department policies intended to ensure appropriate approval and oversight where certain constitutionally protected activity is concerned. Examples include the FBI's heightened approval requirements for sensitive UDP that is likely to affect the exercise of First Amendment rights by members of an organization, the FBI's definition of "Sensitive Investigative Matters" (which includes domestic political candidates and prominent members of domestic political organizations), the Department's approval requirements for consensual monitoring when investigating alleged misconduct by a senior member of the executive branch or a Member of Congress, and the Department's requirement for Attorney General approval for toll record subpoenas and search warrants directed at members of the media. We believe the same considerations that resulted in the adoption of these provisions to protect the exercise of constitutional rights similarly apply to the situation present in Crossfire Hurricane, where the Department and FBI were conducting CHS operations of officials affiliated with a major party candidate's national political campaign.

G.   Participation in ODNI Strategic Intelligence Briefing

As described in Section V of Chapter Ten, we learned during the course of our review that in August 2016, the supervisor of the Crossfire Hurricane investigation, SSA 1, participated on behalf of the FBI in an ODNI strategic intelligence briefing given to candidate Trump and his national security advisors, including Flynn, and in a separate briefing given to candidate Clinton and her national security advisors. The stated purpose of the FBI's counterintelligence and security portion of the briefings was to provide the recipients "a baseline on the presence and threat posed by foreign intelligence services to the National Security of the U.S." However, we found the FBI also had an investigative purpose when it specifically selected SSA 1, a supervisor for the Crossfire Hurricane investigation, to provide the FBI briefings. SSA 1 was selected, in part, because Flynn, who would be attending the briefing with candidate Trump, was a subject in one of the ongoing investigations related to Crossfire Hurricane. SSA 1 told us that the briefing provided him "the opportunity to gain assessment and possibly some level of familiarity with [Flynn]. So, should we get to the point where we need to do a subject interview...I would have that to fall back on."

After the meeting, SSA 1 drafted an Electronic Communication (EC) documenting his participation in the ODNI strategic intelligence briefing attended by Trump, Flynn, and another advisor, and added the EC to the Crossfire Hurricane investigative file. The EC described the purpose, location, and attendees of the briefing, and recounted in summary fashion the portion of the briefing SSA 1 provided. Woven into the briefing summary were questions posed to SSA 1 by Trump and Flynn, and SSA 1's responses, as well as comments made by Trump and Flynn. SSA 1 told us that he documented those instances where he was engaged by the attendees, as well as anything related to the FBI or pertinent to the Crossfire Hurricane investigation, such as comments about the Russian Federation. SSA 1 said that he also documented information that may not have been relevant at the time he recorded it, but might prove relevant in the future. SSA 1 told us that he did not memorialize in writing the briefing he participated in of candidate Clinton and her national security advisors because the attendees did not include a subject of an FBI investigation, and because there was nothing from the other briefings that was of investigative value to the Crossfire Hurricane team.

As we described earlier in connection with the FBI's decision not to conduct defensive briefings to the Trump campaign about the information the FBI received from the FFG, we did not identify any Department or FBI policy that applied to that decision and determined that those decisions are judgment calls left to the discretion of FBI officials. Similarly, we did not identify any Department or FBI policy or guidance that specifically addresses using FBI counterintelligence and security briefings to members of political campaigns for investigative purposes, as occurred in Crossfire Hurricane. We believe there should be.

Baker told us that the decision to select SSA 1 to participate in the ODNI briefing because of his involvement with Crossfire Hurricane was reached by consensus among a group that he recalled involved multiple FBI officials, including McCabe.[530] If accurate, SSA 1's selection at least was discussed and approved by high-level officials at the FBI, which we believe should occur in advance of such activity. However, there is nothing in FBI policy requiring high-level approval. Further, the Department was not informed that the FBI was using the ODNI briefing of a presidential candidate for investigative purposes, nor was ODNI made aware that the individual providing the FBI's portion of the briefing would be

---

[530] McCabe told us that it was possible he participated in conversations about whether SSA 1 should conduct the briefings, but could not recall any.

memorializing information from the briefing into an FBI case file for investigative purposes.

ODNI strategic intelligence briefings of the type that were provided to candidates Trump and Clinton convey sensitive information to familiarize the recipients with certain national security issues; and the FBI's counterintelligence and security portion of the briefings highlights why the recipients, once given access to such information, should assume they will be targets of foreign intelligence services. The briefings are important because they attempt to prepare both national political party candidates, on an equal footing, for the national security threats facing them if elected. The transfer of information, the exchanges of questions and answers that can occur, and the effectiveness of this process rely on an expectation of trust and good faith among the participants. The FBI's use of such briefings for investigative purposes potentially interferes with this expectation and could frustrate the purpose of future counterintelligence briefings. For this reason, we recommend that any decision to use FBI counterintelligence and security briefings to members of political campaigns for investigative purposes should require the approval of senior leaders at both the FBI and the Department, and approval should be documented and based on factors set forth in FBI policy.

CHAPTER TWELVE
CONCLUSIONS AND RECOMMENDATIONS

I.   Conclusions

In July 2016, 3 weeks after then FBI Director James Comey announced the conclusion of the FBI's "Midyear Exam" investigation into presidential candidate Hillary Clinton's handling of government emails during her tenure as Secretary of State, the FBI received reporting from a Friendly Foreign Government (FFG) that, in a May 2016 meeting with the FFG, Trump campaign foreign policy advisor George Papadopoulos "suggested the Trump team had received some kind of a suggestion" from Russia that it could assist in the election process with the anonymous release of information during the campaign that would be damaging to candidate Clinton and President Obama. Days later, on July 31, the FBI initiated the Crossfire Hurricane investigation that is the subject of this report.

As we noted last year in our review of the Midyear investigation, the FBI has developed and earned a reputation as one of the world's premier law enforcement agencies in significant part because of its tradition of professionalism, impartiality, non-political enforcement of the law, and adherence to detailed policies, practices, and norms. It was precisely these qualities that were required as the FBI initiated and conducted Crossfire Hurricane. However, as we describe in this report, our review identified significant concerns with how certain aspects of the investigation were conducted and supervised, particularly the FBI's failure to adhere to its own standards of accuracy and completeness when filing applications for Foreign Intelligence Surveillance Act (FISA) authority to surveil Carter Page, a U.S. person who was connected to the Donald J. Trump for President Campaign. We also identified what we believe is an absence of sufficient policies to ensure appropriate Department oversight of significant investigative decisions that could affect constitutionally protected activity.

The Opening of Crossfire Hurricane and the Use of Confidential Human Sources

The decision to open the Crossfire Hurricane investigation was made by the FBI's then Counterintelligence Division (CD) Assistant Director (AD), E.W. "Bill" Priestap, and reflected a consensus reached after multiple days of discussions and meetings among senior FBI officials. We concluded that AD Priestap's exercise of discretion in opening the investigation was in compliance with Department and FBI policies, and we did not find documentary or testimonial evidence that political bias or improper motivation influenced his decision. While the information in the FBI's possession at the time was limited, in light of the low threshold established by Department and FBI predication policy, we found that Crossfire Hurricane was opened for an authorized investigative purpose and with sufficient factual predication.

However, we also determined that, under Department and FBI policy, the decision whether to open the Crossfire Hurricane counterintelligence investigation, which involved the activities of individuals associated with a national major party campaign for president, was a discretionary judgment call left to the FBI. There was no requirement that Department officials be consulted, or even notified, prior to the FBI making that decision. We further found that, consistent with this policy, the FBI advised supervisors in the Department's National Security Division (NSD) of the investigation only after it had been initiated. As we detail in Chapter Two, high-level Department notice and approval is required in other circumstances where investigative activity could substantially impact certain civil liberties, and that notice allows senior Department officials to consider the potential constitutional and prudential implications in advance of these activities. We concluded that similar advance notice should be required in circumstances such as those that were present here.

Shortly after the FBI opened the Crossfire Hurricane investigation, the FBI conducted several consensually monitored meetings between FBI confidential human sources (CHS) and individuals affiliated with the Trump campaign, including a high-level campaign official who was not a subject of the investigation. We found that the CHS operations received the necessary approvals under FBI policy; that an Assistant Director knew about and approved of each operation, even in circumstances where a first-level supervisory special agent could have approved the operations; and that the operations were permitted under Department and FBI policy because their use was not for the sole purpose of monitoring activities protected by the First Amendment or the lawful exercise of other rights secured by the Constitution or laws of the United States. We did not find any documentary or testimonial evidence that political bias or improper motivation influenced the FBI's decision to conduct these operations. Additionally, we found no evidence that the FBI attempted to place any CHSs within the Trump campaign, recruit members of the Trump campaign as CHSs, or task CHSs to report on the Trump campaign.

However, we are concerned that, under applicable Department and FBI policy, it would have been sufficient for a first-level FBI supervisor to authorize the sensitive domestic CHS operations undertaken in Crossfire Hurricane, and that there is no applicable Department or FBI policy requiring the FBI to notify Department officials of a decision to task CHSs to consensually monitor conversations with members of a presidential campaign. Specifically, in Crossfire Hurricane, where one of the CHS operations involved consensually monitoring a high-level official on the Trump campaign who was not a subject of the investigation, and all of the operations had the potential to gather sensitive information of the campaign about protected First Amendment activity, we found no evidence that the FBI consulted with any Department officials before conducting the CHS operations—and no policy requiring the FBI to do so. We therefore believe that current Department and FBI policies are not sufficient to ensure appropriate oversight and accountability when such operations potentially implicate sensitive, constitutionally protected activity, and that requiring Department consultation, at a minimum, would be appropriate.

The FISA Applications to Conduct Surveillance of Carter Page

One investigative tool for which Department and FBI policy expressly require advance approval by a senior Department official is the seeking of a court order under the Foreign Intelligence Surveillance Act (FISA). When the Crossfire Hurricane team first proposed seeking a FISA order targeting Carter Page in mid-August 2016, FBI attorneys assisting the investigation considered it a "close call" whether they had developed the probable cause necessary to obtain the order, and a FISA order was not requested at that time. However, in September 2016, immediately after the Crossfire Hurricane team received reporting from Christopher Steele concerning Page's alleged recent activities with Russian officials, FBI attorneys advised the Department that the team was ready to move forward with a request to obtain FISA authority to surveil Page. FBI and Department officials told us the Steele reporting "pushed [the FISA proposal] over the line" in terms of establishing probable cause. FBI leadership supported relying on Steele's reporting to seek a FISA order targeting Page after being advised of, and giving consideration to, concerns expressed by a Department attorney that Steele may have been hired by someone associated with a rival candidate or campaign.

The authority under FISA to conduct electronic surveillance and physical searches targeting individuals significantly assists the government's efforts to combat terrorism, clandestine intelligence activity, and other threats to the national security. At the same time, the use of this authority unavoidably raises civil liberties concerns. FISA orders can be used to surveil U.S. persons, like Carter Page, and in some cases the surveillance will foreseeably collect information about the individual's constitutionally protected activities, such as Page's legitimate activities on behalf of a presidential campaign. Moreover, proceedings before the Foreign Intelligence Surveillance Court (FISC)—which is responsible for ruling on applications for FISA orders—are *ex parte*, meaning that unlike most court proceedings, the government is present but the government's counterparty is not. In addition, unlike the use of other intrusive investigative techniques (such as wiretaps under Title III and traditional criminal search warrants) that are granted in *ex parte* hearings but can potentially be subject to later court challenge, FISA orders have not been subject to scrutiny through subsequent adversarial proceedings.

In light of these concerns, Congress through the FISA statute, and the Department and FBI through policies and procedures, have established important safeguards to protect the FISA application process from irregularities and abuse. Among the most important are the requirements in FBI policy that every FISA application must contain a "full and accurate" presentation of the facts, and that agents must ensure that all factual statements in FISA applications are "scrupulously accurate." These are the standards for all FISA applications, regardless of the investigation's sensitivity, and it is incumbent upon the FBI to meet them in every application. That said, in the context of an investigation involving persons associated with a presidential campaign, where the target of the FISA is a former campaign official and the goal of the FISA is to uncover, among other things, information about the individual's allegedly illegal campaign-related activities, members of the Crossfire Hurricane investigative team should have

412

anticipated, and told us they in fact did anticipate, that these FISA applications would be subjected to especially close scrutiny.

Nevertheless, we found that members of the Crossfire Hurricane team failed to meet the basic obligation to ensure that the Carter Page FISA applications were "scrupulously accurate." We identified significant inaccuracies and omissions in each of the four applications—7 in the first FISA application and a total of 17 by the final renewal application. For example, the Crossfire Hurricane team obtained information from Steele's Primary Sub-source in January 2017 that raised significant questions about the reliability of the Steele reporting that was used in the Carter Page FISA applications. But members of the Crossfire Hurricane team failed to share the information with the Department, and it was therefore omitted from the three renewal applications. All of the applications also omitted information the FBI had obtained from another U.S. government agency detailing its prior relationship with Page, including that Page had been approved as an operational contact for the other agency from 2008 to 2013, and that Page had provided information to the other agency concerning his prior contacts with certain Russian intelligence officers, one of which overlapped with facts asserted in the FISA application.

As a result of the 17 significant inaccuracies and omissions we identified, relevant information was not shared with, and consequently not considered by, important Department decision makers and the court, and the FISA applications made it appear as though the evidence supporting probable cause was stronger than was actually the case. We also found basic, fundamental, and serious errors during the completion of the FBI's factual accuracy reviews, known as the Woods Procedures, which are designed to ensure that FISA applications contain a full and accurate presentation of the facts.

We do not speculate whether the correction of any particular misstatement or omission, or some combination thereof, would have resulted in a different outcome. Nevertheless, the Department's decision makers and the court should have been given complete and accurate information so that they could meaningfully evaluate probable cause before authorizing the surveillance of a U.S. person associated with a presidential campaign. That did not occur, and as a result, the surveillance of Carter Page continued even as the FBI gathered information that weakened the assessment of probable cause and made the FISA applications less accurate.

We determined that the inaccuracies and omissions we identified in the applications resulted from case agents providing wrong or incomplete information to Department attorneys and failing to identify important issues for discussion. Moreover, we concluded that case agents and SSAs did not give appropriate attention to facts that cut against probable cause, and that as the investigation progressed and more information tended to undermine or weaken the assertions in the FISA applications, the agents and SSAs did not reassess the information supporting probable cause. Further, the agents and SSAs did not follow, or even appear to know, certain basic requirements in the Woods Procedures. Although we did not find documentary or testimonial evidence of intentional misconduct on the part of the case agents who assisted NSD's Office of Intelligence (OI) in preparing the applications, or the agents and supervisors who performed the Woods Procedures, we also did not receive satisfactory explanations for the errors or missing information. We found that the offered explanations for these serious errors did not excuse them, or the repeated failures to ensure the accuracy of information presented to the FISC.

We are deeply concerned that so many basic and fundamental errors were made by three separate, hand-picked investigative teams; on one of the most sensitive FBI investigations; after the matter had been briefed to the highest levels within the FBI; even though the information sought through use of FISA authority related so closely to an ongoing presidential campaign; and even though those involved with the investigation knew that their actions were likely to be subjected to close scrutiny. We believe this circumstance reflects a failure not just by those who prepared the FISA applications, but also by the managers and supervisors in the Crossfire Hurricane chain of command, including FBI senior officials who were briefed as the investigation progressed. We do not expect managers and supervisors to know every fact about an investigation, or senior leaders to know all the details of cases about which they are briefed. However, especially in the FBI's most sensitive and high-priority matters, and especially when seeking court permission to use an intrusive tool such as a FISA order, it is incumbent upon the entire chain of command, including senior officials, to take the necessary steps to ensure that they are sufficiently familiar with the facts and circumstances supporting and potentially undermining a FISA application in order to provide effective oversight consistent with their level of supervisory responsibility. Such oversight requires greater familiarity with the facts than we saw in this review, where time and again during OIG interviews FBI managers, supervisors, and senior officials displayed a lack of understanding or awareness of important information concerning many of the problems we identified.

In the preparation of the FISA applications to surveil Carter Page, the Crossfire Hurricane team failed to comply with FBI policies, and in so doing fell short of what is rightfully expected from a premier law enforcement agency entrusted with such an intrusive surveillance tool. In light of the significant concerns identified with the Carter Page FISA applications and the other issues described in this report, the OIG today initiated an audit that will further examine the FBI's compliance with the Woods Procedures in FISA applications that target U.S. persons in both counterintelligence and counterterrorism investigations. We also make the following recommendations to assist the Department and the FBI in avoiding similar failures in future investigations.

II. Recommendations

For the reasons fully described in previous chapters, we recommend the following:

1. The Department and the FBI should ensure that adequate procedures are in place for the Office of Intelligence (OI) to obtain all relevant and accurate information, including access to Confidential Human Source

(CHS) information, needed to prepare FISA applications and renewal applications. This effort should include revising:

a. the FISA Request Form: to ensure information is identified for OI: (i) that tends to disprove, does not support, or is inconsistent with a finding or an allegation that the target is a foreign power or an agent of a foreign power, or (ii) that bears on the reliability of every CHS whose information is relied upon in the FISA application, including all information from the derogatory information sub-file, recommended below;

b. the Woods Form: (i) to emphasize to agents and their supervisors the obligation to re-verify factual assertions repeated from prior applications and to obtain written approval from CHS handling agents of all CHS source characterization statements in applications, and (ii) to specify what steps must be taken and documented during the legal review performed by an FBI Office of General Counsel (OGC) line attorney and SES-level supervisor before submitting the FISA application package to the FBI Director for certification;

c. the FISA Procedures: to clarify which positions may serve as the supervisory reviewer for OGC; and

d. taking any other steps deemed appropriate to ensure the accuracy and completeness of information provided to OI.

2. The Department and FBI should evaluate which types of Sensitive Investigative Matters (SIM) require advance notification to a senior Department official, such as the Deputy Attorney General, in addition to the notifications currently required for SIMs, especially for case openings that implicate core First Amendment activity and raise policy considerations or heighten enterprise risk, and establish implementing policies and guidance, as necessary.

3. The FBI should develop protocols and guidelines for staffing and administrating any future sensitive investigative matters from FBI Headquarters.

4. The FBI should address the problems with the administration and assessment of CHSs identified in this report and, at a minimum, should:

a. revise its standard CHS admonishment form to include a prohibition on the disclosure of the CHS's relationship with the FBI to third parties absent the FBI's permission, and assess the need to include other admonishments in the standard CHS admonishments;

b.	develop enhanced procedures to ensure that CHS information is documented in Delta, including information generated from Headquarters-led investigations, substantive contacts with closed CHSs (directly or through third parties), and derogatory information. We renew our recommendation that the FBI create a derogatory information sub-file in Delta;

c.	assess VMU's practices regarding reporting source validation findings and non-findings;

d.	establish guidance for sharing sensitive information with CHSs;

e.	establish guidance to handling agents for inquiring whether their CHS participates in the types of groups or activities that would bring the CHS within the definition of a "sensitive source," and ensure handling agents document (and update as needed) those affiliations and any others voluntarily provided to them by the CHS in the Source Opening Communication, the "Sensitive Categories" portion of each CHS's Quarterly Supervisory Source Report, the "Life Changes" portion of CHS Contact Reports, or as otherwise directed by the FBI so that the FBI can assess whether active CHSs are engaged in activities (such as political campaigns) at a level that might require re-designation as a "sensitive source" or necessitate closure of the CHS; and

f.	revise its CHS policy to address the considerations that should be taken into account and the steps that should be followed before and after accepting information from a closed CHS indirectly through a third party.

5.	The Department and FBI should clarify the following terms in their policies:

a.	assess the definition of a "Sensitive Monitoring Circumstance" in the AG Guidelines and the FBI's DIOG to determine whether to expand its scope to include consensual monitoring of a domestic political candidate or an individual prominent within a domestic political organization, or a subset of these persons, so that consensual monitoring of such individuals would require consultation with or advance notification to a senior Department official, such as the Deputy Attorney General; and

b.	establish guidance, and include examples in the DIOG, to better define the meaning of the phrase "prominent in a domestic political organization" so that agents understand which campaign officials fall within that definition as it relates to "Sensitive Investigative Matters," "Sensitive UDP," and the designation of "sensitive sources." Further, if the Department expands the scope of "Sensitive Monitoring Circumstance," as recommended above, the FBI should apply the guidance on "prominent in a domestic political organization" to "Sensitive Monitoring Circumstance" as well.

6. The FBI should ensure that appropriate training on DIOG § 4 is provided to emphasize the constitutional implications of certain monitoring situations and to ensure that agents account for these concerns, both in the tasking of CHSs and in the way they document interactions with and tasking of CHSs.

7. The FBI should establish a policy regarding the use of defensive and transition briefings for investigative purposes, including the factors to be considered and approval by senior leaders at the FBI with notice to a senior Department official, such as the Deputy Attorney General.

8. The Department's Office of Professional Responsibility should review our findings related to the conduct of Department attorney Bruce Ohr for any action it deems appropriate. Ohr's current supervisors in the Department's Criminal Division should also review our findings related to Ohr's performance for any action they deem appropriate.

9. The FBI should review the performance of all employees who had responsibility for the preparation, Woods review, or approval of the FISA applications, as well as the managers, supervisors, and senior officials in the chain of command of the Carter Page investigation, for any action deemed appropriate.

WOODS PROCEDURES[531]
FIRST FISA APPLICATION

Factual Assertion in FISA Application	Page # or FN	No supporting documentation	Supporting documentation does not state this fact	Supporting document shows that the factual assertion is inaccurate
The DNI commented that this influence included providing money to particular candidates or providing disinformation.	5		X	
Although Page did not provide any specific details to refute, dispel, or clarify the media reporting, he made vague statements that minimized his activities.	27			X
In or about May 2016, Buryakov was sentenced to 30 months in prison.	FN 6	X		
[Steele] is a former ███████ ████████ and has been an FBI source since in or about October 2013. [Steele's] reporting has been corroborated and used in criminal proceedings and the FBI assesses [Steele] to be reliable. [Steele] has been compensated approx. $95,000 by the FBI and the FBI is unaware of any derogatory information pertaining to [Steele].[532]	FN 8	X		
[Steele] reported the information contained therein to the FBI over the course of several meetings with the FBI from in or about June 2016 through August 2016.	FN 8	X		
[Steele] told the FBI that he/she only provided this information to the business associate and the FBI.	FN 18			X
Since that time, Source #2 has routinely provided reliable information that has been corroborated by the FBI.	FN 20	X		
Source #2 has been compensated in excess of ███████ since 2008.	FN 20	X		

---

[531] This Appendix describes errors we identified in the Woods process for the four Carter Page FISA applications. We did not examine the "facilities" section of the applications. This Appendix does not include non-Woods-related errors in the applications described in Chapters Five and Eight. As described in Chapter Two, the Woods Procedures seek to ensure the accuracy of every factual assertion in a FISA application. These procedures require that the case agent who requests an application create and maintain a "Woods File" that contains: (1) supporting documentation for every factual assertion contained in the application, and (2) results and supporting documentation of the required searches and verifications. In this appendix, we identify each factual assertion in the FISA applications for which we found (1) no supporting documentation in the Woods File, (2) purported supporting documentation in the Woods File that did not state the fact asserted in the FISA application, or (3) purported supporting documentation in the Woods File that actually indicates the fact asserted is inaccurate.

[532] The Woods Procedures require that when an application contains reporting from a Confidential Human Source (CHS), the Woods File must contain documentation from the CHS handling agent verifying that the handling agent has reviewed the facts on the CHS's background and reliability and that the representations in the FISA about the CHS are accurate.

WOODS PROCEDURES
RENEWAL APPLICATION NO. 1

Factual assertion in FISA Application	Page # or FN	No supporting documentation	Supporting documentation does not state this fact	Supporting document shows that the factual assertion is inaccurate
The DNI commented that this influence included providing money to particular candidates or providing disinformation.	6		X	
Although Page did not provide any specific details to refute, dispel, or clarify the media reporting, he made vague statements that minimized his activities.	29			X
According to Source #2, Page initially attempted to distance the think tank from Russian funding.	35	X		
Papadopoulos is a current subject of an FBI investigation.[533]	FN 3	X		
In or about May 2016, Buryakov was sentenced to 30 months in prison.	FN 7	X		
[Steele] is a former ███████████████ ███████████████] and has been an FBI source since in or about October 2013. [Steele] has been compensated approx. $95,000 by the FBI. [T]he FBI assesses [Steele] to be reliable as previous reporting from [Steele] has been corroborated and used in criminal proceedings.	FN 9	X		
[I]n or about October 2016, the FBI suspended its relationship with [Steele] due to [Steele's] unauthorized disclosure of information to the press.	FN 9		X	
[Steele] reported the information contained therein to the FBI over the course of several meetings with the FBI from in or about June 2016 through August 2016.	FN 9	X		
[Steele] told the FBI that he/she only provided this information to the business associate and the FBI.	FN 19			X
Since that time, Source #2 has routinely provided reliable information that has been corroborated by the FBI.	FN 21	X		
Source #2 has been compensated in excess of ███████ since 2008.	FN 21	X		

---

[533] Although the Crossfire Hurricane team knew the FBI had an ongoing investigation of Papadopoulos, the Woods File did not contain documentation supporting this factual assertion. The Woods Procedures do not exempt information known to the case agent from having supporting documentation.

WOODS PROCEDURES
RENEWAL APPLICATION NO. 2[534]

Factual assertion in FISA Application	Page # or FN	No supporting documentation	Supporting documentation does not state this fact	Supporting document shows that the factual assertion is inaccurate
The DNI commented that this influence included providing money to particular candidates or providing disinformation.	6		X	
Although Page did not provide any specific details to refute, dispel, or clarify the media reporting, he made vague statements that minimized his activities.	30			X
According to Source #2, Page initially attempted to distance the think tank from Russian funding.	35	X		
Page stated that he believed that he was the subject of electronic surveillance by the U.S. government.	35	X		
The FBI's ongoing investigation has revealed that Page has moved out of his New York City residence and does not currently maintain a permanent address; rather Page lives in and out of hotels inside New York City and other cities.	36	X		
Court-authorized ██████████ revealed a document titled ████████ ." The document outlines what appear to be talking points that are meant to counter media reports that cast Page in a negative light.	42	X		
At a later point in the interview, after the FBI explained to Page how Page could be viewed as having a source-handler or co-optee relationship with the Russian intelligence officers, Page claimed that he believed that he was "on the books," but that he only provided the Russian intelligence officers with "immaterial non-public" information.	46-7	X		
Also during the interviews, Page denied ever meeting with Sechin or Divyekin.	47	X		

---

[534] The Woods File for Renewal Application No. 2 contains a piece of paper that states "Strat Plan" and another piece of paper that states "New 302," "Feb. Article," and "March Article." The case agent who compiled the Woods File for this application told us that these pieces of paper were "placeholders" he inserted into the file to indicate to the SSA reviewer that a supporting document existed, but that a copy of it was not placed into the file. We do not believe these placeholders met the Woods requirements because the descriptions of the referenced documents were vague and it was not clear to us why the actual documents could not have been included in the Woods File. We also observed that there was no notation or other record indicating that the agent and supervisor performing the factual accuracy review in fact examined the documents identified by the placeholders.

Factual assertion in FISA Application	Page # or FN	No supporting documentation	Supporting documentation does not state this fact	Supporting document shows that the factual assertion is inaccurate
As of March 2017, the FBI has conducted several interviews with Papadopoulos. During these interviews, Papadopoulos confirmed that he met with officials from the above-referenced friendly foreign government, but he denied that he discussed anything related to the Russian Government during these meetings.	FN 4			X
In or about May 2016, Buryakov was sentenced to 30 months in prison.	FN 8	X		
[Steele] is a former ▮▮▮▮▮▮▮▮▮▮ ▮▮▮▮▮▮▮▮▮▮ and has been an FBI source since in or about October 2013. [Steele] has been compensated approx. $95,000 by the FBI. [T]he FBI assesses [Steele] to be reliable as previous reporting from [Steele] has been corroborated and used in criminal proceedings.	FN 10	X		
[I]n or about October 2016, the FBI suspended its relationship with [Steele] due to [Steele's] unauthorized disclosure of information to the press.	FN 10		X	
[Steele] reported the information contained therein to the FBI over the course of several meetings with the FBI from in or about June 2016 through August 2016.	FN 10	X		
[Steele] told the FBI that he/she only provided this information to the business associate and the FBI.	FN 20			X
Since that time, Source #2 has routinely provided reliable information that has been corroborated by the FBI.	FN 22	X		
Source #2 has been compensated in excess of ▮▮▮▮▮ since 2008.	FN 22	X		

WOODS PROCEDURES
RENEWAL APPLICATION NO. 3[535]

Factual assertion in FISA Application	Page # or FN	No supporting documentation	Supporting documentation does not state this fact	Supporting document indicates the factual assertion is inaccurate
The DNI commented that this influence included providing money to particular candidates or providing disinformation.	6		X	
Russian President Vladimir Putin said in or about September 2016 that Russia was not responsible for the hack, but that the release of the DNC documents was a net positive: "The important thing is the content that was given to the public."	7	X		
U.S. Person #1 recalled an instance where Page was picked-up in a chauffeured car and it was rumored at that time that Page had met with Igor Sechin.	21		X	
Although Page did not provide any specific details to refute, dispel, or clarify the media reporting, he made vague statements that minimized his activities.	33			X
Court-authorized ██████████ that appears to confirm that Page did, in fact, meet with such officials.	35	X		
Court-authorized ██████████, Page planned to visit members or employees of "Inter RAO."	42	X		
According to Source #2, Page initially attempted to distance the think tank from Russian funding. When Source #2 reminded Page of his previous statement regarding the "open checkbook," Page did not refute his previous comment and provided some reassurance to Source #2 about the likelihood of Russian financial support.	44	X		
Court-authorized ██████████ The document outlines what appear to be talking points that are meant to counter media reports that cast Page in a negative light.	47-8	X		

[535] Similar to the Woods File for Renewal Application No. 2, the file for Renewal Application 3 contains a "placeholder" piece of paper that states "Strat Plan," indicating to the SSA reviewer that a supporting document existed for the factual assertion, but that it was not placed into the Woods File. For the reasons noted above, we do not believe this placeholder met the Woods requirements.

Factual assertion in FISA Application	Page # or FN	No supporting documentation	Supporting documentation does not state this fact	Supporting document indicates the factual assertion is inaccurate
Page downplayed his interactions with Dvorkovich during his March 2017 interviews with the FBI. During these interviews, Page characterized his interaction with Dvorkovich in July 2016 as a simple introduction in passing and a brief handshake.	53		X	
[Steele] is a former ████████ ████████ and has been an FBI source since in or about October 2013. [Steele] has been compensated approx. $95,000 by the FBI. [T]he FBI assesses [Steele] to be reliable as previous reporting from [Steele] has been corroborated and used in criminal proceedings.	FN 10	X		
[I]n or about October 2016, the FBI suspended its relationship with [Steele] due to [Steele's] unauthorized disclosure of information to the press.	FN 10		X	
[Steele] reported the information contained therein to the FBI over the course of several meetings with the FBI from in or about June 2016 through August 2016.	FN 10	X		
In or about December 2008, Source #2 was opened as an FBI source. In or about January 2011, Source #2 was closed as an FBI source for, among other things, motivation for reporting, but not for validity of reporting. Source #2 was reopened in or about March 2011. Since that time, Source #2 has routinely provided reliable information that has been corroborated by the FBI.	FN 21	X		
Source #2 has been compensated in excess of ████████ since 2008.	FN 21	X		
[Steele] told the FBI that he/she only provided this information to the business associate and the FBI.	FN 22			X
According to information on its website, Gazprombank was founded by Gazprom to provide banking services for gas industry enterprises.	FN 26	X		

FBI'S RESPONSE

U.S. Department of Justice

Federal Bureau of Investigation

Office of the Director   Washington, D.C. 20535-0001

December 6, 2019

The Honorable Michael Horowitz
Inspector General
U.S. Department of Justice
Washington, D.C. 20530

Dear Inspector General Horowitz:

Thank you for the opportunity to respond to the Office of the Inspector General (OIG) Report titled, *"Review of Four FISA Applications and Other Aspects of the FBI's Crossfire Hurricane Investigation"* (Report).

The Federal Bureau of Investigation (FBI) appreciates the OIG's crucial independent oversight role and the thoroughness and professionalism your office brought to this work. The Report's findings and recommendations represent constructive criticism that will make us stronger as an organization. We also appreciate the Report's recognition that the FBI cooperated fully with this review and provided broad and timely access to all information requested by the OIG, including highly classified and sensitive material involving national security.

The Report concludes that the FBI's Crossfire Hurricane investigation and related investigations of certain individuals were opened in 2016 for an authorized purpose and with adequate factual predication. The Report also details instances in which certain FBI personnel, at times during the 2016-2017 period reviewed by the OIG, did not comply with existing policies, neglected to exercise appropriate diligence, or otherwise failed to meet the standard of conduct that the FBI expects of its employees — and that our country expects of the FBI. We are vested with significant authorities, and it is our obligation as public servants to ensure that these authorities are exercised with objectivity and integrity. Anything less falls short of the FBI's duty to the American people.

Accordingly, the FBI accepts the Report's findings and embraces the need for thoughtful, meaningful remedial action. I have ordered more than 40 corrective steps to address the Report's recommendations. Because our credibility and brand are central to fulfilling our mission, we are also making improvements beyond those recommended by the OIG. And where certain individuals have been referred by the OIG for review of their conduct, the FBI will not hesitate to take appropriate disciplinary action if warranted at the completion of the required procedures for disciplinary review.

Below is a summary of the actions we are taking, which we describe in more detail in the attachment to this letter.

First, we are modifying our processes under the Foreign Intelligence Surveillance Act (FISA), both for initial applications and renewals, to enhance accuracy and completeness. The FBI relies on FISA every day in national security investigations to prevent terrorists and foreign intelligence services from harming the United States. We are making concrete changes to ensure that our FISA protocols, verifications, layers of review, record-keeping requirements, and audits are more stringent and less susceptible to mistake or inaccuracy. These new processes will also ensure that the FISA Court and the Department of Justice (DOJ) are apprised of all information in the FBI's holdings relevant to a determination of probable cause.

Second, we undertook an extensive review of investigative activity based out of FBI Headquarters. The FBI is a field-based law enforcement organization, and the vast majority of our investigations should continue to be worked by our field offices. Moving forward, in the very rare instance when FBI Headquarters runs a sensitive investigation, we are requiring prior approval by the FBI Deputy Director and consultation with the Assistant Director in Charge or Special Agent in Charge of the affected field offices.

2

Third, we are making significant changes to how the FBI manages its Confidential Human Source (CHS) Program. Many FBI investigations rely on human sources, but the investigative value derived from CHS-provided information rests in part on the CHS's credibility, which demands rigorous assessment of the source. The modifications we are making to how the FBI collects, documents, and shares information about CHSs will strengthen our assessment of the information these sources are providing.

Fourth, I am establishing new protocols for the FBI's participation in Office of the Director of National Intelligence (ODNI)-led counterintelligence transition briefings (*i.e.*, strategic intelligence briefings) provided to presidential nominees. The FBI's role in these briefings should be for national security purposes and <u>not</u> for investigative purposes. Continued participation by the FBI in these transition briefings is critical to ensuring continuity in the event of a change in administrations. The new FBI protocols about transition briefings will complement procedures already implemented by the FBI earlier this year to govern the separate category of defensive briefings. The FBI gives defensive briefings, which are based on specific threat information, in a wide variety of contexts and for myriad federal, state, and other public and private individuals and entities. The procedures we recently established for defensive briefings regarding malign foreign influence efforts have brought a new rigor and discipline to whether and how such briefings should proceed.

Fifth, I am mandating a specialized, semiannual training requirement for FBI personnel at all levels who handle FISA and CHS matters. This training will be experience-based, and it will cover specific lessons learned from this Report, along with other new and revised material. Earlier in my tenure as Director, I reinstated an annual ethics training program for all FBI employees, because I learned the training had been discontinued in prior years. While that training was not introduced in response to this Report, all current FBI employees involved in the 2016-2017 events reviewed by the OIG have since completed this additional training in ethics and professional responsibility.

Finally, we will review the performance and conduct of certain FBI employees who were referenced in the Report's recommendations — including managers, supervisors, and senior

3

officials at the time. The FBI will take appropriate disciplinary action where warranted. Notably, many of the employees described in the report are no longer employed at the FBI.

*   *   *

I want to emphasize that the FBI's participation in this process was undertaken with my express direction to be as transparent as possible, while honoring our duty to protect sources and methods that, if disclosed, might make Americans less safe. Where protection of certain sensitive information is well-founded, I remain committed to upholding the laws and longstanding policies governing classification and public release. I am just as committed to the principle that possible embarrassment and chagrin to the FBI or its employees is not, and should never be, the basis of a decision not to divulge FBI information. The FBI has worked closely with the OIG and DOJ on the classification issues implicated by the Report. Our joint process with the OIG and DOJ has ensured all material facts could be presented in this Report, with redactions carefully limited and narrowly tailored to specific national security and operational concerns. I am grateful for the mutual assistance of the OIG and DOJ in responsible presentation of this extremely sensitive information.

Since becoming FBI Director in August 2017, I have emphasized to FBI agents, analysts, and staff the importance of doing things the right way, by the book. I am humbled to serve alongside these dedicated men and women, and I am confident that the actions we are taking will strengthen our historic institution, ensure that we continue to discharge our responsibilities objectively and free from political bias, and better position us to protect the American people against threats while upholding the Constitution.

Sincerely,

Christopher A. Wray
Director

Enclosure

4

The Federal Bureau of Investigation's Response to the Report
December 6, 2019

[Recommendations from the OIG appear verbatim in *italics*.]

1. *The Department and the FBI should ensure that adequate procedures are in place for the Office of Intelligence (OI) to obtain all relevant and accurate information, including access to Confidential Human Source (CHS) information, needed to prepare FISA applications and renewal applications. This effort should include revising:*

   a. *the FISA Request Form: to ensure information is identified for OI: (i) that tends to disprove, does not support, or is inconsistent with a finding or an allegation that the target is a foreign power or an agent of a foreign power, or (ii) that bears on the reliability of every CHS whose information is relied upon in the FISA application, including all information from the derogatory sub-file, recommended below;*

   b. *the Woods Form: (i) to emphasize to agents and their supervisors the obligation to re-verify factual assertions repeated from prior applications and to obtain written approval from CHS handling agents of all CHS source characterization statements in applications, and (ii) to specify what steps must be taken and documented during the legal review performed by an FBI Office of General Counsel (OGC) line attorney and SES-level supervisor before submitting the FISA application package to the FBI Director for certification;*

   c. *the FISA Procedures: to clarify which positions may serve as the supervisory reviewer for OGC; and*

   d. *taking any other steps deemed appropriate to ensure the accuracy and completeness of information provided to OI.*

The FBI fully accepts these recommendations and is taking the following actions, many of which exceed the OIG's specific recommendations:

1. Supplementing the FISA Request Form with new questions, including a checklist of relevant information, which will direct agents to provide additional information and to collect all details relevant to the consideration of a probable cause finding, emphasizing the need to err on the side of disclosure;

2. Requiring that all information known at the time of the request and bearing on the reliability of a CHS whose information is used to support the FISA application is captured in the FISA Request Form and verified by the CHS handler;

3. Adding reverification directives to the FISA Verification Form, known as the Woods Form, which will require agents and their supervisors to attest to their diligence in re-verifying facts from prior factual applications and to confirm that any changes or clarifying facts, to the extent needed, are in the FISA renewal application;

4. Improving the FISA Verification Form by adding a section devoted to CHSs, including a new certification related to the CHS-originated content in the FISA application by the CHS handler, and CHS-related information that requires confirmation by the CHS handler, which will be maintained in the CHS's file;

5. Adding an affirmation to the FISA Verification Form that, to the best of the agent's and supervisor's knowledge, OI has been apprised of all information that might reasonably

The Federal Bureau of Investigation's Response to the Report, *continued from previous page*
December 6, 2019

call into question the accuracy of the information in the application or otherwise raise doubts about the requested probable cause finding or the theory of the case;

6. Adding a checklist to the FISA Verification Form that walks through the new and existing steps for the supervisor who is affirming the case agent's accuracy review prior to his or her signature, affirming the completeness of the accuracy review;

7. Formalizing the role of FBI attorneys in the legal review process for FISA applications, to include identification of the point at which SES-level FBI OGC personnel will be involved, which positions may serve as the supervisory legal reviewer, and establishing the documentation required for the legal review;

8. Creating and teaching a case study based on the OIG Report findings, analyzing all steps of that particular FISA application and its renewals to show FBI personnel the errors, omissions, failures to follow policy, and communication breakdowns, and to instruct where new or revised policies and procedures will apply, so that mistakes of the past are not repeated;

9. Requiring serialization of completed FISA Verification Forms in the FBI's case management system to increase accountability and transparency;

10. Developing and requiring new training focused on FISA process rigor and the steps FBI personnel must take, at all levels, to make sure that OI and the FISC are apprised of all information in the FBI's holdings at the time of an application that would be relevant to a determination of probable cause;

11. Identifying and pursuing short- and long-term technological improvements, in partnership with DOJ, that will aid in consistency and accountability; and,

12. Directing the FBI's recently expanded Office of Integrity and Compliance to work with the FBI's Resource Planning Office to identify and propose audit, review, and compliance mechanisms to ensure the above changes to the FISA process are effective. In addition, OIC has been directed to evaluate whether other compliance mechanisms would be beneficial to the implementation of the changes detailed below.

2. *The Department and FBI should evaluate which types of Sensitive Investigative Matters (SIM) require advance notification to a senior Department official, such as the Deputy Attorney General, in addition to the notifications currently required for SIMs, especially for case openings that implicate core First Amendment activity, and establish implementing policies and guidance, as necessary.*

The FBI fully accepts this recommendation and is taking the following actions:

1. Identifying, in consultation with the DOJ, which types of SIMs warrant coordination with a senior Department official, implementing heightened FBI approval requirements for the opening of these SIMs, and establishing related processes; and,

2. Training FBI personnel on the changes to ensure that the FBI workforce is consistently recognizing and applying the new requirements and processes for the identified types of SIMs.

2

The Federal Bureau of Investigation's Response to the Report, *continued from previous page*
December 6, 2019

3. *The FBI should develop protocols and guidelines for staffing and administrating any future sensitive investigative matters from FBI Headquarters.*

The FBI fully accepts this recommendation. Prior to receiving this recommendation, the FBI established a working group that reviewed all FBI Headquarters investigations. This review resulted in the closing of those investigations not falling within certain limited exceptions or transferring those cases to the appropriate field offices. In addition, the FBI is taking the following actions, affecting all potential FBI Headquarters investigations:

1. Establishing protocols and guidelines for the rare circumstance when a FBI Headquarters-led investigation might be appropriate;
2. Requiring consultation with the Assistant Director(s) in Charge or Special Agent(s) in Charge of all affected field offices prior to the opening of any FBI Headquarters investigation;
3. Requiring FBI Deputy Director approval prior to opening any FBI Headquarters SIM;
4. Developing and implementing protocols to ensure FBI Headquarters-led investigations follow the structure of field-led investigations, apply the same investigative rigor, and engage in timely and relevant information sharing with the appropriate field offices; and,
5. Instituting an annual audit of investigative files opened at FBI Headquarters during the previous year. The purpose of the audit will be to determine whether each investigation complies with policy and if it should remain an FBI Headquarters-run investigation.

4. *The FBI should address the problems with the administration and assessment of CHSs identified in this report and, at a minimum, should:*
   a. *revise its standard CHS admonishment form to include a prohibition on the disclosure of the CHS's relationship with the FBI to third parties absent the FBI's permission, and assess the need to include other admonishments in the standard CHS admonishments;*
   b. *develop enhanced procedures to ensure that CHS information is documented in Delta, including information generated from Headquarters-led investigations, substantive contacts with closed CHSs (directly or through third parties), and derogatory information. We renew our recommendation that the FBI create a derogatory sub-file in Delta;*
   c. *assess VMU's practices regarding reporting source validation findings and non-findings;*
   d. *establish guidance for sharing sensitive information with CHSs;*
   e. *establish guidance to handling agents for inquiring whether their CHS participates in the types of groups or activities that would bring the CHS within the definition of a "sensitive source," and ensure handling agents document (and update as needed) those affiliations and any other voluntarily provided to them by the CHS in the Source Opening Communications, the "Sensitive Categories" portion of each CHS's Quarterly Supervisory Source Report, the "Life Changes" portion of the CHS Contact Reports, or as otherwise directed by the FBI so that the FBI can assess whether active CHSs are engaged in activities (such as political campaigns) at a level that might require re-designation as a "sensitive source" or necessitate closure of the CHS; and*

3

The Federal Bureau of Investigation's Response to the Report, *continued from previous page*
December 6, 2019

> *f. revise its CHS policy to address the considerations that should be taken into the account and the steps that should be followed before and after accepting information from a closed CHS indirectly through a third party.*

The FBI fully accepts these recommendation and is taking the following actions, which also include improvements separately identified in the OIG's parallel review of CHS validation or by the FBI's own analysis:

1. Creating a new admonishment to sources relating to the confidential nature of the FBI-CHS relationship;
2. Adopting additional admonishments, as necessary, to manage the FBI's relationship with the CHS and to improve the FBI's ability to identify when the CHS's status has changed or should be reevaluated;
3. Creating a new subfile, which will supplement the existing Validation subfile created in 2013, specifically dedicated to holding certain information, including derogatory information, necessary for consideration when CHS-originated information is relied on;
4. Creating a mandatory checklist for CHS handlers so that, in instances where CHS-originated information is used in legal process, relevant information from the new subfile is properly disclosed to the attorneys relying on such CHS-originated information;
5. Adding new documentation requirements to ensure that CHS-originated information and contact with a CHS is captured in the correct FBI recordkeeping system(s), even when it occurs in an atypical circumstance or as part of a separate investigation;
6. Updating and modifying the Validation Management Unit's current practices regarding reporting source validation findings and non-findings to ensure all relevant information is shared with FBI and DOJ personnel;
7. Modifying policy and clarifying guidance for both new and long-term CHSs with a focus on source validation;
8. Revising the policy related to potentially higher-risk CHSs to enhance the scrutiny of those CHSs, including periodic reevaluation for potential closure of the CHS;
9. Establishing guidance and mandatory training for FBI personnel on sharing sensitive information or classified information with CHSs;
10. Expanding the definition of a sensitive source that requires additional approval, scrutiny, and oversight to include CHSs who may have access to certain categories of individuals, such as national-level campaign staff, or who report on subjects in a SIM investigation;
11. Revising policy and adding guidance for handling agents so they know when to ask a CHS about participation in the types of groups or activities that would bring the CHS within the newly expanded definition of a "sensitive source" or require their closure;
12. Requiring agents to update the designation of the CHS to a sensitive CHS if, over the course of the CHS relationship with the FBI, the CHS's position or access changes, triggering a need for additional approvals and oversight;
13. Clarifying documentation and updating requirements related to a CHS's status;
14. Clarifying and enhancing guidance on how to respond in the situation where a CHS, acting independently and not in response to an FBI tasking, provides information about a sensitive target or operation;

4

The Federal Bureau of Investigation's Response to the Report, *continued from previous page*
December 6, 2019

15. Revising policy to establish the requirements and procedures for receiving information
    from a closed source, whether directly or through a third party, and the necessary
    approvals and processes to permit or preclude acceptance of such information; and,

16. Creating a CHS Management Working Group directed to identify and deliver additional
    improvements to FBI CHS policies and procedures.

5. *The Department and FBI should clarify the following terms in their policies:*

   a. *assess the definition of a "Sensitive Monitoring Circumstance" in the AG
      Guidelines and the FBI's DIOG to determine whether to expand its scope to
      include consensual monitoring of a domestic political candidate or an individual
      prominent within a domestic political organization, or a subset of these persons,
      so that consensual monitoring of such individuals would require consultation with
      or advance notification to a senior Department official, such as the Deputy
      Attorney General; and*

   b. *establish guidance, and include examples in the DIOG, to better define the
      meaning of the phrase "prominent in a domestic political organization" so that
      agents understand which campaign officials fall within that definition as it relates
      to "Sensitive Investigative Matters," "Sensitive UDP," and the designation of
      "sensitive sources." Further, if the Department expands the scope of "Sensitive
      Monitoring Circumstance," as recommended above, the FBI should apply the
      guidance on "prominent in a domestic political organization" to "Sensitive
      Monitoring Circumstance" as well.*

The FBI fully accepts these recommendation and is taking the following actions:

1. Assessing, in consultation with the DOJ, the current definition of a "Sensitive
   Monitoring Circumstance" and determining whether to expand the definition;

2. Identifying, in consultation with the DOJ, the appropriate level of coordination for a
   Sensitive Monitoring Circumstance;

3. Establishing guidance and, to the extent necessary, adding or modifying the DIOG,
   including by introducing examples, to better define and explain the phrase "prominent in
   a domestic political organization";

4. Making any further changes to FBI policy that are required upon an expansion of the
   definition of a Sensitive Monitoring Circumstance; and,

5. Ensuring that training and guidance are enhanced and provided to FBI personnel
   pursuant to any revised or expanded definitions.

6. *The FBI should ensure that appropriate training on DIOG § 4 is provided to emphasize the
   constitutional implications of certain monitoring situations and to ensure that agents account
   for these concerns, both in the tasking of CHSs and in the way they document interactions
   with and tasking of CHSs.*

The FBI fully accepts this recommendation and is taking the following actions:

1. Establishing and providing at least semiannual, mandatory training for all relevant
   personnel on CHS handling, source sensitivities, and other source-related topics, such

5

The Federal Bureau of Investigation's Response to the Report, *continued from previous page*
December 6, 2019

as the constitutional implications of certain monitoring situations. Part of this training will include discussion of the constitutional implications of certain monitoring situations, how to approach these considerations, and how to document situations where core constitutional issues, such as First Amendment activity, may be present; and,

2. Instituting regular and mandatory continuing legal training for FBI personnel at all levels and in all investigative roles, in addition to already existing legal and ethics training, to make sure that FBI personnel fully understand and apply their obligations as required by policy and law, including an emphasis on privacy and civil liberties.

7. *The FBI should establish a policy regarding the use of defensive and transition briefings for investigative purposes, including the factors to be considered and approval by senior leaders at the FBI with notice to a senior Department official, such as the Deputy Attorney General.*

The FBI fully accepts this recommendation and is taking the following actions:

1. Instituting a policy that the FBI's counterintelligence and security portion of the Office of the Director of National Intelligence-led strategic intelligence briefings (also known transition briefings) are solely intended to provide candidates and elected officials with relevant intelligence and threat awareness, and thus FBI briefers will not be associated with any ongoing FBI investigation related to any reasonably foreseeable attendee at the strategic intelligence briefing, will be selected based on their knowledge of the threat or threats to be briefed, and to the extent feasible, the same team of briefers will be used for all recipients of a particular strategic intelligence briefing; and,

2. Continuing to refine the FBI's newly implemented review process for malign foreign influence defensive briefings, and in particular briefings to Legislative and Executive Branch officials. This will encompass actions taken after receipt of specific threat information that identifies malign foreign influence operations – that is, foreign operations that are subversive, undeclared, coercive, or criminal – including convening the FBI's Foreign Influence Defensive Briefing Board (FIDBB) to evaluate whether and how to provide defensive briefings to affected parties. To determine whether notification is warranted and appropriate in each case, the FIDBB uses consistent, standardized criteria guided by principles that include, for example, the protection of sources and methods and the integrity and independence of ongoing criminal investigations and prosecutions.

8. *The Department's Office of Professional Responsibility should review our findings related to the conduct of Department attorney Bruce Ohr for any action it deems appropriate. Ohr's supervisors in the Department's Criminal Division should also review our findings related to Ohr's performance for any action they deem appropriate.*

This recommendation is directed to the DOJ, thus the FBI is taking the following action:

With regards to Mr. Ohr, an employee of the DOJ, the FBI respectfully defers to the DOJ for addressing the OIG's recommendation.

6

The Federal Bureau of Investigation's Response to the Report, *continued from previous page*
December 6, 2019

9. *The FBI should review the performance of all employees who had responsibility for the preparation, Woods review, or approval of the FISA applications, as well as the managers, supervisors, and senior officials in the chain of command of the Carter Page investigation, and take any action deemed appropriate.*

The FBI fully accepts this recommendation and is taking the following actions:

Recognizing that many of the individuals involved in this matter are no longer with the FBI, undertaking the review of FBI personnel and taking actions as appropriate.

7

[PAGE INTENTIONALLY LEFT BLANK]

The Department of Justice Office of the Inspector General (DOJ OIG) is a statutorily created independent entity whose mission is to detect and deter waste, fraud, abuse, and misconduct in the Department of Justice, and to promote economy and efficiency in the Department's operations.

To report allegations of waste, fraud, abuse, or misconduct regarding DOJ programs, employees, contractors, grants, or contracts please visit or call the **DOJ OIG Hotline** at oig.justice.gov/hotline or (800) 869-4499.

U.S. DEPARTMENT OF JUSTICE OFFICE OF THE INSPECTOR GENERAL
950 Pennsylvania Avenue, Northwest
Suite 4760
Washington, DC 20530-0001

Website	**Twitter**	**YouTube**
oig.justice.gov	@JusticeOIG	JusticeOIG

Also at Oversight.gov

www.ingramcontent.com/pod-product-compliance
Lightning Source LLC
Chambersburg PA
CBHW080616030426
42336CB00018B/2991